To Stir a Restless Heart

THOMISTIC RESSOURCEMENT SERIES

Volume 14

To Stir a Restless Heart

Thomas Aquinas and
Henri de Lubac on Nature, Grace, and
the Desire for God

JACOB W. WOOD

The Catholic University of America Press
Washington, D.C.

The paper used in this publication meets the minimum
requirements of American National Standards for Information
Science—Permanence of Paper for Printed Library Materials,
ANSI Z39.48–1984.
∞

Library of Congress Cataloging-in-Publication Data
Names: Wood, Jacob W., author.
Title: To stir a restless heart : Thomas Aquinas and Henri de Lubac
on nature, grace, and the desire for God / Jacob W Wood.
Description: Washington, D.C. : The Catholic University of America
Press, 2019. | Series: Thomistic ressourcement series ; Volume 14 |
Includes bibliographical references and index.
Identifiers: LCCN 2019018409 | ISBN 9780813231839
(cloth : alk. paper)
Subjects: LCSH: Thomas, Aquinas, Saint, 1225?–1274. | Lubac,
Henri de, 1896–1991. | Desire for God—History of doctrines.
Classification: LCC B765.T54 W63 2019 | DDC 230/.2092—dc23
LC record available at https://lccn.loc.gov/2019018409

For my wife,
Heather

Contents

Figures and Tables

Acknowledgments

The research that led to this book began a decade ago and has benefited from the advice, encouragement, and support of more people than I can name. Dr. C. C. Pecknold first introduced me to Henri de Lubac and Augustinian Thomism, and has been a guiding light to my thought ever since, while Rev. Thomas Joseph White, OP, first introduced me to the Thomistic commentatorial tradition, and helped me to find my footing within it. Dr. Frederick Bauerschmidt and Dr. Brian Carl provided numerous suggestions and corrections in my research on Thomas Aquinas, while Dr. R. Trent Pomplun did the same for my research on Giles of Rome and the "Aegidian" tradition. Dr. Stephen Metzger assisted me with dates, texts, and editions of Thomas Aquinas's interlocutors in the second Parisian period. All the participants in the Wednesday seminars at the St. Paul Center for Biblical Theology have deepened my knowledge of and appreciation for the context of Thomas Aquinas's work, the significance of Giles of Rome's influence on the theological tradition, and the political-theological implications of the nature/grace debate: Dr. John Bergsma, Dr. Scott Hahn, Dr. Stephen Hildebrand, Dr. Andrew Jones, Dr. John Kincaid, Dr. James Merrick, Dr. William Newton, Dr. Michael Sirilla, Dr. Michael Waldstein, and Mr. Robert Corzine.

This book would not have been possible without generous material assistance. The Catholic University of America supported the beginning of my research with a Hubbard Dissertation Fellowship, while Franciscan University of Steubenville supported the completion of the manuscript with a Faculty Development Grant. Dr. Jay Hammond, Dr. C. C. Pecknold, and Dr. Rega Wood allowed me to consult pre-publication copies of their work. The library staff at the Catholic University of America, Loyola University Maryland, Villanova University, the University of Dallas, and Franciscan University of Steubenville all spent significant portions of their time helping me to locate important but obscure texts in the Thomistic tradition. The entire team at the Catholic University of America Press provided invaluable assistance in giving the book its final shape.

I am indebted to the publishers of some of my previous work for permission to republish that work here: portions of "Recasting Augustine to Look Like Aristotle: Philip the Chancellor, Natural Desire, and the Advent of *potentia obedientiae*," *Nova et Vetera* (English) 13, no. 3 (2015): 815–36, are reprinted in chapter 1 by permission of Emmaus Academic; portions of "Kataphasis and Apophasis in Thirteenth Century Theology: The Anthropological Context of the Triplex Via in the Summa fratris Alexandri and Albert the Great," *The Heythrop Journal* 57, no. 2 (2016): 293–311, are reprinted in chapter 1 by permission of Wiley-Blackwell; portions of "Henri de Lubac, Humani Generis, and the Natural Desire for a Supernatural End," *Nova et Vetera* (English) 15, no. 4 (2017): 1209–41, are reprinted in the introduction and in chapter 6 by permission of Emmaus Academic. In all cases, I have taken the liberty of correcting mistakes, updating references, and making such other emendations as seemed necessary.

I owe the largest debt of gratitude to my wife, Heather, to whom this book is dedicated. For every hour of labor I have devoted to it, she has devoted one or more to making it possible. "Give to her the fruit of her hands, and let her works praise her in the gates" (Pv 31:31).

Abbreviations

Works of Thomas Aquinas

De an.	*Quaestiones disputatae de anima*
De pot.	*Quaestiones disputatae de potentia*
De ver.	*Quaestiones disputatae de veritate*
In I–IV Sent.	*Scriptum super sententiis*
SCG	*Summa contra Gentiles*
ST	*Summa theologiae*

Other Works

CCCM	Corpus Christianorum Continuatio Mediaevalis (Turnhout)
CCSL	Corpus Christianorum Series Latina (Turnhout)
Col.	Albert the Great, *Opera Omnia* (Editio Coloniensis)
CSEL	Corpus Scriptorum Ecclesiasticorum Latinorum (Vienna)
Leon.	Thomas Aquinas, *Opera Omnia* (Editio Leonina)
Leon. Man.	Thomas Aquinas, *Summa Contra Gentiles* (Editio Leonina Manualis)

PG Patrologia Cursus Completus: Series Graeca, ed. J.-P. Migne (Paris)

PL Patrologia Cursus Completus: Series Latina, ed. J.-P. Migne (Paris)

Sent. Peter Lombard, *Sententiae in IV Libros Distinctae*

Vat. John Duns Scotus, *Opera Omnia* (Editio Vaticana)

To Stir a Restless Heart

Introduction

To Stir a Restless Heart

> Great are you, O Lord, and highly to be praised: great is your power and your wisdom is infinite. And man wants to praise you, though he is but a portion of your creation. But as man carries about his mortality, he carries about a witness to his sin—a witness, because you resist the proud. And still, man wants to praise you, though he is but a portion of your creation. You stir him up that he may rejoice to praise you, because you have made us for yourself, and our heart is restless until it rests in you.
>
> —Augustine, *Confessions* 1.1[1]

AUGUSTINE'S DESIRE FOR HAPPINESS

At the beginning of the *Confessions*, Augustine's restless heart struggles with a paradox at the center of fallen humanity: we are made to praise God and long to do so, but we have been estranged through pride from the one whom we were made to praise. Augustine's primary goal in describing this paradox is to give a prayerful testimony

1. Augustine, *Confessionum libri XIII*, ed. L. Verheijen (Turnhout: Brepols, 1981), 1.1 [CCSL 27:1]: "Magnus es, domine, et laudabilis ualde: magna uirtus tua et sapientiae tuae non est numerus. Et laudare te uult homo, aliqua portio creaturae tuae, et homo circumferens mortalitatem suam, circumferens testimonium peccati sui et testimonium, quia superbis resistis: et tamen laudare te uult homo, aliqua portio creaturae tuae. Tu excitas, ut laudare te delectet, quia fecisti nos ad te et inquietum est cor nostrum, donec requiescat in te." All translations are the author's unless otherwise noted.

to its resolution in his own life: while he was "yet at a distance" like the Prodigal Son (Lk 15:20), the Lord stirred up his restless heart by grace so that he, who had longed to praise God, might at last rejoice in doing so.[2] He describes this process particularly in Books 7–9. In Book 7, he tells us about how, under the tutelage of the Neo-Platonists, he first rose above the level of his own imagination to seek his heart's desire in an "immutable light above ... [his] soul."[3] One would think that this initial taste of divinity would sate Augustine's desire for God,[4] but in fact it only increases it on account of a

2. Any discussion of nature and grace in Augustine's *Confessions* has to come to terms with Augustine's seeming admission in *De praedestinatione sanctorum* 3.7–4.8 that from the start of his career until *Ad Simplicianum de diversis quaestionibus* 1.2 he had seen the act of faith as coming from human initiative. Most contemporary scholars follow J. Patout Burns, *The Development of Augustine's Doctrine of Operative Grace* (Paris: Études Augustiniennes, 1980), in not taking Augustine at his word here, but in seeing the decisive turning point in Augustine's thought much later, in *De gratia Christi et de peccato originali*. The principal exception to this rule is Carol Harrison, *Rethinking Augustine's Early Theology: An Argument for Continuity* (New York: Oxford University Press, 2006), 149–50, who sees a consistent emphasis on grace before and after *Ad Simplicianum de diversis quaestionibus* 1.2. Robert Dodaro, *Christ and the Just Society in the Thought of Augustine* (New York: Cambridge University Press, 2004), 83–86, offers us a *via media*, conceding that *Ad Simplicianum de diversis quaestionibus* represents a "watershed" moment in Augustine's thinking on grace, in which Augustine first begins to emphasize both the priority of God's grace in the act of faith as well as the idea that nature receives grace communally in the form of a "city," but allowing that there was still significant development in Augustine's thought throughout the anti-Pelagian period, particularly with regard to the exegesis of Rom 7:15–24.

English translations often miss the distinction between nature and grace in *Confessiones* 1.1 by translating *laudare te uult homo* literally as "man wants to praise you," but translating *ut laudare te delectet* more freely. Ordinarily, such freedom is warranted in rendering an infinitive when it is used as a predicate accusative. However, in this context it obscures the rhetorical parallelism. Without grace, man *wants* to praise God; having been stirred up by grace, man *rejoices* to do what he previously wanted to do but could not. Among all the English translators of the last century (Boulding, Chadwick, Helms, Outler, O'Rourke, Ryan, and Sheed), only Albert Outler captures the parallel completely, though in an admittedly antiquated manner.

3. Augustine, *Confessiones* 7.10.16 [CCSL 27:103]. "Intraui et uidi qualicumque oculo animae meae supra eundem oculum animae meae, supra mentem meam lucem incommutabilem ..."

4. Alongside developments in Augustine's thinking about nature and grace, scholars typically discuss developments in Augustine's thinking on reason and faith, especially his relationship to Neo-Platonism. At the beginning of the twentieth century, the dominant view was that of Prosper Alfaric, *L'évolution intellectuelle de Saint Augustin* (Paris: Noury,

twofold limitation.[5] First, it falls short. Although he "saw with his mind the invisible realities [of God] through those things which have been made,"[6] the dependence of his contemplation on himself and on the created world highlights the distance between creatures and their immutable Creator.[7] Second, it is short lived. Although his intellect had already been healed to a certain extent by grace, his will remained yet unhealed, preferring sensual pleasure to the immaterial joy of contemplation. Only after Augustine is "pierced" by

---

1918), according to whom Augustine was simply a Neo-Platonist. In the mid-twentieth century, Alfaric's view was amended by that of Pierre Courcelle, *Recherches sur les* Confessions *de saint Augustin* (Paris: Boccard, 1950), who sees Augustine as a Christian heavily indebted to Neo-Platonism. Courcelle's outlook predominates English scholarship through James O'Connell, *St. Augustine's Early Theory of Man* (Cambridge, Mass.: Harvard University Press, 1968). Recognizing the continued influence of Courcelle and O'Connell, Mark Boone, *The Conversion and Therapy of Desire* (Cambridge: J. Clark and Co., 2017), 4–5, highlights two recent exceptions: Catherine Conybeare, *The Irrational Augustine* (New York: Oxford University Press, 2006), who separates Augustine from Neo-Platonism, and Harrison, *Rethinking Augustine's Early Theology*, who gives greater emphasis to the uniquely Christian elements of his thought, without altogether rejecting the influence of Neo-Platonism.

The main questions at stake in the interpretation of the vision at Milan are why Augustine found it ultimately unsatisfying, and how it compares to the vision at Ostia. Courcelle, identifying both visions with a Neo-Platonic framework of ascent, locates the source of Augustine's dissatisfaction in an "oeil … insuffisamment purifié" (*Recherches sur les* Confessions, 166), and sees a similar dissatisfaction in Ostia (ibid., 224). While acknowledging that "Augustine obviously thought that Christianity and Platonic (Neoplatonic) philosophy were complementary and ultimately reconcilable," Harrison observes that Augustine sees Christ as the hinge around which these two visions turn, and that Augustine's references to Christ are not reducible in their entirety to a Neo-Platonic framework (*Rethinking Augustine's Early Theology*, 36). James O'Donnell, *Confessions*, 3 vols. (Oxford: Clarendon Press, 1992), 3:128, is more emphatic: "It is scarcely credible that after showing how his difficulties in Bk. 7 were the result of an inadequate knowledge of and acceptance of Christ; and after showing in Bk. 8 how he acquired that knowledge and acceptance; and after showing in early Bk. 9 that new life in action—that he would then describe an event like that of Ostia in terms that showed no sign of progress or development over what he described in Bk. 7."

5. Augustine, *Confessiones* 8.20 [CCSL 27:126].

6. Ibid., 7.17.23 [CCSL 27:107], quoting Rom 1:20: "inuisibilia tua per ea quae facta sunt intellecta conspexi …"

7. Harrison, *Rethinking Augustine's Early Theology*, 54–55, sees the need for "divine initiative" as what sets Augustine's understanding of contemplation apart from Neo-Platonism.

the Lord's love, and purified by baptism in Book 9,[8] can he stand in communion with his mother, Monica, at Ostia, and can his heart be elevated with hers to a contemplative union with God.[9] This mystical participation in the Church Triumphant is as close a resolution to the paradox of desire that Augustine recounts in this life.[10] For it is only in the next life that Augustine expects to find the complete satisfaction and everlasting joy of union with God in Christ.[11]

Although the *Confessions* focuses on Augustine's concrete experience of redemption, he does acknowledge in his spiritual autobiography that his experience raises certain speculative questions which are difficult to answer. Which is prior in our response to the desire for God: prayer or praise, knowledge or prayer?[12] If God is already present to all things, how can we desire him as though he were absent?[13] Given that we depend on God for everything, how can we long to give him anything?[14] At this point in his career, Augustine treats these questions more as mysteries to be pondered than as problems to be solved. But as his life progressed into the Pelagian controversy, he came to see that the questions he raised in the *Confessions* about our longing for the praise of God all point to a single,

8. In Augustine, *Confessiones* 9.2.3 [CCSL 27:134], Augustine proclaims, "Sagittaueras tu cor nostrum caritate tua . . ." He is baptized in ibid., 9.6.14 [CCSL 27:141].

9. Ibid., 9.10.23 [CCSL 27:147]: "Sed inhiabamus ore cordis in superna fluenta fontis tui, fontis uitae, qui est apud te, ut inde pro captu nostra aspersi quoquo modo rem tantam cogitaremus." Brian Dobell, *Augustine's Intellectual Conversion: The Journey from Platonism to Christianity* (New York: Cambridge University Press, 2009), 215–16, following O'Donnell, *Confessions*, 3:128, sees one of the fundamental differences between the Neo-Platonic ascent of Book 7 and the Christian ascent of Book 9 in the fact that the Neo-Platonic ascent is kataphatic, while the Christian ascent is apophatic. The Neo-Platonic ascent involves a vision mediated through Creation in the intellect, but pride in the will. The Christian ascent involves unmediated darkness in the intellect in which the intellect attempts to move from creatures to their Creator, and is spurred on by the presence of charity in the will, which alone can bridge the gap between man and God.

10. On the ecclesial character of Augustine and Monica's experience at Ostia in their union with the communion of saints, see Dobell, *Augustine's Intellectual Conversion*, 219–20; Harrison, *Rethinking Augustine's Early Theology*, 53–54.

11. Augustine, *Confessiones* 9.10.26 [CCSL 27:148].

12. Ibid., 1.1.1 [CCSL 27:1].

13. Ibid., 1.2.2 [CCSL 27:1–2].

14. Ibid., 1.4.4 [CCSL 27:3].

more basic question, which is so central to the Christian life that the integrity of any spiritual biography stands or falls on answering it correctly: what is the relationship between fallen human nature, which unceasingly desires to know and to love the God who sustains it in being, and the grace of Christ by which God ultimately satisfies that desire?

In his polemics with the Pelagians, Augustine explores how giving the wrong answer to the "nature/grace question" risks making the Passion of Christ superfluous to human flourishing. In *De peccatorum meritis et remissione et de baptismo paruulorum,* he explores the woundedness of fallen nature, explaining that Adam passes on to his descendants not only the guilt of original sin,[15] but also the concupiscence that results from it.[16] The whole of the Christian life is thus marked by a struggle between the flesh and the spirit, in which it is possible for a person to avoid all sin,[17] but in which it is nearly impossible that a given person actually will.[18] Fallen human nature therefore has a twofold need for Christ: first, as savior, to forgive the guilt of original sin and restore it to the glory of divine filiation;[19] second, as physician, to strengthen it against concupiscence so that it may pick up its cross and follow Christ.[20]

In *De spiritu et littera,* Augustine explains how his teaching on the woundedness of human nature affects our understanding of human freedom. On the one hand, he vigorously denies that the fallen will can move toward God at all without grace.[21] That does not mean that the will lacks freedom; the choices that the weakened will

15. Augustine, *De peccatorum meritis et remissione et de baptismo parvulorum,* in *De peccatorum meritis et remissione et de baptismo parvulorum, De spiritu et littera, De natura et gratia, De natura et origine animae, Contra duas epistulas Pelagianorum,* ed. K. F. Urba and J. Zycha (Vienna: F. Tempsky, 1913), 1.13.16 [CSEL 60:16].

16. Ibid., 1.39.70 [CSEL 60:70–71].

17. Ibid., 2.6.7 [CSEL 60:77].

18. Ibid., 2.7.8 [CSEL 60:79], 2.20.34 [CSEL 60:105].

19. Ibid., 1.28.56 [CSEL 60:55], 2.24.38 [CSEL 60:109–11].

20. Ibid., 1.23.33 [CSEL 60:32–33], 3.12.21 [CSEL 60:148].

21. Augustine, *De spiritu et littera* 2.4 [CSEL 60:156]. "Sed illis acerrime ac uehementissime resistendum est, qui putant sine adiutorio dei per se ipsam uim uoluntatis humanae uel iustitiam posse perficere uel ad eam tendendo proficere...."

makes still follow the character of its freedom. Rather, it means that the will stands in need of Jesus, who strengthens it in such a way that it can once again make the choices for which God made it.[22] Only by the gift of his Holy Spirit does there arise:

in our mind a joy in and love of that highest and unchangeable good, which is God; this happens even now, when we walk by faith and not yet by sight, so that with this faith, given to us as the pledge of a gratuitous gift, we may yearn to inhere in the Creator, and burn to draw near to a participation in the true light, so that we may receive our well-being from the one who gave us being.[23]

The need for this gift applies to every stage of our motion toward God; even the will to believe results from having first received it.[24] If there were a motion toward God in us without grace, then grace would be a reward for our merits. But, as Augustine goes on to observe in *De natura et gratia,* the whole reason that God's favor is called grace (*gratia*) is that it is given freely (*gratis*).[25] If fallen nature could merit grace from God without the Cross, what need would there have been for Jesus to die on it?[26]

In the second half of *De Trinitate,* which was authored in part during the Pelagian controversy, Augustine returns to some of the speculative questions he had raised in *Confessions* about knowledge, desire, prayer, and praise, having realized that he could not avoid an-

22. Ibid., 30.52 [CSEL 60:208–9].

23. Ibid., 3.5 [CSEL 60:157]: "[Voluntas humana] . . . debeat accipiat spiritum sanctum, quo fiat in animo eius delectatio dilectioque summi illius atque incommutabilis boni, quod deus est, etiam nunc cum per fidem ambulatur, nondum per speciem, ut hac sibi uelut arra data gratuiti muneris inardescat inhaerere creatori atque inflammetur accedere ad participationem illius ueri luminis, ut ex illo ei bene sit, a quo habet ut sit." I have benefited from consulting the translation of Roland Teske: Augustine, *Selected Writings on Grace and Pelagianism,* trans. Roland Teske (Hyde Park, N.Y.: New City Press, 2011), 231.

24. Augustine, *De spiritu et littera* 33.57–59 [CSEL 60:215–21].

25. Augustine, *De natura et gratia* 4.4 [CSEL 60:235]. "Haec igitur Christi gratia . . . non meritis redditur, sed gratis datur, propter quod gratia nominatur."

26. Augustine's accusation that the Pelagians "make the Cross of Christ vain" (cf. 1 Cor 1:17–18) functions as a refrain throughout the work. See ibid., 6.6, 7.7, 9.10, 19.21, 40.47 [CSEL 60: 236, 237, 239, 246, 268].

swering them any longer if he did not want to jeopardize the cross of Christ. In Book 8, he discusses how it is that we can call upon a God whom we do not know.[27] Consistent with his experience at Ostia and his reasoning throughout the Pelagian controversy, Augustine acknowledges the limits of human reason to bring us into a personal relationship with God. It is only by first coming to know God through the gift of faith that we are ultimately moved to call upon him in hope.[28] Faith may not give us the vision of God which we long to enjoy in heaven—faith, after all, is "of things *not* seen"[29]— but it does open the door to a Christian analogy of the Triune God, which supersedes the Neo-Platonic analogy of the One drawn from Creation: once we have been roused by grace from the torpor of self-love,[30] we can experience true love for our fellow wayfarers on the road to heaven,[31] such as Augustine experienced for Monica at Ostia; since that love is itself a gift from God, turning our gaze toward it can reveal to us a *vestigium* of its Triune Giver in the lover, the beloved, and love itself,[32] a *vestigium* which constitutes the starting point for the rest of Augustine's mystical ascent in the books that follow.

While Augustine thus answers the question of how we can rejoice in praising God *after* we receive the gift of faith, he leaves another, more difficult question unanswered until Book 13 (written ca. 415–18):[33] why would we even want to have faith in God, if God is—

27. Augustine, *De Trinitate libri XV*, ed. W. J. Mountain and F. Glorie (Turnhout: Brepols, 1968), 8.3.6 [CCSL 50:274–75].

28. ibid.

29. Heb 11:1 (emphasis added).

30. Augustine, *De Trinitate* 8.7.10 [CCSL 50:284–85].

31. Ibid. 8.8.12 [CCSL 50:286]. In this analogy of charity, Augustine is drawing upon 1 Jn 4:20.

32. Augustine, *De Trinitate* 8.10.14 [CCSL 50:290].

33. Concerning the dependence of Book 13 on the anti-Pelagian controversy, see Lenka Karfíková, *Grace and the Will according to Augustine* (Boston: Brill, 2012), 240. Karfíková notes that with the exception of E. Hendrikx, "La date de composition du *De Trinitate* de saint Augustin," *L'année théologique augustinienne* 12 (1952): 305–16, most scholars agree that Book 13 of the *De Trinitate* dates to the latter part of the 410s, just prior to the work's final redaction in 419.

Whatever one may make about development (or a lack thereof) in Augustine's thinking on nature and grace (about which, see note 3 above), Wetzel is correct to high-as Augustine argues—unknown to us in a personal sense before we receive the gift of faith? True to the *Confessions*, Augustine begins his answer with a story; true to his anti-Pelagian works, he uses that story to set up the priority of grace:

> They laud the humor of a certain comedian as the funniest around. One time, he promised in the theater that he would tell them at future shows what they were all thinking about and what they all wanted. Then, on the appointed day an even greater crowd came together, filled with eager anticipation. When everyone was silent and all eyes were fixed on him, they maintain that he said: "You want to buy things cheap and sell them dear."
>
> Although this line was expressed in the silliest of performances, all the theatergoers recognized their own sentiments in it, and they warmly applauded him for laying such true but unexpected facts before their eyes.[34]

As much as the crowd marveled to hear its common avarice reflected back to it, Augustine does not think that the comedian was as successful in capturing the essence of human desire as he was in capturing the good humor of his audience. The comedian failed to take into account exceptions to the universal desire for profit, which prove that there is something else at the basis of human desire: the man who justly informed the seller that a book was worth much more than the asking price, the man who pawned his inheritance to finance expensive pleasures, the man who took a loss on the sale of food in order to win political support from the poor. Nevertheless, Augustine sees a kernel of truth in the comedian's reply. The mistake was not to suggest that there is something universal in hu-

---

light that the "efficacy [of grace in Augustine's thought at this time] depends crucially on introducing new desires to the unconverted will." James Wetzel, *Augustine and the Limits of Virtue* (New York: Cambridge University Press, 2008), 187.

34. Augustine, *De Trinitate* 13.3.6 [CCSL 50:387]. "illa cuiusdam mimi facetissima praedicatur urbanitas qui cum se promisisset in theatro quid in animo haberent et quid uellent omnes aliis ludis esse dicturum, atque ad diem constitutum ingenti exspectatione maior multitudo conflueret suspensis et silentibus omnibus, dixisse perhibetur: 'uili uultis emere et caro uendere.' In quo dicto leuissimi scenici omnes tamen conscientias inuenerunt suas, eique uera ante oculos omnium constituta et tamen improuisa dicenti admirabili fauore plauserunt." I have benefited from consulting the translation of Edmund Hill: Augustine, *On the Trinity* (Brooklyn, N.Y.: New City Press, 1991), 346. Hill's translation, though otherwise excellent, omits the phrase "quid in animo haberent."

man desire; it was merely to assign that universal desire the wrong object. A given human person may select virtue, pleasure, power, or honor as the object of his desire, but each person seeks his chosen object because he thinks it will make him happy.[35] "Whatever else anyone may wish for secretly, he never forgoes this wish [for happiness] which is well known to all and in all."[36]

Augustine acknowledges that the desire for happiness is unique among all other forms of human desire. When we desire virtue, pleasure, power, or honor, we know what we seek; and we seek it because we think that we can obtain it for ourselves. But happiness is not an object of our desire, properly speaking; happiness is the result in us of enjoying the object of our desire.[37] The true paradox of fallen humanity is that we all have a sense of what it would be like to be completely happy, but we are not born knowing what we need to enjoy in order to make us completely happy. We often seek our happiness among the material goods of this world, whose goodness is more apparent to us than the immaterial good of virtue. Yet if we have all we want, and fail to refer our material goods to the spiritual ends for which they and we were made, then the satisfaction of our desires will make us miserable.[38] Only by having all we want, *and* wanting nothing wrongly, only by using the things of this world to seek rest in the Lord alone, will we ultimately come to that complete happiness which we sense is possible every time we lose ourselves among the lesser goods of this world.[39]

Properly speaking, then, Augustine thinks that our wounded hearts desire the self-fulfillment that complete happiness would entail but do not know where to find it; we have a desire for happiness, but not quite a "desire for God" in the strict sense. This distinction

35. Augustine, *De Trinitate* 13.4.7 [CCSL 50:389–90].

36. Ibid., 13.3.6 [CCSL 50:389; Hill 347]: "Quidquid enim aliud quisquam latenter uelit, ab hac uoluntate quae omnibus et in omnibus satis nota est non recedit."

37. Ibid., 13.4.7 [CCSL 50:390].

38. Ibid., 13.5.8 [CCSL 50:392].

39. Ibid., 13.5.8 [CCSL 50:393]: "Beatus igitur non est nisi qui et habet omnia quae uult et nihil uult male."

is important.[40] Were Augustine to admit that the soul moved at all toward God without grace, he risked coming under his own condemnation for doing away with the Cross of Christ. Yet this does not mean that there was no longer any place for God in Augustine's account of our restless heart. Since it so happens that God alone can satisfy us, whenever and in whatever object our fallen souls seek fulfillment, they are always implicitly seeking a happiness which can only be found by grace in the joy of praising God, even if they lack the resources on their own to know about or to achieve that happiness.

Augustine's anti-Pelagian account of the fallen individual in *De Trinitate*, Book 13, is a microcosm of his account of the fallen community in Books 6–8 of *De civitate Dei*, which were also written in the midst of the anti-Pelagian controversy.[41] In Book 8, Augustine

40. Burns, *Development of Augustine's Doctrine of Operative Grace*, 111n117, uses the distinction to argue for a "shift [at this time] from the natural desire for God to an orientation to personal beatitude." A more synthetic view of these two aspects of desire, relying in part on Maurice Blondel and Henri de Lubac, can be found in Isabelle Bochet, *Saint Augustin et le désir de dieu* (Paris: Études Augustinennes, 1982).

41. Contemporary discussions of Augustine's political theology vary widely in their readings of the *City of God*. For intentionally anti-Pelagian readings of the *City of God*, see Robert Dodaro, *Christ and the Just Society in the Thought of St. Augustine*; C. C. Pecknold, "Church and Politics," in *The Oxford Handbook of Catholic Theology* (New York: Oxford University Press, 2019), 457–75. I am indebted to Pecknold for drawing my attention to the role of sacrifice and of δαιμόνια in Augustine's discussions of true justice in relation to Rome and the Neo-Platonists, and for showing how the concept of sacrifice directs Augustine's use of the definitions of a *respublica* in Books 2 and 19.

Without the anti-Pelagian historical contextualization, sympathetic readings of the *City of God* can be found in William Cavanaugh, *The Myth of Religious Violence: Secular Ideology and the Roots of Modern Conflict* (New York: Oxford University Press, 2009), as well as *Migrations of the Holy: God, State, and the Political Meaning of the Church* (Grand Rapids, Mich.: Eerdmans, 2011); Oliver O'Donovan, *The Desire of Nations: Rediscovering the Roots of Political Theology* (New York: Cambridge University Press, 1996); Andrew Jones, *Before Church and State: A Study of the Social Order in the Sacramental Kingdom of St. Louis IX* (Steubenville, Ohio: Emmaus Academic, 2017); John Milbank, *Beyond Secular Order: The Representation of Being and the Representation of the People* (Malden, Mass.: Wiley Blackwell, 2013). These works reverse to varying degrees the liberal democratic reading of the *City of God* given by Robert Markus, *Saeculum: History and Society in the Thought of St. Augustine* (New York: Cambridge University Press, 1970). For readings of the *City of God*, which maintain a more positive connection to Markus, see Eric Gregory, *Politics and the Order of Love: An Augustinian Ethic of Democratic Citizenship* (Chicago:

praises the Neo-Platonists for their natural theology. Consistent with the *Confessions,* he acknowledges their preeminence among the schools of philosophy, because in his estimation, they alone used Creation to come to the knowledge of its immaterial Creator,[42] and they alone sought union with God through virtue as the source of true happiness.[43] Yet in spite of their affinities with Christianity, Augustine does not let them rest on their laurels, any more than he himself could rest in the knowledge and love to which they brought him in *Confessions,* Book 7. Owing to the wound of ignorance, he is suspicious of the idea that they came to the knowledge of the true God on their own. Developing an idea to which he had first alluded in *De doctrina christiana,* he now allows that perhaps what they knew of the one God was borrowed from the Hebrews, who had already received a Revelation of God's unity.[44] Owing to the wound of pride, he is also suspicious of the idea that the Neo-Platonists' knowledge of the one, true, God—however they acquired it—led to a participation in true contemplation. The Neo-Platonists were, as a matter of historical record, polytheists,[45] who looked not directly to the One in their worship, but to δαιμόνια (demons) as mediators.[46]

By seeking sacrificial fellowship with the δαιμόνια, the Platonists forwent any chance of obtaining the true happiness which they

University of Chicago Press, 2010); Benjamin Wood, *The Augustinian Alternative: Religious Skepticism and the Search for a Liberal Politics* (Minneapolis: Fortress, 2017).

42. Augustine, *De civitate Dei,* ed. B. Dombart and A. Kalb (Turnhout: Brepols, 1955), 8.5–6 [CCSL 47:221–24].

43. Ibid., 8.8 [CCSL 47:225].

44. Ibid., 8.11 [CCSL 47:228]. In *De doctrina christiana* 2.28.43 [CSSL 32.63], Augustine recounts an argument that Ambrose had with the Neo-Platonists. They had alleged that Christ used Plato as a source of his teachings. Ambrose rebutted that Plato must have encountered Jeremiah the Prophet on his journey to Egypt. Augustine does not embrace Ambrose's view; he merely says that it is "more likely" (*probabilius*). In *De civitate Dei* 8.11, he returns to Ambrose's view, but now recognizes that it is historically impossible because Jeremiah was dead by the time that Plato arrived in Egypt. Instead, Augustine embraces a more limited view: Plato probably learned what he could of the Hebrew Scriptures orally through an interpreter.

45. Augustine, *De civitate Dei* 8.1, 8.10 [CCSL 47:216–17, 226–27].

46. Ibid., 8.16–18 [CCSL 47:233–35].

had otherwise discovered. Sacrificial worship brings a person into communion with the object of that worship, and by sacrificing to δαιμόνια, the Platonists received a share in the unhappiness which they knew to be the perpetual lot of creatures who were subject to passion and change in a manner similar to human beings.[47] This unhappiness, amplified among those pagans who lacked even the Neo-Platonists' philosophical knowledge of the one, true God,[48] not only led to the disintegration of paganism on an individual level, but also to the disintegration of paganism on a communal level. For a true republic (*res publica*), as Augustine quotes Cicero, can only exist where the leaders and people together live as "a multitude bound together by consent to what is right [*iuris consensu*] and participation in what is good [*utilitatis communione*]."[49] If the leaders were to lack justice, the *res publica* would become a matter of their own selfish concern rather than that of the people. If the people were to lack

47. Ibid., 8.17 [CCSL 47:234].

48. See ibid., 6.5–12 [CCSL 47:172–84], where Augustine engages Varro's distinctions among the theology of the poets, the philosophers, and the politicians. While Augustine exalts the theology of the philosophers in Book 8 (within the limits explained above), here he reduces the theology of the politicians to that of the poets, and dismisses both as mere fables.

49. Cicero, *De rep.* 1.25.39, cited in Augustine, *De civitate Dei* 2.21 [CCSL 47:53–54]: "Populum ... iuris consensu et utilitatis communione sociatum esse determinat." Just like *Confessions*, Book 1, this phrase is extremely difficult to translate. Dodds, Bettenson, Dyson, and Babcock each relativize the first requirement of the definition by treating *ius* as an indefinite noun. They thereby remove any reference to an objective sense of right and wrong from the word. This is a reasonable way of rendering the Latin, and it can also explain why Augustine says in the course of the chapter that a community with corrupted *leaders* is not a republic, but it cannot make sense of why Augustine says that a community with a corrupted *people* is not a republic (i.e., because it does not fit the definition quoted here). If *ius* is an indefinite noun, why would not any given people with common agreement as to what is right satisfy the definition, no matter what they happen to think is right? Only if *ius* and *utilitas* imply some objective content in Augustine's thinking can his denial that a corrupted people constitute a republic according to Cicero's definition be coherent. Both Markus, *Saeculum*, 64–66, and Dodaro, *Christ and the Just Society in Augustine*, 11–12, make a similar observation, pointing out that Augustine's contrast between Rome and the Church hinges on a word play in Cicero between "right" (*ius*) and "justice" (*iustitia*), both of which imply objective content. The difference between Markus and Dodaro is that Markus finds Augustine's definition impracticable except in heaven, while Dodaro thinks that the healing grace of Christ makes it possible to instantiate it on earth within the Church.

justice, they would no longer be bound together as a people (*populus*) by consent to what is right or participation in what is good, and so there could be nothing truly public (*publica*) about the object of their concern. But since, as a matter of fact, the leaders and people alike had placed themselves in communion with δαιμόνια, Augustine's judgment on Rome is severe: "[Rome] was never a republic, because there was never true justice in it.... rather, there is only true justice in that republic, whose founder and leader is Christ."[50] Seen within an anti-Pelagian context, Augustine's political theology is thus as consciously Christocentric as his theological anthropology.

However bleak Augustine's outlook on Rome may seem, the earthly city in *De civitate Dei* need not be thought of as closed to grace any more than the individual in *De Trinitate*. If we return to Augustine's treatment of the Platonists, we find that he follows *De Trinitate* on the implicit manner in which fallen human desire anticipates a happiness which can only be found in God.

> For now, let it suffice to recall Plato's conclusion that the end of the good is to live according to virtue, and that it can come about for he alone, who not only knows God but also imitates him. Nor is there anything else that can make him happy. That is why he had no doubt that to love God, whose nature is incorporeal, is truly what it means to philosophize. Indeed, that is why he figured that someone intent on wisdom (for that is what a "philosopher" is) will be happy when he begins to enjoy God. That said, he who enjoys what he loves is not continually happy, for many are made wretched by loving those things which ought not be loved, and even more wretched when they enjoy them. And yet, no one is happy who does not enjoy what he loves. For even those, who love things which should not be loved, do not think that they are happy in loving them, but in enjoying them.[51]

50. Augustine, *De civitate Dei* 2.21 [CCSL 47:55]: "numquam [Romam] fuisse rem publicam, quia numquam in ea fuerit uera iustitia.... uera autem iustitia non est nisi in ea re publica, cuius conditor rectorque Christus est."

51. Ibid., 8.8 [CCSL 47:225]: "Nunc satis sit commemorare Platonem determinasse finem boni esse secundum uirtutem uiuere et ei soli euenire posse, qui notitiam Dei habeat et imitationem nec esse aliam ob causam beatum; ideoque non dubitat hoc esse philosophari, amare Deum, cuius natura sit incorporalis. Vnde utique colligitur tunc fore beatum studiosum sapientiae (id enim est philosophus), cum frui Deo coeperit. Quamuis enim

As the desire of the fallen individual anticipates the desire of the saints, because it seeks a happiness that can only be found in God, so does the love of the fallen community anticipate the love of the communion of saints, because it seeks the same happiness.[52] This anticipation can happen in greater and lesser degrees, because the objects of the community's love can approach by varying degrees the object of true enjoyment, the Trinity.[53] Hence, when Augustine says that Rome was not a true republic because the only true republic is Christ's, he nevertheless admits that "[Rome] was a sort of republic in its own way,"[54] because a "people" can also be thought of as "a group of a rational multitude bound together by a harmonious sharing [*concordi communione*] in the objects which it loves."[55] Comparing the Romans to this second definition, he grants them some leeway: "according to this definition of ours, the Roman people is a people [*populus*] and its community [*res*] is without a doubt a republic [*res publica*]."[56] Nevertheless, he hastens to remind the reader that their seeming virtues, directed as they were toward δαιμόνια, were really vices, which needed to be healed by the grace of Christ through true sacrificial and sacramental worship.[57]

Thus, while saying that fallen communities seek the objects of their fallen love seems to imply, as it did for fallen individuals, that there is no place for God in their restless hearts, the contour of Au-

---

non continuo beatus sit, qui eo fruitur quod amat (multi enim amando ea, quae amanda non sunt, miseri sunt et miseriores cum fruuntur): nemo tamen beatus est, qui eo quod amat non fruitur. Nam et ipsi, qui res non amandas amant, non se beatos putant, amando, sed fruendo."

52. Ibid., 8.25, 8.27 [CCSL 47:207, 209–10].

53. The importance of degrees of participation in the nature of a republic is explained in Pecknold, "Church and Politics," 461.

54. Augustine, *De civitate Dei* 2.21 [CCSL 47:55]: "pro suo modo quodam res publica fuit."

55. Ibid., 19.24 [CCSL 47:695]: "Populus est coetus multitudinis rationalis rerum quas diligit concordi communione sociatus."

56. Ibid.: "Secundum istam definitionem nostram Romanus populus populus est et res eius sine dubitatione res publica." On the juxtaposition of the two definitions of a *res publica*, see Pecknold, "Church and Politics," 460–61.

57. Augustine, *De civitate Dei*, 19.25 [CCSL 47:696]. Pecknold, "Church and Politics," 460.

gustine's teaching on nature, grace, and the desire for God is similar in *De Trinitate* and *De civitate Dei.* Where fallen man is trapped in a world of self-desire in *De Trinitate,* the fallen community is shaped by self-love in *De civitate Dei.* Where fallen man organizes his life around the search for the fulfillment of his desire in *De Trinitate,* the fallen community organizes its life around—indeed is defined by—the object of its love in *De civitate Dei.* Where grace converts the heart to long for true happiness in *De Trinitate,* the same grace converts the community to love the source of true happiness in *De civitate Dei.* Where that grace blossoms in a communal, analogical ascent to its Triune Giver in *De Trinitate,* the same grace frees the heavenly city from the lust for power, and draws it upwards in *De civitate Dei* into the very mystical participation in the Church Triumphant which Augustine himself experienced at Ostia.

THE THOMISTIC TRADITION'S NATURAL DESIRE FOR GOD

By the time that Thomas Aquinas became a bachelor of the Sentences at the University Paris in 1252,[58] significant discussions of nature, grace, and the desire for God had already been underway at the university for approximately twenty years. At the heart of those discussions lay the challenge of integrating two very different starting points for the conversation: the Latin Augustinian tradition, received from the Carolingian monasteries through the cathedral schools of the twelfth century,[59] which from the late 1220s quickly began to dominate theological speculation at the University of Paris in the form given it by Peter Lombard's *Book of Sentences,*[60] and

58. On the dates associated with Thomas's life and work, I follow Jean-Pierre Torrell, *The Person and His Work,* vol. 1 of *Saint Thomas Aquinas,* trans. Robert Royal (Washington, D.C.: The Catholic University of America Press, 2000).

59. The classic text on this period of transition is Beryl Smalley, *The Study of the Bible in the Middle Ages* (Notre Dame, Ind.: University of Notre Dame Press, 1989). Smalley's historiography, as well as recent criticisms of it, will be discussed in chapter 1.

60. The *Sentences* will be discussed in detail in chapter 1. On the significance of the

the Greek, Arabic, and Hebrew Aristotelian traditions, which were gradually assimilated into Latin theology from the twelfth century onwards.[61]

However individual scholastics responded to the challenge of appropriating this double tradition—and we shall see in the chapters that follow that their responses were not at all uniform—"natural desire" remained for them, as it had been for Augustine, a central component of any account of the experience of humanity before God. For this reason, the discussion of natural desire sparked repeated controversies over the next eight hundred years, whether in thirteenth- and fourteenth-century debates about matter, form, and the temporal power of the papacy,[62] sixteenth- and seventeenth-century debates about grace, free will, and the divine right of kings,[63] or

Sentences and of Peter Lombard's theology more generally, see Marcia Colish, *Peter Lombard*, 2 vols. (Boston: Brill, 1994); Philipp Rosemann, *Peter Lombard* (New York: Oxford University Press, 2004); Philipp Rosemann, *The Story of a Great Medieval Book: Peter Lombard's* Sentences (New York: Broadview Press, 2007).

61. The entry of Aristotle into the Latin West will be discussed in detail in chapter 1. For a general overview, see Fernand van Steenberghen, *La philosophie au xiiie siècle*, 2nd ed. (Louvain: Peeters, 1991), 75–82; Robert Pasnau, "The Latin Aristotle," in *The Oxford Handbook of Aristotle*, ed. Christopher Shields (New York: Oxford University Press, 2012), 666–85.

62. In the debate between King Philip IV and Pope Boniface VIII over the temporal power of the papacy, theologians on both sides used natural desire to explain the relationship between kings and priests. Giles of Rome argued for Boniface that man has an exclusively supernatural end, so human community has an exclusively ecclesial character. When Giles used the relationship between matter and form as an analogy to explain how kings have an absolute dependence on priests, his student James of Viterbo had to argue for matter's quasi-independent existence from form in order to explain the historical fact—somewhat embarrassingly brought up by John of Paris (Jean Quidort)—that there have been kings in history apart from priests. The key texts in the controversy are Giles of Rome, *De ecclesiastica potestate*, in *Giles of Rome's On Ecclesiastical Power: A Medieval Theory of World Government*, trans. and ed. Robert Dyson (New York: Columbia University Press, 2004); Jean Quidort, *De potestate regia et papali* in *Jean de Paris et l'ecclésiologie du XIIIe siècle*, ed. Jean Leclercq (Paris: J. Vrin, 1942), translated by J. A. Watt as John of Paris, *On Royal and Papal Power* (Toronto: PIMS, 1971); James of Viterbo, *De regimine christiano: A Critical Edition and Translation*, ed. Robert W. Dyson (Boston: Brill, 2009). Giles's understanding of natural desire will be explored in chapter 6.

63. In the debate between King James I and Francisco Suárez over the divine right of kings, Suárez used his understanding of the congruence of divine and human action, together with his understanding of an innate, natural desire for a natural end, to explain

nineteenth- and twentieth-century debates about nature, natural rights, and liberal democracy.[64]

One of the topics that came to occupy a central place in discussions of nature, grace, and the desire for God from the thirteenth century onwards is the historical question of what Thomas Aquinas thought about the subject. So pivotal had been his synthesis of the Augustinian and Aristotelian traditions when he lived, that—notwithstanding the early controversies shortly after his death over his opinions on the unicity of substantial form and the complete pas-

---

the relationship among kings, communities, and the Church. Suárez argued that human community, like the human individual, possesses an inherent and inviolable freedom, which is naturally ordered toward God as first cause, but which has an indirect duty to submit itself to the Church so that it can be elevated to its supernatural end. For a summary of the debate between Suárez and James I, and of the political and anthropological consequences of the *De auxiliis* controversy more generally, see Jacob Wood, "The 500th Anniversary of the Reformation: A Catholic Perspective," in *Reformation Observances: 1517–2017*, ed. Philip Krey (Eugene, Ore.: Cascade, 2017), 69–93. Suárez's understanding of natural desire will be explored in chapter 6.

64. In the debate between Maurice Blondel and Pedro Descoqs over Charles Maurras and *Action Française*, Blondel used his understanding of a natural desire for a transcendent end to argue that any political system which wed Catholicism to a particular form of a government compromised the supernatural end of man. Descoqs used his understanding of a natural desire for a natural end to argue that it was Blondel's natural desire for a transcendent end which compromised the supernatural end of man by destroying the gratuity of grace. For a summary of the debate between Blondel and Descoqs, see Peter Bernardi, *Maurice Blondel, Social Catholicism, and Action Française: The Clash over the Church's Role in Society during the Modernist Era* (Washington, D.C.: The Catholic University of America Press, 2009), 89–118.

In Blondel and Descoqs, the medieval debate between Giles of Rome and John of Paris gets reversed. For Giles, the natural desire for a supernatural end supports a maximalist view of the integration of Church and State; for Blondel, a similar desire leads to their separation. This reversal took place gradually through nineteenth-century French responses to the Revolution. See my "Ressourcement," in *The T&T Clark Companion to Henri de Lubac*, ed. Jordan Hillebert (New York: T&T Clark, 2017), 93–119. The shift has not gone entirely unnoticed in contemporary scholarship. Although he does not document how or when it took place, John Milbank, *The Suspended Middle: Henri de Lubac and the Debate concerning the Supernatural* (Grand Rapids: Eerdmans, 2005), 59, notes that it has occurred, and, although he is speaking of de Lubac rather than Blondel, attempts to return the discussion to its medieval terms. Perceiving the integralist consequences of Milbank's reversal, Bernard Mulcahy, *Aquinas's Notion of Pure Nature and the Christian Integralism of Henri de Lubac: Not Everything Is Grace* (New York: Peter Lang, 2011), 194–96, 209–12, criticizes Milbank for compromising the integrity of human nature both in theological anthropology and in political theology.

sivity of matter[65]—Thomas became a widely reputed, and, in a couple of cases, legally mandated, theological authority within a few decades.[66] Ultimately, Thomas's thought came to achieve, for most of the second millennium of the Church, a prominence analogous to—though admittedly not equal with—that which Augustine's enjoyed by the end of the first. Thus it was that Thomas came to share Augustine's theological fate, and there arose in the second millennium a variety of Thomisms to complement the even greater variety of Augustinianisms.[67] This was particularly the case concerning Thom-

65. The principal source of the controversy shortly after Thomas's death was the condemnation in 1277 of 219 propositions by the bishop of Paris, Étienne Tempier. As Torrell, *Saint Thomas Aquinas*, 1:300–303, observes, the condemnations do not contain any extracts from Thomas's works, but they do contain fifty-one extracts from the works of his student, Giles of Rome, used in such a way that the thought of Thomas himself could be indirectly condemned through the thought of Giles.

The condemnations remained in effect into the 1280s, and when the papal legate to France, Simon de Brion, who had played a pivotal role in bringing them about, was elected pope as Martin IV, there was little chance of Giles appealing against them until after the conclusion of his pontificate. Almost immediately after the election of his successor, Honorius IV, Giles of Rome presented himself to Honorius and promised to submit himself to Honorius's judgment. Honorius remanded the question to the theologians at Paris, who exonerated Giles, and Giles began his regency as a master of theology that year. Honorius's letter, which mentions Giles's visit, can be found in *Chartularium Universitatis Parisiensis*, vol. 1, ed. Heinrich Denifle (Paris: Delalain, 1889), 633.

66. There were two decrees concerning the status of Thomas within the Dominican Order at the time. While the censure of 1277 was still in force, it was decreed in 1279 that no one could disparage his writings. After the censure was lifted, it was decreed in 1286 that everyone had to show that his opinions were defensible. See Torrell, *Saint Thomas Aquinas*, 1:309.

The Augustinian Order followed suit in 1287. They adopted Giles of Rome as their official doctor in 1287, decreeing that all the members of the Order had not only to show that Giles's opinions were defensible, but to defend them actively, and to have recourse to Thomas's opinions whenever there was a question as to what Giles intended. See David Gutiérrez, *The Augustinians in the Middle Ages, 1256–1356*, vol. 1, pt. 1, of *History of the Order of St. Augustine* (Villanova, Penn.: Augustinian Historical Institute, 1984), 139.

67. On the variety of Augustinianisms that developed in this period, see Eric Saak, *Creating Augustine: Interpreting Augustine and Augustinianism in the Later Middle Ages* (Oxford: Oxford University Press, 2012); on the variety of Thomisms that would ultimately develop, see *Aquinas as Authority: A Collection of Studies Presented at the Second Conference of the Thomas Instituut te Utrecht, December 14–16, 2000*, ed. Paul van Geest, Harm Goris, and Carlo Leget (Leuven: Peeters, 2002); Fergus Kerr, *After Aquinas: Versions of Thomism* (New York: Wiley Blackwell, 2008); Gerald McCool, *From Unity to Pluralism: The Internal Evolution of Thomism* (New York: Fordham University Press, 2002); Brian Shanley, *The Thomist Tradition* (London: Springer, 2011).

as's understanding of the desire for God. As Lawrence Feingold observes, the texts of Thomas discussing natural desire are easy enough to locate, but notoriously difficult to make sense of.[68]

Thomists never did come to an agreement about how Thomas himself understood natural desire, although, as Feingold also observes, the majority of theologians in the Thomistic tradition came to agree more or less with the interpretation given by Francisco Suárez, SJ (1548–1617).[69] According to Suárez, there are actually two kinds of desire in the human person that can be called "natural." One is innate, absolute, and non-free; by this desire the human will is oriented toward an end which it can naturally achieve: the philosophical knowledge of God as first cause. The other is elicited, conditional, and free; by this desire the human will is oriented toward an end which it cannot naturally achieve: the vision of the divine essence, to which grace alone can raise us. Suárez's synthesis had a number of benefits: it accounted for the integrity of human nature as a created good; it gave nature a way to desire a supernatural end; it accounted for the gratuity both of our supernatural end and of the grace which raises us to it; and it laid the groundwork—as Suárez himself recognized—for an understanding of political theology which balanced the integrity of human communities with their openness to the Church.[70]

Yet however much Suárez seemed to have captured the essence of Thomism, he never quite succeeded in convincing everyone that he had captured the essence of Thomas himself. There was always a contingent of theologians who accepted Thomas as a patron of their thought, who saw in nature *itself* a desire for the vision of God, and

68. Lawrence Feingold, *The Natural Desire to See God according to St. Thomas Aquinas and His Interpreters*, 2nd ed. (Naples, Fla.: Sapientia Press, 2010), 44.

69. Ibid., 276: "Suárez completed the work of forming a classical synthesis concerning the interpretation of the natural desire to see God that remained basically unchanged for over three hundred years." For a summary of his view, see ibid., 221–59, 263–67. Suárez's understanding of natural desire will be discussed in chapter 6.

70. On the political implications of Suárez's anthropology, see Suárez, *Defensio Fidei Catholicae Adversus Anglicanae Sectae Errores*, in *Opera Omnia* (Paris: Vivès, 1859), 3.2 [24:206–12], 3.5–6 [24:224–38].

who therefore saw Christ and the Church as indispensable mediators of human happiness. That tradition had its origin in a student of Thomas, Giles of Rome (Aegidius Romanus), the first Parisian master of theology from the Order of the Hermits of St. Augustine (OESA). Giles's religious order may be much better known for the other movement of thought that arose within it, a radical Augustinianism which developed from the time of Gregory of Rimini and which ultimately nurtured a young friar, Martin Luther, to the point that he broke with Rome.[71] But there never ceased to exist within the Augustinian Order a tradition of appealing to Thomas through Giles, a tradition which we might call "Aegidian Thomism," and which—though it was often confused by Thomists of other traditions with heterodox Augustinianisms of one form or another—was never proscribed by ecclesiastical authority as in any way compromising the Christian vision of nature, grace, and the desire for God.[72]

Aegidian Thomism was never as popular as its alternatives. In the fourteenth and fifteenth centuries, it lived in the shadow of Domin-

71. The connection between Martin Luther and the Order of the Hermits of St. Augustine has received a significant amount of scholarly attention over the last century. The debate concerns whether it is accurate to identify an "Augustinian School" in the fourteenth and fifteenth centuries, and is summarized in Denis Janz, *Luther and Late Medieval Thomism: A Study in Theological Anthropology* (Waterloo, Ont.: Wilfrid Laurier University Press, 1983), 158–65. While avoiding any naïveté about any supposed uniformity among "schools" in the Middle Ages or their association with particular religious orders, we can at least identify a general trend in Gregory toward a radical Augustinianism which juxtaposes Augustine and Thomas rather than reading the two together, and which is not shared uniformly among the members of the Order.

72. An excellent introduction to the tradition and its major thinkers can still be found in E. Portalié, "Augustinianisme," in *Dictionnaire de théologie catholique*, vol. 1, no. 2, ed. Alfred Vacant, E. Mangenot, and Emile Amann (Paris: Letouzey et Ané, 1903) cols. 2485–2501. More recently, see Agostino Trapè, "Scuola teologica e spiritualità nell'Ordine Agostiniano," in *S. Augustinus vitae spiritualis magister* (Rome Analecta Augustiniana, 1956), 2:7–75; Eric Saak, *High Way to Heaven: The Augustinian Platform between Reform and Reformation, 1292–1524* (Boston: Brill, 2002). For an introduction to the pre-Reformation tradition, see Adolar Zumkeller, *Theology and History of the Augustinian School in the Middle Ages*, trans. John Rotelle (Villanova, Penn.: Augustinian Press, 1996); concerning the post-Reformation tradition, see Winfried Bocxe, *Introduction to the Teaching of the Italian Augustinians of the 18th Century on the Nature of Actual Grace* (Louvain: Augustinian Historical Institute, 1958); Léon Renwart, "Augustiniens du XVIIIe siècle et 'Nature Pure,'" (S.T.D. diss., Institut Catholique de Paris, 1948).

ican Thomism; in the sixteenth and seventeenth centuries, it lived in the shadow of Jesuit Thomism; in the eighteenth century, it lived in the shadow of Jansenism, with which it was often associated, but with which it was never condemned. Yet from the mid-nineteenth century, it began to attract a slow and steady following from outside the religious order which had been its traditional home: first, in Auguste Gratry (1805–72), the re-founder of the Oratorians in France, who looked to it in order to recover the transcendence of humanity and human society amidst the empiricism of the Industrial Revolution, and whose student, Léon Ollé-Laprune (1839–98), passed on a similarly transcendent intellectual orientation to Maurice Blondel (1861–1949);[73] then in Gioacchino Sestili (1862–1939), a lay theologian and later third-order Servite, whose doctorate on the natural desire for God began the early twentieth-century scholastic debate that culminated in *Surnaturel*;[74] next in Hippolyte Ligeard (1878–1916), a Jesuit who appealed directly to the Aegidian tradition as a way to harmonize scholasticism with Blondel;[75] then at last in a young Jesuit scholastic, who followed Ligeard in seeking among the

73. Gratry's defense of the Aegidian tradition can be found in Auguste Gratry, *De la connaissance de Dieu*, 2nd ed. (Paris: C. Douniol, 1854), 2:416–20. On the connection between Gratry and Blondel, see Jacob Wood, "Ressourcement," 106–7.

74. Gioacchino Sestili, *In Summam theologicam S. Thomae Aquinatis Ia. Pe., Q. XII, A. I.: De naturali intelligentis animae capacitate atque appetitu intuendi divinam essentiam: Theologica disquisitio* (Rome: A. and Salvatore Festa, 1896). See also Gioacchino Sestili, *Il desiderio naturale d'intuire la divina essenza, in risposta ad una critica della Civiltà Cattolica* (Rome: F. Setth, 1897), which is a response to Salvatore Brandi, Review of *In Summam Theologicam S. Thomae Aquinatis I. P. Q. XII a. I–De naturalis intelligentis animae capacitate atque appetitu intuendi divinam essentiam, Theologica disquisitio*, by Gioacchino Sestili, *Civiltà Cattolica* 6, no. 1125 (May 1, 1897): 323–26, as well as Gioacchino Sestili, *De possibilitate desiderioque primae caussae [sic] substantiam videndi a criticis animadversionibus vidiciae* (Rome: Hospitii S. Hieronymi Aemiliani, 1900), which is a response to Carlo Ramellini, Review of *In Summam Theologicam S. Thomae Aquinatis I. P. Q. XII a. I–De naturalis intelligentis animae capacitate atque appetitu intuendi divinam essentiam, Theologica disquisitio*, by Gioacchino Sestili, *Divus Thomas* 6 (1897): 273–75, 327–31, 355–60, 423–27, 515–20.

75. Hippolyte Ligeard, "Le rapport de la nature et du Surnaturel d'après les théologiens scolastiques du XIIIe au XVIIIe siècles," *Revue Pratique de l'Apologétique* 5 (1908): 543–51, 621–48, 773–84, 861–77. Ligeard makes explicit appeals to the Aegidian tradition on pp. 773–76, 778–79, and 782–84.

theologians of the Aegidian tradition the scholastic formulation of a natural desire for a supernatural end, Henri de Lubac (1896–1991).[76] De Lubac's 1946 book, *Surnaturel,*[77] would give the Aegidian tradition's doctrine, if not its name, the greatest prominence it had ever known in its 700-year history.

HENRI DE LUBAC'S NATURAL DESIRE FOR A SUPERNATURAL END

It is hard to say why de Lubac's "natural desire for a supernatural end"—something which had been hiding in plain sight continuously from the thirteenth century to the twentieth—would cause such a significant uproar upon being publicized more widely.[78] Perhaps it was the contentious atmosphere of a Europe which had just concluded, but by no means recovered from, a second world war. Perhaps it was the increasingly polemical tone which the nature/grace debate had acquired after the First World War.[79] Perhaps it was something about the style of de Lubac's writing: the imposing array of sources, the agile but coy deployment of them to state "unstatable" criticisms of revered scholastic figures, the youthful exuberance and occasional excesses which belied the author's true age (he turned fifty in the year of its publication). Whatever the case may be, the publication of *Surnaturel* caused a revolution in Thomistic theology by making two fundamental claims. The first was that

76. The standard introduction to de Lubac's life and work is Georges Chantraine, *Henri de Lubac,* 4 vols. (Paris: Cerf, 2007–), of which the third volume has yet to appear. See also Antonio Russo, *Henri de Lubac: Biographie* (Turin: San Paolo, 1994); Rudolf Voderholzer, *Meet Henri de Lubac: His Life and Work,* trans. Michael J. Miller (San Francisco: Ignatius Press, 1988); Jean-Pierre Wagner, *Henri de Lubac* (Paris: Cerf, 2001).

77. Henri de Lubac, *Surnaturel: Études historiques* (Paris: Aubier, 1946).

78. For an account of the initial controversy, see Joseph Komonchak, "Theology and Culture at Mid-Century: The Example of Henri de Lubac," *Theological Studies* 51, no. 4 (1990): 579–602.

79. The contributions to that period of the nature/grace debate are too numerous to list here. A bibliography of them can be found in Heinrich Lennerz, *De deo uno,* 5th ed. (Rome: Gregorian University, 1955), 119n24, 128n28. Lennerz's two footnotes list nearly four pages of contributions to the debate in the sixteen-year period from 1924 to 1939.

Suárez, and with him nearly the entire Thomistic tradition of the several hundred years since, was wrong about natural desire. The tradition had unduly restricted humanity's innate, non-free desire to a naturally achievable end. Returning to the Augustinian experience of *Confessions*, Book 1, de Lubac argued that however estranged we may be from our God, "the desire to *see* him ... constitutes our very selves,"[80] in such a way that human nature has a "natural desire for a supernatural end." The second was that Suárez was wrong about Thomas Aquinas.[81] Following an exegetical mistake made originally by Tommaso de Vio "Cajetan," Suárez had wrongly restricted Thomas's account of desire to a naturally achievable object, the philosophical knowledge of God as First Cause. By placing the end of man within the unassisted reach of human nature, Cajetan, Suárez, and the Thomisms which followed from them realized Augustine's fundamental anti-Pelagian fear: by placing the object of human happiness within the reach of human nature, they opened the door to a secular vision of man,[82] who as an individual could pridefully rejoice in self-fulfillment apart from the Passion of Christ, and who as a community could dangerously assemble in a parody of the *communio sanctorum*, seeking universal human flourishing apart from the Church.[83]

In spite of the initial controversy surrounding its publication, de Lubac's "natural desire for a supernatural end" ultimately became the generally accepted basis of theological anthropology among Catholic theologians from the Second Vatican Council until the

80. Henri de Lubac, "Le mystère du surnaturel," *Recherches de Science Religieuse* 36 (1949): 111: "Le désir de Le *voir* ... il est nous-mêmes" (emphasis added).

81. De Lubac, *Surnaturel*, 431: "'Désir naturel du surnaturel': la plupart des théologiens qui repoussent cette formule, repousse avec elle la doctrine même de saint Thomas d'Aquin." Guy Mansini, "The Abiding Theological Significance of Henri de Lubac's *Surnaturel*," *The Thomist* 73, no. 4 (2009): 599, notes that this exegetical claim is part of what makes de Lubac's thesis so controversial.

82. De Lubac, *Surnaturel*, 153–54. See Mansini, "Abiding Theological Significance of Henri de Lubac's *Surnaturel*," 601; Christopher Malloy, "De Lubac on Natural Desire: Difficulties and Antitheses," *Nova et Vetera* (English)9, no. 3 (2011): 568–70.

83. The political-theological dimension of de Lubac's anthropological concerns were the subject of Henri de Lubac, *Le drame de l'humanisme athée* (Paris: Spes, 1944).

close of the twentieth century.[84] It stood behind the eschatological orientation of *Lumen gentium*,[85] the post-conciliar theology of the *Communio* movement,[86] and it bears an important relationship to the Augustinianism of Joseph Ratzinger, as found throughout curial documents published under Ratzinger's tenure as prefect for the Congregation for the Doctrine of the Faith, as well as his pontifical documents as Pope Benedict XVI.[87] Nevertheless, the consen-

84. For a summary of the consensus surrounding de Lubac's thesis, see Edward Oakes, "The *Surnaturel* Controversy: A Survey and a Response," *Nova et Vetera* (English) 9, no. 3 (2011): 627–34. For bibliographies of recent contributions to the nature/grace debate, which are too numerous to list here, see Thomas Bushlack, "The Return of Neo-Scholasticism? Recent Criticisms of Henri de Lubac on Nature and Grace and Their Significance for Moral Theology, Politics, and Law," *Journal of the Society of Christian Ethics* 35, no. 2 (2015): 83n2; Patrick Gardner, "Thomas and Dante on the *Duo Ultima Hominis*," *The Thomist* 75, no. 3 (2011): 416n2; Aaron Riches, "Christology and *duplex hominis beatitudo*: Re-sketching the Supernatural Again," *International Journal of Systematic Theology* 14, no. 1 (2012): 44n1.

85. See Joseph Ratzinger, "The Ecclesiology of the Second Vatican Council," in *Church, Ecumenism, and Politics: New Endeavors in Ecclesiology*, trans. Michael Miller et al. (San Francisco: Ignatius Press, 1987), 17; Jacques Prévotat, introduction to Henri de Lubac, *Vatican Council Notebooks*, vol. 1, trans. Andrew Stefanelli and Anne Englund Nash (San Francisco: Ignatius Press, 2015), 41n104; Hans Boersma, *Nouvelle Théologie and Sacramental Ontology: A Return to Mystery* (New York: Oxford University Press, 2012), 242.

86. De Lubac was a founding member of the journal *Communio* and of the theological movement associated with it. See Mansini, "Abiding Theological Significance of Henri de Lubac's *Surnaturel*," 596; Joseph Ratzinger, "Communio: A Program," *Communio* 19, no. 3 (1992): 439; David Schindler, *Heart of the World, Center of the Church: Communio Ecclesiology, Liberalism and Liberation* (Grand Rapids: Eerdmans, 2001), 30n48; Antonio Sicari, "'Communio' in Henri de Lubac," *Communio* 19, no. 3 (1992): 450–64. Mansini in particular notes how Catholic theology in the post-conciliar period can be categorized in terms of those who agree with de Lubac's theological anthropology (whether or not they follow other twentieth-century developments, such as the thought of Marie-Dominique Chenu on dogma) and those who do not (Mansini, "Abiding Theological Significance," 598).

87. See Pope Benedict XVI, *Spe salvi*, encyclical letter (November 30, 2007), no. 12. I am also grateful to Matthew Gonzalez, who made me aware of an important discrepancy between the *Catechism of the Catholic Church* and its *Compendium*. While the *Catechism of the Catholic Church*, published under Pope John Paul II, describes only a "desire for God" (CCC, no. 27), and thus prescinds from debates in the schools over whether the formal *terminus* of this desire is the natural knowledge of God, the vision of God as First Cause, or the beatific vision, the *Compendium of the Catechism of the Catholic Church*, published under Benedict XVI, speaks of a "desire to *see* God" (*Compendium*, nos. 2, 533; emphasis added). *Catechism of the Catholic Church*, second ed. (Vatican City:

sus on de Lubac's natural desire for a supernatural end has begun to wane since the beginning of the twenty-first century.[88] Few disagree that de Lubac's thought remains one of the guiding lights of theological anthropology in the post-conciliar Church.[89] But beginning with the completion of Lawrence Feingold's dissertation in 2001 and its subsequent publication in a second edition in 2010, a number of scholars have begun to question the consistency and accuracy of de Lubac's thought.[90] These criticisms come from two opposite directions. Neo-Thomistic scholars claim that de Lubac went too far. Appealing to the Dominican and Jesuit Thomistic traditions, they argue that the natural desire for a supernatural end compromises the integrity of nature and the integrity of the natural law. It therefore jeopardizes the normativity of theism in human society, which is derived from the natural law; the integrity of the liberal democratic state, which is founded ideally upon the natural virtue of religion, ordered toward a theistic end; and the mission of the Church, whose Sacraments perfect a theistic nature by setting it by grace on the road to glory. As a matter of history, they claim that de Lubac's denial of a natural end is a misrepresentation of the thought of Thomas Aquinas. Thomas never challenged Augustine's fundamental insight that human persons and human communities are by nature *capax dei*,[91] but he did repeatedly emphasize that man is absolutely passive with respect to grace, and that grace is absolutely gratuitous with respect

Libreria Editrice Vaticana, 2000); *Compendium: Catechism of the Catholic Church* (Washington, D.C.: U.S. Conference of Catholic Bishops, 2006).

88. Malloy, "De Lubac on Natural Desire," 567; Oakes, "*Surnaturel* Controversy," 626.

89. On the contemporary significance of de Lubac's thesis, see Mansini, "Abiding Theological Significance of Henri de Lubac's *Surnaturel*," 593–619. More recently, one may also consult the essays in *The T&T Clark Companion to Henri de Lubac*, ed. Jordan Hillebert (Edinburgh: T&T Clark, 2017).

90. See Lawrence Feingold, *The Natural Desire to See God according to St. Thomas Aquinas and His Interpreters* (Rome: Apollinare Studi, 2001); Feingold, *Natural Desire to See God* (2010). See also Steven Long, *Natura Pura: On the Recovery of Nature in the Doctrine of Grace* (New York: Fordham, 2010); Malloy, "De Lubac on Natural Desire"; Mulcahy, *Aquinas's Notion of Pure Nature*.

91. Feingold, *Natural Desire to See God* (2010), 395.

to nature. If there were a motion in nature toward grace and/or glory, that would make grace and glory a *debitum naturae*, a debt which God himself would be obliged to pay.

Theologians of the Radical Orthodoxy movement, by contrast, claim that de Lubac did not go far enough. John Milbank, in particular, argues that de Lubac's revolution was limited by the constraints of his day, especially those of ecclesiastical authority and patriarchy.[92] Had de Lubac carried his thinking about nature's active relationship to grace far enough, he would have seen that the very division between passive and active, between nature and grace, is itself an imposition on the self-gift which God gives Creation. This gift endows Creation with its own sphere of activity by means of "influence," in which God, as the primary cause, is understood to act *within* secondary causes, without there being any competition between the two.[93] The rigorous distinction between nature and grace that we find in Dominican and Jesuit Thomism is the result of a fourteenth-century revolution in metaphysics, in which a "concursus" theory of secondary causality replaced the older, influence theory.[94] A concursus theory introduces competition between primary and secondary causes, such that what is attributed to one cannot be attributed to the other. In this way, what is attributed to nature cannot be attributed to grace and vice versa. The scholastic emphasis on man's ability to achieve a natural end therefore leads to a secular vision of man, in which the human person is thought to be sufficient apart from God's grace, and human community, apart from the Church.[95]

92. Milbank, *Suspended Middle*, 107: "De Lubac belonged to a particular generation and within that generation he was incomparable. Yet this generation scarcely prepared him to deal with all the many problematic dimensions of patriarchal authority that I have indicated above."

93. Ibid., 90–92.

94. Ibid., 92–94.

95. See John Milbank, Catherine Pickstock, and Graham Ward, introduction to *Radical Orthodoxy: A New Theology*, ed. John Milbank, Catherine Pickstock, and Graham Ward (New York: Routledge, 2006), 2; Milbank, *Suspended Middle*; Mansini, "Abiding Theological Significance of Henri de Lubac's *Surnaturel*," 608. For a critical evaluation of Milbank's reading of de Lubac, see Reinhard Hütter, *Dust Bound for Heaven: Explorations in the Theology of Thomas Aquinas* (Grand Rapids: Eerdmans, 2012), 136–44.

Each side of the debate accuses the other of being responsible for modern man's, and modern society's, estrangement from God. Neo-Thomists accuse de Lubac of compromising the integrity of nature by denying that nature has a natural end, of compromising the gratuity of grace by denying that nature is passive toward grace, and of compromising the integrity of human nature and of human community by allowing human individuals and communities to see their perfection as a debt which God is obliged to pay them. Radical Orthodoxy accuses Neo-Thomism of compromising the integrity of nature by denying that nature has a supernatural end, of compromising the gratuity of grace by denying that divine influence infuses into nature a natural desire for a supernatural end, and of compromising the integrity of human nature and human community by allowing human individuals and communities to see their own achievement of perfection as competitive with God's gift thereof. This is a disadvantageous situation for the Church. If the Church is to continue to preach Christ crucified to the world today, then in her attempt to describe the situation of man before the crucified God, she cannot risk making the grace which flows from the cross superfluous.

Many theologians argue that the two sides of the contemporary nature/grace debate are simply irreconcilable with one another, and so the Church must ultimately choose between them in her mission of evangelization. Michel Sales, for example, argues that de Lubac's natural desire for a supernatural end saved theology from the Thomistic commentators' "extrinsicist" account of grace, which so separated man from God that it "risked leading nature and grace, human and divine life, the temporal and the spiritual, from separation to confusion."[96] On the opposite side of the debate, Feingold is equally certain of the irreconcilability of the two positions. It is simply "impossible" to reconcile de Lubac's innate, unconditional desire to see

96. Michel Sales, preface to de Lubac, *Surnaturel: Études historiques* (Paris: Lethielleux, 2010), xii: "Le point de doctrine que touchait le Père de Lubac . . . était bien à même de . . . montrer les conséquences ruineuses d'une théorie risquant de conduire de la séparation à la confusion de la nature et de la grâce, de la vie humaine et de la vie chrétienne, du temporel et du spirituel."

God with the commentators' elicited, conditional desire to see God. The two are diametrically opposed: innate is the opposite of elicited, and unconditional is the opposite of conditional.[97]

There are a few scholars who have proposed that some sort of rapprochement is possible. Reinhard Hütter thinks that de Lubac rightly insists on man's active capacity for the vision of God.[98] While he continues to reject, with Feingold, the idea of an innate, unconditional desire for the vision of God, Hütter advances a step closer to the Lubacian thesis by grounding man's capacity for the beatific vision in the *activity* of the powers of intellect and will. Nicholas Healy is similarly conciliatory. Allowing for a *penultimate* end to human nature would preserve de Lubac's fundamental commitment to a single, *ultimate* end for man, while supplying what is necessary to meet the criticisms of his detractors.[99] With Hütter and Healy, contemporary critics and supporters of de Lubac have come close to one another. Nevertheless, Hütter's intellect still has a complete natural finality; Healy's penultimate end is still not enough to satisfy human nature. Either human nature's constitutive desire seeks a natural or a supernatural end; either it can be explained without reference to Revelation and the vision of God, or it cannot; either our restless hearts seek the knowledge of God or the vision of him; either our communities are complete in themselves or they yearn for the completeness of the heavenly city.

97. Feingold, *Natural Desire to See God*, 428.

98. Hütter, *Dust Bound for Heaven*, 242–44. While insisting on the necessity of a finality proportioned to the natural powers of the soul, Hütter avoids using the language of "ultimate end" with respect to this natural finality. "Without a proportionate proximate finality of human nature toward which humans are able to move on the basis of their nature, there would exist no active potency for sanctifying grace to presuppose and to perfect" (ibid., 243).

99. Nicholas Healy, "Henri de Lubac on Nature and Grace: A Note on Some Recent Contributions to the Debate," *Communio* 35, no. 4 (2008): 553; Malloy, "De Lubac on Natural Desire," 576n39.

A THIRTEENTH-CENTURY RESOLUTION?

In spite of the difficulties at which the debate has arrived, I would like to suggest that it is not necessarily as intractable as it may seem. If we take a step back and a closer look at how Thomas Aquinas handled the Augustinian and Aristotelian traditions in his day, Thomas himself may offer us the *via media* between de Lubac and his critics.[100] When Thomas began his career, questions of Augustine's desire were often thought through on analogy with Aristotle's claim that matter desires form.[101] Thomas thought that matter is absolutely passive with respect to form, and yet that it also has what he called a natural "appetite" for form, a purely passive receptivity for it; by analogy, he affirmed that human nature is absolutely passive with respect to grace, and yet that it has a natural appetite for the vision of God. At the beginning of his career, he taught that when our natural appetite is actualized and given motion in the form of a natural desire, our natural desire does indeed seek God as its object, but it seeks only the analogical knowledge of God as First Cause such as Augustine experienced among the Neo-Platonists, not the beatific vision of God by grace, such as Augustine longed to experience at Ostia. But by the end of his career, Thomas had found a way to bring the two together, and in so doing to capture the essence of Augustine's anti-Pelagian anthropology in an Aristotelian mode: in yearning for its own fulfillment, even our natural *desire* seeks at least implicitly the complete fulfillment of our natural appetite in the vision of God, insofar as is possible.

The principal challenge in giving a consistent interpretation of the Thomistic corpus lies not so much in identifying the texts of the Thomistic corpus that touch upon natural desire or in placing them on a timeline. Even if some of our editions could be improved, we

100. Hütter, *Dust Bound for Heaven*, 138–40, notes that the lack of consideration for such historical approaches to the question is among the reasons that Feingold's work produced such a dramatic reaction among some of his critics.

101. Aristostle, *Physica*, ed. David Ross (New York: Oxford, 1951), 1.9 [192a22].

possess editions of every known work of Thomas, and since the days of Mandonnet we have developed an ever-increasing level of accuracy in dating them. Rather, as Feingold intimates, even when we locate the texts and place them on a timeline, the challenge remains of explaining how they fit with Thomas's other teachings, as well as how they answer the difficult questions they seem to raise about matter and form, intellect and will, and nature and grace.[102] The principal obstacle in meeting this challenge has until recently been our lack of an account of the contemporary sources upon which Thomas was drawing, and the contemporary interlocutors with whom he was interacting. But with the rapid progress of historical-textual scholarship in the last century, it has now become possible to revisit the question of identifying Thomas's sources, and to ask whether the story of the development of Thomas's understanding of natural desire, which connects his seemingly inconsistent comments about natural desire with one another, may yet be brought to light.

This book attempts to fill that lacuna. It tells the story of the development of Thomas's understanding of natural desire in connection with his three major theological syntheses, the *Commentary on the Sentences,* the *Summa contra Gentiles,* and the *Summa theologiae.* In each case, it will seek to establish the historical setting of Thomas's teaching on natural desire, the broader set of concerns within which he was thinking about it, the principal interlocutors with whom he was thinking about it, and the ways in which he developed his thinking about it since the last time he had considered it, insofar as our current knowledge of thirteenth-century figures will allow. It will do the same for other works among the Thomistic corpus which touch upon natural desire, and whose dating is known with enough certainty and accuracy to place them on the timeline between the three aforementioned works.[103] Having told the story of how Aqui-

102. Feingold, *Natural Desire to See God,* 45.

103. Since the contours along which Thomas's thought developed concerning natural desire have not previously been shown, this methodology is necessary in order to allow us to begin to establish them for the first time with sufficient accuracy, especially since Thomas's thought often undergoes significant developments within the space of a

nas's thought on nature, grace, and the desire for God developed, it will then offer a rereading of de Lubac's thought and that of certain pivotal figures from the Thomistic tradition in light of that story.[104]

Chapter 1 begins the process of unearthing the conversation about natural desire at the University of Paris in the 1230s and 1240s. It looks at the reception of the Augustinian tradition mediated through Peter Lombard's *Sentences,* which followed Book 13 of Augustine's *De Trinitate,* as well as Philip the Chancellor's *Summa de bono,* which set the tone for the decades that followed in attempting to harmonize Augustine's understanding of nature, grace, and the desire for God with Aristotle. It then looks at subsequent figures, who approached the Aristotelian tradition mediated through the Arabic philosophers Avicenna and Averroes: Richard Rufus, Roger Bacon, William of Auvergne, the *Summa fratris Alexandri,* Albert the Great, and Bonaventure. Almost all of them utilized Avicenna's account of natural motion to posit some active principle in nature toward God. Bonaventure was the great synthesizer of their thought, teaching that our natural desire tends beyond the limits of our nature toward its complete perfection in the vision of God. Albert was their principal exception, teaching that our natural desire finds its fulfillment in the analogical knowledge of God as First Cause.

---

few years. This means that, among the works which are generally regarded as having been composed at least partially between the *Commentary on the Sentences* and the *Prima secundae,* it will not be possible to include a discussion of the following works in this study: 1) the *Compendium,* since it can be dated anywhere from 1265 to 1273 (see Torrell, *Saint Thomas Aquinas,* 1:146); and 2) the *lectura* on the Pauline Epistles, since these are dated anywhere from 1259 to 1273 (see Torrell, *Saint Thomas Aquinas,* 1:250–52). For a discussion of a key passage in the former, see Hütter, *Dust Bound for Heaven,* 244–46; for some of the key passages about natural desire in the latter, see Hütter, *Dust Bound for Heaven,* 150–54.

104. Of necessity, any such rereading must be provisional for two reasons. The first is that each of the figures discussed in this book properly deserves a book-length study in his own right. The second is that, while this book will propose a way of harmonizing the two sides of the nature/grace debate based upon a certain reading of Thomas Aquinas, the bulk of its text must of necessity be taken up with establishing that reading of Thomas. Thus, there will remain the task of giving a broader and more comprehensive commentary on the nature/grace debate as it unfolded throughout the twentieth century based upon the findings of this book, both before *Surnaturel* and afterwards. I hope to take up that commentary in future publications.

Chapter 2 looks at how Thomas engaged the existing conversation about natural desire at the University of Paris in his *Commentary on the Sentences*, giving evidence of how he used Bonaventure's work as an index to the recent Parisian conversation. Thomas's principal contribution to that conversation was the idea that one need not posit any activity in human nature oriented toward the vision of God in order for its reception to be considered "natural." Describing human nature's receptivity to the vision of God on analogy with Averroes's understanding of the receptivity of heavenly bodies for changes of place, Thomas argues that our passive potency is like a "second nature" within us, according to which we receive motion caused in us by God. Thomas calls the passive ordering of this second nature toward the vision of God a natural "appetite." Alongside our passive, natural appetite for the vision of God, Thomas also identifies in us an active, Albertine natural "desire" for happiness, which reaches its terminal development in the analogical contemplation of God as First Cause. If we consider human nature on the part of its active potency, we have a natural desire for a natural end. If we consider human nature on the part of its passive potency, we have a natural appetite for a supernatural end.

Chapter 3 traces the development of Thomas's thought at Orvieto in the *Summa contra Gentiles,* where he gained a foothold on the Parisian tradition independent of Bonaventure through a deeper reading of such sources as Moses Maimonides, William of Auvergne, and Jean de la Rochelle. In general, Thomas distinguished himself sharply from the Avicennianism of these three figures so as to avoid saying that there is any active motion in us which is unconditionally oriented toward the vision of God. But Thomas also adopted one rather curious feature of Avicenna's thought in order to bring natural desire into alignment with natural appetite, and so to reconcile what the Aristotelian tradition says about nature and natural desire with what Augustine says about grace and the desire for God. Avicenna thought that the heavenly bodies had souls, and that the souls of heavenly bodies have a natural appetite for complete assimilation with their first cause. Since they cannot achieve such an assimilation by their natural power, Avicenna says that they desire the fulfillment of their natural appetite "insofar as is possible." Thomas, having thus located within the philosophical tradition an example of a supposed creature whose passive potency exceeds its active power in a manner analogous to human nature, incorporates Avicenna's condition into human natural desire. By means of this condition, Albert's "natural desire for happiness" becomes in effect a "natural desire for the fulfillment of our natural appetite insofar as is possible." Like Augustine's restless heart, it is explicitly a natural desire for happiness and implicitly a natural desire for the vision of God. That same natural desire can come to rest in a natural end or a supernatural end depending on what sort of motion God chooses to communicate to it in a given order of Providence: the knowledge of God, were it left to itself; or the vision of God, in the present order of Providence in which God has chosen to offer us the grace of Christ.

Chapter 4 identifies the beginning of a turn in Thomas's understanding of natural desire during his Roman period, which takes place when he encounters two of William of Moerbeke's newest works: the so-called *translatio nova* of Aristotle's *De anima,* as well as a Latin translation of Themistius's paraphrase of Aristotle's *De anima.* Before Thomas encountered these translations, he had followed Maimonides in teaching that our natural desire is caused by a long chain of causality: God enlightens the agent intellect; the agent intellect moves the possible intellect; and the possible intellect moves the will. William's translation of the *De anima* upset this chain of causality by attributing to Aristotle the view that the appetible object (the *bonum apprehensum*) is the unmoved mover of both the intellect and the will together. Thomas adopts this view as his own, but it caused a difficulty in his account of natural desire: how would he preserve the role of God as the first cause of motion in the soul, if it now seemed as though the *bonum apprehensum* was the first cause of motion in the soul? He solved the problem by appealing to a solution drawn from what William's translation made Themistius appear to say, even if it was not quite what Themistius actually said: a single, superior agent intellect (which Thomas identifies with God) directly illumines the agent intellect within the human soul; this illumination is necessary in order for the possible intellect to apprehend the appetible object in such a way as to cause motion in the will. This account of the origin of motion in the soul would enable Thomas to maintain his existing account of natural desire in the *Prima pars* of the *Summa theologiae* with very few changes, but it would set the stage for a significant development in the *Prima secundae.*

Chapter 5 documents how, in his second Parisian period, Thomas developed the way in which he described natural desire in order to respond to criticisms of his use of Moerbeke's translations of Aristotle's *De anima* and of Themistius's paraphrase of it. The Franciscan master Walter of Bruges and the secular master Gerard of Abbeville both alleged that Thomas compromised the freedom of the will by making it deterministically subject to the *bonum apprehensum* in the intellect. Although the criticism was not entirely fair, because Thomas had already anticipated and responded to it in his *Sententia libri Physicorum,* Thomas nevertheless took the criticism to heart in the *Prima secundae.* Returning to some of the same questions he had already raised in the *Prima pars,* Thomas now gave greater emphasis to the absolute freedom of the will in the order of exercise: the will is a self-mover, moved directly by God, and God moves the intellect indirectly through the will. The motion with which God moves the will is received by the will according to the same Avicennian condition to which Thomas had subjected the intellect in the *Summa contra Gentiles* and the *Prima pars* of the *Summa theologiae*: the natural desire of the will seeks the fulfillment of its corresponding natural appetite *insofar as is possible*; thus, one and the same natural desire can terminate in a natural end or a supernatural end, depending on what sort of motion God chooses to communicate to it.

Chapter 6 offers a re-reading of de Lubac and of a selection of scholastic figures in light of the foregoing, proposing a way forward for the nature/grace debate in the twenty-first century based upon the way in which Thomas relates natural appetite and natural desire. It shows how Cajetan and Suárez mistakenly restrict Thomas's natural desire to a natural end, and how de Lubac tries to respond to this misinterpretation through an appeal to the Aegidian tradition of the Order of the Hermits of Saint Augustine. While de Lubac correctly imputes to Thomas the idea of a natural desire for the vision of God, he mistakenly imputes to Thomas the view that nature is somehow active with respect to grace. If we return to Thomas's Augustinian understanding of natural appetite and natural desire, as expressed in its more definitive form in the *Prima secundae,* Thomas offers us a way of articulating the intelligibility of human nature, the coherence of human community, and the gratuity of grace, without therefore supporting the rise and/or spread of a secular worldview. For while our "first nature," which is active, and which can be understood with reference to natural reason, can furnish us with a philosophical anthropology, a philosophical ethics, and a theological defense of the gratuity of grace, our first nature is always implicitly in search of the fulfillment of our "second nature," which is completely passive, which cannot be understood apart from Christ, and whose fulfillment takes place in that Trinitarian vision of the *communio sanctorum,* which is the gratuitous hope of the City of God *in via,* and its gratuitous reward *in patria.*

NOTES ABOUT THE TEXT

Wherever possible, critical editions of primary sources have been used. Where these are not yet available, or where the work in question was originally available in print, those printed editions have been used which are commonly cited as editions of reference. Quotations of the Greek texts of Aristotle and his Greek commentators are taken from the online version of the *Thesaurus Linguae Graecae.* Quotations from the *Aristoteles Latinus* are taken from the online Brepolis database. Editions of primary sources which have not been assigned a special abbreviation will be referred to by the name of the editor, publisher, or place of publication, as appropriate. Complete bibliographical details for each edition referenced are available in the bibliography.

Since Latin orthography and punctuation vary widely from edition to edition, no attempt has been made to standardize them. In the case of critical editions, the orthographical conventions and punctuation of the edition cited have been preserved, even where these vary from one work to another of the same author; in the case of printed editions from the fifteenth through eighteenth centuries, abbreviations have been expanded, orthography has been corrected and emended, and punctuation has been corrected as needed for the ease of the contemporary reader.

All translations are the author's unless otherwise noted.

1

The Parisian Conversation (1231–1252)

THEOLOGY AT THE TURN OF THE THIRTEENTH CENTURY

The threefold task of the theologian in the Middle-Ages century is commonly summarized by the triad of Peter Cantor (d. 1197): *lectio, disputatio, praedicatio*.[1] To lecture was to read a work carefully and to comment on questions that could be raised in relation to it. To dispute was to apply dialectic to the resolution of those questions, whether in a classroom setting or in a public form. To preach was to apply the understanding reached through dialectic to the lives of Christian people, so that one's studies might not become walled up in decadent abstraction, but might contribute to one's own and others' progress toward Christian perfection.

Ironically, Peter Cantor does not introduce his triad as "theology" (*theologia*); his term for it is "training in Sacred Scripture" (*ex-*

1. Peter Cantor, *Verbum abbreviatum: Textus conflatus*, ed. M. Boutry (Turnhout: Brepols, 2004), 1.1 [CCCM 196:9]: "In tribus autem consistit exercitium sacre Scripture: in lectione, disputatione, predicatione." On the triad that Peter describes, see Smalley, *Study of the Bible in the Middle Ages*, 208–11. On its influence in thirteenth-century theology, see Torrell, *Saint Thomas Aquinas*, 1:54–74; Michael Sirilla, *The Ideal Bishop: Aquinas's Commentaries on the Pastoral Epistles* (Washington, D.C.: The Catholic University of America Press, 2017), 85–95.

ercitium sacrae Scripturae). The training was needed to get in shape for preaching, a task which Pope Innocent III would call upon the whole Church to support at the Fourth Lateran Council (1215).[2] In this sense theology was, as Beryl Smalley observes, a public form of monastic *lectio divina*, designed to lead from the reading of Scripture, through the contemplation of the Christian mysteries, to the building up of Christian lives, and ultimately to communion with God now and in the life hereafter.[3]

Smalley intended her description of theology as public *lectio divina* to apply only to a limited range of theologians. Following Martin Grabmann,[4] she distinguishes between a "biblical moral school," which emphasized *lectio* and *praedicatio*, and a "speculative" school, which emphasized *disputatio*.[5] On this reading, the rise of speculative theology in the mid-twelfth century corresponds with a gradual separation of biblical and speculative theology.[6] However, Alexander Andrée and Mark Clark have recently suggested that this distinction, along with the historiography based upon it, is somewhat inaccurate.[7] While some twelfth- and early thirteenth-century

2. On the orientation of Peter Cantor's understanding of theology toward preaching, see Bert Roest, *A History of Franciscan Education (c. 1210–1517)* (Boston: Brill, 2000), 227. On the importance of preaching in Innocent III, see Andrew Jones, "The Preacher of the Fourth Lateran Council," *Logos* 18 (2015): 121–49.

3. Smalley, *Study of the Bible in the Middle Ages*, 1–36, 196, 214–63. This pattern deliberately follows the four senses of Scripture: literal, allegorical, moral, and anagogical. The classic twentieth-century work on the four senses in the Middle Ages is Henri de Lubac, *Exégèse médiévale: Les quatre sens de l'Écriture*, 4 vols. (Paris: Aubier, 1959–64); translated by E. M. Macierowski as *Medieval Exegesis*, 3 vols. (Grand Rapids: Eerdmans, 1998–2009). More recently, see Ian Levy, *Introducing Medieval Biblical Interpretation: The Senses of Scripture in Premodern Exegesis* (Grand Rapids: Baker, 2018).

4. Martin Grabmann, *Die Geschichte der scholastischen Methode*, 3 vols. (Freiburg im Breisgau: Herder, 1909–11), 2:476–501.

5. Smalley, *Study of the Bible in the Middle Ages*, 197. Also see Mark Clark, "Peter Lombard, Stephen Langton, and the School of Paris: The Making of the Twelfth-Century Scholastic Biblical Tradition," *Traditio* 72 (2017): 83.

6. Smalley, *Study of the Bible in the Middle Ages*, 209. The separation between *lectio* and *disputatio* is thus said to have "relieved [the scholar of Scripture] of his burden" because "theological questions were no longer his subject."

7. See, in addition to the work of Clark already cited, Alexander Andrée, "Peter Comestor's Lectures on the *Glossa 'Ordinaria'* on the Gospel of John: The Bible and

theologians certainly went too far, seeing *disputatio* as an end in itself, many integrated it into a holistic framework, using *disputatio* as an indispensable bridge between *lectio* and *praedicatio*. As Peter the Chanter himself put it: "You should preach after you have studied the Sacred Scripture and disputed the questions that arise therein, *and not before*."[8]

Andrée gives us an example from the School of Laon of the way in which an early twelfth-century classroom might combine *lectio* and *disputatio*: earlier in the day, the *magister* held a *lectio* on a biblical text, where he would assemble Patrisic and Carolingian commentaries on that text, and then give his own, authoritative interpretation; later in the day, he would supervise a sort of *disputatio*, where his students collated contrasting opinions that arose from the *lectio*, and he himself would resolve the discrepancies.[9] At any stage of development, written artifacts of these oral sessions could be produced. When lectures were written down, they would usually take the form of a report (*reportatio*).[10] A *reportatio* could either be in the

---

Theology in the Twelfth-Century Classroom," *Traditio* 71 (2016): 1–32; Mark Clark, *The Making of the Historia Scholastica, 1150–1200* (Toronto: PIMS, 2015).

8. Peter Cantor, *Verbum abbreviatum* 1.1 [CCCM 196:9]: "Post lectionem igitur sacre Scripture et dubitabilium disputationum inquisitionem, *et non prius*, est predicandum" (emphasis added). Peter compares the tasks of a theologian to the construction of a house: lecture is the foundation; disputation is the wall; preaching is the roof. Just as you need a foundation and walls to support a roof, one should not preach without first having read the Scriptures and answered the questions that one has encountered there in disputation.

9. Alexander Andrée, "Magisterial *auctoritas* and Biblical Scholarship at the School of Laon in the Twelfth Century," in *Auctor et Auctoritas in Latinis medii aevi litteris. Author and Authorship in Medieval Latin Literature*, ed. E. D'Angelo and J. Ziolkowski (Florence: Edizioni del Galluzzo, 2014), 6–9; Smalley, *Study of the Bible in the Middle Ages*, 66–82.

10. On *reportatio* as a genre, see Smalley, *Study of the Bible in the Middle Ages*, 200–208. Smalley repeatedly emphasizes the deficiency of the *reportatio*, and notes on pp. 205–6 the possibility of having multiple *reportationes* of varying degrees of quality from the same *lectio*. Clark, "Peter Lombard, Stephen Langton, and the School of Paris," observes throughout that the primacy of oral teaching has two further consequences: first, that multiple *reportationes* of lectures on the same text may result from different lectures on the same text; second, that since lectures might be handed down orally rather than in writing, a written account of one lecture may transmit oral accounts of multiple other lectures from multiple other authors within it.

form of a continuous transcript or paraphrase of what the lecturer said (a *glosula*), or in the form of short comments (each called a *glossa*) written on the text itself, whether between lines (a *glossa interlinearis*) or in the margins (a *glossa marginalis*).[11] The primary written product of the oral teaching at Laon was the *Glossa* on the Bible, which came to be known as "*ordinaria*."[12] Disputations also had a variety of written forms. While they could be included as part of a biblical *glossa*, they could circulate as collections of disputed questions associated with a particular author; they could also be arranged topically into a single collection known as a *summa*.[13]

The great master of both *lectio* and *disputatio* in the twelfth century was Peter Lombard (d. 1160).[14] Peter Lombard was so influential on subsequent medieval theology that when Thomas Aquinas began his studies at the University of Paris almost a century later, Peter Lombard was still known simply as "the Master," without further qualification. At Paris, Peter employed similar methods to those of Laon.[15] He based his *lectio* mainly on the *Glossa ordinaria*, which he

11. Smalley, *Study of the Bible in the Middle Ages*, 66–67.

12. On the *Glossa ordinaria* in general, see ibid., 46–66; Lesley Smith, *The Glossa Ordinaria: The Making of a Medieval Bible Commentary* (Boston: Brill, 2009); as well the works of Andrée cited above. On the school of Laon and its impact, see Alexander Andrée, "Magisterial *auctoritas*," 3–16; Mark Clark, "The Biblical Gloss, the Search for the Lombard's Glossed Bible, and the School of Paris," *Mediaeval Studies* 76 (2014): 57–114; Cédric Giraud, *Per verba magistri: Anselme de Laon et son école au xiie siècle* (Turnhout: Brepols, 2010).

Both the authorship and the location of the composition of *Glossa ordinaria* are subjects of debate. On the importance of both Laon and Paris in the composition of the *Glossa ordinaria*, see Andrée, "Peter Comestor's Lectures," 207–8; on the question of authorship, see Alexander Andrée, "Anselm of Laon Unveiled: The *Glosae super Iohannem* and the Origins of the *Glossa Ordinaria* on the Bible," *Mediaeval Studies* 73 (2011): 223–29.

13. In spite of her reliance on Grabmann's distinction between biblical-moral and speculative theology, Smalley, *Study of the Bible in the Middle Ages*, 73, acknowledges the association between *lectio* and *disputatio* when she admits that the scholastic *quaestio* arose from the biblical exegesis of Laon, as well as on p. 49 when she says for similar reasons that "the *Summa theologica* traces its formal pedigree back to Laon."

14. For introductions to Peter's life and work, see Ignatius Brady, *prolegomena* to Peter Lombard, *Sententiae in IV libris distinctae*, vol. 1, 3rd ed. (Grottaferrata: Editiones Collegii S. Bonaventurae ad Claras Aquas, 1971), 8*–136*, as well as Colish, *Peter Lombard*; and Rosemann, *Peter Lombard*.

15. Peter studied at Rheims prior to Paris, but as Colish, *Peter Lombard*, 1:17,

amplified and emended as he saw fit for the benefit of his students,[16] and he based his *disputatio* mainly on the questions that arose from the *Glossa ordinaria,* as well as the questions which had arisen in recent *summae.*[17] Current research suggests that his *lectio* was preserved in three forms: in the oral teaching of his students,[18] in *glossae* on the Psalms and Epistles, which circulated widely,[19] as well as a single glossed bible, which he bequeathed to his Cathedral chapter upon his death.[20] His *disputatio* was preserved in two forms: within the oral and written accounts of his biblical lectures,[21] as well as in the *Sententiae in IV libris distinctae* for which he is most well-known.

Although it had earlier antecedents,[22] the tradition of commenting upon Peter Lombard's *Sentences* as a formal stage of theological formation gained traction at Paris in the late 1220s and early 1230s. The tradition is often associated with the then-secular master, Alexander of Hales, who in the late 1220s gave a *lectio* on Peter Lombard's

observes, the teaching at the cathedral school in Rheims was significantly influenced by the teaching in Laon.

16. Andrée, "Peter Comestor's Lectures," 209.

17. On the *Sentences* as a "taught text," see Clark, "Peter Lombard, Stephen Langton, and the School of Paris," 80–81; Colish, *Peter Lombard,* 1:25. On its relationship to other *summae,* see Colish, *Peter Lombard* 1:18; Marcia Colish, "From the Sentence Collection to the Sentence Commentary and the Summa: Parisian Scholastic Theology, 1130–1215," in *Manuels, programmes de cours et techniques d'enseignement dans les universités médiévales,* ed. Jacqueline Hamesse (Louvain-la-Neuve: Université Catholique de Louvain, 1994), 9–29.

18. On the preservation of Peter Lombard's biblical lectures in those of Stephen Langton, see Clark, "Peter Lombard, Stephen Langton, and the School of Paris."

19. The *Magna glossatura* on the Psalms and the Pauline Epistles was reprinted in PL 191.

20. On this codex and its significance, see Brady, *prolegomena* to Peter Lombard, *Sententiae in IV libris distinctae,* 2:19*–23*; Clark, "Biblical *Gloss,*" 57–113; Colish, *Peter Lombard,* 1:28–30.

21. As Peter taught both Scripture and the *Sentences* repeatedly over the course of his career, there was a healthy "cross-polinization" between his *lectio* and his *disputatio.* See Clark, "Peter Lombard, Stephen Langton, and the School of Paris," 4n7; Colish, *Peter Lombard,* 1:24–25.

22. See Colish, "Parisian Scholastic Theology, 1130–1215," 20–26; Marcia Colish, "The Development of Lombardian Theology, 1160–1215," in *Centres of Learning and Location in Pre-modern Europe and the Near East,* ed. Jan Willem Drijvers and Alasdair A. MacDonald (Boston: Brill, 1995), 207–16.

Sentences in place of the traditional *lectio* on Scripture.[23] But it was the Dominican master, Hugh of St. Cher, who helped the *Sentences* commentary become the center of Parisian education. Although he is best known for his *postilla* on the entire Bible, in which he amplified and emended the tradition associated with the *Glossa ordinaria* and Peter Lombard,[24] he also gave a *lectio* on Peter Lombard's *Sentences* in a manner similar to that of Alexander. What makes Hugh of St. Cher different is that he went back to the report (*reportatio*) of his *lectio* on the *Sentences* and edited it into a deliberate literary composition (an *ordinatio*), adding authorities, arguments, and questions, which had never come up in class. It was thus that the oral tradition of the previous centuries began the very gradual transition to a written tradition, and that the "*Sentences* commentary" as we know it was born.[25]

The *Sentences* commentary became a standard part of theological education at Paris from the 1240s until the Reformation.[26] After giving lectures on Sacred Scripture, and before being licensed as a *magister in sacra pagina,* the aspiring theologian would spend several years lecturing on Peter Lombard's *Sentences.* In this way, his formation would follow Peter Cantor's program: *lectio* (which he would learn by commenting on Scripture), *disputatio* (which he would learn by commenting on the *Sentences*), and *praedicatio,* which he would perform at the

23. Alexander's *glossa* can be found in Alexander of Hales, *Glossa in quatuor libros Sententiarum Petri Lombardi* (Quaracchi: Collegium S. Bonaventurae, 1951–57).

24. On Hugh's relationship to the *Glossa ordinaria,* see Smith, *Glossa Ordinaria,* 220–23; on his relationship to Peter Lombard, see Clark, "Peter Lombard, Stephen Langton, and the School of Paris," 98–99.

25. The text of Hugh's commentary is as yet unedited, and it is difficult to establish even an edition of reference because the text went through two or three stages of redaction and was diffused at each stage. See Barbara Faes de Mottoni, "Les manuscrits du commentaire des *Sentences* d'Hugues de Saint-Cher," in *Hugues de Saint-Cher (+1263): Bibliste et théologien,* ed. Louis-Jacques Bataillon, Gilbert Dahan, and Pierre-Marie Gy (Turnhout: Brepols, 2004), 273–98. For now, ms. Vat. Lat. 1098 can be used as one of the more reliable sources, although a critical edition remains a significant *desideratum.*

26. Nancy Spatz, "Approaches and Attitudes to a New Theology Textbook: The Sentences of Peter Lombard," in *The Intellectual Climate of the Early University: Essays in Honor of Otto Gründler,* ed. Nancy van Deusen (Kalamazoo: Medieval Institute Publications, 1997), 27–52.

commencement of his theological career.[27] It is true that there were those who thought that the *Sentences* commentary detracted from the biblical orientation of medieval theological education. Roger Bacon (c. 1220–92), for example, complained that the attention given to the *Sentences* was eclipsing the attention given to the Scriptures, and consequently that *disputatio* was getting in the way of *lectio.*[28] Yet while there were certainly excesses—as one would expect in any culture—Bacon's confrère among the Franciscans, Bonaventure, disagreed on the fundamental outlook of this aspect of thirteenth-century theological education: the *Sentences* summarizes biblical questions in such a way that it can be seen as "subalternated" to the Bible; by reflecting upon those questions, a person is better able to bear witness to the biblical faith which is pondered in them.[29] In order, then, to understand how a *magister in sacra pagina* such as Thomas Aquinas resolved the biblical questions about nature, grace, and the desire for God, which the theological tradition bequeathed to him, we may begin by a careful examination of Peter Lombard's treatment of these questions in the *Sentences.*

TWELFTH-CENTURY LATIN AUGUSTINIANISM: PETER LOMBARD

According to Peter Lombard's *Sentences,* any theological account of our natural desire has to come to terms with three questions. First, what does it means for a motion to be called "natural"? Second, what

27. Torrell, *Saint Thomas Aquinas,* 1:55–74.

28. Roger Bacon, *Opus Minus,* in *Quaedam hactenus inedita,* vol. 1, ed. J. Brewer (London: Longman, Green, Longman, and Roberts, 1859), 328–29.

29. Speaking of its relationship to Scripture, Bonaventure, *In I Sent.,* in *Opera Omnia,* vol. 1 (Quaracchi: Collegium S. Bonaventurae, 1882), proem., q. 2, ad 4 [Quaracchi 1:11] says that "liber iste ad sacram Scripturam reducitur per modum cuiusdam subalternationis" and gives as evidence of this fact the witness of Peter Lombard's repeated appeals to Scripture. Speaking possibly of its relationship to preaching, he says in the *corpus* of the same question [Quaracchi 1:10–11], that "modus perscrutatorius convenit huic doctrinae sive libro. Cum enim finis imponat necessitatem his quae sunt ad finem; quia, sicut dicit Pliilosoplus, 'Serra est dentata, quia est ad secandum'; sic iste liber, quia est ad promotionem fidei, habet modum inquisitivum."

is the end of the will's natural motion? Third, what is the relationship of the natural end of the will with that end which is posited for human nature by Scripture? In his response to each of these questions, the authority of Scripture, read through the lens of Augustine, is at the forefront of his mind.[30]

In answer to the first question, Peter turns to the biblical story of Creation in Genesis 2. Relying on Augustine's *De genesi ad litteram* he asks a simple question about one of the mysteries recounted there: how could Eve be formed from Adam's rib? In response, he distinguishes between changes that occur according to the ordinary course of nature and changes that occur according to the marvelous intervention of God.

We should bear in mind that the causes of all things are in God from eternity . . . while, as Augustine says, the causes of some, but not all things, are in creatures, because God placed germinatory properties [*rationes seminales*] in things according to which some things arise from others, as is the case when such a grain comes from such a seed, or such a fruit comes from such a tree, and so on and so forth. . . . Those things which happen according to a germinatory cause are said to be done naturally, because when they happen this way they follow the course of nature known to men; but other things, whose causes are in God alone, are said to be done beyond nature [*praeter naturam*].—Augustine, *On Genesis*. Moreover, Augustine says that the latter are those things which are done by grace, or done to signify things which are done by grace—they do not happen naturally; they happen marvelously [*mirabiliter*]. He places the creation of woman from the rib of man among these things, speaking thus: "It had not been established among things that it would be necessary for woman to be made thus; rather, it had been hidden in God. Every course of nature has natural laws. Above this natural course, the Creator has within himself the ability to make of all things something other than their respective natural properties contain: like, for example, that a dry rod should suddenly flower and bear fruit; and that a woman who was barren in her youth should bear a child in her old age; that an ass should speak, and so on and so forth. For

30. See Eric Saak, "Augustine in the Western Middle Ages to the Reformation," in *A Companion to Augustine*, ed. Mark Vessey (Somerset: Wiley-Blackwell, 2012), 468. Saak points out that Augustine is the most commonly cited author in the *Sentences*, receiving over ten times as many citations as the next most commonly cited author, Ambrose.

he afforded to the natures of things that these things could be caused from them [*ex his*], not that they would have them in their natural motion."[31]

Changes which follow *rationes seminales* are natural; they happen according to the ordinary course of nature as God created it. Changes which happen above or beyond *rationes seminales* are marvelous.[32] When God wants to effect one of these changes, Peter quotes Augustine saying that God places a primordial cause (*causa primordialis*) in the creature, which is not a cause properly speaking; rather, it is something in the creature, by which the creature responds to what God chooses to do in it.[33]

31. Peter Lombard, *II Sent.*, 18.5–6 [Quaracchi 1:418–20]: "Ad quod sciendum est, omnium rerum causas in Deo ab aeterno esse.... In creaturis vero quarundam rerum, sed non omnium causae sunt, ut ait Augustinus, quia inseruit Deus seminales rationes rebus, secundum quas alia ex aliis proveniunt, ut de hoc semine tale granum, de hac arbore talis fructus, et huiusmodi.... Et illa quidem quae secundum causam seminalem fiunt, dicuntur naturaliter fieri, quia ita cursus naturae hominibus innotuit; alia vero praeter naturam, quorum causae tantum sunt in Deo.—Augustinus, *Super Genesim*. Haec autem dicit Augustinus esse illa quae per gratiam fiunt, vel ad ea significanda non naturaliter, sed mirabiliter fiunt. Inter quae mulieris facturam de costa viri ponit, ita dicens: 'Ut mulierem ita fieri necesse foret, non in rebus conditum, sed in Deo absconditum erat. Omnis naturae cursus habet naturales leges. Super hunc naturalem cursum Creator habet apud se posse de omnibus facere aliud quam eorum naturalis ratio habet: ut virga scilicet arida repente floreat, fructum gignat; et in iuventute sterilis femina in senectute pariat; ut asina loquatur, et huiusmodi. Dedit autem naturis ut ex his etiam haec fieri possent, non ut in naturali motu haberent.'" Compare this to Peter's commentary on Eph. 3:9 [PL 192:189D].

32. Peter Lombard, *II Sent.*, 18.6, no. 2 [Quaracchi 1:419–20]. The distinction seems to be taken from the *Glossa ordinaria* on Gn 2:20, Biblia sacra cum glossa ordinaria (Strassburg: A. Rusch, 1480), 1:12va–b: "Omnia ergo quae ad gratiam significandam non naturali motu rerum, sed mirabiliter facta sunt, eorum absconditae causae in Deo fuerunt." The *Glossa* is quoting Augustine, *De Genesi ad litteram* 9.18.34 [CSEL 28.1:293]. Also see Peter Lombard, *Glossa in Rom.* [PL 191:1488B].

33. Peter Lombard, *II Sent.*, 18.5, no. 4 [Quaracchi 1:419]; 18.6, no. 2 [Quaracchi 1:419–20]. The distinction between *rationes seminales* and *causae primordiales* is taken from Augustine, *De Genesi ad litteram* 5–6 [CSEL 28:137–200]. While the latter term (*causae primordiales*) appears to be unique to Augustine, the former term (*rationes seminales*) may have entered Latin theology through Jerome's discussions of Origen. See Jerome, *Contra Iohannem*, ed. J. L. Feiertag (Turnhout: Brepols, 1999), 26 [CCSL 79A:43–44].

Peter's use of Augustine, *De Genesi ad litteram*, is not entirely direct, relying in part on the *Glossa ordinaria* on Gen. 2:5 [Rusch 1:10ra]. The Glossa, in turn, is an abbreviated

In order to explain what it means for a desire to follow the ordinary course of events, Peter educes the words of the *Glossa ordinaria* on Romans 7:15, where Paul notes the dichotomy between what he wills and what he does. The *Glossator* had observed that "man, having been subjected to sin, does what he does not want to do, because he naturally wants what is good, but this will always fails to achieve its effect except by the grace of God."[34] Peter perceives in this comment a distinction between what is willed naturally (*naturaliter*) and what is willed freely (*libenter*).[35] What is willed naturally is what Adam would have willed at Creation, because God made him morally upright. Subsequently, whatever sins we may happen to commit freely, a trace (*scintilla*) of that natural will remains in us after the Fall.[36] Grace, according to this view, frees us from freely choosing sin, and allows us to make free choices in accord with our natural will.[37]

If the role of grace is to heal fallen nature from the free choice of evil so that it may freely pursue the goal of its natural will, this raises a second question: whether the natural goal of the will is that end which is posited for human nature by Scripture. The importance of this question arises from the fact that, if Adam could choose freely in accord with his natural will without the need for grace to heal him from sin, and if Adam's natural will was ordered toward the beatific vision, then it would seem that Adam could choose the beatific vi-

---

and somewhat corrupted version of *De Genesi ad litteram* 6.9.16–6.10.17 [CSEL 28.1: 182–83].

34. Peter Lombard, *II Sent.*, 39.3, no. 1 [Quaracchi 1:555]: "Dicit enim quod 'homo subiectus peccato facit quod non vult, quia naturaliter vult bonum, sed voluntas haec semper caret effectu, nisi gratia Dei.'"

35. Ibid., 39.3, no. 3 [Quaracchi 1:555–56]. Peter does acknowledge later in this chapter that there are others who deny this distinction (no. 4).

36. See ibid., 35.2 [Quaracchi 1:530–34]. Here, with respect to sinful acts, Peter distinguishes between acts considered insofar as they are acts (*inquantum actus sunt*), in which case he says that they are always good, and acts insofar as they are evil (*inquantum mala sunt*), in which case he says that they are sins.

37. Ibid. The editors of the Quaracchi edition note the dependence of Peter on the school of Anselm of Laon. See the note to cap. 3 on p. 1:452. Peter's distinction of wills parallels that of the *Glossa ordinaria* on Rom. 7:15 [Rusch 4:1064vb].

sion without the help of grace. Aware of the Pelagian danger in such a consequence, Peter is keen to point out that in no sense does the human will suffice to achieve the final end posited for it by Scripture without the help of grace.[38] If it did, then grace (*gratia*) could nowise be called gratuitous (*gratuita*), because it would be due the merits of our previous actions.[39] There are some basic goods toward which our will might tend even without the aid of grace, such as cultivating a field and building a dwelling, but these do not suffice to merit our final end.[40]

In order to avoid anachronism by reading later categories and distinctions into the text of the *Sentences,* we should note that Peter does not predicate the word, "natural," of those basic goods which are willed freely without the help of grace. Rather, he distinguishes first between what is willed naturally and what is willed freely, and then between what is willed freely with the help of grace and what is willed freely without the help of grace. Cultivating a field and building a house are not willed naturally for Peter; they are willed freely *without* the help of grace. Neither is charity willed naturally; it is willed freely *with* the help of grace (see figure 1).[41]

On account of the fact that Peter primarily distinguishes between what is willed naturally and what is willed freely, when Pe-

38. Peter Lombard, *II Sent.,* 26.4, no. 5 [Quaracchi 1:475–76].

39. Ibid., 26.7, no. 1 [Quaracchi 1:477]. Quoting Augustine's *Epistula* 194.3.7, Peter's text reads, "'Illius enim gratiae percipiendae, quae voluntatem hominis sanat, ut sanata legem impleat, nulla merita praecedunt. Ipsa est enim qua iustificatur impius, id est fit iustus qui prius erat impius; meritis autem impii non gratia, sed poena debetur; nec ista esset gratia, si non daretur gratuita.' Datur autem gratuita, quia nihil ante feceramus unde hoc mereremur." The last sentence is not from Augustine, but it does appear in Peter's commentary on Rom 3:22–26 [PL 191:1361C].

Peter's commentary, in turn, is based on the *Glossa ordinaria* of the passage in question [Rusch 4:1061ra], which uses the text from Augustine in a slightly different form. The discrepancy between the text of the *Glossa ordinaria* and Lombard's use of it, as well as Peter's expansive use of it in the *Sentences,* suggests that Peter actually knew and read the text from Augustine alongside the *Glossa ordinaria,* and that while the *Glossa ordinaria* influenced his application of this text from Augustine to this question, Peter did not merely repeat what he had learned from the school of Laon here.

40. Peter Lombard, *II Sent.,* 26.7, no. 2 [Quaracchi 1:477].

41. See ibid., 29.1, no. 2 [Quaracchi 1:492].

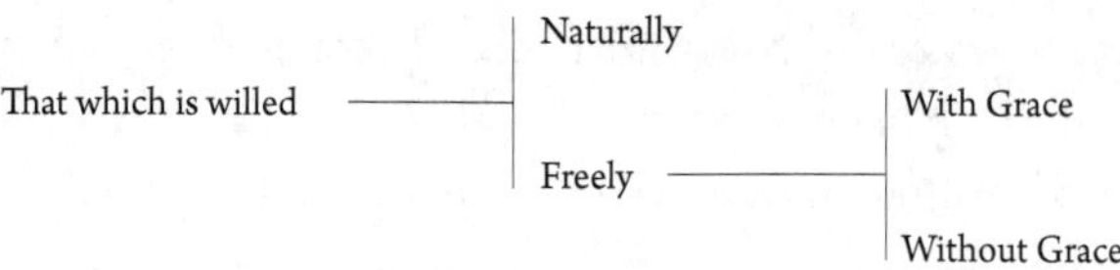

FIGURE 1. Willing according to Peter Lombard

ter discusses the will's end in the context of drawing the aforementioned distinctions, he only discusses the end of what is willed freely, not the end of what is willed naturally. The goal of the will's free action, Peter argues, is not the ultimate end of man. Free action concerns the means to our end, not the end itself.[42]

Speaking, then, of means toward our end, Peter describes a twofold proximate end of the will: good delight (*delectatio bona*) for those who choose good means to their end; evil delight (*delectatio mala*) for those who choose evil means to their end.[43] Explaining what constitutes an object of good delight, Peter acknowledges that "good" can be said in several senses: "as useful, as it can be rewarded, as a sign of the good, as an appearance of good, as licit, and in perhaps other ways."[44] But for the purposes of selecting the means to our end, all that matters is the sense in which our actions can be said to be rewardable.[45] Only those who freely will here and now to take good delight in actions which are rewardable with good, a choice that cannot be made without grace,[46] will be rewarded with the ultimate end of man, the never-ending enjoyment (*fruitio*) of God.[47]

This understanding of the proximate and remote ends of the free will could lead to some confusion, because Peter uses the adverb,

42. Ibid., 26.11, no. 1 [Quaracchi 1:479].
43. Ibid., 38.4, no. 3 [Quaracchi 1:551].
44. Ibid., 41.2 [Quaracchi 1:564]: "Bonum enim multipliciter accipitur, scilicet pro utili, pro remunerabili, pro signa boni, pro specie boni, pro licito, et aliis forte modis."
45. Ibid., 41.1, no. 8 [Quaracchi 1:563].
46. Ibid., 41.1, no. 4 [Quaracchi 1:562–63].
47. Peter Lombard, *I Sent.*, 1.2–3 [Quaracchi 1:56–61].

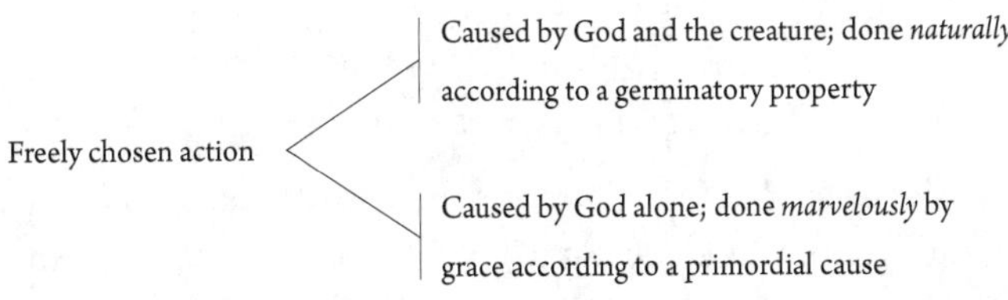

FIGURE 2. Freely chosen action according to Peter Lombard

"naturally," equivocally in his discussions of natural change and of the will. When speaking of natural change, "naturally" describes that which follows from a *ratio seminalis*; when speaking of the will, "naturally" describes that which is willed non-freely. This leads to a difficulty with regard to the will's free action without the aid of grace. It is natural in the first sense, but it is not natural in the second sense (see figure 2).

Although Peter distinguishes between natural and free will in Book 2, he saves a more detailed discussion of the end of natural will for Book 4. In Book 4, distinction 49, he brings up the universal desire for happiness. Instead of offering his own commentary on the subject, he quotes lengthy passages of *De Trinitate*, Book 13.[48] Peter's conclusion, spoken through the mouth of Augustine, is that all people know the basic contour of a happy life, "having all you want, and not wanting anything wrongly," but not all people realize that the only possible possession of this happiness is in God.[49] In short, as Peter elaborates in his own words, we have a natural desire for a happiness which is only found in God, though a given individual, who is unaware of God's existence, might not experience this as a natural desire for *God*, and might freely seek happiness elsewhere.[50]

48. Peter Lombard, *IV Sent.*, 49.1, nn. 4–5 [Quaracchi 2:549–50].

49. Ibid., 49.1, no. 7 [Quaracchi 2:550]. Also see Peter's commentary on Rom 4:1–8 [PL 191:1369D–1370A].

50. Peter Lombard, *IV Sent.*, 50.2, no. 3 [Quaracchi 2:556]: "in hac vita nullus adeo malus est ut penitus secludatur a cogitatione Dei, qui nec perdit appetitum beatitudinis et quendam boni amorem, quem naturaliter habet rationalis creatura."

THE RISE OF ARISTOTLE AND THE ARISTOTELIAN TRADITION

Alongside the study of Scripture and the Latin theological tradition, thirteenth-century theologians also had to come to grips with the Aristotelian tradition. Not that earlier Latin scholastics had been total strangers to it—but over the course of the twelfth century, a flood of Aristotelian texts entered the Latin West, which changed the face of scholarship over the course of the following century. Van Steenberghen offers us a succinct snapshot of the state of Aristotelian texts around the year 1200:

> The greater part of [Aristotle's] writings were accessible to Latin readers in 1200. The *Organon* was translated completely: the *Logica vetus* (the *Categories, De interpretatione*, and the *Isagoge* of Porphyry) had been in circulation since Boethius; the *Logica nova* (*Analytica, Topica, Sophistici elenchi*) became widespread in the twelfth century. A good part of the *Libri naturales* had been translated from Arabic by Gerard of Cremona (d. 1187): the *Physics*, the *De generatione*, the *De caelo*, Books 1–3 of the *De meteora*. Book 4 of *De meteora* had been translated from Greek by Enrico Aristippo (d. 1162), as well as the *De generatione*. Furthermore, they were indebted to anonymous translators from the twelfth century for Greco-Latin translations of the *Physics*, the *De anima*, and the *Parva naturalia*. The *Metaphysics* existed partially in Latin (Books 1–4.4).... Finally, the twelfth century also witnessed a partial translation—equally anonymous—of the *Nicomachean Ethics* ... which includes Books 1 and 2.[51]

51. Van Steenberghen, *La philosophie au xiii*ᵉ *siècle*, 77–78: "la majeure partie de [les] écrits [d'Aristote] était accessible aux lecteurs latins en 1200. L'*Organon* est traduit tout entier: la *Logica vetus* (*Categoriae, De interpretatione* et l'*Isagoge* de Porphyre) est en circulation depuis Boèce, la *Logica nova* (*Analytica, Topica, Sophistici elenchi*) se répand au XIIe siècle. Une bonne partie des *Libri naturales* a été traduite de l'arabe par Gérard de Crémone († 1187): la *Physique*, le *Traité de la génération*, le *Traité du ciel*, les livres I à III du *Traité des météores*. Le livre IV du *Traité des météores* a été traduit du grec par Henri Aristippe († 1162), de même que le *Traité de la génération*. En outre, on doit à des traducteurs inconnus du XIIe siècle la traduction gréco-latine de la *Physique*, du *Traité de l'âme* et des *Parva naturalia*. La *Métaphysique* existe partiellement en latin (livres I à IV, chap. 4).... Enfin le XIIe siècle a connu une traduction partielle, également anonyme, de l'*Éthique à Nicomaque* ... qui comporte les livres II et III."

In addition to these works of Aristotle, other works were to varying degrees influenced by Aristotle. John Damascene's *De fide orthodoxa* mediated Aristotelian moral psychology to the medievals through his use of Maximus the Confessor, a text which we will discuss in relation to Philip the Chancellor below. Any number of philosophers and theologians from the Arabic and Hebrew traditions also mediated Aristotelian doctrine, and at times Aristotelian texts, to the Latin scholastics: Al-Kindī (ca. 800–70), Al- Fārābī (c. 870–950/51), Avicenna (Ibn-Sīnā; ca. 970–1037), and Avicebron (Ibn-Gabirol; ca. 1021–ca. 1057) were all available at the beginning of the thirteenth century;[52] texts from Averroes (Ibn Rushd; 1126–98) would shortly become available;[53] and texts from Moses Maimonides (Moses ben Maimon; 1135–1204) followed not long thereafter.[54]

The three most important Aristotelian works for the study of natural desire in the early thirteenth century were the *Physics*, the *De anima*, and the *Nicomachean Ethics*. While the *Physics* and the *De anima* had been available in a complete translation since the late twelfth century,[55] there were repeated ecclesiastical prohibitions against their use. The *Nicomachean Ethics*, by contrast, did not exist in the Latin West in a complete translation until the third quarter of the 1240s.[56] In order to understand how these texts of Aristotle, as well as related texts from the Aristotelian tradition, came to be used in the early thirteenth century in discussions of nature, grace, and the desire for God, we must therefore first turn our attention to the

52. Van Steenberghen, *La philosophie au xiiie siècle*, 79–80.

53. See below, pp. 71–73.

54. Van Steenberghen, *La philosophie au xiiie siècle*, 107.

55. On Latin translations of the *Physics*, see Vernon Bourke, introduction to Thomas Aquinas, *Commentary on Aristotle's Physics*, trans. Kenneth Thomas (Notre Dame, Ind.: Dumb Ox Books, 1999), xviii. On Latin translations of the *De anima*, see Carlos Bazán, "13th Century Commentaries on *De anima*: From Peter of Spain to Thomas Aquinas," in *Il commento filosofico nell'occidente latino (secoli XIII–XV), atti del colloquio Firenze-Pisa, 19–22 ottobre 2000, organizzato dalla SISMEL*, ed. Gianfranco Fioravanti, Claudio Leonardi, and Stefano Perfetti (Turnhout: Brepols, 2002), 119–20.

56. See István P. Bejczy, introduction to *Virtue Ethics in the Middle Ages: Commentaries on Aristotle's Nicomachean Ethics, 1200–1500*, ed. István P. Bejczy (Boston: Brill, 2008), 3; van Steenberghen, *La philosophie au xiiie siècle*, 107.

three so-called "condemnations" of Aristotle that were issued in the first half of the thirteenth century: those of 1210, 1215, and 1231.

In 1210, a provincial synod in Paris decreed: "Neither the books of Aristotle on natural philosophy nor commentary on them may be read publicly or secretly in Paris; we enjoin this under pain of excommunication."[57] In 1215, Cardinal Robert de Courçon, who had been charged by Pope Innocent III with the reorganization of Parisian studies, added, "They may not read the books of Aristotle about metaphysics and natural philosophy, nor summaries of them."[58] In 1231, Pope Gregory IX weighed in as well: "We command that masters of arts ... not use those books of natural [philosophy] in Paris, which were prohibited for a good reason at the provincial council, until such time as they have been examined and purged from every suspicion of error."[59] Gregory did assemble the promised committee within a few weeks,[60] but its most prominent member died later that year, and the committee's work seems to have died with him.[61] The condemnations were not completely lifted until March 19, 1255, when the Aristotelian *corpus* was officially adopted into the standard philosophical curriculum in the Faculty of Arts at the University of Paris.[62]

For a long time, scholars have struggled to explain the observable fact that the influence of Aristotle and of the Aristotelian tradition continued to grow steadily throughout the period from 1210 to 1255, seemingly in spite of the prohibitions. Many interpret this

57. Denifle, *Chartularium Universitatis Parisiensis,* 1:70, quoted in van Steenberghen, *La philosophie au xiiie siècle,* 83: "Nec libri Aristotelis de naturali philsoophia nec commenta legantur Parisius publice vel secreto et hoc sub pena excommunicationis inhibemus."

58. Denifle, *Chartularium Universitatis Parisiensis,* 1:78–79, quoted in van Steenberghen, *La philosophie au xiiie siècle,* 83: "Non legantur libri Aristotelis de methaphisica et de naturali philosohpia nec summe de eisdem."

59. Denifle, *Chartularium Universitatis Parisiensis,* 1:138, quoted in van Steenberghen, *La philosophie au xiiie siècle,* 98: "Iubemus ut magistri artium ... libris illis naturalibus, qui in Concilio provinciali ex certa causa prohibiti fuere, Parisius non utantur, quousque examinati fuerint et ab omni errorum suspitione purgati."

60. Van Steenberghen, *La philosophie au xiiie siècle,* 99.

61. Ibid., 101.

62. Ibid., 322–23.

to mean that they were ineffective and blithely ignored. Why else would they have to be repeated?[63] This interpretation is sufficient for explaining the general use of Aristotle's work, but it does not necessarily make sense of all the historical evidence we have from the period surrounding the condemnations.

1) There is documentary evidence in the *Chartularium* suggesting that the prohibitions of 1210 and 1215 were, in fact, enforced until 1231 with the sentence of excommunication, and that those excommunications were absolved in connection with the condemnation of 1231.
2) There is testimony from Roger Bacon suggesting that the so-called condemnation of 1231 actually corresponded with permission to use the works of Aristotle and the Aristotelian tradition more widely.
3) There is evidence in philosophical and theological works from the period after 1231 that there was a dramatic increase in the use of Aristotle and the Aristotelian tradition during that time.

In light of these facts, I would like to suggest that the prevailing interpretation of the condemnations is incomplete. If we place each of the three so-called "condemnations" in context, a different picture emerges: the condemnations should be viewed more as prudential prohibitions. The prohibition of 1210 sought to proscribe a heretical reading of Aristotle by prohibiting a limited range of his works; the prohibition of 1215 added a few provisions to that of 1210 in order to prevent pastors of parishes as well as monastics from neglecting their duty to study the Scriptures; and the prohibition of 1231 was scarcely a prohibition in any meaningful sense: it walked back the provisions of 1215 to those of 1210, with a view toward eliminating them altogether. In the period from 1231 to 1255, therefore,

63. See, for example, G. R. Evans, *Philosophy and Theology in the Middle Ages* (New York: Routledge, 1993), 20; Edward Grant, *The Nature of Natural Philosophy in the Late Middle Ages* (Washington, D.C.: The Catholic University of America Press, 2010), 230.

the study of Aristotle and of the Aristotelian tradition was actually encouraged at the University of Paris, and so we witness a tremendous growth in the study of Aristotle and of the Aristotelian tradition, particularly on the questions of nature, grace, and the desire for God. Since this interpretation of the prohibitions cannot be assumed, however, it will be beneficial to make a brief *excursus* in order to show how we may arrive at it.[64]

The prohibition of 1210 concerned heresies associated with two figures, Amaury of Bène and David of Dinant. Amaury receives far greater attention in the text.[65] Although he had died in 1206, the condemnation of 1210 begins by decreeing that he be posthumously excommunicated, and that his body be exhumed from the cemetery and cast onto unblessed ground. Ten of his followers are to be handed over to the secular authorities to be burnt at the stake, while another four of them are sentenced to life in prison. The reason for such a serious sentence is given in the entry in the *Chartularium* following the one that contains the prohibition.[66] They were accused of holding a long list of heretical propositions, mainly about the Trinity and the Sacraments, which were very close to those held by Joachim of Fiore and his followers.[67]

Instead of connecting the prohibition on the study of Aristotle with its principle business, the prohibition of 1210 is annexed to a secondary decree in which David of Dinant's *Quaternuli* is condemned.[68] David had evidently travelled near Sicily, where in "Great-

64. A definitive interpretation of the prohibitions would require more space than we can devote to the subject here. Accordingly, the following interpretation is presented by way of a hypothesis, and nothing that is said below about works dating from the period of 1231 to 1252 will rely exclusively on it.

65. Van Steenberghen, *La philosophie au xiii*[e] *siècle*, 84; Spencer Young, *Scholarly Community at the Early University of Paris: Theologians, Education, and Society, 1215–1248* (New York: Cambridge University Press, 2014), 48.

66. Denifle, *Chartularium Universitatis Parisiensis*, 1:71–72.

67. Whether one influenced the other or they were both influenced by a common source is difficult to determine. See G. C. Capelle, *Amaury de Bène: Étude sur son panthéisme formel* (Paris: J. Vrin, 1931), 81–85. Joachimism would be definitively condemned at Lateran Council IV in 1215.

68. Denifle, *Chartularium Universitatis Parisiensis*, 1:70: "Quaternuli magistri David

er Greece" he had encountered Greek texts which were not yet available in Latin translation elsewhere in the Latin West.[69] David's principle error, an idea which he may have taken from Alexander of Aphrodisias, was the idea that God should be identified with prime matter.[70] Van Steenberghen notes that the prohibition of Aristotle attached to this condemnation seems to have been something of a "prudential measure."[71] In an atmosphere where the works of Aristotle and of the Aristotelian tradition were not yet as widely known and disseminated as they would later be, the bishops observed how one person who gained wider access to them was led into heresy and so sought to prevent similar cases from arising.

The prohibition of Aristotle attached to David of Dinant concerned not only the words of the Stagirite, but also "*commenta*" on them. Unfortunately, the text does not specify what these *commenta* are. Amos Bertolacci argues that the *commenta* are the works of Avicenna, because John Blund, writing at Paris around the time of the condemnation, called Avicenna's *Prima philosophia* a *commentum* on Aristotle's *Metaphysics*.[72] However, Dag Niklaus Hasse has shown

de Dinant infra natale episcopo Parisiensi afferantur et comburantur, nec libri Aristotelis de naturali philosophia nec commenta legantur Parisius publice vel secreto, et hoc sub penae excommunicationis inhibemus. Apud quem invenientur quaternuli magistri David a natali Domini in antea pro heretico habetur." For the text of the *Quaternuli*, see David of Dinant, *Quaternulorum fragmenta*, ed. Marian Kurdziałek (Warsaw: Polska Akademia Nauk, 1963). Pasnau, "Latin Aristotle," 666, does not distinguish the decrees, giving the perhaps unintentional impression in his treatment of the decree that the dramatic actions of the first part had to do with the influence of Aristotle.

69. See Henryk Anzulewicz, "Person und Werk des David von Dinant im literarischen Zeugnis Alberts des Grossen," *Mediaevalia Philosophica Polonorum* 24 (2001): 38–39.

70. The association between David and Alexander comes from Albert the Great. Anzulewicz, "Person und Werk des David von Dinant," 42, notes that this may not indicate any dependency of David on Alexander. Albert evidently encountered a copy of Alexander's *De intellectu* prior to his arrival at Paris, and so may have merely noted a purely coincidental correspondence between what he found in David and what he had earlier found in Alexander.

71. Van Steenberghen, *La philosophie au xiiie siècle*, 84, describes it as a "une mesure de prudence et de défense provoquée par l'usage abusif que David, et d'autres peut-être avec lui, avaient fait de [les] écrits [d'Aristote]."

72. Amos Bertolacci, "On the Latin Reception of Avicenna's Metaphysics before

convincingly that *commentum* is not a term with a definite meaning during this period; it could just as conceivably refer to any work in the tradition of a work of Aristotle.[73] We may thus imagine two other possible scenarios: 1) that the *commenta* refer to the works which David himself read in Sicily, such as that of Alexander; or 2) that the *commenta* refer to other contemporary Latin works that are now lost, since they were burnt following his condemnation. There does not exist sufficient evidence to decide the matter with certainty. Nevertheless, if we hypothesize from the context of the prohibition that the *commenta* envisioned are either ancient Greek or contemporary Latin works, not Arabic works of the intervening centuries, it becomes possible to see why a broadening of the prohibition might have become necessary in 1215.

The condemnation of 1215 had much more pastoral character than the condemnation of 1210. Already since 1213, Cardinal Robert de Courçon had been struggling to get clerics in Paris to stop attending lectures in philosophy. Evidently he felt that it was leading pastors of parishes to neglect their duties toward their parishioners, since by spending their time in the *lectio* of philosophers, they were neglecting the *lectio* of Scripture, which was the ultimate basis of *praedicatio*.[74] It was having a similar effect on members of religious orders: they were neglecting the duties of their interior prayer, spending their time listening to *lectiones* on philosophy in the schools when they should have been practicing *lectio divina* in the cloister.[75] It is not that Robert was against all philosophical study,

---

Albertus Magnus: An Attempt at Periodization," in *The Arabic, Hebrew and Latin Reception of Avicenna's Metaphysics*, ed. Dag Nikolaus Hasse and Amos Bertolacci (Boston: De Gruyter, 2012), 212. Van Steenberghen, *La philosophie au xiii*[e] *siècle*, 85, shares this conclusion.

73. Dag Nikolaus Hasse, *Avicenna's* De anima *in the Latin West: The Formation of a Peripatetic Philosophy of the Soul 1160–1300* (London: The Warburg Institute, 2000), 20.

74. It is easy to overlook the significance of the pastoral context and to take concern for preaching as a pretext for a concern about heresy. But the concern for preaching was a genuinely integral part of the pastoral program of the period. See Jones, "Preacher of the Fourth Lateran Council."

75. Denifle, *Chartularium Universitatis Parisiensis*, 1:77. Concerning pastors of parishes, he ordered "ut nulli habenti curam parochialem liceat seculares scientias addiscere,

or even specifically against the study of Aristotle. In the statutes he erected for the Faculty of Arts at Paris in 1215, wherein he issued the prohibition of 1215, he actually *commands* that students read the logical works of Aristotle, and places the *Nicomachean Ethics* on a shortlist of books that they are permitted to read on feast days.[76] The Aristotelian prohibition is limited in scope and tied, as it was in 1210, to the works of Amaury of Bène and David of Dinant. Robert adds only three things to the provisions of 1210: first, he adds metaphysics to the list of topics which cannot be studied; second, he adds a certain Mauricius of Spain to the list of persons whose works may not be studied; third, he prohibits the reading of *summae* of Aristotle's natural philosophy and metaphysics.

Denifle, following Renan, gives the identity of Mauricius as Averroes. Renan had argued that it resulted from a corruption of Averroes's name.[77] While that may seem admittedly far-fetched (notwithstanding that Renan adduces some extremely wide-ranging examples of such corruptions from manuscripts of the period), Mandonnet suggests a simpler and more elegant solution with which to arrive at the same conclusion: Mauricius ("Maurice") is a corruption of Maurus ("The Moor").[78] Mauricius of Spain would thus be "the Spanish Moor."[79]

---

ex quibus nullatenus possit subditorum suorum saluti prodesse. Immo si a prelato suo licentiam adeundi scolas obtinuerit, nihil nisi veram litteram aut sacram paginam ad informationem parochianorum suorum addiscat." Concerning religious, he permitted them to study within the cloister, but ordered that they return from the schools within two months under pain of excommunication.

76. For this reason, we cannot follow van Steenberghen, *La philosophie au xiiie siècle*, 88, when he concludes that "les interdictions de 1210 et de 1215 touchant la philosophie naturelle d'Aristote, ont été inspirées par la faculté de théologie de Paris; il faut y voir des mesures de défense en vue de protéger la science sacrée contre les infiltrations païennes du nouvel Aristote." Van Steenberghen's interpretation relies upon Grabmann's biblical-moral/speculative distinction, and so needs to be revised in light of the work of Andée and Clark, cited above.

77. Denifle, *Chartularium Universitatis Parisiensis*, 1:80n4; Ernest Renan, *Averroès et l'Averroïsme*, vol. 3 of *Oeuvres Complètes* (Paris: Calmann-Lévy, 1949), 179.

78. Pierre Mandonnet, *Siger de Brabant et l'averroïsme latin* (Fribourg: Librairie de l'Université, 1899), xxxn2.

79. While not agreeing that Mandonnet's conclusion rests on perfect reasoning, van Steenberghen, *La philosophie au xiiie siècle*, 86–87, allows that it is a reasonable hypothesis.

Mandonnet's theory is plausible, but it suffers from one difficulty. Hasse has shown recently that the translations of Averroes's works of natural philosophy and metaphysics were almost certainly translated by Michael Scot, as has long been thought;[80] Michael did not begin translating the works of Averroes until 1217, two years after the condemnation.[81] We may respond to this difficulty by suggesting that the prohibition of 1215 had a pre-emptive nature like the prohibition of 1210.[82] Latin scholars were aware of Averroes in 1215, even if they did not have large access to his works. Thus, just as the bishops sought to prohibit the spread of false ideas taken from Aristotle and his Greek or Latin commentators in 1210, so likewise did Robert seek to prohibit the spread of potentially false ideas from Averroes in 1215.

Identifying the *summae* is a far less controversial task than identifying Mauricius. Van Steenberghen and Bertolacci both present compelling arguments that they can be identified with the works of Avicenna.[83] Since a portion of Avicenna's *Physics* and all of his *De anima* and *Prima philosophia* had been available from the late twelfth century in Latin translation,[84] there is no textual or historical reason to prevent us from following their conclusion on this point.[85]

80. Dag Nikolaus Hasse, "Latin Averroes Translations of the First Half of the Thirteenth Century," in *Università della Ragione, Pluralità delle Filosofie nel Medioevo. XII Congresso Internazionale di Filosofia Medievale, Palermo 17–22 settembre 2007*, ed. A. Musco (Palermo: Officina di Studi Medievali, 2012), 1:149–78.

81. Van Steenberghen, *La philosophie au xiii*[e] *siècle*, 103; Bertolacci, "On the Latin Reception of Avicenna's Metaphysics," 216.

82. Van Steenberghen, *La philosophie au xiii*[e] *siècle*, 87, already envisioned this possibility, highlighting that "la mention d'Averroès dans le statut de 1215 n'impliquerait pas l'existence de traductions latines de ses écrits à cette date."

83. Ibid., 85; Bertolacci, 'On the Latin Reception of Avicenna's Metaphysics," 215–17.

84. The Latin translation of Avicenna's *Physics* was known as the *Liber primus naturalium*. See Gérard Verbeke, introduction to Avicenna, *Liber primus naturalium*, ed. S. van Riet (Leiden: Brill, 1996), 53*–54*. Verbeke observes that although we lack the complete text of the *Liber primus naturalium*, it is possible that a completed Latin text existed, but was destroyed around the time of the initial condemnations. On the Latin text of Avicenna's *De anima*, see Hasse, *Avicenna's* De anima *in the Latin West*, 7–8. On the Latin text of Avicenna's *Prima philosophia*, see Gérard Verbeke, introduction to Avicenna, *Liber de philosophia prima*, ed. S. van Riet (Leuven: Peeters, 1977–80), 1:123*–24*. On the general influence of these texts prior to the prohibitions, see van Steenberghen, *La philosophie au xiii*[e] *siècle*, 90.

85. I part company from Bertolacci in one major respect: Bertolacci also wants to

While absolute certainty in the interpretation of the prohibitions of 1210 and 1215 is impossible because of a lack of evidence from the period, we can at least propose the following provisional conclusions:

1) The condemnation of David of Dinant in 1210 stemmed from his heretical use of Greek sources which were not necessarily available throughout the Latin West.
2) The prohibited *commenta* of 1210 are either Greek commentaries that David knew or Latin ones which were presumably destroyed.
3) The Mauricius of 1215 is Averroes.
4) The *summae* of 1215 are the works of Avicenna.

In short, the condemnation of 1210 prohibited Latin and Greek natural philosophy, while the condemnation of 1215 prohibited Latin, Greek, *and Arabic* natural philosophy and metaphysics. The differences between the two prohibitions are important, because we shall see in a moment that they play an essential role in bringing us to an interpretation of the condemnation of 1231 which accords with the available evidence.

The prohibition of 1231 is nestled within Gregory IX's bull, *Parens scientiarum,* which he issued to facilitate the reopening of the University of Paris after the Great Dispersion during the strike of 1229. The occasion of the strike was the use of secular force against students who rioted after a dispute at a tavern. The masters at the university went on strike to protest this use of force and to uphold their right to independence from the secular authority. Unfortunately for the masters, their plan backfired in two ways. First, other universities where the works of Aristotle and his commentators could be studied freely benefited from the influx of masters and students.[86]

identify the *commenta* of 1210 with the *summae* of 1215. See Bertolacci, "On the Latin Reception of Avicenna's Metaphysics," 215–17.

86. Torrell, *Saint Thomas Aquinas,* 1:37; van Steenberghen, *La philosophie au xiii*[e] *siècle,* 96. Van Steenberghen notes the existence of what amounts to a recruitment flyer from the University of Toulouse advertising that students at that university can read the

Second, the members of the mendicant orders declined to strike, gaining seats on the university faculty and allowing classes to continue.[87] Gregory sought to diffuse the situation by inducing the masters who were on strike to return. He upheld their right to exemption from civil prosecution as well as their right to go on strike if needed, and sought to compel other masters (like the mendicants) to comply with legitimate statutory decisions made by the masters as a whole.[88]

Notwithstanding the fact that Gregory had previously expressed support for the prohibitions of 1210 and 1215,[89] it would make little sense for Gregory to reassert the Aristotelian bans gratuitously if his goal were to induce the masters who were on strike to come back; they were already growing used to their newfound freedom at other institutions. Gregory's actions instead suggest that he took three steps toward undoing the prohibitions as part of his general effort to reopen the university. First, he walked back the prohibition of 1215 to that of 1210. Notice how when Gregory supposedly "reinstates" the prohibitions, he refers only to the "books of natural [philosophy] ... prohibited ... *at the provincial council.*" This is a direct reference to the prohibition of 1210, which was issued by a provincial synod; it cannot refer to the prohibition of 1215, which was issued by the papal legate alone. Next, seven days after *Parens scientiarum*, and as a sign of his good will, he wrote to the Abbot of St. Victor and to the Prior of the Dominican convent in Paris granting them faculties to absolve anyone under them who had incurred excommunication for reading the works of natural philosophy under the terms of either the 1210 or the 1215 ban. Here he deliberately mentions both bans, re-

books which they cannot read at the University of Paris. Unfortunately, the "advertising campaign" could not last forever. In 1245, Pope Innocent IV extended the Parisian prohibition to Toulouse as well, a few years after Peter of Spain had given a course on Aristotle's *De anima* there. On the Toulouse ban, see van Steenberghen, *La philosophie au xiiie siècle*, 101. On Peter's commentary, see Bazán, "13th Century Commentaries on *De anima*," 126–32.

87. See Torrell, *Saint Thomas Aquinas*, 1:38.

88. See Young, *Scholarly Community at the Early University of Paris*, 41.

89. See van Steenberghen, *La philosophie au xiiie siècle*, 93.

ferring to the 1210 ban as the one given "in a provincial council," and the 1215 ban as the one given by "Cardinal . . . Robert," which prohibited the books that had been banned "in the provincial council."[90] This confirms for us that Gregory distinguished the two condemnations in his own mind, and that his choice to omit reference to the condemnation of 1215 in *Parens scientiarum* was deliberate. Another three days later, Gregory took a third step: he formed a committee to examine and expurgate the prohibited books, so that even the prohibition of 1210 could be lifted and all the works of Aristotle and his commentators could once again be read at Paris.[91]

While any interpretation of the prohibitions of 1210, 1215, and 1231 must engage in a high degree of speculation, it is therefore plausible that, although *Parens scientiarum* upheld the terms of the prohibition of 1210, it had the effect of eliminating the three provisions which the prohibition of 1215 had added to the prohibition of 1210: the prohibition of Aristotle's *Metaphysics*, as well as on the works of Avicenna and Averroes.[92] This accounts for the dramatic increase in

90. Denifle, *Chartularium Universitatis Parisiensis*, 1:143; Pasnau, "Latin Aristotle," 667; Young, *Scholarly Community at the Early University of Paris*, 48n121.

91. Denifle, *Chartularium Universitatis Parisiensis*, 1:143–44; Pasnau, "Latin Aristotle," 667.

92. This seems to accord with Roger Bacon's later memory which may possibly suggest that the "principal works" of natural philosophy and metaphysics were prohibited until the conclusion of the strike. See Bacon, *Opus minus*, 326: "Et si ipse [Alexander] eam [Summam fratris Alexandri] fecisset vel magnam partem, tamen non legit naturalia nec metaphysica nec audivit ea, quia non fuerunt libri principales harum scientiarum nec commentarii translati quando rexit in artibus. Et diu postea fuerunt excommunicati et suspensi Parisius, ubi ipse studuit. Unde citius ordinem intravit antequam fuerunt hi libri semel perlecti. Istud notum est per ejus ingressum in ordinem, et per dispersionem universitatis parisiensis nam usque ad eum fuerunt libri prohibiti, et usque quod rediit universitas, post quem reditum ipse intravit in religionem, jam senex et magister in theologia."

Richard Lemay, "Roger Bacon's Attitude toward the Latin Translations and Translators of the Twelfth and Thirteenth Centuries," in *Roger Bacon and the Sciences: Commemorative Essays*, ed. Jeremiah Hackett (Leiden: Brill, 1997), 27–29, reads Bacon as definitively stating that the proscribed books were permitted after the strike, and then criticizes Bacon harshly for what he calls an "arbitrary" recollection of the facts of history. Yet if we take into account the context of 1231, perhaps Bacon's memory need not appear so arbitrary after all.

Avicennianism at the University of Paris throughout 1230s, an empirical fact which we will observe through the study of texts from the period in a moment.[93]

Apart from the possibility that the effects of the prohibitions were already in the process of being revoked by 1231, we may note another reason for the increase of Aristotelianism at the University of Paris in the 1230s and 1240s. If we read the condemnations of 1210 and 1215 carefully, it says that one may not "*legere*" the prohibited works. As van Steenberghen points out, *legere* is the verbal cognate of the first noun of Peter Cantor's triad of magistral duties: *lectio, disputatio,* and *praedicatio*. To prohibit that a book be "read" is not to prohibit that it be perused in one's private study; it is to prohibit that it be "lectured upon," as the primary text in a classroom setting. Since such lectures could be given publicly or privately, the reference to public or private "reading" refers to public or private *lectures*.[94] Thus, notwithstanding the possibility that the use of certain books was actually permitted again after 1231, we can imagine a variety of ways in which even the books which remained prohibited could potentially still be used:

93. Early in the twentieth century, Étienne Gilson described an "Avicennianizing Augustinianism" at work in this period. See Étienne Gilson, "Pourquoi saint Thomas a critiqué saint Augustin," *Archives d'Histoire Doctrinale et Littéraire du Moyen Âge* 1 (1926): 111–27; Gilson, "Les sources gréco-arabes de l'augustinisme avicennisant," *Archives d'Histoire Doctrinale et Littéraire du Moyen Âge* 4 (1929): 5–149; Gilson, "Roger Marston: Un cas d'augustinisme avicennisant," *Archives d'Histoire Doctrinale et Littéraire du Moyen Âge* 8 (1933): 37–42. Hasse, *Avicenna's* De anima *in the Latin West,* v–vi, summarizes the reception of Gilson's thesis; he then gives a detailed exposition of the use of Avicenna in Roland of Cremona, William of Auvergne, Jean de la Rochelle, the *Summa fratris Alexandri,* Peter of Spain, and Albert the Great (ibid., 36–68).

Since the rise of Avicennian influence at Paris in the 1230s and 1240s is an empirical fact, its veracity does not rest on the interpretation that one gives to the prohibitions of 1210, 1215, and 1231. The interpretation I have suggested is merely one way of reading the texts which seems to accord with the fact that Avicenna and Averroes were used widely throughout this period.

94. Van Steenberghen, *La philosophie au xiii*[e] *siècle,* 85.

1) They could be used for private study.
2) They could be used in a *lectio* upon some other text, provided that one did not lecture directly upon a prohibited book.
3) They could be used in *disputatio*.
4) They could be used in the written artifacts of lectures and disputations, provided that the lectures in question were given on approved books.
5) They could be used in written compositions which did not arise from *lectio* or *disputatio*.

In light of these limitations to the three prohibitions, we can see why the practical effect of the prohibitions would be small after 1231. The letter of the condemnations exercised control over the *curriculum* of the Faculty of Arts at Paris, not the specific *content* of individual courses taught there,[95] and after 1231, the spirit of the prohibitions

95. If this is the case, then there may be reason to challenge the prevailing assumption that the condemnations were not taken seriously. We have already averted to the fact that one of Gregory IX's gestures in 1231 was to absolve members of the Abbey of St. Victor and of the Dominican convent of Saint-Jacques of the excommunication they had incurred for lecturing upon the prohibited books. This means that such lectures did in fact occur, and that the masters who gave them were in fact excommunicated. This would make sense of Roger Bacon's later comment in *Opus maius*, Ia.10 [Bridges 20]. Contrasting the reception of Averroes in the 1260s, which we will discuss in chapter 5, with the reception of his work in the 1210s–1220s, Bacon observes: "Nam Averroes major post eos et alii condemnaverunt Avicennam ultra modum; sed his temporibus gratiam sapientum obtinuit quicquid dicit Averroes, qui etiam diu neglectus fuit et repudiatus ac reprobatus a sapientibus famosis in studio, donec paulatim patuit ejus saptientia satis digna, licet in aliquibus dixit minus bene. *Scimus enim quod temporibus nostris Parisiis diu fuit contradictum naturali philosophiae et metaphysicae Aristotelis per Avicennae et Averrois expositores, et ob densam ignorantiam fuerunt libri eorum excommunicati, et utentes eis per tempora satis longa.* Cum igitur haec ita se habent, et nos moderni approbamus viros praedictos tam philosophos quam sanctos; et scimus quod omnis additio et cumulatio sapientiae quas dederunt, sunt dignae omni favore, licet in multis aliis diminuti sint, et in pluribus superflui, et in quibusdam corrigendi, et in aliquibus explanandi, manifestum nobis est quod illi, qui per aetates singulas impediverunt documenta veritatis et utilitatis quae oblata fuerunt eis per viros praedictos, nimis erraverunt, et vitiosi plurimum fuerunt in hac parte; sed hoc fecerunt propter scientiae extollentiam et propter ignorantiam" (emphasis added). Lemay, "Roger Bacon's Attitude," 28, quotes only the italicized portion of this passage, and finds Bacon's assertion "arbitrary" and "contradicted by the actual facts as we know them," because it seems to make too little of the use of Aristotle in the previous period. But if we compare the use of Avicenna and Averroes in the 1210s–20s

sought the annulment of the letter. If we turn, then, to the discussion of nature, grace, and the desire for God in the 1230s–50s, we should not be surprised to see a great diversity of attempts to incorporate the Aristotelian tradition within the existing Augustinian conversation bequeathed to the thirteenth century by Peter Lombard.

LATIN ARISTOTELIAN-AUGUSTINIANISM: PHILIP THE CHANCELLOR

One of the scholars at the University of Paris who made significant use of Aristotle in the period right around 1230 is Philip the Chancellor.[96] In his *Summa de bono*, Philip takes Peter's Augustinian understanding of natural desire as a starting point, but then develops Peter's understanding subtly but significantly in order to incorporate questions raised by what Aristotle says about nature.[97] His considerations can be framed around the same three questions as Peter's. First, what does it means for a motion to be called "natural"? Second, what is the end of the will's natural motion? Third, what is the relationship of the natural end of the will with that end which is posited for human nature by Christian Revelation?

Philip begins by grounding his reflections on nature in the text of Peter through a comparison of Peter Lombard's *Glossa* on Romans 11:24 with the text of Book 2 of the *Sentences*. Peter's text of Paul read, "against your nature, you were grafted onto the good olive tree."[98] On this, Peter had commented in his *Glossa*:

---

with the use of these same authors 1230s–40s, or even the 1260s (during the time when this text was composed and Latin Averroism was reaching its peak), Bacon's text is not altogether inaccurate, notwithstanding the author's tendency toward hyperbole.

96. On the details of Philip's life, see Nicolai Wicki, introduction to Philip the Chancellor, *Summa de bono* (Bern: Editiones Francke, 1985), 11*–28*. On the dating of the *Summa de bono*, see pp. 63*–66*.

97. Mansini, "Abiding Theological Significance of Henri de Lubac's *Surnaturel*," 612, notes the importance that Philip the Chancellor would have for later discussions of nature and the supernatural.

98. Philip the Chancellor, *Summa de bono* [Wicki 468:173]: "Contra naturam insertus es in bonam olivam."

> Since God is the one who creates and establishes all natures, he does nothing contrary to nature, since what he, from whom comes every mode, number, and order of nature, does, is what belongs to nature or is natural for any sort of thing. Nevertheless, it is not unreasonable to say that [God] does something contrary to nature when he acts contrary to that which we know in nature.... Yet he never acts contrary to that highest law of nature, which is far from the knowledge of we who are wicked and weak, because he no more does these things than he acts contrary to himself.[99]

We may note how Peter's text weds two ideas: the first is the historical act of Creation revealed in Genesis, whereby God creates and establishes natures; the second is the structure of a given nature on account of God's choice to create it as such. There is a dependency of the second upon the first—God's creative act fixes, in a historical moment, the bounds of a given nature. There is also a certain plasticity and contingency with respect to the word "nature." The ordinary course of events, according to which we understand and experience our human nature, occurs in our nature's fallen state, not the state of its first creation. When God justifies a sinner, he acts contrary to the ordinary course of events for a nature wounded and weakened by sin, but he does not act contrary to human nature according to its primary institution.

When Philip quotes this passage of Peter, he abstracts it from the historical context of Creation and the Fall, leaving out the part of Peter's text which discusses God as the one who creates and establishes all natures, and thereby obscures the distinction between original and fallen nature. Of course, it is not that Philip does not think that God is the one who creates and establishes all natures; rather, the historical context of Creation and Fall is not as determinative of Philip's approach to the structure of nature as such. A closer look at

99. Peter Lombard, *Glossa in Rom.* [PL 191:1488B]: "Deus ... creator et conditor omnium naturarum, nil contra naturam facit, quia id est naturae, vel naturale cuique rei quod facit, a quo est omnis modus, numerus, ordo naturae, sed tamen non incongrue dicitur aliquid facere contra naturam, quando facit contra id quod novimus in natura.... Contra vero illam summam naturae legem a notitia remotam, sive impiorum, sive infirmorum, tam Deus nullo modo facit, quam contra seipsum non facit."

Philip's discussion of nature reveals the shifting basis from which he considers it. Responding to the question of whether it is of the essence of a miracle that it be done contrary to nature, Philip observes:

Nature is taken in many senses. For sometimes the natural course of events [for a given creature], as known to man, is called "nature," as is said in the aforesaid authority [that is, Peter's gloss].... Sometimes a certain possibility belonging to that creature, which God has given to it so that what he wills may be done from it, is called "nature," and nature is defined in this way by the gloss on the passage from Romans 11[:24] ... which says, "what belongs to each thing's nature is what God, from whom comes every mode, number, and order of nature, makes of it." And in Book 2 of the *Sentences,* d. 18 [it likewise says]: "Moreover, [God] gave to natures that [what God wills] could be educed from them, not that they would have it by a natural motion...." Sometimes the highest law of nature is called "nature," namely, God himself. [Thus] the gloss on the [aforesaid] passage from Romans 11 [says] ... "But he never acts contrary to that highest law of nature, which is far from the knowledge of we who are wicked and weak, because he does not act contrary to himself."[100]

Philip goes on to argue that miracles are contrary to nature only in the first sense, not the other two.[101] But since not everything that is done contrary to the ordinary course of nature is a miracle, Philip distinguishes further. Some things which are done contrary to the ordinary course of nature have an end result entirely in accord with it, such as the healing of the blind. These are miracles, but they are beyond nature (*preter naturam*) rather than contrary to nature (*contra naturam*), because there is nothing contrary to nature about a man who sees.[102] Some things, which are done contrary to the or-

100. Philip the Chancellor, *Summa de bono* [Wicki 468:183]: "Natura accipitur multipliciter. Dicitur enim quandoque naturalis cursus hominibus notus, ut in predicta auctoritate dicitur.... Quandoque dicitur natura possibilitas quedam ipsius creature, quam dedit ei Deus, ut ex ea fiat quod ipse vult, et sic accipitur super illud ad Rom. XI.... Glosa: 'Id nature est cuique rei quod de ea facit Deus, a quo omnis modus, numerus et ordo nature.' Et II Sententiarum XVIII: 'Dedit autem naturis ut ex eis hoc fieri posset, non ut naturali motu haberent....' Quandoque dicitur natura summa lex nature, ipse scilicet Deus, super illud ad Rom. XI.... Glosa: 'Contra illam summam nature legem a notitia remotam sive impiorum sive infirmorum tam Deus nullo modo facit quam contra se ipsum non facit.'"

101. Ibid. [Wicki 468:195].

102. Ibid. [Wicki 471:273, 280].

dinary course of nature, have an end result which is entirely above nature, such as the justification of sinners,[103] or the assumption of a human nature by the Word.[104] These things are not contrary to nature so much as they are above nature (*supra naturam*).[105]

Whereas Peter's primary factor in determining what is natural is how a motion relates to God's institution of a nature at Creation, Philip's is how a motion relates to the ordinary course of events. This has a significant influence on how Philip appropriates Peter's understanding of the relationship between what is done freely with the help of grace and what is done without it. By decoupling reasoning about nature from an account of Creation, Philip is able to attempt a synthesis of Augustinian causes, as described by Peter, with Aristotelian causes, the knowledge of which had recently become available in the time between the completion of Peter's *Sentences* and the composition of the *Summa de bono*.

There are two Aristotelian texts that seem to have influenced Philip in particular. The first is *Physics* 2.1.[106] In that text, Aristotle gives two accounts of nature. The first is less a definition than an indication of how to begin thinking of nature: everything with a nature has an intrinsic principle of motion and rest.[107] The second relates nature to each of the four causes. Aristotle begins from material causality: "nature … is the immediate material substratum of things which have in themselves a principle of motion or change."[108] In terms of formal causality, "nature is … the shape or form (not separable except in statement) of things which have in themselves a source

103. Ibid. [Wicki 469:214].

104. Ibid. [Wicki 471:268].

105. Ibid. [Wicki 469:218, 471:268].

106. See Wicki, introduction to Philip the Chancellor, *Summa de bono*, 46*. Wicki comments that Philip knew Aristotle's *Physics* in the translation of James of Venice, which was completed ca. 1170, and which included only Books 1 and 2.

107. Aristotle, *Physics* 2.1 [192b13–14]. Philip alludes to this passage and actually uses it as a definition of nature in *Summa de bono* [Wicki 486:134]: "natura est intrinsecum principium motus et quietis."

108. Ibid. [193a28–30]. All translations from Aristotle's Greek are taken from *The Basic Works of Aristotle*, ed. Richard McKeon (New York: Modern Library, 2001).

of motion."[109] In terms of efficient and final causality, nature is that from which and toward which generation and corruption tend.[110] Of all the four causes, a thing's formal cause is most properly called its "nature," because form brings the potency of matter into act, and is that which governs the transmission of nature in generation.[111]

The second text of which Philip makes use is *Metaphysics* 9.8, in which Aristotle develops the account of nature given in *Physics* 2.1, by expounding upon the teleology of nature as a formal cause.[112] Aristotle first associates nature with potency. Every principle of movement or rest is a potency (δύναμις), and thus nature is a potency in a thing for movement with respect to itself.[113] As with any potency, the actuality of nature is prior to its potentiality in three senses: meaning (λόγος), because potency is ordered to act;[114] time (χρόνος) with respect to form but not with respect to number, because any existing potency or act always comes to be from something in act, even if the source of that act is another individual;[115] and finally being (οὐσία), for the same reason that it is prior in time, and also because an existing potency, like all existing things, is ordered toward a principle, and act is its principle.[116] By thus classing nature as a species of potency and defining every potency by the act toward which it is ordered, Aristotle suggests that every nature, as a potency, is ordered toward act as its teleological perfection.

The encounter with Aristotle left Philip with a dilemma. From Peter's reading of Augustine, Philip received an account of nature that was dependent on God's will as the cause of nature; from Aris-

109. Ibid. [193b3–5].
110. Ibid. [193b12–18].
111. Ibid. [193b6–7].
112. Philip references a variety of translations of the *Metaphysics*, but it is likely that he at least consulted Aristotle's *Metaphysics* in the *translatio media*, which included most of the *Metaphysics*, save for Book XI. See Wicki, introduction to Philip the Chancellor, *Summa de bono*, 46*, especially, note 2.
113. Aristotle, *Metaphysics* 9.8 [1049b5–8].
114. Ibid. [1049b12–14].
115. Ibid. [1049b17–29].
116. Ibid. [1050a3–10].

totle, he received an account of nature that was dependent on some act as nature's end. In order to harmonize these two accounts of nature, Philip looked to the first of the three arguments from Aristotle's *Metaphysics,* where Aristotle argues that act is prior in meaning (λόγος) to potency because potency is ordered to act. A subtle linguistic coincidence allowed him to bring Aristotle and Peter together. Λόγος was rendered by the Latin translator as *ratio,* the very same word that Peter had taken from Augustine to describe the properties that God had placed within creatures at Creation. Philip availed himself of this coincidence to unite the two ideas by means of a single definition: "A potency ordered to an end is called a *ratio*; for an end orders every cause."[117] This definition gave Philip the necessary conceptual tools to describe Augustine's *rationes* in terms of Aristotle's potencies.

As Philip attempts to harmonize Augustine and Aristotle, he makes more distinctions from Augustine's text than did Peter. For Philip, there is a germinatory property (*ratio seminalis*) in every creature, which corresponds to a material cause, a natural property (*ratio naturalis*) which corresponds to a formal cause, a causal property (*ratio causalis*) which corresponds to an efficient cause, and all of these are ordered toward a final property (*ratio finalis*) as to a final cause. The germinatory and natural properties are intrinsic to a thing; the causal property is extrinsic.[118] Primordial properties (*rationes primordiales*) are either in God as the causes of things, or identical to the germinatory and natural properties of a creature.[119]

117. Philip the Chancellor, *Summa de bono* [Wicki 481:9]: "ratio dicitur potentia ordinata per finem; finis enim ordinat causas omnes."

118. Ibid. [Wicki 481:13]. As an antecedent to this attempted harmonization, we may highlight Alexander of Hales, *Glossa in II Sent.* [Quaracchi 2:162]: "Quatuor sunt genera causarum, et ideo ratio dicitur quadrupliciter. Aliquando enim dicitur in comparatione ad causam finale, et sic accipitur ratio simpliciter; aliquando autem respicit causam formalem, et sic dicitur ratio naturalis; aliquando autem respicit causam materialem dispositam, et sic dicitur ratio seminalis; aliquando respicit causam efficientem, et sic dicitur ratio primordialis." Philip's association of *ratio* and potency is anticipated here, but not in the complete sense in which Philip discusses it.

119. Ibid. [Wicki 482:18].

Philip's association of Augustine's primordial properties with Aristotle's material and formal causes created a problem that had existed neither for Peter nor for Aristotle: how does one give a teleological account in terms of material and formal causes of that property of human nature in virtue of which God causes effects in it which human nature cannot cause of its own accord? Philip's solution was to develop a new kind of potency. Grounding himself in the association in *Metaphysics* 9.8 between nature and potency, he states:

A potency for obedience [*potentia obedientie*] toward every divine work was created from the beginning, whether nature mediates it as a principle, or whether the will of the Creator does it immediately. But while there is the same potency for obedience toward every work, there is not a potency in the same degree to one or another work. Rather, for some [works] it is called a potency in the second or third degree, while for miraculous works [*opera miraculosa*] it is only called a possibility. However, since that possibility arises from the creature's obedience, God can make of it what he wills; and since it is a passive possibility, it does not therefore follow that [the possibility] is a potency for an act.[120]

By his recourse to the term, "potency for obedience," Philip intentionally recasts Peter's Augustinian distinctions in Aristotelian language without changing their underlying meaning. A potency for obedience sounds Aristotelian, but insofar as an Aristotelian potency is immediately ordered to an act, a potency for obedience in the utmost degree is not a potency properly speaking, because it is not ordered immediately to any particular act at all. That is why Philip calls it only a "possibility."[121]

120. Ibid. [Wicki 483:69]: "potentia obedientie a principio creata est ad omnia opera divina, sive mediante natura principio, sive voluntate creatoris immediate. Et est eadem potentia obedientie ad omnia opera, sed non est potentia in eodem gradu ad hec opera et ad alia; sed ad alia dicitur potentia in secundo gradu vel tertio, ad opera vero miraculosa possibilitas tantum. Sed non ideo sequitur quod potentia sit ad actum, quia illa possibilitas est secundum obedientiam creature, de qua potest Deus facere quod vult, et est possibilitas passiva."

121. In fact, keenly aware of this difference between Aristotelian potency and what he is proposing, Philip goes on to call the Aristotelian potency, "active potency" (*potentia activa*), and the Augustinian possibility, "receptive potency" (*potentia susceptiva*). See Ibid. [Wicki 484:90].

Philip's account of natural desire is eclectic like his account of nature, drawing from Augustine, Peter, and Aristotle as before, and adding to them the authority of John Damascene. With Peter, Philip distinguishes in general between a natural desire by which we desire what is good in general, and a free desire for any particular good.[122] Philip also identifies that natural desire with a spark (*scintilla*),[123] which was part of Adam's upright nature at Creation,[124] and cannot be extinguished completely, even by sin.[125] However, Philip's thought adds to these Augustinian distinctions taken from Peter several Aristotelian distinctions taken from Damascene.

In chapter 36 of *De fide orthodoxa*,[126] Damascene distinguishes two aspects of the will: natural willing (θέλησις, transliterated by the medieval translators as *thelisis*), which concerns in general everything that pertains to a creature's natural existence,[127] and deliberative will-

122. Ibid. [Wicki 199:105].

123. Ibid. [Wicki 192:3].

124. Ibid. [Wicki 197:65].

125. Ibid. [Wicki 204:50].

126. Damascene explains his philosophical psychology in chap. 36, and applies it to the two wills of Christ in chap. 56. The translation of *De fide orthodoxa* which Peter used for the *Sentences*, from the twelfth-century Venetian theologian, Cerbanus, starts at chap. 45 and only continues until chap. 52. A translation by Burgundio of Pisa would later include the complete text. Circumstances appear to have been such that Peter may have had only a brief time to copy out the texts he considered to be most important from a complete edition, and he evidently judged Damascene's philosophical psychology not to be among the most important passages. Philip, however, shows a thorough acquaintance with the complete translation and is able to incorporate Damascene's moral psychology more thoroughly into his reflections on the natural desire for God. See Rosemann, *Peter Lombard*, 38; Colish, *Peter Lombard*, 1:22.

Both translations are available in a modern critical edition in John Damascene, De Fide Orthodoxa: *Versions of Burgundio and Cerbanus*, ed. Eligius M. Buytaert (St. Bonaventure, N.Y.: The Franciscan Institute, 1955).

127. John Damascene, *De fide orthodoxa*, trans. Burgundio, 36, no. 8 [Buytaert 135–36]: "Oportet scire quoniam animae inserta est naturaliter virtus, 'appetitiva eius quod secundum naturam est, et omnium quae substantialiter naturae adsunt contentiva,' quae vocatur voluntas. Nam 'substantia quidem esse et vivere et moveri secundum intellectum et sensum appetit, propriam concupiscens naturalem et plenam essentiam.' 'Ideoque' et sic determinant hanc naturalem voluntatem: 'thelima (id est voluntas) est appetitus rationalis et vitalis, ex solis dependens naturalibus.' 'Quare thelisis (id est voluntas) quidem est ipse' naturalis et 'vitalis et rationalis appetitus' omnium naturae constitutivorum, 'simplex virtus.' Qui aliorum enim appetitus, non existens rationalis, non dicitur thelisis

ing (βούλησις, transliterated by the translators as *bulisis*), which concerns some "particular thing."[128] θέλησις is in us prior to any actual determined intention, whereas βούλησις is the beginning of any action and concerns the end in view.[129] As compared with Peter's Augustinian psychology, we may note one significant similarity and one significant difference in Damascene's distinction of wills. The similarity concerns θέλησις, which is the "simple power of willing."[130] Like Peter's natural willing, it is not the subject of free will; it seeks the satisfaction of human nature in general.[131] The difference concerns βούλησις. While Peter's freely willed actions concern the means to a pre-determined end, βούλησις also concerns the very end itself.

Philip tries to harmonize Damascene's moral psychology with that of Peter. In order to do this, he adopts Damascene's distinction between θέλησις and βούλησις, but maps onto it Peter's distinction between natural and free will. This posed no particular difficulty as concerns θέλησις.[132] However, it posed a set of difficult questions concerning βούλησις.

First, Damascene explicitly states that βούλησις primarily concerns the end, not the means to the end, while Peter says the opposite about what is willed freely.[133] Second, since Peter thought the

---

(id est voluntas)." The passages in single quotes are taken by Damascene from Maximus the Confessor, *Opusculum I ad Marinum* [PG 91:12C–13A].

128. John Damascene, *De fide orthodoxa*, trans. Burgundio, 36, no. 9 [Buytaert 136]: "'Bulisis (id est voluntas) autem est qualitativa naturalis thelisis' (id est voluntas), scilicet naturalis et rationalis appetitus 'alicuius rei.' Nam iniacet quidem hominis animae virtus rationaliter appetendi. Cum igitur naturaliter motus fuerit ipse rationalis appetitus ad aliquam rem, dicitur bulisis (id est voluntas). Bulisis (id est voluntas) enim est appetitus et desiderium cuiusdam rei rationalis.'" The quoted passages are taken by Damascene from Maximus the Confessor, *Opusculum I ad Marinum* [PG 91:13B].

129. John Damascene, *De fide orthodoxa*, trans. Burgundio, 36, no. 11 [Buytaert 137]. Damascene is relying here on Maximus the Confessor, *Opusculum I ad Marinum* [PG 91:13–16].

130. John Damascene, *De fide orthodoxa*, trans. Burgundio, 36, no. 15 [Buytaert 140–41].

131. Ibid., 36, no. 8 [Buytaert 135–36].

132. Philip the Chancellor, *Summa de bono* [Wicki 160:29]: "Dividit autem [bulisim] contra voluntatem naturalem, que thelisis dicta est."

133. Philip the Chancellor, *Summa de bono* [Wicki 73:32]: "Est enim voluntas secundum duos modos. Primo modo dicitur voluntas finis quod est summum bonum, et sic ponitur voluntas cum tria anime assignantur secundum conversionem eius ad essentiam

end of the natural will was fixed, it was sufficient for Peter to define *beatitudo* as "having all you want, and not wanting anything wrongly": the first part of Augustine's phrase pertained to man's fixed end, and the second to the freely chosen means toward that end. Since, however, Philip follows Damascene's moral psychology, he had to make room in Peter's description of happiness for an explanation of why any person would *want* to choose human nature's ultimate end for himself. In short, Philip had to distinguish the *object* of human happiness, the subjective *dispositions* which cause a person to desire that object freely, and a person's choice of *means* toward that object.

The necessity of distinguishing the object of happiness from the subjective dispositions which lead a person to choose it freely was made all the more important in light of Aristotle's *Nicomachean Ethics*. In Philip's day, only the first three books of the *Nicomachean Ethics* were available to Latin readers,[134] and in Book 1 of the *Nicomachean Ethics*, Aristotle defines happiness as "an activity of the soul according to perfect virtue."[135] Philip, aware of this text, sought a way of distinguishing the good, as the end of human nature, from virtue, which leads us to choose the good as our particular end. He did this by leaving aside Augustine's definition of happiness and preferring one taken from Boethius: "happiness ... is 'a state made perfect by the amalgamation of everything that is good.'"[136] Philip, like Boe-

divinam per illa tria intelligentia, memoria et voluntas que sunt trinitas creata. Secundo modo dicitur eorum que sunt ad finem que ex iudicio et deliberatione procedunt, ut II Damasceni XXII, et huiusmodi dicitur liberum arbitrium facultas sive ipsa voluntas facilis. Primam vocat Iohannes Damascenus thelisim, secundam que est liberum arbitrium bulisim. Prima est in bonum tantum, secunda est declinans in bonum vel in malum."

134. István P. Bejczy, introduction, 3. The translation of Books 2–3 was known as the *ethica vetus*, while the translation of Book 1 was known as the *ethica nova*. Both are presumed to have been made by Burgundio of Pisa, the same translator who completed John Damascene's *De fide orthodoxa*.

135. Aristotle, *Nicomachean Ethics*, 1.13 [1102a5]: "Ἐπεὶ δ᾽ ἐστὶν ἡ εὐδαιμονία ψυχῆς ἐνέργειά τις κατ᾽ ἀρετὴν τελείαν." Burgundio's translation reads, "est felicitas anime actus quis secundum virtutem perfectam."

136. Philip the Chancellor, *Summa de bono* [Wicki 527:37]. The definition is taken from Boethius, *De consolatione philosophiae*, in *Opuscula theologica*, ed. Claudio Moreschini. Münich: K. G. Saur, 2000), 3, pros. 2 [Moreschini 60]: "Liquet igitur esse beatitudinem statum bonorum omnium congregatione perfectum."

thius, identifies the amalgamation of everything that is good with God as an object, and so is able to distinguish virtue from it as the subjective disposition which disposes a subject for the enjoyment of God.[137]

Philip the Chancellor thus made two contributions to reflection on natural desire in the second quarter of the thirteenth century. The first concerned what it means to be natural. By redefining "natural" as that which happens according to the ordinary course of events, Philip developed an account of nature more directly receptive to philosophical analysis through detachment from any explicit reference to the biblical narrative of creation, fall, redemption, and glorification. This had the benefit of bringing Christian reflection on nature into more explicit dialogue with non-Christian reflection, and of allowing for a rich flowering of philosophical analysis of human nature in the decades that would follow. But it also had the perhaps unintended consequence of distinguishing two questions which had previously been united in the Augustinian tradition: the question of how grace heals fallen nature from its woundedness, and the question of how grace elevates healed nature to the vision of God. Although the two questions remained closely related, arguments about the desire for God subsequently tended to be considered in light of nature's elevation to the vision of God, not its healing from sin.

By distinguishing the question of nature's elevation from the question of its healing, Philip was able to make a second contribution to reflection on natural desire in the second quarter of the thirteenth century with regard to Peter Lombard's category of free desire without the aid of grace. Through an appropriation of John Damascene's moral psychology, Philip extended free desire to include the end of human nature, not just the means of achieving that end. The legacy of this contribution was ambiguous, in light of two questions that Philip left unanswered. First, what is the ultimate end of man's free desire without the aid of grace? Peter had not asked

137. Philip the Chancellor, *Summa de bono* [Wicki 528:83]. Philip expresses a similar idea to that of Boethius in *De consolatione philosophiae* 3, pros. 10 [Moreschini 80–86].

this question, because he did not think that man's ultimate end was the subject of free desire without the aid of grace—he spoke only of proximate and immediate ends for such a desire, such as those associated with the sustenance of human life. Even though Philip's thought allowed for this question, Philip did not resolve it either, as his speculation on man's freely chosen end focused on the end of man's free desire *with* the aid of grace. Nevertheless, standing in the background to subsequent reflection on the desire for God was Peter Lombard's comment that whatever is willed freely without the help of grace can be said to be desired "naturally," even if in an equivocal sense.

This leads to a further question: what is the relationship between the ultimate end of man's natural desire (as contrasted with free desire), and the ultimate end of man's free desire without the aid of grace (as contrasted with the ultimate end of man's free desire with the aid of grace)? Is the end of both "natural" desires the same, or is there a different end for each? If they are the same, then an infelicitous consequence could arise for theological anthropology: how can man be said to desire the vision of God freely without the aid of grace? If they are different, then Philip's appropriation of Damascene's distinction between θέλησις and βούλησις planted the seed for a contrast between the ultimate end of our free desire *with* the aid of grace and our free desire *without* the aid of grace. If Philip did not call this a distinction between "natural" and "supernatural" desire, Peter had at least already called the former—in a certain sense—"natural."

LATIN AVICENNIAN-AUGUSTINIANISM

The appropriation of Aristotle that we find in Philip the Chancellor was only the beginning of a larger trend in the 1230s and 1240s toward the ever greater appropriation of the Aristotelian tradition in discussions of nature, grace, and the desire for God. Whatever one may make of the prohibitions of 1210, 1215, and 1231, it is an observable fact that other philosophers and theologians in the years that followed made particular use not only of Aristotle, but also of his Arabic commentators, Avicenna and Averroes. Here we will examine three witnesses to the use of Avicenna: Richard Rufus, William of Auvergne, and the *Summa fratris Alexandri*. Each engages some aspect of the discussion of nature, grace, and the desire for God by way of an analogy. Rufus discusses nature by an analogy with the relationship between matter and form; William discusses the desire for God by an analogy with the relationship between the intellect and the will; and the *Summa fratris Alexandri* discusses the desire for God by an analogy with the relationship between nature and grace. Rufus and the *Summa fratris Alexandri* will both become influential in the discussion of Bonaventure below, whose *Commentary on the Sentences* formed the basis for Thomas's initial engagement with the Parisian conversation on nature, grace, and the desire for God, as we will see in the next chapter; William will become influential in the discussion of Thomas's *Summa contra Gentiles,* which we will address in chapter 3.

Richard Rufus

Philip the Chancellor's detachment of nature from the historical context of Creation and the Fall set the stage for a flowering of philosophical and theological speculation on nature in the decades that followed. One such example can be found in the work of Richard Rufus (fl. 1231–56).[138] In the 1230s, Rufus was a secular master lecturing in the arts faculty at the University of Paris. He wrote a treatise, *Contra Averroem,* the second part of which was intended to oppose Averroes's doctrine of individuation,[139] and which would set

138. On Rufus's life, see Peter Raedts, *Richard Rufus of Cornwall and the Tradition of Oxford Theology* (New York: Oxford University Press, 1987), 1–13.

139. On the treatise and its dating, see Rega Wood, "Richard Rufus and English Scholastic Discussion of Individuation," in *Aristotle in Britain during the Middle Ages: Proceedings of the International Conference at Cambridge 8–11 April 1994; Organized by the Société Internationale pour l'Étude de la Philosophie Médiévale,* ed. John Marenbon

the stage for him to incorporate Aristotle and the Arabic Aristotelian tradition into the Augustinian discussion about nature.

In *Metaphysics* 7.8, Aristotle claims that matter is the principle of individuation in things.[140] This raises the question of *how* matter functions as the principle of individuation, since in *Metaphysics* 7.3, Aristotle also claims that when one substance changes to another, the *substratum*, if stripped of all form, is matter "which in itself is neither a particular thing nor of a certain quantity nor assigned to any other of the categories by which being is determined."[141] How, then, can that which is undetermined in itself be the principle of individual determination in things? The medievals of the thirteenth century inherited two general approaches to this question: that of Avicenna and that of Averroes. Avicenna proposed that matter, insofar as it constitutes the principle of individuation in things, must have at least a *forma corporeitatis* (a form of corporeity), which adds three dimensional existence of an undetermined quantity and quality to completely undetermined matter.[142] Matter informed by corporeity can then be determined more completely through receiving subsequent, more specific forms,[143] which are received extrinsically from a "giver of forms" (*dator formarum*).[144] Avicenna unfortunately left

(Turnhout: Brepols, 1996), 117–43. For the dating of Rufus's work, see pp. 118–21; for the content, see pp. 121–22. Wood discusses Rufus's influence on John Duns Scotus in "Individual Forms: Richard Rufus and John Duns Scotus," in *John Duns Scotus: Metaphysics and Ethics*, ed. Ludger Honnefelder, Rega Wood, and Mechthild Dreyer (New York: Brill, 1996), 251–72. More recently, one may also consult Wood's "Indivisibles and Infinites: Rufus on Points," in *Atomism in Late Medieval Philosophy and Theology*, ed. Christophe Grellard and Aurélien Robert (Boston: Brill, 2009), 39–64.

140. Aristotle, *Metaphysics* 7.8 [1034a5–8].

141. Ibid. 7.3 [1029a20–22; McKeon 785].

142. Avicenna, *Prima philosophia* 2.2 [van Riet 1:73]. Also see ibid. [van Riet 1:82].

143. On this question, see Allan Bäck, "The Islamic Background: Avicenna (b. 980; d. 1037) and Averroes (b. 1126; d. 1198)," in *Individuation in Scholasticism: The Later Middle Ages and the Counter-Reformation 1150–1650*, ed. Jorge Gracia (Albany, N.Y.: SUNY Press, 1994), 47.

144. On the place of the *dator formarum* in Avicenna's metaphysics, see Dag Nikolaus Hasse, "Avicenna's 'Giver of Forms' in Latin Philosophy, Especially in the Works of Albertus Magnus," in *The Arabic, Hebrew and Latin Reception of Avicenna's Metaphysics*, ed. Dag Nikolaus Hasse and Amos Bertolacci (Boston: Walter de Gruyter, 2012), 225–49.

a note of ambiguity as to whether he conceived the *forma corporeitatis* as a substance or an accident, and consequently how the *forma corporeitatis* interacts with the form(s) that matter receives when it is further determined.[145]

Responding to Avicenna, Averroes criticized both possibilities.[146] If the *forma corporeitatis* is a substance, then Avicenna begs the question because he assumes a substantial form in matter in order to show how substantial form comes to be in matter.[147] If the *forma corporeitatis* is an accident (a view which Averroes discusses but does not attribute to Avicenna, even if modern scholars recognize it as a legitimate interpretation of his thought),[148] then one must still postulate a substantial form in matter, because accidents can only inhere in a substance.[149] Instead, Averroes argues that corporeity is "the most general genus" (the *genus generalissma*, as the Latin scholastics would call it), which mediates a kind of incomplete existence

145. However Avicenna conceived the *forma corporeitatis* and the process of subsequent determination, the process never resulted in a creature having more than one substantial form at one time. See John Wippel, "Thomas Aquinas and the Unity of Substantial Form," in *Philosophy and Theology in the Long Middle Ages: A Tribute to Stephen F. Brown*, ed. Kent Emery et al. (Boston: Brill, 2011), 121–22.

146. Averroes's explicit treatment of Avicenna's ambiguity can be found in his *Epitome of the Metaphysics*. This text was only available in the thirteenth century in two Hebrew translations. It was not translated into Latin until the sixteenth century, and then only from one of the Hebrew versions. On the transmission of the text in the Middle Ages and early modern period, see the introductory remarks by Rüdiger Arnzen to Averroes, *On Aristotle's "Metaphysics": An Annotated Translation of the So-called "Epitome,"* ed. Rüdiger Arnzen (Berlin: Walter de Gruyter, 2010), 8–9. Averroes's critique of Avicenna is on pp. 89–93.

Even if the medievals lacked Averroes's explicit critique of Avicenna, they nevertheless possessed a critique of Avicenna's position in Averroes's long commentary on Aristotle's *Metaphysics*. See Averroes, *Commentarium magnum in libros Metaphysicorum*, in *Opera Omnia* (Venice: Giunti, 1562), 7.2, com. 5 [Giunti 8:156vk–l], and com. 8 [Giunti 8:158vm–159ra].

147. I infer this from Averroes's comment in the *Epitome*, 92. Averroes argues that if Avicenna is correct, then the coming to be of simple corporeal bodies (the elements) constitutes an instance of alteration. Averroes calls this "preposterous," because the elements would no longer be elemental if they were made from some more elemental substance.

148. See Marie-Dominique Roland-Gosselin, "Le principe de l'individualité," in *Le "De ente et essentia" de St. Thomas d'Aquin: Texte établi d'après les manuscrits parisiens: Introduction, Notes et Études historiques* (Paris: J. Vrin, 1948), 62–65.

149. Averroes, *Epitome*, 91–92.

to prime matter "between potentiality and actuality," and enables it to desire form naturally, without yet being completely informed.[150] Individuation occurs when a substantial form completes the process begun by corporeity, actualizes matter's potential for definite determination, and so communicates both substantiality and individuality to it.[151] On this view, substantial form is not placed in matter (*in materia*) from a *dator formarum*; it is drawn out from the matter itself (*ex materia*) in which it pre-exists potentially.[152]

One of the most significant elements of Averroes's account of individuation, to thirteenth-century theologians, was the fact that Averroes describes the eduction of form from matter as a gradual process:

Genus differs from matter. For Genus is a universal form, while matter should not be something in act at all, and possesses no form whatsoever, neither universal nor particular, from those things which it receives. Rather, it first receives a universal form, and then, by the mediation of its universal form, it receives other forms all the way to individual ones. It is both one in number, according as it is the subject of individual forms, and many in its forms, because it is divided by them. Also, if you consider [matter] in its universality, it is similar to genus, but it differs from it [as well], because it is one in number among many [forms], insofar as its being is in potency; genus, on the other hand, is one in form, midway between act and potency among many forms.[153]

150. Ibid., 92.

151. Averroes, *Commentarium magnum in libros Metaphysicorum* 7.2, com. 8 [Giunti 8:159rd].

152. See ibid., 12.3, com. 18 [Giunti 8:305vh–i]. Averroes twice criticizes Avicenna explicitly on the question of the *dator formarum*. See 304ra–b, where the doctrine of a *dator formarum* is attributed to "some people" (*quidam*), and 304vg, where it is attributed explicitly to Avicenna.

153. Ibid., 1.8, text 17 [Giunti 8:14vk]: "Genus est aliud a materia. Genus enim est forma universalis: materia autem secundum quod in ea non debet esse in actu aliquid omnino, et ex eis, quae recipit, nullam habet formam omnino neque universalem, neque particularem: sed primo recipit formam universalem, et postea mediante forma universali recipit formas alias usque ad individuales. Et est una in numero, secundum quod est subiectum formarum individualium, et multa secundum formas, quia dividitur per eas. Et est universaliter similis generi, sed differt a genere, quia est una in numero in multis, secundum quod esse eius est in potentia, genus autem est unum in forma media inter actum et potentiam in multis."

Averroes therefore differs from Avicenna in four principal respects: matter is the principle of individuation; forms are educed from matter and are not placed in matter; the primary form educed from matter must always be a substantial form; there can, and indeed must, be multiple substantial forms in an individual composite.

Rufus raises eleven objections against the position that matter is the principle of individuation.[154] The most significant of these concerns the same basic question that faced Avicenna and Averroes: if individuation supposedly comes from matter, how does that which is in pure potentiality to everything become determined to one individual thing? Since matter which has already been determined can still receive a variety of forms, Rufus argues that individuation must arise from a single, individual form. This form, imparted to the composite by its efficient cause, contracts the form to the point of creating an individual composite, without the need to posit a variety of substantial forms arriving in succession and co-existing once arrived.[155]

Since Rufus wrote *Contra Averroem* while he was lecturing in the arts faculty, he did not comment in the treatise about the implications of his thought for Augustine's *rationes seminales*. However, Ru-

154. I am grateful to Rega Wood for permitting me to consult her unpublished transcription of this text. Since the work remains unpublished, I will cite it in substance without any arguments that depend upon technical textual questions, which might be subject to future revision.

The objections mentioned in the body of this chapter begin at line 125 of Wood's transcription. Rufus's eleven objections proceed as follows: The first two (ll. 125 and 130 respectively) hinge more on the question hylomorphism than individuation, arguing that immaterial being cannot be individuated if matter is the cause of individuation, since immaterial being lacks matter. Rufus dismisses the first of these, since he assents to universal hylomorphism. The third (ln. 133) begs the question, arguing that individuation by matter alone would deny any individual character to form. The fourth through seventh (ll. 139, 142, 147, 158), as well as the ninth (ln. 169), all hinge on some form of the argument that since even designated matter can receive a variety of forms, it must be form that communicates individuality. The eighth and tenth (ll. 162, 175) make the argument that since matter, taken in itself, is pure potency, it requires some level of actuality for designation, which it can only receive from form. The eleventh (ln. 180) argues that since corporeity, according to Averroes, is the *genus generalissima*, all that could individuate something further would be form.

155. Rufus, *Contra Averroem* II, 224–33, and again at 239–44.

fus left the arts faculty in 1238 to become a Franciscan friar and was sent for studies in theology at Oxford.[156] Around 1250 he lectured on Peter Lombard's *Sentences* and applied his theory of individuation to the question of *rationes seminales*, which Peter had used as the basis for his understanding of nature, grace, and the desire for God.[157] In that text, Richard explains that the point of the doctrine of *rationes seminales* in the theological tradition is to account for the multifaceted potentiality of created existence. For this reason, *rationes seminales* cannot be associated with the substantial forms of things, since these forms are determined all the way to the point of individuality.[158] Instead, they must be associated with matter's corporeity, its most generic form, since this leaves matter open to formation by a variety of individual forms.[159]

While we await the publication of critical editions of Rufus's theological works, we can at least draw some preliminary conclusions about the significance of his reflections on nature in the works referred to above. Rufus is dealing with the same question that faced Philip: once we detach the study of nature from the historical context of Creation and the Fall, how do we give an account of it which balances the normativity of the teleology of its formal cause with its openness to grace? Philip looked on the side of potency; his "potency for obedience" expressed Augustine's *capacitas Dei* in Aristotelian language, but since it lacked a determined teleological act, it could

156. Rega Wood, "Richard Rufus," in *A Companion to Philosophy in the Middle Ages*, ed. Jorge J. E. Gracia and Timothy B. Noone (Malden, Mass.: Blackwell, 2006), 579.

157. Ibid. I am grateful to Rega Wood for permitting me to consult her unpublished transcription of this text as well.

158. Richard Rufus, *In II Sent.*, d. 18 [Rega Wood 1711–12].

159. Ibid. [Rega Wood 1712]. My claim that Rufus's thoughts on *rationes seminales* in the 1250s are consistent with his views on individuation in the 1230s should not be interpreted as precluding the observation by R. James Long that Rufus's *Commentary on the Sentences* is also much indebted to that of Richard Fishacre. See R. James Long, "Adam's Rib: A Test Case for Natural Philosophy in Grosseteste, Fishacre, Rufus, and Kilwardby," in *Robert Grosseteste and His Intellectual Milieu: New Editions and Studies*, ed. John Flood, James Ginther, and Joseph Goering (Toronto: PIMS, 2013), 160. Fishacre's influence was negative; Rufus mainly clarified his own views by contrasting them with those of Fishacre (161).

not be classified among Aristotle's potencies per se. Rufus, by contrast, gives *rationes seminales* a home within the Aristotelian tradition by identifying them with corporeity. Corporeity is, for Avicenna, the broadest and most indeterminate of forms that a creature can possess. In that sense it is among the closest concepts within the Aristotelian tradition to Philip's *potentia obedientiae.* But corporeity has one principal difference from *potentia obedientiae*: Since it is communicated to matter by a form, and since an Aristotelian formal cause has some definite, teleological act, this means that for all its indeterminacy, it is not *completely* indeterminate; it is merely the least determinate form that Rufus identifies.

Rufus's identification of *rationes seminales* with corporeity would give him a unique place in discussions of nature in the 1230s–1250s. On the one hand, in the debates in the 1240s and 1250s over whether *rationes seminales* should be identified with a creature's material or formal cause, his decision to identify them with corporeity would mark him out among contemporaries as a partisan of formal causality. In this respect, Rufus was to become nearly identified with Avicenna, and to bear the brunt of the criticism of those who followed Averroes's account of individuation. But on the other hand, his decision to identify *rationes seminales* with corporeity *rather than* a more specific form would also make Rufus a moderate by comparison with other partisans of formal causality. William of Auvergne was to take a more radical step. Where Philip associated our *capacitas Dei* with a *potentia obedientiae,* and Rufus made it the most general of forms that a composite can receive, William would simply identify our *capacitas Dei* with the formal cause of the human person, that is, the rational soul. But since every Aristotelian formal cause has some act as its teleological perfection, we will now proceed to see how William assigns nature and natural desire a teleological act which can only be reached by grace: the beatific vision in heaven.

William of Auvergne

We find another example of the use of Avicenna in the work of William of Auvergne, the bishop of Paris from 1228 to 1251. Some time in the second half of the 1230s, William authored a treatise, *De anima*, in which he mirrored very closely the style and tone of Avicenna's treatise by the same name.[160] In it, William takes Avicenna's understanding of natural motion in corporeal bodies, applies it to the intellect and the will, and adjusts the resulting account of nature, grace, and the desire for God to harmonize it with what Christian Revelation says about the perfection of the human person.[161]

Avicenna's primary instance of natural motion is that of simple, earthly bodies toward what Avicenna calls their "natural place." To the extent that a simple, earthly body is located anywhere other than its natural place, it has a natural motion toward that place, and will move toward that place unless prevented by some other motion impressed upon it.[162] The soul functions analogously to a simple body. Just as a body naturally desires some place, so likewise the will naturally desires some end.[163] But since "that which is made acquires its perfection from that by which it is made," the end of the soul is to know the first principle from which it came.[164]

Avicenna encountered a difficulty in his theory of natural motion when it came to explaining the motion of the heavenly bodies. According to Aristotle's *De caelo* 1.2, the simplest kinds of bodies in the universe are divided according to the simplest kinds of motion in the universe, straight (rectilinear) and circular. Straight motion comes

160. Hasse, *Avicenna's* De anima *in the Latin West*, 43.

161. Gilson, "Pourquoi Saint Thomas a critiqué Saint Augustin," 48–49: "L'attitude qu'il adopte à l'égard du philosophe arabe [that is, Avicenna] est déjà celle que conserveront après lui nombre de théologiens scolastiques: rejet énergetique de sa cosmologie, et spécialement de sa doctrine de l'intelligence séparée, mais sentiment d'être en accord intime avec lui touchant la nature de l'âme et l'origine de nos connaissances."

162. Ibid., 81.

163. Avicenna, *Prima philosophia* 9.2 [van Riet 2:455].

164. Ibid. [van Riet 2:456]: "Id enim quod factum est acquirit suam perfectionem ab eo a quo factum est."

from a simple, earthly body, which moves up or down according as it is heavy or light. The simple, earthly bodies are fire, air, water, and earth; the former two move upwards by nature, while the latter two move downwards by nature. Circular motion comes from a simple, heavenly body, which circles the heavens. The difficulty is that heavenly bodies circle the heavens unceasingly, and since they therefore never come to rest in a single place the way that simple, earthly bodies do, how can we say that they have a natural place? Moreover, if natural motion is defined as a motion toward a natural place, how can we say that their motion is natural at all? To solve the problem, Avicenna posits that the simple, heavenly bodies are ensouled; they are moved voluntarily by their souls out of a desire to reach the first cause insofar as they are able.[165]

Averroes was critical of Avicenna's theory of motion in the simple, heavenly bodies.[166] By positing a composition in them of mover (soul) and moved (body), Avicenna was able to preserve Aristotle's dictum that what is moved is moved by something.[167] However, precisely by positing such a composition, Avicenna failed to preserve their simplicity.[168] In order to preserve Aristotle's dictum *as well as* their simplicity, Averroes suggests that one may consider the ability of a simple body to receive motion, which is caused in it by another mover, as a separate principle of motion or rest in that simple body (that is, as a second "nature").

Averroes notes that there are two possible ways of rendering an account of this second nature. The first is to say that the second nature is actually the subject of an external mover. This would be an equivocal use of the term "nature," since it would denote a principle in the mover for moving a simple body, not a principle of motion in

165. Ibid. [van Riet 2:449]. See Silvia Donati, "Is Celestial Motion a Natural Motion?" in *Averroes' Natural Philosophy and Its Reception in the Latin West*, ed. Paul Bakker (Leuven: Leuven University Press, 2015), 96.

166. Donati, "Is Celestial Motion a Natural Motion?" 97–98.

167. For a detailed study of Averroes's treatment of this axiom, see Ruth Glasner, *Averroes' Physics: A Turning Point in Medieval Philosophy* (New York: Oxford University Press, 2012), 141–71.

168. Averroes, *Commentarium magnum in libro De coelo* 1.2, com. 5 [Giunti 5:5vc–f].

the simple body. This might lead, in turn, to the mistaken assumption that the mover's nature was actually the form of the simple body being moved, and that the two had entered into composition with one another, such as Avicenna had supposed. The second possibility, which Averroes considers more consistent, is to say that it belongs to the nature of the mover that, when it moves itself, it causes motion in the simple body. The matter of the simple body could then be called the simple body's "nature" in an analogical sense, insofar as it is the principle by which it receives motion or rest from the natural motion of an external mover.[169]

William follows the general contour of Avicenna's understanding of natural motion with one important caveat: William believes that the role envisioned by Avicenna for the *dator formarum* is actually performed directly by God.[170] According to William, when God makes a corporeal creature, he impresses upon it a natural inclination toward some one fixed place. As long as it is at a distance from that place, its natural inclination moves it toward that place; it will not rest until it reaches it.[171] It is similar with the soul, because "spiritual substances are related to their ends in a manner proportionate to the way in which natural bodies are related to their places."[172] But since the human soul is created by God and for God, it possesses a natural inclination toward God that nothing in all this world can satisfy. Only by the grace of God, elevating the soul to the vision of himself, can our soul's natural inclination be satisfied.[173]

Although it might seem that William places humanity in a metaphysically precarious position, since it has a natural inclination that cannot in any way be naturally satisfied, William senses no difficulty in this situation. Foreseeing some of the contours of future debates

169. See Averroes, *Commentarium magnum in libro Metaphysicorum* 7.5, com. 21 [Giunti 8:171vk].

170. William of Auvergne, *De anima*, in *Opera Omnia*, (Orleans: F. Hotot, 1674), 7.6 [Hotot 2:211b].

171. Ibid., 5.21 [Hotot 2:146b].

172. Ibid.: "Proportionaliter autem se habent corpora naturalia ad loca sua, et spirituales substantiae ad fines suos."

173. Ibid., 6.25 [Hotot 2:185a].

over the gratuity of grace (though perhaps not offering an entirely adequate solution), he argues that human nature is not at a loss, because we can always ask God for our perfection through prayer. Grace remains gratuitous, because God, who sees the moral blemishes on our souls, is always free to refuse our prayer if he sees fit.[174]

In supporting the claim that we have a natural inclination that can only be satisfied by the vision of God, William specifically distinguishes the natural inclination of the intellect from the natural inclination of the will. As with any natural inclination, the natural inclination of the intellect has one single, fixed end, just like a bodily creature has one single, fixed resting place: "this [act] ... is the most lucid and immediate vision of the creator."[175] In support of this idea, William gives an argument that anticipates one which Thomas Aquinas will later use in the *Summa contra Gentiles*,[176] by appealing to the beginning of Aristotle's *Metaphysics*:

> Aristotle's observation, when he says that "all men by nature desire to know," is certain as can be. Since, therefore, a desire of this sort is a spiritual hunger, it is also equally a natural hunger. But a hunger placed within us is vain if it is impossible for it to be satisfied naturally. [Therefore] it is necessary that it be possible to satisfy the human soul's hunger for knowing. And since the human soul only has a hunger of this sort according to its intellective power, it is necessary that the intellective power be satiable by a satisfaction which completely fills this sort of hunger, and leaves no vestige of it in the intellective power. And since there is no satisfaction of our hunger for knowledge except that which feasts on the fullness of knowledge, it is necessary that the knowable [object], by the knowledge of which our intellective power enjoys complete satisfaction, also possess such a luminosity as to leave no darkness at all in the intellective power (I mean the darkness of ignorance, opinion, and doubt), but to satisfy and fulfill the whole of it with its illumination [*irradiatio*].
>
> Furthermore, only the blessed creator can be a knowable [object] of this sort. For however well known by however much knowledge ev-

174. Ibid.

175. Ibid., 7.1 [Hotot 2:203b]: "Haec ... [operatio] est visio lucidissima et immediate creatoris." 7.7 [Hotot 2:212b].

176. Thomas's relationship to William on this point will be discussed in chapter 3.

ery other knowable [object] may be known, if [God] alone is unknown, there remains in the human soul in its intellective power the darkness of not knowing the creator, and the most vehement hunger to know him.[177]

William still has yet to conclude his argument, but if we pause for a moment and place to one side the influence of Avicenna on what William means by "natural inclination," the text could be given a much less extreme interpretation than an Avicennian reading might suggest. It is said that we have a "natural hunger" to know God. This could be interpreted as a natural inclination of the intellect. It is said that the natural hunger must be fulfillable "naturally," and that it terminates in the "creator." This could be interpreted as a reference to the knowledge of God through creatures. Can we not therefore say that William has in a mind a natural inclination to know God as first cause? William does not think so. When he goes on to conclude that "only the knowledge of the creator satisfies us," he is thinking specifically of our intellect being "joined to him with the most fitting and immediate union."[178]

177. Ibid., 7.2 [Hotot 2:204b]: "certissimus est sermo Aristotelis quo dicit quod omnes homines natura scire desiderant. Quia igitur desiderium hujusmodi fames spiritualis est, pariter et naturalis; frustra autem indita est fames, cujus naturaliter impossibilis est satietas, necesse est satietatem sciendi possibilem esse apud animam humanam: et quoniam hujusmodi fames non est animae humanae nisi secundum virtutem intellectivam, necesse est virtutem intellectivam satiabilem esse satietate quae famem hujusmodi plane repleat, nullumque ejusdem vestigium in virtute intellectiva relinquat: et quoniam fames scientiae non habet satietatem, nisi ipsam quae esuritur scientiae plenitudinem; necesse est scibile illud, cujus scilicet scientia satietas est plena virtutis intellectivae nostrae, ejus luminositatis esse ut nihil omnino tenebrarum, et intendo tenebrarum ignorantiae, opinionis, et dubitationis in virtute intellectiva relinquat, sed eam irradiatione sua totam satiet ac repleat.

"Porro scibile hujusmodi non potest esse nisi creator benedictus, omnibus enim aliis scibilibus quantacumque perfectione cognitionis notissimis, illo autem solo ignorato remanet apud animam humanam in virtute intellectiva ipsius tenebrositas ignorantiae creatoris, et fames vehementissima cognitionis illius."

A similar argument appears in William of Auvergne, *De anima* 6.25 [Hotot 2:184a]: "Amplius inter scibilia omnia nobilissimum etiam est creator, et scientia ejus tanto amplius aliis desiderabilis, quanto ipse omnibus scibilibus supereminet, aliorum igitur scibilium scientiis si esset possibile acquisitis restaret desiderium, et fames cognitionis ipsius creatoris: absque cognitione igitur ipsius non est possibile naturaliter ut quiescat desiderium hujusmodi vel sedetur fames, vel antedicta vacuitas impleatur."

178. Ibid.: "Quia igitur est per se quo posito ponitur, et quo remoto removetur

Several chapters later, William recapitulates his argument with an even greater emphasis on the specificity of our final end:

In the manner in which our noble motive power [that is, the will] is inclined naturally and tends toward a good object [*bonum*] which is the creator (for it is not possible that there be any rest or satisfaction for it in another), our intellective power is naturally inclined toward a true object [*verum*] (and when I say "toward a true object," I do not mean with a universal intention, but toward a particular true object, and a particular truth [*veritas*]). For the end of a natural inclination and intention cannot be vague and indeterminate, likewise neither can a natural motion. Wherefore it is clear that the natural intention and inclination of our intellect power is the first true object.[179]

If we read the first argument in light of the second, it is evident that William's natural inclination for the vision of God is an Avicennian motion, impressed upon the soul, with a specific and determinate end: the beatific vision, nothing short of which can constitute the soul's "natural place."[180]

By locating an Avicennian natural motion in the soul toward the beatific vision, William goes a step further than either Philip or Rufus toward the incorporation of Augustinian potency within the Aristotelian tradition. Like Rufus, he associates nature's *capacitas Dei* with a formal cause; unlike Rufus, he simply identifies that formal cause with the rational soul. Guided by Aristotle's understanding

aliquid, manifestum est tibi quod scientia creatoris sola satietas est, ac plenitudo virtutis nostrae intellectivae. Causa autem in hoc est quoniam creator est universum intelligibile, exemplum lucidissimum et distinctissimum universi, in quo relucet universum, et apparet apparitione lucidissimae expressionis; propter quod et virtus nostra intellectiva, si conjuncta ei fuerit conjunctione convenientissima et immediata, erit juxta congruentiam suae possibilitatis, et inferioritatis secundum intelligibile."

179. Ibid., 7.7 [Hotot 2:212a]: "Quemadmodum virtus nostra motiva nobilis est inclinata naturaliter, et propondens in bonum quod est creator; in alio enim non est possibile ut si[t] ei quies neque satietas: sed virtus nostra intellectiva est naturaliter inclinata in verum, et non in verum intentione universali, sed in quoddam verum, et in quandam veritatem. Non enim potest esse vagus, et indeterminatus finis naturalis inclinationis, et intentionis, similiter neque motus naturalis. Quapropter manifestum est quod intentio naturalis, et inclinatio virtutis nostrae intellectivae est primum verum."

180. William has a similar argument for the natural inclination of the will. See *De anima* 7.7 [Hotot 2:213a].

that every formal cause has some act as its teleological perfection, and Avicenna's teaching that this act is found in conjunction with a thing's natural place, William identifies God as the soul's natural place, and the beatific vision as its teleological perfection. Moreso than any other author whom we have encountered thus far, William thus turns the Augustinian desire for happiness, which Peter Lombard mediated to the thirteenth century, into a desire for God, properly speaking.

While William's teaching that the soul's teleological perfection is the beatific vision went further in harmonizing the Aristotelian and Christian traditions than any other thinker we have discussed so far, it raised questions for both traditions which subsequent theologians would have to resolve. On the part of the Aristotelian tradition, it raised the question of nature's integrity. If the soul can never reach its natural place *naturally*, to what extent is that place *natural* for it in any meaningful sense of the word? On the part of the Christian tradition, it raised the question of the gratuity of grace. If the beatific vision really is the soul's *natural* perfection, how can we say that the grace by which God admits the saints to it is gratuitous? Although William is thus an early adherent to the "natural desire for a supernatural end," his answer to these questions is ironically similar to that of the later Thomistic commentators: grace is gratuitous, because God is always free to withhold it. One might be tempted to think that William thus squares the circle, but his justification of God's freedom in this regard—while well-intentioned—is problematic: we are never so free from sin that God could not choose to hold our sins against us. While William was thus able to think through an account of nature that resulted in a Christian view of natural desire, he hit a roadblock on the question of grace, which subsequent thinkers, such as those who contributed to the *Summa fratris Alexandri*, would have to avoid by paying more careful attention to the relationship between nature and grace.

The *Summa fratris Alexandri*

The *Summa* in four books which bears the name of Alexander of Hales (the "*Summa fratris Alexandri*" or "*Summa Halensis*"), represents the work of several figures.[181] While its fourth book was an addition by William of Melitona in the mid-1250s, the first three books were at least to some extent compiled under the supervision of Alexander from Alexander's *Quaestiones disputatae*, the works of Alexander's student, Jean de la Rochelle, and the works of several other contemporary scholars. This gives it a curious character as concerns its teaching on nature, grace, and the desire for God. It certainly bears witness to a unified teaching on the matter influenced by Avicenna, although how or to what extent that teaching could be said to be Alexander's is a matter of dispute.

Presumably owing to the peculiar circumstances of its composition, the *Summa fratris Alexandri* copies *verbatim* large tracts from Philip's *Summa de bono* when discussing the relationship between nature and grace.[182] For both *Summae*, what is "natural" is what occurs according to the ordinary course of nature. When it is said that man has a "natural" desire, this means that there is a desire that occurs in all men according to the ordinary course of nature. Following John Damascene, this natural desire, θέλησις, can be distinguished from free desire, βούλησις.[183]

The *Summa fratris Alexandri* parts company from Philip concerning the *terminus* of natural desire. For Philip, following Boethi-

181. On the composition of the work, see Victorin Doucet, Prolegomena to Alexander of Hales, *Summa theologica*, vol. 4 (Quaracchi: College of St. Bonaventure, 1948), lix–lxxxi. Doucet argues that of the four books of the *Summa*, books 1–3 were mostly in existence by 1245 and were compiled mainly from the *Quaestiones disputatae* of Alexander, as well as the works of Jean de la Rochelle, while book 4 was composed by William of Melitona.

182. The copied sections are *Summa fratris Alexandri*, Ia-IIae, nos. 230–34 [Quaracchi 2:285–89]. The editors note the corresponding sections in the *Summa de bono*.

183. The *Summa fratris Alexandri* tends to distinguish these terms in Latin as *voluntas naturalis* and *voluntas deliberativa*, but it clearly attributes the distinction to Damascene. See *Summa fratris Alexandri*, Ia-IIae, no. 418, obj. E [Quarrachi 2:493]; Ia-Iae, no. 108, ad 1 [Quarrachi 1:169].

us, the end of natural desire is "happiness … 'a state made perfect by the amalgamation of everything that is good.'"[184] The *Summa fratris Alexandri,* however, adopts Avicenna's epistemology,[185] as well as the *triplex via* of the Greek theologian, Pseudo-Dionysius,[186] in order to turn a natural desire for happiness in general into a natural desire specifically for God.

In his *Prima philosophia,* Avicenna claims that metaphysics must begin with the apprehension of certain first principles, impressed upon the mind, which are neither demonstrated nor learned.[187] This is not an un-Aristotelian supposition; Aristotle says in *Metaphysics* 4.3 that certain principles cannot be proved or denied in the order of speculative judgment; chief among these is the principle of non-contradiction.[188] Avicenna agrees with Aristotle, but adds that

184. Philip the Chancellor, *Summa de bono* [Wicki 527:37]. The definition is taken from Boethius, *De consolatione philosophiae* 3, pros. 2 [Moreschini 60]: "Liquet igitur esse beatitudinem statum bonorum omnium congregatione perfectum."

185. Bertolacci, "On the Latin Reception of Avicenna's Metaphysics," 197–223, criticizes the previously held concensus, drawn from Gilson and van Steenberghen, that the reception of Avicenna's *Metaphysics* did not occur widely until the second half of the thirteenth century, and argues that its reception was more gradual. The unmistakable influence of Avicenna on Alexander would seem to support Bertolacci's view.

186. Overviews of the Dionysian corpus can be found in Jean Leclercq, "Influence and Non-influence of Dionysius in the Western Middle Ages," introduction in *Pseudo-Dionysius: The Complete Works,* trans. Colm Luibheid (New York: Paulist Press, 1987), 25–32; Paul Rorem, *Pseudo-Dionysius: A Commentary on the Texts and an Introduction to Their Influence* (New York: Oxford, 1993). In terms of the Middle Ages, H. F. Dondaine, *Le corpus dionysien de l'Université de Paris au XIIIe siècle* (Rome: Edizioni di storia e letteratura, 1953), remains invaluable for its research into the manuscripts available at the University of Paris, while several of the essays in *Re-Thinking Dionysius the Areopagite,* ed. Sarah Coakley and Charles M. Stang (Malden, Mass.: Wiley-Blackwell, 2009), provide chronologically successive perspectives on Dionysius's reception.

187. Avicenna, *Prima philosophia* 1.5 [van Riet 1:32–33]: "Dicemus igitur quod res et ens et necesse talia sunt quod statim imprimuntur in anima prima impressione, quae non acquiritur ex aliis notioribus se, sicut credulitas quae habet prima principia, ex quibus ipsa provenit per se, et est alia ab eis, sed propter ea." On Avicenna's doctrine of first impressions, see Jan Aertsen, "Avicenna's Doctrine of the Primary Notions and Its Influence on Medieval Philosophy," in *Islamic Thought in the Middle Ages: Studies in Text, Transmission and Translation, in Honour of Hans Daiber,* ed. Anna Akasoy and Wim Raven (Boston: Brill, 2008), 21–42. Avicenna's doctrine is drawn from his application of Aristotle's principle that every science assumes the existence of its principles (*Posterior Analytics* 1.10 [76a31]).

188. Aristotle, *Metaphyiscs* 4.3 [1005a17–b33].

there must be first principles in the order of concepts as well; otherwise there would be a reduction *ad infinitum* in the principles of first philosophy.[189] Avicenna therefore claims that the concepts of being (*ens*), thing (*res*), necessity (*necesse*), one (*unum*), and other such realities are "impressed" upon the mind in a non-demonstrable way.[190] Avicenna does not intend to provide an exhaustive list of these impressed principles; rather, he gives examples of how to identify them. The key factor for identifying such a principle is that it must be "common to all things," and unable "to be demonstrated … by a proof which is not circular, or through something which is better known."[191]

The *Summa fratris Alexandri* adopts from Avicenna the idea that certain basic concepts are impressed upon the mind. However, it differs from Avicenna on how to determine which particular concepts are impressed upon the mind. It agrees with Avicenna that being (*ens*) is one such concept, but it also adds the "first determinations of being": one, true, and good:[192]

Although the divine essence is ineffable, as is the most high Trinity, nevertheless it has *rationes* in itself, like that it is the highest, that it is the high-

189. The Latin Avicenna refers to the order of judgment, in which the first principles are axioms like the principle of non-contradiction, as *credulitas*; it refers to the order of concepts, in which the first principles are impressed notions of being and other concepts, as *imaginatio*. See John Wippel, "The Latin Avicenna as a Source for Thomas Aquinas's Metaphysics," in *Metaphysical Themes in Thomas Aquinas II* (Washington, D.C.: The Catholic University of America Press, 2007), 31–64.

On the reduction of the order of concepts to primary principles, see Avicenna, *Prima philosophia* 1.5 [van Riet 1:33], quoted in Aertsen, "Avicenna's Doctrine of the Primary Notions," 24n11: "Si autem omnis imaginatio egeret alia praecedente imaginatione, procederet hoc in infinitum vel circulariter."

190. Avicenna gives two lists of such concepts. The first includes being, thing, and necessity [van Riet 1:31]; the second includes being, thing, and one, but suggests that there are others of this kind [van Riet 1:33]. The plasticity of this category is important for the *Summa fratris Alexandri*, because it allows it to adapt Avicenna's primary notions for its understanding of the natural desire for God.

191. Avicenna, *Prima philosophia* 1.5 [van Riet 1:33]: "Quae autem priora sunt ad imaginandum per seipsa, sunt ea quae communia sunt omnibus rebus, sicut res et ens et unum, et cetera. Et ideo nullo modo potest manifestari aliquid horum probatione quae non sit circularis, vel per aliquid quod sit notius illis."

192. *Summa fratris Alexandri*, Ia-Iae, no. 72, co. [Quaracchi 1:113].

est truth, and that it is the highest good. Although these [*rationes*] are the same in God, they are nevertheless distinguished in a given created thing. Thus, [the *rationes*] have a certain similitude with their cause, as though they were impressions [of it]. On account of this they are called by the name of "footprint" [*vestigium*], not on account of imaging [the divine essence], but on account of their *ratio*.[193]

Since every cause leaves an imprint like itself on its effect, when God impresses his image on a rational creature, he impresses a threefold *vestigium* corresponding to the three *rationes* mentioned here. These impressions are of the concepts one, true, and good.[194] They correspond with humanity's relationship to God as its efficient, formal, and final cause,[195] and they likewise correspond with the faculties of memory, reason, and will.[196]

The impressions of true and good upon the mind play a particularly important role in the *Summa fratris Alexandri*'s understanding of natural desire. Since God is the first truth, the impression of 'true' upon the mind constitutes an impression of the knowledge of God. "There is a twofold knowledge of God: actual knowledge and habitual knowledge. Habitual knowledge ... is in us naturally as an impressed habit, namely, as a similitude of the first truth in the intellect, whereby the rational soul can adduce that God exists and cannot be

193. Ibid., Ia-IIae, no. 35, co. [Quaracchi 2:45]: "Licet divina essentia sit infigurabilis et similiter summa Trinitas, nihilominus habet in se rationes, ut quod summe est et quod summe verum est et quod summe bonum est, quae licet idem sint in Deo, nihilominus tamen distinguuntur in re creata, et sic quamdam habent similitudinum respectu suae causae quasi essent quaedam impressiones, et propter hoc dicuntur nomine vestigii, non propter figurationem, sed propter ipsam rationem."

194. Ibid., Ia-Iae, no. 72, co. [Quaracchi 1:113]. The *Summa*'s list of ideas is not completely foreign to Avicenna. See Avicenna, *Prima philosophia* 8.6 [van Riet 2:412–13]. There, good and true are the first names attributed to the first being. However, even if Avicenna grants that "one" is one of the concepts impressed upon the mind, he never would have granted it for the reason that Alexander gives. For Avicenna, the whole point of the first impressions is that they are *not* determined. However, Alexander's association of the first impressions with the *vestigia trinitatis* was necessary in order to allow him to broaden the category of impressed knowledge, as we shall see below.

195. *Summa fratris Alexandri*, Ia-Iae, no. 73, pars 4, co. [Quaracchi 1:115].

196. Ibid. [Quaracchi 1:113–16], cited in Aertsen, *Medieval Philosophy as Transcendental Thought*, 144. Aertsen includes a helpful chart on being's determinations in the *Summa fratris Alexandri* on p. 146.

unaware of that fact."[197] Corresponding to this innate knowledge of the first truth is an innate knowledge of the highest good. It is on account of this innate knowledge of the highest good that all rational creatures have a natural desire for the highest good.[198] Since man has a habitual knowledge of God as the highest truth and the highest good impressed upon the soul, no one can fail to know inwardly that God exists or to desire God with natural desire.

Although the *Summa fratris Alexandri* identifies four impressed concepts, it says that only one of them, that of being, is impressed upon the mind in such a way that it can be recognized without any reference to creatures.[199] This is because there is no impressed notion prior to the other notions by which we can distinguish them from being (one of Avicenna's conditions for identifying an impressed notion is that it cannot be known through something better known). For this reason, we must make some comparison between being and creatures in order to distinguish the other notions from being.[200] In practice, therefore, there are not two kinds of actual knowledge, but three: 1) that which begins from the notions impressed upon our soul alone (the knowledge of being); 2) that which begins with the notions impressed upon our soul and includes some references to creatures (the knowledge of one, true, and good); 3) that which begins from creatures.[201]

197. *Summa fratris Alexandri*, no. 26, co. [Quaracchi 1:43]: "Est cognitio de Deo duplex: cognitio actu, cognitio habitu. Cognitio de Deo in habitu ... naturaliter est in nobis habitus impressus, scilicet similitudo primae veritatis in intellectu, quo potest conicere ipsum esse et non potest ignorari ab anima rationali." See ibid., IIa-Iae, no. 345 [Quaracchi 1:513].

198. See ibid., Ia-Iae, no. 108 [Quaracchi 1:169]. Note particularly the *corpus* and the reply to the first objection, in which Alexander associates natural knowledge of the highest good specifically with our natural will (vis-à-vis Damascene) for the highest good. See also ibid., IIa-Iae, no. 450, co. [Quaracchi 1:646].

199. *Summa fratris Alexandri*, IIa-Iae, no. 345 [Quaracchi 1: 513]: "Notio tamen entis sive essentiae absolvit ab omni comparatione [eorum quae facta sunt]."

200. Ibid., Ia-Iae, no. 72, co. [Quaracchi 1:113]: "Si ergo notificatio fiat eorum, hoc non erit nisi per posteriora, ut per abnegationem vel effectum consequentem."

201. Rahim Acar actually locates the same threefold epistemological schema in Avicenna. See Rahim Acar, *Talking about God and Talking about Creation: Avicenna's and Thomas Aquinas's Positions* (Boston: Brill, 2005), 32–34.

Granted that only one impressed notion can be recognized without any reference to creatures, it would seem that the actual knowledge available directly through impressed, habitual knowledge would be of limited significance. This would be true if the *Summa fratris Alexandri* were only concerned with establishing the basis of metaphysical reasoning, like Avicenna was. However, the *Summa fratris Alexandri* uses all three categories of actual knowledge to establish that we can know God by natural reason. In order to explain how we may come to actual knowledge of God without the aid of grace, the *Summa fratris Alexandri* turns to the writings of Pseudo-Dionysius.

In a Neo-Platonic framework of *exitus* and *reditus*,[202] Dionysius describes how every creature desires to return to the God, from which it has come, insofar as it is possible for that creature. This means that rational creatures desire to achieve true union with God through contemplation.[203] The ascent to unitive contemplation occurs through a twofold path of purification and illumination.[204] Purification is the liturgical and sacramental path of the mind and the will toward God; illumination, which follows upon purification, is the path toward ever more appropriate means of praising the One with whom we seek union through purification.[205]

In the path of illumination, we make use of two kinds of words: symbolic and mystical.[206] Symbolic language is metaphoric; it speaks of God primarily with reference to creatures and is intended to represent the things of God in a way that the average person can understand.[207] Mystical language is analogical; it begins from creatures but

202. See Aertsen, *Medieval Philosophy as Transcendental Thought*, 185.

203. See Pseudo-Dionysius, *Divine Names* 4 [700A–B]. See also *Divine Names* 4 [696A, 700B, 712A, 736B], 11 [952C]; *Celestial Hierarchy* 2 [141D].

204. Pseudo-Dionysius, *Celestial Hierarchy* 3 [165B–168B], 8 [240C], 10 [272D–273A]; *Ecclesiastical Hierarchy* 5 [504A–C, 508Dff], 6 [532A–533A, 536D–537C].

205. Pseudo-Dionysius, *Divine Names* 4 [693C], *Mystical Theology* 3 [1000C], *Celestial Hierarchy* 3 [165D], *Ecclesiastical Hierarchy* 2 [392A], 5 [504A–505A, 508D, 516B, 536D].

206. Pseudo-Dionysius, Epistle 9 [1105D]. Another good description of this contrast is to be found in *Mystical Theology* 3 [1033A–C].

207. Pseudo-Dionysius, Epistle 9 [1108A–B].

speaks primarily of God.[208] As we ascend closer to union with God, we make a transition from symbolic to mystical language.[209] The embrace of mystical language, moreover, entails a threefold path (*triplex via*) of negation, causality, and eminence. We begin with negation, denying of God those words which are most dissimilar to him.[210] But since God, as the cause of all, is not simply the opposite of what we find in creatures[211]—indeed, since he is beyond our denials[212]—we can rightly seek him preeminently above any affirmation or denial.[213]

Dionysius did not use the *triplex via* to establish a framework for the natural knowledge of God and natural desire for God. One could perhaps extract from Dionysius a very limited concept of natural desire, but it would have to be confined to a general, Neo-Platonic *reditus*. For Dionysius, even language which seems "philosophical" when predicated of God is only achieved through sacramental purification and grace.[214] Dionysius's writings about the *triplex via* thus presuppose the Christian economy of salvation.

Despite the fact that Dionysius's framework for knowing and naming God presupposes grace, the *Summa fratris Alexandri* adopts it to describe how we know and name God according to nature. Like Dionysius, the *Summa fratris Alexandri* divides our names for God into symbolic and mystical.[215] Since the symbolic names are said metaphorically, they can be used without grace because even Diony-

208. Pseudo-Dionysius, *Mystical Theology* 1 [1000A–B]. See *Celestial Hierarchy* 2 [141A–B].

209. Pseudo-Dionysius, *Mystical Theology* 3 [1033B].

210. Ibid. [1033C].

211. Ibid. 4 [1040D].

212. Ibid.

213. Ibid. 5 [1048B]: "We make assertions and denials of what is next to [the Cause of all], but never of it, for it is both beyond every assertion, being the perfect and unique cause of all things, and, by virtue of its preeminently simple and absolute nature, free of every limitation, beyond every limitation; it is also beyond every denial." The translation is from Pseudo-Dionysius, *The Complete Works*, trans. Colm Luibheid (Mahwah, N.J.: Paulist Press, 1987), 141.

214. On the ascent to purified language being a gift of grace, see Pseudo-Dionysius, *Divine Names* 1 [588C–589A]. Also see *Divine Names* 3 [680C], 4 [693B–693C], 7 [872B]; *Mystical Theology* 1 [1000A]; *Celestial Hierarchy* 1 [121B]; *Eccliastical Hierarchy* 1 [376B], 2 [397D, 440B, 476B], 5 [504C–D].

215. *Summa fratris Alexandri*, IIa-Iae, no. 366, ad a–c [Quaracchi 1:544].

sius placed them at the bottom of the ascent to naming God, before the reception of sacramental purification. However, since the mystical names follows only after sacramental purification, their natural use requires a new analogical framework.

In order to adopt mystical names for use outside the context of sacramental purification and grace, the *Summa fratris Alexandri* develops a doctrine of analogy with respect to priority and posteriority, which is based upon that of Avicenna. For Avicenna, the fact that God causes creatures establishes an ontological relationship of priority and posteriority between God and creatures.[216] This relationship allows us to affirm that God exists and that there is only one God.[217] Since there is an ontological relationship between God and creatures, we can make three further kinds of statements about God, which follow from these affirmations. First, we can deny anything in God which pertains to multiplicity or change.[218] For Avicenna, this includes calling God "one," which negates division, and "intelligence," which negates matter.[219] Second, we can speak about God with some reference to that which is subject to multiplicity or change. For Avicenna, this includes calling God "first," which implies his order with respect to creatures, and "powerful," which implies the fact that God causes creatures.[220] Third, we can attribute to God what limited perfections we find in that which is subject to multiplicity and change, provided that we omit any reference to limitation or defect.[221]

216. See Avicenna, *Prima philosophia* 4. One of the main focuses of this book is establishing the difference between ontological priority and temporal priority. Ontological priority follows the order of efficient causes with respect to act and potency, and may exist even when there is simultaneity in a chain of causality. In *Prima philosophia* 8.3, Avicenna applies this thinking at the level of being, and it grounds his discussion of the properties of the first principle in subsequent chapters of Book 8.

217. Avicenna, *Prima philosophia* 8.3 [van Riet 2:393–97].

218. Ibid. 8.7 [van Riet 2:423–33].

219. Ibid. [van Riet 2:430].

220. Ibid.

221. This is the subject of the whole of *Prima philosophia* 8.6 [van Riet 2:412–22]. It is too long to quote here in full. We should note, however, that Avicenna's eminence is still a form of apophasis, because it is based on negation. Such will not be the case, however, for the *Summa fratris Alexandri*.

Although the *Summa fratris Alexandri* does not say so explicitly, it follows Avicenna by associating the first group of Avicenna's names with Dionysius's *via negativa*, the second with Dionysius's *via causalitatis*, and the third with Dionysius's *via eminentiae*.[222] Moreover, in order to distinguish the *via negativa* from the *via eminentiae*, and so attribute a more kataphatic character to the *via eminentiae* than we find in Avicenna's third group, it points to two aspects of a given name: there is the character of its expression (*proprietas dicendi*), and there is the ontological character of its meaning (*veritas essendi*). If we consider the character of its expression, then since words signify things in a concrete mode, it is more appropriate to speak of God by way of a negation, which denies what is concrete. If, on the other hand, we consider the ontological character of its meaning, then it is more appropriate to speak of God by way of an affirmation, which attributes whatever perfection we find in creatures *per prius* of God. Names said according to the *via causalitatis* simply combine what is said according to one of the other two *viae* and include some notion about a creature's relationship to God.[223]

The complete actualization of our impressed, habitual knowledge of God occurs in the *Summa fratris Alexandri* through the *via eminentiae*. This is fitting, since for Dionysius the *via eminentiae* is the summit of Christian life, in which God is praised in a mystical union which transcends affirmation and negation. Yet the *Summa fratris Alexandri*'s *via eminentiae* corresponds more with the third of Avicenna's ways of speaking about God than it does to anything in the writings of Dionysius. Specifically, the *via eminentiae* begins with the recognition of the notion of being, impressed upon the soul. Having

222. *Summa fratris Alexandri*, IIa-Iae, no. 334, co. [Quaracchi 1:435]. The *Summa fratris Alexandri* also distinguishes a class of names called "names of operation" (*nomina operationis*). Effectively, these names either signify the divine power directly, and are similar to the names said according to the *via eminentiae*, or they signify the divine power with respect to creatures, and then they are similar to the *via causalitatis*. See ibid., no. 356, ad 3 [Quaracchi 1:532]. In actual fact, however, the *Summa fratris Alexandri* only identifies one name that falls under this category, namely, "God" (*Deus*).

223. Ibid., no. 373, co. [Quaracchi 1:551].

recognized the existence of being simply speaking, we can proceed from it to recognize various levels of multiplicity in individual beings. There is, for example, the multiplicity of individuals, the multiplicity in a given individual of its existence and its essence, and the multiplicity in a given individual of what is possible for it and what is actual in it. By the negation of each of these kinds of multiplicity, we come by a *via negativa* to apprehend the first determinations of being impressed upon the soul: one (the indivision of a being, by which it corresponds with its efficient cause), true (the indivision of existence and essence in a being, by which it corresponds with its formal exemplar cause), and good (the indivision of act and potency in a being, by which it corresponds with its final cause).[224] Once we have recognized the first determinations of being, it becomes possible for us to predicate them of God by Avicenna's analogy of ontological priority and posteriority.[225]

By appropriating an Avicennian epistemology and combining it with a Dionysian *triplex via*, the *Summa fratris Alexandri* assigned a more definite term to natural desire than had Philip and Rufus, linking our natural desire for God with two kinds of natural knowledge of God: the impressed, habitual knowledge of God common to all rational creatures, as well as actual knowledge, which proceeds by analogy from that impressed, habitual knowledge. The *Summa fratris Alexandri* thus gives an account of nature that is as concretely teleological as William of Auvergne's, but does not go as far as William in saying that this natural desire is for God as a supernatural end. In one sense, it therefore shows how we can turn a natural desire for happiness into a natural desire for God without running into Wil-

224. On the fact that it is a *via negativa* applied to creatures which brings us to actual knowledge of the first determinations of being, see ibid., Ia-Iae, no. 72, co. [Quaracchi 1:114–15]. On the actual negations required to reach that knowledge, see ibid., no. 88, co. [Quaracchi 1:140]. On the desirability of the good, see ibid., no. 102, co. [Quaracchi 1:161].

225. See again ibid., IIa-Iae, no. 368, co. [Quaracchi 1:546]. We note here that, because of the assumption of the impressed knowledge of being on the soul, the *Summa fratris Alexandri*'s recension of Avicenna turns the apophaticism of Avicenna into a radical kataphaticism.

liam's double difficulty concerning the integrity of nature and the gratuity of grace. However, its solution to William's problem raises a question about the limits of formal causality as a mechanism for incorporating Augustinian potency into Aristotelian categories: if the human soul has a concrete, teleological act which it can achieve naturally, and that act is *not* the vision of God (which it cannot be, since it is naturally achieved), where in the soul shall we locate the unlimited openness to God's creative action which Philip identified with *potentia obedientiae*? That difficulty would in some respects constitute the fundamental basis for an Averroistic-Augustinian critique of the Avicennian-Augustinian tradition, and so it is to the figures associated with that critique that we now turn.

LATIN AVERROISTIC-AUGUSTINIANISM

Roger Bacon

As noted above, the rise of the Latin Avicennian-Augustinianism of the 1230s–1240s also coincided with beginning of the availability in the Latin West of Michael Scot's translations of the works of Averroes. We should not be surprised to find, therefore, that among the philosophers and theologians making use of the Aristotelian tradition, some would draw more on Averroes than on Avicenna when considering nature, grace, and the desire for God. One such example is Roger Bacon (c. 1220–92).[226]

Roger Bacon, who like Rufus began his career in the arts faculty of Paris before entering the Franciscan Order, took Rufus's thought into account when dealing with the question of individuation, but sought to defend Averroes where Rufus had critiqued him. In Bacon's *Questiones secunde supra undecimum prime philosophie Aristo-*

226. For introductions to the life and works of Roger Bacon, see Jeremiah Hackett, "Roger Bacon: His Life, Career, and Works," in *Roger Bacon and the Sciences: Commemorative Essays*, ed. Jeremiah Hackett (Kinderhook, N.Y.: Brill, 1997), 9–23; David Linberg, introduction to *Roger Bacon's Philosophy of Nature: A Critical Edition, with English Translation, Introduction, and Notes, of* De multiplicatione specierum *and* De speculis comburentibus (New York: Oxford, 1983), xv–xxvi.

telis,[227] which were perhaps held sometime around the middle of 1245,[228] he discusses the same sets of questions as Averroes concerning the relationship between matter and form. Bacon begins by criticizing Avicenna, and with him the Latin Avicennian-Augustinian tradition: there are those who say that since matter is infinitely potential, it requires extrinsic information by a *dator formarum* of infinite potency, since otherwise there is no way to determine which form matter *would* receive out of the infinite number of forms it *could* receive.[229] Bacon replies: "Although [the first cause's] power or potency is infinite in itself and for its part, nevertheless it is not received insofar as it is infinite in the production of natural things, but rather according to the requirements of what receives it. And since nature is a finite power, therefore [the first cause's power] is received [by nature] in a finite manner."[230] For Bacon, the fact *that* the first cause is omnipotent does not mean that there must exist a correspondingly omni-potential entity in nature. All created nature is finite, and so the infinite power of God is received into nature in a finite manner.

The principle that matter receives power and form according to its own manner offered Bacon the possibility of developing an alternative solution to the problem that Rufus posed in *Contra Averroem* II

227. Roger Bacon, *Questiones secunde supra undecimum prime philosophie Aristotelis*, in *Opera hactenus inedita*, ed. Robert Steele et al. (Oxford: Clarendon Press, 1909–1940), 7:125–51. Steele observes that since at the time when Bacon was commenting on the *Metaphysics*, Book 11 was not known, Bacon treats our Book 12 as his Book 11.

Silvia Donati, "Pseudoepigrapha in the *Opera hactenus inedita Rogeri Baconi*? The Commentaries on the *Physics* and on the *Metaphysics*," in *Les débuts de l'enseignement universitaire à Paris (1200–1245 environ)*, ed. Jacques Verger and Olga Weijers (Turnhout: Brepols, 2013), 153–203, has challenged the authenticity of three works previously attributed to Bacon in the area of natural philosophy and metaphysics, but our analysis here will not depend absolutely on the authenticity of any potentially inauthentic works.

228. Steele, introduction to Roger Bacon, *Questiones secunde supra undecimum prime philosophie Aristotelis*, iv.

229. The objections run from Bacon, *Questiones secunde*, 128:26–129:2.

230. Ibid., 129:8–13: "Licet sua [that is, causae primae] virtus vel potentia sit infinita secundum se et a parte sua, non tamen in productione rerum naturalium secundum quod infinita, set secundum exigentiam ipsius recipientis, et quia natura est virtus finita, ideo recipitur modo finito."

about individuation. Bacon notes that there are three possibilities concerning how forms relate to matter: either forms are completely extrinsic to matter, they are completely intrinsic to matter, or they are somewhere in between.[231] He dismisses the first possibility outright, because it would mean re-proposing Avicenna's *dator formarum*.[232] Bacon observes that the second is the doctrine of "the hiddenness of forms [in matter]" (*latitatio formarum*), which he attributes to the ancient Greek philosopher Anaxagoras.[233] The *latitatio formarum* can be distinguished again, depending on whether the forms are present in the matter actually or potentially.[234] If they are present in the matter actually, they either inform some part of the matter, in which case some part of the matter would have contrary forms, or each among the plethora of forms informs a different part of the matter, which destroys matter's substantial unity. Neither of these possibilities is metaphysically acceptable. Therefore, forms must be present in matter potentially. If that is so, they can be present either according to an active potency, which makes matter the efficient cause of its own information, or according to a receptive potency, which requires the existence of a *dator formarum*. Neither of these possibilities is metaphysically acceptable either.

In order to overcome this impasse, Bacon developed a novel idea, which he attributes to Aristotle, but which is difficult to prove from the Stagirite's *ipsissima verba*. Bacon suggests that forms are present in matter in an active potency, that this active potency is itself conferred upon matter by a form, but that the presence of forms in this active potency is *incomplete*, because the form communicating actuality to the matter is incomplete.[235] The solution owes

231. Ibid., 131:6–8: "Consequenter queritur utrum forme rerum naturalium producantur penitus ab intrinseco, vel ab extrinseco omnino, vel modo medio."

232. Ibid., 131:8–10.

233. Ibid., 131:10–11. The *latitio formarum* is also discussed in the Commentary on *Physics* I–IV attributed to Bacon. See Roger Bacon, *Opera hactenus inedita,* 8:21. For the relative dating of the two works, I rely on Ferdinand Delorme's introduction to *Opera hactenus inedita,* 13:xxx.

234. These distinctions are found in Bacon, *Quaestiones secundae,* 131:11–35.

235. Ibid., 132.1–6: "Quantum autem ad illud quod producitur in esse, est ab extrinseco

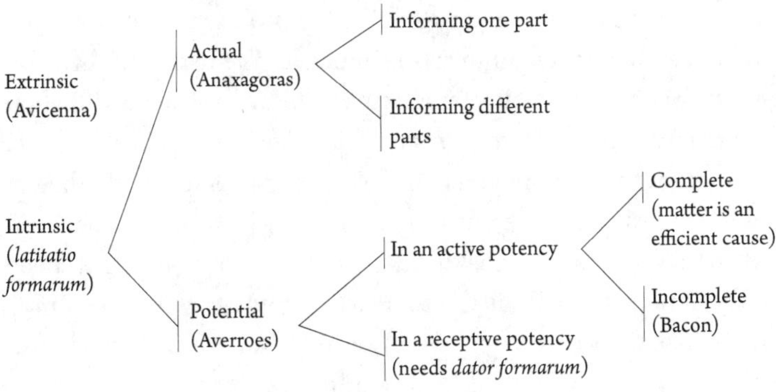

FIGURE 3. The relationship of form to matter according to Bacon

something both to Rufus and to Averroes. With Rufus, Bacon avoids saying that a doctrine of active potency in matter makes a thing's material cause its efficient cause, because an incomplete active potency still requires the power of an extrinsic agent in order to turn it into a complete form. Matter is thereby able to serve as the principle of individuation through the incomplete determination that it possesses in virtue of its incomplete active potency.[236] With Averroes, Bacon seems to accept that the process of individuation occurs successively. The hypothesis of incomplete potency simply posits that the process of individuation can be interrupted after the actualization of generic form but before individuation (see figure 3).

Unlike Rufus, who went off to teach theology and so made the

omnino, non sicut posuit Anaxagoras, ita quod sunt ibi in actu, set in potentia activa, que est forma incompleta que, excitata per illud quod immittitur extra ab agente universali vel particulari vel utroque, fit forma rei completa." See Günther Mensching, "Metaphysik und Naturbeherrschung im Denken Roger Bacons," in *Mensch und Natur im Mittelalter*, vol. 1, ed. Albert Zimmermann and Andreas Speer (Berlin: Walter de Gruyter, 1991), 132–35; Silvia Donati, "Pseudoepigrapha in the *Opera hactenus inedita Rogeri Baconi?*" 173–85.

236. Ibid., 134.2–17.

connection between his theory of individuation and *rationes seminales* explicit prior to Thomas Aquinas's period as a bachelor of the Sentences, Bacon taught in arts faculties for the rest of his life, and so did not draw the connections between his theory of individuation and *rationes seminales* except in an off-hand remark in his *Communia naturalia* at the end of the 1260s.[237] Discussing his understanding of the relationship between matter and form, which had not changed substantially since the *Questiones secunde,* Bacon notes that, "deep down, a *ratio seminalis* is the same as a potency, wherefore a *ratio seminalis* is the very incomplete essence of matter which can be advanced into completion, like a seed into a tree."[238]

Bacon thus serves as a counterpoint to Rufus, both in terms of individuation as well as *rationes seminales.* In terms of individuation, Bacon provides one possible response to Rufus's critique of Averroes's doctrine of individuation: since whatever is received is received according to the mode of the receiver, there is no need to posit an individual form in order to account for the possibility of individuation. A form is contracted sufficiently by being received into matter, which has a limited potential for information. This limited potential is grounded in the matter's incomplete active potency, communicated to it by an incomplete form, which confers on matter a tendency toward complete form.

While Bacon's appeal to a unique form of material causality was a creative solution to the challenge of incorporating Augustinian po-

237. Donati, "Pseudoepigrapha in the *Opera hactenus inedita Rogeri Baconi?*" 173. For the dating of the *Communia naturalia,* see Lindberg, *Roger Bacon's Philosophy of Nature,* xxv–xxvi. Some of the outlines of these conclusions, without the explicit reference to *rationes seminales,* are discussed in Bacon's second commentary on Aristotle's Physics. See Roger Bacon, *Questiones supra libros octo Physicorum Aristotelis* [Steele 13:56–69].

238. See Roger Bacon, *Communia naturalia,* pars 2, 2.4 [Steele 2:84–85]: "racio seminalis et potencia idem est penitus, unde racio seminalis est ipsa essencia materie incompleta que potest promoveri in complementum, sicut semen in arborem."

Even if Bacon would not make clear the connection between incomplete active potencies in matter and *rationes seminales* until much later, others would explicitly draw the connection sooner. Robert Kilwardby is one such example. See José Sílva, *Robert Kilwardby on the Human Soul: Plurality of Forms and Censorship in the Thirteenth Century* (Boston: Brill, 2012), 56.

tency into an Aristotelian framework, and suggested a general direction in which the limitations of appeals to formal causality might be overcome, it was subject to one textual ambiguity and two metaphysical difficulties, which would mark it for criticism in the scholarly generation immediately before Thomas Aquinas. The textual ambiguity concerns whether the incomplete active potency in matter belongs to matter in virtue of itself, or in virtue of its form. Earlier in the *Questiones secunde,* Bacon had argued that since potency comes from matter, and actuality from form, matter does not differ from its potency.[239] Yet he subsequently suggests that matter has a twofold potency: receptive and active. No problem arises in the present context with saying that matter is identical with its receptive potency. But saying that matter is identical with its active potency entails either one of two problematic claims: first, that matter possesses in itself some degree of actuality apart from form, something which Bacon had explicitly denied; second, that something in matter is identical with form. Bacon seems to be inclined to this latter view, observing at one point that whether you associate the active potency in matter with matter or form depends on your perspective. Compared with matter, the active potency is supposed to be identical with the essence of matter; compared with form, it is supposed to be an incomplete substantial form and not identical with matter.[240] But if matter's incomplete active potency is identifiable with form, then do we not ultimately come full circle and return to the limitations of an Avicennian appeal to formal causality which Bacon's incomplete active potency was supposed to overcome?

Albert the Great

When Thomas's own *magister,* Albert the Great, arrived at Paris in the early 1240s,[241] Philip the Chancellor's influence had over a de-

239. Bacon, *Questiones secunde* [Steele 7:9].

240. Ibid.

241. See James A. Weisheipl, "The Life and Works of Saint Albert the Great," in

cade to make itself sufficiently felt,[242] the work William of Auvergne was still a matter of recent memory, and the work of Rufus and Bacon was ongoing. Albert's earliest systematic presentation of nature, grace, and the desire for God in the treatises, *De IV coaequaevis* and *De homine*, together comprising the *Summa de creaturis*,[243] suggests a thorough familiarity and engagement with Philip's work,[244] while his work later in the decade engages more with Rufus and Bacon. The early works of Albert are of particular importance, because when Albert composed his *Commentary on the Sentences* he thought his treatment of some topics in these treatises so complete that he

---

Albertus Magnus and the Sciences: Commemorative Essays (1980), ed. James A. Weisheipl (Toronto: PIMS, 1980), 21. There is no hard evidence for assigning Albert's arrival at Paris to a particular year, but Weisheipl notes that Albert would have had to have spent several years as a bachelor of the Sentences before becoming a master of theology at Paris in 1245, so we may safely assume that he spent most of the first half of that decade in Paris. More recently, Henry Anzulewicz has suggested on the basis of the date of Albert's early treatises that he would have come to Paris in 1241 (Col. 27.2:xiv).

242. For evidence of that influence, which can be used in dating the *Summa de bono*, see Nicolai Wicki, introduction to Philip the Chancellor, *Summa de bono*, 63*–66*.

243. There has been some confusion in recent years about the status of the *Summa de creaturis*. Formerly, it was thought that Albert composed a large *Summa* at Paris before completing his *Commentary on the Sentences*. The treatises of this *Summa* were thought to be *De sacramentis, De incarnatione, De resurrectione, De IV coaequaevis, De homine*, and *De bono*. An example of this older view can be found in Col. 28:x–xi. Subsequently, it was thought the treatises must all be taken independently. This view can be seen in Stanley Cunningham, *Reclaiming Moral Agency: The Moral Philosophy of Albert the Great* (Washington, D.C.: The Catholic University of America Press, 2008), 31–32. Most recently, however, Henryk Anzulewicz has shown from mid-thirteenth-century manuscript evidence that there was indeed a *Summa de creaturis*, but that it only included *De IV coaequaevis*, as its first part, and *De homine*, as its second part, the other treatises being more or less independent. Thus, for example, our oldest manuscript of *De homine* is inscribed, "Pars Secunda de Creaturis Alberti …" and concludes, "… haec de creaturis dicta sufficiant" (Ann Arbor, Mich.: Alfred Taubman Medical Library, Ms. 201, cited in Col. 27.2:xvii). Anzulewicz has also published these findings in English. See Henryk Anzulewicz, "The Systematic Theology of Albert the Great," in *A Companion to Albert the Great: Theology, Philosophy, and the Sciences*, ed. Irven Resnick (Boston: Brill, 2013), 42.

244. For references to Albert's works, I will use the best critical editions available. In the case of *De homine* and *De bono*, references will be to the Cologne edition (*Opera Omnia. Editio Coloniensis*, ed. Bernhard Geyer et al., 41 vols. [Münster: Aschendorff, 1951–]). In the case of *De IV coaequaevis*, the Cologne edition of which is still under preparation, and of Albert's *Commentary on the Sentences*, of which only the first book is even in preparation, reference will be made to the Borgnet edition (*Opera Omnia*, ed. Auguste Borgnet, Jacques Echard, and Jacques Quétif, 38 vols. [Paris: Vivès, 1890–99]).

decided to refer the reader back to them, rather than repeating the material they contained.[245]

In the *De IV coaequaevis,* Albert inquires about Damascene's distinction between θέλησις and βούλησις, asking how either desire is "natural" in the angels. Albert begins by assigning Damascene's distinction of wills to the angels in the same way that Philip had assigned it to humanity,[246] but then he raises a new question about the distinction: can we call the end of that which is freely willed without the aid of grace "natural"? Albert responds by distinguishing three ways of calling something natural: 1) what follows from nature alone (*ex solis naturalibus*); 2) what nature can arrive at it by its own operation; 3) what an individual is habituated into by custom.[247] The first two senses of "natural" apply to the present question. We may note that they correspond, in substance, with θέλησις and βούλησις. The angels cannot love God for his own sake and above all things with θέλησις, but they can with βούλησις. In order to avoid Pelagianism, Albert adds that their love for God, according to the βούλησις, is not the love of charity, since it is not caused by God as an efficient cause, only as a final cause.

Turning to the consideration of humanity in *De homine,* Albert expands his engagement with Philip's understanding of nature by bringing Averroes's *Long Commentary* on Aristotle's *Metaphysics* to

245. There are two passages in Book II of Albert's *Commentary on the Sentences* that refer to a "*Tractatus noster de Anima,*" *In II Sent.*, d. 24, a. 5, q. 2, resp. [Borgnet 27:402], and *In II Sent.*, d. 26, a. 12, ad 2/3 [Borgnet 27:468], as well as another which refers to certain "*quaestiones de anima,*" *In II Sent.*, d. 42, a. 6, q. 3, ad 3 [Borgnet 27:664]. This cannot refer to Albert's commentary on Aristotle's *De anima,* because the latter can be reliably dated to the late 1250s. See Clemens Stroick, *prolegomena* to Col. 7.1:v. Nor can it refer to another treatise of Albert's, *De natura et origine animae,* because this must be dated after his commentary on Aristotle's *De anima*. See Bernhard Geyer, *prolegomena* to Col. 12:ix. Given the content ascribed to this treatise by Albert in the aforesaid passages, it seems likely that Albert has in mind what we now call his *De homine*. This hypothesis can be confirmed by a reference within the *De IV coaequaevis* wherein Albert refers to the *De homine* in terms of a "*tractatus de anima hominis.*" See *De IV coaequaevis*, q. 25, a. 1, ad 2 [Borgnet 34:488]. The Cologne edition of the *De bono* points to a number of similar references [Col. 28:x].

246. Albert the Great, *De IV coaequaevis*, q. 25, a. 1, co. [Borgnet 34:487].

247. Ibid., q. 25, a. 2 [Borgnet 34:489].

bear on the discussion. In his commentary on *Metaphysics* 9.8, Averroes posits that something possesses a potency for a particular act when some agent can bring forth that act from it by one motion.[248] Albert uses this text to address an ambiguity in Philip's understanding of receptive potency: while Philip had observed a receptive potency for obedience in nature, he had not distinguished that potency for obedience as clearly as it might have been distinguished from receptive potencies that can be actualized by connatural agents. Albert uses Averroes's understanding of potency to make that distinction: there is one kind of receptive potency which can be actualized by one motion of a connatural agent acting in virtue of its own *ratio seminalis*; there is another, a potency for obedience, which can only be actualized in one motion by God.[249]

Concerning the will, Albert continues to follow Peter by adopting the distinction between θέλησις and βούλησις as he had in the *De IV coaequaevis*, yet with some terminological differences.[250] The terminological differences seem to have come from his reading of *De fide orthodoxa* 36.10. There, Damascene argues that βούλησις can will impossibles and conditionals, alongside possibles. Albert adopts the Greek term προαίρεσις, which he renders in Latin as *voluntas rationalis*,[251] for the act by which we will possibles, while he retains

248. Averroes, *Commentarium magnum in libros Metaphysicorum* 9.8, comm. 12 [Giunti 8:238vk].

249. Albert the Great, *De homine* [Col. 27.2:563]: "Similiter vim facit Augustinus inter hoc quod aliquid sit in materia, ut ex ipsa fiat et quod aliquid sit in ipsa quod non ex ipsa fiat, sed quod fieri possit. Primo modo in materia est, cuius causas sufficientes ad actum materia habet in seipsa, sive in naturalibus sive in artificiatis. Dico autem causas efficientes, formales, materiales, finales, et hoc modo naturalia sunt in materia. Secundo vero modo est in materia, cuius causas sufficientes ad actum non habet materia, sed oboedientes; efficiens enim est extra in virtute divina, quali modo, ut dicit Augustinus, de quinque panibus satiata sunt quinque milia hominum, et de aqua factum est vinum. Et hoc modo dicit mulierem fuisse in latere viri."

250. See ibid. [Col. 27.2:488ff].

251. Aristotle discusses προαίρεσις in *Nicomachean Ethics* 3.2 [1111b5–1112a17]. The word does not appear in Burgundio's translation of Damascene's *De fide orthodoxa*, but it does appear briefly in the *Ethica vetus* several times at 1111b5–13: "Determinatis autem voluntario et involuntario, de proereseos sequitur ut dicamus. Valde proprium enim videtur esse virtuti, et magis consuetudines iudicare operacionibus. Proeresis autem,

βούλησις for the act by which we will conditionals or impossibles. Nevertheless, the distinction between natural and deliberative willing remains intact.[252]

In the consideration of natural willing, Albert seems to have sensed an inconsistency in Philip: God is not "a state made perfect by the amalgamation of all that is good"; such a "state" describes our possession of God in the beatific vision (that is, our happiness), not God himself. In *De homine,* Albert criticizes but does not overcome this limitation. He distinguishes two kinds of happiness: perfect and imperfect. Perfect happiness is that of which Boethius speaks, which the soul receives upon exiting this life. Imperfect happiness can be possessed in this life, and corresponds to Aristotle's definition of happiness in Book 1 of the *Nicomachean Ethics,* "an act of the soul which is done according to virtue."[253] In both cases, whether speaking of Boethius or Aristotle, Albert makes it clear that he is speaking of a subjective state in which the soul receives the object of its desire, and not of the object whose possession causes that state. He leaves open the question of whether the goal of natural desire is happiness in general, or God specifically.

In the *De IV coaequaevis* and the *De homine,* therefore, Albert

---

voluntarium quidem videtur. Non autem illud idem, set maius voluntarium. Voluntarii quidem enim et pueri et alia animalia communicant ; proeresi autem, non. Et repentina voluntaria quidem dicimus ; secundum proeresim autem, non. Qui autem dicunt eam, desiderium, aut iram, aut voluntatem, aut aliquam opinionem, non videntur dicere recte. Non enim commune proeresis et irracionabilium, desiderium autem et ira." Thereafter, the text switches from the Greek transliteration, *proeresis,* to the Latin translation, *electio.*

If we look ahead in Albert's writings, he makes his dependence on Aristotle's *Nicomachean Ethics* 3.2 explicit in an entire article that he devotes to προαίρεσις in the *De bono.* See *De bono,* q. 4, a. 6 [Col. 28:59–62].

252. Albert the Great, *De homine* [Col. 27.2:498].

253. Ibid. "Beatitudo accipitur in via et in patria, perfecta et imperfecta. Perfecta est, quae amputat et poenam et culpam, et hanc recipit anima secundum se, quando est separata. Imperfecta est, quae tollit culpam, sed non omnem poenam, et hanc recipit in corpore existens. Boethius autem diffinit beatitudinem secundum quod est in ultimo et optimo statu. Sed beatitudo quae est viae, magis proprie dicitur felicitas, secundum quod dicit Philosophus, quod 'felicitas est actus animae qui est secundum virtutem perfectam.'"

problematizes Philip's account of natural desire without solving the problem it raises. It remained for Albert to give an account of nature, grace, and the desire for God that was more objectively teleological than the one he had criticized. For this account, we must turn to his *Commentary on the Sentences.*

Perhaps aware of the teleological vacuum opened by his treatment of natural desire in the *Summa de creaturis,* Albert revised his thought about natural desire in his *Commentary on the Sentences.*[254] That Albert intended to give a more complete account of nature in his *Commentary on the Sentences* is clear from the way he treats happiness at the beginning of the commentary. In Book 1, distinction 1, question 1, he asks the simple question, "Whether happiness ought to be enjoyed?" (*An beatitudine sit fruendum*).[255] Augustine had famously asserted that only that which is our final end ought to be enjoyed.[256] The question at stake in Albert's commentary is whether we have a natural desire for the subjective state of happiness, or whether God himself is the *terminus* of natural desire.

Although Albert had only distinguished two kinds of happiness in the *De homine,* both of which were subjective, in his *Commentary on the Sentences* he distinguishes three kinds of happiness, one of which is objective. First, there is created happiness, which prepares us to be joined with God. This is a subjective happiness to be had in this life. Beyond this, there is also uncreated happiness, which is God himself. Uncreated happiness can be considered in two ways: either God as he dwells in the hearts of the saints and the blessed,

254. It used to be thought that the dating of Albert's *Summa de creaturis* and of his *Commentary on the Sentences* overlapped. This view can be found (or at least not ruled out) in the prolegomena to the *De bono* [Col. 28:xi–xiii], as well as in Weisheipl, "Life and Works of St. Albert," 22. That hypothesis rests in part upon the assumption that the *De bono,* whose composition may have overlapped with some portion of Albert's *Commentary on the Sentences,* should be included in the *Summa de creaturis.* More recently, Anzulewicz has shown that that Albert must have completed the *De homine* before the first book of his *Commentary on the Sentences,* because at several points in the first book of the *Commentary on the Sentences,* he refers back to the *De homine.* See Col. 27.2:ix.

255. Albert the Great, *In I Sent.,* d. 1, q. 1, a. 9 [Borgnet 25:25].

256. The distinction colors Augustine's writings throughout, but the most important discussion of it begins at *De doctrina christiana* 1.3.3 [CCSL 32:8].

in which case God's presence is a subjective presence, or God as he is considered in himself, in which case God is considered objectively.[257] Like Philip, Albert identifies Boethius's definition of happiness with uncreated happiness. However, Albert explicitly aligns Boethius's happiness not with God as he is considered in himself objectively, but rather with the indwelling of God in the hearts of the saints and the blessed.[258]

To connect natural desire to the objective knowledge of God, Albert turns to the *corpus* of Pseudo-Dionysius, but he does not utilize Dionysius in the same way as the *Summa fratris Alexandri*, which developed a doctrine of analogy based upon God's efficient causality. Albert thinks that if we consider God as efficient cause, there is an insurmountable gap between God and creatures because there is no proportion whatsoever between God's power and creaturely power.[259] The same is not true concerning God's formal and final causality. When God makes a creature, something of the divine idea of that creature, together with the perfections implied by that idea, is "reflected" in the creature.[260] Moreover, since God is the final cause of creation, every creature seeks God insofar as it is able.[261]

Since Albert does not admit any proportion between God and creatures according to efficient causality, he could not rely on an Avicennian reworking of the *vestigia trinitatis* to establish a correspondence between Creation and the impressed notions of being, one, true, and good, as the *Summa fratris Alexandri* had done. Albert found a different way forward by rethinking Philip's account of nature more thoroughly than he had in *De homine*. Continuing to use Averroes's "one motion" rule for distinguishing between a potency for natural receptivity and a potency for obedience,[262] Albert applies

257. Albert the Great, *In I Sent.*, d. 1, a. 9, co. [Borgnet 25:25].

258. Ibid., ad 1. [Borgnet 25:26].

259. Ibid., d. 3, a. 7 [Borgnet 25:97].

260. Ibid., a. 2, ad 1 [Borgnet 25:93].

261. Ibid., d. 10, a. 6, ad 3 [Borgnet 25:320].

262. Albert the Great, *In II Sent.*, d. 18, a. 6, qc. 1, ad 1–2 [Borgnet 27:321]. Here Albert acknowledges Peter's two ways of speaking about nature, and distinguishes the ordinary

the distinction to a theological question about the Resurrection. If we define nature as that which happens according to the ordinary course of events, then we are bound to say that not only are those things "natural," which all the members of a given species tend to do, but also those which God happens to do to them over and above what they can do of themselves, provided that God does it ordinarily and to most or all of them. For example, since the Scriptures reveal that God has decided to resurrect the body of every member of the human species, it follows from Philip's definition that the resurrection of bodies is natural.[263]

Albert responds that everything that a creature does must follow from the form of its nature.[264] This means that among the things which happen to a creature in the ordinary course of nature we can distinguish those things which proceed immediately from the form of its nature from those which require the addition of a form in order to produce the effect.[265] Aligning the definition of "natural" with the first member of this distinction enabled Albert to say that the resurrection of bodies is not natural, because it does not follow from some form intrinsic to a creature.

Albert's solution to the problem of "natural" resurrection gave rise to another question similar to those asked by Rufus and Bacon. If matter has a desire for form, does the soul have a natural desire only for those forms which can be acquired naturally, or does it also have a natural desire for those forms which God can cause in it, but which cannot be acquired naturally? When Albert had previously addressed the question of matter's desire for form in the *Summa de*

---

course of events, which occur according to *rationes causales* and *rationes primordiales*, and contrary to which God can act, from the natures of things, which occur according to *rationes seminales* and *rationes naturales*, and which God does not violate. Concerning our receptive potency, he goes on in qc. 2 to use Averroes's "one motion" rule to distinguish between a receptive potency for an act caused in accord with the *ratio seminalis* of a connatural agent, and a potency for obedience which can only be actualized by God.

263. Albert the Great, *In IV Sent.*, d. 43, a. 3, obj. 3–4 [Borgnet 30:506].

264. Ibid., co. [Borgnet 30:507].

265. For the response to Augustine and Philip, see ibid., ad 9 [Borgnet 30:508]; for the response to Boethius, see ad 8.

creaturis, the question centered on a text attributed to Boethius's *De hebdomadibus* stating that "nothing desires something unless it is similar to it."[266] This rule seemed to preclude the possibility of matter desiring form, since it implies that matter must already have some form in it in order to desire the acquisition of a form. Albert had responded that matter's desire for form "is nothing other than the privation of form with a potency for having it," and that this potency can be called "a desire or an appetite."[267] But to have continued to do so in the *Commentary on the Sentences* would have led him to say that there is a natural desire for resurrection in the body.

Perhaps in order to avoid the consequence of saying that resurrection is naturally desired, Albert changed his perception of the aforementioned text attributed to Boethius when he returned to it in his *Commentary on the Sentences*:

Appetite is twofold in matter: One of these is only a susceptibility to form; this one is not an appetite properly speaking, because Boethius says in his book *On the Hebdomads* that one thing only desires another because it is similar to it in some way, since appetite does not only mean [something]

266. Albert the Great, *De IV coaequaevis*, q. 2, a. 4, s.c. 2 [Borgnet 34:328]: "Dicit Boetius in libro de Hebdomadibus: 'Nihil appetit aliquid nisi per hoc quod est simile:' materia appetit formam: et ergo per hoc quod est simile: sed similitudo est convenientia duorum in una forma." The rule that Boethius had laid down undergirding the text that Albert attributes to him is, "Omnis diversitas discors, similitudo vero appentenda est; et quod appetit aliud, tale ipsum esse naturaliter ostenditur quale est illud hoc ipsum quod appetit" (*Quomodo substantiae* 44–46 [Moreschini 188]). Boethius will go on, in the course of argumentation, to remark that, "omne . . . tendit ad simile" (Quomodo substantiae, 50–52 [Moreschini 188]). The connection between these two texts had already been made by Gilbert of Poitiers. See Gilbert of Poitiers, *De hebdomadibus*, in *The Commentaries on Boethius by Gilbert of Poitiers*, ed. Nikolaus Häring (Toronto: PIMS, 1966), no. 94 (p. 208).

On the reception of *Quomodo substantiae* along with Boethius's other theological treatises in the Middle Ages, see Margaret Gibson, "The *Opuscula Sacra* in the Middle Ages," in *Boethius: His Life, Thought, and Influence* ed. Margaret Gibson (Oxford: Basil Blackwell, 1981), 214–34.

267. Albert the Great, *De IV coaequaevis*, q. 2, a. 4, ad 1 [Borgnet 34:330]: "materia seipsa est principium desiderii: desiderium enim illud nihil aliud est nisi privatio formae cum potentia habendi illam, quae potentia est ipsa materia: ipsa enim entitas materiae est subjectum subjicibile formae: quae subjicibilitas est potentia et desiderium sive appetitus, et non differt ab ipsa nisi secundum rationem dictam." Albert reaffirms this position in the *De bono* [Col. 28:4].

passive, but also [something] in some way active, while this susceptibility adds nothing to the substance of matter. Since [appetite of this sort] is therefore ordered to anything, it can be reduced to act by the divine will. In that case, [its reduction to act] is a miracle, since there is only a potency for obedience in matter such that what God wills may occur in it. But natural eduction is not caused by this process. There is also an appetite in matter which is the beginning of generic or specific form. This appetite is coactive, not merely passive, and is not present unless the forms required for it [are present].... But the form of a body rising [from the dead] is not present in ashes in this way; rather [it is present] only by way of obedience.[268]

By changing the manner in which he viewed the aforementioned text attributed to Boethius, and consequently the way in which he evaluated Aristotle's claim about matter desiring form, Albert was able to avoid saying that the resurrection of the body is natural.[269] His solution paid deference to Averroes, to Bacon, and to Philip. With Averroes, he posits that matter is purely passive, and that individuation occurs through the reception of successively more determined forms into matter. With Bacon, he seems to suggest that this process can be interrupted: there can be a composite with a form that does not determine the composite to the level of an individual, and so confers upon the composite an incomplete active potency, whereby it desires the forms it does not yet have by means of the form which it already has. With Philip, he continues to distinguish between two kinds

268. Albert the Great, *In IV Sent.*, d. 43, a. 3, ad 5 [Borgnet 30:508]: "Appetitus duplex est in materia: quorum unus est susceptibilitas formae tantum, et iste proprie non est appetitus: quia dicit Boethius in libro de Hebdomadibus, quod nihil appetit aliud nisi quod aliquo modo similis est illi: quia appetitus non sonat tantum passivum, sed etiam activum aliquo modo: haec autem susceptibilitas nihil addit supra substantiam materiae: et ideo cum ad quodlibet ordinetur, potest reduci in actum per voluntatem divinam: et tunc est miraculum: quia non est ita in materia, nisi potestas obedientiae, ut in ea fiat quod Deus vult: et ex hoc non causatur naturalis eductio. Est iterum appetitus in materia, qui est formae inchoatio in genere vel specie: et ille appetitus non est, nisi formae sibi debitae in genere vel specie, et coactivus, non tantum passivus.... Sed forma resurgentis corporis non est per hunc modum in cineribus, sed per modum obedientiae tantum."

269. Albert's decision to embrace the text attributed to Boethius becomes even more evident in the *Super Dionysium De divinis nominibus*, where he makes consistent use of it as an authority. See Albert the Great, *Super Dionysium De divinis nominibus* 1 [Col. 37:37], and 4 [Col. 37:160, 209]. Also see *Super Ethica* 6, lect. 2 [Col. 14:403].

of potencies: an Augustinian potency for obedience, which results from God's will for a creature at Creation, and an Aristotelian nature, which is limited to a specific range of ends which are achieved by the powers which flow from the creature's substantial form.[270]

Albert's solution also raises an important point which he does not fully explain, but which will become a foundational principle in Thomas's commentary on the same distinction in the *Sentences*, as we shall see in the next chapter: the idea that some creatures reach their perfection not only by actions which follow from their own *ratio seminalis*, but also by means of effects caused in them by actions which follow from the *ratio seminalis* of another creature.[271] This idea—which reflects Averroes's account of "second nature" in the simple, heavenly bodies, but expresses it in an Augustinian mode—would become a central point of departure for the young Thomas.

Albert would consider the *terminus* of natural desire more fully in Book 4, distinction 49. Following his distinctions of happiness from Book 1, Albert begins in Book 4, distinction 49, by distinguishing uncreated and created happiness. Uncreated happiness is God himself; created happiness is the effect in us of possessing God.[272] But created happiness, Albert now suggests, can be considered in two ways: either we can consider *that* something is good and makes us happy, or we can consider *what about it* is good and makes us happy (the *ratio* of its goodness). If we consider the latter, then anything which makes us happy does so because it is an imitation and example of God, who, as the primary instance of happiness, is the exemplar cause of all instances of happiness.[273] A given person may be mistaken about where true happiness is to be found; nevertheless, that person desires what he desires because he at least thinks that it will lead him to the happiness which is actually found in God.

270. Albert's solution follows that of his Dominican predecessor Hugh of St. Cher, *In IV Sent.*, d. 43 [ms. Vat. Lat. 1098, 192v].

271. Albert the Great, *In II Sent.*, d. 18, a. 6, qc. 2, sol. [Borgnet 27:321].

272. Albert the Great, *In IV Sent.*, d. 49, a. 2, co. [Borgnet 30:678].

273. Ibid. Also see Albert the Great, *Super Dionysium De divinis nominibus* 1 [Col. 37:37].

In order to explain how it is that we desire God implicitly in whatever we desire, Albert at last turns to Dionysius's *triplex via*, which, like the *Summa fratris Alexandri*, he uses outside of its native framework of sacramental purification.[274] In order for us to know God through a creaturely effect, there must be some proportion between the creaturely effect and God. Although there is no strict proportion between God and creatures according to efficient causality, there is a certain proportion between God and creatures on account of formal exemplar causality. When God creates a creature, the formal *ratio* of goodness in that creature (what about it is good) reflects the goodness of the idea in the mind of God according to which the creature is fashioned.[275] That having been said, the proportion between the *ratio* of goodness in the creature and the goodness of God's idea is not a perfect proportion, since the creature can only exhibit God's perfection in a limited manner. Knowledge of a creature can only lead to knowledge *that* God exists, and that he has attributes corresponding with the perfections found in creatures.[276]

The fact that we can only know that God exists and that he has attributes corresponding with the perfections found in creatures does not prevent us from saying a number of things about God without the aid of grace. Albert thinks that philosophers, not just theologians, can speak of God according to each of Dionysius's three ways.[277] Philosophers can speak symbolically of God when they use

274. Here I should voice general agreement with Henryk Anzulewicz, "Pseudo-Dionysius Areopagita und das Strukturprinzip des Denkens von Albert dem Grossen," in *Die Dionysius-Rezeption im Mittelalter: Internationales Kolloquium in Sofia vom 8. Bis 11. April 1999 unter de Schirmherrschaft de Société Internationale pour l'Étude de la Philosophie Médiévale*, ed. Tzotcho Boiadjiev, Georgi Kapriev, and Andreas Speer (Turnhout: Brepols, 2000), 251–95, that Albert's thought must be read in light of the Dionysian influence on it, but disagree with the level to which Anzulewicz views Dionysius as more of a Neo-Platonic philosopher and less of a Christian theologian.

275. See Albert the Great, *Super Dionysium De divinis nominibus*, 1, no. 16, ad 5 [Col. 37:11].

276. Albert the Great, *In I Sent.*, d. 3, a. 2, co. [Borgnet 25:93].

277. Ibid., a. 10, co. [Borgnet 25:99]: "Illae tres viae accipiuntur secundum ea in quibus relucet Creator: aut enim illa sunt symbolice sive figurative convenientia tantum, et in illis est propria via negationis sive oblationis [sic; perhaps this should read 'ablationis'],

metaphors which are said *per prius* of creatures and negate in their language what is improperly said of God; they can speak mystically of God when they use language in which the words are taken from creatures, but the reality indicated by the words is said *per prius* of God by eminence; or they can do both in succession, on account of the quasi-proportion of formal, exemplar causality between God and creatures. Albert's last of the three ways is particularly significant, because it provides the philosophers with a way to make positive affirmations about God without the aid of grace.[278] In so doing, it bridges the gap between natural desire and free desire without the aid of grace by making the proximate term of natural desire the starting point for free desire.[279]

Like the *Summa fratris Alexandri*, Albert's use of the Dionysian *triplex via* enables him to give an account of human nature and natural desire which includes reference to the philosophical knowledge of God as its teleological act, and so turns a natural desire for happiness into a natural desire for God. Also like the *Summa fratris Alexandri*, Albert was thus challenged to give an account of how a human nature, which possesses such a naturally achievable end, relates to grace. Albert's use of Averroes helped him to surpass the limitations of an Avicennian account of nature which Bacon sensed, but was not ultimately able to overcome. By appealing to material potency, and

---

ut lapis, leo et hujusmodi: aut secundum rem per prius in Deo, licet secundum nomen non ita perfecte possint significari, et sic sunt per eminentiam exponenda, ut est vita, essentia, intellectus, et caetera hujusmodi, et haec vocantur mystica, ut dicit Dionysius: aut quantum ad utraque conveniunt, secundum quod ab illo sunt, et sic via est a causato in causam."

278. See ibid., ad 2 [Borgnet 25:100].

279. It would be useful here to avert to a comment in Albert the Great, *Super Ethica* 7, lect. 14 [Col. 14:580], which is clearly not the *ipsissima verba* of Aristotle: "Illud unum divinum quod est in omnibus inclinans ipsa ad desiderium optimi, est refulgentia causae primae, quae etiam est una in omnibus secundum analogum. Cum enim, sicut dicit Boethius, nihil desideret aliquid nisi secundum quod habet aliquam similitudinem ipsius, cum omnia quodam modo desiderent optimum, oportet, quod similitudo optimi sit aliquo modo in omnibus, quae inclinat ad hoc desiderium, sicut materia desiderat formam, secundum quod in ipsa est aliqua similitudo formae. Unde ista similitudinis analogia, secundum quod omnia participant divinum quoddam, erit ex parte appetentium quocumque modo, sed primo dicta erit ex parte appetibilis."

maintaining the strict passivity of matter, Albert could incorporate Philip's *potentia obedientiae* as a passive potency, open to the beatific vision, which stands alongside the active potency conferred upon the soul by its nature. Albert thus suggests the direction in which a solution to Philip's challenge might ultimately be found. But Albert, too, falls short of the goal. While he was able to incorporate Philip's Augustinian potency within the soul in such a way that—within the framework of Aristotelian philosophy—it could credibly be considered a potency in more than just name, he did not ultimately describe how the two sets of potencies—Aristotelian and Augustinian—relate to one another in the same soul. The challenge of figuring out how to relate those two sets of potencies to one another fell to another, and it would be among the questions that Bonaventure of Bagnoregio would take up when he entered into the conversation about nature, grace, and the desire for God.

A MID-THIRTEENTH-CENTURY SYNTHESIS: BONAVENTURE OF BAGNOREGIO

When Bonaventure set about the composition of his own *Commentary on the Sentences* from 1250 to 1252, he did not have access to Bacon's later writings on *rationes seminales,* since Bonaventure's work pre-dates Bacon's *Communia naturalis* by over a decade. At Paris in the early 1250s, he would nevertheless have had access to all of the works from the 1230s to the 1240s that we have examined so far. Among the authors whose *Sentences* commentaries have been published, he appears to make the first to attempt at a comprehensive synthesis of the tradition of the 1230s and 1240s. Bonaventure was uniquely positioned to undertake such a synthesis. His academic career had coincided nearly perfectly with the composition of the texts reviewed thus far.[280] He was a student in the faculty of arts from 1235 to 1243; he was a student in the faculty of theology from 1243 to 1248,

280. Here I follow the chronology of Jacques Bougerol, *Introduction à Saint Bonaventure,* 2nd ed. (Paris: J. Vrin, 1988), 4–5.

and he commented on the *Sentences* from 1250 to 1252, evidently with a copy of Albert's *Commentary on the Sentences* by his side.[281]

Following Peter Lombard, Bonaventure approaches the question of what is natural through the Augustinian concept of *rationes seminales*. Yet when Bonaventure turns to the recent tradition on *rationes seminales*, he observes a problem: although the concept of *rationes seminales* had a theological provenance in the works of Augustine, the ends for which the concept had been used had in recent years had come to be dominated by philosophical speculation.[282] Bonaventure sought to purify the use of *rationes seminales* in discussions of nature, grace, and the desire for God, and so overcome certain theological limitations which he thought the concept had accrued in previous thinkers.

Bonaventure's use of the recent tradition focuses particularly on Rufus and Bacon, both of whom had entered the Franciscan Order by this time. Observing that "there was a dispute among philosophical men about individuation,"[283] he begins by summarizing and criticizing Averroes's (that is, Bacon's) and Avicenna's (that is, Rufus's) views on individuation: "either one of these positions has something [in it] which could seem reasonably improbable to a man without too much thought."[284] Matter, *pace* Averroes, "is common for all things," while form, *pace* Avicenna, "is made to have another like

281. Marianne Schlosser, "Bonaventure: Life and Works," in *A Companion to Bonaventure*, ed. Jay Hammond, Wayne Hellmann, and Jared Goff (Leiden: Brill, 2014), 12, averts to Bougerol's observation that Bonaventure actually composed his *Commentary on the Sentences* with a copy of Albert's commentary in front of him.

282. Bonaventure, *In II Sent.*, d. 18, a. 1, q. 1 [Quaracchi 2:436]: "Notandum, quod cum de his rationibus seminalibus egregius doctor Augustinus in quinto et sexto super Genesim ad litteram ambigue loquatur, et ab ipso potissime habeamus horum nominum usum; non est facile inter huiusmodi vocabula recte distinguere."

283. Ibid., d. 3, p. 1, a. 2, q. 3, co. [Quaracchi 2:109]: "Haec eadem est quaestio de individuatione, quae nunc movetur de personali discretione; et de ipsa fuit contentio inter philosophicos viros." I take this to refer to masters of arts at the University of Paris. It may, however, simply be a paraphrase of a comment that appears in Rufus's *Contra Averroem*. This is suggested in Rega Wood, "Richard Rufus and English Scholastic Discussion," 127.

284. Bonaventure, *In II Sent.*, d. 3, p. 1, a. 2, q. 3, co. [Quaracchi 2:109]: "Quaelibet istarum positionum aliquid habet, quod homini non multum intelligenti rationabiliter videri poterit improbabile."

it," and is not reintroduced anew in all cases of individuality.[285] Attempting to mediate the disagreement between members of the Arabic Aristotelian tradition and the members of his own religious order, Bonaventure proposes a middle way: matter and form mutually individuate one another under the influence of an efficient cause.[286] Matter makes a thing to be *this* (*hoc*), while form makes it to be *something* (*aliquid*). Together, they make it to be *this thing* (*hoc aliquid*).[287]

Bonaventure then engages in a commentary on Bacon's *Questiones secunde*, following the outline of the text and making distinctions at each stage of Bacon's reasoning.[288] Like Bacon, Bonaventure begins with Anaxagoras's *latitatio formarum*. According to Bonaventure, there are really two ways of understanding the *latitatio formarum*: either forms are hidden in matter *actually*, which is what Anaxagoras had held, or they are hidden in matter *potentially*, in which case nothing problematic follows.[289] Also like Bacon,

285. Ibid.: "Quomodo enim materia, quae omnibus est communis, erit principale principium et causa distinctionis, valde difficile est videre. Rursus, quomodo forma sit tota et praecipua causa numeralis distinctionis, valde difficile est capere, cum omnis forma creata, quantum est de sui natura, nata sit habere aliam similem, sicut et ipse Philosophus dicit etiam in sole et luna esse. Vel quomodo dicemus, duos ignes differre formaliter, vel etiam alia, quae plurificantur et numero distinguuntur ex sola divisione continui, ubi nullius est novae formae inductio?"

286. Ibid.: "Individuatio consurgit ex actuali coniunctione materiae cum forma, ex qua coniunctione unum sibi appropriat alterum; sicut patet, cum impressio vel expressio fit multorum sigillorum in cera, quae prius erat una, nec sigilla plurificari possunt sine cera, nec cera numeratur, nisi quia fiunt in ea diversa sigilla."

287. Ibid. [Quaracchi 2:109–10]: "Quod sit hoc, principalius habet a materia, ratione cuius forma habet positionem in loco et tempore. Quod sit aliquid, habet a forma. Individuum enim habet esse, habet etiam existere. Existere dat materia formae, sed essendi actum dat forma materiae—Individuatio igitur in creaturis consurgit ex duplici principio." See Averroes, *Commentarium magnum in libros Metaphysicorum* 7.7, com. 27 [Giunti 8:177rd].

288. The relevant passage is Bonaventure, *In II Sent.*, d. 7, p. 2, a. 2, q. 1, co. [Quaracchi 2:197–98]. What follows is a summary of that passage.

289. Ibid.: "Quidam enim posuerunt latitationem formarum, sicut imponitur Anaxagorae. Et illud potest dupliciter intelligi: aut quod ipse poneret, formas actualiter existere in materia, sed non apparere extrinsecus, sicut pictura operta panno; et iste modus impossibilis est omnino, quia tunc contraria simul ponerentur in eodem. Alio modo potest intelligi sic, ut essentiae formarum sint in materia in potentia non solum latentes, sed entes in potentia, ut materia habeat in se seminales omnium formarum rationes, sibi a primaria conditione inditas—et illud concordat et philosophiae et sacrae Scripturae—

Bonaventure highlights Avicenna's *dator formarum* as the counterpoint to Anaxagoras. Here too, Bonaventure makes a distinction: if one really means that God is the sole cause of every instance of form in matter—and Bonaventure takes this to have been Avicenna's position—then one would have to say that created agents do absolutely nothing in the manner of efficient causes, which is false. Nevertheless, Bonaventure concedes that there is nothing wrong with saying that God is the *principal* agent in any instance of efficient causality, provided that we make room for creatures as secondary causes acting under the power of God as primary cause.

When Bonaventure arrives at Bacon's conclusion (incomplete active potencies), he attempts to distance himself from Bacon by a further distinction: to say that something is present in an active potency is nothing other than to say that it is present actually in virtue of a form.[290] If Bacon were correct, and forms were in matter as in

et per actionem agentis educerentur in actum. Sed hic intellectus non fuit huius positionis, sed primus, secundum quod expositores dicunt. Haec enim positio fuit, quod agens particulare nihil agat, sed tantum detegat."

290. Ibid.: "Nam quidam dicunt, quod huiusmodi formae sunt in materia in potentia receptiva et quodam modo activa sive cooperativa; quoniam materia et habet possibilitatem ad recipiendum, et etiam inclinationem ad cooperandum, et in agente est huiusmodi forma producenda sicut in principio effectivo et originali, quia omnis forma per naturam suae speciei recipit virtutem multiplicandi se; unde inductio formae est ab agente formam suam multiplicante. Et ponunt exemplum in candela, quo modo una inflammat multas, et ab uno obiecto relucent multae imagines in pluribus speculis. Et huiusmodi formae, ut dicunt, non habent, ex quo sint materialiter, sed ex quo originaliter; et ideo non dicuntur creari nec dicuntur esse ex nihilo. Illud enim creatur, quod nullo modo est; sed talis forma sic producta aliquo modo est, tum ratione agentis tum ratione materiae."

Here, a question arises concerning the identity of Bonaventure's interlocutor. As mentioned above, Bacon defended the idea of forms existing in an active, but incomplete potency in matter in his *Questiones secunde*. Bonaventure is also at the point in his discussion of the topic where, if he were following Bacon, we might expect him to treat Bacon's work. Yet while Bonaventure makes it clear that he has a very specific text in mind when he references the example of the candle, that example is nowhere to be found in the *Questiones secunde*. It appears that Bonaventure changed tack here, and completes a discussion of Bacon's views with an example taken from some early recension of Bacon's *De multiplicatione specierum*, or another work which stood as a precursor to that one.

Scholars of Bacon might object to this hypothesis, because *De multiplicatione specierum*, although it did go through several editions, was not begun until the late 1250s or early 1260s, well after the composition of the second book of Bonaventure's *Commentary on the Sentences*. These are the dates assigned for the work's composition in David

an active potency, then forms would be received *in* the receptive potency of matter, and they would be caused *by* the active potency in matter, but in no sense could they be drawn *out of* or *educed from* the matter by an efficient cause,[291] as Averroes had stated and as Bacon had supposed.[292] Bacon's doctrine of incomplete active potency is actually a combination of the two doctrines that Bacon rejects. Insofar as his active potency is complete, it is simply the actuality communicated to matter by form. Insofar as it is incomplete, it is simply matter's receptive potency.

Bonaventure does not deny that there is something intrinsic in matter from which forms are educed. His disagreement with Bacon concerns whether that from which form is educed can be said to be "incomplete":

> There is something cocreated [*concreatum*] with matter out of which an agent, when it acts upon it, educes a form. I do not say "out of which" as meaning out of something that is like some part of the form that is going to be produced; rather, [I say it] because [that something] can be form and becomes form, just as a rosebud becomes a rose. [My] position posits that the truths of all forms that are going to be produced are in matter naturally, and that when a form is produced, no quiddity, no truth of essence is induced anew, but rather a new disposition is given to it, so that what was in potency may be in act.[293]

Lindberg's introduction to *Roger Bacon's Philosophy of Nature*, xxxiii. Lindberg may be correct about the dating of the formal undertaking which is now known as *De multiplcatione specierum*. However, the text of Bonaventure which appears here, exactly where one would expect him to discuss Bacon's position, is a direct summary of the most important points and distinctions of *De multiplicatione specierum*, p. 1, chap. 3. That chapter makes all of the claims that Bonaventure attributes to his interlocutor, and defends them finally with the example of the candle.

291. Bonaventure, *In II Sent.*, d. 7, p. 2, a. 2, q. 1, co. [Quaracchi 2:198]: "Alia via est, quod formae sunt in potentia materiae, non solum in qua et a qua aliquo modo, sed etiam ex qua." *In qua* refers to the reception of form in a receptive potency, *a qua* refers to the causing of form by an active potency.

292. Roger Bacon, *De multiplicatione specierum* 1.3 [Lindberg 46:50–53]: "Cum igitur nullo predictorum modorum fiat generatio speciei, manifestum est quod quinto modo oportet fieri, scilicet per veram immutationem et eductionem de potentia activa materie patientis, non enim est aliquis alius modus excogitabilis preter dictos."

293. Bonaventure, *In II Sent.*, d. 7, p. 2, a. 2, q. 1, co. [Quaracchi 2:198]: "In ipsa materia aliquid est concreatum, ex quo agens, dum agit in ipsam, educit formam; non inquam ex illo tanquam ex aliquo, quod sit tanquam aliqua pars formae producendae,

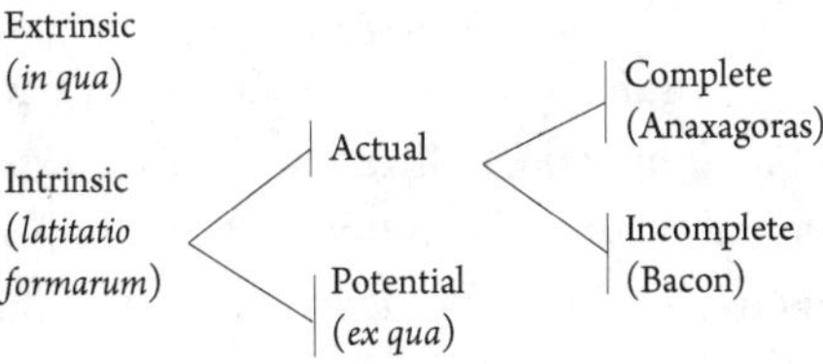

FIGURE 4. The relationship of form to matter according to Bonaventure

Bacon was on to something when he asserted that forms must be educed from matter, and this transition can be likened to the transition from a seed into a tree, but he did not go far enough. Taken to its logical conclusion, Bacon's doctrine results in a form which is partially hiding (*latens*) and partially given (*data*), but in no sense educed (*educta*) (see figure 4).

At this point, one might ask why Bonaventure went to such great lengths to involve himself in the philosophical disputations of the arts faculty concerning the questions of individuation and information, if his original contention was to restore *rationes seminales* to theology. As if anticipating the objection, Bonaventure replies by recalling us to the doctrine of Creation, which gave rise to Augustine's doctrine of *rationes seminales* and Peter Lombard's use of that doctrine in the first place.

Rather than descend to the particular question of Adam's rib, Bonaventure enlarges his discussion of Creation to encompass the whole structure of the material universe.[294] He observes that there

sed quia illud potest esse forma et fit forma, sicut globus rosae fit rosa. Et ista positio ponit, quod in materia sint veritates omnium formarum producendarum naturaliter; et cum producitur, nulla quidditas, nulla veritas essentiae inducitur de novo, sed datur ei nova dispositio, ut quod erat in potentia fiat in actu."

294. Ibid.: "Hanc positionem credo esse tendendam, non solum quia eam suadeat ratio, sed etiam quia confirmat auctoritas Augustini super Genesim ad litteram, quam Magister allegat: quod 'quae producuntur a natura secundum rationes seminales producuntur.'"

are two ways of considering matter at Creation: in its concrete, historical existence (*secundum esse*), and in itself as abstracted from history (*secundum essentiam*).[295] The distinction between these two ways of viewing matter arises out of a seeming discrepancy in the texts of Augustine. In the *Confessions*, Augustine argues that matter was created at first without form, and only subsequently received form.[296] Later, in *De genesi ad litteram*, he maintains that form is "something cocreated" (*aliquid concreatum*) with matter.[297] By the time of the composition of Peter Lombard's *Sentences*, both these views had their adherents, with some espousing that matter was created before form, and others espousing that they were created simultaneously.[298]

Whether Bonaventure wanted to reflect upon matter *secundum esse* (in the concrete) or *secundum essentiam* (in the abstract), he faced implicit criticism from Bacon. Two works attributed to Bacon that predated Bonaventure referenced the idea that matter *secundum esse* was created at first without form, and that this unformed matter could rightly be called "confusion" or "chaos."[299] In the earlier of the

295. Ibid., 12, a. 1, q. 1, co. [Quaracchi 2:294]: "dupliciter est loqui de materia: aut secundum quod existit in natura, aut secundum quod consideratur ab anima."

296. Augustine outlines this position beginning at *Confessiones* 12.3.3 [CCSL 27:217], and summarizes it at *Confessiones* 12.13.16 [CCSL 27:223–24]. Technically, Augustine never says that there was a period *in time* in which matter existed without form, because, he notes, form is required in order that something be subject to time. For that reason, he thinks that when matter was created without form it participated in eternity, and only later became subject to time with its reception of form. See *Confessiones* 12.9.9 [CCSL 27:221]: "ista uero informitas terrae inuisibilis et incomposita, nec ipsa in diebus numerata est. ubi enim nulla species, nullus ordo, nec uenit quidquam nec praeterit, et ubi hoc non fit, non sunt utique dies nec uicissitudo spatiorum temporalium."

297. Augustine, *De Genesi ad litteram* 1.15 [CSEL 28.1:21]: "Non quia informis materia formatis rebus tempore prior est, cum sit utrumque simul concreatum… sed quia illud, unde fit aliquid, etsi non tempore, tamen quadam origine prius est, quam illud, unde fit aliquid, etsi non tempore."

298. See Peter Lombard, *II Sent.*, 12.2 [Quaracchi 2:384–85]. Peter mentions that, while Augustine was generally ascribed the view from *De Genesi ad litteram*, there were others expounding the view that matter was created at first without any form.

299. The works are *Questiones supra libros quatuor Physicorum Aristotelis* [Steele 8:19–20], and *Questiones altere supra libros prime Philosophie* [Steele 10:61–63]. Donati, "Pseudoepigrapha in the *Opera hactenus inedita Rogeri Baconi?*" 153–203, challenges the

two works, the *Questiones supra libros quatuor Physicorum Aristotelis,* Bacon defended the view, arguing that since matter of itself desires greater perfection, it is fitting for it to be created in a confused state without form; otherwise, as it already possesses form, it has no further perfection to desire.[300] In the later of the two works, the *Questiones altere supra libros prime philosophie,* he opposed the position, arguing that such a sort of confused matter would be impossible on account of the mutually opposed motions of the potencies in it.

Having evidently read both works, Bonaventure repeats Bacon's philosophical criticism of the idea that Creation began with a metaphysical *chaos,* but develops his own critique of it along the lines of his previous criticisms of Bacon. Just as Bonaventure had earlier denied that Bacon's incomplete active potency was anything more than actuality, and had argued that matter with an incomplete active potency is really one part of matter awaiting another part, so here Bonaventure suggests that the incomplete active potencies of *chaos* would have to be actualized "parts" of it. These parts would have to pre-exist the *chaos* into which they were integrated, and such preexistent, confused elements are nowhere to be found in Scripture as part of the Creation narrative.[301]

Bonaventure affirms that there is something cocreated (*concreatum*) with matter which communicates existence to it but still allows it further potentiality toward subsequent and more specific forms. But he makes a distinction in order to avoid Bacon's later criticism of the hypothesis of *chaos.* The distinction is reminiscent of Albert's embrace of Averroes's generic and specific forms: he takes Bacon's

---

authenticity of both these works. But since, as Donati herself says, "the results presented here cannot be considered as the final answer to the question," we are not yet justified in concluding with certainty that they are inauthentic. If they prove ultimately to be inauthentic, what is of principal importance to this chapter is how Bonaventure responds to the challenge before him, not that this specific challenge arose from works attributed to Bacon.

300. Roger Bacon, *Questiones supra libros quatuor Physicorum Aristotelis* [Steele 8:19–20].

301. Bonaventure, *In II Sent.,* d. 12, a. 1, q. 3, co. [Quaracchi 2:300].

idea of an incomplete form *with* an incomplete active potency in matter and reworks it so that it becomes an incomplete form *without* an incomplete active potency in matter:

There is another way of speaking, which is more reasonable, that matter [at Creation] was produced under some form, but that it was not a complete form, nor did it give matter complete being. Wherefore matter was not informed in such a way that it could not be said to be "unformed," nor was the desire of matter fulfilled to such an extent that the matter could not still desire other forms. And therefore there was a disposition toward further forms, not complete perfection.[302]

Bonaventure's incomplete form does two things which an incomplete active potency could not do for Bacon. First, since Bonaventure's incomplete form allows for the pure passivity of matter taken of itself (*secundum essentiam*), it clears up any ambiguity about the origin of actuality in matter; any and all actuality must come from form. Second, since the actuality that form confers upon matter in actual existence (*secundum esse*) remains distinct from the potentiality of the matter, the incompleteness of the form allows for the incompletely formed matter to retain its pluripotentiality toward other forms.

Bonaventure's approach to the question of how form comes to be in matter afforded him the possibility of explaining *rationes seminales* in a way that was manifestly different from Bacon's.[303] Since

302. Ibid.: "Et ideo est alius modus dicendi rationabilior, quod materia illa producta est sub aliqua forma, sed illa non erat forma completa nec dans materiae esse completum; et ideo non sic formabat, quin adhuc materia diceretur informis, nec appetitum materiae adeo finiebat, quin materia adhuc alias formas appeteret; et ideo dispositio erat ad formas ulteriores, non completa perfectio."

303. In *In II Sent.*, d. 18, a. 1, q. 3, co. [Quaracchi 2:440–42], Bonaventure summarizes Bacon's position and critiques it at length, but he seems to have the text of the *Questiones supra libros prime philosophie Aristotelis* attributed to Bacon in front of him, rather than the *Questiones secunde* or the *Questiones altere*, since he paraphrases several sections from the *Questiones supra libros prime philosophie Aristotelis*. Here is the text of Bonaventure's summary; the numbers in brackets, which I have added, refer to the source text for Bonaventure's understanding of Bacon, as printed in Roger Bacon, *Questiones supra libros prime philosophie Aristotelis* [Steele 10]. "Quidam enim dicere voluerunt, quod cum universalia non sint fictiones, realiter et secundum veritatem non solum sunt in anima, sed etiam in natura; et quia omne quod est in natura, habet fundari in materia, tam formae

matter is purely potential and undetermined in itself, as in Rufus, but is partially and incompletely determined in virtue of its incomplete form, similar to Bacon, it is the form, not the matter, which serves as the principle according to which matter is enabled to be formed by any number of subsequent substantial forms.[304] A *ratio seminalis* is therefore an incomplete form, not an active potency in the matter into which that incomplete form is received.

The doctrine of incomplete forms led Bonaventure to an important insight in his understanding of nature and natural desire. Returning to the text of Augustine's *De genesi ad litteram,* Bonaventure goes on to explain that Augustine actually uses three distinct terms: *ratio causalis, ratio seminalis,* and *causa primordialis.* Although both God and creatures can be called "causes," we call the rule according to which God acts a *ratio causalis.*[305] The uncreated *ratio causalis* is the

universales quam singulares in materia habent esse [241–42]. Et ita non differunt forma universalis et singularis per abstractionem a materia, et concretionem in materia, sed differunt per additionem unius ad alteram [253], et per magis completum et minus completum [256]. Cuius signum est, quia in coordinatione generum et specierum forma speciei est completissima et compositissima. Forma vero generis respectu illius est ens in potentia, et fit magis in actu per differentiam sibi superadditam [232, 284]. Et ita, cum ratio seminalis dicat formam ratione incompleta, dixerunt, nihil aliud esse rationem seminalem quam formam universalem." The last sentence does not come from the *Questiones supra libros prime philosophie Aristotelis.* Bonaventure seems to have referenced some writing of Bacon that I have not found or that we do not possess, to have referenced some thought that Bacon conveyed to him personally, or to have simply drawn what he considered the logical conclusions of Bacon's thought.

304. Bonaventure, *In II Sent.,* d. 18, a. 1, q. 3. [Quaracchi 2:440]. Here Bonaventure co-opts Bacon's language of "active potency," but locates its origin in form, not in matter. Bonaventure concludes, "si … dicatur forma universalis forma existens secundum esse incompletum in materia et indifferens et possibilis ad multa producenda; sic potest dici ratio seminalis forma universalis" (ibid. [Quaracchi 2:442]).

305. Bonaventure, *In II Sent.,* d. 18, a. 1, q. 2 [Quaracchi 2:436]: "Causa enim communis est ad principium intrinsecum et extrinsecum, similiter et ratio causalis, quantum est de vi nominis; semen vero dicit principium intrinsecum. Et ita ratio causalis se extendit ad rationes creatas et increatas; ratio vero seminalis solum ad rationes creatas. Quantum ergo est de vi nominis, unum est commune respectu alterius; in quantum autem ad invicem distinguuntur et connumerantur, sic causa et causalis ratio accipitur quantum ad principium increatum, semen vero et seminalis ratio spectat ad principium creatum— Differunt autem causa et ratio causalis, quia causa dicit principium productivum, ratio vero causalis dicit regulam dirigentem illud principium in sua operatione. Similter per hunc modum differt semen et ratio seminalis. Regula autem agentis increati est forma

divine idea that serves as a creature's formal exemplar cause; this corresponds in a creature with its natural form (*forma naturalis*). But a creature's natural form can be considered in two ways. As it causes something to be done by the creature (*ab illo*), the creature is said to act according to a *ratio naturalis*; as it causes something to be done from within the creature (*ex illo*), it is said to act according to a *ratio seminalis*.[306]

There are three basic ways in which the various *rationes* enumerated above can interact. In one way, God can act according to a *ratio causalis*, to which nothing in a creature corresponds (that is, God actualizes a receptive potency in the creature, to which no active tendency in its form corresponds). In that case, the creature is said to respond according to a potency for obedience (*potentia obedientiae*); acts of this kind include Creation and the multiplication of one thing from another. In a second way, God acts according to a *ratio causalis*, to which a *ratio seminalis* corresponds in a creature (that is, God communicates actuality to the creature's receptive potency through the mediation of its form). In that case, a creature is said to act as one might ordinarily expect; acts of this kind include ordinary generation of like from like. In a third way, God acts according to a *ratio causalis*, to which a whole series or chain of *rationes seminales* correspond, but God skips the ordinary chain of events and causes the thing to happen immediately; here again, creatures possess only a potency for obedience with respect to God's action.

On the question of which of the above three aforementioned kinds of interaction is "natural," Bonaventure makes a distinction which parallels the one he had made in the case of the creation of

---

exemplaris sive idealis, regula vero agentis creati est forma naturalis: et ita rationes causales sunt formae ideales sive exemplares, rationes vero seminales sunt formae naturales."

306. Ibid.: "Naturales rationes et seminales re idem sunt, ratione vero differunt. Quia enim semen dicit ut ex quo, et natura dicit ut a quo, ratio seminalis attenditur, in quantum dirigit potentiam naturae, ut ex aliquo fiat aliquid; naturalis vero, ut ab aliquo fiat aliquid—Vel ratio seminalis respicit inchoationem et intrinsecam virtutem, quae movet et operatur ad effectus productionem; naturalis vero concernit producentis ad productum assimilationem et modi agendi assuetudinem."

matter, and which is evocative of Philip's distinction between the Augustinian and Aristotelian senses of nature.

> Nature can be said in two ways. In one way, nature means "everything that befits something from its natural origin"; and in this way it befits a creature that everything that God wants should be produced from it [*ex ea*]. For a work has in itself a potency for perfect obedience [*potentia perfectae obedientiae*] with respect to its maker, since it is subject to his will in all things ... God does nothing against this [sort of] nature; much rather, whatever he does with a creature, he does according to this nature [*secundum hanc naturam*].... In another way, nature means "the power instilled properly into things, according to which natural things pursue their courses and their customary motions." And if we understand nature in this way, sometimes God acts against nature [*contra naturam*], sometimes above nature [*supra naturam*]. He acts against nature, when he does something, to which something similar can be produced in nature and by nature, but in an altogether different way ... and then it is called a miracle. But when God produces an effect to which nature can do nothing similar, and toward which nature has no ordering of its own power, like when God was made man, or when a mortal body is made glorious; then God acts above nature [*supra naturam*], and that work is properly called "marvelous" [*mirabile*], not a "miracle" [*miraculum*].[307]

If we compare the three kinds of actions described here to the three categories of interaction among the *rationes* described above, we can say that when God actualizes a receptive potency in a creature for which there does not correspond any active potency in the creature's form, then God acts *supra naturam*; when God actualizes a recep-

307. Ibid., ad 5 [Quaracchi 2:437–38]: "Dupliciter dicitur natura. Uno modo dicitur natura omne illud quod competit rei a sua naturali origine; et sic competit creaturae, ut ex ea producatur omne quod Deus vult. Opus enim respectu sui artificis habet in se potentiam perfectae obedientiae, cum per omnia subiaceat eius voluntati ... et contra hanc naturam Deus nunquam facit, immo quidquid facit de creatura, secundum hanc naturam facit. Alio modo dicitur natura proprie vis insita rebus, secundum quam res naturales peragunt cursus suos et motus solitos; et hoc modo accipiendo naturam, aliquando Deus facit contra naturam, aliquando supra naturam.—Tunc facit contra naturam, quando facit aliquid, cuius simile in natura et a natura produci habet, tamen alio modo omnino diverso ... et tunc dicitur miraculum. Quando vero Deus facit aliquid, cuius simile natura facere non potest, et ad quod natura non habet ordinem secundum propriam virtutem, sicut quando Deus factus est homo, vel quando corpus mortale fit gloriosum; tunc facit supra naturam, et illud opus proprie dicitur mirabile, non miraculum."

tive potency through the mediation of a creature's form, then God acts *secundum naturam*; when God actualizes a receptive potency in a creature to which some remote form in nature corresponds, but he does so immediately, then God acts *contra naturam*.

Bonaventure's deference to Philip's two senses of the word, "natural," has important consequences when it comes to his explanation of natural desire. Just as matter's incomplete information does not exhaust, but rather enables matter's desire for subsequent formation, so neither does nature's complete formation exhaust its desire for subsequent formation. In the case of an incomplete substantial form, matter continues to desire complete substantial form; in the case of a complete substantial form, matter continues to desire accidental form. Consequently, since the perfection by which we are joined with God is accidental, not substantial, there is no reason that human persons, informed by the soul as their substantial form, cannot desire a union with God which they cannot achieve of their own accord.[308] "Since ... the rational soul is created after the image and likeness of God, it is also made capable of the most fulfilling good; and [happiness] is not enough for [a rational soul], when it is vain and defective; therefore I say that [a rational soul] desires true happiness naturally."[309] As William of Auvergne had said, following Avicenna: since the soul is *created* for God, therefore it is natural that the soul *desire* God. Yet the soul does not desire God because it can achieve God according to the active potential of its substantial form *secundum naturam*—that would capitulate too much to the opposite sense of nature, in which nature is bound by the ends it can achieve by its active potency—the soul desires to be united with God as by an accidental form above its own principles.[310] The desire is natural in one sense because it flows from God's intention for us at Creation; it can proceed from our soul in the other sense because it is a de-

308. Bonaventure, *In IV Sent.*, d. 49, p. 1, a. un., q. 1, ad 4 [Quaracchi 4:1001].

309. Ibid., q. 2, co. [Quaracchi 4:1003]: "Quoniam igitur anima rationalis creata est ad Dei imaginem et similitudinem et facta est capax boni sufficientissimi; et ipsa non sufficit sibi, cum sit vana et deficiens: ideo dico, quod veram beatitudinem appetit naturaliter."

310. Ibid., q. 5, ad 4 [Quaracchi 4:1009].

sire for the actualization of a receptive potency for accidental form.

In elaborating this position on natural desire, Bonaventure observes three properties concerning man's relationship to happiness: "all believe that happiness is good, that it satisfies [us], and everyone desires this."[311] As with Peter Lombard, people may seek happiness in a variety of particular goods. But our natural desire is not for that reason purely subjective. Bonaventure thinks that there is only one good that is truly "the most satisfying."[312] Everyone desires the effect in themselves of possessing this good, even if not everyone identifies the true nature of this good in actual fact.

When pressed to explain how exactly it is that we have a natural desire for the happiness caused in us by the vision of God, Bonaventure admits that he cannot say with absolute certainty. He gives three possible answers, without determining the question, each drawn from a different aspect of Dionysius's *triplex via*. First, he appeals to the *via negativa*. He draws a parallel between the soul and matter, and he asks us to engage in a thought experiment: imagine that matter had the power of knowing; could it know form? Bonaventure thinks that it could, because from the combination of its lack of form and its inclination toward form, it would know what it is to be informed and would desire it. Second, he appeals to the *via causalitatis*, and asks us to follow the sort of Avicennian psychology which undergirds the *Summa fratris Alexandri*: maybe the knowledge of perfect happiness is simply impressed upon our minds. Lastly, he appeals to the *via eminentiae*. Perhaps the knowledge of perfect happiness is not impressed upon our minds, but we can know it by extrapolating from something that is.[313]

311. Ibid., q. 2, co. [Quaracchi 4:1003]: "Omnes . . . credunt, quod beatitudo sit bonum, quod sufficit, et omnes istud appetunt."

312. Ibid.: "Quoniam igitur anima rationalis creata est ad 'Dei imaginem et similitudinem' et facta est capax boni sufficientissimi; et ipsa sibi non sufficit, cum sit vana et deficiens: ideo dico, quod veram beatitudinem appetit naturaliter."

313. Ibid. [Quaracchi 4:1004]. He distinguishes the three explanations here, and explains the first two in detail. For the third, he refers us to a similar explanation with regard to the knowledge of charity in *In I Sent.*, d. 17, pars 1, a. un., q. 4, resp. [Quaracchi 1:301–2].

CONCLUSION

Bonaventure's failure to propose a definitive answer as to how we can have a natural desire for a supernatural end highlights for us a fundamental difficulty that Latin Christian philosophers and theologians encountered in the second quarter of the thirteenth century: in their attempt to articulate an Augustinian understanding of nature within the Aristotelian tradition, they came to seemingly irreconcilable conclusions. Those who followed Avicenna's understanding of natural desire, especially William of Auvergne, the *Summa fratris Alexandri,* and in some respects Bonaventure (if we consider his three possible explanations for how we can have a natural desire for the vision of God), turned Augustine's desire for happiness into a positive motion toward God. This desire was either rooted in the nature of the intellect itself, as in William and in Bonaventure's first possibility, or predicated upon knowledge which God impresses there, as in the *Summa fratris Alexandri* and Bonaventure's second and third possibilities.

In its most extreme form, that of William of Auvergne, an Avicennian-Augustinian doctrine of desire had the benefit of easily reconciling what the Christian Faith reveals about the final end of man with what the philosophers say about natural desire, but it struggled to reconcile what the Christian Faith reveals about the woundedness of nature in search of that end, and about the gratuity of that end when it is offered to us by grace. William sensed this difficulty. If man has a natural desire for an end that he cannot naturally achieve, is our natural desire therefore vain? William's response was in the negative: we always have the opportunity to ask God for it as a gift, and God is always free to deny the request because our souls are never so perfect that God could not find some reason to deny if he so chose. But is William's answer truly adequate? If, *ex parte creaturae,* the gratuity of the vision of God is predicated on our ability to pray, what shall we make of Albert's observation that, in order to conform to the principles of philosophy, a natural desire is *supposed* to have a naturally achievable end? More significantly, if *ex parte Dei*, the gratuity of the vision of God is predicated on God's ability to hold our sins against us, even after they have been sacramentally forgiven, does this not raise some troubling questions with regard to the definitiveness of God's forgiveness, the distinction between mortal and venial sin, and/or the doctrine of Purgatory?

Even with the more moderate forms of an Avicennian-Augustinian doctrine of desire, which suggest that the end of natural desire may be in some way natural, we may observe two unresolved difficulties during this period. First, there is a struggle to show how nature maintains that fundamental openness to God's action which Philip the Chancellor described with the term *potentia obedientiae*. By describing a creature's openness to divine action in terms of formal causality, Avicennian-Augustinian doctrines of desire tended to limit a creature's openness to divine action within the boundaries of the form with which they were associated. This was clearest with William of Auvergne, who posited a positive motion toward the beatific vision, but it was also present in Richard Rufus, who identified nature's openness to change with the most general form it possesses. Second, for those less radical than William of Auvergne, there is a struggle to describe the relationship between any naturally achievable end associated with the desire for God (as in the *Summa fratris Alexandri*) and the supernaturally achievable end available to humanity by the grace of Christ. A natural desire with a natural end easily reconciles what the Christian Faith reveals about the gratuity of man's final end with what the philosophers say about natural desire, and just as easily protects the supernatural gifts of God from any creature claiming them by rights, but if the act which satisfies human desire is an act that it can achieve without the grace of God, what shall we make of Augustine's fundamental concern, evident throughout his anti-Pelagian works, to protect the Christocentricity of human perfection?

An Averroistic-Augustinian doctrine of desire shared the benefit of protecting the gratuity of grace and the integrity of nature with a moderate Avicennian-Augustinian doctrine of desire. It had the further benefit of safeguarding nature's openness to God by associating that openness with material rather than formal causality, but it raised the seemingly insoluble question of explaining how these two sets of potencies, that which is perfected by a natural end and that which is perfected by the vision of God, relate to one another in the same soul. Roger Bacon related them by means of the dubious idea of an "incomplete active potency" in matter. Albert the Great more consistently upheld the complete passivity of matter, and with it the limitless nature of nature's openness to God, but in so doing he seemingly avoided the question altogether which Bacon was trying to resolve. Bonaventure maintained the absolute passivity of matter with Albert and transferred Bacon's incomplete active potency to an "incomplete form." But speaking strictly in theological terms of nature's openness to grace, and prescinding from other questions that might be raised about their respective differences in natural philosophy, does this not represent in a certain sense a return to Rufus, whose corporeity does the same theological work as Bonaventure's incomplete forms? Yes and no. It does in the sense that it represents the limitation of a creature's openness to divine action in the most general sense, provided that we are speaking of divine action which occurs *through* a creature's *ratio seminalis* (what Bonaventure describes as actions that are *secundum naturam*). But it does not if we are speaking of divine action which has no corresponding *ratio seminalis* (what Bonaventure describes as actions that are *supra naturam*). Yet once we admit that there are certain actions which occur in a creature that do not correspond with its *ratio seminalis*, Bonaventure leaves us with the same question that Albert did: what is the relationship between these two kinds of actions *in the creature in whom they take place*?

We see, then, in the second quarter of the thirteenth century the same basic positions as we find in the contemporary nature/grace debate. Both the Avicennian-Augustinians and the Averroistic-Augustinians were concerned to give a philosophically comprehensible account of nature by assigning nature some definite act as its teleological perfection. We see in the most radical form of the Avicennian side a natural desire for a supernatural end; while in the moderate Avicennians and the Averroists we see a natural desire for a natural end. All parties to the debate tried to give a philosophically comprehensible account of grace. On the Avicennian side, there was a general tendency to see in nature an active orientation toward grace. The Avicennians were aware of the danger that a natural desire for a supernatural end may compromise the gratuity of grace, but were unable to give a satisfactory defense of it. On the Averroistic side, there was a general tendency to see in nature a passive ordering toward grace. The Averroists were aware of the danger that a natural desire for a natural end may compromise nature's openness to grace, but they, too, struggled to give an adequate explanation of it. As much as these are the questions that face theologians in the present, they were among the unresolved questions that Thomas Aquinas would inherit as a bachelor of the Sentences in the year 1252. In order to begin to see how Thomas began to formulate an answer to them—a process which would ultimately take nearly his entire theological career—we turn now to consider his *Commentary on the Sentences*.

2

Thomas's First Parisian Period (1252–1259)

THOMAS'S ENCOUNTER WITH THE PARISIAN CONVERSATION

Thomas Aquinas came late to the discussions of nature, grace, and the desire for God, which were taking place at the University of Paris in the 1230s and 1240s. It was not until 1239 that he began his university education, and even then, his initial formation took place at Naples, not at Paris.[1]

The University of Naples was rather different from the University of Paris. For a start, it had never been hindered by the prohibitions against Aristotle and the Aristotelian tradition affecting the University of Paris, such as they were; and there is every reason to believe that Aristotle and Averroes were taught there at the time. Michael Scot, the great translator of Averroes, had died only four years previously, and had been active at Naples during his lifetime.[2] Thomas himself may have studied natural philosophy there under the Averroist Peter of Ireland.[3]

1. Torrell, *Saint Thomas Aquinas,* 1:6.

2. Ibid.

3. Ibid., 7–8. It cannot be proven with absolute certainty that Thomas studied under Peter, however. See A. A. Robiglio, "'Neapolitan Gold': A Note on William of Tocco

Because no prohibition on the study of Aristotle existed at the University of Naples, one often hears that Thomas somehow had privileged access to the Aristotelian tradition while studying there.[4] Sometimes this is even connected with the fact that the University of Naples had a civil charter from Emperor Frederick II, rather than an ecclesiastical charter.[5] Yet as we saw in chapter 1, the prohibitions of Aristotle and the Aristotelian tradition at the University of Paris were much more limited than is commonly supposed. The more restrictive prohibitions were effectively repealed from 1231 onwards, and those that may have existed controlled the curriculum of the university, but not the works that could be privately studied, or referenced in individual courses that were already part of the curriculum, in disputations, in written works which were the products of legitimate lectures or disputations, or in written compositions. In this sense, Aristotle and his Arabic commentators were studied freely at

---

and Peter of Ireland," *Bulletin de Philosphie Médiévale* 45 (2002): 107–11. Robiglio was opposed in this opinion by Michael Dunne. For a bibliography of the exchange between them, see Pasquale Porro, *Thomas Aquinas: A Historical and Philosophical Profile*, trans. Joseph Trabbic and Roger Nutt (Washington, D.C.: The Catholic University of America Press, 2016), 4n3. To that list may be added Michael Dunne, "Peter of Ireland, the University of Naples and Thomas Aquinas' Early Education," *Yearbook of the Irish Philosophical Society* 3 (2006): 84–96.

4. See, for example, Alasdair MacIntyre, *God, Philosophy, and Universities: A Selective History of the Catholic Philosophical Tradition* (Lanham, Md.: Rowman and Littlefield, 2011), 75: "[Aquinas's] early education at the University of Naples had introduced him to Aristotle's scientific texts at a time when they were not yet taught at the University of Paris." Or more dramatically, see Brian Davies, *The Thought of Thomas Aquinas* (Oxford: Clarendon Press, 2009), 2: "During this time, [the works of Aristotle] were disapproved of in some powerful academic quarters. They were, for example, banned in the Faculty of Arts at the University of Paris in 1215. So Aquinas was treading on controversial ground in finding himself in a place where Aristotle was known and appreciated for more than his logic. Intellectually speaking, he was entering a new world."

5. This is insinuated by Stephen Brock, *The Philosophy of Saint Thomas Aquinas: A Sketch* (Eugene, Ore.: Cascade Books, 2015), 2: "Only very recently had the bulk of Aristotle's writings been translated into Latin. They were causing a stir throughout the continent, and Church authorities regarded them with some suspicion.... When Thomas began his philosophical studies, ecclesiastical universities such as the one at Paris did not allow the official teaching of any but a fraction of Aristotle's works, those on logic and ethics. Frederick's civil university had no such restrictions." See also Davies, *Thought of Thomas Aquinas*, 2.

the University of Paris throughout the 1230s and 1240s, as evidenced by written works produced by philosophers and theologians at Paris during this period. Since, moreover, it was during this period that Thomas matriculated at the University of Naples, it would be more accurate to say that Thomas was at somewhat of a distance from the Aristotelian renaissance already underway at the University of Paris, rather than that he somehow had privileged access to that tradition. We shall see below that one of his principal challenges upon arriving at Paris was to catch up on the Aristotelian conversation that had begun at least a quarter of a century before he arrived.

Thomas studied at Naples for five years before entering the Order of Preachers toward the end of the 1243–44 academic year.[6] His mother, displeased because she had destined him for the Abbatial See of Monte Cassino, had him apprehended and placed under house arrest for the 1244–45 academic year.[7] Upon his release in the summer of 1245, Thomas was sent for his continued studies—as well as his continued safety—to the University of Paris, where he remained until the conclusion of the 1247–48 academic year.[8]

There is a significant controversy as to what Thomas did during his initial stay at Paris. Weisheipl marks out three possible options: Thomas studied under Albert the Great; Thomas matriculated into the arts faculty to finish the studies which had been interrupted at Naples; or Thomas underwent religious formation.[9] Weisheipl rejects the first on the basis that the Dominican convent in Paris, Saint Jacques, was not yet a *studium generale*; since Albert was a *magister regens* in theology, only students who had formally matriculated into the theology faculty at the university would have been able to attend his lectures.[10] Weisheipl rejects the second on the basis that reli-

6. Torrell, *Saint Thomas Aquinas*, 1:8–9. Michèle Mulchahey, *"First the Bow Is Bent in Study . . ." Dominican Education before 1350* (Toronto: PIMS, 1998), 75–78, gives a description of the process and ceremony for receiving Dominican postulants at this time.

7. Torrell, *Saint Thomas Aquinas*, 1:11–12.

8. Ibid., 1:18–19.

9. James Weisheipl, *Friar Thomas d'Aquino: His Life, Thought and Works* (Washington, D.C.: The Catholic University of America Press, 1983), 37–38.

10. Ibid., 37.

gious were prohibited from matriculating in faculties of arts.[11] Accordingly, he concludes that Thomas underwent religious formation and engaged in private study for the entire three years.[12]

Thomas must have spent at least some time in religious formation. Although postulants in the mendicant orders could often be dispensed from the novitiate in the 1220s and 1230s, Innocent IV issued a bull in 1244, *Non solum in favorem*, requiring that a postulant spend at least one year in formation as a novice before making his religious profession.[13] Assuming that Thomas's entrance into the order followed the prescriptions of this bull, and that he could not receive credit toward his religious formation for the time spent under house arrest, Torrell would be correct in supposing that Thomas's first academic year at Paris (1245–46) would have to have been spent in the novitiate.[14]

As for the second two years (1246–47 and 1247–48), Torrell differs sharply from Weisheipl: it was possible to obtain a dispensation from the prohibition on studying the arts, and it is likely that Thomas would have obtained such a dispensation.[15] It is also possible that Thomas would have begun the study of theology early—otherwise we have difficulty accounting for the full five years that it ordinarily took to complete theological studies.[16] For these reasons, Torrell embraces the idea that Thomas studied theology during that period by being assigned as Albert's *socius*,[17] a companion who functioned as Albert's scribe, secretary, and research assistant. This is plausible from what little evidence we have from the period. We know that later in the thirteenth century, an assignment as a *socius* to a licensed preacher was the last stage of formation for a Dominican brother,[18] and we possess copies in Thomas's own handwriting of two works

11. Ibid., 37–38.
12. Ibid., 38.
13. Mulchahey, *First the Bow Is Bent in Study*, 82.
14. Torrell, *Saint Thomas Aquinas*, 1:24.
15. Ibid., 1:23.
16. Ibid., 1:24.
17. Ibid., 1:20–21.
18. Mulchahey, *First the Bow Is Bent in Study*, 193.

that Albert taught during this period, commentaries on the *De divinis nominibus* and *De caelesti hierarchia* of Pseudo-Dionysius.[19]

In 1248, Albert was tasked with forming a *studium generale* at Cologne, and Thomas was sent with him. Whatever may have been the case when Thomas arrived at Paris, we know for a fact that Thomas served as Albert's *socius* from that point until he returned to Paris,[20] enjoying the opportunity outside Paris to hear Albert give a lecture on Aristotle's *Ethics*.[21] He may also have served as a biblical bachelor at this time, giving short lectures on the literal sense of Isaiah, Jeremiah, and Lamentations.[22]

In 1252, Thomas was sent, at Albert's suggestion, to the University of Paris to study as a bachelor of the Sentences under Albert's successor, Elias Brunet de Bergerac.[23] As a bachelor of the Sentences, he would be required to give regular lectures on Peter Lombard's text, and in so doing to determine theological and philosophical questions that arose from it. Given that the prohibition against lecturing on Aristotle and his commentators did not affect one's ability to discuss Aristotle and his commentators in the course of lecturing on other works, Thomas would be expected not only to show a mastery of the Augustinian tradition mediated through Peter, but also the burgeoning Aristotelian conversation that had been developing at Paris since at least 1231.

In all likelihood, Thomas's formal education had not prepared him well for the duties of his new position. It is not that Thomas's educational formation was poor; he had received seven years of formal training in philosophy (if we count Torrell's hypothetical two years in Paris), as well as four years of training in theology under Albert at Cologne. But be that as it may, Thomas was not expected merely to give

19. Torrell, *Saint Thomas Aquinas*, 1:20–21. Torrell provides a helpful list of sources establishing the Thomistic origin of the manuscripts in question.

20. Weisheipl, "Life and Works of Albert the Great," 29; on Aquinas's role, see also Torrell, *Saint Thomas Aquinas*, 1:21.

21. See Weisheipl, "Life and Works of Albert the Great," 29, 39.

22. Torrell, *Saint Thomas Aquinas*, 1:21.

23. Ibid., 1:37.

evidence of his personal brilliance at Paris; he needed to show a mastery of the philosophical and theological questions under discussion at the university, and he had had only had two years at the university (1246–47 and 1247–48) in which to familiarize himself with that discussion. Moreover, if we assume that during those two years Thomas was acting as Albert's *socius,* then a curious fact presents itself: prior to being named a bachelor of the Sentences, Thomas had never actually heard an entire set of lectures on the *Sentences.* By 1246, Albert had already finished Books 1 and 3 of his *Commentary on the Sentences* and was working on Book 2. At most, Thomas would have heard Albert's lectures on the latter part of Book 2 and on Book 4.

We should not be surprised to find, therefore, that Thomas's own *Commentary on the Sentences* is somewhat eclectic. On the one hand, Thomas occasionally (and sharply) distinguishes himself from some common Parisian positions on questions related to natural desire. On the other hand, he also relies for his understanding of those Parisian positions, at this early stage, on the work of Bonaventure, whose years of experience of the Parisian academic community, together with his synthesizing spirit, provided Thomas with the perfect inroad to an academic conversation to which he was very much still an outsider.

THE *COMMENTARY ON THE SENTENCES*

Nature

Thomas's approach to questions of nature, grace, and the desire for God in his *Commentary on the Sentences* is grounded in a conceptual framework that he establishes for considering matter and form in the *De principiis nature,* which was written either prior to or contemporary with his *Commentary on the Sentences,* and in which Thomas brings some of the uniqueness of his study and formation to bear on questions related to nature and natural desire.[24] In this text, Thomas acknowledges, with Bonaventure, two ways of con-

24. On the dating of this treatise, see Torrell, *Saint Thomas Aquinas,* 1:349.

sidering matter: one in which matter is considered in its abstract essence, and one in which matter is considered in its concrete existence at Creation in Genesis 1. Matter in its abstract essence is completely devoid of form, while matter in its concrete existence is never without form, since it requires form to mediate being to it.[25] When substantial form comes to be in matter, it does so by actualizing the receptive potency in matter. Following Bonaventure's use of Averroes, Thomas therefore says that matter can be said to be that out of which (*ex qua*) form arises.[26]

Thomas disagrees with Bonaventure that the reception of a complete substantial form would exhaust the potentiality of matter for subsequent forms. On the contrary, a created substance is never without some privation whereby it might receive a substantial form other than it has (and thereby undergo substantial change), or subsequent accidental forms consequent to its substantial form (and thereby undergo accidental change).[27] Otherwise, ordinary generation would be impossible, because ordinary generation involves a transformation of matter with one substantial form into matter with another. Thomas develops this line of thinking further in his *Commentary on the Sentences*. Since matter retains its pluripotentiality toward other forms even after formation by a complete substantial form, there is no need to hypothesize an incomplete active potency in matter with Bacon, nor an incomplete substantial form in matter with Bonaventure, in order to secure the pluripotentiality of created existence in Genesis 1.[28]

25. Thomas Aquinas, *De principiis nature*, §2 [Leon. 43:41]. Here, one should note Thomas's treatment of the same subject in *In II Sent.*, d. 12, q. 1, a. 4, co. [Mandonnet 2:313–15], where Thomas acknowledges explicitly his agreement with Bonaventure. Noting the difficulty with Bacon's position, which Bonaventure had criticized, Thomas says, "Et ideo, tenendo viam aliorum sanctorum [that is, Bonaventure], qui ponunt successionem in operibus sex dierum, videtur mihi dicendum quod prima materia fuit creata sub pluribus formis substantialibus, et quod omnes formae substantiales partium essentialum mundi in principio creationis productae sunt: et hoc sacra Scriptura ostendit, quae caelum et terram et aquam in principio commemorat."

26. Thomas Aquinas, *De principiis nature*, §1 [Leon. 43:39].

27. Ibid. [Leon. 43:40]. See John Wippel, *The Metaphysical Thought of Thomas Aquinas* (Washington, D.C.: The Catholic University of America Press, 2000), 298.

28. Thomas Aquinas, *In II Sent.*, d. 18, q. 1, a. 2, co. [Mandonnet 2:451].

Thomas's account of Creation formed the basis from which he interacted with Bonaventure's and Bacon's respective understandings of Augustine's *rationes seminales.*[29] With these Parisian predecessors, Thomas observes that the correspondence between creatures and their Creator is found in one sense through formal exemplar causality.[30] When God makes a creature, the creature is fashioned after a divine idea or "primordial form" (*forma primordialis*), a limited similarity of which is received in the creature as its single, natural form (*forma naturalis*).[31] This reception of a limited similarity of a divine idea imparts to the creature two sets of powers. The first is the power to produce an effect like itself; this occurs according to a germinatory form (*forma seminalis*). The second is the power to receive what further effects God might choose to cause in it; this occurs according to obediential properties (*rationes obedientiales*).[32]

Since Thomas disagrees with Bacon and Bonaventure on the question of incomplete active potencies and incomplete forms, since the hypothesis of an incomplete substantial form arose from

29. Ibid., aa. 2–3 [Mandonnet 2:450–57].

30. On the place of exemplar causality in Thomas's thought, see Gregory Doolan, *Aquinas on the Divine Ideas as Exemplar Causes* (Washington, D.C.: The Catholic University of America Press, 2008). More recently, John Meinert has added to Doolan's thought the idea that exemplar causality implies instrumental causality for Aquinas. See John Meinert, "In Duobus Modis: Is Exemplar Causality Instrumental according to Aquinas?" *New Blackfriars* 95, no. 1 (2014): 57–70. Meinert provides a contemporary bibliography on Thomas's doctrine of exemplar causality on p. 58n2.

31. Thomas Aquinas, *In II Sent.*, d. 18, q. 1, a. 2, co. [Mandonnet 2:451]: "Emanatio creaturarum a Deo est sicut exitus artificiatorum ab artifice; unde sicut ab arte artificis effluunt formae artificiales in materia, ita etiam ab ideis in mente divina existentibus fluunt omnes formae et virtutes naturales. Sed quia, ut Dionysius dicit in II cap. De div. nom., col. 635, t. I, 'ea quae sunt causatorum abundanter praeinsunt causis,' formae receptae in materia non adaequant virtutem vel artem increatam a qua procedunt; unde apud artificem remanet ex arte sua virtus aliquid aliter operandi circa ipsa artificiata, quibus virtus artis alligata non est."

32. Ibid.: "Formae autem rerum secundum quod in arte divina existunt primordiales esse dicuntur, eo quod ipsae sunt prima principia simpliciter rerum producendarum: potentia autem quae rebus indita est ad suscipiendum illud in se quod voluntas Dei disponit, rationes obedientiales a quibusdam dicuntur, secundum quas inest materiae ut fieri possit ex ea quod Deus vult. Ipsae autem virtutes in materia positae, per quas naturales effectus consequuntur, rationes seminales dicuntur."

a discussion of Augustine's *rationes seminales,* and since Bonaventure's treatment of *rationes seminales* was framed as an exegesis of Augustine, Thomas then goes on to clarify what he thinks Augustine actually meant by the term, calling into question the entire Avicennian-Augustinian tradition. According to Thomas's reading of Augustine, which closely follows that of Albert, *rationes seminales* denote principles that actually bring about their effects in nature. If something could exist merely with a generic form, such a thing would possess the possibility of receiving a specific form, but not the ability to bring about a specific form as its effect.[33]

Apart from questions of Augustinian exegesis, Thomas also sees two speculative problems with incomplete substantial forms. First, in *De anima* 2.1, Aristotle says that a thing's substantial form gives it the specific character of its existence. Aristotle uses the example of an axe: an axe's substantial form makes it to be an axe; without the substantial form of an axe, one may have a body, but one does not have an axe.[34] According to Thomas, the hypothesis of incomplete substantial forms implies just such an impossibility. Every substantial form has to communicate both generic and specific existence to the individual of which it is the form. Consequently, a supposedly "incomplete" substantial form is really just a complete substantial form by another name.[35] Even though incomplete forms were thought to be necessary in order to safeguard the potentiality for development in Creation, they are not. All form actualizes the potency of matter incompletely anyway, and so all substantial form allows for the possibility of substantial change.

33. Ibid. [Mandonnet 2:452]: "Nec etiam hoc convenit secundum intentionem Augustini: quia ex virtute formae generalis non necessario sequitur forma specialis; unde non est talis virtus secundum quam necesse sit fieri; sed secundum quam fieri potest."

34. Aristotle, *De anima* 2.1 [412b10–18].

35. Thomas Aquinas, *In II Sent.,* d. 18, q. 1, a. 2, co. [Mandonnet 2:452]. Writing at Oxford around the time that Thomas was writing at Paris, Robert Kilwardby allowed for the possibility of an individual *secundum universalem* in his *Commentary on the Sentences,* but he denied that such an individual could ever be actualized without a species. See Graham McAleer, "The Presence of Averroes in the Natural Philosophy of Robert Kilwardby," *Archiv für Geschichte der Philosophie* 81, no. 1 (1999): 50.

On the basis that incomplete substantial forms are really just complete substantial forms by another name, Thomas advances to a second criticism of them: even if it *were* granted that matter, formed by an incomplete substantial form, could receive a more complete substantial form, then the same composite would have two substantial forms, communicating two acts of existence to it, which is impossible. Thomas sees in this a reformulation of Avicenna's *forma corporeitatis*, merged with the Averroistic idea that such a form could co-exist when a subsequent substantial form were received.[36]

36. Thomas Aquinas, *In II Sent.*, d. 18, q. 1, a. 2, co. [Mandonnet 2:452]. There is a wide-ranging debate on the extent to which individual theologians in the thirteenth century held the view that there were a plurality of substantial forms in one substance. Contemporary scholarship falls generally into two camps on the origin and influence of the thesis. The one is typified by David Callus, "The Origin of the Problem of the Unity of Form," *The Thomist* 44 (1961): 257–85. Callus argues that the doctrine of substantial forms originated with Dominicus Gundissalinus, whose *De anima* transferred to the West the doctrine of a plurality of substantial forms from Avicebron (Ibn-Gebirol). Gundissalinus's text is available as Dominicus Gundissalinus, "The Treatise De anima of Dominicus Gundissalinus," ed. J. T. Muckle, *Mediaeval Studies* 2 (1940): 23–103. For Avicebron, see *Avicebrolis Fons Vitae*, vol. 1, nos. 2–3 of *Beiträge zur Geschichte der Philosophie des Mittelalters*, ed. Clemens Baeumker (Münster: Aschendorff, 1895). Callus's position seems to be inspired by Thomas's own remark in *In II Sent.*, d. 3, q. 1, a. 1, co. [Mandonnet 2:86]: "Quidam enim dicunt quod in omni substantia creata est materia, et quod omnium est materia una; et hujus positionis auctor videtur Avicebron, qui fecit librum Fontis vitae, quem multi sequuntur." See Wippel, "Thomas Aquinas and the Unity of Substantial Form," 117–54.

The other hypothesis is typified by Graham McAleer, "Who Were the Averroists of the Thirteenth Century?: A Study of Siger of Brabant and Neo-Augustinians in respect of the Plurality Controversy," *The Modern Schoolman* 76, no. 4, (1999): 273–92, esp. 281: "Classic studies of the 'plurality of forms' thesis have identified Neo-Platonic thinkers [including Avicebron] as the source of Latin pluralism. . . . A certain reserve is necessary in relation to these studies . . . because pluralism had a source indigenous to the Latin tradition. Augustinian Platonism had long articulated plurality theses which received further confirmation from the recently translated Arabic and Jewish sources."

What is at issue here is whether the "plurality of forms" thesis is intrinsic to the Christian tradition via Augustine, or extrinsic to it via Avicebron. I do not intend to solve this question. However, I will say that although Thomists—and on my reading, Thomas himself—tend to attribute the "plurality of substantial forms" thesis to Bonaventure, a closer look at Bonaventure's *Commentary on the Sentences* suggests otherwise. For Bonaventure, as noted above, the incomplete form of a body *becomes* a complete form under the power of an external agent. There are never two substantial forms in the same composite co-existing at the same time. For an overview of the problem and a defense of the unicity of substantial form in Bonaventure, see John Francis Quinn, *The Historical Constitution of St. Bonaventure's Philosophy* (Toronto: PIMS, 1973), 219–319.

Having excluded the possibility of incomplete forms, Thomas advances to Bacon's incomplete active potency in matter. Thomas's critique of Bacon proceeds along a much different line than Bonaventure's. In the *Questiones supra libros prime philosophie,* attributed to Bacon, the text that Bonaventure had used to summarize Bacon's position at this point in his own *Commentary on the Sentences,* Bacon had argued that the active potency in matter is that according to which like generates like in natural generation, and that generation which does not proceed in accordance with the active potency in matter is violent.[37] If you deny an active potency in matter, any introduction of motion into it (such as that proposed by generation) would be contrary to its natural state. Thus, if matter were purely passive, as Thomas holds,[38] then Bacon's thought would suggest that no natural motion or change is possible in matter at all.

In order to overcome the objection that could be raised by Bacon's *Questiones supra libros prime philosophie,* Thomas adopts Averroes's solution to the problem of natural motion in simple bodies, and applies it to the general structure of all Creation. We may recall from chapter 1 that Averroes says that one may consider the ability of simple bodies to receive what is caused in them by another as a second "nature" in them.[39] Thomas now says that creatures do not always achieve all the perfection that pertains to their nature by an activity originating from their own *ratio seminalis;* sometimes they receive a perfection of their nature in virtue of an activity originating *completely* in another.

Not all motions are called natural in the same way, as the Commentator says in *Physics* 2, and *De caelo et mundo* 1, … rather, some motions are

37. Aristotle, *Physics* 8.4 [255a28].

38. Thomas begins his criticism of Bacon by reaffirming this passivity. See *In II Sent.,* d. 18, q. 1, a. 2, co. [Mandonnet 2:452]: "Quamvis formae educantur de potentia materia, illa tamen potentia materiae non est activa, sed passiva tantum."

39. See Averroes, *Commentarium magnum in libros Metaphysicorum* 7.5, com. 21 [Giunti 8:171vk]. Although Dennis Bradley does not avert to this specific source, he seems to touch upon the same issues that it raises in *Aquinas on the Twofold Human Good: Reason and Human Happiness in Aquinas's Moral Science* (Washington, D.C.: The Catholic University of America Press, 1997), 462–63.

called natural on account of an active principle which exists interiorly, like changes of place in heavy and light [bodies], and some are called natural on account of a passive principle, which exists according to a potency made to be educed into act by a natural agent, as in the generation and alteration of simple bodies: accordingly, nature is also divided into matter and form.[40]

Just because a creature receives some perfection from another, even though there may be no activity in the creature advancing it toward that perfection, does not mean that the perfection is received violently, "since matter assists generation not by acting, but rather insofar as it is able to receive such an action. This ability is also called the 'appetite of matter' and the 'inchoation of form.'"[41]

Although the ability to receive natural motion from another is called an "appetite" or "inchoation," Thomas does not think that it entails any active motion in the receiver toward what is received; it merely designates the potential to receive it. The presence of that potential is enough to make the perfection which the creature receives a *natural* perfection, even though the creature possesses no formal motion toward it.

And therefore I concede that there is no active potency in matter, but rather a purely passive one; and that active powers [*virtutes activae*], comple-

40. Thomas Aquinas, *In II Sent.*, d. 18, q. 1, a. 2, co. [Mandonnet 2:453]: "Non enim eodem modo omnes motus naturales dicuntur, ut in II Physic. et I Caeli et mundi, com. III, Commentator dicit; sed quidam propter principium activum intus existens, ut motus localis gravium et levium; et quidam propter principium passivum quod est secundum potentiam ab agente naturali natam in actum educi, ut in generatione et alteratione simplicium corporum: unde et natura dividitur in materiam et formam." The reference to comment 3 in Averroes, which I have omitted in the translation, is both ambiguous and incorrect. Mandonnet takes it directly from the text of the Parma edition without comment. However, not only is it unclear to which Aristotelian text the citation of comment 3 refers (the *Physics* or the *De caelo*), but the actual content under discussion is found in Averroes, *In II Physic.*, com. 1 [Giunti 4:23rb], and is scattered about in *In I De coelo et mundo*, from comments 5–21 [Giunti 5:3vb–8vb].

41. Thomas Aquinas, *In II Sent.*, d. 18, q. 1, a. 2, co. [Mandonnet 2:453]: "Nec tamen sequitur, si in materia est potentia passiva tantum, quod non sit generatio naturalis: quia materia coadjuvat ad generationem non agendo, sed inquantum est habilis ad recipiendum talem actionem, quae etiam habilitas appetitus materiae dicitur et inchoatio formae."

mented in nature by their passive counterparts, are called *rationes seminales* ... and they are called "germinatory" [*seminales*] not on account of any imperfect being that they have, like the formative power in a seed, but because powers of this sort were bestowed throughout the activity of the six days upon the first created individuals of things, so that natural things might be produced and multiplied from them as from certain seeds.[42]

For Thomas, no longer are nature and what is natural confined to what a given creature can achieve from its own active principle, whether that active principle be its complete substantial form, as with Albert, its incomplete substantial form (as with Bonaventure), or the incomplete active potency of its matter (as with Bacon). Nature and what is natural include both what a creature can achieve from its form, as well as what it can receive in its "material" potency.[43]

Thomas's adoption of Averroes's "second nature" had an important effect on how he received Philip the Chancellor's idea of a potency for obedience (*potentia obedientiae*). Thomas certainly pays deference to this traditional concept with his mention of *rationes obedientiales*, "according to which there is in matter the possibility that God can do what he wills."[44] Yet Thomas places a certain distance between himself and the tradition here. When Albert adopted Philip's *potentia obedientiae*, he was looking for separate potency within nature by which it might be open to the influence of grace, because he still thought of nature primarily in terms of active potency. However, Thomas's use of Averroes's second nature gave him a way of accounting for creation's openness to divine action without

42. Ibid.: "Et ideo concedo quod in materia nulla potentia activa est, sed pure passiva; et quod rationes seminales dicuntur virtutes activae completae in natura cum propriis passivis ... et dicuntur seminales non propter esse imperfectum quod habeant, sicut virtus formativa in semine, sed quia rerum individuis primo creatis hujusmodi virtutes collatae sunt per opera sex dierum, ut ex eis quasi ex quibusdam seminibus producerentur et multiplicarentur res naturales."

43. See ibid., ad 4 [Mandonnet 2:454]: "Sub rationibus seminalibus comprehenduntur tam virtues activae quam etiam passivae, quae perfici possunt per agentia naturalia."

44. Ibid. [Mandonnet 2:451]: "Potentia ... quae rebus indita est ad suscipiendum illud in se quod voluntas Dei disponit, rationes obedientiales a quibusdam dicuntur, secundum quas inest materiae ut fieri possit ex ea quod Deus vult."

needing to posit a separate potency for it. Since no substantial form exhausts the potency of the matter that it informs, what Albert called a potency for obedience is for Thomas contained among the properties of our material potency, broadly conceived.[45]

Grace

For confirmation of the idea that Thomas includes Philip's potency for obedience within an Averroistic second nature one may look to Thomas's comments on the relationship between acts of nature and acts of grace, especially the grace of justification. Like Bonaventure, Thomas classifies actions that occur in nature but do not result from nature according to whether they are above nature (*supra naturam*), beyond nature (*praeter naturam*), or against nature (*contra naturam*).[46] Something is above nature (*supra naturam*) if God causes that which no active principle in nature could ever cause; something is beyond nature (*praeter naturam*) if an active principle in nature could cause it, but God causes it in a manner that nature cannot; something is against nature (*contra naturam*), when it is done opposite to the natural motion of a thing.[47] Thomas differs from his predecessors in terms of how he accounts for grace within this threefold distinction. He says that the acts which human nature performs *secundum naturam* are the "matter" out of which acts under the influence of grace are performed.[48] Consequently, an act under the influence of grace proceeds partly from nature in its material principle, and partly from grace in its formal principle.

Since God considers all things equally, it is necessary that the diversity of gifts received from him be sought on the part of the diversity of their re-

45. A similar remark with regard to Christ's grace of union can be found in Jean-Miguel Garrigue, "The 'Natural Grace' of Christ in St. Thomas," in *Surnaturel: A Controversy at the Heart of Twentieth-Century Thomistic Thought*, ed. Serge-Thomas Bonino, trans. Robert Williams, rev. Matthew Levering (Ave Maria, Fla.: Sapientia Press, 2009), 109.

46. Thomas Aquinas, *In II Sent.*, d. 18, q. 1, a. 3 [Mandonnet 2:454–57].

47. Ibid. [Mandonnet 2:456]. On what is *contra naturam* with respect to the natural desire of the will, see *In IV Sent.*, d. 49, q. 1, a. 3, qc. 2, ad 2 [Parma 7.2:1192B].

48. See Hütter, *Dust Bound for Heaven*, 237.

cipients. Now, a diversity of recipients is sought according as something is more apt and prepared for receiving [what God offers]. For, just as one sees in natural forms that matter is made more or less disposed to receive a form by accidental dispositions, like hot and cold and things of this sort, so also in the perfections of the soul, the soul is made more or less able to achieve its perfection by its actions. And yet, the soul is ordered differently toward infused and acquired [accidental] perfections. For acquired perfections are in the very nature of the soul in a potency that is not purely material, but also active, as something is in germinatory causes [*causae seminales*]. It happens in this way that all acquired knowledge is in the knowledge of the first principles, which are naturally known, as in active principles from which conclusions can be drawn. And likewise moral virtues are in the rectitude and order of reason itself, as in a certain germinatory principle [*principium seminale*].... And therefore, the operations of the soul are oriented toward acquired perfections not only by way of a disposition, but also as active principles. However, infused perfections are in the nature of the soul itself as in a potency *which is material and in no way active,* since they elevate the soul above all of its natural action [*supra omnem ... actionem naturalem*]. Accordingly, the operations of the soul are ordered toward infused perfections only as dispositions.[49]

49. Thomas Aquinas, *In I Sent.*, d. 17, q. 1, a. 3, co. [Mandonnet 1:400–401]: "Cum Deus habeat se aequaliter ad omnia, oportet quod diversitas donorum receptorum ab ipso, attendatur secundum diversitatem recipientium. Diversitas autem recipientium attenditur, secundum quod aliquid est magis aptum et paratum ad recipiendum. Sicut autem videmus in formis naturalibus, quod per dispositiones accidentales, sicut calorem et frigus et hujusmodi, materia efficitur magis vel minus disposita ad suscipiendum formam; ita etiam in perfectionibus animae ex ipsis operibus anima efficitur habilior vel minus habilis ad consequendum perfectionem suam. Sed tamen differenter se habent operationes animae ad perfectiones infusas vel acquisitas. Acquisitae enim perfectiones sunt in natura ipsius animae in potentia, non pure materiali, sed etiam activa, secundum quod aliquid est in causis seminalibus. Sicut patet quod omnis scientia acquisita est in cognitione primorum principiorum, quae naturaliter nota sunt, sicut in principiis activis ex quibus concludi potest. Et similter virtutes morales sunt in ipsa rectitudine rationis et ordine, sicut in quodam principio seminali .... Et ideo operationes animae se habent ad perfectiones acquisitas, non solum per modum dispositionis, sed sicut principia activa. Perfectiones autem infusae sunt in natura ipsius animae sicut in potentia *materiali et nullo modo activa,* cum elevent animam supra omnem suam actionam naturalem. Unde operationes animae se habent ad perfectiones infusas solum sicut dispositiones" (emphasis added).

Thomas repeats the language of "material potency" and "material dispositions" in *In II Sent.*, d. 28, q. 1, a. 4, co. [Mandonnet 2:728]: "Non opportet ut actus quibus homo se ad gratiam habendam praeparat sint naturam humanam excedentes; sicut enim natura

Just like matter is completely passive with respect to form, so also do natural acts in no way advance us toward grace. If they did, that would be Pelagianism in theology, not to mention Baconism in philosophy. Nature has a capacity for grace, it can be well-disposed toward grace, but it has no active motion toward grace (as the analogy would suggest if Bacon had applied it), nor does it have some sort of antecedent, incomplete possession of grace (as the analogy would suggest if Bonaventure had applied it).

Precisely because nature relates to grace as matter relates to form, several consequences follow. The first is that, since *rationes seminales* are in nature as a combination of material and formal principles, acts performed under the influence of grace are partly *secundum naturam* in their material principle, and partly *supra naturam* in their formal principle.[50] They are *secundum naturam* in the sense that they presuppose an active power for operation in the natural order; they are *supra naturam* insofar as they take that action as a material principle, and formally elevate it toward an end which it cannot achieve of its own power. Second, since for Thomas there is only one substantial form in a creature, grace can only constitute the formal element of an action by inhering in the soul as an accidental form.[51] Third, without the ability to perform the natural acts which serve a material principle for grace, human nature would be unable to receive the effects of grace. Thomas confirms this thinking by considering the fate of children who die unbaptized and in original sin only.[52] Al-

humana se habet *in potentia materiali* ad gratiam, ita actus virtutum naturalium se habent ut *dispositiones materiales* ad ipsam ; unde non exigitur ad hoc ut homo ad gratiam se praeparet, aliquod aliud lumen gratiae praecedens" (emphasis added).

50. Cf. ibid., *In II Sent.*, d. 28, q. 1, a. 1, co. [Mandonnet 2:719]. Also see *In IV Sent.*, d. 49, q. 1, a. 4, qc. 4, ad 1 [Parma 7.2:1196A].

51. Ibid., *In II Sent.*, d. 26, q. 1, a. 2 [Mandonnet 2:671].

52. It is not my intention to enter into current theological discussions about whether the *limbus infantium* actually exists, merely to observe the place that it holds in Thomas's thought, and the consequence of what Thomas says about it for his doctrine of natural desire. For a sympathetic view of Thomas's thought, see Serge-Thomas Bonino, "The Theory of Limbo and the Mystery of the Supernatural in St. Thomas Aquinas," in his *Surnaturel: A Controversy at the Heart of Twentieth-Century Thomistic Thought*, 117–54;

though they do not enjoy the beatific vision, these souls do not suffer because they never had the material principle (the use of their free will) whereby they might have disposed themselves for grace and glory.[53] They do not despair at having not received a perfection in their material principle that they are were unable to cause by motion following from their formal principle.

The Desire for God

Thomas applies his matter/form analogy for nature and grace to his account of the desire for God. He does this with both the intellect and the will. Since the intellect can grow naturally in knowledge and the will can grow naturally in virtue throughout the course of one's life, and since *rationes seminales* serve as principles of natural change, Thomas identifies in each of these two powers the same constitutive elements as he identifies in nature broadly speaking.

In the intellect, the material, passive principle is the possible intellect, and the formal, active principle is the agent intellect.[54] The possible intellect is in potency to all intelligible form; Thomas likens it to prime matter, which allows him to preserve the limitless character of its openness to change, without introducing the limitations that Avicennian-Augustinian appeals to formal causality tended to introduce in the 1230s–1240s.[55] The agent intellect actualizes and determines the possible intellect by two degrees of habits: natural knowledge, which consists of an "innate" knowledge of the first principles of speculative and practical reason,[56] and acquired knowledge, which is deduced from natural knowledge; a third degree of knowledge, infused knowledge, can be given directly by God in the possible intellect and supersedes the power of the agent intellect.[57]

---

for a critical view, framed as a criticism of Feingold, see Oakes, "*Surnaturel* Controversy," 639–44.

53. Thomas Aquinas, *In II Sent.*, d. 33, q. 2, a. 2 [Mandonnet 2:863].

54. Ibid., d. 17, q. 2, a. 1, co. [Mandonnet 2:428].

55. Thomas Aquinas, *In III Sent.*, d. 23, q. 1, a. 1, co. [Moos 3:699].

56. For knowledge of the first principles of speculative and practical reasoning described as "innate," see Thomas Aquinas, *In II Sent.*, d. 24, q. 2, a. 3 [Mandonnet 2:610].

57. Thomas Aquinas, *In III Sent.*, d. 23, q. 1, a. 1, co. [Moos 3:699].

With Peter Lombard, Thomas usually calls the natural knowledge of the first principles a "spark" of reason (*scintilla rationis*),[58] although sometimes he uses this term only for the first principles of speculative reasoning;[59] he calls the first principles of practical reasoning *synderesis*.[60] The determination of the possible intellect by these three degrees of knowledge is called "assent."[61]

In affirming a natural knowledge of the first principles of speculative and practical reasoning, Thomas reservedly follows Avicenna, the *Summa fratris Alexandri*, and potentially Bonaventure. As we saw in chapter 1, for Avicenna and the *Summa fratris Alexandri* (as well as for Bonaventure, if we consider the second and third of his ways of accounting for our natural desire for a supernatural end), there cannot be a *reductio ad absurdum* in the principles of knowledge; something must be naturally known in order for our reasoning to have an appropriate starting point.[62] Thomas agrees in part. In a power of the soul which undergoes only accidental change by growing in knowledge or virtue, the material principle lies open to subsequent accidental formation only within the boundaries of the determinate perfection already communicated to it by the formal principle. If we were to have a specific, natural knowledge of God impressed upon the intellect, our possible intellect would not be open to subsequent accidental formation to the contrary; we could never err concerning God's existence because our speculation would always proceed from that natural knowledge. But since people do, in fact, err in such matters—because there are, as a matter of observable fact, atheists—it must be the case that the first principles of reason are undetermined.[63]

Thomas's treatment of the *ratio seminalis* in the will is modeled

58. See Thomas Aquinas, *In II Sent.*, d. 39, q. 3, a. 1, ad 2 [Mandonnet 2:997].

59. See ibid., obj. 1 and ad 1 [Mandonnet 2:995, 997].

60. Ibid., co. [Mandonnet 2:996].

61. Thomas Aquinas, *In III Sent.*, d. 23, q. 2, a. 2, qc. 1, ad 1 [Moos 3:726].

62. Avicenna, *Prima philosophia*, 1.5 [van Riet 1:31–42].

63. Thomas Aquinas, *In II Sent.*, d. 39, q. 3, a. 1, co. [Mandonnet 2:997]. Hütter, *Dust Bound for Heaven*, 234.

upon his treatment of the *ratio seminalis* in the intellect: it includes a formal active principle, a material passive principle, and three levels of habituation in the material passive principle. The material passive principle is the free will. Thomas uses similar language to describe the free will as he does the possible intellect: it is a passive potency, of itself undetermined, which is open to determination by means of habits.[64] The formal, active principle is the natural will. In discussing the natural will, Thomas inherits Albert's use of Philip's use of Damascene's distinction between θέλησις or *voluntas ut natura* for natural will, and βούλησις or *voluntas ut deliberata* for free will:

There is something naturally known in reason as an indemonstrable principle among matters pertaining to activity, which is oriented by way of an end, because in matters pertaining to activity the end takes the place of a principle, as is stated in *Ethics* 6.2. Accordingly, that which is man's end is naturally known in his reason to be good and to be desirable, and the will is called "will as nature" when it follows this knowledge. On the other hand, both in matters pertaining to activity as well as to speculation, something is known in reason by investigation. And it happens in both cases (namely, in matters pertaining to speculation and activity), that reason can err in its investigation. Accordingly, the will, which follows reason's knowledge of this sort, is called "deliberate" [*deliberata*], and can tend toward good and evil, but not from the same inclination, as was said.[65]

When Thomas describes the determination of the free will by the natural will, he can point to three degrees of habituation that parallel the three degrees of habituation that determine the intellect: "natural virtue" parallels natural knowledge of the first principles,[66]

64. Thomas Aquinas, *In II Sent.*, d. 24, q. 1, a. 1, s.c. [Mandonnet 2:589–90].

65. For the Latin text, see ibid., d. 39, q. 2, a. 2, ad 2 [Mandonnet 2:994]. See also *In IV Sent.*, d. 49, q. 1, a. 3, qc. 2, co. [Parma 7.2:1192A–B]; Odon Lottin, *Psychologie et morale aux XIIe et XIIIe siècles*, vol. 1 (Gembloux: J. Duculot, 1957), 227.

66. For the conceptual distinction between *voluntas ut natura* and what Thomas calls "natural virtue," see *In II Sent.*, d. 39, q. 2, a. 1, co. [Mandonnet 2:991]. At times Aquinas seems to deny the existence of natural virtues. See *In III Sent.*, d. 23, q. 1, a. 4, qc. 3, ad 3 [Moos 3:715]. Yet at other times he clearly affirms their existence. See *In III Sent.*, d. 23, q. 3, a. 4, qc. 3, co. [Moos 3:755]: "Sicut dicit Philosophus in VI *Ethicorum* in homine ante completum esse virtutis moralis, existit quaedam naturalis inclinatio ad virtutuem illam quae dicitur virtus naturalis; et haec eadem virtutis rationem sumit, secundum quod a superiori potentia, scilicet ratione, perfectionem accipit."

acquired virtue parallels acquired knowledge, and infused virtue parallels infused knowledge.[67] The determination of the will in act according to these three degrees of habit is called "consent."[68]

Thomas's distinction between the natural will and natural virtue is not always clear. Part of the reason for this lack of clarity is that, while Thomas distinguishes conceptually between the will as nature and the will insofar as it follows a motion that parallels the first principles of speculative and practical reasoning in the intellect, he does not always distinguish terminologically between these concepts.[69] Sometimes, he refers to the *voluntas ut natura* as a "natural inclination" (*inclinatio naturalis*),[70] in such a way as seems to impute the motion of natural desire to natural will. That would certainly capture the ordinary sense of the English word "inclination," but it would not always capture the technical sense that Thomas gives his Latin. As was the case above with reference to the terms "appetite" and "inchoation," Thomas does not think that "inclination" *necessarily* implies motion. As an indication of this intention, we may highlight two instances in the *Commentary on the Sentences* in which Thomas speaks of a natural inclination apart from any motion at all: the natural inclination of the damned toward the good,[71] and the natural inclination of prime matter for form.[72] In both these cases, Thom-

67. See Thomas Aquinas, *In III Sent.*, d. 23, q. 1, a. 1, co. [Moos 3:699]; *In III Sent.*, d. 23, q. 1, a. 3, qc. 1, co. [Moos 3:707]; *In II Sent.*, d. 39, q. 2, a. 1, ad 2 [Mandonnet 2:992].

68. Thomas Aquinas, *In III Sent.*, d. 23, q. 2, a. 2, qc. 1, ad 1 [Moos 3:726].

69. See, for example, ibid., *In II Sent.*, d. 39, q. 2, a. 2, co. [Mandonnet 2:993]: "Voluntas ... rationalis, prout est natura hominis, sive prout consequitur naturalem apprehensionem universalium principiorum juris, est quae in bonum inclinat."

70. See, for example, Thomas Aquinas, *In I Sent.*, d. 48, q. 1, a. 4, ad 1 [Mandonnet 1:1090]; *In II Sent.*, d. 39, q. 2, a. 1, ad 1 [Mandonnet 2:991]; *In II Sent.*, d. 39, q. 2, a. 1, ad 5 [Mandonnet 2:992]; *In II Sent.*, d. 39, q. 3, a. 1, ad 5 [Mandonnet 2: 998]; *In II Sent.*, d. 41, q. 2, a. 1, ad 5 [Mandonnet 2:1041–42]; *In III Sent.*, d. 23, q. 1, a. 4, qc. 3, ad 2 [Moos 3:715]; *In III Sent.*, d. 27, q. 1, a. 2, co. [Moos 3:860–62]; *In III Sent.*, d. 27, q. 1, a. 4, ad 12 [Moos 3:871]; *In III Sent.*, d. 29, q. 1, a. 7, ad 1 [Moos 3:942]; *In III Sent.*, d. 33, q. 2, a. 4, qc. 4, co. [Moos 3:1066]; *In IV Sent.*, d. 49 q. 1 a. 3 qc. 3 co. [Parma 7.2:1192–93].

71. In Thomas Aquinas, *In II Sent.*, d. 39 q. 3 a. 1 ad 5 [Mandonnet 2:998], Thomas clarifies explicitly that in this case, "Haec inclinatio non dicit actum aliquem, sed solum ordinem naturae ad actum."

72. Thomas Aquinas, *In IV Sent.*, d. 17, q. 1, a. 3, qc. 2, co. [Moos 4:840].

as uses the word *inclinatio* to indicate the relationship of a potency to its act antecedent of any motion toward that act. In the second of these two instances, he even uses the word to refer to the orientation of a *purely* passive potency toward its act. Consequently, if we consider Thomas's usage of the term with technical rigor, "inclination" is closer to "appetite" (*appetitus*) at this point in Thomas's career.

Even if Thomas does not employ consistent terminology for the will's orientation toward its end or for the motion in it which parallels the natural knowledge of the first principles of speculative and practical reason, Thomas does at least provide some resources to suggest how such a terminological distinction might be made. In his discussion of love, Thomas explains that an appetite is a passive power, ordered toward an act, which requires the presence of an appetible object in order to be actualized.[73] Thomas distinguishes an "appetite" from a "desire" (*desiderium*), because a desire is an appetite which has been actualized and set in motion, but which has yet to attain its object.[74] Consequently, if the *voluntas ut natura* is a "rational appetite," we may say that it has a "natural desire" for its end when that appetite has been set in motion by the presence of an appetible object which has yet to be obtained.

Theological Challenges

Although Thomas makes every effort in the *Commentary on the Sentences* to draw as close a parallel as possible between the *ratio seminalis* in the intellect and the *ratio seminalis* in the will, there remains one significant difference between them: the *ratio seminalis* in the will is dependent upon the *ratio seminalis* in the intellect. Thomas arrives at a description of this dependence in working out his understanding of Providence. Providence, Thomas says, pertains to God's knowledge insofar as he orders things toward their end.[75] This happens on analogy with an artist. First, an artist considers the end, then he con-

73. See Thomas Aquinas, *In III Sent.*, d. 27 q. 1 a. 1 co. [Moos 3:854–55].
74. Ibid., d. 26 q. 2 a. 3 qc. 2 co. [Moos 3:840].
75. Thomas Aquinas, *In I Sent.*, d. 39, q. 2, a. 1, co. [Mandonnet 1:927–28].

siders the ordering of what he intends to make to the end, then he considers how to move the means toward the end and remove what stands in the way of that end.[76]

Thomas works out how creatures are subject to this Providence in dialogue with Arabic and Hebrew recensions of the Aristotelian tradition. According to Shlomo Pines, this branch of the Aristotelian tradition was based on a now-lost treatise by Alexander of Aphrodisias titled *On Providence.* Alexander's text probably discussed three positions: the opinion of Epicurus, according to which there is no Providence and so all things occur by chance; an opinion attributed to Aristotle, whereby God's knowledge and Providence extend to universals and incorruptible beings, but not to corruptible, sublunary bodies; and an opinion attributed to Plato, whereby God's knowledge and Providence extend to all things, even singular, corruptible things.[77]

In the mid-thirteenth century, one recension of the Alexandrian tradition could be found in the work of Averroes. In Book 12 of Averroes's *Long Commentary on the Metaphysics,* Averroes rehearses four positions on Providence: the first corresponds with the position that Alexander would have attributed to Plato: all things happen according to the wisdom of the first cause such that there are no evils; the second corresponds with the position that Alexander would have attributed to Epicurus, that all things happen according to chance; the third corresponds with the position that Alexander would have attributed to Aristotle, that the celestial bodies are subject to Providence but the sublunary bodies are subject to chance on account of their matter; a fourth takes an extreme view with regard to the third: that there are actually two first principles, one of which created the celestial bodies as good, the other of which created the sublunary bodies as evil.[78]

76. Ibid. [Mandonnet 1:928].

77. Ibid. See Shlomo Pines, translator's introduction to Moses Maimonides, *The Guide of the Perplexed,* trans. Shlomo Pines, vol. 1 (Chicago: University of Chicago Press, 2010), lxv.

78. Averroes, *Commentarium magnum in libros Metaphysicorum* 12.10, com. 52 [Giunti 8:338rd–f].

A second recension of the Alexandrian tradition could be found in the work of the Jewish scholar, Moses ben Maimon (commonly referred to among the Latins as "Maimonides"; 1138–1204).[79] As Maimonides receives the Alexandrian tradition, he rehearses the same three positions.[80] Those of Epicurus and Aristotle he merely repeats. That of Plato he subdivides into three positions based on positions he finds among contemporary medievals of the Arabic and Hebrew traditions: a voluntarist school, that of the Ash'arites, according to which all singular events occur on account of the divine will; an intellectualist school, that of the Mu'tazilites, according to whom all singular events occur according to the plan of divine wisdom; and a moralist school, which he understands to be taught by the Torah, according to which man acts by a general influence such as Alexander understands Aristotle to have envisioned, but in which all singular events among human persons happen as rewards or punishments for individual moral choices that are made according to that general influence.

According to Maimonides, the opinions he enumerates all result in different answers to the question of why bad things happen to good people. For Aristotle, as Alexander would have read him, since human beings are among the earthly creatures which are not subject to Providence, bad things happen to good people by pure chance. For the Ash'arites, bad things happen to good people happen simply because God wills for them to happen. For the Mu'tazilites, bad things happen to good people only insofar as God will restore the balance of justice in the universe by rewarding good people at some future time. For the scholars of the Torah, they happen because the people to whom they happen deserve them. Maimonides himself opts for a harmony of the views he attributes to Aristotle and to the Torah: ordinarily, sublunary bodies are not subject to Providence, but it is not so with human persons, who benefit from a share in

79. Moses Maimonides, *Dux dubitantium* (Venice: Iodoco Badio Ascensio, 1520).
80. Ibid., 3.18 [Ascensio 80r–81r]. See Pines, translator's introduction, 1:lxv.

God's providential concern—they are rewarded and punished for their merits.[81]

Maimonides gives two reasons for his belief that man receives an exemption from the general rule that sublunary bodies are not subject to Providence. The first is theological: he argues that he cannot find it said anywhere in the Hebrew Scriptures that God exercises Providence over another sublunary creature. The second is philosophical: Providence is an act of intellect, which shines forth from the Creator into created intellects; consequently, all and only those creatures which participate in intellect are governed by Providence.[82] He takes this last principle even further. Among the members of the human species, those who have achieved a higher degree of intellectual perfection are subject to a greater degree of Providence; those who have achieved a lesser degree of intellectual perfection are subject to a lesser degree of Providence.[83] Those who reach the highest degree of intellectual perfection are so subject to God's Providence that they experience continual joy no matter what may befall them.[84]

Maimonides applies his thinking about Providence to an exegesis of the Book of Job, by assigning the various viewpoints on Providence to the main characters in that book.[85] To Job, expressing despair at God's actions, he assigns the opinion of Aristotle; to Zophar, the voluntarist opinion of the Ash'arites; to Bildad, the intellectualist opinion of the Mu'tazilites; to Eliphaz, the opinion of the Torah. The purpose of the Book of Job is to serve as a parable of these opinions, and to demonstrate that God did no real injustice to Job: although God permitted Job's temporal welfare to be sorely afflicted, he never

81. Ibid. [Ascensio 81v].

82. Ibid. [Ascensio 81v–82r].

83. Ibid. 3.19 [Ascensio 82r].

84. Ibid. 3.52. [Ascensio 112r]. For a helpful discussion of the degrees of Providence in Maimonides, see Charles Raffel, "Providence as Consequent Upon the Intellect: Maimonides' Theory of Providence," *AJS Review* 12, no. 1 (1987): 25–71. See also David Burrell, "Maimonides, Aquinas and Gersonides on Providence and Evil," *Religious Studies* 20, no. 3 (1984): 335–51.

85. Moses Maimonides, *Dux dubitantium*, 3.24 [Ascensio 86r].

took away the one thing that could constitute true happiness for Job, the knowledge of God; much to the contrary, God demonstrated the incomprehensibility of the divine wisdom to Job, and in so doing caused Job to repent of Aristotle's position and accept the wisdom by which God governs human affairs.[86]

When Thomas discusses Providence, he shows himself familiar with both the Arabic and Hebrew recensions of the Alexandrian tradition.[87] He begins by rehearsing the opinion which sees everything as subject to chance; he attributes it to "almost all the ancient natural philosophers." Like Averroes and Maimonides had done, Thomas dismisses this view as incoherent.[88] Then Thomas discusses the view of Averroes, which Maimonides had attributed to Aristotle. Rather than raising any philosophical objection against it, Thomas addresses it exegetically and theologically: exegetically, he distances Aristotle from this view;[89] theologically, he criticizes it from the standpoint of Maimonides: if God does not exercise Providence over sublunary bodies, "this opinion expressly takes away [the possibility of] God's judging human actions."[90]

Third, Thomas addresses the view of Maimonides. Here Thomas *does* offer a philosophical critique, which applies equally to Averroes as well as to Maimonides:

But since God knows singulars and universals alike, as was shown above, and [since] it belongs to him, who is good in the highest manner, to order

86. On Job's repentance, see ibid. [Ascensio 85v].

87. Thomas Aquinas, *In I Sent.*, d. 39, q. 2, a. 2 [Mandonnet 1:929–36].

88. Ibid., co. [Mandonnet 1:930]: "Sciendum est ergo primo, quod quidam posuerunt nullius rei esse providentiam, sed omnia casu contingere: et ista fuit positio Democriti, et quasi omnium antiquorum naturalium, qui negaverunt causam agentem, et posuerunt tantum causam materialem. Sed haec positio satis efficaciter improbata est etiam ab ipsis philosophis."

89. Ibid.: "Alii posuerunt . . . quod providentia Dei non se extendit nisi ad species, et non ad individua, nisi quae necessaria sunt; eo quod ponebant, illud quod exit cursum suum, providentiae legibus non subjacere . . . et ista opinio imponitur Aristoteli: quamvis ex verbis suis expresse haberi non possit."

90. Ibid. [Mandonnet 1:931]: "Sed haec opinio expresse tollit judicium Dei de operibus hominum."

> all things toward the end for which they were made, it does not seem fitting for there not to be Providence over all things, even singulars. And besides, this is expressly contrary to what the Lord spoke, when he said that "not one of the sparrows falls to the earth without the heavenly Father," (Mt 10) that is, without his Providence.[91]

Since God knows singular things, and since God is good, God cannot but exercise Providence over all singulars, even those of the sublunary world.

Next, Thomas considers the fourth opinion recounted by Averroes, in which the heavenly bodies and the sublunary bodies are said to have different first causes, good and evil respectively. From the standpoint of Christian history Thomas attributes this position to the Manichees, and dismisses it quickly on the philosophical basis that evil has no efficient cause.[92] Afterwards, Thomas considers the third and fourth opinions recounted by Maimonides: the voluntarist position of the Ash'arites, and the intellectualist position of the Mu'tazilites. The former he dismisses out of hand as ridiculous; the latter he dismisses on theological grounds because he thinks it implies that it would be a sin to kill an animal.[93]

Finally, Thomas arrives at his own position, which he aligns with Dionysius: "all things lie under Providence, but not in the same way."[94] Natural things seek ends in accord with their nature; the heavenly bodies always achieve this end, while the sublunary bodies achieve this end insofar as the destruction of one irrational creature leads to the generation of another. Rational creatures achieve this by their will,

91. Ibid. [Mandonnet 1:931]: "Sed quia divina cognitio aequaliter est singularium et universalium, ut supra habitum est, et ejus qui summe bonus est, est ordinare omnia ad finem, secundum quod nata sunt: non videtur conveniens non omnium etiam singularium providentiam esse. Et praeterea hoc est expresse contra sententiam Domini, Matth., X, dicentis, quod 'unus ex passeribus non cadit in terram sine Patre caelesti,' id est sine providentia ejus."

92. Ibid.: "Et haec positio sufficienter a sanctis et philosophis improbata est: quia malum non habet causam efficientem, nec potest esse intentum."

93. Ibid. [Mandonnet 1:931–32].

94. ibid. [Mandonnet 1:932]: "omnia providentiae subjacent, sed non eodem modo ... Sicut ... dicit Dionysius, iv cap. *De div. nom.*, non est providentiae naturas rei destruere, sed salvare."

which, as Boethius observes, is freer insofar as it is closer to God.[95]

The two authorities which Thomas cites, Dionysius and Boethius, are each cited as incipits to an opinion more fully expressed in the context of the text quoted, rather than as a citation complete in itself. If we follow up those references, Dionysius's opinion turns out to be the general basis of Thomas's interactions with Averroes and Maimonides.

> "Given the fact of Providence, how can there be evil?" But evil as such has no being nor is it inherent in the things that have being. However, nothing possessed of being lies outside the workings of Providence, and evil has no share of being except in an admixture with the Good. So, if no being is without some share in the Good and if evil is a deficiency of the Good and if no being is completely devoid of the Good, the Providence of God must then be in all beings and nothing can be lacking it.[96]

Dionysius is also a source for the idea that rational creatures are led to God by their will.

> [Providence] provides for each particular being. Therefore, we should ignore the popular notion that Providence will lead us to virtue even against our will. Providence does not destroy nature. Indeed, its character as Providence is shown by the fact that it saves the nature of each individual, so that the free may freely act as individual or as groups, insofar as the nature of those provided for receives the benefactions of this providing power appropriate to each one.[97]

But in spite of the fact that the text of Dionysius correlates closely with the argument of Thomas, we may note a curious fact about Thomas's use of Dionysius. Even though support for both claims that Thomas wants to make can be found in this paragraph of Dionysius's writing, Thomas cites Dionysius only for the first claim and not for the second. The reason for this has to do with Thomas's philosophical psychology. Dionysius's text omits any reference to the intellect when accounting for the will's motion; he focuses on the relationship

95. Ibid. [Mandonnet 1:932–33].
96. Pseudo-Dionysius, *Divine Names* [Rorem 733A–B].
97. Ibid. [Rorem 733B–C].

between God, whose primary attribute is his goodness, and the will, which is attracted to that goodness. Boethius, by contrast, emphasizes the role of the intellect:

"Freedom there is," she said, "for there could not be any rational nature, did not that same nature possess freedom of the will. For that which can by its nature use reason, has the faculty of judgment, by which it determines everything; of itself, therefore, it distinguishes those things which are to be avoided, and those things that are to be desired. Now what a man judges is to be desired, that he seeks; but he runs away from what he thinks is to be avoided. And therefore those who have in themselves reason have also in them freedom to will or not to will."[98]

If we take Thomas's reference to Boethius in context, then while it is true that having the ability to will makes human beings closer to God, Thomas's use of Boethius brings him into a close association with Maimonides's idea that Providence is consequent upon the intellect, and with the possibility noted above and expressed only once in the *Commentary on the Sentences* that there is a natural appetite in the intellect which is oriented toward God antecedent of the will.

If we apply what Thomas says about Providence to the question of the relationship between the *ratio seminalis* in the intellect and the *ratio seminalis* in the will, we may conclude that the consent which determines the free will has three limiting factors at this stage of Thomas's career: it is limited by the will's natural orientation toward the good, similar to how the possible intellect is limited by the agent intellect's natural orientation toward the truth; it is limited by the free will's natural virtue, similar to how the possible intellect is limited by its habitual knowledge of the first principles of speculative

98. Boethius, *De consolatione philosophiae* 5, pros. 2, trans. H. F. Stewart, E. K. Rand, and S. J. Tester, Loeb Classical Library 74 (Cambridge, Mass.: Harvard, 1973), 391–93: "'Est,' inquit, 'neque enim fuerit ulla rationalis natura quin eidem libertas adsit arbitrii. Nam quod ratione uti naturaliter potest id habet iudicium quo quidque discernat; per se igitur fugienda optandave dinoscit. Quod vero quis optandum esse iudicat petit; refugit vero quod aestimat esse fugiendum. Quare quibus in ipsis inest ratio, inest etiam volendi nolendique libertas.'"

and practical reasoning; finally, the will's *consent* is limited by the intellect's *assent,* which the intellect reaches in an act of judgment, and determines what will be presented to the will as good, and hence as desirable.

There do exist exceptions to the ordinary structure of the will's determination by the assent of the intellect. Boethius hints at this fact in the words immediately following the passage just quoted:

> But this freedom is not, I am sure, equal in all [rational creatures]. For heavenly, divine substances possess penetrating judgement, an uncorrupted will, and the ability to achieve what they desire. But human souls must indeed be more free when they preserve themselves in the contemplation of the divine mind; less free, however, when they slip down to the corporeal, and still less free when they are bound into earthly limbs.[99]

To say that the will can be made "less free" is not to say that it can be coerced. For Thomas, the free will can never be coerced, because no creature possesses the means of moving the will of another.[100] Rather, since the freedom of the will is based upon the judgment of the intellect, the will becomes less free insofar as the intellect's judgment becomes less clear when obscured by a movement of passion.

In explaining how the passions can interfere with the judgment of reason, Thomas follows Aristotle's account of incontinence in *Nicomachean Ethics,* Book 7.[101] There, Aristotle recounts the opinion

99. Ibid.: "Sed hanc non in omnibus aequam esse constituo. Nam supernis divinisque substantiis et perspicax iudicium et incorrupta voluntas et efficax optatorum praesto est potestas. Humanas vero animas liberiores quidem esse necesse est cum se in mentis divinae speculatione conservant, minus vero cum dilabuntur ad corpora, minusque etiam cum terrenis artubus colligantur." See also Thomas Aquinas, *In II Sent.,* d. 24, q. 1, a. 3, co. [Mandonnet 2:596–97], where Thomas takes a similar view of free will.

100. Thomas Aquinas, *In II Sent.,* d. 25, q. 1, a. 2 [Mandonnet 2:647–50].

101. On Thomas's engagement with the Aristotelian tradition on incontinence, see Bonnie Kent, *Virtues of the Will: The Transformation of Ethics in the Late Thirteenth Century* (Washington, D.C.: The Catholic University of America Press, 1995), 150–75; Peter Eardley, "Giles of Rome's Theory of the Will" (Ph.D. diss., University of Toronto, 2003), 71–81; Dennis Bradley, "Thomas Aquinas on Weakness of the Will," in *Weakness of Will from Plato to the Present,* ed. Tobias Hoffmann (Washington, D.C.: The Catholic University of America Press, 2008), 82–114, particularly for references to the secondary literature; Tobias Hoffmann, "Aquinas on the Moral Progress of the Weak Willed," in *The Problem of Weakness of Will in Medieval Philosophy,* ed. Tobias Hoffman, Jörn Müller, and Matthias

of Socrates, who had said that there is no such thing as incontinence: every person who acts contrary to virtue in the will first errs in the reason.[102] Although Aristotle initially rejects Socrates's opinion on the grounds that no one actually thinks that all their vicious actions *ought* to be pursued as a universal premise, Aristotle eventually embraces Socrates's opinion in part by making a distinction between two kinds of universal premises: those which concern the subject (I ought not to eat sweets) and those which concern the object (every sweet food is tasty).[103] The continent man reasons thus: I ought not to eat sweet foods; but this food is sweet; therefore I ought not to eat it. The incontinent man's knowledge of that universal principle is clouded by passion; he becomes, according to Aristotle, as someone asleep or intoxicated.[104] Lacking access to his knowledge of universal moral principles on account of his passion, he reasons only with reference to the particular object of the passion: every sweet food is tasty; but this food is sweet; therefore this food is tasty.[105] Having reached the conclusion that the food is tasty, the incontinent man must taste it, because passion for the particular has become the principle of his action, rather than knowledge of the universal; the only difference between him and an animal is that passion first had to sway his mind to the consideration of a different universal principle, whereas an animal would lack all access to a universal principle in the first place.[106]

Thomas follows Aristotle's account of incontinence almost to the letter. He recounts the opinion of Socrates, rejects it with Aristotle, and then proposes Aristotle's quasi-Socratic solution. The only change that he makes to the argument is in the example: rather than

Perkams (Leuven: Peeters, 2006), 221–47; Tobias Hoffmann, "Aquinas and Intellectual Determinism: The Test Case of Angelic Sin," *Archiv für Geschichte der Philosophie* 89, no. 2 (2007): 122–56.

102. Aristotle, *Nicomachean Ethics* 7.2 [1145b22].

103. Ibid., 7.3 [1147a1–7].

104. Ibid. [1147a17].

105. Ibid. [1147a28–32].

106. Ibid. [1147b4].

using Aristotle's example about sweets, Thomas uses the Sixth Commandment ("Thou shalt not commit adultery").[107] By all outward appearances, the change is inconsequential to the flow of the argument. It results in the same explanation of incontinence by means of the same substitution of a syllogism about the particular object for a syllogism about the universal principles which ought to govern the subject's action. However, the substitution of one of the Ten Commandments for a general rule of healthy eating does add some significant theological consequences to the philosophical ones noted by Aristotle, because it turns Aristotle's philosophical question about incontinence into a theological question about sin.

Considering Aristotle's argument within the theological framework of sin meant that Thomas had to consider two things which Aristotle did not address. First, Thomas needed to consider whether reason was implicated in sin if the sin only took place on account of reason's having started with a premise about the object rather than a premise about the subject. Second, Thomas needed to consider whether sin enters the action only at the moment of choice, or whether any sin precedes the will's choice, while the subject is still deliberating.

With regard to the first, Thomas denies that any sin enters the reason, properly speaking. Sin is an evil moral choice, and good and evil exist only in the will, not in the intellect. Sin can only be "in the reason" to the extent that reason is acting at the command of the will,[108] and with the will's consent.[109] Yet this leads us to a seeming paradox: according to Thomas's understanding of Providence at this point in his career, the will can only choose sinfully to the extent that it is acting under the influence of mistaken reason,[110] and yet, according to Thomas's understanding of sin, the reason only directs the will to choose sinfully to the extent that it is guided by the will to do so.

107. Thomas Aquinas, *In II Sent.*, d. 24, q. 3, a. 3, co. [Mandonnet 2:623–24].

108. Ibid. [Mandonnet 2:623]. See also *In II Sent.*, d. 41, q. 2, a. 1, ad 1 [Mandonnet 2:1043].

109. Thomas Aquinas, *In II Sent.*, d. 21, q. 1, a. 2, co. [Mandonnet 2:528].

110. Ibid., d. 24, q. 3, a. 3, ad 1 [Mandonnet 2:623].

One way in which Thomas resolves the seeming paradox is to reduce many sins to the interference of the passions, and so to use Aristotle's account of incontinence to explain them. To do this, he appeals to the Augustinian concept of the *primi moti*, the "first movements" of inordinate passions. While affirming that sin only lies in the will, properly speaking,[111] and so acknowledging that only movements of the soul that somehow lie under the influence of the will can be sinful,[112] Thomas argues that the first movements of inordinate passions do lie within the power of the will because the will has the power to stop them. To the extent that the will does nothing to stop them, its silence implies consent.[113] So, when an unchecked passion occludes the reason's consideration of subjective universal premises (such as "Thou shalt not commit adultery"), the subsequent error in the intellect which determines the will to choose adultery can be ascribed to the will's prior choice not to inhibit the passion which led to the error in the first place.[114]

Thomas's description of the role of passion in sin could account for many instances of sin, but there are two sins for which it could not account: the sin of the angels, and the sin of Adam and Eve. It could not account for the sin of the angels, because angels do not have bodies and so they do not have passions; it could not account for the sin of Adam and Eve, because they were preserved from the influence of their passions by the gift of original justice.

111. See ibid., d. 21, q. 1, a. 2, ad 4 [Mandonnet 2:528], where Aquinas clearly states that a representation that remains solely in the apprehension, without affecting the will, lacks the *ratio peccati*.

112. Ibid., d. 24, q. 3, a. 2, co. [Mandonnet 2:620]. Attempting to save the Augustinian terminology of "first movements," while preserving the moral quality of sin insofar as it is rooted in the will, Thomas distinguishes between "first-first movements" and "second-first movements." The former are mere natural responses to external stimuli, and carry no moral quality; the latter are inordinate responses to internal deliberations. Thomas makes a similar distinction, without the Augustinian terminology, in *In II Sent.*, d. 21, q. 1, a. 2, ad 5 [Mandonnet 2:529].

113. Thomas Aquinas, *In II Sent.*, d. 40, q. 1, a. 4, ad 3 [Mandonnet 2:1021]. Also see *In III Sent.*, d. 23, q. 1, a. 3, qc. 2, ad 3 [Moos 3:708].

114. Thomas Aquinas, *In II Sent.*, d. 24, q. 3, a. 2, co. [Mandonnet 2:620]. Also see *In II Sent.*, d. 39, q. 2, a. 1, ad 3 [Mandonnet 2:992].

Concerning the angels, Thomas attempts to preserve as much of Aristotle's account of incontinence as possible. While acknowledging that in this case Aristotle's reasoning does not apply in the strict sense, there is nevertheless the possibility that an angel's reasoning about some particular conclusion of a known universal premise might be reached without due attention to all the relevant circumstances of that particular conclusion.[115] For example, although angels do not reason cogitatively, we can reconstruct the following hypothetical syllogism from what Thomas says about their sin: "I ought to pursue happiness where it is to be found; but happiness is to be found in God; therefore I will seek happiness in God."[116] There is nothing wrong with this act of moral reasoning as it stands, except that it overlooks the most important circumstance: that God has decided to offer happiness not as the reward of nature but as a free gift of grace in reward for meritorious action.

Thomas reasons similarly concerning the devil's interaction with Adam and Eve in Genesis 3. God had given Adam and Eve a universal premise: "of the Tree of the Knowledge of Good and Evil thou shalt not eat" (Gn 2:17). Again appealing to *Nicomachean Ethics*, Book 7, Thomas says that in order for Adam and Eve to sin, the devil needed to convince them to substitute an objective premise for the subjective one that God had given them.[117] The difficulty for the devil was that, on account of original justice, Adam and Eve were preserved from any inordinate passion that might lead them to make that substitution on their own.[118] Consequently, the devil had to convince them by purely intellectual means to somehow give up the divinely revealed premise. He did this by convincing them

115. Thomas Aquinas, *In II Sent.*, d. 5, q. 1, a. 1 [Mandonnet 2:144].

116. See ibid., a. 2, co. [Mandonnet 2:147].

117. Ibid., d. 21, q. 2, a. 1, ad 5 [Mandonnet 2:534].

118. Ibid. [Mandonnet 2:533]; *In II Sent.*, d. 21, q. 2, a. 3, co. [Mandonnet 2:538]. Thomas is aware that this puts him at odds with Augustine, who thought that Adam and Eve were induced to sin by passion. Not wishing to exclude the Augustinian tradition on this question entirely, Thomas allows the possibility that Augustine may yet be correct. See the second half of ad 5 [Mandonnet 2:534], and again the second half of *In II Sent.*, d. 22, q. 1, a. 1, ad 1 [Mandonnet 2:550].

that the subjective premise should be taken metaphorically and not literally.[119] Thus, "the tempter relegated the precept to memory,"[120] and substituted another universal premise with another syllogism following from it: similarity with God is had in knowing good and evil; but if you eat of the Tree of the Knowledge of Good and Evil, you will know good and evil; therefore, if you eat of that tree "you will be as gods."[121] Seeking in pride the particular object of this new syllogism (namely, similarity with God), Adam and Eve fell.[122]

If we compare the devil's syllogism in Genesis 3 to Aristotle's syllogism about sweets in *Nicomachean Ethics*, Book 7, or to the syllogism about adultery which Thomas substitutes for Aristotle's, we see that it takes roughly the same form. Rather than starting from a universal precept about what a person ought to do or ought not to do (for example, "You should not eat the fruit of the Tree of the Knowledge of Good and Evil"), it begins with a universal premise about the object of another power of the soul ("similarity with God is had in knowing good and evil"). The new syllogism can only induce the agent to moral action because the agent has, in the act of permitting the substitution of a new universal premise for the one already known, tacitly consented to have his or her reason subordinated to that power.

Yet there is one major difference between gluttony/adultery on

119. Thomas Aquinas, *In II Sent.*, d. 22, q. 1, a. 1, ad 1 [Mandonnet 2:550]: "Non crediderunt Deum falsum dixisse, hoc enim simpliciter infidelitatis fuisset, sed crediderunt forte alio modo intelligendum fore et metaphorice, et ad aliud significandum dictum."

120. Ibid., d. 21, q. 2, a. 1, ad 5 [Mandonnet 2:534]: "Rectam autem aestimationem in particulari corruptit delectatio, ut Philosophus, in VI *Ethic.*, cap. vi, dicit; et etiam aliae passiones, quae tunc inesse homini non poterant praeter regulam rationis; et ideo oportuit ut in universali aestimatio corrumperetur; et ideo praeceptum ad memoriam reduxit tentator, ut aestimationem rectam falsis suasionibus corrumperet, et sic ad peccandum inclinaret."

121. See Gn 3:5. Aquinas points to this passage in *In II Sent.*, d. 22, q. 1, a. 1, co. [Mandonnet 2:550]; he alludes to a syllogism like this in *In II Sent*, d. 22, q. 1, a. 2, co. [Mandonnet 2:552–53].

122. Aquinas says that Eve's sin took place in this more purely rational mode, while Adam still left the matter in doubt but had "quaedam amicabilis benignitas ad uxorem" impelling him on. See Thomas Aquinas, *In II Sent.*, d. 22, q. 1, a. 3, co. [Mandonnet 2:555].

the one hand, and pride on the other. In the case of gluttony (Aristotle's example) and of adultery (Thomas's initial example), the reason is conquered by a passion in one of the lower appetites. The will is complicit in the act, because the will had a duty to hold the passions in check and it willingly failed to do so. But in the case of Adam and Eve, where the lower appetites were held in check through original justice, things are different. The object sought (similarity with God) is a rational good, not a corporeal good. As such it pertains to the will directly rather than to one of the lower appetites. The substitution of a new universal premise about this object takes place not when the will fails through passion to hold some lower power of the soul in check, but rather when the will fails through pride to hold *itself* in check. In this way the sin of pride takes place a little differently than sins of gluttony or adultery: the will latches onto a particular rational good which reason has not fully considered (similarity to God); the will, failing to hold itself in check, conquers the reason and forces it to begin a line of moral reasoning from a new universal premise which includes reference to the object to which it has already adhered itself through pride; when the intellect concludes this new line of reasoning with assent to its conclusion ("you will be as gods"), actions follows ("she took of its fruit and ate").[123] While the will is implicated in Aristotle's example and in the sin of Adam and Eve, it is therefore implicated differently in each case. In Aristotle's example, the will is implicated through omission; in Adam and Eve, it is implicated through commission.

There is a difficult question that arises from Thomas's account of the sin of Adam and Eve in light of his understanding of how Providence acts upon the intellect and the will: *commission* requires *consent,* and Aquinas had said that *consent* in the will normally follows *assent* in the intellect. But the first commission in the case of Adam and Eve's sin takes place in the middle of an act of reasoning, as the will directly forces the intellect to substitute one universal premise

123. Gn 3:6. See Thomas Aquinas, *In II Sent.*, d. 21, q. 1, a. 2, ad 1 [Mandonnet 2:553].

for another. How is it that the consent of the will, which normally follows the assent of the intellect, can occur prior to the conclusion of the syllogism in the intellect which causes that assent? Thomas gives the beginnings of an answer here, which he does not fully develop: "the will itself commands the other powers, including the intellect; for this reason, the acts of the other powers (that is, only those which obey reason) as well as their defects are in the power of the will."[124] This suggests that there is a deeper reciprocity between the intellect and the will than Thomas otherwise describes in the *Commentary on the Sentences*. Unfortunately, he does not explain that reciprocity any further in his discussion of the sin of Adam and Eve. In order to see him explain it more fully, we have to turn from considering the sin of Adam and Eve toward the initial healing of that sin in the act of faith.

The act of faith presents a special case like the sin of Adam and Eve. It cannot follow the ordinary course of nature such as Thomas describes it at this point in his career, in which the will's consent follows the intellect's assent, because the object of faith is "not apparent," and so supersedes the powers of human understanding.[125] Consequently, in the act of faith the will's consent moves the intellect to assent, rather than the reverse. In attempting to explain how the will's consent can move the intellect to assent, Thomas notes that there are two kinds of voluntary actions: those that are *elicited* and those that are *commanded*.[126] Elicited acts are those in which the will moves itself; commanded acts are those in which the will moves an-

124. Thomas Aquinas, *In II Sent.*, d. 22, q. 2, a. 1, ad 1 [Mandonnet 2:558]: "Ipsa enim voluntas imperat aliis viribus et intellectui: unde actus aliarum virium sunt in potestate voluntatis, et defectus earum, scilicet solum illi qui rationi obediunt." See also *In III Sent.*, d. 23, q. 1, a. 2, ad 3 [Moos 3:704].

125. Thomas Aquinas, *In III Sent.*, d. 23, q. 2, a. 1, co. [Moos 3:719]: "Habitus autem quilibet per actum cognoscitur et actus ex objecto specificatur et ex fine bonitatem habet. Et ideo Apostolus definit fidem per duo, scilicet per comparationem ad objectum, quod est res non apparens, scilicet secundum naturalem cognitionem; et per comparationem ad finem, in hoc quod dicit: 'substantia rerum sperandarum.'" Also see In *III Sent.*, d. 23, q. 1, a. 4, qc. 3, co. [Moos 3:715].

126. Thomas Aquinas, *In III Sent.*, d. 23, q. 1, a. 4, qc. 2, co. [Moos 3:713–14].

other power. These two different kinds of acts are good in two different ways.

> Since an act receives its form from its proper object, we call that act "formally good" whose object is the good according to the *ratio* of good. Since, moreover, the good is the object of the will, for this reason an act cannot be called good like this unless it is an act of the will, or of the appetitive part. However, [any] act is called "materially good" which is congruous with the power performing it, even though its object is not good under the *ratio* of good, as when someone correctly understands and when someone's eye sees clearly.[127]

On this basis, Thomas says that "the will commands the acts of the other powers insofar as their acts are materially oriented toward the *ratio* of good, which is the object of the will. And according to this, something of the formal goodness of the will arrives in those actions which are commanded by the will."[128] Thus, each power of the soul can be subject to two kinds of good actions. It can be subject to materially good actions when it seeks an object that is congruent with itself; it can be subject to formally good actions when the will commands it. In the former case, Thomas imputes the role of "first mover" to the agent intellect.[129] In the latter case, Aquinas also imputes to the will, on the authority of Pseudo-Anselm, the role of "first mover" among the powers of the soul.[130]

127. Ibid., qc. 1, co. [Moos 3:711–12]: "Quia enim actus a proprio objecto formam recipit, ille actus formaliter bonus dicitur cujus objectum est bonum secundum rationem boni. Et quia bonum est objectum voluntatis, ideo per modum istum actus bonus dici non potest nisi actus voluntatis, aut appetitivae partis. Materialiter autem actus bonus dicitur qui congruit potentiae operanti, quamvis objectum ejus non sit bonum sub ratione boni, sicut cum quis recte intelligit et oculus clare videt."

128. Ibid. [Moos 3:712]: "Et inde est quod voluntas imperat actus aliarum potentiarum inquantum actus earum materialiter se habent ad rationem boni, quod est voluntatis objectum. Et secundum hoc aliquid de formali bonitate voluntatis pervenit ad alios actus qui a voluntate imperantur."

129. Ibid., d. 14, q. 1, a. 1, qc. 2, co. [Moos 3:436]: "Sicut autem in sensu visus est duplex activum: unum quasi primum agens et movens, sicut lux; aliud quasi movens motum, sicut color factus visibilis actu per lucem; ita in intellectu est quasi primum agens lumen intellectus agentis; et quasi movens motum, species per ipsum facta intelligibilis in actu."

130. Ibid., d. 23, q. 3, a. 1, qc. 1, co. [Moos 3:743]: "Cum ergo in viribus animae

Even though the consent of the will normally follows the assent of the intellect, Thomas does not exempt the intellect from the primary influence of the will in actions that can be commanded. "Truth itself," he says, "is the good of the intellect materially."[131] For this reason the intellect is subject to the command of the will in those actions which concern its pursuit of truth, that is, in acts of assent and of reasoning toward assent, but not acts of apprehension.[132] Provided that the intellect does not immediately see the truth of a matter either in its first principles or in what it has deduced from them, the will can command the intellect to consider the matter,[133] or even to assent to a conclusion about it, so long as doing so first appears to the will as consonant with the perfection of the intellect.[134]

The will's command is necessary in the act of faith because the intellect lacks the means of arriving at that assent by its natural powers. Reason cannot prove faith; faith entails knowledge which is subalternated to God's knowledge of himself and to the beatific vision shared by the saints, of which no comprehension is possible.[135] Thus, if the intellect is going to assent to the articles of faith, the will must move the intellect to make that assent. But it is also the case that if the will is going to move the intellect to assent, it must first appear good to the will to do so. On what basis does the will apprehend the act of faith as good? Thomas suggests that, upon hearing the faith

voluntas habeat locum primi motoris, actus ejus est prior quodammodo actibus aliarum virium, inquantum imperat eos secundum intentionem finis ultimi et utitur eis in consecutione ejusdem." In *In III Sent.*, d. 17, a. 1, qc. 3, s.c. 2 [Moos 3:530], Aquinas attributes this position to Anselm of Canterbury. Moos identifies the reference as *De casu diaboli* 1, but this is a bit of a stretch. As the editor of the Leonine edition of the *De veritate* notes [Leon. 22:436, note on line 96], a better reference would be Pseudo-Anselm, that is, Eadmer of Canterbury, *De similitudinibus* 2–4 [PL 159:605C–606B]. Aquinas explicitly attributes the quote to [Pseudo-]Anselm in *De ver.*, q. 22, a. 12, s.c. 1 [Leon. 22:641], and again in *ST*, Ia, q. 82, a. 4, co. [Leon. 5:303].

131. Thomas Aquinas, *In III Sent.*, d. 23, q. 1, a. 4, qc. 1, ad 3 [Moos 3:712]: "Ipsa veritas est materialiter bonum intellectus, cum sit finis ejus: finis enim habet rationem boni, ut dicitur in III Metaphysicorum."

132. Ibid., q. 2, a. 4, qc. 1, co. [Moos 3:736].

133. Ibid., q. 1, a. 4, qc. 2, co. [Moos 3:713].

134. Ibid., q. 2, a. 2, qc. 1, co. [Moos 3:725].

135. Thomas Aquinas, *In IV Sent.*, d. 49, q. 2, a. 3 [Parma 7.2:1202–4].

preached, the intellect assents to the proposition that it would be a good idea to make an act of faith. This initial assent inclines the will to command the intellect to make an act of faith. We can thus outline the act of faith in the following five stages:[136]

1) God speaks through a human person.
2) Reason, recognizing through some fallible sign or person that God has spoken,[137] inclines the will to want the things about which God has spoken,[138] by judging that an assent to them would be prudent.
3) The will, inclined by prudence in the intellect, commands the intellect to assent to God and to the things that God says, because it sees that to achieve them it must love God, that to love God it must hope in God, and that to hope in God it must believe in God.[139]
4) The intellect, commanded by the will, makes an act of faith.
5) The will, informed by the intellect's assent, moves toward the object of faith with hope and charity.[140]

In this way, Thomas acknowledges a reciprocal relationship between the intellect and the will, which nevertheless preserves the priority of the intellect. The intellect assents to the idea that an act of faith is prudent; the will commands the act; the intellect performs the act. This allows the act of faith not only to be good for the intellect *materially* (because it orders the intellect to first truth) but also *formally*, because it makes the act of faith voluntary and so meritorious.[141]

136. This is the pattern envisioned in Thomas Aquinas, *In III Sent.*, d. 23, q. 2, a. 2, qc. 2, co. [Moos 3:727]. Also see q. 2, a. 3, qc. 1, ad 2 [Moos 3:732]; q. 2, a. 2, qc. 3, co. [Moos 3:728]; q. 3, a. 2, ad 2 [Moos 3:748]. The *responsio* of q. 2, a. 2, qc. 2, does not mention the human agency involved in bearing witness to Revelation; this is spelled out in ad 3 of the same *quaestiuncula* [Moos 3:728].

137. This dynamic is spelled out in Thomas Aquinas, *In III Sent.*, d. 23, q. 2, a. 4, qc. 1, ad 2 [Moos 7:737]. Also see *In III Sent.*, d. 23, q. 3, a. 3, qc. 1, co. [Moos 3:750].

138. See Thomas Aquinas, *In III Sent.*, d. 23, q. 2, a. 5, ad 5 [Moos 3:740].

139. Ibid., ad 4 [Moos 3:740].

140. Ibid.

141. Ibid., a. 3, qc. 1, ad 3 [Moos 3:732].

The sin of Adam and Eve and the act of faith thus give us two different examples of how the will can move the intellect. In the sin of Adam and Eve the will neglects to restrain itself, and so commands the intellect to begin a line of reasoning from one premise rather than another. In the act of faith, the intellect assents to a prudent course of action and directs the will to command the intellect to make an assent that the intellect cannot make of its own accord. In each case, the will moves the intellect; but in the first case it does so contrary to the better judgment of the intellect; in the second case, it does so in accord with the better judgment of the intellect.

One may question whether what Thomas says about the relationship between the intellect and the will in the sin of Adam and Eve and in the act of faith is entirely consistent with what he otherwise says about Providence. In the sin of Adam and Eve, where the will's pride directs the intellect to reason from a different premise than the one revealed by God, Thomas never does suggest, as he does in the act of faith, that there is a prior judgment of the intellect indicating to the will that it would be prudent (even if only apparently) to command the will to reason from a different first premise. We may extend this critique to other sins, which are influenced by a movement of passion. If omission is imputed to the will similarly to commission, then on what basis can Thomas say that the will can culpably omit to restrain the passions without a prior judgment of the intellect?

Thomas's account of the act of faith manages to preserve the ordering of the intellect and the will by an appeal to the intellect's judgment that the act of faith would be prudent. However, since this prior judgment is motivated by prudence, since the ground of that prudence is a judgment reached on the basis of signs and/or people whom Thomas admits to be fallible, and since the judgment of prudence is *ipso facto* not the motive of faith, is the prior judgment of the intellect really a sufficient basis for the subsequent action of the will? Thomas does not suggest an answer to these questions in the *Commentary on the Sentences*, but we will return to them in his subsequent works.

The Natural Desire for God

The manner in which Thomas explains the *rationes seminales* of the intellect and will directly affects the way in which Thomas discusses natural desire. As indicated above, Thomas affirms that when the will is set in motion (that is, when it "desires"), the motion of the will ordinarily follows the knowledge of the intellect.[142] Since, however, Thomas denies the *Summa fratris Alexandri*'s teaching that the intellect possesses determined natural knowledge, Thomas likewise denies its idea that the will possesses a pre-determined natural desire.

> Although the will may be borne by its natural inclination toward happiness according to a general notion, nevertheless, the fact that it is borne unto this or that happiness does not come from the inclination of nature, but rather through the discretion of reason, which devises that the highest good of man consists in this or in that. Therefore, whenever someone desires happiness, his natural appetite and his rational appetite are joined together in act. On the part of the natural appetite there is always rectitude in that act, but on the part of the rational appetite sometimes there is rectitude in that act, when, for instance, happiness is desired where it truly is; sometimes, however, there is perversity, when [happiness] is desired where in actual fact it is not.[143]

In saying generally that the motion which follows from our natural appetite leads toward happiness, Thomas is first and foremost

142. See also *In IV Sent.*, d. 33, q. 1, a. 1, ad 9 [Parma 7.2:968b]: "naturalis inclinatio in appetitiva sequitur naturalem conceptionem in cognitione." There are texts in which Thomas seems to anticipate later developments in his thought and to suggest that natural inclination does not need to follow natural knowledge. See, for example, ibid., d. 49, q. 3, a. 1, qc. 1, co. [Parma 7.2:1214].

143. Ibid., q. 1, a. 3, qc. 3, co. [Parma 7.2:1193A]: "Quamvis autem ex naturali inclinatione voluntas habeat ut in beatitudinem feratur secundum communem rationem, tamen quod feratur in beatitudinem talem vel talem, hoc non est ex inclinatione naturae, sed per discretionem rationis, quae adinvenit in hoc vel in illo summum bonum hominis constare; et ideo quandocumque aliquis beatitudinem appetit, actualiter conjungitur ibi appetitus naturalis, et appetitus rationalis; et ex parte appetitus naturalis semper est ibi rectitudo; sed ex parte appetitus rationalis quandoque est ibi rectitudo, quando scilicet appetitur ibi beatitudo ubi vere est; quandoque autem perversias, quando appetitur ubi vere non est." Also see ibid., d. 49, q. 2, a. 1, ad 1 [Parma 7.2:1192B]: "Ista naturalis inclinatio in bonum invenitur in hominibus omnibus, sed quia . . . voluntas non est necessario determinata ad unum, non oportet quod omnes actu bonum velint."

inspired by Augustine's *De Trinitate* 13, mediated through Peter Lombard. Yet in his particular formulation, he is also inspired by Bonaventure. As we saw in chapter 1, Bonaventure thinks that we seek the perfect actualization of the passive potency of our nature, but since only God can fulfill that potency, our subjective desire for actualization is ordered toward God as the object of that actualization. Thomas agrees that human nature is only fully actualized by God, but he disagrees that our natural desire (natural as distinguished from "free") moves toward the vision of God *as to a terminus*. For Thomas, "the per se object of the will is the good; but *per accidens* it is this or that good;"[144] Thus, since the active principle in the will is indeterminately ordered toward the good, "although the vision of God is happiness itself, it does not therefore follow that whoever desires happiness desires the vision of God, since happiness ... implies the per se object of the will, but the vision of God does not."[145]

Thomas denies that the vision of God lies under the per se object of the will for two principal reasons. First, since what previous generations of theologians had called a potency for obedience is but one property of a creature's material potency, since matter is purely passive in relation to form, and since any substantial form communicates complete substantial existence to matter while determining the range of its subsequent activity, the exercise of an appetite as a desire requires two things: first, that the matter be actualized by some form; second, that the actualized desire operate within the range of activity communicated by the form to the matter. Human nature can by all means be said to have a natural *appetite* for the vision of God, because it is passively capable of receiving the vision of God, but it cannot be said to have a natural *desire* to see God in the *Commentary*

144. Ibid., q. 1, a. 3, qc. 1, ad 1 [Parma 7.2:1192A]: "Per se objectum voluntatis est bonum; sed per accidens est hoc vel illud bonum."

145. Ibid., qc. 4, ad 2 [Parma 7.2:1192A]: "Quamvis divina visio sit ipsa beatitudo, non tamen sequitur quod quicumque appetit beatitudinem, appetat divinam visionem: quia beatitudo, inquantum hujusmodi, importat per se objectum voluntatis, non autem ipsa divina visio."

on the Sentences, because that would require that the vision of God fall within the range of activity which the human soul can perform of its own accord.

The second reason that Thomas opposes a direct association between the per se object of the will and the vision of God is much simpler. Since Thomas thinks that the motion of the will follows knowledge of the intellect, to say that the per se object of the will is the vision of God would require that the intellect have a natural knowledge of that vision. But this is impossible in two ways: first, because as we have seen, Thomas denies that the intellect has natural concepts; second, because no concept of God that we form can ever comprehend the divine essence.[146]

If Thomas's account of nature includes a natural desire which does not advance toward the vision of God, a merely passive receptivity to that vision, and no motion beyond the limits of nature toward that vision, does this mean that Thomas's account of nature is closed off to grace? It does not. In human nature's material principle, it always has a natural ordering toward and *appetite* for the vision of God, even if in the *Commentary on the Sentences* it does not possess a principle which actualizes this appetite so that it causes a natural *desire* for the vision of God. This appetite is that out of which (*ex qua*) grace is caused in human nature, and so human nature is never closed off to grace, even if it lacks a first motion toward grace.

The fact that Thomas identifies a natural appetite for a supernatural end, but not a natural desire for a supernatural end, means that Thomas's understanding of natural desire in the *Commentary on the Sentences* does not have the same theological consequences as Bonaventure's. It cannot and is not intended to be used to prove by natural reason that the actual, historical end of man *in this state* is the vision of God. To do so would require that we be able to locate in human nature some natural motion (as distinguished from "free" motion) whose *terminus* was the vision of God. But that is impossi-

146. See ibid., q. 2, a. 3 [Parma 7.2:1202B–1204B].

ble for the reasons already enumerated. If we were to find a person whose soul experienced such a motion, we would have to conclude that such a person actually happened to be in possession of grace, or, if such a person lacked grace, that such a person was God because he possessed by nature an act which is only proper to the divine nature. For this reason, the doctrine that Thomas sets forth in the *Commentary on the Sentences* cannot prove that the end of human nature in this concrete state is the vision of God. However, that does not mean that Thomas thinks that natural desire tells us nothing about our final end. In the *Commentary on the Sentences,* it has one very important use, and that is in proving—in support of the Christian faith—that man's ultimate happiness is to be found after this present life.

In order to explain what we can learn about human happiness from an account of natural desire, Thomas relies at the beginning of the *Commentary on the Sentences* upon the definition of happiness taken from Aristotle's *Nicomachean Ethics,* Book 10.4, where Aristotle observes that happiness is "for each thing, the best activity of the most well-disposed [power] toward the most powerful of those [objects] which fall under it."[147] Based on this text, Thomas explains, like Bonaventure, that our desire for happiness is a desire for the perfection of our highest faculty by its highest act; he adds to these subjective conditions an orientation of that highest act toward its highest object.[148] He follows Albert in identifying the highest faculty of the human person with the intellect. He then concludes that the happiness of the human person is in the highest act of the intellect, oriented toward its highest object.[149]

But in Book 4 of his *Commentary on the Sentences,* Thomas notes a certain tension in human nature: since the objects of the human

147. Aristotle, *Nicomachean Ethics* 10.4 [1174b15]. My translation is from Grosseteste's Latin translation, which Thomas would have used at this point in his career: "secundum unumquodque optima est operacio optime dispositi ad potentissimum eorum que sub ipsam. Hec autem utique perfectissima erit et delectabilissima."

148. *In I Sent.,* d. 1, q. 1, a. 1, co. [Mandonnet 1:33]. Also see *In IV Sent.,* d. 49, q. 1, a. 4, qc. 2, co. [Parma 7.2:1195B]; *In IV Sent.,* d. 49, a. 2, a. 7, co. [Parma 7.2:1210B].

149. *In I Sent.,* d. 1, q. 1, a. 1, co. [Mandonnet 1:33].

intellect are among spiritual goods, not corporeal goods,[150] one may ask whether or to what extent a rational creature with a body can ever really attain the object of its intellectual potential. To partake fully of spiritual goods would require "immobility … and perpetuity," neither of which the vicissitudes of bodily existence afford in this life.[151] Thomas responds by drawing on an axiom from Aristotle's *De anima,* Book 3.9: "nature does nothing in vain, neither does it fail in necessary matters, except among those things which are incomplete and imperfect."[152] If we have a natural appetite for a happiness that includes the complete possession of a spiritual good, it must be possible for us to attain that good, otherwise our natural appetite would be vain.

> Since reason and intellect belong to man … in his essence, it would be necessary to posit that man can arrive at true happiness at some point, and not only to some participation of happiness; otherwise the natural appetite of the intellectual nature, which is in man, would be frustrated. But we cannot posit true happiness in this life on account of the various changes to which man is subject; accordingly, it is necessary that the happiness which is the end of human life be after this life.[153]

We may note three things about Thomas's argument here. First, it is an argument from our natural *appetite* and not our natural *desire,* which is to say that it depends upon the receptive, material potency

150. *In IV Sent.,* d. 49, q. 1, a. 1, qc. 1, ad 2 [Parma 7.2:1183B].

151. Ibid., qc. 4, co. [Parma 7.2:1185A–B]: "Beatitudo ergo cum sit finis ad quem referuntur omnia desideria, oportet quod sit tale aliquid, quo habito nihil ulterius desiderandum restet. Quilibet autem naturaliter esse desiderat, et permanere in bono quod ipse habet; et ideo ab omnibus beatitudo tale aliquid esse ponitur quod immobilitatem habeat et perpetuitatem."

152. Aristotle, *De anima* 3.9 [432b1]. The Latin translation of James of Venice reads, "natura neque facit frustra nichil neque deficit necessariis nisi in non completis et inperfectis."

153. Thomas Aquinas, *In IV Sent.,* d. 49, q. 1, a. 1, qc. 4, co. [Parma 7.2:1185B–86A]: "Cum in homine … est … ratio et intellectus per essentiam; oporteret ponere quod ad veram beatitudinem quandoque pervenire possit, et non tantum ad aliquam beatitudinis participationem; alias appetitus naturalis intellectualis naturae quae est in homine frustraretur. Beatitudo autem vera non potest poni in hac vita propter mutabilitates varias quibus homo subjacet; unde necesse est beatitudinem quae est finis hominae vitae, esse post hanc vitam."

in human nature, not the active, formal potency in human nature. Second, because it is about appetite and not desire, Thomas's argument touches only upon what it is possible for human nature to receive, not what it will actually achieve.[154] Third, because Thomas's argument does not touch upon the question of whether we will ever receive the complete actuality of our material potency, Thomas's argument does not alter his teaching that the active potency in human nature is undetermined; simply put, it does not say anything about the active potency in human nature at all.

When it comes to the end of our natural *desire*, Thomas avoids saying that our natural desire is oriented toward the vision of God, because the vision of God lies outside the reach of the active principles of our nature. Indeed, he follows the letter of Albert and the spirit of the *Summa fratris Alexandri* in identifying the end of our natural desire with the terminal development of our analogical knowledge.

A potency and its proper act are always taken in the same genus; wherefore a potency and its act divide any and all genera of being, as is clear in *Physics* 3. And therefore, a faculty or potency of a creature does not extend to anything beyond the form of its genus. And in this way the divine essence, which is outside every genus, exceeds the natural faculty of any created intellect. And therefore, the final disposition for union of the intellect with such an essence exceeds every faculty of nature. For this reason, it cannot be natural; rather, it is above nature [*supra naturam*]. This disposition is the light of glory, about which it is written in Psalm 35:10: "In your light we shall see light."

However, a created intellect can, by its natural faculty, come to the knowledge of God by created forms instilled in or acquired by it. But this knowledge is not the vision of God's essence, as is clear from what was said, nor is *what he is* known by it, but only *that he is*, and *what he is not*.[155]

154. Hütter, *Dust Bound for Heaven*, 236, makes a similar remark about a later text.

155. Thomas Aquinas, *In IV Sent.*, d. 49, q. 2, a. 6, co. [Parma 7.2:1208B]: "Potentia enim et proprius ejus actus semper accipiuntur in eodem genere; unde potentia et actus dividunt quodlibet genus entis, ut patet in 3 Physic.; Facultas sive potentia creaturae non

As Thomas makes clear, since the vision of God is something *supra naturam*, created nature cannot arrive at it by a motion arising from any of its active potencies. If a human person is going to receive the vision of God, that person has to be prepared to do so by the reception of a new form, which actualizes material potential in human nature, which the human soul was unable to actualize on its own. Since, moreover, the active potency in the intellect can only achieve knowledge abstracted from creatures and represented by a similitude taken from them, our unassisted intellect can at best—as Albert had said—reach an analogical knowledge of God, not the vision of God.[156] However, since, as was stated above, acts of nature are the "matter" out of which acts of grace are made, the very fact that the intellect has a formal principle in it which can *know* of God

se extendit nisi ad sui generis formam: et sic essentia divina, quae est extra omne genus, excedit naturalem facultatem cujuslibet intellectus creati; et ideo dispositio ultima quae est ad unionem intellectus cum tali essentia, excedit omnem facultatem naturae; unde non potest esse naturalis, sed supra naturam; et ista dispositio est lumen gloriae, de quo dicitur ibi, Psalm 35, 10: 'In lumine tuo videbimus lumen.' Secundum autem naturalem facultatem potest intellectus creatus pervenire ad cognitionem Dei per formas creatas ei inditas vel acquisitas; sed haec cognitio non est visio ejus per essentiam, sicut ex dictis patet, nec per eam scitur quid est, sed solum quia est, et quid non est."

156. See ibid., a. 7, co. [Parma 7.2:1210B]; a. 1, ad 3 [Parma 7.2:1199B]. Studies of Thomas's doctrine of analogy abound, and it would be impossible to give a complete account of them here. In general, contemporary scholars tend to disagree as to whether Thomas can best be understood through the lens of Pseudo-Dionysius as teaching a radical apophaticism, through the lens of Cajetan as teaching an analogy of proportionality, or through the lens of Aristotle and Averroes as teaching an analogy of one to another. For the first view, some of the most important works are David Burrell, *Aquinas: God and Action*, 2nd ed. (Scranton, Penn.: University of Scranton Press, 2008); John Milbank and Catherine Pickstock, *Truth in Aquinas* (London: Routledge, 2001); Denys Turner, *Faith, Reason and the Existence of God* (New York: Cambridge University Press, 2004). For the second, the most important work is Joshua Hochschild, *The Semantics of Analogy: Rereading Cajetan's* De nominum analgoia (Notre Dame, Ind.: University of Notre Dame Press, 2010). For the third, some of the most important works are Ralph McInerny, *Aquinas and Analogy* (Washington, D.C.: The Catholic University of America Press, 1996); Bernard Montagnes, *The Doctrine of the Analogy of Being according to Thomas Aquinas*, trans. M. Macierowski, ed. Andrew Tallon (Milwaukee: Marquette University Press, 2004); John Wippel, *The Metaphysical Thought of Thomas Aquinas* (Washington, D.C.: The Catholic University of America Press, 2000). For a discussion of the differences among members of the first group, see D. Stephen Long, *Speaking of God: Theology, Language, and Truth* (Grand Rapids: William B. Eerdmans, 2009).

requires that the intellect be open to the possibility of receiving the ability to *see* God.

At this point, one might object that Thomas seems to prove too little. What would be the point of proving the mere possibility of the vision of God without also speculating as to whether someone will actually see God? Surely the question of metaphysical "vanity" concerns what will actually take place, not what may or may not hypothetically be the case?[157] If we look at Thomas's argument in its historical context, however, we find that there was very good reason to make an argument that touched only upon the possibility of the vision of God. As Reinhard Hütter notes, there was a long apophatic tradition in Latin theology going back to John Scotus Eriugena, which denied that very possibility.[158] According to Dondaine, it arrived in the Middle Ages through an appropriation of John Chrysostom and Gregory of Nyssa.[159] In the first half of the thirteenth century, a long line of authors tried to grapple with this Eastern tradition. More than a few adhered to it.

In the late 1230s, at least two Dominican masters had defended the Eastern tradition to the point of denying that it is *possible* for the created intellect to see God: Guerric of Saint-Quentin and Hugh of Saint-Cher. Hugh uses Chrysostom to distinguish between the essence and the attributes of God. He thinks we will see the attributes but not the essence.

What does it mean when 1 John [3:2] says "we will see him as he is?" Concerning this, we should say that John does not intend to say that we would in some way behold the substance of God in heaven, because this is im-

157. We will see in chapter 6 that this concern is central to Cajetan, and to the commentatorial tradition after him.

158. See Hütter, *Dust Bound for Heaven*, 227–28. See also H.-F. Dondaine, "L'objet et le 'medium' de la vision béatifique chez les théologiens du XIIIe siècle," *Recherches de Théologie Ancienne et Médiévale* 19, no. 1 (1952): 63–66. This article updates and significantly expands upon Dondaine's previous observations in "Hugues de Saint-Cher et La Condamnation de 1241," *Revue des Sciences Philosophiques et Théologiques* 33 (1949): 170–74.

159. On Chrysostom, see Dondaine, "L'objet et le 'medium' de la vision béatifique," 73–74. Nyssa was mediated through Eriugena (ibid., 63).

possible for every creature. For this reason, Chrysostom [says]: "what sort of thing is there among that which can be created that it can see what cannot be created?" as if to say: absolutely none. Therefore, [1] John [3:2] means [that we will see him through] a mirror and an enigma [cf. 1 Cor. 13:12], because in heaven we will see God (not his essence, but as he is glory, and goodness, and truth) openly through an immediate reception of light.[160]

Guerric of Saint-Quentin is even more restrictive. In a *quaestio disputata* on the beatific vision held prior to 1241, he distinguishes between God's power and his goodness. God's power is that by which he causes an influx into other creatures; God's goodness is that by which he draws people to himself. If we saw God's goodness, we would be joined with his essence,[161] which is impossible for a creature.[162] Rather, we are joined to him by his power which impresses a form on us through which he is seen.[163] In another *quaestio disputata* from the same period, Guerric explains what that form is:[164]

As for the question, "will God be seen by a medium which is himself": [I answer] no; [he will be seen] by a medium which comes from him; for he will be seen through a form impressed by the one who is impressing the

160. Hugh of Saint-Cher, *Postilla in Evangelium Iohannis*, cited in Dondaine, "L'objet et le 'medium' de la vision béatifique," 120: "Sed quid est quod dicitur I Joh.: ... *videbimus sicuti est*? —Ad hoc dicendum quod Iohannes non intendit dicere quod nos aliquo modo consideremus Dei substantiam in patria, quia hoc est impossibile omni creaturae. Unde Crisostomus: 'quod creabilis nature est, qualiter uidere poterit quod increabile est?' quasi dicat: nullo modo. Intendit ergo Iohannes speculum et enigma, quia in patria per immediatam acceptionem luminis aperte videbimus Deum, non tamen essentiam, sed ut gloriam, bonitatem, et veritatem."

161. Guerric of Saint-Quentin, *Quaestio* I, cited in Dondaine, "Guerric de Saint-Quentin et La Condamnation de 1241," *Revue des Sciences Philosophiques et Théologiques* 44, no. 2 (1960): 234.83–89.

162. Ibid., 231.35–37. Among the long list of authorities cited by Guerric to this point, we find the same quotation from Chrysostom, with the same gloss, "Quasi dicat: nullo modo" (230.14–15).

163. Ibid., 233.134–36.

164. In *Quaestio* I, Guerric himself may refer us to *Quaestio* II: "Dilectio et fides sunt formae impressae et ideo per se videntur. Deus autem est forma imprimens, non impressa; unde non per se videtur, sed per formam impressam. Quae sit ista forma, *alias quaeretur*" (emphasis added).

form. But what is that medium? Charity, or something else? And how is it common [to both]? [Is it] because there is an assimilation of the knower and the known, such that it is necessary that it be common to both? Solution: it is necessary that that medium be a similitude which is both assimilating and assimilated; but the most assimilating [form] is love, because it has a motive power by which it assimilates. It is assimilated because it is an example of essential and not personal love.[165]

For Hugh, then, we will see God's attributes but not his essence. For Guerric, we will see at most God's power, to which we are joined by the form of charity impressed upon our souls.

In 1241, Odo Chateauroux (d. 1273), then chancellor at the University of Paris, condemned, on William of Auvergne's authority, a syllabus of errors on a range of theological topics. The Eastern tradition about the beatific vision, as understood by medieval scholastics, was first on the list:

First, that the divine essence will not be seen in itself neither by man nor by an angel. We condemn this error, and, by the authority of Bishop William, we excommunicate both those who assert it, and those who defend it. For we firmly believe and assert that God will be seen in his essence or substance by all holy angels and persons, and that he is seen by glorified souls.[166]

The Dominican Order moved swiftly to ensure compliance. It mandated twice in successive years (1243 and 1244) that all theologians

165. Guerric of Saint-Quentin, *Quaestio* I, cited in Dondaine, "Guerric de Saint-Quentin et La Condamnation de 1241," 238.189–96: "Quod queritur 'videbiturne Deus per medium quod est ipse': non, sed per medium quod erit ab ipso; videbitur enim per formam impressam ab ipso qui est forma[m] imprimens. Sed quid est illud medium utrum caritas vel aliud et quomodo sit commune quod est assimilatio cognoscentis et cogniti unde oportet quod sit commune cum utroque?—Solutio: oportet quod illud medium sit similitudo assimilans et assimilata; sed maxime assimilans est amor quia habet vim motivam et ita assimilat. Assimilatur quia est exemplum amoris essentialis et non personalis."

166. Denifle, *Chartularium Universitatis Parisiensis*, 1:170: "Primus, quod divina essentia in se nec ab homine nec ab angelo videbitur. Hunc errorem reprobamus et assertores et defensores auctoritate Wilhermi episcopi excommunicamus. Firmiter autem credimus et asserimus, quod Deus in sua essentia vel substantia videbitur ab angelis et omnibus sanctis et videtur ab animabus glorificatis."

follow the condemnation.[167] The text of Hugh was corrected and/or suppressed as needed.[168] Guerric publicly repudiated the *quaestio* quoted above in person,[169] by holding another in which he determined that we see God immediately.[170]

In light of the aforementioned controversy, we can see why Thomas would find it useful to develop an argument that merely proved the possibility of the beatific vision, without speculating as to whether anyone actually sees God: he was correcting a recent error among the theologians of his order, and following the ecclesiastical authority of both the bishop in whose diocese he resided as well as the religious order of which he was a member.[171]

DE VERITATE

Thomas's treatment of nature, grace, and the desire for God in the *Quaestiones disputatae de veritate* is very similar to his treatment of them in the *Commentary on the Sentences,* although it admits of several changes in terminology, and occasional developments in the concepts to which his terms refer. Thomas makes only terminological adjustments to his discussions of nature and grace, as well as to his discussions of the intellect and the will taken as separate powers. He develops his teaching on natural desire by clarifying three important points in relation to God's Providence: first, that the intellect is the first mover among the powers of the soul; second, that the intellect is moved directly by God as its first mover; third, that

167. Dondaine, "L'objet et le 'medium' de la vision béatifique," 83.

168. Ibid., 83–84.

169. B.-G. Guyot, "Trois Questiones Guerriciennes sur la vision béatifique," cited in H.-F. Dondaine, "Guerric de Saint-Quentin et la condamnation de 1241," 226.

170. Guerric of Saint Quentin, *Quaestio* III, cited in Dondaine, "Guerric de Saint-Quentin et la Condamnation de 1241," 240.79–242.194.

171. That we should read this text in light of that controversy can also be gathered from Thomas Aquinas, *De ver.,* q. 8, a. 1 [Leon. 22:217], where Thomas treats the same question and mentions explicitly: "circa hanc quaestionem quidam erraverunt dicentes Deum per essentiam a nullo umquam intellectu creato videri posse, attendentes distantiam quae est inter divinam essentiam et intellectum creatum; sed haec positio sustineri non potest cum sit haeretica."

the motion of the will is caused by God indirectly through the motion of the intellect.

Nature and Grace

As in the *Commentary on the Sentences,* God makes all creatures according to a divine idea, a limited similarity of which is received in a given creature as the creature's single substantial form.[172] In a human being, this substantial form is the soul,[173] which confers upon the human person a certain realm of activity.[174] This realm of activity includes a formal, active and a material, passive principle.[175] Together, these principles constitute a *ratio seminalis.*[176]

In the *Commentary on the Sentences,* Thomas had attributed *rationes seminales* to the intellectual powers of the soul analogous to the one possessed by human nature itself. In the intellect, he had associated the formal, active principle with the "spark of reason" and the material, passive principle with the possible intellect. In *De veritate,* Thomas makes the same association. He is even more explicit than before about how thinking about matter and form can help us think about the *rationes seminales* in the intellect and the will: "the same differences of opinion are found in three questions: in the eduction of forms into being, in the acquisition of the virtues, and in the acquisition of knowledge."[177]

As in the *Commentary on the Sentences,* Thomas places his reflection about the relationship between matter and form, as well as the principles in the intellect and the will which are analogous to mat-

172. Ibid., q. 3, aa. 1–3, 8 [Leon. 22:99–109, 115–16]. See also Doolan, *Aquinas on the Divine Ideas as Exemplar Causes,* 6–11, 50–53, 88–93, 124–27, 160.

173. Thomas Aquinas, *De ver.,* q. 15, a. 2, ad 11 [Leon. 22:488].

174. Ibid., q. 10, a. 11, co. [Leon. 22:335]. Also see q. 27, a. 1, ad 1 and ad 3 [Leon. 22:791].

175. Ibid., q. 18, a. 2, co. [Leon. 22:536]; q. 18 a. 4, co. [Leon. 22:546]. See also q. 15, a. 1, co. [Leon. 22:436].

176. Ibid., q. 5, a. 9, ad 8 [Leon. 22:166].

177. Ibid., q. 11, a. 1, co. [Leon. 22:349]: "In tribus eadem opinionum diversitas invenitur, scilicet in eductione formarum in esse, in acquisitione virtutum et in acquisitione scientiarum."

ter and form, in the tradition of discourse reflected in Bonaventure's *Commentary on the Sentences.* Thomas even rehearses the same diversity of opinions which had framed his discussion of nature in *In II Sent.*, d. 18, q. 1, a. 2: Avicenna (the *dator formarum*), which he associates with radical illuminationism and the extrinsic influence of virtue; Anaxagoras (the *latitatio formarum*), which he associates with Platonic reminiscence and innate virtues; and Bacon (incomplete active potency), whose specific consequences for knowledge and virtue he does not specify.[178]

Passing over a critique of Bonaventure's incomplete forms, Thomas resumes his reiteration of concepts from the *Commentary on the Sentences* by discussing Averroes's two ways that a change can be considered natural: when a creature has an active potency capable of causing the eduction of a form, and when a creature has a passive potency capable of having the form educed from it by another.[179] In the intellect there is an active potency, the agent intellect, according to which the intellect educes knowledge from its passive potency, the possible intellect;[180] in the will, there is an active potency, the natural will, which educes virtue from a passive potency, the free will.[181]

Although Thomas is thus far conceptually consistent with the

178. Ibid. [Leon. 22:349–50].

179. Ibid. [Leon. 22:351]: "Sciendum tamen est quod in rebus naturalibus aliquid praeexistit in potentia dupliciter: uno modo in potentia activa completa, quando scilicet principium intrinsecum sufficienter potest perducere in actum perfectum, sicut patet in sanatione: ex virtute enim naturali quae est in aegro aeger ad sanitatem perducitur; alio modo in potentia passiva, quando scilicet principium intrinsecum non sufficit ad educendum in actum, sicut patet quando ex aere fit ignis: hoc enim non poterat fieri per aliquam virtutem in aere existentem."

180. Ibid., q. 15, a. 2, co. [Leon. 22:486]; ad 13 [Leon. 22:488]; q. 20, a. 4, co. [Leon. 22:583–84].

181. Ibid. q. 11, a. 1, co. [Leon. 22:350]: "similiter etiam secundum ipsius [that is, Aristotelis] sententiam in VI *Ethicorum* virtutum habitus ante earum consummationem praeexistunt in nobis in quibusdam naturalibus inclinationibus quae sunt quaedam virtutum inchoationes, sed postea per exercitium operum adducuntur in debitam consummationem; similiter etiam dicendum est de scientiae acquisitione quod praeexistunt in nobis quaedam scientiarum semina, scilicet primae conceptiones intellectus quae statim lumine intellectus agentis cognoscuntur per species a sensibilibus abstractas ... *in istis autem principiis universalibus omnia sequentia includuntur sicut in quibusdam rationibus seminalibus ...*" (emphasis added). Also see ibid., ad 5 [Leon. 22:352].

Commentary on the Sentences, he does make one very important terminological change: instead of speaking of "material potency" in the intellect, he now prefers to speak of "passive potency." The cause of this terminological development appears to have been Thomas's greater familiarity with the use of the term "material intellect" (*intellectus materialis*) among the Arabic commentators on Aristotle, particularly Book 5 of Avicenna's *De anima,* as well as Book 3 of Averroes's *Long Commentary* on Aristotle's *De anima.*[182] In itself, the term "material intellect" posed no difficulty for Thomas, since he had described the possible intellect in the *Commentary on the Sentences* as "material" only by way of analogy. However, the text of Averroes's commentary related to him that Alexander of Aphrodisias (fl. c. 200) and Avempace (Ibn Bâjja; c. 1085–1138) taught that the possible intellect was material in the *literal* sense, that is, that it was corporeal, and therefore corruptible;[183] and there is evidence that certain early thirteenth-century scholastics followed this opinion.[184] Thomas had known about these commentators when he wrote his *Commentary on the Sentences,*[185] but had avoided the language of "material intellect" in the discussion of their positions. It is otherwise in *De veritate.* Thomas expressly refers to Alexander's doctrine of a "material possible intellect," and discusses the consequences of Alexander's teaching about the possible intellect in direct relation to its supposed materiality.[186]

182. Richard Taylor, "Aquinas and 'the Arabs': Aquinas's First Critical Encounter with the Doctrines of Avicenna and Averroes on the Intellect: *In 2 Sent.,* d. 17, q. 2, a. 1," in *Philosophical Psychology in Arabic Thought and the Latin Aristotelianism of the 13th Century,* ed. Luis Xavier López-Farjeat and Jörg Alejandro Tellkamp (Paris: J. Vrin, 2013), 144–45.

183. See Averroes's commentary on *De anima* 3.5, in *Commentarium magnum in Aristotelis De anima libros,* ed. F. Stuart Crawford (Cambridge, Mass.: Medieval Academy of America, 1953), 387–413.

184. See, for example, the anonymous *Lectura in librum de anima a quodam discipula reportata,* ed. R.-A. Gauthier (Grottaferrata: Collegium S. Bonaventurae ad Claras Aquas, 1985), cited in Christian Trottmann, *La vision béatifique: Des disputes scolastiques à sa définition par Benoît XII* (Rome: École française de Rome, 1995), 218–29.

185. See Thomas Aquinas, *In II Sent.,* d. 17, q. 2, a. 1 [Mandonnet 2:423–24]; Taylor, "Aquinas and 'the Arabs,'" 141–296.

186. See Thomas Aquinas, *De ver.,* q. 18, a. 5, ad 8 [Leon. 22:548].

Although Thomas is careful to avoid any language that might confuse his understanding of the possible intellect with that of Alexander of Aphrodisias or Avempace, Thomas does not altogether abandon the analogy between matter and the possible intellect,[187] and so the change in terminology does not occasion any significant change in Thomas's teaching about the agent intellect's relationship to the possible intellect or his teaching about the stages of habituation that determine the possible intellect. As in the *Commentary on the Sentences,* since each level of habituation in the possible intellect restricts the realm of its subsequent information,[188] the first principles of demonstration do not include the knowledge of God; otherwise there could be no atheists.[189] In this life, God's existence has to be demonstrated by means of those first principles,[190] although in the next life, when the saints see God, they are more certain of his existence than of these principles,[191] because God becomes the intelligible species informing their intellects.[192]

Turning his attention toward the will, Thomas clarifies that since the intellect has to propose a specific end to the will in order to move it, and since the first principles of demonstration are only the pattern by which the intellect arrives at specific conclusions (not specific conclusions in themselves), the first principles of demonstration are not sufficient to set the will in motion. Just as the first principles of demonstration are only the pattern by which the intellect arrives at specific knowledge, so also the natural appetite of the will is only the pattern by which the will tends toward the specific good presented to it by the intellect, when and only when the intellect presents such a good to it in act. Natural desire is therefore not a

187. Thomas expressly compares the possible intellect with prime matter in *De ver.,* q. 14, a. 1, co. [Leon. 22:436].

188. Ibid., q. 15, a. 2, co. [Leon. 22:485].

189. Ibid., q. 10, a. 12, co. [Leon. 22:341]. On these first principles, also see q. 15, a. 1, co. [Leon. 22:480].

190. Ibid., q. 10, a. 13, co. [Leon. 22:345].

191. Ibid., a. 12, co. [Leon. 22:341]; q. 24, a. 9, co. [Leon. 22:701].

192. Ibid., q. 10, a. 11, co. [Leon. 22:336].

sort of first movement of the will antecedent of a specific conclusion in the intellect. Indeed, there are times when the will is not in motion toward anything at all:

> The first good is willed of itself, and the will wills it of itself and naturally. Yet [the will] does not always will [the first good] in act; for it is not necessary that those things which naturally befit the soul be always in act in the soul, just like the principles which are naturally known are not always considered in act.[193]

Since the will has freedom to act or not to act, the intellect must determine the will to act not simply by presenting it with something good (a concrete *bonum*), but by presenting it with a good that corresponds with the will's natural appetite (a *bonum conveniens*).[194] When the intellect does determine the will toward a specific end in this way, the choice of a specific action toward that end can happen in one of two ways. In the first way, the intellect can direct the will toward an end which is proportionate to the active principles in the intellect and in the will. In this case, the person performs a free action which can be called "natural" in the sense that it is *secundum naturam*, such as giving money to a beggar out of kindness, because the action can be naturally known to be good by reasoning from the first principles of practical reason, and can be naturally accomplished by acting from the first motion of the will.[195] In a second way, the intellect can direct the will toward an action whose *substance* follows from the active principle in both powers, but which is done *in a manner* that exceeds either or both of their respective active principles, like giving money to a beggar out of the theological virtue of charity, by which we love God above all things and our

193. Ibid., q. 22, a. 5, ad 11 [Leon. 22:625]: "Primum bonum est per se volitum, et voluntas per se et naturaliter illud vult. Non tamen semper illud vult in actu; non enim oportet ea quae sunt naturaliter animae convenientia semper actu in anima esse, sicut principia quae sunt naturaliter cognita non semper actu considerantur."

194. Ibid., co. [Leon. 22:624]: "Voluntati ipsi inest naturalis quidam appetitus boni sibi convenientis."

195. Ibid., q. 24, a. 14, co. [Leon. 22:723]. See also Thomas, Aquinas, *In IV Sent.*, d. 49, q. 1, a. 3 [Parma 7.2:1190B–1196A].

neighbor as ourselves. In the second case, as in the *Commentary on the Sentences,* the act performed under the influence of grace is neither *secundum naturam* nor *supra naturam* simply speaking; it is *secundum naturam* in the sense that it presupposes an active power for operation in the natural order (that is, giving); it is *supra naturam* insofar as grace takes that action as a material principle, and formally elevates it toward an end which it could not achieve of its own power (that is, giving out of the virtue of charity).[196]

The Natural Desire for God

While Thomas's teaching about the intellect and the will remains fairly consistent, his teaching on the relationship between them develops significantly. This development is evident in two further changes in terminology. The first is the assertion that the intellect "moves" the will; the second is the identification of a "natural appetite" in the intellect, apart from the will, as the pattern according to which the intellect moves the will.

Thomas's teaching that the intellect moves the will is reflected in his treatment of Providence. In *De veritate,* Thomas continues to locate Providence in the divine intellect.[197] He develops his thinking from the *Commentary on the Sentences* by describing Providence on analogy with prudence rather than art. The reason for this development is Thomas's appropriation of the distinction between prudence and art in Book 6 of Aristotle's *Nicomachean Ethics.* In this text, Aristotle draws a firm distinction between the two: art is the habit that gives rise to making and is only concerned with bringing things into being;[198] prudence is the habit that gives rise to action.[199] Since Providence is concerned with the governance of things that already exist, Thomas says that it should be located under the habit of prudence. Since, moreover, it is concerned with the means of

196. Ibid. See also Thomas Aquinas, *De ver.,* q. 10, a. 11, ad 7 [Leon. 22:337]; q. 14, a. 2, ad 9 [Leon. 22:444]; q. 27, a. 1, co. [Leon. 22:790–91].

197. *De ver..,* q. 5, a. 2, co. [Leon. 22:144].

198. Aristotle, *Nicomachean Ethics* 6.4 [1140a11–16].

199. Ibid., 6.5 [1140b4–7].

bringing creatures to their end and not with their end itself, Thomas more specifically associates it with the act of counsel, whereby we determine the appropriate means to an end with our intellect, and secondarily with the act of choice, whereby we select the means determined by counsel.[200]

In deference to Maimonides, Thomas continues to distinguish between the way in which human nature is subject to Providence and the way in which other sublunary creatures are subject to it, even though Thomas will never abandon his contention that God both knows and is provident over all singulars.[201] The distinction in Providence over singulars concerns not *whether* a given creature is subject to Providence, but *why*. Rational creatures are subject to Providence on account of *themselves*; they have a direct share in God's providential care for the universe by participating in the powers of intellect primarily and also will. Non-rational creatures, by contrast, are subject to Providence on account of their *species*.[202] Continuing to follow Maimonides's understanding of the manner in which God relates to human persons, Thomas even goes so far as to say that the primary mode through which God exercises Providence on rational creatures is through reward and punishment.[203] Thomas also continues to agree that those who are more perfect have a greater share in Providence.[204]

The direct share that rational creatures have in God's Providence over themselves happens in virtue of their intellect, which "moves" the will in the manner of a final cause by its assent.[205] But

200. Thomas Aquinas, *De ver.*, q. 5, a. 1, co. [Leon. 22:139].

201. Ibid., a. 4, co. [Leon. 22:149–50].

202. Ibid., a. 2, co. [Leon. 22:144]; a. 6. [Leon. 22:153–54].

203. Ibid., a. 6, co. [Leon. 22:154].

204. Ibid., a. 7, co. [Leon. 22:155]. Thomas explicitly likens the exercise of Providence over the wicked to the exercise of Providence over the brutes, but qualifies that this is merely a "lower mode" of Providence, not a different kind of Providence.

205. Ibid., q. 15, a. 3, co. [Leon. 22:491]: "aliquis actus rationi attribuitur dupliciter: uno modo quia est immediate eius, utpote ab ipsa ratione elicitus, sicut conferre de agendis vel scibilibus; alio modo quia eius est mediante voluntate, quae per eius iudicium movetur." See also a. 2, ad 6 [Leon. 22:488]: "Non autem dicuntur in ratione superiori esse plures potentiae, quasi in plures potentias ipsa rationis potentia dividatur, sed

here a question arises. If the will is moved by the intellect as by a final cause, what moves the intellect to make a judgment so that the will may move, and how do we avoid a regress to infinity in reciprocal causality between the intellect and the will?[206] Thomas places this difficulty in the mouth of an objector in *De veritate,* q. 22, a. 12;[207] the reply is abrupt: "That does not lead to a regress to infinity; for [the regress] is brought to a halt in the natural appetite whereby the intellect is inclined toward its act."[208] The intellect moves itself when it deliberates; it moves the will when it reaches a judgment in the practical order.[209] This leads to another, subtle shift in Thomas's terminology. Where previously Thomas had attributed consent to the will, he now attributes it to the intellect: consent is a form of assent, in which the reason judges that a particular act is to be done; the corresponding act of the will is *choice,* not consent, and it is assumed that an act of choice will follow an act of assent in the practical order.[210]

Latent in Thomas's description of the intellect's motion is an allusion to a second significant development in Thomas's understanding of the relationship between the intellect and the will: the ascription of a natural appetite to the intellect independent of the will. In the *Commentary on the Sentences,* Thomas had implicitly ascribed a natural appetite to the intellect by ascribing one to every power of the

---

secundum quod voluntas sub intellectu comprehenditur, non quod sint una potentia sed quia ex apprehensione intellectus voluntas movetur."

206. This question is raised by Lottin, *Psychologie et morale aux XIIe et XIIIe siècles,* 1:235. On the fact that intellectual activity constitutes a "motion," even though it is only connected *per accidens* with the movement of the heavenly bodies, see Thomas Aquinas, *De ver.,* q. 28, a. 2, ad 10 [Leon. 22:823].

207. Thomas Aquinas, *De ver.,* q. 22, a. 12, obj. 2 [Leon. 2:641].

208. Ibid., ad 2. "Non est procedere in infinitum; statur enim in appetitu naturali quo inclinatur intellectus in suum actum."

209. Ibid.

210. Ibid.: "In speculativis autem scientiis non perficitur iudicium rationis nisi quando conclusiones resolvuntur in prima principia, unde nec in operabilibus perficietur nisi quando fiet reductio usque ad ultimum finem: tunc enim solummodo ratio ultimam sententiam de operando dabit et haec sententia est consensus in opus." Thomas connects this idea to an etymology of the word "consent" in q. 14, a. 1, ad 3 [Leon. 22:438].

soul, even though he had not explicitly applied that statement to the intellect. We find the same general principle in *De veritate*, q. 2, a. 3:

It is necessary that everything that naturally tends toward another have this [property] from another which directs it toward its end, otherwise it would tend toward it by chance. However, we find among natural things that there is a natural appetite by which each thing tends toward its end. For this reason, it is necessary that we posit an intellect above every natural thing which orders natural things toward their ends and places within them a natural inclination or appetite.[211]

If we follow the logic of this description, and we do so in light of what Thomas had said about natural appetites in the *Commentary on the Sentences*, then the meaning of Thomas's abrupt reply about reciprocal causality between the intellect and the will in *De veritate*, q. 22, a. 12, ad 2, becomes clear: Thomas solves the problem of reciprocal causality between the intellect and the will by appealing to God, who acts as the first, unmoved mover of the intellect; God moves the intellect by actualizing the natural appetite of the intel-

211. Ibid., q. 2, a. 3, co. [Leon. 22:50–51]: "omne enim quod naturaliter in alterum tendit oportet hoc habeat ex aliquo dirigente ipsum in finem, alias casu in illud tenderet; in rebus autem naturalibus invenimus naturalem appetitum quo unaquaeque res in finem suum tendit, unde oportet supra omnes res naturales ponere aliquem intellectum qui res naturales ad suos fines ordinaverit et eis naturalem inclinationem sive appetitum indiderit."

We should note here the association between inclinations and appetites. As noted above, Thomas uses the term "natural inclination" in a variety of senses, but one of the more common senses denotes the orientation of the formal, active principle in a nature toward its perfection. Thomas seems to have the same sense in mind in ibid., q. 2, a. 3, as well as in q. 11, a. 1, co. [Leon. 22:350]; q. 14, a. 3, ad 9 [Leon. 22:448]; q. 15, a. 3, co. [Leon. 22:491]; q. 22, a. 1, co. [Leon. 22:613–14]; q. 22, a. 5 [Leon. 22:621–26]; q. 22, a. 6, co. [Leon. 22:627]; q. 22, a. 8, co. [Leon 22:631]; q. 22, a. 9, co. [Leon. 22:632–33]; and q. 24, a. 8, co. [Leon 22:700].

Toward the end of *De veritate*, Thomas also uses "natural inclination" to describe the ordering of a passive principle toward its perfection. See q. 24, a. 10, ad 1 [Leon. 22:701]; q. 25, a. 1, co. [Leon. 22:728–30]; and possibly ad 2 [Leon. 22:700–701]; q. 27, a. 2, co. [Leon. 22:793–94]. In these texts, Thomas tends to be careful to distinguish the inclination *qua* ordering toward an end from the motion which actualizes the inclination.

Once, that I have found, Thomas uses the term "inclination" in a non-technical sense, meaning simply the concupiscible desires that people with a fallen human nature tend to experience. See q. 5, a. 10, ad 7 [Leon. 22:171].

lect, and God communicates motion to the will by means of the motion which he communicates to the intellect.[212]

Theological Challenges

Thomas's recourse to God as the first mover of the intellect avoided a regress to infinity in reciprocal causality between the intellect and the will, but it did not solve the existing problems from the *Commentary on the Sentences* concerning the sin of Adam and Eve as well as the act of faith. Thomas seems to have been aware of this fact. Concerning the sin of Adam and Eve, Thomas now fully admits that the will's pride, which preceded the actual taking of the fruit, constituted the first sin.[213] In order to explain how the will could sin without a previous error in the intellect, Thomas places Adam and Eve in a morally exceptional situation: on account of their pre-existing union with God, in which their souls were subject to God as part of original justice, they were uniquely capable of withdrawing from God in the will before they withdrew from him in the intellect:

> From the fact that the soul of man in the state of innocence was conjoined to the highest good, it was not possible for any defect to arise in man as long as such a conjunction continued. But this conjunction was caused

212. We should also clarify that even if there is a motion in the intellect leading to the act whereby the intellect moves the will, the intellect does not move the will as though the intellect or its motion were the efficient cause of the motion of the will. Rather, the intellect, at the instigation of God, undertakes a process of motion which culminates in a judgment. The object of that judgement, which is the result of a motion rather than a motion in itself, moves the will as a final cause.

It is understandable that Lottin, *Psychologie et morale aux XIIe et XIIIe siècles,* 1:235, would wonder why Thomas does not make a direct appeal here to God as the first mover of the intellect in order avoid a regress to infinity. However, seeing that Thomas says, in *De ver.,* q. 2, a. 3, co. [Leon. 22:50–51], that having a natural appetite entails being moved by God, it is safe to say that Thomas does make such a direct appeal to God, even if that appeal can only be understood by a wider study of his use of the term "natural appetite."

Even if Thomas does not make his appeal to God as the first mover of the *intellect* as explicit as he could have, that does not justify us in concluding with Lottin that there is some first motion of the *will,* caused by God, which sets the intellect in motion before it determines the will. That is an anachronistic interpretation, even if by only a few years in Thomas's career. For now, Thomas understands God to move the will indirectly by means of the intellect, not directly.

213. Thomas Aquinas, *De ver.,* q. 18, a. 6, ad 5 [Leon. 22:553].

chiefly by the affect. Wherefore deception could not occur in the intellect nor could some defect occur in the body before the affect was corrupted, even though—on the contrary—there could be a defect in the affect without a pre-existing defect in the speculative intellect, because conjunction with God is not perfected in the intellect but in the affect.[214]

Rather than explaining the sin of Adam and Eve consistently with other sins, as he does in the *Commentary on the Sentences,* Thomas deliberately carves out an exception for it. On account of their pre-existing union with God, it was only possible for them to withdraw from God by a direct motion of the will, unaffected by passion. After that withdrawal, every other sin (including the "seduction" by which they ate the fruit) requires some form of preceding error in the intellect at the least, whether through the intellect's complete obfuscation toward universal principles (as in drunkenness) or whether through its inability to reason from a known universal principle to a particular conclusion on account of a passion.[215]

Concerning the act of faith, Thomas now admits that it would be disordered for the intellect to be moved by some fallible sign, because the proper object of the intellect is infallible truth.[216] Instead, the prudential judgment that immediately precedes the act of faith is based on *what* is said, not on *who* says it or how it is confirmed. The intellect judges that it would be good to receive the rewards promised, and that making an act of faith is the necessary means to receive those re-

214. Ibid., ad 10 [Leon. 2:554]: "Ex hoc quod anima hominis in statu innocentiae coniuncta erat summo bono, non poterat aliquis defectus in homine esse quandiu talis coniunctio continuaretur. Haec autem coniunctio facta erat principaliter per affectum, unde antequam affectiva corrumperetur nec deceptio in intellectu nec aliquis defectus in corpore esse poterat, quamvis e converso potuerit esse defectus in affectu non praeexistente defectu in speculativo intellectu, eo quod coniunctio non perficitur ad Deum in intellectu sed in affectu."

215. Thus, although Thomas seems to suggest in ibid., ad 1–2 [Leon. 22:552–53], that the actual "seduction" by which Adam and Eve ate the fruit occurred as a result of a movement of passion, he later explains in ad 8 [Leon. 22:554] that they could only have that passion as a result of their having previously been stripped of the state of innocence through the sin of pride in the will.

216. Ibid., co. [Leon. 22:552].

wards.[217] On the basis of this judgment, the will commands the intellect to grant its assent. That command is rooted in the will's ability to move any power toward the material good of that power.[218]

One may question whether the developments in Thomas's teaching on the sin of Adam and Eve and on the act of faith resolve all the difficulties that could be raised in relation to them. Concerning the sin of Adam and Eve, one may ask whether the special exception that Thomas develops is really as unique as Thomas makes it out to be. After all, Adam and Eve were not in a state of complete union with God, such as the saints possess. As Thomas himself acknowledges, their union was a union of charity, which is formally the same as the union with charity that post-lapsarian persons in a state of sanctifying grace possess. The unique characteristic of the union with God which Adam and Eve possessed was in the initial submission of their souls to God by the gift of original justice. It is possible that this union might constitute a unique enough case to exempt Adam and Eve from the general rules of Thomas's philosophical psychology, but it is also possible that it might not. Does Thomas's account of the consequences of their union at this stage of his career perhaps presuppose a fullness which is really only possible in the vision of God?

Concerning the act of faith, one may ask whether there is a sufficient basis in the intellect's judgment that "those who believe God will be rewarded" to move the will to command the intellect to make an act of faith. Even if we grant that this judgment is sufficient to ground the prudence of the act of faith, one may still ask about the structure of the act in itself. If the intellect moves the will as its final cause by the conclusion of a practical syllogism in every other act (except the sin of Adam and Eve), is it not contrary to the fundamental Thomistic theological axiom that "grace does not destroy nature, but perfects it,"[219] and to the anthropological principle, ex-

217. Thomas spells this out in ibid., q. 14, a. 2, co. [Leon. 22:441]. For a quick summary, see ad 10 [Leon. 22:444]. In ad 13, Thomas goes on to call the apprehended good of eternal life the "first mover" in the act of faith [Leon. 22:444].

218. Ibid., a. 2, ad 6 [Leon. 22:443].

219. See Thomas Aquinas, *ST*, Ia, q. 1, a. 8, ad 2 [Leon. 4:22]: "Cum enim *gratia non*

pressed in the *Commentary on the Sentences* and in *De veritate,* that nature is oriented toward grace like matter toward form, to say that God circumvents the order of nature in the act of faith by infusing the will with grace to move the intellect?

If Thomas's account of the relationship between the intellect and the will in the act of faith encountered significant difficulties, it should not for that reason be entirely discounted. As Thomas had already observed in the *Commentary on the Sentences,* there is an essential *theological* reason to preserve the role of the will in the act of faith: it is a truth of the Christian faith that the act of faith is a meritorious act.[220]

An act cannot be called meritorious unless it is grounded in the power of the one who performs it, because a person who merits has to be able to show forth something, and he can only show forth what is in some way his, that is, [because it] comes from him. However, an act lies in our power insofar as it belongs to the will, whether it belongs [to the will] as elicited by it, like loving and wanting, or as commanded by it, like walking and speaking. For this reason, no matter what sort of act we consider, we can posit a power eliciting perfect acts in that category of action. So then, belief, as was said above, only derives its assent from the command of the will. Therefore [belief] depends on the will in its essence [*secundum id quod est*]. And for this reason, belief itself can be meritorious.[221]

---

tollat naturam, sed perficiat, oportet quod naturalis ratio subserviat fidei; sicut et naturalis inclinatio voluntatis obsequitur caritati" (emphasis added). On the history of this axiom, see Jean-Pierre Torrell, *Spiritual Master,* vol. 2 of *Saint Thomas Aquinas,* trans. Robert Royal (Washington, D.C.: The Catholic University of America Press, 2003), 228n2.

220. The paradigmatic example is the faith of Abraham. See Gn 15:16; Rom 4:3. Thomas had made a similar point about faith in *In IV Sent.,* d. 49, q. 1, a. 3, qc. 3, ad 3 [Parma 7.2:1193A].

221. Thomas Aquinas, *De ver.,* q. 14, a. 3, co. [Leon. 22:447]: "Aliquis actus meritorius dici non potest nisi secundum quod est in potestate operantis constitutus quia qui meretur oportet quod aliquid exhibeat, nec exhibere potest nisi quod aliquo modo suum est, id est ex ipso; actus autem aliquis in potestate nostra consistit secundum quod est voluntatis, sive sit eius ut ab ipsa elicitus, ut diligere et velle, sive ut ab ipsa imperatus, ut ambulare et loqui; unde respectu cuiuslibet talis actus potest poni aliqua virtus eliciens actus perfectos in tali genere actuum. Credere autem, ut supra dictum est, non habet assensum nisi ex imperio voluntatis, unde secundum id quod est a voluntate dependet; et inde est quod ipsum credere potest esse meritorium."

A Christian theologian *must* preserve the idea that the intellect is moved to believe by the will, otherwise the freedom to believe is lost, along with the merit in doing so. That is not to say that the motion in the will by which a person is led to faith is the same as the motion of the will by which a person believes meritoriously. As Thomas also rightly notes, the perfection of the will by which a person is motivated to anything meritorious at all is charity.[222] But it is to say that unless the will has a role in the act of faith *from the beginning*, there will be no way to introduce the will into the act of faith subsequently. If Thomas was not sure as of yet how best to articulate that role, still he was certain that a Christian theologian must.

CONCLUSION

In the *Commentary on the Sentences,* Thomas attempts to chart a course through the theological and philosophical tradition concerning nature, grace, and the desire for God, which had matured in the quarter of a century prior to the beginning of his term as a bachelor of the Sentences. We saw at the end of chapter 1 that the principal difficulty facing theologians in discussions of nature, grace, and the desire for God just before Thomas arrived at Paris was figuring out how to give an account of the relationship between nature and grace in a given individual. Thomas's principal contribution to that conversation was his application of Averroes's concept of a "second nature" in the heavenly bodies for the passive reception of motion in the interpretation of Augustine's and Peter's *rationes seminales.* For Thomas, creatures possess a "material" passive potency which is distinct from their formal, active potency. This passive potency does not correspond in every respect with its active counterpart. Just as matter possesses a potential which cannot be actualized completely by any one form, so does the material potency in a creature exceed what can be actualized by its form. The fact that a creature's material

222. Ibid., a. 5, co. [Leon. 22:453].

potency exceeds its formal potency is the basis of the possibility of natural motion and natural change.

The use of Averroes's second nature helped Thomas to propose an initial solution to the unresolved problem of nature's relationship to grace. With Albert, Thomas argues that human nature has a natural desire for a natural end: the activity of our nature, which follows from our substantial form, terminates in the analogical knowledge of God as first cause. With Bonaventure, Thomas argues that human nature is still "naturally" open to grace, because it has a natural appetite for a supernatural end: its "material" potency is always open to the vision of God, which alone can confer upon it complete perfection. Nature is, as it were, the matter out of which grace is educed,[223] and so "graced actions" are *secundum naturam* in their material principle and *supra naturam* in their formal principle. Nature's openness to grace can therefore be described as an "obediential property" (*ratio obedientialis*) of its material potency, rather than a separate "potency for obedience" (*potentia obedientiae*) within it. We see an example of the relationship between natural appetite and natural desire in the souls that Thomas supposes to be in limbo. They reach an end, because they reach the terminal development of their natural *desire*, but they do not reach their *ultimate* end, because they do not reach the terminal development of their natural appetite. Their lack of sorrow is based upon the fact that God has not withheld from them the fulfillment of their natural desire, only the fulfillment of their natural appetite.

In the *Commentary on the Sentences,* Thomas struggles to describe consistently the origin of the motion by which our natural appetite is transformed into a natural desire. In some places, he describes the intellect as the first cause of motion within the soul; in other places, the will. In *De veritate* Thomas resolves this seeming discrepancy in favor of the intellect: God moves the intellect directly and the will by means of the intellect. In order to account for

223. Hütter, *Dust Bound for Heaven*, 237.

the ways in which these powers operate distinctly from one another, Thomas identifies parallel and distinct *rationes seminales* in each power. In the intellect, the active principle is the agent intellect and the passive principle is the possible intellect; the agent intellect determines the possible intellect by the first principles of demonstration and by acquired knowledge. In the will, the active principle is the natural will, and the passive principle is the free will; the natural will determines the free will by natural virtue and by acquired virtue. When the agent intellect causes the conclusion of a practical syllogism in the possible intellect, the conclusion of that syllogism determines the motion of the will.

Given the way in which Thomas understands the intellect and the will at this stage of his career, he struggles to give a consistent account of the sin of Adam and Eve, as well as the act of faith. Concerning the sin of Adam and Eve, Thomas tries to say in the *Commentary on the Sentences* that the devil induced them to sin by convincing them first to misinterpret God's prohibition against eating of the forbidden fruit. In the *De veritate,* by contrast, Thomas exempts Adam and Eve from the general priority of the intellect over the will by suggesting that, on account of their union with God, they were uniquely capable of withdrawing from God in their wills before they withdrew from God in their intellects. Concerning the act of faith, Thomas tries to say in the *Commentary on the Sentences* that the practical intellect establishes that such an act would be prudent on the basis of fallible testimony and signs; the will, directed by the intellect, in turn commands the intellect to make an act of faith. In the *De veritate* he acknowledged that the intellect is not perfected by judgments based on fallible things; instead, he bases the judgment of prudence solely on the desirability of the object promised as a reward for faith.

In these early works, then, Thomas already makes a unique and important contribution to the thirteenth-century discussion of nature, grace, and the desire for God by suggesting the analogy of matter and form as a way of explaining how nature and grace relate in a given individual. But when he applied this teaching to the desire for God, the difficulties he encountered in harmonizing his psychology with his understanding of Providence, the sin of Adam and Eve, and the act of faith could not be ignored. Those difficulties would be at the top of his agenda at the next stage of his career.

In addition to these more technical questions, there is also a more general question that Thomas left unresolved at this point in his career: if our second "nature" is truly part of human nature, how do we balance Augustine's anti-Pelagian concern to ensure that there is no motion in human nature toward the beatific vision, with Aristotle's philosophical concern to ensure that every nature has a motion toward some act as its end? In one sense, the complete passivity of Thomas's second nature protected humanity from claiming the grace of God by any right. But is humanity as such purely indifferent to the possibility of its supernatural end? This question also would be on Thomas's agenda in the next stage of his career; it would find its initial resolution in the *Summa contra Gentiles*.

3

Orvieto (1259/61–1265)

Sometime between 1259 and 1261—we do not know the exact date—Thomas relocated to Italy.[1] What we do know is that in September of 1261 he was appointed as a conventual lector in the priory at Orvieto.[2] This position marked a contrast from the position he had held at Paris. In Paris, he had studied with and taught the best and brightest students that the Church and her religious orders had to offer. At Orvieto, he found himself in charge of the intellectual formation of the *fratres communes*, religious brothers who were destined not for advanced studies in philosophy and theology, but for the ordinary mission of preaching and hearing confessions.[3]

The teaching of *fratres communes* was governed by statutes which Thomas himself helped to draw up in 1259.[4] Those statutes made it

1. Torrell, *Saint Thomas Aquinas*, 1:98–101.

2. Ibid., 1:118.

3. Ibid., 1:118–19; Mary O'Carroll, *A Thirteenth Century Preacher's Handbook: Studies in MS Laud Misc. 531* (Toronto: PIMS, 1997), 46; Mulchahey, *First the Bow Is Bent in Study*, 130. On the education of the *fratres communes* in general, see Leonard Boyle, "Notes on the Education of the *Fratres communes* in the Dominican Order in the Thirteenth Century," in *Xenia medii aevi historiam illustrantia oblata Thomae Kaeppeli, O.P.*, ed. Raymond Creytens and Pius Künzel (Rome: Edizioni di storia e letteratura, 1978), 249–67; Michèle Mulchahey, "More Notes on the Education of the *fratres communes* in the Dominican Order: Elias de Ferreriis of Salagnac's *Libellus de doctrina fratrum*," in *A Distinct Voice: Medieval Studies in Honor of Leonard E. Boyle, O.P.*, ed. Jacqueline Brown and William Stoneman (Notre Dame, Ind.: University of Notre Dame Press, 1997), 328–69.

4. Torrell, *Saint Thomas Aquinas*, 1:96–98. For the text of the statutes, see Denifle,

clear that one of the most important priorities for the conventual *scholae* was study.[5] However, the precise means by which the *scholae* were to achieve their educational goals had not yet been established by the time that Thomas took up his post.[6] What we know is limited: in 1249 it had been established that the lectors should lecture primarily on the Bible; in 1271, it would subsequently be established that they should lecture on Peter Lombard's *Sentences* as well.[7] Sometime after 1265 but before 1277, it was recommended by a former master of the Order that the lectors stay close to the texts upon which they were lecturing, and that those texts should be the Bible, the *Sentences*, and the *Historiae Scholasticae* of Peter Comestor.[8] There is also evidence that the *fratres communes* would have been the recipients of moral manuals to direct them in hearing confessions.[9] Given the nature of the evidence we can only conclude that there was a certain fluidity to the curricula of the *scholae*, provided that one chose to teach from among those "texts which [were] esteemed better by common judgment."[10] It seems reasonable to conclude that Thomas, as a *magister in sacra pagina*, could have made prudent use of that fluidity in order to bring the conventual *schola* to as high a level of intellectual formation as possible.[11]

Chartularium Universitatis Parisiensis, 1:385. On Thomas's role in drafting them, see O'Carroll, *A Thirteenth Century Preacher's Handbook*, 46; Mulchahey, *First the Bow Is Bent in Study*, 168–69.

5. Mulchahey, *First the Bow Is Bent in Study*, 134–35.

6. Ibid., 134.

7. Ibid., 135.

8. Humbert of Romans, *De officiis ordinis* 11, in *Opera Omnia* (Rome: A. Befani, 1889), 2:254, cited in Boyle, "Notes on the Education of the *Fratres communes*," 257n27: "Dare operam ... litteram tantum legere, relicta multitudine eorum quae dici possunt ad singula; quod auditores sub eo proficiant ad sciendum *Bibliam*, et *Historias*, et *Sententias*: maxime lectiones, aut omnes, aut saltem unam continuare libenter."

9. Boyle, "Notes on the Education of the *Fratres communes*," 253–54.

10. Humbert of Romans, *De officiis ordinis* 11 [Befani 2:254]. Speaking of the books which the lector himself ought to study, Humbert notes, "Ut autem melius et fructuosus officium suum exequatur, debet studere diligenter, et precipue in scriptis quae communi judicio meliora reputantur."

11. In attempting to understand the customary course of study in a conventual *schola* at this time, we must avoid the mistake of generalizing exceptions to the rule. One such exception is that which is contained in the *ratio studiorum* of 1259: "Item, quod si inveniri

THE LITERAL COMMENTARY ON JOB

To the mind of a thirteenth-century theologian such as Thomas, the challenge of shaping a conventual *schola* would have seemed spiritual as well as academic. Let us recall from chapter 1 Dionysius's association between advancement in the spiritual life and the manner in which we speak about God. As we progress through the spiritual life, we move from symbolic to mystical language, to the praise of God beyond all affirmations and negations. One could almost suggest a certain correspondence among this Dionysian ascent, the four senses of Scripture, and the duties of a *magister*: symbolic theology being associated with the literal sense (*lectio*); mystical theology with the allegorical sense (*disputatio*), and the praise of God with the moral sense (*praedicatio*).[12] If Thomas were going to introduce the *fratres communes* to the study of theology, he had to find a way of taking beginners—who were better suited to symbolic theol-

non possunt lectores sufficientes ad legendum publice, saltem provideatur de aliquibus qui legant privatas lectiones, vel ystorias, vel summam de casibus, vel aliud hujusmodi, ne fratres sint otiosi." This rule should not be taken as stipulating the texts that should be read if a suitable public lecturer can be found; at most it tells us what texts were thought safe enough to be taught by less capable lecturers. Consequently, we cannot conclude with Torrell, *Saint Thomas Aquinas*, 1:120, that Thomas devoted this period of his teaching to "pastoral morals." Much to the contrary, as we shall see below, the evidence suggests that Thomas taught dialectical theology, albeit through Scripture.

12. This is how it might have seemed to a medieval author reading that "symbolic theology is not argumentative" in Dionysius, *Epistle* 9 [1105D], cited in Rorem, *Pseudo-Dionysius*, 37. Peter Lombard alludes to a similar rule in *III Sent.*, d. 11, cap. 2 [Quaracchi 2:80]. Peter's text is following Augustine, who warns in *Ep.* 93 [CSEL 34.2:470], "quis autem non inpudentissime nitatur aliquid in allegoria positum pro se interpretari, nisi habeat et manifesta testimonia, quorum lumine inlustrentur obscura?"

As Rorem notes, Thomas quotes this text of Dionysius throughout his career. At the beginning, see *In I Sent.*, prol., a. 5, co. [Mandonnet 1:18], where Thomas weds the texts of Dionysius and Peter together: "Ad destructionem autem errorum non proceditur nisi per sensum litteralem, eo quod alii sensus sunt per similitudines accepti et ex similitudinariis locutionibus non potest sumi argumentatio; unde et Dionysius dicit in *Epistola ad Titum*, quod symbolica theolgia non est argumentativa." Later, see *ST*, Ia, q. 1, a. 10, ad 1 [Leon. 4:25]: "Et ita etiam nulla confusio sequitur in sacra Scriptura: cum omnes sensus fundentur super unum, scilicet litteralem; ex quo solo potest trahi argumentum, non autem ex his quae secundum allegoriam dicuntur, ut dicit Augustinus in epistola contra Vincentium Donatistam [*Ep.* 93]."

ogy, the literal sense, and *lectio*—and advancing them as quickly as possible to the stage of proficients, so that they might be introduced to the mystical language with which theological argumentation is made in *disputatio*.

Given this general goal, Thomas's choice to lecture upon the literal sense of Job was a natural fit. For Thomas, the Book of Job occurs among the "hagiographical" books, which encompass what contemporary Christian scholars tend to think of as the historical books and wisdom literature.[13] The hagiographical books are more straightforward than other books: the literal sense of the historical books among the hagiographical books are the historical facts they narrate, while the literal sense of the wisdom literature among the hagiographical books are the teachings they expound.[14] The hagiographical books are therefore free from some of the more complex questions about genre that the other books can raise.[15] Given the choice between a historical book and a wisdom book, Thomas chose from among the latter; had he chosen a historical book, he would have had to have first spent time establishing the historical record; and only then would he have been able to draw theology from it by means of disputation. Teaching from a wisdom book meant simply introducing students to the teaching contained in the book without the need for an extra layer of interpretation.

Job had a further benefit: not only did Thomas think that its literal sense is contained simply in the speeches it narrates, he also thought that those speeches narrate the sort of disputation proper to mystical theology.[16] By lecturing on Job in the literal sense, Thomas

13. Thomas Aquinas, *Hic est liber*, in *Opuscula Theologica*, vol. 2, ed. Raymundo Verardo (Turin: Marietti, 1954), 436.

14. Ibid. [Verardo 2:438].

15. For an indication of some of those questions, see Thomas Aquinas, *Quodlibet* 7, q. 6, a. 2, ad 5 [Leon. 27.1:31].

16. Thomas Aquinas, *Hic est liber* [Verardo 438]: "Libri autem agiographi et apocryphi, qui tantum instruunt verbo, distinguuntur secundum quod verbum dupliciter ad instructionem operatur: uno modo petendo sapientiae donum.... Secundo modo sapientiam docendo, et hoc dupliciter, secundum duplex opus sapientis; *quorum unum est mentientem manifestare posse: et quantum ad hoc est liber Iob, qui per modum disputationis*

could satisfy all of his pedagogical needs. Not that the actual work involved in producing a literal commentary was in any way facile—the task of commenting literally on Job was so difficult that it was assumed by Thomas's contemporaries to be impossible[17]—but if it could be done, it would serve as an excellent introduction to the study of theology in general, as well as to the theological question at the center of the book, the doctrine of Providence.[18]

The significance of Thomas's *Literal Exposition on Job* for our study of nature, grace, and the desire for God lies in the way in which Thomas develops his discussion of the doctrine of Providence. This doctrine, as we may recall from chapter 2, plays a central role in his understanding of the desire for God. In *In I Sent.*, d. 39, Thomas had opposed Maimonides's idea that Providence does not extend to sublunary bodies, save those of human beings, by juxtaposing it with God's knowledge of singulars. Since God knows singulars, and since God is good, God orders all singulars (including irrational, sublunary creatures), toward the good as an end. In the *Literal Exposition on Job*, Thomas explains God's Providence over irrational creatures not only by means of God's knowledge of singulars, but also by means

errores elidit, Iob XIII: 'Disputare cum Deo cupio.' Aliud opus eius est non mentiri de quibus novit; et sic dupliciter instruituimur," etc. (emphasis added).

Seeing Thomas's *Literal Commentary on Job* as an introduction to scholastic theology has a number of benefits. First, it fits the available historical data: we know that Thomas had to lecture on Scripture, but it cannot be established that he had to lecture on the *Sentences* and there is no record of his having done so at Orvieto—only at Rome when he had more capable students at the *studium generale* would he again turn to the *Sentences*. Second, it explains why we lack any evidence of further teaching from this period. Third, it helps why Thomas would have had time to compose his immense literary output during this period, including the *Summa contra Gentiles*.

17. Antoine Dondaine, preface to *Expositio super Iob ad litteram* [Leon 26.1:26*].

18. Thomas Aquinas, *Expositio super Iob ad litteram*, prol. [Leon. 26.2:3]: "Post Legem datam et Prophetas, in numero hagiographorum, idest librorum per Spiritum Dei sapienter ad eruditionem hominum conscriptorum, primus ponitur liber Iob, cuius tota intentio circa hoc [that is, Providentiam] versatur ut per probabiles rationes ostendatur res humanas divina providentia regi." The idea that the *Literal Exposition on Job* is intended as a textbook on disputation was first suggested in Martin Yaffe, "Interpretive Essay," in Thomas Aquinas, *The Literal Exposition on Job: A Scriptural Commentary Concerning Divine Providence*, trans. Anthony Damico (Atlanta: Scholars Press, 1989), 28.

of the natural motion which God gives those creatures as a consequence of their having been ordered by divine wisdom.

Commenting on Job 9:5–6, which attributes to God the movement of the earth and of the mountains, Thomas explains:

> It is not unreasonable for [Job] to attribute those things which happen naturally to divine power. For since nature acts for an end, but everything which is ordered to a particular end either directs itself toward the end or is ordered by another who directs it toward the end, it is necessary that a natural thing, which has no knowledge of its end such that it might be able to direct itself toward it, be ordered toward its end by some higher intelligence. For this reason, the whole activity of nature can be compared to an intellect directing natural things toward their end, which we call God.... Wherefore, just as the motion of an arrow is fittingly attributed to the archer, so is the whole operation of nature fittingly attributed to divine power.[19]

God's providence over all creatures includes his providential care over the powers of the soul, which are inclined to their respective ends just like nature in general.[20] This applies to both the intellect and the will, and even to their relationship with one another, because the intellect has priority over the will; the intellect "distinguishes evil from good, so that, having avoided evil, [a person] may arrive at a participation of divine wisdom by the performance of good works."[21] In human beings, the wisdom that leads the intellect

19. Thomas Aquinas, *Expositio super Iob ad litteram*, cap. 9, l. 1 [Leon. 26.2:59]: "Nec autem irrationabiliter ea quae naturaliter continguunt divinae virtuti attribuit: cum enim natura agat propter finem, omne autem quod ad finem certum ordinatur vel se ipsum dirigit in finem vel ab alio dirigente in finem ordinatur, necesse est quod res naturalis, quae finis notitiam non habet ut se in ipsum dirigere possit, ab aliquo superiori intelligente ordinetur in finem. Comparatur igitur tota naturae operatio ad intellectum dirigentem res naturales in finem, quem Deum dicimus.... Unde sicut motus sagittae convenienter sagittatori attribuitur, ita convenienter tota naturae operatio attribuitur virtuti divinae." On God as the cause of natural motion creatures, see also cap. 26, l. 1 [Leon. 26.2:145].

20. On God's inclining the will, see ibid., cap. 12, l. 5 [Leon. 26.2:83].

21. Ibid., cap. 28, l. 2 [Leon. 26.2:155]: "Intelligentia ad hoc praecipue est homini necessaria ut per intelligentiam discernat a bonis mala, quibus evitatis per executionem bonorum operum ad sapientiae divinae participationem perveniat."

to proper moral judgments can be achieved through the sort of intellectual investigation in which Thomas was leading the *fratres communes*.[22] The performance of good works happens in virtue of the will, whose motion can be attributed to God as a primary cause operating through a secondary cause,[23] and which does not rest until it has reached its final end after this life.[24] Even though bad things happen to good people, divine Providence is shown forth among human affairs because of the eternal, spiritual rewards which God gives to the upright after this life, even if he allows the wicked some flitting temporal goods in this life.[25]

Thomas's exegesis of the Book of Job tells us as much about the development of Thomas's thought as it does about Job. It bears a number of similarities with his teaching in *De veritate*: Providence is located in the divine wisdom; it is exercised over rational and non-rational creatures; rational creatures share in God's Providence primarily through the intellect and secondarily through the will, because God acts on the human soul first by moving the intellect, which in turn moves the will by a practical judgment. It also develops his teaching in *De veritate* by emphasizing more rigorously the idea that the powers of the soul, and in particular the intellect, have a particular nature and natural motion. This emphasis on the distinction of God's providential motion within the powers in the soul would pave the way for a breakthrough in Thomas's understanding of the desire for God in the *Summa contra Gentiles*.

22. Ibid.: "Homines ... non per simplicem apprehensionem percipiunt sapientiam veritiatis, sicut angeli quibus enarratur, sed per inquisitionem rationis ad eam perveniunt."

23. Ibid., cap. 10, l. 1 [Leon. 26.2:70–71]. Although the principal point of discussion concerns the process of human generation, Thomas goes on to speak of "seeds of virtue" implanted in the will by God: "simul autem cum anima rationali infunduntur homini divinitus quaedam seminaria virtutum, aliqua quidem communiter omnibus, aliqua vero specialiter aliquibus secundum quod homines quidam sunt naturaliter dispositi ad unam virtutem, quidam ad aliam." Although Thomas does not speak specifically of an "inclination" in the will, we should recall that the conceptual framework of *rationes seminales*, of which the *semina virtutum* are a part, entails such a framework.

24. Ibid., cap. 7, l. 1 [Leon. 26.2:46].

25. Ibid., cap. 28, l. 2 [Leon. 26.2:155].

THE *SUMMA CONTRA GENTILES*

The *Summa contra Gentiles* was a massive undertaking, the beginnings of which overlap with the end of the *De veritate,* but the end of which is roughly contemporaneous with the conclusion of Thomas's stay at Orvieto.[26] Scholars of the last century have disputed at length its scope and purpose. Torrell helpfully summarizes the development of its twentieth-century reception thus: classically it was thought to be a missionary treatise, aimed at Muslim lands;[27] in the mid-twentieth-century Gauthier proposed instead that it was a theological text aimed at Christians;[28] in the 1980s, Patfoort proposed a *via media*: it is a text aimed at the formation of Christian missionaries.[29]

Some version of Patfoort's view seems preferable for two reasons. First, given Thomas's intellectual abilities, it is hard to believe that he would have laid to rest the "synthesizing spirit" that Torrell describes, and not carved out at least some time for more advanced study when he was teaching the *fratres communes.*[30] As we shall see below, he took advantage of the time to catch up on the history of Aristotelian influence at the University of Paris, and so to gain a foothold on the Parisian conversation about nature, grace, and the desire for God independent of the one which Bonaventure's *Commentary on the Sentences* initially afforded him. Second, at least as concerns the desire for God, the *Summa contra Gentiles* is—as we shall see—the most advanced and nuanced work of any that Thomas had pro-

26. Torrell, *Saint Thomas Aquinas,* 1:101–4.

27. Marie-Dominique Chenu, *Toward Understanding Saint Thomas,* trans. A.-M. Landry and D. Hughes (Chicago: Henry Regnery and Co., 1964), 247–48, cited in Torrell, *Saint Thomas Aquinas,* 1:105.

28. R. A. Gauthier, "Introduction historique à S. Thomas d'Aquin," in *Contra Gentiles: Texte de l'édition Léonine,* trans. Réginald Bernier and Maurice Coverz (Paris: Lethielleux, 1961), 1:60–87, cited in Torrell, *Saint Thomas Aquinas,* 1:105.

29. Albert Patfoort, "Le Somme contre les Gentils, école de présentation aux infidèles de la foi chrétienne," in *Saint Thomas d'Aquin. Les clefs d'une théologie* (Paris: FAC, 1983), 103–30, cited in Torrell, *Saint Thomas Aquinas,* 1:105–6.

30. See Torrell, *Saint Thomas Aquinas,* 1:116.

duced to date on the subject. It takes major strides in terms of Thomas's understanding of natural desire in general, and of the natural desire of the intellect in particular.

However much the *Summa contra Gentiles* may stand on its own as a theological synthesis, the missionary character of the synthesis also cannot be denied. In addition to the explanatory character of the theological developments in the *Summa contra Gentiles* for Christians *ad intra*, many of these developments also had an important apologetical function *ad extra*. In the introduction to the work, Thomas says that, when proposing the Christian faith to those who do not share a common belief in any Revelation with Christians, one must appeal to reason.[31] In previous discussions of the desire for God, Thomas had argued that reason could establish that man has a natural desire for happiness, and that this desire must be fulfilled in the next life. In the *Summa contra Gentiles*, Thomas shifts from a temporal argument to a structural argument: examining more carefully and more deeply the structure of the natural desire of the intellect, he now says that reason can prove not only that human beings have a natural desire for beatitude in general, but also that we have a natural desire for the vision of God.

Nature

In *Summa contra Gentiles* 3.97–102, Thomas discusses nature and grace in a very similar way to his treatment of those topics in Book 2 of his *Commentary on the Sentences* and in *De veritate*.[32] At Creation, God communicates to each creature a form, which constitutes that creature's limited participation in a divine idea.[33] On account of that form, the creature possesses actuality, as well as a limited range of

31. Thomas Aquinas, *SCG* 1.2 [Leon. Man. 2]: "quia quidam eorum [Gentilium], ut Mahumetistae et pagani, non conveniunt nobiscum in auctoritate alicuius Scripturae, per quam possint convinci, sicut contra Iudaeos disputare possumus per Vetus Testamentum, contra haereticos per Novum. Hi vero neutrum recipiunt. Unde necesse est ad naturalem rationem recurrere, cui omnes assentire coguntur."

32. Ibid., 3.97–102 [Leon. Man. 343–51].

33. Ibid., 3.97 [Leon. Man. 343–44].

activity flowing from the active powers communicated to the creature by its form.[34] In addition to that limited range of activity, the creature remains susceptible to accidental change through acquiring or receiving accidental forms within the limits of the actuality conferred on the creature by its substantial form.[35] Alluding to the doctrine of *rationes seminales,* Thomas explains that the limited range of activity that the creature possesses by its form is like a seed, from which all its other activity develops. The creature possesses this seed of activity from God. Yet just because God has placed a seed of activity in the creature does not mean that God is bound always and everywhere to act *through* that seed. Sometimes God acts through it, and the creature constitutes an active participant in God's activity; while sometimes God acts directly on creatures, and they become merely passive recipients of his actions.[36]

As in the *Commentary on the Sentences* and *De veritate,* a creature's passive receptivity to accidental change is analogous to Averroes's second nature in simple bodies.[37] For this reason, although creatures remain completely passive with respect to the activity they receive from God above their natural activity, the activity they receive from God is not therefore violent.[38] Since all created nature is in potency to God's action, nothing that God does in nature is against nature (*contra naturam*). Here, Thomas speaks even more strongly than be-

34. Ibid. [Leon. Man. 344].

35. Ibid. [Leon. Man. 344–45].

36. Ibid., 3.99 [Leon. Man. 347]: "Virtus divina comparatur ad omnes virtutes activas sicut virtus universalis ad virtutes particulares, sicut per supra dicta patet. Virtus autem activa universalis ad particularem effectum producendum determinari potest dupliciter. Uno modo, per causam mediam particularem: sicut virtus activa caelestis corporis determinatur ad effectum generationis humanae per virtutem particularem quae est in semine; sicut et in syllogismis virtus propositionis universalis determinatur ad conclusionem particularem per assumptionem particularem. Alio modo, per intellectum, qui determinatam formam apprehendit, et eam in effectum producit. Divinus autem intellectus non solum est cognoscitivus suae essentiae, quae est quasi universalis virtus activa; neque etiam tantum universalium et primarum causarum; sed omnium particularium, sicut per supra dicta patet. Potest igitur producere immediate omnem effectum quem producit quodcumque particulare agens."

37. Ibid. [Leon. Man. 348]. See also 3.23 [Leon. Man. 248].

38. Ibid., 3.99 [Leon. Man. 349]. See also 3.23 [Leon. Man. 249].

fore: even if God's action results in the corruption of a form already in a creature, this would still be "natural corruption," since the creature was in potency to undergo such a corruption.[39]

Since what God does immediately in nature is not against nature, Thomas suggests that one can distinguish three ways in which God acts in nature but beyond nature (*praeter naturam*) when he performs a miracle. Sometimes he acts completely above the potential of nature, as when he makes two bodies exist in the same place, or makes the sun stop in its place; sometimes he achieves an end which nature could bring about but causes it immediately by circumventing the natural means to that end, like when he makes the blind see or the lame walk; sometimes he achieves an end which nature *could* achieve by the means that nature would employ to achieve it, but does so when nature was not going to achieve that effect on its own, as when he heals the sick.[40] In all of these cases, even the last one, only God can work a miracle. If a creature were to do so, the so-called miracle would fall within the range of that creature's natural activity and would by definition constitute a natural action, not a miracle.[41]

Grace

As in the *Commentary on the Sentences* and *De veritate*, the reception of grace is not a miracle, even if it is in some way beyond the power of nature to perform acts under the influence of grace. Rather, the reception of grace involves the reception of an accidental form which exceeds the active potential of nature, but not its passive, or "material" potential.

39. Ibid., 3.100 [Leon. Man. 349] "Quod . . . est in potentia secundum ordinem naturalem in respectu alicuius agentis, si aliquid imprimatur in ipsum ab alio agente, non est contra naturam simpliciter, etsi sit aliquando contrarium particulari formae quae corrumpitur per huiusmodi actionem: cum enim generatur ignis et corrumpitur aer igne agente, est generatio et corruptio naturalis. Quicquid igitur a Deo fit in rebus creatis, non est contra naturam, etsi videatur esse contra ordinem proprium alicuius naturae."

40. Ibid., 3.101 [Leon. Man. 350].

41. Ibid., 3.102 [Leon. Man. 350–51].

Now, from what has been said it is clear that man cannot merit the help of God. For everything is oriented *materially* toward that which is above it [*supra ipsam*]. But matter cannot move itself to its own perfection; rather, it is necessary that it be moved by another. Man, therefore, does not move himself to acquire the help of God, which is above him [*supra ipsum*], but rather he is moved by God to acquire this.[42]

If human nature has no active potential to acquire grace, that does not mean that grace is violent (similar to what Thomas had Bacon objecting in the *Commentary on the Sentences*). It belongs to human nature to receive grace, just as it belongs to an element's nature to receive change. Humans receive grace in accordance with human nature, not against it.[43] But since the form by which grace is conferred upon a human person orients that person toward an end that is above the natural activity of human nature,[44] that form can be said to be a "supernatural form" (*forma supernaturalis*) which "is superadded" (*superaddatur*) to nature, even if it is not above the passive principle of human nature.[45] The reception of a supernatural form enables a human person to achieve an end which is completely above the natural activity of human nature, conferring perfections which are "above our natural potencies" (*super naturales potentias*).[46]

42. Ibid., 3.149 [Leon. Man. 407]: "Ex dictis autem manifeste ostenditur quod auxilium divinum homo promereri non potest. Quaelibet enim res ad id quod supra ipsam est, *materialiter* se habet. Materia autem non movet seipsam ad suam perfectionem, sed oportet quod ab alio moveatur. Homo igitur non movet seipsum ad hoc quod adipiscatur divinum auxilium, quod supra ipsum est, sed potius ad hoc adipiscendum a Deo movetur" (emphasis added).

43. Ibid., 3.148 [Leon. Man. 406].

44. Ibid., 3.150 [Leon. Man. 409].

45. Ibid.: "Unumquodque ordinatur in finem sibi convenientem secundum rationem suae formae: diversarum enim specierum diversi sunt fines. Sed finis in quem homo dirigitur per auxilium divinae gratiae, est supra naturam humanam. Ergo oportet quod homini superaddatur aliqua supernaturalis forma et perfectio, per quam convenienter ordinetur in finem praedictum."

46. Ibid.: "Divina providentia omnibus providet secundum modum suae naturae, ut ex supra dictis patet. Est autem hic modus proprius hominum, quod ad perfectionem suarum operationum oportet eis inesse, super naturales potentias, quasdam perfectiones et habitus, quibus quasi connaturaliter et faciliter et delectabiliter bonum et bene operen-

Natural Desire

As in the *Commentary on the Sentences* and *De veritate,* Thomas uses the term "natural appetite" in a variety of ways. Sometimes he uses it to describe the ordering of non-rational creatures as directed toward their perfection by the divine intellect.[47] This includes the desire of matter for form.[48] At other times, natural appetite describes the ordering of rational and non-rational creatures alike toward their highest perfection.[49] In rational creatures, this includes the activity of the will when it has been directed by the intellect.[50] It also includes each of the powers of the soul considered in themselves and not in relation to one another.[51]

As in *De veritate,* Thomas expressly states that "natural inclination" can be used in some ways interchangeably with "natural appetite."[52] Accordingly, we find him using the term "natural inclination" to refer to many of the same realities as "natural appetite" does.[53] Yet if we examine his use of terms closely, Thomas also introduces a new way of using the term "natural inclination," which does not correspond to any of his uses of the term "natural appetite": to denote the

tur. Igitur auxilium gratiae, quod homo a Deo consequitur ad perveniendum in ultimum finem, aliquam formam et perfectionem homini inesse designat."

47. Ibid., 1.72 [Leon. Man. 69]; 2.47 [Leon. Man. 140]; 3.24–26 [Leon. Man. 250–56]; 3.95 [Leon. Man. 341]; 3.108 [Leon. Man. 359].

48. Ibid., 2.83 [Leon. Man. 197]; 3.23 [Leon. Man. 249].

49. Ibid., 2.55 [Leon. Man. 149]. See also 1.91 [Leon. Man. 82], 2.79 [Leon. Man. 188]; 2.82 [Leon. Man. 194]; 3.19 [Leon. Man. 243]; 3.48 [Leon. Man. 277]; 3.59 [Leon. Man. 290].

50. Of the texts mentioned in the previous footnote, see specifically ibid., 2.55 [Leon. Man. 149]; 2.79 [Leon. Man. 188]; 2.82 [Leon. Man. 193–95].

51. Ibid., 4.36 [Leon. Man. 490]. On the intellect specifically, see 1.4 [Leon. Man. 4], 1.61 [Leon. Man. 57]; 3.59 [Leon. Man. 290]; 3.88 [Leon. Man. 331]. On the will, see 4.19 [Leon. Man. 461].

52. See, for example, ibid., 1.68 [Leon. Man. 64]; 2.55 [Leon. Man. 149]; 3.88 [Leon. Man. 331]; 4.19 [Leon. Man. 461].

53. Sometimes "natural inclination" refers to the ordering of non-rational creatures toward their end, especially as distinct from the "rational inclination" in rational creatures, which is the will; see ibid., 3.24 [Leon. Man. 250]; 3.26 [Leon. Man. 255]; 3.85 [Leon. Man. 327]; 3.114 [Leon. Man. 366], 3.143 [Leon. Man. 401], 4.19 [Leon. Man. 461]. Sometimes it refers to the ordering of the will toward its end; see 3.109 [Leon. Man. 361].

ordering of an individual member of a species to the good of the species as such, not the good of the specific individual as such.[54] This suggests that Thomas thinks of inclination as a broader category than appetite. This will become important later in his career, but for now we may note that the underlying structure of Thomas's thought about the ordering of material principles in nature toward their perfection remains the same as it was in chapter 2: both appetite and inclination indicate a passive ordering in nature toward an end as distinct from the motion by which a nature moves toward that end. Adding motion to an appetite or inclination transforms it into a desire.[55]

As in the *Commentary on the Sentences*, Thomas's treatment of natural change and natural desire corresponds with his treatment of nature and grace, because just as all creatures have a certain range of natural activity on account of their form, so also do they possess a natural inclination by which they always tend toward the good of their nature. In connection with his emphasis on Providence in the *Commentary on Job*, Thomas explains that this tendency is evident in nature even among those things which receive the perfection of their nature from another, and can be accounted for in the following way: all creatures are subject to the providence and influence of God; but God is an agent who acts for an end; therefore the fact that all things in nature seek their good is the effect of God's directing

54. See ibid., 3.113 [Leon. Man. 365]; [Leon. Man. 394]. This meaning of the term "natural inclination" is particularly germane to Thomas's teaching about natural law. See Fulvio di Blasi, "Natural Law as Inclination to God," *Nova et Vetera* (English) 7, no. 2 (2009): 344–47.

55. Unlike in the *Commentary on the Sentences* and the *De veritate*, Thomas does not explicitly state this difference in the *Summa contra Gentiles*. However, the way in which he speaks about desire makes a consistent association between desire and motion. See, for example, *SCG* 3.88 [Leon. Man. 330–31]: "Ab illo agente aliquid natum est moveri et pati per cuius formam reduci potest in actum: nam omne agens agit per formam suam. Voluntas autem reducitur in actum per appetibile, quod motum desiderii eius quietat. In solo autem bono divino quietatur desiderium voluntatis sicut in ultimo fine, ut ex supra dictis patet. Solus igitur Deus potest movere voluntatem per modum agentis."

For other examples of the association between motion and desire, see *SCG* 1.20 [Leon. Man. 22]; 1.37 [Leon. Man. 35–36]; 1.42 [Leon. Man. 38]; 1.101 [Leon. Man. 91]; 2.70 [Leon. Man. 169]; 3.48 [Leon. Man. 277]; 3.50 [Leon. Man. 281–82]; 3.62 [Leon. Man. 293–94]; 3.64 [Leon. Man. 296]; 3.95 [Leon. Man. 340–41]; 4.95 [Leon. Man. 565].

them toward himself as that end.[56] Since God's direction of all creatures toward himself occurs *through* the substantial forms of those creatures,[57] each creature seeks God naturally in accordance with the potential conferred upon it by its form.[58]

As in the *Commentary on the Sentences* and the *De veritate,* Thomas identifies a natural appetite or inclination in the intellect as well as the will. Following the *De veritate,* Thomas is clear that among these two, the intellect is the "superior mover" (*superior motor*) in the soul,[59] and within the intellect, the agent intellect.[60] The agent intellect moves the possible intellect and causes an intelligible species to be actualized in it; the possible intellect, formed by that intelligible species, moves the will.[61]

Concerning the manner in which the agent intellect serves as the superior mover in the soul, Thomas develops his thinking from the *Commentary on the Sentences* and the *De veritate.* In both of those texts, Thomas was clear that the formal, active principle of the *ratio seminalis* in the intellect is the agent intellect, and that the agent intellect impresses upon the possible intellect an innate knowledge of the first principles of speculative and practical reasoning as the possible intellect's first habitual determination. In the *Summa contra*

56. Ibid., 3.17 [Leon. Man. 241–42]. That the end that God intends is himself, see 3.18–21 [Leon. Man. 242–46]. On the motion of irrational creatures toward their end, see 3.24 [Leon. Man. 250]. Thomas explicitly connects his thoughts about inclinations and ends with the doctrine of Providence in 3.65–67 [Leon. Man. 297–301].

57. Ibid., 3.67 [Leon. Man. 300–301].

58. Ibid., 3.25 [Leon. Man. 261]: "Cum autem omnes creaturae, etiam intellectu carentes, ordinentur in Deum sicut in finem ultimum; ad hunc autem finem pertingunt omnia inquantum de similitudine eius aliquid participant."

59. Ibid., 3.25 [Leon. Man. 253]: "In omnibus agentibus et moventibus ordinatis oportet quod finis primi agentis et motoris sit ultimus finis omnium: sicut finis ducis exercitus est finis omnium sub eo militantium. Inter omnes autem hominis partes, intellectus invenitur superior motor: nam intellectus movet appetitum, proponendo ei suum obiectum; appetitus autem intellectivus, qui est voluntas, movet appetitus sensitivos .... Finis igitur intellectus est finis omnium actionum humanarum.... Et per consequens ultimus finis primum verum. Est igitur ultimus finis totius hominis, et omnium operationum et desideriorum eius, cognoscere primum verum, quod est Deus." See Hütter, *Dust Bound for Heaven*, 220.

60. Thomas Aquinas, *SCG* 2.76 [Leon. Man. 183–84].

61. Ibid.

Gentiles, he still speaks of the agent intellect as the formal active principle of the *ratio seminalis* in the intellect, but he emphasizes more clearly the distance between the agent intellect and the first principles of demonstration. The reason for this distance, he tells us, is that there were some people (that is, William of Auvergne, to whom we will return in a moment) who thought that the active principle in the soul *was* the habit of the first principles.[62] In response, Thomas notes that the habit of the first principles is not impressed by the agent intellect on the possible intellect immediately; it is caused by the agent intellect in the possible intellect according to forms which are received from sensible objects.[63]

Rather than explain more directly how the impression of the first principles of speculative and practical reasoning upon the possible intellect occurs, Thomas refers us to Book 2 of Aristotle's *Posterior Analytics.*[64] There, Aristotle considers whether our knowledge of the first principles is innate or acquired. If those principles are innate, how do some people not notice them? But if they are acquired, how can they be acquired without the assistance of prior knowledge? Aristotle's conclusion about the intellect is very similar to what Thomas had said about the natural appetite of the will in *De veritate*: it is part of the structure of the agent intellect that, when it abstracts universals from particular sense objects, it abstracts them according to the pattern of the first principles. The knowledge of those first principles is the first habit which the agent intellect educes from the possible intellect when a person begins to think.[65]

62. See William of Auvergne, *De anima,* 7.5–6 [Hotot 2:210–12]. It is not that William assents to the proposition "the agent intellect is the habit of the first principles," but that William has the habit of the first principles function in the soul in the place that Thomas assigns to the agent intellect. See Gilson, "Pourquoi saint Thomas a critiqué saint Augustin," 62: "Guillaume d'Auvergne ne se passe d'intellect agent que parce que Dieu sera là pour conférer à notre intellect les premiers intelligibles par mode d'illumination." Roger Bacon followed William here. See the texts referenced by Gilson on p. 81n1, as well as Gilson's comments on pp. 106–9.

63. Thomas Aquinas, *SCG* 2.78 [Leon. Man. 186].

64. Aristotle, *Posterior Analytics* 2.19 [99b14–100b17].

65. See especially ibid., 2.19 [100b3–17].

Although Thomas discusses how the intellect acts as first mover in the soul, he does not dwell at length in the *Summa contra Gentiles* about the difficult theological questions that arise from this teaching such as those concerning the sin of Adam and Eve and the act of faith. When he speaks of the sin of Adam and Eve, he merely assumes from Revelation the historical fact that it happened; the rest of his argument is an apologetic for the Christian belief that original sin is transmitted to posterity by the process of generation.[66] When he speaks of the act of faith, he does make one small adjustment. In the *De veritate* he had backed away from the idea that a judgment about signs and/or people could ground the prudence of the act of faith, because both signs and people are fallible. This had the benefit of providing a more solid basis for the prudence of the act of faith, but it also compromised the central role of the preacher in inviting people to that faith. No doubt aware of the negative implications that this would have for missionary activity, Thomas returns in the *Summa contra Gentiles* to the idea that human testimony grounds the prudence of the act of faith. However, instead of basing that prudence on the immediate authority of the fallible preacher bearing witness to the faith, Thomas now recognizes in his argument that a person who bears witness to the Christian faith today will have himself received a testimony of that faith from someone else. Tracking this line of preaching backwards, and forming what we might call a chain of "predicatory causality," he argues that the authority of human testimony given today is itself grounded historically in the person from whom that testimony was originally received. Ultimately, therefore, the authority of human preaching is grounded in two sources: Christ, who is infallible of himself, and who alone among men comprehends the truth of the mysteries he revealed; as well as the prophets and apostles, who received their testimony directly from God and so participate by grace in the infallibility which he possesses by nature.[67]

66. Thomas treats original sin in *SCG* 4.50 [Leon. Man. 505–6], and then responds to objections against the idea that it is transmitted to posterity in 4.51 and 4.52 [Leon. Man. 506–10].

67. Ibid., 3.40 [Leon. Man. 265].

The Natural Desire for God

As in the *Commentary on the Sentences,* the final end of an intellectual creature occurs in the highest act of its highest potency (intellectual understanding) ordered toward the highest object (God, as "the most perfect of intelligibles"). This means that the ultimate end of an intellectual creature's natural appetite is to know God.[68] But also as in *De veritate,* we can imagine two ways in which an intellectual creature could be said to have a natural appetite to know God: 1) in its intellect, as perfected materially by knowing God directly; 2) in its will, as perfected formally by knowing God indirectly through the intellect.[69]

Although Thomas had acknowledged a natural appetite in the intellect in *De veritate,* he had not devoted significant attention to explaining what the natural desire following from that appetite looks like. Here it is otherwise. Thomas makes the natural desire of the intellect the center-piece of his discussion of human happiness.[70]

There was precedent in the thirteenth century for conceiving of a natural desire in the intellect as distinct from the natural desire of the will. As we saw in chapter 1, the distinction is found in the *De anima* of William of Auvergne, the same bishop of Paris who, as we saw in chapter 2, condemned Guerric of Saint-Quentin and Hugh of Saint-Cher in 1241 for holding that the intellect cannot see God in the next life. Dondaine has already observed that William's *De anima* was something of a proving ground, where William worked out

68. Ibid., 3.25 [Leon. Man. 251].

69. Ibid., 3.88–89 [Leon. Man. 330–32], especially 3.89 [Leon. Man. 332]. See also Lottin, *Psychologie et morale,* 1:258. Thomas makes a similar comment with regard to the way in which faith interacts with the other theological virtues in *SCG* 3.149 [Leon. Man. 407]; 3.152 [Leon. Man. 410].

70. Hütter, *Dust Bound for Heaven,* 188: "the *desiderium naturale visionis Dei* as considered in Book 3 of the *Summa contra Gentiles* belongs to the principle of nature in its relative integrity as it pertains to the metaphysical constitution of the *intellectus.*" Hütter's subsequent account of *intellectus* (ibid., 208–15) draws significantly on the *Summa theologiae,* but he still preserves Thomas's account of the motive priority of the intellect in the *Summa contra Gentiles* (ibid., 220).

the reasoning behind the condemnation as well as the text of it.[71] Evidently reading more widely into the context of the condemnation, which had already influenced Thomas's thought in the *Commentary on the Sentences*, Thomas appropriated William's argument concerning the natural desire of the intellect, although he purged it of almost—but not all—of its Avicennian influence.

William's text was quoted in chapter 1. However, it will be useful to repeat a portion of it here so that it may be compared more easily to the text of the *Summa contra Gentiles*:

Aristotle's observation, when he says that "all men by nature desire to know," is certain as can be. Since, therefore, a desire of this sort is a spiritual hunger, it is also equally a natural hunger. But a hunger placed within us is vain if it is impossible for it to be satisfied naturally. [Therefore] it is necessary that it be possible to satisfy the human soul's hunger for knowing. And since the human soul only has a hunger of this sort according to its intellective power, it is necessary that the intellective power be satiable by a satisfaction which completely fills this sort of hunger, and leaves no vestige of it in the intellective power. And since there is no satisfaction of our hunger for knowledge except that which feasts on the fullness of knowledge, it is necessary for that knowable, by the knowledge of which our intellective power enjoys complete satisfaction, also to possess such a luminosity as to leave no darkness at all in the intellective power (I mean the darkness of ignorance, opinion, and doubt), but to satisfy and fill the whole of it, with its illumination [*irradiatio*].

Furthermore, only the blessed creator can be a knowable of this sort. For however well known by however much knowledge every other knowable may be known, if he alone is unknown, there remains in the human soul in its intellective power the darkness of not knowing the creator, and the most vehement hunger to know him.[72]

71. Dondaine, "L'objet et le 'medium' de la vision béatifique," 93.

72. William of Auvergne, *De anima*, cap. 7, pars 2 [Hotot 2:204b]: "certissimus est sermo Aristotelis quo dicit quod omnes homines natura scire desiderant. Quia igitur desiderium hujusmodi fames spiritualis est, pariter et naturalis; frustra autem indita est fames, cujus naturaliter impossibilis est satietas, necesse est satietatem sciendi possibilem esse apud animam humanam: et quoniam hujusmodi fames non est animae humanae nisi secundum virtutem intellectivam, necesse est virtutem intellectivam satiabilem esse satietate quae famem hujusmodi plane repleat, nullumque ejusdem vestigium in virtute intellectiva relinquat: et quoniam fames scientiae non habet satietatem, nisi ipsam quae

At this point, we can pause and compare William's argument to an argument which Thomas makes for the first time in the *Summa contra Gentiles,* based upon the natural desire of the intellect:

There is a desire, which is in all men naturally, of knowing the causes of the things they see. According to this principle, men first began to philosophize on account of their wonder at the things they saw, whose causes remained hidden, while they would rest when they discovered a cause. But this investigation did not stop until it arrive at the *first* cause: and "we consider ourselves to know perfectly when we arrive at the first cause" [Aristotle, *Metaphysics* 1.3 (983a24–26)]. Therefore, man naturally desires to know the first cause as his ultimate end. But the first cause of all things is God. Therefore, the ultimate end of man is to know God.[73]

Thomas's argument reads like a streamlined version William's. It focuses exclusively on the natural desire of the intellect, it takes as its starting point the text from Aristotle's *Metaphysics* with which William had begun his argument, and it concludes, as had William, that the intellect can only be satisfied by knowledge of the first cause.

However, if we read Thomas's argument *solely* as a more succinct version of William's, we risk overlooking a profound difference between the two arguments. As we saw in chapter 1, William goes on to argue that the natural inclination of the intellect indicates that it finds its perfection in the beatific vision. Thomas had previous-

---

esuritur scientiae plenitudinem; necesse est scibile illud, cujus scilicet scientia satietas est plena virtutis intellectivae nostrae, ejus luminositatis esse ut nihil omnino tenebrarum, et intendo tenebrarum ignorantiae, opinionis, et dubitationis in virtute intellectiva relinquat, sed eam irradiatione sua totam satiet ac repleat.

"Porro scibile hujusmodi non potest esse nisi creator benedictus, omnibus enim aliis scibilibus quantacumque perfectione cognitionis notissimis, illo autem solo ignorato remanet apud animam humanam in virtute intellectiva ipsius tenebrositas ignorantiae creatoris, et fames vehementissima cognitionis illius. . . ."

73. Thomas Aquinas, *SCG* 3.25 [Leon. Man. 253]: "Naturaliter inest omnibus hominibus desiderium cognoscendi causas eorum quae videntur: unde propter admirationem eorum quae videbantur, quorum causae latebant, homines primo philosophari coeperunt, invenientes autem causam quiescebant. Nec sistit inquisitio quousque perveniatur ad primam causam: et 'tunc perfecte nos scire arbitramur quando primam causam cognoscimus.' Desiderat igitur homo naturaliter cognoscere primam causam quasi ultimum finem. Prima autem omnium causa Deus est. Est igitur ultimus finis hominis cognoscere Deum."

ly argued against the idea of a determinate natural inclination toward God (it would, on Thomas's understanding, make error about God impossible, as well as sin), but there was one thing that William's understanding of the natural inclination of the intellect could do that Thomas's previous arguments could not. William had correctly observed that the Aristotelian tradition, broadly conceived, posited man's highest happiness in a return to the soul's origin. William then almost undercut the entire Aristotelian tradition by arguing that the soul comes from God, that the soul has a capacity for God, and that the soul cannot be satisfied by anything less than the complete fulfillment of that capacity in the vision of God. While Thomas had agreed with the first two of those points, he had disagreed with the last point; he had thus left room for the possibility that, should God choose not to fulfill the passive potency of the soul completely, its active principle might reach a resting place short of the complete fulfillment of the passive principle.

In subsequent chapters of the *Summa contra Gentiles*, Thomas looks for a way to exclude the possibility that human happiness might occur in something less than God, without abandoning his basic understanding of matter, form, appetite, and desire. In this regard, he considers the range of opinions among the Aristotelian commentators about how human nature reaches its final end:[74] as the *terminus* of speculation (Avempace),[75] as the perfection of generation (Alexander of Aphrodisias),[76] as union with a separate intellect which all intellectual creatures share in common (Averroes),[77] as union with separate substances (Themistius),[78] or whether, adding a Latin theologian to the list of Greek and Arabic philosophers, it comes through an intuition of the soul (as Thomas reports that

74. See Hütter, *Dust Bound for Heaven*, 228.
75. Thomas Aquinas, *SCG* 3.41 [Leon. Man. 265–67].
76. Ibid., 3.42 [Leon. Man. 267–69].
77. Ibid., 3.43 [Leon. Man. 269–71].
78. Ibid., 3.45 [Leon. Man. 273–74].

some reputed to have gathered from the words of Augustine).[79] Like William, Thomas wanted to dispense with all of these arguments on an *a priori* basis. But since Thomas understood natural desire differently than William, Thomas had to find a different argument. His solution was to fault the array of opinions just mentioned not for positing man's perfection in an object other than the vision of God, but for positing it in an act which is metaphysically impossible: each one placed the happiness of man in this life in a direct knowledge of a separated substance; but since all human knowledge in this life is drawn from our understanding of material things, we cannot understand separated substances;[80] nor for the same reason can we see God in this life.[81] We can have in this life a certain knowledge of immaterial substance through analogy,[82] but this analogy is imperfect. The object of our knowledge always remains unknown to us to a certain extent.[83]

By arguing that the Aristotelian commentators all proposed something impossible as man's final end, Thomas undercut *almost* the entire Aristotelian tradition almost as effectively as William had. I say "almost," because unlike William, Thomas left Aristotle himself unscathed. As we saw in chapter 2, Thomas understood Aristotle to teach that the perfection of man is in analogical knowledge of God as first cause that can be had in this life.[84] Since this sort of knowledge is possible—unlike the various forms of knowledge posited by the Aristotelian commentators—Thomas's argument did not exclude it *a priori* the way that William's had.

79. Ibid., 3.46 [Leon. Man. 274–75].

80. Ibid., 3.45 [Leon. Man. 273]. Thomas dismisses the possibility of knowing separate substances though an intuition of the human soul in 3.46 [Leon. Man. 274].

81. Ibid., 3.47 [Leon. Man. 275]: "Si autem alias substantias separatas in hac vita intelligere non possumus, propter connaturalitatem intellectus nostri ad phantasmata, multo minus in hac vita divinam essentiam videre possumus, quae transcendit omnes substantias separatas."

82. Ibid., 1.36 [Leon. Man. 34].

83. Ibid., 3.39 [Leon. Man. 263].

84. Ibid., 3.44 [Leon. Man. 272].

The Natural Desire for the Vision of God

In *Summa contra Gentiles* 3.39, Thomas gives, among other considerations, three versions of an argument based upon the desire of a potency for actualization to show why, although Aristotle's analogical knowledge of God is metaphysically possible, it cannot be our final end.[85] The general contour of all three arguments is this: our final end is not reached until our natural desire is fulfilled, and our natural desire is not sated until our highest potency is completely actualized; but the analogical knowledge of God leaves some potency of our intellect in some manner unactualized; therefore, the analogical knowledge of God cannot be our final end.

The first of the three arguments does not suggest anything which we have not encountered in Thomas's previous work. It restates what Thomas had said in the *Commentary on the Sentences* and in *De veritate* about the fact that man's ultimate happiness requires the fulfillment of the soul's natural appetite. There is something new about the second and third arguments, however. They both seem to borrow from William, and they both presuppose some motion toward our final end. That is to say, they begin from our natural *desire* rather than our natural *appetite*; on the basis of our natural desire, they both conclude that the analogical knowledge of God is not a sufficient final end for man.

Since the third argument is more detailed than the second, and since it restates and includes what is covered by the second, it will be useful to review the text of the third argument here:

> The end of anything that exists in potency is to be led into act; for it tends toward this through the motion whereby it is moved toward its end. Moreover, each and every being which is in potency tends toward being in act *insofar as is possible* [*secundum quod est possibile*]. Now, there is one sort of thing which exists in potency whose whole potency can be reduced into act; wherefore the end of this [sort of creature] is to be totally reduced into act; like a heavy thing is in potency toward its proper place when it

85. Ibid., 3.39 [Leon. Man. 263–64].

exists outside the center. But there is another sort of thing whose whole potency cannot be reduced into act at the same time, as is the case with prime matter; wherefore by its motion it desires to come forth into the act of different forms successively (on account of the differences among these forms, they cannot be in it at the same time). Now then, our intellect is in potency to everything that can be understood, as was said in Book 2. But in the intellect's first act, which is knowledge, two intelligible things can exist in it at the same time, although perhaps not in its second act, which is consideration. From this line of reasoning it is clear that the whole potency of the possible intellect can be reduced into act at the same time. Therefore, this [simultaneous reduction into act] is required for its ultimate end, which is happiness. But the aforementioned knowledge which can be had of God by demonstration does not do this, since when we have it, we still do not know many things. Therefore, this sort of knowledge of God is not sufficient for our ultimate happiness.[86]

In terms of the metaphysics of matter and form, as well as the metaphysics of natural desire, this argument marks a significant development over Thomas's previous work. Where previously Thomas had assigned our natural appetite and natural desire two different ends, he unites them here by introducing the condition "insofar as is possible" into natural desire.

The source of the condition appears to have been Avicenna. For Avicenna, as we saw in chapter 1, the souls of the heavenly bodies desire to be assimilated to their respective first causes, but, being tied

86. Ibid., 3.39 [Leon. Man. 364]: "Finis cuiuslibet existentis in potentia est ut ducatur in actum: ad hoc enim tendit per motum, quo movetur in finem. Tendit autem unumquodque ens in potentia ad hoc quod sit actu *secundum quod est possibile*. Aliquid enim est existens in potentia cuius tota potentia potest reduci in actum: unde huius finis est ut totaliter in actum reducatur; sicut grave, extra medium existens, est in potentia ad proprium ubi. Aliquid vero cuius potentia tota non potest simul in actum reduci, sicut patet de materia prima: unde per suum motum appetit successive in actum diversarum formarum exire, quae sibi, propter earum diversitatem, simul inesse non possunt. Intellectus autem noster est in potentia ad omnia intelligibilia, ut in Secundo dictum est. Duo autem intelligibilia possunt simul in intellectu possibili existere secundum actum primum, qui est scientia: licet forte non secundum actum secundum, qui est consideratio. Ex quo patet quod tota potentia intellectus possibilis potest reduci simul in actum. Hoc igitur requiritur ad eius ultimum finem, qui est felicitas. Hoc autem non facit praedicta cognitio quae de Deo per demonstrationem haberi potest: quia, ea habita, adhuc multa ignoramus. Non est igitur talis cognitio Dei sufficiens ad ultimam felicitatem" (emphasis added).

to their bodies, they cannot. Consequently, they exist in a situation analogous to human nature: as spiritual substances, they are capable of union with a higher spiritual substance, but their nature does not confer upon them an active power capable of causing that union. In order to explain the discrepancy between their active and passive powers, Avicenna had introduced a condition into their natural desire; in Latin it was rendered the same way as Thomas's condition: "its intention is to be assimilated to its first [cause], insofar as is possible [*secundum quod possibile est*]."[87] If the soul of the heavenly body were able to perform some action by which it might be assimilated completely to the heavenly body, it would perform that action unhesitatingly; but since it lacks an active potency adequate to that assimilation, it contents itself with the highest perfection which it is capable of causing in itself, the unceasing orbit of its body.

Although Thomas avoided Avicenna's account of motion generally speaking, Avicenna's account of the natural desire of the souls of the heavenly bodies thus provided the key for Thomas to harmonize the Aristotelian and Augustinian traditions, and so to balance Augustine's anti-Pelagian concern about the motion of the human soul toward the vision of God with Aristotle's concern about the teleology of natural desire. The soul, for Augustine, seeks its own happiness first and foremost. For Thomas, relying on Avicenna, this means that it seeks with a natural desire the fulfillment of its natural appetite insofar as is possible. When the intellect receives a motion that is insufficient to cause or lead to the vision of God, the soul uses that motion to pursue the highest happiness that it can achieve with that motion. But when the human intellect receives by grace a motion that is sufficient to cause or lead to the vision of God, it will use that motion, according to *that very same desire*, to reach its ultimate end. The soul can therefore be said to have a natural desire for the vision of God, in such a way that respects the teleology of natural motion, without therefore

87. Avicenna, *Prima philosophia*, 9.2 [van Riet 2:459]: "intentio eius est assimilari primo, secundum quod possibile est." See Donati, "Is Celestial Motion a Natural Motion?" 97.

asserting, contrary to Augustine, that the soul moves toward the vision of God without grace.[88]

The idea that we have in some sense a natural desire for the vision of God necessitated a reworking of Thomas's previous teaching that our natural desire terminates in the analogical knowledge of God through demonstration. He reworks this teaching in *Summa contra Gentiles* 3.48 by updating his argument from the *Commentary on the Sentences* about how natural desire cannot be satisfied in this life.[89] First he uses the argument about the natural desire of the intellect from *Metaphysics* 1.3 to show that man's final happiness cannot be in this life. Then he adds to it the argument from the *Commentary on the Sentences* that our beatitude cannot be found in this life because our natural desire would be frustrated by the vicissitudes of this life. On the basis of these arguments, Thomas reaches the same conclusion as he had in the *Commentary on the Sentences*, but adds to it a consideration of the separate substances: "the final happiness of man will be in the knowledge of God which the human mind has after this life, in the manner in which the separate substances know God."[90]

The introduction of the separate substances into Thomas's argument about man's final end raised a question which Thomas had not

88. William's *De anima* 6.25 [Hotot 2:184a], makes a similar, but not identical argument: "Amplius inter scibilia omnia nobilissimum etiam est creator, et scientia ejus tanto amplius aliis desiderabilibus, quanto ipse omnibus scibilibus supereminet, aliorum igitur scibilium scientiis *si esset possibile* acquisitis restaret desiderium, et fames cognitionis ipsius creatoris: absque cognitione igitur ipsius non est possibile naturaliter ut quiescat desiderium hujusmodi vel sedetur fames, vel antedicta vacuitas impleatur." William uses the condition, *si esset possibile* differently than Thomas uses Avicenna's *secundum quod est possibile*. For Thomas, it refers to a condition built into our natural desire. For William it merely sets up a counter-factual: if it were possible to attain all the knowledge of the sciences, then we would still have a desire to see God.

William was fiercely critical of Avicenna's account of the souls of the heavenly bodies. See Gilson, "Pourquoi Saint Thomas a critiqué Saint Augustin," 49–51.

89. Thomas Aquinas, *SCG* 3.48 [Leon. Man. 277–79]. The first and fourth arguments of this chapter fall into this category.

90. Ibid. [Leon. Man. 279]: "Erit igitur ultima felicitas hominis in cognitione Dei quam habet humana mens post hanc vitam, per modum quo ipsum cognoscunt substantiae separatae."

addressed in the *Commentary on the Sentences*: since after this life the separated soul possesses a mode of existence which is analogous to that of the angels, are there any grounds for saying that separated souls and angels cannot be fully satisfied by the analogical knowledge of God as first cause? Thomas makes two observations in this regard. First, although the angels know God in a different manner than us because they can have intuitive self-knowledge, nevertheless without grace their intellects still only know God analogically.[91] Hence, although their natural knowledge of God is better than ours, it does not fulfill their natural appetite for knowing God any more than our natural knowledge fulfills ours.[92] Thomas even goes so far as to deploy his new argument from *Metaphysics* 1.3 in the service of angelic felicity: since the angels have a natural desire to know the cause of things, their intellectual desire is not satisfied until they know the cause of their own being in its essence; anything less only increases their desire to know.[93]

On the basis that men and angels have a natural desire to know God and that nothing that men or angels can achieve from their natural motion in this life or in the next can completely fulfill that desire, Thomas concludes at length that it must be possible for us to see God, and that the vision of God is the only possible final end for human nature. "Since … it is impossible that a natural desire be in vain, which it would indeed be if it were not possible to arrive at an understanding of the divine essence, which all minds naturally desire, it is necessary to say that it is possible for the substance of God

91. Ibid., 3.49 [Leon. Man. 280]: "Cognoscit tamen substantia separata per suam substantiam de Deo quia est; et quod est omnium causa; et eminentem omnibus; et remotum ab omnibus, non solum quae sunt, sed etiam quae mente creata concipi possunt. Ad quam etiam cognitionem de Deo nos utcumque pertingere possumus: per effectus enim de Deo cognoscimus quia est, quod causa aliorum est, aliis supereminens, et ab omnibus remotus. Et hoc est ultimum et perfectissimum nostrae cognitionis in hac vita, ut Dionysius dicit." He continues: "Quia vero natura inferior in sui summo non nisi ad infimum superioris naturae attingit, oportet quod haec ipsa cognitio sit eminentior in substantiis separatis quam in nobis."

92. Ibid., 3.50 [Leon. Man. 281].

93. Ibid. [Leon. Man. 281–82].

to be seen by both the intellect of the separate substances and by the intellect of our souls."[94] A *caveat* is necessary here, lest we interpret Thomas's use of the axiom that "nature does nothing in vain" as similar to William's use of it. As in the *Commentary on the Sentences,* the argument concludes only that it is *possible* for us to see God, not that anyone actually *will* see God.[95] A natural appetite can tell us what is possible, but it cannot tell us what will actually happen. A natural desire that seeks the perfection of a natural appetite insofar as it is possible is in a similar situation. Since it cannot achieve the end of our natural appetite of its own accord, it cannot tell us any more than our natural appetite can about whether God has offered, is offering, or will offer us the superior motion we need in order to receive its ultimate fulfillment.[96]

As a corollary to Thomas's argument about the natural desire of the intellect, we may also consider what Thomas says about the natural desire of the will. In the course of proving that the soul is incorruptible in *Summa contra Gentiles* 2.79, Thomas offers a supporting argument from the will's natural inclination for the perpetual existence of being. The argument runs thus:

> It is impossible for a natural appetite to be frustrated. But man naturally desires [*appetit*] to remain forever. This is clear from the fact that being is what is desired by everything. But through his intellect man apprehends being not only as it exists now, like the brute animals do, but *simpliciter*. Therefore, man pursues perpetuity in his soul, by which he apprehends being *simpliciter* and according to every time.[97]

94. Ibid., 3.51 [Leon. Man. 282]: "Cum ... impossibile sit naturale desiderium esse inane, quod quidem esset si non esset possibile pervenire ad divinam substantiam intelligendam, quod naturaliter omnes mentes desiderant; necesse est dicere quod possibile sit substantiam Dei videri per intellectum, et a substantiis intellectualibus separatis, et ab animabus nostris."

95. See Hütter, *Dust Bound for Heaven,* 236.

96. Thomas Aquinas, *SCG* 3.52 [Leon. Man. 283].

97. Ibid., 2.79 [Leon. Man. 188]: "Impossibile est appetitum naturalem esse frustra. Sed homo naturaliter appetit perpetuo manere. Quod patet ex hoc quod esse est quod ab omnibus appetitur: homo autem per intellectum apprehendit esse non solum ut nunc, sicut bruta animalia, sed simpliciter. Consequitur ergo homo perpetuitatem secundum animam, qua esse simpliciter et secundum omne tempus apprehendit."

When Thomas says that the soul has a natural appetite for perpetuity, an interpretive question arises. Is Thomas speaking of a natural appetite in the intellect or in the will? It seems initially that he is speaking of a natural appetite in the intellect. If we follow the argument in *Summa contra Gentiles* 2.79 carefully, Thomas builds his case for the incorruptibility of the soul on the basis of the intellect's apprehension of *esse*. The intellect apprehends *esse* in itself; it beholds its perpetuity; and it identifies that perpetuity as desirable. Yet here a difficulty arises. We saw above that Thomas argues that the ultimate end of the intellect's natural inclination is to know God, the first cause of being, not to know being in itself. The intellect certainly attains knowledge of being in its quest for the knowledge of God, but since the intellect's proper object is what is true *sub ratione veri*, the natural desire of the intellect only concerns speculative truths, such as "being in itself is perpetual," not practical truths such as "being's perpetuity is good and to be pursued." According to its own natural desire, then, the intellect continues from the speculative proposition "being in itself is perpetual" to seek true knowledge of the first cause of perpetual being, not to seek being's perpetuity for itself.

When the intellect assents to the speculative proposition, "being in itself is perpetual," Thomas seems to imply that the intellect is quickly led to assent to the practical proposition, "the perpetuity of being is a good thing to pursue." He does not specify at this point what drives the intellect to make that secondary assent; he will do so in the *Quaestiones disputatae de anima,* as we shall see in chapter 4. But be that as it may, when the intellect assents to that practical proposition, Thomas thinks that the will cannot but choose to pursue it, because the pursuit of perpetuity is part of the pattern according to which the will wills whenever it wills. This gives us the answer to our first question: the natural appetite in question here is the natural appetite of the will.

Having identified the natural appetite for perpetuity as a natural appetite in the will, we may now compare how Thomas expresses the will's natural appetite for perpetuity in *Summa contra Gentiles* 2.79 with how he expresses it in *Summa contra Gentiles* 3.48. In both texts, Thomas uses the axiom that "nature does nothing in vain" as a key component of his argument. However, he uses it to prove a different conclusion in each argument.

We can outline Thomas's argument from *Summa contra Gentiles* 3.48 thus:

1) Man has a natural appetite for the perfect possession of the highest good; but the perfect possession of the highest good entails perpetuity; therefore, man has a natural appetite to possess the perfect good perpetually.
2) Man has a natural appetite to possess the perfect good perpetually; *but a natural appetite cannot be vain*; therefore, it must be possible at some point for man to possess the perfect good perpetually.
3) It must be possible at some point for man to possess the perfect good perpetually; but it is not possible in this life; therefore, there must be another life, after this one, where it is possible.

The conclusion of the argument, that it must be possible for man to possess the perfect good in the next life, does not entail that anyone does or will in actual fact possess that good.

In *Summa contra Gentiles* 3.48, Thomas is merely repeating an argument he had made in the *Commentary on the Sentences*. But Thomas's argument in *Summa contra Gentiles* 2.79 seems to show an awareness of a possible exegetical concern with the use of Aristotle's axiom in *Summa contra Gentiles* 3.48. The source of the axiom is Book 3 of Aristotle's *De anima*.[98] In that text, Aristotle uses the axiom very differently than Thomas had initially used it in the *Commentary on the Sentences*. Where Thomas had used it to prove that *a future act is possible*, prescinding from the question of whether anyone does or will perform it, Aristotle uses the axiom to prove that *a*

98. Aristotle, *De anima* 3.12 [434a22–434b6].

power of the soul actually exists here and now. We may outline Aristotle's argument thus:

1) Everything that lives has a nutritive soul by which it lives; but animals live; therefore, they have a nutritive soul.
2) Everything that has a nutritive soul requires nourishment to sustain life; but *nature does nothing in vain*; therefore, everything that has a nutritive soul actually has some means of obtaining nourishment.
3) Anything that can move around requires some means of apprehending nourishment in order to obtain it; but animals move around; therefore, animals have an apprehensive power which enables them to apprehend nourishment.

Thomas's argument in *Summa contra Gentiles* 2.79 is modeled on the structure of Aristotle's argument in *De anima,* rather than his previous argument in the *Commentary on the Sentences.* He argues that it is built into the structure of the will to seek perpetual possession of the perfect good, just like Aristotle argues that it is built into the structure of the nutritive soul to seek nutrition. If the human soul were to lack a power which was capable of possessing the perfect good, it would be in the same situation as an animal that lacked a power capable of obtaining nutrition. Just as animals must have the powers of sensation to find food, so must human persons have a power capable of obtaining the good perpetually. But if the human soul lacked any incorruptible powers, it would be unable to obtain the good perpetually. Therefore, the human soul must possess incorruptible powers. Therefore, it must be incorruptible.

There was precedent in the thirteenth century for distinguishing two arguments of this sort that we find in *Summa contra Gentiles* 2.79 and 3.48 respectively. We find it in Jean de la Rochelle's *Summa de anima,* which was likely composed in the mid-1230s.[99] Jean's text contains versions of both arguments that Thomas employs, one im-

99. See Jacques Bougerol, introduction to Jean de la Rochelle, *Summa de anima,* ed. Jacques Bougerol (Paris: J. Vrin, 1995), 12.

mediately following the other.[100] First he gives the argument that we see in *Summa contra Gentiles* 3.48. His argument is almost exactly the same as Thomas's in structure. It concludes from Aristotle's axiom that the soul is incorruptible because it must be possible for man to be happy after this life.[101] Second he gives the argument that we see in *Summa contra Gentiles* 2.79. While he does not use Aristotle's axiom, the structure of his thought assumes it: the soul has a natural inclination toward perpetual rest; therefore, it must be able to attain it; therefore, it must be incorruptible.

If we do not distinguish the argument in *Summa contra Gentiles* 3.48 from the argument in *Summa contra Gentiles* 2.79, there is a danger that we might reach a conclusion that Thomas never intended to draw. What would happen if we took Thomas's understanding of Aristotle's axiom from *Summa contra Gentiles* 2.79 (where it proves the actual existence of a power) and merged it with the interpretation of the axiom in *Summa contra Gentiles* 3.48 (where it proves the possibility of an act), so as to suggest that the axiom ought to prove the actual existence of an act? We would be left with something like this: "Man has a natural desire to possess the perfect good perpetually; *but a natural desire cannot be vain*; therefore, man must at some point actually possess the perfect good perpetually." Thomas does not make an argument like this in either text, although as we will see

100. See Jean de la Rochelle, *Summa de anima*, cap. 44 [Bougerol 139]. While much of Jean's text was incorporated into the *Summa fratris Alexandri*, these particular arguments do not appear to be reproduced there. This suggests that Thomas read Jean directly. Similar arguments to Jean's can be found in William of Auvergne's *De anima*, 6.1 [Hotot 2:156] and 6.13 [Hotot 2:169].

101. Jean de la Rochelle, *Summa de anima*, cap. 44 [Bougerol 139]: "Item ostenditur immortalitas eius per comparacionem ad finem, sic : omne quod naturaliter mouetur, non est naturali possibilitate prohibitum a fine ad quem mouetur, quia nullus motus nature naturaliter frustra est; sed anima racionalis naturaliter mouetur per appetitum ad felicitatem et beatitudinem; non ergo naturaliter prohibetur ab illo ; sed si esset mortalis, naturaliter prohiberetur ab illo; ergo est immortalis. Quod autem si esset mortalis prohiberetur, probatur sic: nam in bonis huius uite non est felicitas uel beatitudo; nichil enim potest conferre beatitudinem quod non potest auferre miseriam; quia miserum est quidquid morti obnoxium est; non est igitur in bonis huius uite felicitas, quia non aufert necessitatem moriendi: erit ergo in bonis post hanc uitam."

in chapter 6, some form of this argument would eventually work its way into the Thomistic commentatorial tradition. The argument in *Summa contra Gentiles* 2.79 stops at the same place at which the argument from *Summa contra Gentiles* 3.48 does concerning our final end, even if it gets to that point by another route. It proves that there is a power in the human soul *capable* of possessing the perfect good, but it does not prove one way or the other whether anyone does or will possess that good *in actual fact.*

Even if Thomas does not attempt to prove from natural desire that anyone has, does, or will receive the vision of God, we may ask whether Thomas's doctrine of natural desire for the vision of God in the *Summa contra Gentiles* implies the abandonment of his commitment to the idea that the active principles of the intellect and the will are by nature undetermined. In the *Commentary on the Sentences,* Thomas had argued that if human natural knowledge were determined, like the *Summa fratris Alexandri* claimed and Bonaventure insinuated, human persons would be unable to err concerning that which they naturally know; likewise, if human natural desire were determined to a specific object, that is, God, human persons would be unable to sin. Thomas omits these arguments from the discussion of natural desire in the *Summa contra Gentiles.* Does Thomas therefore abandon the principle entirely?

There are several reasons why one ought not to conclude that Thomas abandoned his teaching that the active principle in a *ratio seminalis* is undetermined, even if he appears to have introduced into it a determination toward the vision of God. First, we may note that although Thomas appears to have introduced a determination into the active principles of the intellect and the will, the determination is not *absolute.* The natural desire that Thomas identifies seeks the highest perfection of its corresponding appetite "insofar as is possible." Human natural *appetite* is determined to the vision of God as its final end, but this does not entail a corresponding absolute determination of human natural *desire.* In the absence of the offer of grace which makes the complete perfection of our appetite possible, the active principle in our nature can come to rest in the terminal development of its active principle *secundum naturam*, just as the active principle in Avicenna's hypothesized soul of a heavenly body comes to rest in the perpetual orbit of its body.

Second, as confirmation of the fact that Thomas did not introduce an absolute determination into the intellect and the will, we may look elsewhere in the *Summa contra Gentiles* to see how Thomas accounts for the possibilities of error and sin. With respect to the intellect, we may look to Thomas's discussion of whether the knowledge of God is self-evident (*per se notum*) to us.[102] With respect to the will, we may look to Thomas's discussion of the possibility of impeccability in this life, which Thomas raises in connection with the Sacrament of Penance.[103]

Concerning whether the knowledge of God is *per se notum* to us, Thomas considers the following objection: "Things which are naturally known are known per se, for we do not come to know them by the labor of inquiry. But that God exists is naturally known, since man's desire tends naturally toward God as toward man's ultimate end, as will be made clear below. Therefore, that God exists is known per se."[104] Against this objection, Thomas replies:

> Man naturally knows God like he naturally desires God. But man naturally desires God inasmuch as he naturally desires happiness, which is a certain similitude of divine goodness. For this reason, therefore, it is not necessary that God himself, considered in himself, be naturally known to man, rather [only] a similitude of him. Wherefore it is necessary that by similitudes of him found in his effects man arrives at the knowledge of him by reasoning.[105]

102. Thomas Aquinas, *SCG* 1.11 [Leon. Man. 9].

103. Ibid., 4.70 [Leon. Man. 533].

104. Ibid., 1.10 [Leon. Man. 8]: "Quae naturaliter sunt nota, per se cognoscuntur: non enim ad ea cognoscenda inquisitionis studio pervenitur. At Deum esse naturaliter notum est: cum in Deum naturaliter desiderium hominis tendat sicut in ultimum finem, ut infra patebit. Est igitur per se notum Deum esse."

105. Ibid., 1.11 [Leon. Man. 9]: "Sic enim homo naturaliter Deum cognoscit sicut naturaliter ipsum desiderat. Desiderat autem ipsum homo naturaliter inquantum desiderat naturaliter beatitudinem, quae est quaedam similitudo divinae bonitatis. Sic igitur non oportet quod Deus ipse in se consideratus sit naturaliter notus homini, sed similitudo

Thomas affirms the correlation between desire and knowledge, but dismisses the conclusion about natural knowledge by denying two premises about natural desire. First, he denies that our natural desire has God as its *terminus*. Strictly speaking, the *terminus* of our desire is *happiness*, not the vision of God. Second, he denies that our natural desire requires natural knowledge of its *terminus*. Thomas had already pointed out in *De veritate* that to have a natural desire for happiness does not require a natural knowledge of happiness. Since the will's natural appetite determines the pattern according to which the will pursues the end presented to it by the intellect, the will's natural appetite is itself sufficient for determining the will to seek whatever in the intellect's judgment appears as a cause happiness. For this reason, instead of saying that having a natural desire for happiness requires "natural" knowledge of happiness, all that Thomas requires is that the intellect attain a really or apparently good object in an act of judgment, that the goodness in that judgment move the will to act, and that, once the will is moved to act, it do so according to the pattern of its natural appetite.

Thomas takes a similar approach to the question of the determination in the will in his discussion of the Sacrament of Penance. Considering the text of 1 John 3:9: "he, who is born of God, cannot sin,"[106] Thomas asks whether a person who has received grace can sin afterwards. Rather than accounting for post-baptismal peccability on the basis of experience, Thomas has to show here that it is necessarily and antecedently the case that man can sin after having received grace, since the objector does not grant the existence of post-baptismal sin.

Among the arguments that Thomas proposes in favor of our post-baptismal peccability is an argument from the indetermination of the will:

---

ipsius. Unde oportet quod per eius similitudines in effectibus repertas in cognitionem ipsius homo ratiocinando perveniat."

106. Ibid., 4.70 [Leon. Man. 533]. Thomas quotes the text as follows: "Qui natus est ex Deo, non potest peccare."

There can be no impeccability in man without immutability of the will. But man cannot have immutability of the will unless he has reached his ultimate end. For the will is rendered immutable from the fact that it is completely fulfilled so that it does not have the wherewithal to turn away from that in which it is fixed. But the fulfillment of the will does not accrue to man unless he reaches his ultimate end: for as long as there remains something to desire, the will has not been fulfilled. Hence, therefore, impeccability does not accrue to man before he arrives at his final end.[107]

As was the case with the intellect, Thomas's doctrine of matter and its relationship to form continues to influence how he treats the will. As long as the will has not been completely actualized by any form in the intellect directing it to an end, it remains in potency to actualization by a different form directing it to a different end. As Thomas had previously noted, only God *could* completely actualize the will, because the complete actualization of the will depends upon the complete actualization of the intellect, and only God can completely fulfill the intellect's desire for knowledge by becoming the form informing the intellect.[108]

While Thomas does not therefore change his teaching on the indetermination of the active principle of the *rationes seminales* in the intellect and the will, his use of Avicenna's conditional natural desire helps to explain a curious fact about the structure of the *Summa contra Gentiles* which Torrell observes: In the *Summa theologiae,* the discussion of Providence (Ia, qq. 103–19) occurs before the discussion of happiness (Ia-IIae, qq. 1–5), while in the *Summa contra Gentiles* the discussion of Providence (3.64–end) comes after the discussion of happiness (3.2–63).[109] Why the difference? We may point out that

107. Ibid.: "Impeccabilitas in homine esse non potest sine immutabilitate voluntatis. Immutabilitas autem voluntatis non potest homini competere nisi secundum quod attingit ultimum finem. Ex hoc enim voluntas immutabilis redditur quod totaliter impletur, ita quod non habet quo divertat ab eo in quo est firmata. Impletio autem voluntatis non competit homini nisi ut finem ultimum attingenti: quandiu enim restat aliquid ad desiderandum, voluntas impleta non est. Sic igitur homini impeccabilitas non competit antequam ad ultimum finem perveniat."

108. Ibid., 3.53 [Leon. Man. 284–85], 3.68 [Leon. Man. 294].

109. Torrell, *Saint Thomas Aquinas,* 1:115. Thomas divides the treatment of Providence

for the first time in his career, Thomas was able to articulate from top to bottom how Providence operates in intellectual creatures: God imparts to them a first motion; this motion is received into their intellects as a natural desire according to the pattern of the natural appetite of the intellect; their intellects, in turn, move their wills, which are similarly moved in the form of a natural desire according to the pattern of their natural appetite; their wills, in turn, move the other powers of their souls. While in the order of being, Providence is prior to happiness, the reverse is true in the order of knowing. We come to know (and as a matter of historical fact, Thomas did come to know) how Providence operates upon us insofar as we come to understand the appetite and the desire of our souls for God.[110] Given the missionary intent of the *Summa contra Gentiles*, explaining beatitude and Providence in the order of knowing would be more effective than explaining them in the order of being.

Thomas's inductive approach to Providence allowed him to distinguish more clearly two related questions that had been bound up together in previous discussions of *rationes seminales*: God in himself as the first mover of creatures,[111] and creatures as the recipients of God's motion when, as moved movers, they engage in the actions associated with their natural appetites and desires.[112] From this point forward in Thomas's work, these questions will be treated separately. The traditional material on *rationes seminales* will be included with the second question, because it concerns the participation of creatures in God's action. It will be merged with the material on Prov-

into two parts. As Torrell notes and as Thomas indicates in *SCG* 3.1 [Leon. Man. 227], 3.64–110 concerns Providence in general; 3.111–end, Providence over rational creatures.

110. See Thomas Aquinas, *SCG* 1.1 [Leon. Man. 1]: "Finis autem ultimus uniuscuiusque rei est qui intenditur a primo auctore vel motore ipsius. Primus autem auctor et motor universi est intellectus, ut infra ostendetur. Oportet igitur ultimum finem universi esse bonum intellectus. Hoc autem est veritas. Oportet igitur veritatem esse ultimum finem totius universi." In 3.64 [Leon. Man. 295], Thomas reiterates, after his treatment of beatitude, "*Ex his autem quae praemissa sunt,* sufficienter habetur quod Deus est rerum omnium finis. Ex quo haberi potest ulterius quod ipse sua providentia gubernet vel regat universa" (emphasis added).

111. Ibid., 3.67 [Leon. Man. 300–301].

112. Ibid., 3.69 [Leon. Man. 301–2].

idence that Thomas received from Maimonides, because this also concerned the manner in which creatures receive God's motion.

In his discussion of the material from Maimonides in the *Summa contra Gentiles,* Thomas begins with the Ash'arites.[113] We may recall from chapter 2 that Maimonides understood the Ash'arites to possess a radical, voluntarist understanding of Providence: all things happen simply and only on account of the divine will. For Thomas, this implies a denial of the participation of creatures in God's motion. Thomas connects it with the views of Plato and Avicenna, which were part of his previous discussions of *rationes seminales.* Plato he associates with the view that God creates all substantial and accidental forms immediately; Avicenna he associates with the view that God creates all substantial forms immediately, but that creatures participate in the actualization of accidental forms.[114] Thomas sees both of these figures undergirding the view of Avicebron, whom he adds to the discussion, and according to whom "no body is active; rather, the power of spiritual substance, passing through bodies, performs the actions which seem to be done by the bodies."[115] Then he returns to the Maimonidian material and discusses the Mu'tazilites. Where the Ash'arites denied the possibility of creatures participating

113. On Thomas's relationship to Maimonides in the *SCG* and the opinions he recounts here, see Gilson, "Pourquoi Saint Thomas a critiqué Saint Augustin," 8–25. Gilson notes on p. 17 that "les termes dans lesquels saint Thomas résume leur doctrine [that is, that of the Mu'tazilites and the Ash'arites] sont presque littéralement empruntés à Maïmonide."

114. This more nuanced view of Avicenna suggests that Thomas has by this point been able to engage with Avicenna's thought directly, rather than merely repeating the Bonaventurean tradition. On the association more generally between Plato and Avicenna in Thomas's thought, see Gilson, "Pourquoi Saint Thomas a critiqué Saint Augustin," 44–45.

115. Thomas Aquinas, *SCG* 3.69 [Leon. Man. 303]: "Propter has igitur rationes ponit Avicebron, in libro *Fontis Vitae,* quod nullum corpus est activum; sed virtus substantiae spiritualis, pertransiens per corpora, agit actiones quae per corpora fieri videntur." See Gilson, "Pourquoi Saint Thomas a critiqué Saint Augustin," 25–35. John Laumakis believes that Aquinas misinterprets Avicebron here, and that Avicebron only posits the passivity of the first intelligible substance. See John Laumakis, "Aquinas' Misinterpretation of Avicebron on the Activity of Corporeal Substances: *Fons Vitae* II, 9 and 10," *The Modern Schoolman* 81, no. 2 (2004): 135–49.

in substantial change, the Mu'tazilites denied the possibility of creatures participating in accidental change.[116]

Thomas rejects all of the aforementioned views. The most significant of his arguments for the present purpose is based upon his previous teaching about *rationes seminales.* He observes that actions in nature take place not in virtue of forms alone, but in virtue of composites of matter and form. A composite causes effects in other creatures in virtue of its form; it receives effects from other creatures in virtue of its matter. There is no difficulty in saying that one creature causes effects in another, because such effects are caused not by the transferal of a form from one creature to another, but by the eduction into act of the second creature's potency for that form.[117] When such an eduction occurs, God is the first cause and the acting creature is the secondary cause; the effect is attributed entirely to both causes.[118]

Next, Thomas continues with the Maimonidian material and rejects the opinion of Averroes, who taught that Providence did not extend to sublunary bodies because natural evils occur among them. Thomas connects this view with a more extreme view, taken from an unnamed philosopher referenced by Boethius, who argued that the existence of any evil negates the existence of Providence. Thomas responds with the argument which he had drawn from Dionysius in the *Commentary on the Sentences*: since evil is merely a privation of the good, the existence of evil bespeaks the existence of the good. Consequently, if evil exists, God exists.[119] Thomas annexes to his refutation of Averroes a refutation of the view that good and evil have different principles. In the *Commentary on the Sentences* Thom-

116. Thomas Aquinas, *SCG* 3.69 [Leon. Man. 303]. See Gilson, "Pourquoi Saint Thomas a critiqué Saint Augustin," 22–25.

117. Thomas Aquinas, *SCG* 3.69 [Leon. Man. 302–5].

118. This is the subject of ibid., 3.70 [Leon. Man. 305–6].

119. Ibid., 3.71 [Leon. Man. 308]: "Boethius ... introducit quendam philosophum quaerentem: *Si Deus est, unde malum?* Esset autem e contrario arguendum: *Si malum est, Deus est.* Non enim esset malum sublato ordine boni, cuius privatio est malum. Hic autem ordo non esset, si Deus non esset."

as had taken this view from a reference in Averroes to an unnamed group of scholars, and then likened that group to the Manichees. Here, Thomas simply attributes the view to the Manichees.[120]

As in the *Commentary on the Sentences*, Maimonides is treated separately from Averroes, even though Maimonides's view that all sublunary creatures *except* human beings are subject to Providence is very similar to that of Averroes. Building on the argument from *De veritate* that Providence can be understood on analogy with prudence, Thomas rejects Maimonides's understanding of Providence with a simple argument about prudence:[121] Prudence involves practical judgments; but practical judgments concern the application of universals to particulars; therefore, if God only had Providence over universals and not particulars for some creatures, God would not be perfectly prudent, let alone provident.[122]

CONCLUSION

At a distance from the intensity of the academic pace at the University of Paris, Thomas spent his time at Orvieto deepening his knowledge of the sources of the arguments he had encountered at Paris, with the result that his own engagement with them was not as immediately dependent on Bonaventure. He devoted a significant amount of time to the reading of Maimonides on Providence, William of Auvergne on natural desire, and Jean de la Rochelle on the soul. He also thought through the consequences of the positions he had taken at Paris, drawing forth their logical conclusions.

The most important development of Thomas's thought during

120. Ibid.

121. That Thomas has Maimonides in view here is clear from the end of the chapter, in which he states, "Per haec autem excluditur opinio quorundam qui dixerunt quod divina providentia non se extendit usque ad haec singularia. Quam quidem opinionem quidam Aristoteli imponunt, licet ex verbis eius haberi non possit." As we saw in chapter 2, Maimonides was among those who imputed this view to Aristotle, together with Averroes.

122. Ibid., 3.75 [Leon. Man. 311–12].

this period occurred through his engagement with William of Auvergne. Thomas took William's argument that there is a natural desire in the intellect for the vision of God and used it to construct an account of intellectual desire that could be used to show that the analogical knowledge of God cannot be our ultimate end. Although Thomas could not assent to William's Avicennian idea that we have an active motion in us that seeks the vision of God as its determinate object, he achieved a similar result by introducing a condition into our natural desire, which he appears to have borrowed from Avicenna's account of the natural desire of the souls of the heavenly bodies: when our natural appetite is actualized in the form of a natural desire, Thomas now says that the resulting desire seeks the perfection of its corresponding appetite "insofar as is possible." Left to itself, the intellect's natural desire terminates in the analogical knowledge of God as first cause. But since a natural desire seeks the highest possible perfection of its corresponding appetite, and since the highest possible perfection of our natural appetite is the vision of God, the end of our natural desire is—at least implicitly—also the vision of God. All motion that the intellect receives from God is devoted to this end, and since the intellect's highest good is the human person's highest good, all motion that the will receives through the intellect is similarly devoted to this end.

Finding a way to say that we have a natural desire for the vision of God was essential for Thomas to be able to achieve the missionary purpose of the *Summa contra Gentiles*. Thomas could show that the various final ends proposed for man by the Aristotelian commentators all entailed an impossible action, but he could not dismiss the final end proposed by Aristotle himself, because Aristotle's act—the analogical knowledge of God as first cause—is possible both in this life and in the next. By arguing that the natural desire of the human intellect seeks the complete fulfillment of its natural appetite insofar as possible, rather than the terminal fulfillment of the motion it possesses by nature, Thomas was able to show how Aristotelian contemplation cannot serve as man's final end.

Given that Thomas identifies a natural desire for a supernatural end in the *Summa contra Gentiles,* we may raise three potential objections against Thomas's teaching here. The first is whether Thomas therefore compromises the gratuity of the vision of God by identifying in us a natural desire for it. William had recognized the potential problem, but as we saw in chapter 1, his solution was not entirely adequate: he appealed to the latent sinfulness of the human soul and the absolute freedom of God as the basis upon which God might refuse to grant us the fulfillment of our natural desire. Thomas's solution is different. Rather than rooting our primary orientation toward the vision of God in an active desire, he appeals to a passive appetite. That being the case, Thomas still thinks that natural desire can only prove the *possibility* of the vision of God, not its *actuality*. Even when he applies Aristotle's axiom that nature does nothing in vain to our natural appetite and natural desire, the same conclusion holds. In *Summa contra Gentiles* 3.48, he repeats his argument from the *Commentary on the Sentences,* showing that our natural desire for happiness proves that it is possible for us to obtain happiness after this life; in *Summa contra Gentiles* 2.79, he adopts a different use of that axiom from Jean de la Rochelle, using it with greater faithfulness to Aristotle to prove that there is a power in us capable of receiving the vision of God, but not that anyone has or will receive it.

The second objection is whether Thomas violates Augustine's anti-Pelagian concern to deny that the fallen soul has any motion in it directed toward the vision of God. There are two ways to respond to this objection. The first is to observe that Thomas's use of Avicenna's account of the natural desire of the souls of the heavenly bodies actually led him to a *more* Augustinian account of natural desire, not less. In the *Commentary on the Sentences,* Thomas had largely followed Albert, who identified in the human soul an Aristotelian natural desire for a natural end. In the *Summa contra Gentiles,* however, Thomas used Avicenna to align Albert's natural desire more closely with that of Augustine. The natural desire for the fulfillment of a natural appetite insofar as it possible is just the sort of subjective fulfillment that Augustine described as the object of the desire for happiness in *De Trinitate,* Book 13. Augustine's language is certainly simpler and easier to understand, but Thomas's had to do three times as much conceptual work. First, it had to preserve the anti-Pelagian patrimony of the Latin Patristic tradition; second, it had to preserve the Aristotelian account of nature; third, it had to achieve the missionary goal of showing from within the Aristotelian tradition broadly conceived that the final end of man cannot merely be that posited by an Aristotelian account of nature. The natural desire for the fulfillment of a natural appetite insofar as possible achieved all three of these goals.

Finally, we saw that in the *Summa contra Gentiles* Thomas considers our knowledge of Providence to be dependent upon our knowledge of the natural desire of the intellect for its fulfillment. This gave Thomas for the first time a way to describe the structure of God's providential action upon intellectual creatures from top to bottom. As significant an advance as this was, however, Thomas still did not resolve the open questions about the sin of Adam and Eve and the act of faith. Concerning the sin of Adam and Eve, the question remained from the *De veritate* as to how/whether it might be consistent for Thomas to say that the will moves the intellect in this particular action without a prior judgment in the intellect. Concerning the act of faith, while Thomas eliminated the problem from the *Commentary on the Sentences* of saying that the judgment establishing the prudence of the act of faith is based on fallible persons by establishing a chain of predicatory causality stretching back to infallible persons (Jesus, the prophets, and the apostles), he still did not address how a natural judgment in the intellect moves the will to command the intellect to perform a supernatural action.

4

Rome (1265–1268)

In 1265, Thomas moved from Orvieto to Rome. He had been tasked by the provincial chapter of Rome with founding a *studium* there and teaching in it.[1] Mulchahey observes that there were three kinds of *studia* in the Dominican Order around this time: those attached to a local priory (*scholae,* such as Thomas had known at Orvieto), those attached to a province (*studia provincialia*), and those attached to a university (*studia generalia,* such as Thomas had known at Paris). The *studia provincialia* were a more recent invention. They functioned as an intermediate network between the *studia generalia* and the local conventual *scholae.* Over the course of the second half of the thirteenth century, the *studia provincialia* were gradually coming to be subdivided into *studia particularia artium,* which taught logic,[2] *studia particularia naturarum,* which taught natural philosophy and metaphysics,[3] and *studia particularia theologiae,* which taught theology.[4] Thomas's Roman *studium* was to be a *studium particulare theologiae,* a sort of proving ground for theologians from which the best and brightest might be sent to a *studium generale,* but most would be

1. Torrell, *Saint Thomas Aquinas,* 1:142.
2. Mulchahey, *First the Bow Is Bent in Study,* 224, 238–39.
3. Ibid., 252, 269–70.
4. Ibid., 277–78.

sent back to a priory to teach as Thomas had done at Orvieto.[5] This was the first time that the Roman province had experimented with one of these specialized provincial schools.[6]

It may be that Thomas himself helped to push for the creation of the *studium*.[7] The academic life in the Roman province was not in a good state,[8] and it would be hard to imagine Thomas sitting idly by while it continued to languish. Yet whether or not Thomas was an immediate cause of the *studium*'s creation, the resulting *studium* was so dependent on his personal genius that Boyle, and Torrell after him, describe it as a sort of *studium personale*.[9] Notwithstanding the anachronism of the term, Mulchahey approves of it on the basis of Thomas's particular responsibilities: he was to found it, to run it, to design its curriculum, and to be the sole person in charge of its students.[10]

At first Thomas tried to replicate the teaching methods of Paris,[11] lecturing to his Roman students on the *Sentences* of Peter Lombard.[12] But Parisian methods were not well suited to this audience, most of whom were destined not for Paris but for the priories. Thomas quickly abandoned his relecture of the *Sentences* and embarked upon the composition of a new pedagogical text better suited to his new students, the *Summa theologiae*.[13]

Thomas was not the only one rethinking pedagogical texts for specialized provincial *studia* at the time. The Franciscans were also

5. Ibid., 278–79.

6. Ibid., 279.

7. Torrell, *Saint Thomas Aquinas*, 1:143–44.

8. Ibid., 1:142–43, describes the general disrepair into which studies in the Roman province had fallen at this time.

9. Leonard Boyle, *The Setting of the Summa theologiae of Saint Thomas* (Toronto: PIMS, 1982), 9; Torrell, *Saint Thomas Aquinas*, 1:144.

10. Mulchahey, *First the Bow Is Bent in Study*, 279.

11. See John Boyle, introduction to Thomas Aquinas, *Lectura romana in primum Sententiarum Petri Lombardi*, ed. Leonard Boyle and John Boyle (Toronto: PIMS, 2006), 3.

12. A *reportatio* of Thomas's lecture can be found in Thomas Aquinas, *Lectura romana*.

13. Leonard Boyle, "Alia lectura fratris Thome," in Thomas Aquinas, *Lectura romana*, 58–69.

in the process of setting up such *studia* (Roest refers to them as "custodial" *studia*),[14] and trying to figure out how best to teach the students in them. Jay Hammond has very recently concluded on the basis of a codicological analysis that Bonaventure's *Breviloquium* was composed as just such a text.[15] Hammond has also suggested, on the basis of his study, that the text was composed after 1262, rather than in 1257 as has long been supposed.[16] While it is too early to tell with absolute certainty, we will see below that internal evidence from the *Prima pars* suggests that Thomas was reading and responding to the *Breviloquium* as he wrote the *Summa theologiae*. Perhaps, then, the *Summa theologiae* may be thought of as Thomas's contribution to a common problem: how to re-invent introductions to theological *disputatio* so that they serve the brethren who are talented enough to be sent to a provincial theological *studium*, but not necessarily so talented as to be sent on to a university.

In anticipation of the *Summa theologiae*, and at times parallel with it, Thomas held various sets of disputed questions. It seems that his intention was not unlike that of the contemporary university professor, who holds a seminar in order to think through, with his students, some of the more important questions pertaining to a book in progress. In order to prepare specifically for the *Prima pars*, he held three sets of disputed questions. The *Quaestiones disputatae de potentia* and the *Quaestiones disputatae de anima* were held in 1265–66.[17] The former were private disputes held for the benefit of students; they reflect a wider variety of subjects and prioritize the themes of biblical events. Related to the subject of natural desire, they discuss questions connected with Creation, Providence, and *potentia obedientiae*. The latter were public disputes held weekly, and organized more tightly around

14. See Roest, *A History of Franciscan Education*, 65–68.

15. Jay Hammond, "The Textual Context," in *Bonaventure Revisited: Companion to the Breviloquium*, ed. Dominic Monti and Katherine Wrisley-Shelby (St. Bonaventure, N.Y.: The Franciscan Institute, 2017), 29–72. I am grateful to Dr. Hammond for suggesting to me the possibility of parallels between the *Breviloquium* and the *Summa theologiae*.

16. Ibid., 45.

17. Torrell, *Saint Thomas Aquinas*, 1:335.

a central theme.[18] Among other things, they apply what Thomas says about Creation, Providence, and *potentia obedientiae* to the specific case of the separated soul. Two academic years later (1267–68) he also composed a commentary on Aristotle's *De anima*, the *Sententia libri de anima*,[19] and held the *Quaestiones disputatae de spiritualibus creaturis*.[20] The *Sententia libri de anima* is of particular interest, because Thomas had access to two new translations from William of Moerbeke when he wrote it: the *translatio nova* of Aristotle's *De anima*, and Themistius's paraphrase of the *De anima*.

While in the *De potentia* and the *Quaestiones disputatae de anima* Thomas stays reasonably close to his previous teaching, his encounter with Moerbeke's recent translations would cause significant developments in his thought on two points. His encounter with the *translatio nova* of the *De anima*, in which Moerbeke apparently mistranslates Aristotle on the object of the will, would cause him to speak of the appetible object as the first mover of both the intellect and the will together, rather than the intellect as the first mover of the will. His encounter with the translation of Themistius, where Moerbeke mistakenly represents Themistius as affirming the existence of individualized agent intellects in human persons, would cause him to adopt a much more conciliatory view toward the Christian Avicennian tradition of the 1230s and 1240s. Together, these two developments would lead Thomas to begin a re-articulation of his understanding of the desire for God. Instead of speaking of a chain of providential motion in which God illumines the agent intellect, the agent intellect moves the possible intellect, the possible intellect moves the will, and the will moves the other powers of the soul, Thomas will now speak of two parallel sources of activity in the human soul, both ultimately rooted in God: God, who stands in the place of Avicenna's *dator formarum*, illumines the agent intellect directly; God is also said to "move" the possible intellect and the will insofar as he is the author of the natu-

18. Carlos Bazán, introduction to *Quaestiones disputatae de anima* [Leon. 24.1:102*].
19. Torrell, *Saint Thomas Aquinas*, 1:341.
20. Ibid., 1:336.

ral appetite according to which these powers are moved when in the presence of their respective objects. When the intellect and the will are moved, the intellect still maintains a structural priority over the will, since the good apprehended by the intellect (the *bonum apprehensum*) is the first cause of motion in the will.

QUAESTIONES DISPUTATAE DE POTENTIA

When Thomas discusses nature in the *Quaestiones disputatae de potentia,* he returns to the scriptural questions about Creation that had informed his discussion of these topics in the *Commentary on the Sentences,* integrating with them the developments in his thought which we observed in *De veritate* and the *Summa contra Gentiles.* Since these questions were held privately for the formation of Dominican brothers, the biblical material would have formed an essential component of the theological consideration, just as it had during the time at Orvieto. However, since these brothers were not *fratres communes,* Thomas was free to work out some of the more difficult problems that occurred to him as he prepared to write the *Summa theologiae.* Chief among these more difficult problems were the doctrines of Creation and miracles. In both cases, Thomas would maintain his commitment to some of the fundamental positions he had taken about *rationes seminales* in the *Commentary on the Sentences.* In the case of Creation, he uses them to critique Bonaventure more sharply than previously. In the case of miracles, he develops an even more radical commitment to the unity of humanity's passive potency in his discussion of our potency for obedience.

In *De potentia,* question 4, Thomas returns to Bonaventure's distinction between matter *secundum esse* and matter *secundum essentiam,* which he had initially discussed in the *Commentary on the Sentences,* and reinterprets it in light of his understanding of Providence from the *Summa contra Gentiles.*[21] Since matter in its abstract essence

21. This is the subject of Thomas Aquinas, *De pot.,* q. 4, a. 1 [Pession 102–10].

is pure potency with no admixture of act, it cannot exist concretely on its own; it only exists insofar as it is actualized by a form.[22] That form is a creature's single substantial form. As was customary by this point in his career, Thomas combines his affirmation of the unicity of substantial form with a rejection of Bacon's incomplete active potencies and Bonaventure's incomplete forms.[23] The question had gained a renewed importance since the last time he had considered it, because the Oxford Dominican Robert Kilwardby (d. 1279) had recently published views on the subject which were nearly identical to Bacon's.[24]

As in Thomas's *Commentary on the Sentences*, the interpretation of Genesis 1 on this question is bound up with biblical hermeneutics. Here Thomas diverges from Bonaventure more sharply than before on the relationship between reason and faith:

> There can be a twofold debate about [creation]: one concerning the truth of the matter; another about the meaning of the text wherein Moses, inspired by God, explains the beginning of the world to us.
>
> With regard to the first debate, we should avoid two [errors]: the first of these is asserting something false in this question, especially something that contradicts the truth of faith; the other is believing that something is true [and] immediately wanting to assert that it pertains to a truth of faith. . . .
>
> With regard to the second debate, we should also avoid two [errors]: The first of these is saying that we should understand among the words of Scripture which teach the creation of things that there is something which is clearly false; for nothing false can be found in Sacred Scripture, because it has been handed down by the Holy Spirit; neither can anything false be found in the Faith which is taught by it. The other is, no one should want to so force Scripture toward one sense that he altogether excludes the other senses which in themselves contain truth, and which can, while preserving the context of the text itself, be accommodated to Scripture;

22. Ibid., co. [Pession 105a].

23. Ibid. [Pession 105a–b].

24. See Sílva, *Robert Kilwardby on the Human Soul*, 56. The similarities between Kilwardby and Bacon may date all the way back to the late 1230s–40s, when the two studied together at Paris (ibid., 9).

for it pertains to the dignity of Scripture both that it contains many senses under one letter so that it adapts itself to people's differing intellectual capacities (so that everyone can marvel at the fact that he can find truth in Sacred Scripture which he may conceive with his mind), and that by this fact it may also be easily defended against those who do not believe: for example, when an idea that a person wants to take from Sacred Scripture appears false, recourse can be made to one of its other senses.[25]

While Thomas certainly does not wish to locate Bonaventure among those "who do not believe," because he does not see anything contrary to the faith about Bonaventure's conclusion,[26] he does think that Bonaventure ascribes to Scripture a teaching which is clearly false according to natural reason. Given the pure passivity of matter and the unicity of substantial form, Thomas sees no coherent way to affirm that matter was created under incomplete substantial forms.[27] This is not a case in which reason must submit to Scripture; it is rather a case in which reason leads us to the correct interpretation of Scripture.

25. Thomas Aquinas, *De pot.*, q. 4, a. 1, co. [Pession 104a–105b]. "Circa hanc quaestionem potest esse duplex disceptatio: una de ipsa rerum veritate; alia de sensu litterae, qua Moyses divinitus inspiratus principium mundi nobis exponit.

"Quoad primum disceptationem duo sunt vitanda; quorum unum est ne in hac quaestione aliquid falsum asseratur, praecipue quod veritati fidei contradicat; aliud est, ne quidquid verum aliquis esse crediderit, statim velit asserere, hoc ad veritatem fidei pertinere. . . .

"Circa secundam disceptationem duo etiam sunt vitanda. Quorum primum est, ne aliquis id quod patet esse falsum, dicat in verbis Scripturae, quae creationem rerum docet, debere intelligi; Scripturae enim divinae a Spiritu Sancto traditae non potest falsum subesse, sicut nec fidei, quae per eam docetur. Aliud est, ne aliquis ita Scripturam ad unum sensum cogere velit, quod alios sensus qui in se veritatem continent, et possunt, salva circumstantia litterae, Scripturae aptari, penitus excludantur; hoc enim ad dignitatem divinae Scripturae pertinet, ut sub una littera multos sensus contineat, ut sic et diversis intellectibus hominum conveniat, ut unusquisque miretur se in divina Scriptura posse invenire veritatem quam mente conceperit; et per hoc etiam contra infideles facilius defendatur, dum si aliquid, quod quisque ex sacra Scriptura velit intelligere, falsum apparuerit, ad alium eius sensum possit haberi recursus."

26. Ibid. [Pession 105a]: "His ergo suppositis, sciendum est quod diversi expositores sacrae Scripturae diversos sensus ex principio Genesis acceperunt; quorum nullus fidei veritati repugnat."

27. Ibid., a. 2, co. [Pession 113b].

Having confirmed his understanding of nature with regard to Creation, Thomas explicitly draws a connection between Creation and the desire for God. As we saw in chapter 3, Thomas had begun in the *Summa contra Gentiles* to distinguish the question of God as the first mover from that of creatures as recipients of that motion in his treatment of natural desire. He discusses God as the first cause of motion in creatures in *De potentia* q. 5, a. 1. He makes a further distinction concerning creatures as recipients of that motion: he treats creatures as secondary causes of accidental change in q. 3, a. 7, and creatures as secondary causes of substantial change in q. 3, a. 8.

In *De potentia* q. 3, a. 7, Thomas returns to the views of the Mu'tazilites and of Avicebron.[28] He rejects the teaching of the Mu'tazilites for the same reason as in the *Summa contra Gentiles*: when it is said that one creature causes an accident in another, it is not that the new accident is the same in number as the old, but that it is merely the same in species; the new accident is reduced to act from the potency of the substance in which it is caused. He also adds a further consideration. Imputing to the Mu'tazilites the view that all forms are accidental, Thomas now argues that they destroy the possibility of substantial change as well, because in their rejection of substantial form they reject the possibility of one substance causing another substance.[29]

Thomas then discusses Avicebron. Where previously Thomas had emphasized Avicebron's teaching on the passivity of material creatures, here he adds that Avicebron merges all corporal being into one substance with only accidental distinctions. Thomas concedes that Avicebron's view of change would be correct if corporeal substances were made up only of matter. However, since corporeal substances are composed of matter *and form*, this means—as Thomas had taught consistently since the *Commentary on the Sentences*—that in their matter they are in potency to all the other forms which they

28. Ibid., q. 3, a. 7 [Pession 56b]. Thomas recycles this view in q. 3, a. 8, obj. 13 [Pession 60b].

29. Ibid., a. 7 [Pession 57a].

do not currently possess, and that those forms can potentially be reduced into act by the forms of other creatures.[30] When an agent educes such a form into act, it participates in a chain of motion that originates in God in a variety of ways: God moves created natures because he gives them the power to move; God moves created natures because he conserves their power to move; God moves created natures because he applies their power to move in the manner of an instrument; God moves created natures because, as the first cause, their actions are more properly his.[31] Thomas's conclusion is sweeping: "God is the cause of every action, insofar as any agent is an instrument of the action of God's power";[32] and "God acts in every sort of thing insofar as it needs his power to act."[33]

Having established in *De potentia* q. 3, a. 7, that God acts through the forms of creatures by moving them as their first cause so that they cause accidental change as secondary causes, Thomas then proceeds to consider, in q. 3, a. 8, how God acts through the forms of creatures to cause substantial change. Here Thomas follows the pattern of discourse established in his previous treatments of *rationes seminales*. He begins by discussing Anaxagoras and Avicenna. Where previously Thomas's primary point of reference for the *latitatio formarum* was the text of Bonaventure's *Commentary on the Sentences*, by this point Thomas has tracked back Bonaventure's and Bacon's discussion of Anaxagoras to its source in Aristotle.[34] With this independent knowledge of the source of the discussion, Thomas is able to reduce the philosophical error in Anaxagoras to another version

30. Ibid.

31. Ibid. [Pession 57b–58a]. The fourth observation seems to have been taken directly from the *Liber de causis*, prop. 1. Although Thomas does not cite that the proposition, he does go on to cite the *Liber de causis* subsequently in the same paragraph, which suggests that he had it in mind when he was composing his response.

32. Ibid. [Pession 58b]: "Sic ergo Deus est causa omnis actionis, prout quodlibet agens est instrumentum divinae virtutis operantis."

33. Ibid.: "Deus in qualibet re operatur in quantum eius virtute quaelibet res indiget ad agendum."

34. Ibid., a. 8, co. [Pession 61b]: "Ex hoc enim aliqui crediderunt quod nulla res fieret aliter nisi per hoc quod extrahebatur a re alia in qua lateat, sicut de Anaxagora narrat Philosophus." The text of Aristotle is *Physics* 1.4 [187a11–188a17].

of the Baconian thesis: "[Anaxagoras] did not distinguish between potency and act; for he thought that that which is generated must exist in act before it is generated, whereas it is necessary that it exist in potency before it is generated, not in act."[35]

Next Thomas discusses Avicenna's *dator formarum.* In the *Summa contra Gentiles* Thomas had already begun to distinguish different versions of this view by contrasting Avicenna with Plato. In the *De potentia,* Thomas continues his research into the sources of the question. The first source is Plato, whom Thomas thinks gave rise to the idea of a *dator formarum.* The second is Avicenna, who identified the *dator formarum* with the "ultimate intelligence among the separated substances." The third are "some modern thinkers, following them, who say that this is God."[36] Given the prolific nature of Latin Avicennianism at the time, any number of contemporary figures could be intended when Thomas speaks of *moderni.*[37]

In the response to *De potentia* q. 3, a. 8, Thomas systematizes this article with the previous one: the errors of article 7 come from mistakes about matter, while the errors in article 8 come from mistakes about form. As in the *Commentary on the Sentences,* the errors about form reduce Avicenna's idea that form comes to be *in* matter rather than *from* matter.[38] *Pace* Avicenna, form is not "what comes to be," that is, the *terminus* of generation; the composite of matter and form is the *terminus* of generation. Form is merely that *whereby* the composite comes to be. The composite itself is not pre-existing or created *de novo*; it is brought into existence when its form actualizes the potency of its matter.[39]

35. Thomas Aquinas, *De pot.* q. 3, a. 8, co. [Pession 61b]: "non distinguebat inter potentiam et actum; putabat enim oportere quod actu praeextiterit illud quod generatur. Oportet autem quod praeexistat potentia et non actu."

36. Ibid.: "Formam vero, quam oportet fieri et non praesupponi, oportet esse ex agente qui non praesupponit aliquid, sed potest ex nihilo facere: et hoc est agens supernaturale, quod Plato posuit dator formarum. Et hoc Avicenna dixit esse intelligentiam ultimam inter substantias separatas. Quidam vero moderni eos sequentes, dicunt hoc esse Deum."

37. See Hasse, *Avicenna's* De anima *in the Latin West,* 203.

38. Thomas Aquinas, *De pot.,* q. 3, a. 8, co. [Pession 62a]: "Et sic non proprie dicitur quod forma fiat in materia, sed magis quod de materiae potentia educatur."

39. The context for this particular observation may be Avicenna's idea that the power

Unlike his *Commentary on the Sentences*, Thomas does not include a critique of Bonaventure in the *corpus* of article 8. By this point he appears to see Bonaventure's hypothesis as but one among many instances of the idea that there can be activity in matter prior to its possession of a complete substantial form. Accordingly, he quickly dispenses with Bonaventure's position in his replies to objections 10 and 11. He now acts as though Bonaventure's position reduces entirely to Bacon's. "Form preexists in matter imperfectly, not because some part of it is in act there and another is not, but because the whole preexists in potency, and afterwards the whole is produced in act."[40]

In *De potentia* q. 5, a. 1, Thomas applies what he had said about creaturely motion in q. 3, aa. 7–8, to a new question arising from the denial of creaturely participation in divine motion which he had taken in the *Summa contra Gentiles* to be implied by the voluntarism of the Ash'arites: if a creature can exist without any participation in the motion of God, could it exist completely and entirely apart from God?[41] In response, Thomas applies what he had said about intellectual creatures in the *Summa contra Gentiles* to all creatures in general. Intellectual creatures depend directly on God not only for their being, but also for their motion. One cannot remove the first cause of their motion without removing the first cause of their being. It might seem at first glance to be otherwise with material creatures, since, while God causes their being directly through their forms he causes their motion indirectly through the mediation of other material creatures. Yet even in the case of motion that is caused indirectly, the same dependence on the first cause applies.[42]

Thomas's treatment of creaturely participation in accidental and

---

to create can be directly communicated to creatures. See Verbeke, introduction to Avicenna, *Prima Philosophia*, 2:66*–68*.

40. Thomas Aquinas, *De pot.*, q. 3, a. 8, ad 10 [Pession 62b]: "forma praeexistit in materia imperfecte; non quod aliqua pars eius sit ibi in actu, et alia desit; sed quia tota praeexistit in potentia, et postmodum tota producitur in actu."

41. Ibid., q. 5, a. 1 [Pession 129a]: "Utrum res conserventur in esse a Deo, an etiam circumscripta omnia Dei actione, per se in esse remaneant."

42. Ibid., ad 2 [Pession 132a].

substantial change in *De potentia*, q. 3, aa. 7–8, together with his treatment of how God imparts motion to creatures in q. 5, a. 1, grounds his treatment of miracles and of *potentia obedientiae* in q. 6, aa. 1–2. In article 1, following the *Summa contra Gentiles*, Thomas argues that God never does anything contrary to nature simply speaking. Even though he can act contrary to (*contra*) or beyond (*praeter*) the customary ordering among creatures, all motion that they receive from him is in some sense natural to them, because it is received in their passive, "material" potency.[43] He supports this argument with a reference to our *potentia obedientiae* in the reply to the eighteenth objection. The eighteenth objection had posited, on the authority of Averroes, that there cannot be a passive potency in nature for an effect that exceeds the active potency available in nature, because every passive potency in nature must have a corresponding active potency in nature.[44] Presuming that this objection arose from a classroom setting, the student who raised it was perceptive. This was, in fact, the very first argument that Thomas *himself* had used to establish the existence of an individualized agent intellect in the human soul in the *Summa contra Gentiles*.[45] In reply, Thomas dispenses with any concern for what Averroes might have meant and sacrifices whatever usefulness his previous argument might have had with regard to the agent intellect: a higher cause can produce a higher effect, and so there is nothing to prevent God, as the highest cause, from producing an effect in a creature that the creature itself or a connatural agent could not produce. Thomas calls the creature's potency for this effect a "potency for obedience" (*potentia obedientiae*).[46]

43. See especially ibid., q. 6, a. 1, ad 1 [Pession 159b–60a]. On the use of the word "material," see q. 6, a. 1, ad 9 [Pession 160b]: "Opera miraculosa materialiter in operibus sex dierum praecesserunt, licet tunc non oportuerit aliquid miraculose fieri contra cursum naturae, quando natura instituebatur."

44. Ibid., q. 6, a. 1, obj. 18 [Pession 158b]: "Cum omne genus per potentiam et actum dividatur, ut patet in III *Physicorum*, ad potentiam autem potentia passiva pertineat, ad actum autem activa; oportet quod illa sola potentia passiva inveniatur in natura ad quae invenitur potentia activa naturalis, hoc enim est eiusdem generis; et hoc etiam dicit Commentator in IX *Metaphysicorum*."

45. Thomas Aquinas, *SCG* 2.76 [Leon. Man. 181–82].

46. Thomas Aquinas, *De pot.*, q. 6, a. 1, ad 18 [Pession 161a]: "Quanto aliqua virtus

If we read *De potentia* a. 1, ad 18, quickly, it is easy to come away with the impression that Thomas uses the idea of a potency for obedience to refer to that subset of passive potency within a creature which cannot be actualized by a connatural agent, as Albert and Bonaventure had done. However, if we pay close attention to the context, Thomas uses the idea of a potency for obedience to refer not only or even primarily to a creature's susceptibility to the eduction of forms which nature could never educe, but also to its susceptibility to the eduction of forms which nature could otherwise educe but was not going to educe. This is an important distinction, for while it is clear that our potency for grace is outside of what the objector calls a "natural passive potency," it is similarly clear for Thomas that our potency for miracles is not. As Thomas had explained in the *corpus* of article 1, a passive potency, which happens to be actualized immediately in a miracle, *could* have been reduced into act mediately by a connatural agent. If the potency actualized in a miracle where not numerically the same as the potency that could be actualized by a connatural agent, then all miracles would be *supra naturam*, something which Thomas had never asserted.

QUAESTIONES DISPUTATAE DE ANIMA

In the *Quaestiones disputatae de anima*, Thomas applies his understanding of *rationes seminales* and of our potency for obedience to the question of the knowledge in the separated soul. Concerning *rationes seminales*, Thomas states that there are in the universe higher powers and lower powers. The higher powers exercise a universal influence on the lower powers and assist the lower powers in the process of natural generation. However, beyond the case of the

activa est altior, tanto eamdem rem potest perducere in altiorem effectum: unde natura potest ex terra facere aurum aliis elementis commixtis, quod ars facere non potest; et inde est quod res aliqua est in potentia ad diversa secundum habitudinem ad diversos agentes. Unde nihil prohibet quin natura creata sit in potentia ad aliqua fienda per divinam potentiam, quae inferior potentia facere non potest: et ista vocatur potentia obedientiae, secundum quod quaelibet creatura Creatori obedit."

smallest, most insignificant creatures, it is necessary that the particular active powers in lower creatures participate in the universal active influence of higher powers. The particular, active power in lower creatures is a seed. Since, moreover, the intellect is the "most perfect" among created powers, it is necessary that it have a seed of action inside it as well. This seed is the agent intellect.[47] The agent intellect is an individual's particular participation in the universal light which enlightens all intellectual creatures. Utilizing the Augustinian language of illumination, Thomas identifies the eternal light with God, who illumines the human intellect, and the agent intellect with a created participation in that eternal light.[48] God is not the agent intellect, as Christian Avicennians had supposed. But the light of God is the light by which each person's agent intellect is enlightened.[49]

Thomas also uses language related to his discussions of *rationes seminales* when speaking about the possible intellect. In order for an act of understanding to take place in our souls, there must be a formal participation in our souls in all of the powers required for understanding. The agent intellect is one such power; the possible intellect is another. Just as, therefore, there is a formal, active principle in the human intellect (the agent intellect), so likewise must there be a receptive principle (the possible intellect).[50] Using seed imagery, Thomas thus establishes the existence of the components which he elsewhere describes as a *ratio seminalis.*

The idea of a *ratio seminalis* in the intellect helped Thomas to engage once again with the thought of William of Auvergne. Let us

47. Thomas Aquinas, *De an.*, q. 5, co. [Leon. 24:41]: "Ad generationem animalium perfectorum, preter uirtutem celestem, requiritur etiam uirtus particularis que est in semine. Cum igitur id quod est perfectissimum in omnibus inferioribus sit intellectualis operatio, preter principia actiua uniuersalia, que sunt uirtus Dei illuminantis uel cuiuscumque alterius substantie separate, requiritur in nobis principium actiuum proprium, per quod efficiamur intelligentes in actu. Et hoc est intellectus agens."

48. Ibid., q. 4, ad 7 [Leon. 24:36].

49. Ibid., q. 5, co. [Leon. 24:40–41]: "Quidam catholici posuerunt quod intellectus agens sit ipse Deus."

50. Ibid. [Leon. 24:42].

recall from chapter 3 that William identified the agent intellect with God, and thought that the proximate active principle in the human intellect was the habit of the first principles of demonstration. In response to this, and drawing on his treatment of motion and being in *De potentia* q. 5, a. 1, Thomas now asks whether the possible intellect can carry on thinking without any further need for the agent intellect once the first principles of demonstration have been actualized.[51] He responds in the negative: just as the soul needs God to move, so likewise does the possible intellect need the agent intellect not only to come to a knowledge of the first principles, but also to use them.[52]

Having established that the possible intellect needs the agent intellect like the agent intellect needs God, Thomas goes on to suggest that there might nevertheless be some ways of appropriating the Christian Avicennian tradition without abandoning Thomas's own understanding of how motion is received into the human soul. This conciliatory direction may have been suggested through a reading of Jean de la Rochelle, who had inspired at least one of Thomas's arguments about the desire for God in the *Summa contra Gentiles,* and upon whose *Summa de anima* the *Quaestiones disputatae de anima* may have been intentionally modeled.[53] Jean posits what we might call three "levels" of agent intellect that influence the human possible intellect.[54] When the human soul knows supernatural mysteries, God is its agent intellect through the infusion of grace. When the human soul knows angels, the angels themselves are its agent intellect through communication. When the human soul knows itself or the things below it, the human soul acts as its own agent intellect.[55] In

51. This is a paraphrase of the objection from Thomas's *De an.*, q. 4, obj. 6 [Leon. 24.1:32].

52. Ibid., ad 6 [Leon. 24.1:36].

53. See Carlos Bazán, "The Human Soul: Form *and* Substance? Thomas Aquinas' Critique of Eclectic Aristotelianism," *Archives d'Histoire Doctrinale et Littéraire du Moyen Âge* 64 (1997): 96.

54. Gilson, "Pourquoi saint Thomas a critiqué saint Augustin," 87.

55. Jean de la Rochelle, *Summa de anima,* cap. 116 [Bougerol 279–80].

Jean's *Tractatus de multiplici divisione potentiarum animae,* he clarifies that when the human soul acts as its own agent intellect, this does not mean that it is somehow independent of God; even in natural knowledge the human agent intellect receives the first principles of demonstration from God, and uses them to cause knowledge in the possible intellect.[56]

Where Thomas had previously said that the agent intellect actualizes the possible intellect directly, he now says that the agent intellect makes use of a *ratio seminalis* when it causes knowledge in the possible intellect: "Just as I claim that superior agents cause natural forms by the mediation of natural agents, so likewise do I claim that the agent intellect causes knowledge in our possible intellect through phantasms rendered actually intelligible by it."[57] There was an important theological reason for Thomas to identify a local combination of an active and passive principle in the possible intellect. If the agent intellect is the only active "seed" of growth in the intellect, what shall we say about Thomas's observation in the *Commentary on the Sentences* that there are perfections of the possible intellect which begin and develop from an active principle that entirely supersedes the first principles caused by the agent intellect, such as belief in the articles of the Creed, the natural knowledge of the separated soul, and the beatific vision? Thomas does not address belief in the articles of the Creed in the *Quaestiones disputatae de anima,* but he does address the natural knowledge of the separated soul and the beatific vision.

When Thomas addresses the natural knowledge of the separated soul, he says that once the soul is loosed from the body it will receive

56. Jean de la Rochelle, *Tractatus de multiplici divisione potentiarum animae,* ed. Pierre Michaud-Quantin (Paris: J. Vrin, 1964), pars 2, cap. 21 [Michaud-Quantin 91].

57. Thomas Aquinas, *De an.,* a. 15, co. [Leon. 24.1:135]: "sicut enim ponimus quod agentia superiora, mediantibus agentibus naturalibus, causant formas naturales, ita ponimus quod intellectus agens, per fantasmata ab eo facta intelligibilia actu, causat scientiam in intellectu possibili nostro."

an influence of knowledge from the separated substances.[58] This is essentially what Jean had said. But Thomas does not merely repeat Jean; he also raises an objection to Jean's teaching based upon Thomas's understanding of a potency for obedience. The objector applies Thomas's teaching from the *De potentia* about our potency for obedience to the natural knowledge of the separated soul: since in this case the actualization of our possible intellect is caused by a higher agent (that is, an angel) rather than a connatural agent (the agent intellect), should this sort of knowledge not be classified as miraculous? If so, then is it not true that the separated soul has no natural knowledge?[59] Thomas responds:

> The possible intellect cannot be reduced into the act of the knowledge of all natural things by the light of the agent intellect alone, but rather through some superior substance, to whom the knowledge of all things in act belongs. And if someone were to consider the matter rightly, the agent intellect (according to those things which the Philosopher teaches about it) is not active directly with respect to the possible intellect, but much rather with respect to the phantasms which it makes intelligible in act, through which the possible intellect is reduced into act.[60]

The solution is similar to the solution he had initially proposed at the beginning of his career to the problem of the relationship of nature and grace. By separating the agent intellect from direct interaction with the possible intellect, Thomas is able to argue that, since forms received into the possible intellect are not above its material potency, any form infused into the possible intellect by the natural act of another creature can be said to result in "natural" knowledge.

58. Ibid., q. 15, co. [Leon. 24.1:136].

59. Ibid., q. 18, obj. 12 [Leon. 24.1:155].

60. Ibid., ad 11 [Leon. 24.1:159]: "Intellectus possibilis non potest reduci in actum cognitionis omnium naturalium per lumen solum intellectus agentis, set per aliquam superiorem substantiam, cui actu adest cognitio omnium naturalium. Et si quis recte consideret, intellectus agens, secundum ea que Philosophus de ipso tradit, non est actiuum respectu intellectus possibilis directe, set magis respectu fantasmatum que facit intelligibilia actu, per que intellectus possibilis reducitur in actum."

The separated soul can therefore receive a natural influx of intelligible species from the angels without that knowledge being classified as miraculous.[61]

When discussing the supernatural knowledge of the separated soul, Thomas uses a similar argument to the one which he uses with regard to its natural knowledge, because, while the beatific vision may involve a knowledge that is *supra naturam* in its active principle, it does not and cannot involve knowledge which is *supra naturam* in its material principle. With a succinct allusion to the argument about our natural desire for the vision of God from the *Summa contra Gentiles*, he argues: "The possible intellect is continually reduced from potency into act by the fact that it understands more and more, yet the end of this sort of reduction or generation will be in understanding the highest intelligible, which is the divine essence; yet it can only arrive at this by grace, not by its natural endowments."[62] Continuing to recognize the ability of higher agents to circumvent our agent intellect when they actualize our possible intellect, Thomas thus reiterates his use of the matter/form analogy to describe the relationship between nature and grace.

Although the bulk of Thomas's text concerns the intellect, since he is working out problems with regard to illumination, we may note for the sake of completeness that he does at least restate the argument taken from Jean de la Rochelle about the natural appetite in the will for perpetual being from *Summa contra Gentiles* 2.79.[63]

61. In ibid., q. 15, co. [Leon. 24.1:136–37], Thomas observes that since the human agent intellect does not possess the same intellective power as an angel, it cannot deduce all that an angel would deduce from the species which it receives from the angels.

62. Ibid., q. 16, ad 3 [Leon. 24.1:146]: "Cum intellectus possibilis continue reducatur de potentia in actum per hoc quod magis ac magis intelligit, finis tamen huiusmodi reductionis siue generationis erit in intelligendo suppremum intelligibile, quod est diuina essentia; set ad hoc non potest peruenire per naturalia, set per gratiam tantum."

63. Ibid., q. 14, co. [Leon. 24.1:127]: "Secundo, ex naturali appetitu qui in nulla re frustratri potest. Videmus enim hominibus appetitum esse perpetuitatis. Et hoc rationabiliter: quia cum ipsum esse secundum se sit appetibile, oportet quod ab intelligente qui apprehendit esse simpliciter, et non hic et nunc, appetatur esse simpliciter, et secundum omne tempus. Unde videtur quod iste appetitus non sit inanis; sed quod homo secundum animam intellectivam sit incorruptibilis."

There is one small development. Where previously Thomas had only implied that it is necessary for the soul to desire being's perpetuity once that perpetuity is apprehended, Thomas now states that necessity explicitly. The observation does not at this point entail any change to what he says in the *Summa contra Gentiles,* but the use of the word "necessity" with regard to the will was going to become a significant point of contention when he returned to Paris for his second regency, as we will see in chapter 5.

SENTENTIA LIBRI DE ANIMA

In 1267, two resources appeared that, as mentioned in the introduction to this chapter, would influence the direction of Thomas's thought on natural desire significantly: William of Moerbeke's translation of Aristotle's *De anima* (the so-called *translatio nova*), and his translation of Themistius's paraphrase of the *De anima.* The latter was completed on November 22, 1267, and there is good reason to believe that both works were made available to Thomas around that time.[64] Each would have an important influence on his thought: the former with respect to his understanding of the object of the will, and the latter with respect to the more conciliatory approach he had taken to the Christian Avicennian tradition in the *Quaestiones disputatae de anima.*

With regard to the object of the will, the *translatio nova* subtly changed the way that the *translatio vetus* rendered Aristotle's discussion of the intellect and the will in *De anima* 3.10. In that text, Aristotle is trying to identify the first mover among the powers of the soul. In the course of his discussion, he distinguishes between the appetitive faculty (τὸ ὀρεκτικόν), and the appetible object (τὸ ὀρεκτόν). Both Latin translators recognize a distinction between these two terms; they render the appetitive faculty (τὸ ὀρεκτικόν) as *appetitivum,* and the appetible object (τὸ ὀρεκτόν) as *appetibile.* But there

64. Torrell, *Saint Thomas Aquinas,* 1:171–75.

TABLE 1. The translation of τὸ ὀρεκτικόν and τὸ ὀρεκτόν in the *translatio vetus* and in the *translatio nova*

De anima 3.10 (433b10–13)	*Translatio vetus*	*Translatio nova*
εἴδει μὲν ἓν ἂν εἴη τὸ κινοῦν, [1] **τὸ ὀρεκτικόν, ᾗ ὀρεκτικόν**—πρῶτον δὲ πάντων [2] **τὸ ὀρεκτόν** τοῦτο γὰρ κινεῖ οὐ κινούμενον, τῷ νοηθῆναι ἢ φαντασθῆναι—ἀριθμῷ δὲ πλείω τὰ κινοῦντα.	specie quidem igitur unum erit movens: [1] **appetitivum secundum quod appetitivum** est (primum autem omnium [2] **appetibile** est; hoc autem movet, cum non movetur, in eo quod sit intellectum aut imaginatum), numero autem plura sunt moventia.	Specie quidem igitur unum erit mouens, [1] **appetibile | aut appetitiuum,** primum autem omnium [2] **appetibile**; hoc | enim mouet cum non mouetur, eo quod sit intellectum aut ymaginatum.

are some anomalies in their translations, which ultimately have a significant effect on the meaning. Consider the example in table 1.

Both translators are very clearly working from a Greek text in which phrase 2 matches the contemporary critical edition of the Greek text. The *translatio vetus,* moreover, is working from a text in which phrase 1 also matches the contemporary critical edition of the Greek. However, something appears to have gone wrong with the *translatio nova.* Either William is working from a text in which phrase 1 has "τὸ ὀρεκτόν, ᾗ ὀρεκτικόν" rather than "τὸ ὀρεκτικόν, ᾗ ὀρεκτικόν," or William's transcription and/or translation is simply inaccurate at this point. However William may have arrived at his translation, William has Aristotle say something different from what Aristotle actually said, and different from what previous generations of Latins who read the *translatio vetus* thought that Aristotle had said. Rather than suggest in phrase 1 with Aristotle and the *translatio vetus* that the primary mover in the soul is the appetitive faculty, William has Aristotle set up a disjunction between the appetible object and the appetitive faculty in phrase 1, and conclude in phrase 2 that the primary mover of the soul is the appetible object *as opposed to* the appetitive faculty.

TABLE 2. Further examples of the translation of τὸ ὀρεκτικόν and τὸ ὀρεκτόν in the *translatio vetus* and the *translatio nova*

De anima 3.10 (433a17–21)	*Translatio vetus*	*Translatio nova*
ὥστε εὐλόγως δύο ταῦτα φαίνεται τὰ κινοῦντα, ὄρεξις καὶ διάνοια πρακτική· [1] **τὸ ὀρεκτὸν** γὰρ κινεῖ, καὶ διὰ τοῦτο ἡ διάνοια κινεῖ, ὅτι ἀρχὴ αὐτῆς ἐστι [2] **τὸ ὀρεκτόν**.	Quare rationabiliter hec duo videntur moventia: appetitus et intelligentia practica; [1] **appetitivum** enim movet, et propter hoc intelligentia movet, quia principium ipsius [2] **appetitivum** est	Quare rationabiliter hec duo uidentur | mouencia, appetitus et intelligencia practica; [1] **appetibile** enim mouet, | et propter hoc intelligencia mouet, quia principium huius est quod | [2] **appetibile**.
καὶ ἡ φαντασία δὲ ὅταν κινῇ, οὐ κινεῖ ἄνευ ὀρέξεως	Et fantasia autem cum moveat, non movet sine appetitu.	Et fantasia autem cum moueat, non mouet sine appetitu.
ἓν δή τι τὸ κινοῦν, [3] **τὸ ὀρεκτικόν**.	Unum igitur quiddam est movens, quod est [3] **appetitivum**.	Vnum igitur mouens, quod [3] **appetibile**.

Setting aside for a moment the consequences of William's translation, to which we will return in a moment, let us consider a wider set of comments that Aristotle makes shortly before the text just quoted about the appetitive faculty and the appetible object. We will see that the same issues of transcription and translation affect these texts as well (see table 2).

Neither Latin translation reproduces the contemporary Greek critical edition of the text. The *translatio vetus* differs from the Greek on phrases 1 and 2, but matches it on phrase 3, while with the *translatio nova* does precisely the reverse. The result is that, while Aristotle speaks of τὸ ὀρεκτὸν (*appetibile*) in phrases 1 and 2, but τὸ ὀρεκτικόν (*appetitivum*) in phrase 3, the *translatio vetus* thinks that Aristotle speaks of τὸ ὀρεκτικόν (*appetitivum*) in every instance, while William thinks that Aristotle speaks of τὸ ὀρεκτὸν (*appetibile*) in every instance. This amplifies the difference noted above between the *translatio vetus* and the *translatio nova*. The *translatio vetus* clearly emphasizes the appetitive power as the first mover of the soul, while the *translatio nova* just as clearly emphasizes the appetible object.

In Thomas's exegesis of Aristotle in the *Sententia libri de anima,* he follows the *translatio nova.* Applying what William has Aristotle say about the appetite in general to the will in particular as a rational appetite, Thomas says that the object of the will is the apprehended good (*bonum apprehensum*).[65] But this leads him to an observation which had not factored significantly into his previous discussions of the will's motion: the good can either be apprehended by the intellect or the imagination. Given that either the intellect or the imagination can apprehend an object in such a way that the object can move the will, Thomas can no longer say that the intellect is the first mover of the will, as he had said in the *De veritate* and the *Summa contra Gentiles.* The appetible object itself, however it may be apprehended, is the first mover of the will.[66] While there remains a *structural* priority of the intellect over the will when the object which moves the will is apprehended by the intellect, no such structural priority exists when the object which moves the will is apprehended by the imagination. Furthermore, when the object which moves the will is apprehended by the intellect, the intellect no longer maintains what might be described as a *temporal* priority over the will, since it is the object itself which moves the will. This change will oc-

65. Thomas Aquinas, *Sententia libri De anima* 3.9 [Leon. 45.1:247].

66. Ibid. [Leon. 45.1:245]: "Et hoc rationabile est quod hec duo mouencia reducantur in unum, quod est appetibile, quia, si ponebantur hec duo, intellectus et appetitus, esse mouencia respectu eiusdem motus, cum unius effectus sit una causa propria, necesse est quod moueant hec duo secundum aliquam speciem communem; non autem dicendum quod appetitus moueat sub specie intellectus, set magis e conuerso intellectus uel intelligibilis <sub specie appetitus>, quia intellectus non inuenitur mouens sine appetitu, quia uoluntas, secundum quam mouet intellectus, est quidam appetitus (et huius ratio assignatur in IX Methaphisice, quia cum ratio sciencie practice se habeat ad opposita, non mouet nisi determinetur ad unum per appetitum). Set appetitus mouet sine ratione, sicut patet in hiis que mouentur ex concupiscencia; concupiscencia enim est appetitus quidam."

This was effectively what Themistius said in Moerbeke's translation: "Unum quidem igitur specie appetitivum, unum autem et quod ante hoc appetibile, quod quidem iam movet non motum eo quod intelligatur aut phantasietur: numero autem esse plura moventia et ut appetibilia et ut appetitiva nihil prohibet" [Verbeke 268].

casion a significant shift in Thomas's explanation of natural desire, as we shall see below with reference to the *Prima pars,* because it upset the tidy chain of causality that Thomas had carefully worked out in dialogue with Maimonides's understanding of Providence, which moved from God, to the agent intellect, to the possible intellect, to the will, to the other powers of the soul.

In Thomas's use of Themistius the central text is *De anima* 3.5, where Aristotle distinguishes what Thomas will call the agent intellect and the possible intellect. In Greek, Aristotle distinguishes between an intellect which is said to become all things (πάντα γίνεσθαι) and one which is said to make all things (πάντα ποιεῖν). Speaking of the intellect that makes all things, Aristotle says that it is a state or habit (ἕξις) like light, that it is separable/separated (χωριστός), impassible (ἀπαθής), and unmixed (ἀμιγής), as well as that it relates to the intellect that becomes all things like form relates to matter.[67]

As we have already seen in previous chapters, *De anima* 3.5 had a long and varied history among the Aristotelian commentators before it was received into Latin theology in the thirteenth century. Thus far we have mainly considered the Arabic commentators, Avicenna and Averroes, as well as those who read and made use of them among thirteenth-century Latins. Yet the early Greek commentators had a similar diversity of thought on how to interpret this passage, and it is important for us to take this diversity into account if we want to understand the significance of Thomas's engagement with Themistius.

Alexander of Aphrodisias, who preceded Themistius, distinguished three kinds of intellect: the "intellect which becomes all things" he called the "material intellect" (ὁ νοῦς ὑλικός),[68] the "in-

67. Aristotle, *De anima* 3.5 [430a14–19]: "καὶ ἔστιν ὁ μὲν τοιοῦτος νοῦς τῷ πάντα γίνεσθαι, ὁ δὲ τῷ πάντα ποιεῖν, ὡς ἕξις τις, οἷον τὸ φῶς·τρόπον γάρ τινα καὶ τὸ φῶς ποιεῖ τὰ δυνάμει ὄντα χρώματα ἐνεργείᾳ χρώματα. Καὶ οὗτος ὁ νοῦς χωριστὸς καὶ ἀπαθὴς καὶ ἀμιγής, τῇ οὐσίᾳ ὢν ἐνέργεια· ἀεὶ γὰρ τιμιώτερον τὸ ποιοῦν τοῦ πάσχοντος καὶ ἡ ἀρχὴ τῆς ὕλης."

68. Alexander of Aphrodisias, *De anima libri mantissa* [*De intellectu*], in *Alexandri*

tellect which makes all things" he called the "agent intellect" (ὁ νοῦς ποιητικός),[69] and the material intellect when actualized by the agent intellect in an act of thought he called the intellect in "habit" (ἕξις).[70] In his explanation of the agent intellect he was the first to take χωριστός to mean "separated" rather than "separable," interpreting it in light of *De generatione animalium* 2.3, which says that "reason alone enters [a newly generated organism] from without."[71] This led Alexander to say that the agent intellect "is called [intellect] from without, not because it is a part and a faculty of our soul, but because it comes to exist in us from outside whenever we think of it . . . and it is itself an immaterial form in that, when thought of, it is never accompanied by matter, nor is it being separated from matter."[72] For Alexander, the agent intellect is identical with God,[73] who, as the highest intellect, is the cause of understanding in all lower intellects, including the material intellect.[74] This occurs when the agent intellect causes a disposition toward thought in the material intellect.[75] When actualized by the agent intellect, the material intellect also attains a certain degree of actuality.[76] However, this actuality does not constitute a power belonging to the human soul properly speaking; it remains a disposition, and so is corrupted at the moment of death.[77]

Although Themistius agrees with the idea that the single, agent intellect is received into a material intellect—he points to the fact

---

Aphrodisiensis praeter commentaria scripta minora, supplement 2.1 to *Commentaria in Aristotelem Graeca*, ed I. Bruns (Berlin: Reimer, 1887), 106.19.

69. Ibid., 107.30.

70. Ibid., 107.25.

71. Herbert Davidson, *Alfarabi, Avicenna and Averroes on Intellect* (New York: Oxford University Press, 1992), 13–14. See Aristotle, *De generatione animalium* 2.3 [736b28], quoted in Davidson, *Alfarabi, Avicenna and Averroes on Intellect*, 11.

72. Alexander of Aphrodisias, *De intellectu*, 108.19–25, trans. Frederic Schroeder (Toronto: PIMS, 1990), 49.

73. Davidson, *Alfarabi, Avicenna and Averroes on Intellect*, 14.

74. Ibid., 9, 20n80.

75. Ibid., 21–22.

76. Ibid., 23.

77. Ibid., 37–38.

that people have a common knowledge of the first principles of reasoning and of philosophical axioms[78]—for our purposes he distinguishes himself from Alexander in two significant ways.[79] First, he denies that the agent intellect is God,[80] although he does say that it should be thought of on *analogy* with God:[81] it is the first efficient cause of thinking,[82] its essence is identical with its activity without any admixture of potentiality,[83] and it can be described as "unceasing, untiring, immortal, and eternal,"[84] knowing all things above composition and division.[85] Since individuation comes from matter,[86] and since the agent intellect is a separate substance, albeit below God, the agent intellect is common to all humanity.[87]

Second, Themistius criticizes the way in which Alexander describes the agent intellect as coming to the potential intellect from "without"; Themistius prefers to speak of the relationship between the agent and the potential intellect on analogy with the relationship between matter and form; form inhabits matter intrinsically rather than extrinsically.[88] This is part of how Themistius construes the powers of the soul more generally speaking. Each power stands in relationship to the one above it as matter and to the one below it as form.[89] Consequently the agent intellect, though single for all human persons, relates to their individual intellects as the form of each.

When William translated the text of Themistius, some of this subtlety appears to have been lost. As a result, he introduces into Themistius's text a distinction that Themistius does not make be-

78. Themistius, *De anima*, 104.1.

79. Ibid., 98.12–23.

80. Ibid., 102.30–103.19; see Davidson, *Alfarabi, Avicenna and Averroes on Intellect*, 14.

81. Themistius, *De anima*, 99.20–21.

82. Ibid., 99.24.

83. Ibid., 99.32–33, and again at 100.7–8.

84. Themistius, *De anima*, 99.39–40, quote from Themistius, *On Aristotle on the Soul*, trans. Robert Todd (New York: Bloomsbury, 2013), 124.

85. Themistius, *De anima* 100.11–14.

86. Ibid., 103.30–31.

87. Ibid., 103.20–103.35.

88. Ibid., 99.15–20.

89. Davidson, *Alfarabi, Avicenna and Averroes on Intellect*, 27.

TABLE 3. Agent intellect in the Greek text of Themistius's *De anima* and William of Moerbeke's Latin translation

	Themistius	Moerbeke's Translation
Text 1	παρὰ μόνου τοίνυν **τοῦ ποιητικοῦ** τὸ ἐμοὶ εἶναι.·... (100.31–32)	A solo igitur **factivo** est mihi esse.... (Verbeke 229:85)
Text 2	ἡμεῖς οὖν **ὁ ποιητικὸς** νοῦς... (101.1–2)	Nos igitur sumus **activus** intellectus. (Verbeke 229:91)
Text 3	ἆρα εἷς **ὁ ποιητικὸς** οὗτος νοῦς ἢ πολλοί; (103.21)	Utrum unus **activus** iste intellectus aut multi? (Verbeke 224.95–96)
Text 4	ἢ ὁ μὲν πρώτως ἐλλάμπων εἷς, οἱ δὲ ἐλλαμπόμενοι καὶ ἐλλάμποντες πλείους ὥσπερ τὸ φῶς. ὁ μὲν γὰρ ἥλιος εἷς, τὸ δὲ φῶς εἴποις ἂν τρόπον τινὰ μερίζεσθαι εἰς τὰς ὄψεις. διὰ τοῦτο γὰρ οὐ τὸν ἥλιον παραβέβληκεν ἀλλὰ τὸ φῶς, Πλάτων δὲ τὸν ἥλιον· τῷ γὰρ ἀγαθῷ ἀνάλογον αὐτὸν ποιεῖ. (103.32–36)	Aut primus quidem illustrans est unus, illustrati autem et illustrantes plures, sicut lumen; sol quidem enim est unus, lumen autem dices utique modo aliquo partiri ad visus; propter hoc enim non solem in comparatione proposuit sed lumen, Plato autem solem: bono enim proportionalem ipsum facit. (Verbeke 235.6–12)
Text 5	εἰ δὲ εἰς ἕνα **ποιητικὸν** νοῦν ἅπαντες ἀναγόμεθα οἱ συγκείμενοι ἐκ τοῦ **δυνάμει** καὶ **ἐνεργείᾳ**, καὶ ἑκάστῳ ἡμῶν τὸ εἶναι παρὰ τοῦ ἑνὸς ἐκείνου ἐστίν, οὐ χρὴ θαυμάζειν. (103.36–38)	Si autem ad unum **activum** intellectum omnes reducimur compositi ex eo qui **potentia** et **actu**, et unicuique nostrum esse ab illo uno est, non oportet mirari. (Verbeke 235.12–14)

tween a separated agent intellect that is one for all persons, and individual agent intellects in each human soul. Consider the examples in table 3.

Once in this series of texts (text 1), when ὁ ποιητικός appears as a substantive, William translates it as *factivum* ("productive"). In that instance, Themistius is describing the separated agent intellect as the active principle according to which individual identity is established. By translating ὁ ποιητικός as *factivum,* Moerbeke makes it seem as though Themistius is simply speaking about the efficient cause of the human individual. In texts 2, 3, and 5, by contrast, Moerbeke translates ὁ ποιητικὸς νοῦς as *intellectus activus* ("active intellect"). Themistius is still talking about what the separated agent intellect does for individual potential intellects, but Moerbeke makes it sound as though he is describing individual agent intellects, illumined by the separated agent intellect. This seems to represent an interpretive move, as evidenced by the fact that Moerbeke also translates ποιητικός as *activus* in the same sentence as he translates ἐνεργεία as *actus*. Thus, while Themistius is actually saying that the potential intellect is the object of the agent intellect's illumination, and that the act caused in it is the actual understanding of the first principles, Moerbeke has Themistius appear to say that the Creator (the *factivus*) causes act (*actus*) in our active intellect (*intellectus activus*), rather than in our potential intellect; the active intellect, in turn, illumines the potential intellect.

Since Thomas read Themistius in Moerbeke's Latin translation, he understood Themistius to be saying what Moerbeke has him appear to say, rather than what Themistius actually said. This is clear from a slightly later text, *De unitate intellectus*, where Thomas discusses text 4. After quoting the text in its entirety, Thomas comments: "Therefore, it is clear *from Themistius's words* that the agent intellect, about which Aristotle is speaking, is not the 'single [intellect] which enlightens,' nor likewise is it the possible intellect, which is enlightened (*illustratus*); yet it is true that the principle of enlightenment (*illustratio*) is one, namely some separated substance: either God according to Catholics, or the last intelligence according to Avicenna."[90] Where the Greek text of Themistius makes it very clear

90. Thomas Aquinas, *De unitate intellectus contra Averroistas*, cap. 5 [Leon. 43.314] (emphasis added): "Et ut Grecos non omittamus, ponenda sunt circa hoc uerba Themistii in Commento. Cum enim quesisset de intellectu agente utrum sit unus aut plures, subiungit soluens 'Aut primus quidem illustrans est unus, illustrati autem et illustrantes sunt plures. Sol quidem enim est unus, lumen qutem dices modo aliquo partiri ad uisus. Propter hoc enim non solem in comparatione proposuit, scilicet Aristotiles, sed lumen; Plato autem solem.' Ergo patet *per uerba Themistii* quod nec intellectus agens, de quo Aristotiles loquitur, est unus qui est illustrans, nec etiam possibilis qui est illustratus; sed

that Themistius *is*, in fact, identifying Aristotle's agent intellect with the single intellect which enlightens, Thomas—reading Themistius through Moerbeke—comes to precisely the opposite conclusion.

If the only consequence of Thomas's Moerbekian reading of Themistius were an error of exegesis, we might be excused for passing over the error as an historical accident of little consequence. But this misread, like the one of *De anima* 3.10, would also have a significant effect on Thomas's future writing. From the *De veritate* to the *Quaestiones Disputatae de anima*, Thomas was careful to oppose the Avicennian idea that there is one agent intellect for all human persons. But henceforth Thomas will take a much more conciliatory approach to this view. Using his previous arguments to safeguard the multiplicity of created agent intellects in individual human souls, Thomas will

---

uerum est quod principium illustrationis est unum, scilicet aliqua substantia separata: uel Deus secundum Catholicos, uel intelligentia ultima secundum Auicennam."

Gilson, "Pourquoi saint Thomas a critiqué saint Augustin," 114, cites this text without an awareness of the difference between the Latin and the Greek, and uses it to show how Thomas is more conciliatory toward Avicenna than toward Averroes: "la doctrine ... d'Avicenne, quoique fausse même une fois ainsi corrigée, n'est pas sans avoir quelque apparence de raison. Et l'on peut aller jusqu'à dire qu'en un certain sens elle est vraie." He goes on to note on p. 118 that although Thomas could not follow an Avicennian-Augustinian account of divine illumination, there was a certain manner in which Thomas himself approved of Augustine's theory of illumination: "Un Dieu qui serait à la fois lui-même et notre propre intellect est radicalement inacceptable pour le thomisme; un Dieu qui illumine notre intellect sans l'être, et qui agit par conséquent pour nous sans se confondre avec nous, n'est aucunement inassimilable pour le thomisme et n'a même dans son fond rien que de vrai." This may help us to understand the apparent tension among interpreters of Thomas's work on the subject of divine illumination. While Thomas certainly opposed himself to the Avicennian-Augustinian illuminationist tradition of the second quarter of the thirteenth century at the beginning of his career, we may make three observations about this opposition. First, we should not assume without evidence that the Avicennian-Augustinian illuminationist tradition of the thirteenth century represents the authentic interpretation of Augustine; second, we should therefore not assume without evidence that by opposing the Avicennian-Augustinian illuminationist tradition of the thirteenth-century Thomas was opposing himself to Augustine; third, whatever we make of the relationship between the Avicennian-Augustinian illuminationist tradition of the thirteenth century and Augustine, Thomas's reading of Moerbeke's translation of Themistius changed his attitude toward that tradition so that he took a more conciliatory stance toward it, even if he was not in every way reconciled to it. This change will be documented in the texts considered below.

even adopt in a certain respect the Christian Avicennian identification of the separated agent intellect with God. Moerbeke's translation of Themistius thus helped him to safeguard the priority of God's illumination in the agent intellect, even as Moerbeke's translation of Aristotle would challenge him to locate the beginning of activity in the possible intellect and the will in the *bonum apprehensum*.

Of course, adopting the Christian Avicennian identification of the separated agent intellect with God would bring Thomas very close to the position of William of Auvergne, which Thomas had just carefully opposed in the *Quaestiones disputatae de anima*, and in which the first principles of demonstration function as an individual's agent intellect. Thomas is careful to avoid that consequence, and so he gives two arguments why one need not identify the agent intellect with the first principles of demonstration. First, he redeploys his argument against William's position from the *Quaestiones disputatae de anima*. Second, he tries to show that Aristotle did not mean what William says. One difficulty with that line of argument is that Aristotle says, as we saw above, that the agent intellect is a "habit" (ἕξις). Thomas's response is less thorough than one might wish: he claims that Aristotle must have meant to use the word "habit" as a substitute for "form" or "nature," "as he is frequently accustomed to do."[91]

QUAESTIONES DISPUTATAE DE SPIRITUALIBUS CREATURIS

In question 1 of the *Quaestiones disputatae de spiritualibus creaturis*, Thomas reconsiders the *ratio seminalis* in the intellect in light of his observation in the *Sententia libri De anima* that the first mover of both the practical intellect and the will is the appetible object. Previously, he had likened the active principles in these powers to form and the passive principles to matter. While acknowledging that this was

91. Thomas Aquinas, *Sententia libri De anima* 3.4 [45.1:219]: "Dicendum est ergo quod 'habitus' hic accipitur secundum quod Philosophus frequenter consueuit nominare omnem formam et naturam habitum."

not a precise analogy, because there is no matter in the intellect,[92] he had not explicitly addressed a key difference between matter/form on the one hand, and passive/active potency in the immaterial soul on the other. In the case of material being, form is separable from matter and can subsist without it. But in the case of created, spiritual being, the formal principle is not separable from the "material" principle and cannot subsist without it, because without that passive principle it would be *ipsum esse subsistens*—God himself.[93]

Thomas's observation concerning the impossibility of separating the active and passive powers of the soul caused a difficulty with his recent reception of Jean de la Rochelle, since Jean had posited a quasi-separability of the agent intellect from the possible intellect when discussing knowledge received into the possible intellect from angels and God in the separated state. Although Thomas had initially addressed this difficulty by suggesting that the agent intellect only acts indirectly on the possible intellect, his even more recent reading of Themistius would have brought to light the support that this leant to William of Auvergne's identification of the individual agent intellect with the first principles of demonstration. Perhaps for this reason, Thomas now emphasizes again the inseparability of the agent and possible intellects, and the fact that the agent intellect acts directly on the possible intellect.

In this respect, when Thomas inquires in article 10 as to whether the agent intellect is single or multiple, he defends the multiplicity of the agent intellect not only on the basis of his previous arguments,[94] but also with an allusion to *rationes seminales*: God does not act directly on the things of nature; rather, on account of his perfect fullness, by which he communicates his power to creation,[95] he places within them "seeds" by which they bring about their proper effects. For God to bring about the perfection of the possible intellect, we

92. See, for example, Thomas Aquinas, *De an.* q. 6, co. [Leon. 24.1:51].

93. Thomas Aquinas, *Quaestiones disputatae de spiritualibus creaturis*, a. 1, co. [Leon. 24.2:14].

94. Ibid., a. 10, co. [Leon.24.2:106].

95. Ibid., ad 16 [Leon. 24.2:114].

must therefore posit a seed of that activity in the human intellect, which is the agent intellect.[96]

Even if Thomas carefully defends the multiplicity of the agent intellect, he does not abandon his conciliatory approach to the Christian Avicennian tradition. Inspired by his reading of Themistius, he now takes the conversation in a new direction. Admitting that there is a difference between proving that the human agent intellect is dependent on a higher intellect and proving that the human agent intellect is dependent on God, he now seeks to demonstrate that that the higher intellect upon which the human agent intellect is dependent is, in fact, God.

We might expect Thomas to continue in this article with a set of proofs from natural reason. This would certainly be consistent with the philosophical mode he had previously adopted for arguments concerning the agent intellect. However, Thomas would in that case upset our expectations. He does not offer a single such philosophical argument in what follows. Instead, he observes that the idea of a created agent intellect above the human intellect is "repugnant to the truth of faith in many ways," and proceeds to make three theological arguments against the idea:

1) Since the cause of the soul's knowing is also the cause of its being, if an angel were the cause of the soul's knowing, then man would have been created by an angel. But Genesis 1 says that God "breathed the breath of life" into man.
2) Since the ultimate perfection of any creature is to reach its principle, if an angel were the cause of the soul's being then human happiness would be found in knowing an angel. But John 17 says "This is eternal life, that they may know you, the only true God."
3) If man received knowing and being from an angel then we would be made in the image of an angel. But Genesis 1 says that man is made in the *imago Dei*.

96. Ibid., co. [Leon. 24.2:105].

Why, we may ask, does Thomas prescind from philosophical arguments here? One possibility is that he simply did not have any such arguments or could not think of any in the moment. This is what he had done as a young scholar in Book 2, distinction 17, of his *Commentary on the Sentences.* Yet while we may make allowances for such gap-filling in his early work, this would be inappropriate for a scholar who by this point had been personally entrusted with the formation of an entire *studium.* Moreover, Thomas possessed an abundance of philosophical arguments which could have served his purposes here. In *De potentia* q. 5, a. 1, as we saw above, he had shown that God, as the cause of the soul's first motion, is the cause of both its knowing and its being; in Book 3 of the *Summa contra Gentiles,* as we saw in chapter 3, as well as question 14 of the *Quaestiones disputatae de anima,* as we saw above, he had shown that the end of man's natural desire is the vision of God. It seems, therefore, that Thomas did not omit philosophical arguments because he lacked them. He must have turned to theological arguments because he thought that theological arguments were needed *as a supplement* to the many philosophical arguments, which were ready to hand. This would make sense if his intended interlocutors were Christian theologians rather than Arabic philosophers.[97] He seems to be demarcating the theological boundaries within which Christian theologians can adopt the Avicennian tradition, if that tradition is understood in light of Moerbeke's translation of Themistius.

THE *SUMMA THEOLOGIAE, PRIMA PARS*

Nature and Grace

In the *Prima pars* of the *Summa theologiae,* Thomas's discussion of nature and grace follows closely his discussion of related topics in the *De potentia,* although he now takes a somewhat softer stance with regard to Bonaventure's view of Creation. Unlike in the *Commentary on the Sentences* and the *De potentia,* where Thomas used his

97. Thomas Aquinas, *SCG* 1.3.

understanding of substantial form to all but accuse Bonaventure of imposing an irrational reading of Creation on Genesis, Thomas now goes out of his way to defend the Christian orthodoxy of Bonaventure's reading, and to harmonize it as far as possible with his own.

The possibility of harmonizing the two views was actually suggested implicitly by Bonaventure. In his *Breviloquium*, Bonaventure returns to the question of Creation and quietly responds to the criticisms Thomas had levied against Bonaventure's *Commentary on the Sentences*. Bonaventure begins by reasserting the idea from his own *Commentary on the Sentences* that reason must submit to Sacred Scripture in relation to Genesis 1.[98] But when it comes to the metaphysical underpinnings of the events that Scripture narrates, Bonaventure suggests a different way to approach the question than asking about matter *secundum esse* and *secundum essentiam*: use a distinction between Creation with regard to becoming and Creation with regard to being.[99] Considered with regard to becoming, Bonaventure says that we must "especially hold" that Creation was brought to be out of nothing gradually over the course of six days.[100] Even though God could have created everything in an instant, he chose to create over six days so that he might show forth his power at the first instant, his wisdom over the first three days during which he distinguished his creation, and his goodness over the second three days during which he decorated his creation.[101] Since God rested from making new species on the seventh day, the antecedents of all things must have been created during the six-day process. Here Bonaventure points to the elements, which represent the activity and passivity of nature in the universe.[102] The elements are the formal an-

98. Bonaventure, *Breviloquium*, prol., in *Opera Omnia*, vol. 5 (Quaracchi: College of St. Bonaventure, 1891), 201. See also 2.2 [Quaracchi 5:219].

99. These are the subjects of ibid., 2.2 [Quaracchi 5:219–20] and 2.3 [Quaracchi 5:220–21] respectively.

100. Ibid., 2.2 [Quaracchi 5:219]: "De natura vero corporea quantum ad fieri haec specialiter tenenda sunt, quod sex diebus sit in esse producta, ita quod 'in principio,' ante omnem diem 'creavit Deus caelum et terram.'"

101. Ibid. [Quaracchi 5:220].

102. Ibid., 2.4 [Quaracchi 5:221].

tecedents to some things and the *rationes seminales* of others.[103] They are the formal antecedents of the elemented spheres: fire, air, water, and earth; they are the *rationes seminales* of others, because each of them admits of a composition of active and passive potencies, and so can "be mixed to introduce multifaceted forms."[104] Following Bacon, Bonaventure rejects the idea that the elements were created in a state of confusion and chaos. Yet Bonaventure insists that they were not created as entirely distinct either. Rather, the first created things were made in an imperfect state, so that they could be brought to perfection over the course of the days narrated in Genesis.[105]

Thomas appears to have read through Bonaventure's revised account of Creation, and to have sensed that Bonaventure's more recent view was not all that far from his own. This was in a way convenient, because Thomas also seems to have sensed his own view, although more in accord with how he understood the principles of metaphysics, was in the minority. Among the Church Fathers, Thomas could claim Augustine as an authority for the idea that God made all things in an instant, but Augustine stood virtually alone; the Fathers, Thomas admits, generally preferred a more literal reading of the six days.[106]

103. Ibid., 2.2 [Quaracchi 5:220].

104. Ibid., 2.3 [Quaracchi 5:220]. "Ratio autem ad intelligentiam praedictorum haec est: quia, cum natura corporalis ad perfectionem sui et expressionem sapientiae multiformis primi principii, requirat multiformitatem foramarum, sicut apparet in mineralibus, plantis et animalibus; necesse fuit ponere aliqua corpora simplicia, quae multiformiter possent misceri ad introductionem formarum multiformium; et talis est natura subiecta contrarietati, et haec est elementaris....

"Et quoniam mixtio fieri non potest nisi per contraria agentia et patientia, ideo necesse fuit, duplicem contrarietatem fieri in elementis, scilicet quantum ad qualitates activas, quae sunt calidum et frigidum; et quantum ad passivas, quae sunt humidum et siccum. Et quia quodlibet elementum agit et patitur, ideo habet duas qualitates, unam activam et alteram passivam."

In the same chapter, Bonaventure also speaks in the allegorical sense of the "seeds of works to be done" being contained in the works of creation.

105. Ibid., 2.5 [Quaracchi 5:223]. As in Bonaventure's *Commentary on the Sentences*, man's desire for the vision of God is fulfilled in a structure analogous to matter's desire for form. See ibid., 7.7 [Quaracchi 5:289].

106. Thomas Aquinas, *ST*, Ia, q. 74, a. 2, co. [Leon. 5:190]: "in hac quaestione

Thomas finds the key to a more literal reading of the six days in the material potency of creatures such as he had expressed it in the *De potentia*. To say that Creation took place all in an instant need not entail that all the diversity of natures that we find today was present in that instant *in act*. Following Bonaventure's *Breviloquium*, Thomas now says that it is sufficient for that diversity to have been present potentially, and for that potency to have been actualized over the course of six days. This safeguards both the literal sense of Scripture as well as the unicity of substantial form. And while some small differences of interpretation might still remain between his and Bonaventure's respective opinions, still "if these two opinions are considered with regard to the mode of the production of things, there is not a great difference between them."[107] So great does Thomas perceive to be the similarity between their views that he refuses to support either view at the expense of the other.

Thomas's conciliatory approach to Bonaventure is reflected throughout his discussion of creatures as causes of change in the *Prima pars*. As in the *De potentia*, Thomas distinguishes the question of how creatures participate in substantial change from how they participate in accidental change. The first question, which corresponds with *De potentia* q. 3, a. 8, is discussed in the treatise on Creation (*Summa theologiae*, Ia, q. 45, a. 8); the second, which corresponds with *De potentia* q. 3, a. 7, is discussed in the treatise on Providence (*Summa theologiae*, Ia, q. 115, a. 2).

As in *De potentia* q. 3, a. 8, the subject of *Summa theologiae*, Ia, q. 45, a. 8, is whether God places any principles in nature as a whole to bring about different substances after the act of Creation. Following the *De potentia*, Thomas reduces the question to a discussion of forms.[108] He then gives a simple summary of the positions he had

Augustinus ab aliis Expositoribus dissentit." In Ia, q. 66, a. 1, co. [Leon. 5:154], he lists Basil, Ambrose, and John Chrysostom among those with whom Augustine disagreed.

107. Ibid., q. 74, a. 2, co. [Leon. 5:190]: "si istae duae opiniones referantur ad modum productionis rerum, non invenitur magna differentia."

108. Ibid., q. 45, a. 8, co. [Leon. 4:476–77]. The question is "utrum creatio admisceatur

discussed in *De potentia,* q. 3, a. 8, leaving out any reference to specific names. First, he discusses Anaxagoras's *latitatio formarum.* As in *De potentia,* he identifies the precise difficulty with Anaxagoras as a failure to distinguish between potency and act; in almost the same language as previously, he says that this failure led to the idea that forms must pre-exist in matter actually. Second, he discusses Avicenna's *dator formarum.* As in *De potentia,* he argues that this idea arose from a failure to understand that the composite, not the form, is the *terminus* of generation.

Also as in the *De potentia,* Thomas treats Bonaventure's incomplete forms apart from Anaxagoras's *latitatio formarum* and Avicenna's *dator formarum.* His treatment of Bonaventure occurs in *Summa theologiae,* Ia, q. 76, a. 4, where Thomas asks about the possibility of a multiplicity of substantial forms inhering in a single substance. Against an objector reasserting some of the same objections from *Summa theologiae,* Ia, q. 45, a. 8,[109] Thomas argues that any substantial form is a complete substantial form, and so to posit a so-called "incomplete" substantial form is really to posit a complete substantial form by another name. Notwithstanding the truth of the matter as such, Thomas does makes a quasi-concession to Bonaventure: Bonaventure's opinion is a legitimate reading of Averroes, even if Thomas thinks that that makes both Averroes and Bonaventure mistaken.[110]

---

in operibus naturae et artis." Thomas begins his response, "Respondeo dicendum quod haec dubitatio inducitur propter formas."

109. Ibid., q. 76, a. 4, obj. 4 [Leon. 5:223].

110. Ibid., ad 4 [Leon. 5:224]. Having discussed and criticized the Avicennian opinion that "formas substantiales elementorum integras remanere in mixto: mixtionem autem fieri secundum quod contrariae qualitates elementorum reducuntur ad medium," Thomas goes on to note: "Averroes autem posuit, in III *De caelo,* quod formae elementorum, propter sui imperfectionem, sunt mediae inter formas accidentales et substantiale; et ideo recipiunt magis et minus; et ideo remittuntur in mixtione et ad medium reducuntur, et conflatur ex eis una forma.—Sed hoc est etiam magis impossibile. Nam esse substantiale cuiuslibet rei in indivisibili consistit; et omnis additio et subtractio variat speciem, sicut in numeris, ut dicitur in VIII *Metaphys.* Unde impossibile est quod forma substantialis quaecumque recipiat magis et minus.—Nec minus est impossible aliquid esse medium inter substantiam et accidens."

In *Summa theologiae,* Ia, q. 115, a. 2, Thomas discusses the question of whether God places any principles in a given creature to bring about accidental perfections in that creature.[111] As with the question of substantial change, this article summarizes and greatly simplifies the corresponding article in the *De potentia.* Instead of engaging the doctrine of the Mu'tazilites and Avicebron, he sets up the question with a simple appeal to the text of Aristotle himself, which would help the students connect Aristotelian and Augustinian terminology more easily. In *Metaphysics* 5.4,[112] Aristotle suggests by etymology that nature is linked with generation.[113] Thomas agrees. But since—according to Aristotelian biology—there is an active principle (the father) and a passive principle (the mother) in all generation,[114] Thomas suggests that Aristotle's active and passive principles are just another way of referring to the same metaphysical principle to which Augustine's *rationes seminales* refer.[115]

Continuing the understanding of nature he had given in *De potentia* in reference to our *potentia obedientiae,* Thomas says that God never does anything beyond *rationes seminales,* because although he can act beyond the active principle in a *ratio seminalis,* he can never act beyond its passive principle. Only if we voluntarily restrict our definition of a *ratio seminalis* in such a way that the passive principle consists only of that portion of passive potency which directly corresponds to that which can be actualized by the active principle, will we be able to say that anything can be done beyond *rationes seminales.*[116]

This understanding of passive potency allows Thomas to bor-

111. Ibid., q. 115, a. 2 [Leon. 5:540–41].

112. Aristotle, *Metaphysics* 5.4 [1014b16–1015a19].

113. Ibid. [1014b19–21].

114. Aristotle, *De generatione animalium,* 2.4 [740b19–741a4].

115. Thomas Aquinas, *ST,* Ia, q. 115, a. 2, co. [Leon. 5:541]. Having summarized Aristotle, Thomas observes: "Manifestum est autem quod principium activum et passivum generationis rerum viventium sunt semina ex quibus viventia generantur. Et ideo convenienter Augustinus omnes virtutes activas et passivas quae sunt principia generationum et motuum naturalium, seminales rationes vocat."

116. Ibid., ad 4 [Leon. 5:541].

row from Bonaventure a way of articulating the gradual reduction of potency to act over the course of the six days of Creation. We saw above that Bonaventure speaks in the *Breviloquium* of the elements possessing *rationes seminales* of other bodies. Thomas works this understanding of the elements into *Summa theologiae,* Ia, q. 115, a. 2. Here he describes a fourfold characterization of *rationes seminales*: they pre-exist by way of origin in the divine ideas; they exist first of all in the elements of the world; they exist second in the particular creatures that are brought to be from those universal causes; they exist finally in the seeds according to which those creatures reproduce.[117] This adoption of Bonaventure's language, albeit with Thomas's particular understanding of *rationes seminales,* allows Thomas to articulate with greater clarity how his own philosophical principles can still allow for a literal reading of the six days.

Thomas's understanding of passive potency is also reflected in his discussion of whether God does anything against, beyond, or above nature. Although God never does anything against nature (*contra naturam*) in a strict sense, God can—and often does—act contrary to the ordinary course of nature. Repeating the three categories for divine intervention in the *Summa contra Gentiles* (*not* the three categories of miracles from the *De potentia,* which Thomas had only reluctantly agreed to use), Thomas states that God's action outside the ordinary course of nature can take place in one of three ways: he can actualize some passive power in nature which nature cannot actualize on its own at all; he can actualize some passive power in nature which nature cannot actualize in the way that he actualizes it; or he can actualize some passive power in nature which it so happened that nature was not going to actualize.[118] The first of these actualizations is said to be "above nature" (*supra naturam*), and includes the reception of grace, while all of them are said to be in some way "beyond nature" (*praeter naturam*).[119] Since, moreover,

117. Ibid., co. [Leon. 5:540–41].

118. See ibid., q. 105, a. 8, co. [Leon. 5:480]. The three grades parallel those expressed earlier in the *Summa contra Gentiles*.

119. On the first class of miracles being above nature, see Thomas Aquinas, *ST*, Ia,

God acts *supra naturam* when he actualizes human nature's passive potency for grace, grace can be said to be "supernatural" (*supernaturalis*) and "superadded" (*superaddita*) to nature.

If grace is supernatural and is superadded to nature, that does not mean that grace in any way adds another substance to nature or imparts what we might call a "second nature" or a "super-nature" in a strict sense. Grace is indeed supernatural with respect to the active principle in nature because the eduction of grace from the passive principle in nature is above the active principle in nature. Nevertheless, grace is not above the passive principle in nature. If it were, grace would be *contra naturam*, not *supra naturam*. This means that grace is not "super-added" because it adds a substantial perfection to nature above that which its active principle confers. Instead, grace is "super-added" because it actualizes a creature's passive potential for *accidental* perfection. Thomas actually describes all accidents as "superadded," because they confer an accidental perfection *above* that which a substance possesses in virtue of its substantial form.[120] The difference between grace and other accidents is that other accidents are superadded naturally, while grace is superadded supernaturally.

As an example of the relationship between nature and grace, Thomas points to the natural knowledge of the separated soul, as he had in the *Quaestiones disputatae de anima*. Although he follows the *De spiritualibus creaturis* in rejecting Jean de la Rochelle's idea that angels can operate as an agent intellect for the soul,[121] Thomas still

q. 105, a. 7, ad 2 [Leon. 5:479]. On all three classes being beyond nature in some way, see a. 6, ad 1, of the same question [Leon. 5:477]. Thomas saves a detailed discussion of grace for the Treatise on Grace in the *Prima secundae*.

120. There are too many passages in the *Prima pars* in which Thomas uses the word "superadditus, -a, -um," to allow adequate space to categorize them all, so let us instead draw attention to *ST*, Ia, q. 6, a. 3, co. [Leon. 4:68]: "Solus Deus est bonus per suam essentiam. Unumquodque enim dicitur bonum, secundum quod est perfectum. Perfectio autem alicuius rei triplex est. Prima quidem, secundum quod in suo esse constituitur. Secunda vero, prout ei aliqua accidentia superadduntur, ad suam perfectam operationem necessaria. Tertia vero perfectio alicuius est per hoc, quod aliquid aliud attingit sicut finem." See also ibid., ad 3: "Bonitas rei creatae non est ipsa eius essentia, sed aliquid superadditum; vel ipsum esse eius, vel aliqua perfectio superaddita, vel ordo ad finem."

121. The skepticism is expressed in ibid., q. 89, a. 1, co. [Leon. 5:370–71]. Along those

observes that an influx of species from a higher agent can be considered natural on account of the unity of the soul's passive potency to receive that influx.[122]

Natural Desire

As in the *Summa contra Gentiles,* Thomas explains that God providentially directs all things by his intellect according to his prudence,[123] and so there is an ordering in every creature toward its perfection which arises from God's direction.[124] God directs a creature toward its perfection through its form, which mediates being and movement to the creature.[125] Consequently, as in *De potentia,* there is no way for a creature to exist without God continually sustaining it in both being and motion.[126] This means that each creature is a moved mover; its motion can be ascribed to the creature as a secondary cause, and to God as a primary cause.[127]

Also as in the *Summa contra Gentiles,* the pattern or order according to which a creature receives motion when it is moved by God can be called an "inclination" in a generic sense, or an "appetite" in a specific sense.[128] Since this ordering occurs in virtue of a form and in accordance with its nature, the ordering can fittingly be called a "natural" appetite.[129] There are two basic ways in which something

lines, one possible way to read q. 89, a. 2, ad 2 [Leon. 5:375] and q. 89, a. 4, co. [Leon. 5:378] is as affirming that the species come directly from God. Even if Thomas denies the idea, inspired by Jean de la Rochelle, that the separated soul receives a direct, natural influx of species from the angels, still he is open to the idea that angels may have a remote participation in the illumination of the intellect (see q. 84, a. 4, ad 3 [Leon. 5:321]), particularly as regards the revelation of supernatural truths in this life (see q. 111, a. 1, ad 2 [Leon. 5:390–91]); and he maintains Jean's understanding that the separated soul must use the natural light of its agent intellect to deduce particulars from the species infused, and that it does so only in a confused manner on account of its weakness.

122. Ibid., q. 89, a. 1, ad 3 [Leon. 5:371].

123. Ibid., q. 22, a. 1, co. [Leon. 4:263].

124. Ibid., q. 59, a. 1, co. [Leon. 5:92].

125. Ibid., q. 104, a. 1, co., and ad 1 [Leon. 5:463–64].

126. Ibid., ad 2 [Leon. 5:464].

127. Ibid., q. 103, a. 6 [Leon. 5:458–59]; q. 105, a. 5, co. [Leon. 5:475–76].

128. Ibid., q. 59, a. 1, co. [Leon. 5:92].

129. Ibid.

can be said to have a natural appetite. First, on the level of substance, natural appetite is the passive receptivity that non-rational creatures have for their perfection insofar as they are ordered toward that perfection by the divine intellect.[130] In this sense natural appetite is distinguished from an appetite that follows some kind of knowledge in a creature. The latter is a rational appetite, or more simply, the will.[131] Second, natural appetite gives rise to an inclination that flows from nature into any power of the soul, which orders that power toward its perfection; this latter inclination can also be spoken of as a natural appetite.[132] As in the *Summa contra Gentiles,* this latter natural appetite is ordered toward the complete actuality of the power in question.[133]

Turning to the powers of the soul, Thomas follows the *Quaestiones disputatae de anima* in describing the intellect as an essentially passive power.[134] The intellect does not so much receive motion and impart motion as it receives light from a higher intellect and illumines, as Thomas—following Moerbeke—had taken Themistius to say.[135] As in the *De spiritualibus creaturis,* this leads Thomas to speculate about the specific identity of the higher intellect that illumines the human intellect. Again he argues from theological principles that the higher intellect is God.[136] God actualizes the agent intellect because he enlightens it and is the formal exemplar cause of the species which it educes from the possible intellect.[137]

As in both the *Quaestiones disputatae de anima* and the *De spiritualibus creaturis,* Thomas supports his understanding of the relation-

130. Ibid.

131. Ibid., q. 60, a. 1, co. [Leon. 5:98]; q. 59, a. 1, co. [Leon. 5:92].

132. Ibid., q. 80, a. 1, ad 3 [Leon. 5:282–83].

133. Ibid., q. 77, a. 3, co. [Leon. 5:241].

134. Ibid., q. 79, a. 2 [Leon. 5:259–60].

135. Ibid., a. 4, co. [Leon. 5:267]; q. 89, a. 1, co. [Leon. 5:370–71]; q. 105, a. 3, ad 2 [Leon. 5:473].

136. Ibid., q. 79, a. 4, co. [Leon. 5:267–68]. For a version of the philosophical argument which stops at the identification of a need for a higher intellect without specifying which higher intellect it is, see a. 5, ad 3, of the same question [Leon. 5:269].

137. Ibid., q. 89, a. 1, co. [Leon. 5:370–71]; q. 105, a. 3, ad 2 [Leon. 5:473].

ship between the agent intellect and the possible intellect with reference to his thought on *rationes seminales.* As in the *De spiritualibus creaturis* specifically, Thomas denies the separability of the agent intellect and possible intellect, and so he identifies the agent intellect as the active principle of the intellect,[138] while he identifies the possible intellect as the passive principle of the intellect,[139] without any intermediary between them.

That the agent intellect is the active principle in the intellect does not mean that it acts exclusively of its own accord. The agent intellect receives light from God and imparts that light to the possible intellect by rendering intelligible species into act.[140] As in the *Quaestiones disputatae de anima,* we cannot sufficiently account for thought in the possible intellect merely by the fact that the agent intellect has actualized the first principles of demonstration in it.[141] Just like the soul is required in order to sustain the body in motion and in being at all times, so likewise the agent intellect is required in order to sustain the possible intellect in actual thought at all times.[142]

Concerning the relationship between the intellect and the will, Thomas says that the will is a moved mover.[143] Since the will is only moved by particular goods, insofar as they have some similarity with and participation in that universal good, which God is,[144] particular goods must be apprehended by the intellect as good in order for them to cause motion in the intellect.[145] As in *De veritate,* God thus moves the will not directly, but *indirectly* through the apprehension of the intellect.[146] God does this as the author of the will's natural inclination, according to which the pattern of its action is to seek the good when it moves.[147] But since the intellect is "like a mover" of

138. Ibid., q. 79, a. 4, co. [Leon. 5:267–68].
139. Ibid., q. 76, a. 2, co. [Leon. 5:216–17].
140. Ibid., q. 79, a. 3, co. [Leon. 5:264].
141. Ibid., a. 4, co. [Leon. 5:267–68]; q. 84, a. 3, ad 2 [Leon. 5:318].
142. Ibid., q. 79, a. 3, ad 3 [Leon. 5:264–65].
143. Ibid., q. 105, a. 4, ad 3 [Leon. 5:474]. See also q. 59, a. 1, ad 3 [Leon. 5:92].
144. Ibid., q. 105, a. 4, co. [Leon. 5:474].
145. Ibid., q. 111, a. 2, co. [Leon. 5:516].
146. Ibid., q. 79, a. 1, ad 2 and ad 3 [Leon. 5:258–59].
147. Ibid., q. 105, a. 4, ad 1 [Leon. 5:474]; q. 111, a. 2, co. [Leon. 5:516]. In q. 106, a. 2,

the will, the intellect's apprehension is sufficient to cause motion in the will without positing a separate active principle in the will. Consequently, Thomas no longer speaks of the free will by analogy with the possible intellect as he had in the *Commentary on the Sentences*; the will as a whole is a passive power, and so there is no reason to postulate a distinct passive power in it.[148]

Even if the movement of the will follows the apprehension of the intellect, and so the intellect is "like a mover," Thomas no longer says in the *Prima pars* that the intellect is a "mover" of the will in the sense in which he had previously said that it was. Following the *translatio nova* of the *De anima*, Thomas now says that the respective objects of the intellect and the will function as their respective first movers, and that these objects are in some sense the same thing. Yet rather than reduce the objects of the intellect and the will to the *bonum apprehensum*, as Moerbeke had Aristotle do, Thomas maintains the intellect's orientation toward the true, while achieving a material commonality of the objects of the two powers in virtue of the transcendental convertibility of the true and the good:

> The true and the good include one another. For the true is a sort of good, otherwise it would not be desirable [*appetibile*]; and the good is a sort of true, otherwise it would not be intelligible. Just as, therefore, the object of an appetite can be true, insofar as it has the *ratio* of good (as when someone desires to know the truth), so likewise the object of the practical intellect is the good, as it may be ordered to an action under the *ratio* of true. For the practical intellect knows truth, just like the speculative; but it orders the known truth to action.[149]

---

co. [Leon. 5:483–84], there is a sense in which God would have to change the natural inclination of the will in order to move it directly.

148. Ibid., q. 83, a. 4, ad 3 [Leon. 5:312]: "Intellectus comparatur ad voluntatem, ut movens; et ideo non oportet in voluntate distinguere agens, et possibile."

149. Ibid., q. 79, a. 11, ad 2 [Leon. 5:279]: "Verum et bonum se invicem includunt. Nam verum est quoddam bonum; alioquin non esset appetibile: et bonum est quoddam verum; alioquin non esset intelligibile: sicut igitur objectum appetitus potest esse verum, inquantum habet rationem boni; sicut, cum aliquis appetit veritatem cognoscere: ita objectum intellectus practici est bonum ordinabile ad opus sub ratione veri: intellectus enim practicus veritatem cognoscit, sicut speculativus; sed veritatem cognitam ordinat ad opus." See also *ST*, Ia, q. 59, a. 2, ad 3 [Leon. 5:94]; q. 80, a. 1, ad 2 [Leon. 5:282]; q. 82, a. 3, ad 3 [Leon. 5:299].

By bringing together the true and the good in virtue of their transcendental convertibility, Thomas pushes the conclusion he drew from the *translatio nova* of Aristotle's *De anima* concerning the object of the will even further. Thomas now speaks of the intellect as merely "directive" of motion which takes place in the will:[150] the object itself apprehended by the intellect, *not the intellect,* is the "unmoved mover" of the will,[151] even if that object could not have that effect on the will were it not apprehended by the intellect.[152] The intellect and the will thus stand in a relationship of mutual, but not reciprocal, causality. By apprehension, the intellect presents to the will the object which serves as the will's final cause; by intention, the will moves the intellect toward the object which serves as the intellect's formal cause.[153]

As the intellect and the will pursue their common material object, each does so according to the pattern of its first habits: the first principles of demonstration in the intellect, and natural virtue in the will. These habits, Thomas continues to say, are undetermined. In the intellect, God's existence is not naturally known to us; if it were, there could be no such thing as an atheist.[154] Similarly, the pattern according to which the will seeks whatever it seeks is the "universal and perfect good," which will completely actualize the potential of the will.[155] We do not necessarily desire to find that universal and

150. Ibid., q. 79, a. 11, ad 1 [Leon. 5:279].

151. Ibid., q. 80, a. 2, co. [Leon. 5:284]: "Potentia enim appetitiva est potentia passiva, quae nata est moveri ab apprehenso; unde appetibile apprehensum est movens non motum: appetitus autem movens motum, ut dicitur in 3 *De anima* et 11 *Metaph.*"

152. Ibid., ad 1 [Leon. 5:284].

153. Ibid., q. 82, a. 4, co. [Leon. 5:303].

154. Ibid., q. 2, a. 1, co. [Leon. 4:27]; q. 83, a. 3, co. [Leon. 5:368]. The text of Ia, 1. 2, a. 1, posits as the first objection the very text from Damascene upon which the *Summa fratris Alexandri* bases its argument for natural knowledge of God. The corresponding treatment of the topic in the *Lectura romana,* which Thomas would have written just prior to beginning the *Prima pars,* also begins with this text from Damascene. See *Lectura romana* 3.1.1 [Boyle 106].

155. Thomas Aquinas, *ST,* Ia, q. 82, a. 2, ad 2 [Leon. 5:296–97]: "Movens tunc ex necessitate causat motum in mobili, quando potestas moventis excedit mobile, ita quod tota eius possibilitas moventi subdatur. Cum autem possibilitas voluntatis sit respectu boni universalis et perfecti, non subiicitur eius possibilitas tota alicui particulari bono. Et

perfect good in this or that object, such as God, any more than we naturally know that God exists; we only desire of necessity what we perceive to have a necessary connection with universal and perfect good, just like we only know of necessity what has a necessary connection with the first principles of demonstration.[156] Since, however, we lack demonstrative certitude in this life of any necessary connection between any object that the will might encounter and the complete fulfillment of its potency, to seek happiness in a specific object is the domain of free choice,[157] depending on how the intellect and the will mutually pursue their respective objects.

In our previous discussions of the inter-relationship between the intellect and the will, we saw how Thomas's treatment of the question at various stages in his career affected his understanding of the sin of Adam and Eve and of the act of faith. Thomas treats these topics in the *Prima secundae* and *Secunda secundae* respectively, and so we will reserve our discussion of those topics for chapter 5.[158]

The Natural Desire for the Vision of God

In the *Summa theologiae,* Ia, q. 12, a. 1, Thomas discusses what natural desire can tell us about the final end of man.[159] The question asks whether a created intellect can see the divine essence. As we saw in chapter 2, the context for such a question was the pre-1241 tradition, evident in the works of Hugh of Saint-Cher and Guerric of Saint-Quentin, which denied this possibility.[160] The first objection of the article references the precise text of Chrysostom that Hugh of

ideo non ex necessitate movetur ab illo." See also a. 4, co., and ad 2 [Leon. 5:303] of the same question.

156. Ibid., q. 82, a. 2, co. [Leon. 5:296]. See Lottin, *Psychologie et morale,* 1:239.

157. Thomas Aquinas, *ST,* Ia, q. 82, a. 2, co. [Leon. 5:296]; See also q. 83, a. 1, co. [Leon. 5:307]; a. 1, ad 4 [Leon. 5:308]; a. 4, co. [Leon. 5:311].

158. Each topic is mentioned, but none in a way that reveals anything consequential about Thomas's thought. We find sins of passion mentioned in ibid., q. 81, a. 3, ad 2 [Leon. 5:291]; and q. 83, a. 1, ad 1 [Leon. 5:307]. We find the sin of Adam and Eve mentioned in q. 81, a. 1, ad 3 [Leon. 5:288]. We find the act of faith mentioned in q. 111, a. 1, ad 1 [Leon. 5:390].

159. Ibid., q. 12, a. 1 [Leon. 4:114–15].

160. See a similar remark in Hütter, *Dust Bound for Heaven,* 227n101.

Saint-Cher had utilized in the text quoted previously in chapter 2.[161]

Given the theological context of the question, it is unsurprising that Thomas aims to establish a theological conclusion: "the blessed see the essence of God." Yet if we compare Thomas's conclusion here to other texts in which Thomas argues from natural desire to establish a conclusion about the vision of God, we find something new. In Thomas's previous treatments of the question, which relied exclusively on natural reason, he was always careful to distinguish the possibility of the vision of God from the revealed fact that there are people who have, do, or will enjoy that vision. Here it is otherwise. Thomas deliberately relies upon Revelation, and so he draws a conclusion about what is actually the case, rather than what is possible.

First, Thomas begins with a theological argument: "Since man's final happiness consists in his highest activity, which is the activity of the intellect, if the created intellect can never see the essence of God, either it will never obtain happiness, or its happiness will consist in something other than God. This is alien from faith."[162] It is tempting to read this as a philosophical argument. After all, it contains two propositions that are very close to ones which Thomas repeatedly refutes with philosophical arguments: 1) That a created intellect cannot obtain happiness; 2) That a created intellect has its happiness in something other than God. Yet there is a subtle difference between the language of the argument and the language in which the question was posed. Although the question asks about whether the created intellect "can" see God,[163] Thomas argues in this first part of the argument solely about whether the human intellect "will" see God. One can only argue about what actually happens if one assumes the revealed fact that God has offered the grace to humanity to actual-

161. See above, p. 184.

162. Thomas Aquinas, *ST*, Ia, q. 12, a. 1 [Leon. 4:114–15]: "Cum enim ultima hominis beatitudo in altissima eius operatione consistat, quae est operatio intellectus, si nunquam essentiam Dei videre potest intellectus creatus, vel nunquam beatitudinem obtinebit, vel in alio eius beatitudo consistet quam in Deo. Quod est alienum a fide."

163. This is the way it is worded in the first objection (ibid., obj. 1): "Videtur, quod nullus intellectus creatus possit Deum per essentiam videre."

ize this possibility. In the condemnation of 1241, the position condemned was framed in just these terms. The censured proposition was that the divine essence "will not" be seen, not that God "cannot" be seen.[164]

Next, Thomas offers a short corollary in support of his initial argument. Again, the argument seems philosophical. "For the ultimate perfection of a rational creature is in that which is its principle of being; for each rational creature is perfected to the extent that it reaches its principle."[165] But let us recall the source of this argument from chapter 1: it was a point that William of Auvergne, the very bishop who condemned the theological positions referenced in the first part of the argument, had drawn from Avicenna to disprove the idea that our beatitude could be in anything less than the vision of God. It is, at it were, a veiled reference to the very authority upon which Thomas's theological argument rests. Although the words can be understood in a purely philosophical mode, they are evidently being deployed as much for their theological authority as for their philosophical effectiveness.

Then Thomas shifts deliberately into a philosophical mode: "Likewise it is also beyond reason. For there is in man a natural desire of knowing the cause when he looks upon an effect; and from this, wonder arises among men. If, therefore, the intellect of a rational creature cannot reach the first cause of things, the desire of its nature will remain in vain."[166] Here again, the source is William; it is the same argument that Thomas had taken from William in the *Summa contra Gentiles*. Yet if we compare the language of this part of the response, where Thomas switches deliberately into a philosophical

164. See above, p. 185.

165. Thomas Aquinas, *ST*, Ia, q. 12, a. 1 [Leon. 4:114–15]: "In ipso enim est ultima perfectio rationalis creaturae, quod est ei principium essendi: intantum enim unumquodque perfectum est, inquantum ad suum principium attingit."

166. Ibid.: "Similiter etiam est praeter rationem. Inest enim homini naturale desiderium cognoscendi causam, cum intuetur effectum; et ex hoc admiratio in hominibus consurgit. Si igitur intellectus rationalis creaturae pertingere non possit ad primam causam rerum, remanebit inane desiderium naturae."

mode, to the language of the first part of the response, where Thomas was speaking in a theological mode, we find that there is an important change in his choice of verb. As soon as Thomas shifts into a philosophical mode, he no longer speaks of what "will" happen; he speaks only of what "can" happen. When arguing in a philosophical mode, he is careful not to assume the revealed fact that God has offered the grace to humanity to actualize the possibility of seeing God.

The conclusion of the argument is based on the combination of both the theological and the philosophical arguments. Consequently it assumes the revealed data of the theological argument. The language of the conclusion makes this clear. Thomas switches again from speaking about what "can" happen to speaking about what is actually the case: "Accordingly it must be conceded simply that the blessed see the essence of God."[167] This is essentially the profession of faith made in the condemnation of 1241: "For we firmly believe and assert that God … is seen by glorified souls."[168] In short, Thomas raises a question about a theological issue condemned by the bishop of Paris in 1241, he utilizes an authority from those condemned by the condemnation as the first objection, he frames his response and his conclusion in the language of the condemnation, and he intersperses his response with arguments drawn from the bishop who authorized the condemnation. Although, therefore, the argument contains certain pieces which can be taken in a philosophical mode, the argument taken as a whole, including its conclusion, is theological in context and theological in structure.

167. Ibid.: "Unde simpliciter concedendum est quod beati Dei essentiam videant."

168. Denifle, *Chartularium Universitatis Parisiensis,* 1:170: "Firmiter autem credimus et asserimus, quod Deus … videbitur … ab animabus glorificatis." Similarly, we may point to the *Super Evangelium S. Matthaei Lectura,* cap. 5, lect. 2, ed. R. Cai (Turin: Marietti, 1951), 69–70. The text was composed in the 1269–70 academic year (Torrell, *Saint Thomas Aquinas,* 1:56). Since it is extremely short and has not yet been dated with reference to the condemnation of 1270, it will not receive its own section in chapter 5. But suffice it to say here that it mimics the text of *ST,* Ia, q. 12, a. 1. Thomas begins by referencing the condemnation of 1241, and then gives a very similar, seemingly philosophical argument. However, assuming the revealed data of the Gospel on which he is commenting, he again concludes with the words of the profession of faith from 1241, "Videbitur ergo per essentiam."

If we overlook the context and the structure of this argument, we run the risk of crossing a boundary that Thomas never crossed. We might extract the philosophical statements from their context and use them to prove the theological conclusion. To do so would be to attempt to prove from natural reason that God has offered us grace. But as we have seen, Thomas consistently denies throughout the course of his career that we can do that. Although the argument from *Summa theologiae,* Ia, q. 12, a. 1, makes use of philosophical language, we can say confidently that it in no way mitigates the idea that natural reason can prove only the *possibility,* not the actuality, of the vision of God.

CONCLUSION

Although Thomas had used his time at Orvieto in part to gain a foothold independent of Bonaventure in the Parisian theological tradition, and had developed during that time his own Augustinian-Aristotelian synthesis of a natural desire for the fulfillment of our natural appetite insofar as is possible, he found himself learning from Bonaventure's writings once again during his Roman period. Having been tasked with the organization of a *studium particularis theologiae,* Thomas studied Bonaventure's *Breviloquium,* which had been destined for a similar *studium* within the Franciscan Order, and composed the *Summa theologiae* as his own contribution to the task of designing a pedagogical text for students who were capable of rising above the level of education in conventual *schola,* but not necessarily capable of the advanced studies available at a *studium generale* like Paris. We see evidence of this interaction with Bonaventure's *Breviloquium* in Thomas's teaching on Creation in the *Prima pars* of the *Summa theologiae.* Where previously Thomas had been a fierce critic of Bonaventure's understanding of Creation, Bonaventure had suggested in the *Breviloquium* a way of bringing the two sides close together: looking to the "second nature" of the elements, one could hold that God made all things with substantial forms, but that those things came into existence gradually through the actualization of the elements' passive potency. Following Bonaventure, Thomas adopts this conciliatory approach to Creation, using it to acknowledge the possibility that Creation took place over a six-day period, and refusing to defend the idea of simultaneous Creation against it.

In preparation for the *Prima pars* of the *Summa theologiae*, Thomas held three sets of disputed questions (*De potentia, De anima,* and *De spiritualibus creaturis*); and he also wrote a commentary on Aristotle's *De anima*. In the *Quaestiones disputatae de potentia* and *de anima*, he developed his thinking from the *Summa contra Gentiles* on nature, grace, and the desire for God. Referencing our *potentia obedientiae* in the *De potentia*, Thomas upheld his previous teaching regarding Averroes's "second nature," and used it to continue to develop his teaching on Providence from the *Summa contra Gentiles*. More so than previously, Thomas emphasized the fact that creatures need to receive an immediate and simultaneous influx of motion from their Creator in order to be moved, a teaching which he upholds in the *Prima pars*. In the *Quaestiones disputatae de anima*, Thomas applied his approach to our "second nature" to the case of the separated soul, arguing that the separated soul can receive natural knowledge from angels and supernatural vision from God in the possible intellect without that knowledge and vision therefore being considered miraculous. He also applied his teaching on Providence to the case of the intellect, arguing against William of Auvergne that the possible intellect requires the immediate and simultaneous action of the agent intellect in order to use the first principles of demonstration.

William of Moerbeke's translations of Aristotle's *De anima* and of Themistius's paraphrase of it caused Thomas to develop his thinking on the relationship between the intellect and the will, as well as the relationship between the agent intellect and God. Whether on account of a corrupted Greek text or inconsistency of transcription or translation, William had Aristotle appear to say that the unmoved mover of the will is the appetible object, not the intellect. Thomas follows William in this interpretation, and in the *Prima pars* Thomas now says that the objects of the intellect and the will are materially the same, since the true and the good are transcendentally convertible. For seemingly more deliberate reasons, William had Themistius appear to say that there are two agent intellects, one in the soul and one above the soul but below God, when in fact Themistius acknowledges only the latter. Thomas also follows William in this interpretation, using theological arguments in the *De spiritualibus creaturis* and the *prima pars* to show how Christians can use Themistius to develop an acceptable reading of Avicenna, provided that they hold that the separated agent intellect is God, rather than something below God. This helped Thomas to preserve the priority of God's illumination in the agent intellect, even as he located the source of the activity of the possible intellect and of the will in the "apprehended good" (the *bonum apprehensum*).

Notwithstanding the inaccuracies of William's translations, Thomas's encounter with them raised a question about the systematic understanding of natural desire and Providence that he had achieved in the *Summa contra Gentiles*. If the appetible object, rather than the intellect, is the unmoved mover of the will, to what extent can we continue to maintain a Maimonidian, intellectualist view of Providence, in which God moves the intellect directly, and God moves the will indirectly *through* the intellect? Thomas's solution to this question in the *Prima pars* is to say that since the object of the will is the *bonum apprehensum*, it follows that even though the object of the will is materially the same as the object of the intellect, the will can only access its object through the intellect. When this happens, the good apprehended by the intellect determines the will to one end, so that the will may pursue that end in act. Here, however, a further question arises: if an undetermined passive power only moves to the extent that it is determined to one thing, does the apprehended good somehow necessitate the motion of the will? Thomas seems to suggest that it does, at least in a very qualified sense. But as we shall see in chapter 5, that necessity would very shortly become a point of significant philosophical and theological controversy at Paris, because it seemed to some scholars to compromise the freedom of the will.

Although Thomas's discussion of the agent intellect and of the possible intellect in reference to Moerbeke's translations separated the activity of the possible intellect from that of the agent intellect, his manner of bringing them back together in the *De spiritualibus creaturis* and the *Prima pars* was sufficient to ensure that his discussion of our natural desire for the vision of God in *Summa theologiae,* Ia, q. 12, a. 1, would not significantly alter his previous teaching about the desire for God. Although the conclusion of his argument is that the blessed do, in fact, see the essence of God, Thomas did not in any way abandon his teaching that arguments from natural desire prove only the possibility of the vision of God. In order to establish what happens in actual fact, Thomas deliberately references Revelation and theological authority. Consequently, he is careful about his language. Whenever he speaks in a philosophical mode, he talks about what "could" happen. But whenever he speaks in a theological mode, he is able to talk about what "will" happen. His response to the controversy about the necessitation of the will would not alter this fundamental position, but it would lead to other, wide-ranging developments in his understanding of our desire for God. Consequently, we turn our attention now to that controversy, and to the developments in Thomas's thought that it occasioned.

5

Thomas's Second Parisian Period (1268–1272)

In 1268, Thomas moved from Rome to Paris to assume a second regency as a master of theology at Paris. The date of his departure is not certain,[1] although it seems highly probable that he arrived at Paris around the start of the 1268 academic year.[2] The reason for his move is similarly uncertain. Torrell thinks that his task was threefold: to oppose recent attacks on the mendicant life, to oppose those who resisted the use of the Aristotelian tradition in theology, and to oppose those who overused the Aristotelian tradition in theology.[3] While the texts of the mendicant controversy are not immediately germane to a discussion of nature, grace, and the desire for God, the texts associated with the Radical Aristotelian controversy are.

Our knowledge of the beginning of Radical Aristotelianism is unclear at best. Our best access to the teaching of its proponents comes to us from Siger of Brabant (d. 1282/84), reputed by contemporary scholars to have been the "leader" of the movement, though

1. On the various proposals concerning his departure, see Torrell, *Saint Thomas Aquinas,* 1:179–82.

2. Ibid., 1:182.

3. Ibid., 1:182–83.

certainly not its only adherent.[4] Our first documented mention of Siger is on August 27, 1266; he appears in a letter from Simon de Brion, the papal legate at Paris, who was attempting to quell disputes in which Siger had evidently been involved for some time within the Faculty of Arts at the University of Paris.[5] This suggests that the movement with which Siger has become associated had been in existence for some years prior to that date. Van Steenberghen places its genesis somewhere between 1260 and 1265, after Thomas left Paris for Italy, but before de Brion's letter.[6]

Unfortunately, we lack any documentary evidence attesting to the doctrinal positions of Radical Aristotelians from the first half of the 1260s. Even in the second half of the 1260s, we possess only one work of Siger, the *Quaestiones in tertium de anima,* which probably dates to the academic year 1269–70, after Thomas had already arrived at Paris.[7] This makes us entirely reliant on the movement's critics for a description of their earlier teaching, which is never an ideal situation as concerns historical accuracy.

Among the movement's earliest and primary critics was Bonaventure. Bonaventure denounced the movement at least twice during Thomas's Roman period: once in his *Conferences on the Decalogue* in 1267,[8] and once in his *Conferences on the Gifts of the Holy*

4. Van Steenberghen, *La philosophie au xiiie siècle,* 342. For the background to this so-called "heterodox" Aristotelianism, see pp. 321–70. On Siger in particular, see pp. 335–60; Fernand van Steenberghen, *Maître Siger de Brabant* (Louvain: Publications universitaires, 1977). Although the movement was formerly called "Latin Averroism," van Steenberghen argues convincingly that it ought not to be because only one of the doctrines professed by the so-called "Averroists" actually came from Averroes.

5. Van Steenberghen, *La philosophie au xiiie siècle,* 337; Mandonnet, *Siger de Brabant et L'averroïsme latin,* 80.

6. Van Steenberghen, *La philosophie au xiiie siècle,* 325.

7. Siger of Brabant, *Quaestiones in tertium de anima,* in *Quaestiones in tertium de anima, de anima intellectiva, de aeternitate mundi,* ed. Carlos Bazán (Louvain: Publications universitaires, 1972). On the dating of the *Quaestiones,* see Bazán, introduction to Siger of Brabant, *Quaestiones in tertium de anima,* 67*–74*. A summary of Siger's teaching on the unicity of the possible intellect can be found in John Wippel, "The Condemnations of 1270 and 1277 at Paris," *Journal of Medieval and Renaissance Studies* 7 (1977): 176–77.

8. Bonaventure, *Collationes in decem praeceptis* 2 [Quaracchi 5:519]. See van Steenberghen, *La philosophie au xiiie siècle,* 386; Kent, *Virtues of the Will,* 44; Wippel, "Condemnations of 1270 and 1277 at Paris," 180.

Spirit in 1268.[9] In the course of his denunciations he gives us a sort of syllabus of the movement's alleged errors: that the world is eternal, that there is only one intellect for all human persons, that there is no Providence, and that there is no resurrection of the body. In Bonaventure's opinion, these philosophers' teaching on the unicity of the human intellect is the "worst" (*pessimum*) of their errors, because without an individual intellect, human persons cannot be held responsible for their actions; human actions would be subject to a fatalistic determinism.[10]

While we cannot confirm with documentary evidence the accuracy of Bonaventure's allegations at the precise moment in which he made them, we can confirm that Siger taught some version of the alleged doctrines in the years that followed. In Siger's *Quaestiones in tertium de anima,* he argues that there is one intellect for all people,[11] the intellect is "probably" eternal,[12] created *de novo* in aveternity,[13] that it perfects the body only by its power and not by its substance,[14] and so is said to "be" in the body like an angel is said to "be" in a place.[15] While again it is never ideal to have to rely on a movement's critics as the chief source of one's knowledge of the movement's thought, it seems safe to say that at least some version of what Bonaventure alleged was being taught at Paris during Thomas's Roman period, and that it had its beginnings at Paris during Thomas's time at Orvieto.

9. Bonaventure, *Collationes de donis Spiritus Sancti* 8 [Quaracchi 5:497]. See van Steenberghen, *La philosophie au xiiie siècle,* 386; Kent, *Virtues of the Will,* 44; Wippel, "Condemnations of 1270 and 1277 at Paris," 180.

10. See Torrell, *Saint Thomas Aquinas,* 1:183. Here again we must question Torrell's interpretation of the controversy, suggesting that "Bonaventure is probably not speaking about contemporaries." See van Steenberghen, *La philosophie au xiiie siècle,* 337.

11. Siger of Brabant, *Quaestiones in tertium de anima,* q. 9 [Bazán 28].

12. Ibid., q. 2 [Bazán 5–6]. While concluding "quod intellectus factum est aeternum et non factum novum" (5), he qualifies "quod licet hoc sit probabile, non tamen hoc est necessarium" (6). Still, it is "probabilior quam positio Augustini [that intellects are created in time]" (7).

13. Ibid., q. 3 [Bazán 10].

14. Ibid., q. 7 [Bazán 23].

15. Ibid., q. 8 [Bazán 25]; q. 10 [Bazán 34].

SENTENTIA LIBRI PHYSICORUM

When Thomas arrived at Paris, he devoted two kinds of labor to meeting the challenge posed by the differing attitudes toward Aristotle which he encountered there. The first and most immediate response was to begin commenting upon the works of Aristotle at an unheard of pace. Within five years, he produced commentaries or partial commentaries on the *De sensu et sensato* (1268–69), *Physics* (1268–69), *Meteora* (1268–69), *Peryermenias* (December 1270–October 1271), *Posterior Analytics* (October 1271–72), *Nicomachean Ethics* (1271–72), *Politics* (1269–72), *Metaphysics* (1270–73), *De caelo et mundo* (1272–73), and the *De generatione et corruptione* (1272–73).[16] Of these, the *Sententia libri Physicorum* is of the most interest to us, because it is the only commentary completed prior to Thomas's discussion of the desire for God in the *Prima secundae,* which directly touches upon the subject of nature.

The *Commentary on the Physics* gave Thomas an opportunity to review and to support his basic positions on matter, form, privation, nature, and motion, before engaging directly in questions about man, the soul, and human happiness in the *Prima secundae.* In Book 1, he rearticulates his basic ideas from the *De principiis naturae* regarding matter, form, and privation. Matter is purely passive; form mediates actuality to matter; matter is that from which (*ex qua*) form is educed; prime matter is never without some privation whereby a composite substance might undergo substantial change, and composite substances are never without some privation whereby they might undergo accidental change.[17] In Book 2, he returns to the basic question about how to account for alteration and generation in simple earthly bodies, and changes of place in simple heavenly bodies.[18] Here again, Thomas references the Baconian posi-

16. See the dating for these commentaries in Torrell, *Saint Thomas Aquinas,* 1:341–46.

17. These are the subjects of Thomas Aquinas, *Sententia libri Physicorum* 1.7, lect. 13 [Leon. 2:45–47]; and 1.8, lect. 14 [Leon. 2:49–50].

18. Ibid., 2.1, lect. 1 [Leon. 2:56].

tion that there may be an imperfect active principle in matter and rejects it on the basis that only a complete active principle could cause those changes; if such an active principle were in the simple bodies, it would be—as Avicenna had supposed concerning the heavenly bodies—their substantial form. Accordingly, Thomas determines the question once again in favor of Averroes: the matter of the simple bodies is the principle by which they naturally receive change which is caused in them by another.[19]

When Thomas discusses this "second nature" in simple bodies, he introduces a distinction, which was not present in his *Commentary on the Sentences,* between a creature's *per se* material potency and its *per accidens* material potency. Anything at all may occur to a creature in virtue of its *per accidens* material potency; it is only through the reception and contraction of a form into matter that matter's potency is in some way limited.[20] A creature's *per se* material potency includes its potency for every accidental perfection that can be caused in it while it still maintains its substantial form; its *per accidens* material potency includes its potency for every substantial or accidental perfection that can be caused in it without maintaining its form. Only changes which accrue to a composite in virtue of its *per se* material potency can be called "natural" or "according to nature" (*secundum naturam*).[21] The reason for this is that "each thing is denominated from its act," and so, since act is communicated to a creature by its form: "form … is nature."[22]

19. Ibid. He addresses the same point again in ibid., 8.4, lect. 7 [Leon. 2:388].

20. Ibid., 2.1, lect. 2 [Leon. 2:59]; 2.3, lect. 6 [Leon. 2:73]. We should note that Thomas is speaking exclusively of corporeal creatures here, because the consideration of incorporeal creatures belongs to the science of metaphysics. See ibid., 2.2, lect. 4 [Leon. 2:66–67]; 2.3, lect. 5 [Leon. 2:69].

21. Ibid., 2.1, lect. 1 [Leon. 2:56–57]. We see in this the seeds of what the Thomistic commentatorial tradition will later refer to as "generic obediential potency" and "specific obediential potency." See Steven Long, "Obediential Potency, Human Knowledge, and the Natural Desire for the Vision of God," *International Philosophical Quarterly* 37, no. 1 (1997): 45–63. More recently, see Steven Long, "Creation *ad imaginem Dei*: The Obediential Potency of the Human Person to Grace and Glory," *Nova et Vetera* (English) 14, no. 4 (2016): 1175–92; Malloy, "De Lubac on Natural Desire," 616–18.

22. Thomas Aquinas, *Sententia libri Physicorum* 2.1, lect. 2 [Leon. 2:60]:

Here a question arises: the human person is unique among corporeal creatures, because the human person has a twofold set of *per se* material perfections: natural perfections which can be caused by the powers of the human soul, and supernatural perfections which can be caused in the human soul by God without therefore changing the soul's substance. If "form is nature," rather than matter, to what extent are those *per se* material perfections which the soul cannot cause in itself "natural"? Thomas does not address that question here, but he will address it in the *Prima secundae* of the *Summa theologiae*, as we will see below.

Thomas also develops his thinking about motion. When motion occurs, he asks whether it happens from chance or in view of an end. If it occurs always or for the most part, Thomas argues that it occurs on account of an end; if it occurs only infrequently, he admits that it happens from chance.[23] Since, moreover, what happens according to nature happens always or for the most part, Thomas argues that nature acts on account of an end.[24] Do the things that occur in nature therefore occur of necessity? Here Thomas makes two distinctions about necessity, which will become important for his subsequent thinking about natural desire. First, he notes that there is a difference between something which merely happens to occur always, and something which "cannot not happen." Only when something "cannot not be" is it truly necessary; that which "could happen not to be," but nevertheless happens, is contingent.[25] Concerning what is truly necessary, Thomas makes another distinction between absolute necessity and necessity on account of a condition (*ex conditione*).[26] Absolute necessity accrues to an effect if it follows directly from a creature's matter, form, or efficient cause. Necessity on ac-

"Unumquodque enim denominatur ab actu, qui est principium actionis et terminus passionis ... unde id quod nascitur, denominatur ab eo in quod, non ab eo ex quo. Id autem in quod tendit nativitas, est forma: forma igitur est natura."

23. Ibid., 2.8, lect. 13 [Leon. 2:93–94]. See also ibid., 2.5, lect. 8 [Leon. 2:79].

24. Ibid., 2.8, lect. 13 [Leon. 2:94].

25. Ibid., 2.5, lect. 8 [Leon. 2:79].

26. Ibid., 2.15, lect. 15 [Leon. 2:98].

count of a condition accrues to an effect to the extent that a creature must possess certain properties or dispositions in order to reach its end.[27]

Here another question arises. In the *Sententia libri De anima* and the *Prima pars* of the *Summa theologiae,* Thomas had described the will as a passive power, which is set in motion by the appetible object as by an unmoved mover, because it is made by God to be set in motion by such an object. Thomas says something similar in the *Sententia libri Physicorum.* Any potency which is of itself undetermined, such as matter or the will, is only reduced to act insofar as it is determined to one thing.[28] Matter is determined to one thing by nature, which it receives through form; the will is determined to one thing by the really or apparently good object proposed to it by the intellect.[29] But if the will is a passive power determined to one thing by the good proposed to it by the intellect, is the will therefore necessitated by its object? Thomas does not give us a direct answer to this question in the *Sententia libri Physicorum,* but his double distinction concerning necessity should at least give us an indication of how he would eventually resolve the question. An appetible object moves a passive power as a final cause. Therefore, the motion by which the appetible object moves the will does not entail absolute necessity. It is a contingent motion and is only subject to necessity *ex conditione.* If the will is to pursue such and such a good, it needs to have such and such a nature; but we cannot say that because it has such and such a nature it will of necessity pursue such and such a good.

The same question about determination and necessity can also be raised about human nature in general. In the *Sententia libri Physicorum,* Thomas distinguishes nature, which determines matter by a formal cause and so imposes absolute necessity upon it, from the good proposed by the intellect, which determines the will by a final cause and so does not impose absolute necessity upon it. Yet there

27. Ibid. [Leon. 2:98–99].
28. Ibid., 2.5, lect. 8 [Leon. 2:79].
29. Ibid., 2.3, lect. 5 [Leon. 2:71]; 2.5, lect. 8 [Leon. 2:79].

are times when this distinction seems to become blurred. Thomas notes, for instance, that nature furnishes each creature with those properties or powers which it needs to achieve its determined end (claws, horns, and the like). Man, on the other hand, lacks such natural tools, because he requires such a variety of them that it would not be feasible for him to possess them all by nature. In place of these, man has reason.[30] The human intellect therefore has a twofold task. As an undetermined power, it must seek contingently its own perfection in knowledge according to its own natural inclination, but as a participant in a determined nature, it also must seek of necessity the determinate goods of that nature. Is there a difference in how the will acts when these different kinds of goods are presented to it by the intellect? Thomas will not address the question until the *De malo*, but his thinking suggests that human nature as a whole may be subject to a more radical determination than the will as a specific power of that nature.

DE UNITATE INTELLECTUS

Thomas also engaged in polemical works upon his arrival at Paris. With regard to the issue of Radical Aristotelianism, Thomas authored a polemical treatise, *De unitate intellectus contra averroistas*, which sought to update his previous arguments about the multiplicity of the agent and possible intellects in light of Bonaventure's critiques of Radical Aristotelianism.[31] In this treatise, Thomas begins by following Bonaventure's theological criticism of the doctrine of

30. Ibid., 3.3, lect. 5 [Leon. 2:115].

31. Thomas Aquinas, *De unitate intellectus contra averroistas* [Leon. 43:243–314]. On the dating of the work, see van Steenberghen, *La philosophie au xiiie siècle*, 389. For a summary of its contents, see pp. 390–91. Also, see Wippel, "Condemnations of 1270 and 1277 at Paris," 181, where Wippel observes that Bonaventure confined himself to a theological critique of heterodox Aristotelianism because of the theological nature of the conferences.

Unlike Bonaventure, Thomas seems to have been able to take cognizance of Siger's *Quaestiones in tertium de anima*. On the dating of the exchanges between Siger and Thomas on the nature of the soul, see the introduction to Leon. 43:249–50.

the unicity of the human intellect: "If you take away a diversity of intellects from the human race, it follows that nothing remains of the souls of men after death but a single intellectual substance, since the intellect is the only incorruptible and immortal part of the soul. Thus, you take away the distribution of rewards and punishments, as well as the difference between them."[32] Granted, then, that the unicity of the possible intellect is contrary to the Christian faith, Thomas seeks to show throughout the rest of the treatise that it is repugnant to natural reason as well.[33]

Thomas's philosophical arguments are characterized by the shifts which we observed in chapter 4 with respect to the object of the will in the *Sententia libri De anima* and the *Prima pars,* as well as by an awareness of Bonaventure's criticisms. For example, in chapter 3 of *De unitate intellectus contra averrositas,* Thomas adds to his standard list of arguments in favor of the multiplicity of the possible intellect a consideration of the relationship between the intellect and the will. Since the will is itself an intellectual power, if you take away the individual intellect you also take away the individual will. While this certainly has theological consequences, such as Bonaventure had enumerated, it also has consequences that can be known by natural reason: since the possible intellect informs the choices of the will, free choice would be destroyed if each soul did not have its own possible intellect.[34] As a result, "the principles of moral philosophy are destroyed."[35]

32. Thomas Aquinas, *De unitate intellectus contra averrositas* 1 [Leonine 43:291]: "Subtracta enim ab hominibus diuersitate intellectus, qui solus inter anime partes incorruptibilis et immortalis apparet, sequitur post mortem nichil de animabus hominum remanere nisi unicam intellctus substantiam; et sic tollitur retributio premiorum et penarum et diuersitas eorundem."

33. Ibid.; and 5 [Leonine 43:314].

34. Ibid., 4 [Leon. 43:308].

35. Ibid., 3 [Leon. 43:306]: "Adhuc, secundum istorum positionem destruuntur moralis philosophie principia." Since this had already come up in questions of faith, he says that "Relinquitur igitur hoc [quod 'intellectus sic uniatur nobis ut uere ex eo et nobis fiat unum ... ut sit scilicet potentia anime que unitur nobis ut forma ...'] absque omni dubtatione tenendum, non propter reuelationem fidei, ut dicunt, sed quia hoc subtrahere est niti contra manifeste apparentia."

The *De unitate intellectus* also takes into account Moerbeke's distinction in the translation of Themistius between a separated agent intellect and individual agent intellects. In fact, exegeses of Themistius occur in nearly every chapter.[36] Since Thomas thinks that Themistius identifies the human person chiefly with the individual agent intellect,[37] he is not overly concerned with philosophers who posit that there is a separated agent intellect below God.[38] In fact, he now even goes out of his way to point out the reasonableness of holding such an opinion.[39] So high is Thomas's philosophical esteem for Themistius that one may wonder at this point whether he thinks that the non-existence of an intermediary agent intellect between the human intellect and God is solely a matter of faith. As a result, the *De unitate* follows the conciliatory tone of the *De spiritualibus creaturis* toward those who acknowledge a single separated agent intellect below God, provided that they at least acknowledge individual possible intellects.

THE CONDEMNATION OF 1270 AND THE *DE MALO*

The controversy over Radical Aristotelianism culminated initially on December 10, 1270, when Étienne Tempier, the bishop of Paris, condemned thirteen propositions that were understood to be held or implied by members of the movement.[40] The propositions concerned the unicity of the human intellect (1–2), the moral determinism which follows from it (3–4, 9), the eternity of the world (5–6), the denial of the immortality of the soul (7–8), the denial of those things which follow death according to the Christian faith (13), and

36. See ibid., 2 [Leon. 43:301]; cap. 3 [Leon. 43:306–7]; cap. 4 [Leon. 43:307]; cap. 5 [Leon. 43:314].

37. Ibid., 2 [Leon. 43:301]; cap. 3 [Leon. 43:306–7].

38. Ibid., 5 [Leon. 43:314].

39. Ibid., 4 [Leon. 43:307].

40. For the text of the propositions, see Denifle, *Chartularium Universitatis Parisiensis*, 1:486–87. For a discussion of their context and contents, see Wippel, "Condemnations of 1270 and 1277 at Paris," 169–82.

the denial of Providence (10–13). Those who knowingly asserted or defended these propositions were henceforth *ipso facto* excommunicated,[41] much like those, in 1241, who denied that the blessed see the essence of God.

The most important of the condemnations for our understanding of Thomas's teaching on natural desire is the ninth: "That free choice is a passive potency, not active; and that it is moved of necessity by the appetible object."[42] Unfortunately, while there has been profuse scholarship on the sources and intended objects of the subsequent condemnation of 1277, scholarship on the condemnation of 1270 has been comparatively thin. If we examine the scholarship on the propositions condemned in 1277 which are closely related in substance and wording to the ninth proposition of 1270,[43] we find that the later condemnations are written from a position on the freedom of the will inspired by the Franciscan tradition after Bonaventure.[44] That tradition thought of the will as an active power, and emphasized the ability of the will to move itself, not just to be moved by its appetible object.[45] The opposite position, that the will is a completely passive power necessitated by the appetible object, can be found clearly represented among the works of Siger that date approximately to this period.[46] But what about Thomas? If we com-

41. Denifle, *Chartularium Universitatis Parisiensis*, 1:486.

42. Ibid., 1:486–87: "Quod liberum arbitrium est potentia passiva, non activa; et quod necessitate movetur ab appetibili."

43. There are three such propositions:

"134. Quod appetitus, cessantibus impedimentis, necessario mouetur ab appetibili. —Error [est] de intellectiuo." *La condamnation parisienne de 1277: Nouvelle édition du texte latin, traduction, introduction et commentaire*, ed. David Piché, (Paris: J. Vrin, 1999), 120.

"135. Quod uoluntas secundum se est indeterminata ad opposita sicut materia; determinatur autem ab appetibili, sicut materia ab agente" [Piché 120].

"194. Quod anima nichil uult, nisi mota ab alio a se. Unde illud est falsum: anima seipsa uult.—Error, si intelligatur mota ab alio scilicet ab appetibili uel obiecto, ita quod appetibile uel obiectum sit tota ratio motus ipsius uoluntatis" [Piché 139].

44. See Roland Hissette, *Enquête sur les 219 articles condamnés à Paris le 7 mars 1277* (Louvain: Publications universitaires, 1977), 232.

45. Ibid.

46. Ibid., 232–33; 251–52.

pare what Thomas says about the relationship between the intellect and the will after his encounter with the *translatio nova* of Aristotle's *De anima* and before the condemnation, with the text of the ninth condemnation and with the text of Siger, Thomas's writing is admittedly ambiguous.

I do not intend to suggest in any sense that Thomas implicitly or explicitly gave his assent to the proposition, "the will is necessitated by its object," or that Bishop Tempier intended to condemn Thomas when he condemned that proposition. As others have observed, and as we have seen above in chapter 2, Thomas acknowledged very clearly in the *De veritate* that the will's natural appetite is not a necessitated, primordial motion; it is merely the pattern or structure according to which the will acts, when it acts.[47] Moreover, as we have observed above in this chapter with regard to the *Sententia libri Physicorum*, Thomas had a set of distinctions to hand which could readily account for the contingency of the will's choices: since the good proposed to the will by the intellect moves the will in the manner of a final cause, the will's motion toward that good is contingent; the only necessity accruing to that motion is necessity *ex conditione*. The sole potential exception to this rule would be the will's desire for the goods of nature, since nature is determined to one thing.

However, to say that Thomas himself did not assent to the idea that the will is necessitated to its object is not the same as saying that others did not impute the view to Thomas. Since Thomas did not address the question directly, we can only piece together a potential answer that he did not actually give, to a question that he did actually not ask, from a variety of distinctions he makes in another context. Therefore, much like Thomas repeatedly has Averroes denying the proposition, "*hic homo intelligit*," even though Averroes never says anything of the sort, because Thomas thinks it is implied by Averroes's position, it would not be difficult to imagine a person or

47. Ibid., 232.

persons either conflating the view of Thomas with that of Siger, or thinking that Siger's view is logically implied by Thomas's.

Bearing the possibility of such an association in mind, let us turn to the *Quodlibets* 4–6 of Walter of Bruges (d. 1307) and to *Quodlibet* 18 of Gerard of Abbeville, all of which were held in the period shortly preceding the condemnation of 1270. Like Bonaventure, both Walter and Gerard oppose the Radical Aristotelian movement by emphasizing the moral consequences of certain Aristotelian teachings. Unlike with Bonaventure, there is good reason to suppose that Thomas fell within the intended scope of their criticism. The issue seems to center around Thomas's use of the *translatio nova* of Aristotle's *De anima*. When in the *Prima pars* of the *Summa theologiae*, Thomas referred to the will as a passive power, which is actualized by the presence of its appetible object, Walter and Gerard may have both thought that this made the will subject of necessity to that appetible object.[48]

Walter was a student of Bonaventure, and a Franciscan regent master from 1267 to 1268. Around 1267–69, he held a set of disputed questions, which touched upon the relationship between the intellect and the will.[49] *Quodlibet* 4 asks specifically, "whether the will is necessitated by its appetible object."[50] William appears to have been very current in the reading of Thomas's work. The very first objection, save for the conclusion which Walter draws from it, could easily be taken from the *Sententia libri Physicorum*:

And it seems that it is. The will, of itself, is undetermined and indifferent to opposites; therefore, in order for it only to want one of [a pair of opposites], it is necessary for it to be determined to want it by something. But that which determines it is not itself, since what is undetermined does not determine. Therefore, [what determines it] will be other than itself: in-

48. Lottin, *Psychologie et morale*, 1:243, 247–48.

49. See ibid., 1:243; Sophie Delmas, *Un franciscain à Paris au milieu du XIIIe siècle: Le maître en théologie Eustache d'Arras* (Paris: Cerf, 2010), 66–67.

50. Walter of Bruges, *Quodlibet* 4, in *Quaestiones disputatae*, ed. E. Longpré (Louvain: Institut Supérieur de Philosophie de l'Université, 1928), 34: "Quaeritur utrum voluntas necessitetur ab appetibili suo."

deed, a good other [than itself] apprehended by reason. Therefore, it is determined to one [of a pair of] opposites or things proposed to it by the appetible good offered to it by reason; but for it to be thus determined to only one thing is for it to be necessitated by that thing. Therefore, the will is necessitated.[51]

Meanwhile, the third objection seems to speak to the position that Thomas takes in the *Prima pars* of the *Summa theologiae*:

> ... and in *De anima* 3: "The will is a moved mover;" therefore the will is a passive potency; but a passive potency necessarily undergoes actualization [*patitur*] by its active potency being applied to it; therefore, when the apprehended appetible good, which is active with respect to the will (as is claimed in *De anima* 3), is applied by reason to the will, it is necessary for it to undergo actualization by willing it.[52]

The twelfth objection is the most striking. Here, Walter seemingly takes Thomas's argument from *Summa theologiae*, Ia, q. 12, a. 1, and interprets it in the light of Thomas's observation that the true and the good are convertible: "Just as all men by nature desire to know (*Metaphysics* 1), so likewise do all desire what is good; but when we see the knowable it necessarily makes us know; therefore, when a man apprehends the good it necessarily makes him desire."[53] In re-

51. Ibid., obj. 1 [Longpré 34]: "Et quod sic videtur. 1. Voluntas de se indeterminata est ad opposita et indifferens; ergo ad hoc quod unum illorum velit tantum, oportet quod per aliquid determinetur ad id volendum; illud autem quod ipsam determinat non est ipsamet, quia indeterminatum non determinat; ergo erit aliud ab ipsa, nonnisi bonum aliud ratione apprehensum; igitur determinatur ad unum oppositorum vel sibi propositorum per bonum appetibile sibi a ratione oblatum; sed quod sic determinatur ad unum tantum necessitatur per illud, ergo voluntas necessitatur." Walter begins the *responsio* with an allusion to contemporaries: "Dicunt quidam quod voluntas necessitatur, pro se allegantes aliquas rationes de praedictis."

52. Ibid., obj. 3 [Longpré 34]: "et III *De anima:* 'Voluntas est movens motum'; ergo voluntas est potentia passiva; sed potentia passiva necessario patitur a suo activo sibi applicato; ergo quando bonum appetibile apprehensum, quod est activum respectu voluntatis, ut habetur III *De anima*, applicatur per rationem voluntati, necesse est quod patiatur volendo illud." Walter also picks up on Thomas's teaching concerning incontinence in obj. 11 [Longpré 36].

53. Ibid., obj. 12 [Longpré 36–37]: "Item, sicut omnes homines natura scire desi[de]rant, I *Metaphysicae*, ita omnia bonum appetunt; sed scibile aspectum necessario facit scire; ergo bonum apprehensum necessario facit hominem appetere."

sponse, Walter turns with Bonaventure to the moral consequences of Radical Aristotelianism. Any necessity on the part of the will, even one that derives from the intellect, compromises the will's freedom and moral responsibility. Ultimately such necessity leads to Pelagianism, because it supposes that we can perform any good work we can cognize.[54] In fact, all the actions of all the powers of the soul lie directly under the influence of the will. Even when presented with an appetible object, the will is still free to desire it or to ignore it.[55]

Replying to the first argument, Walter suggests that there is a parallel between the first principles of demonstration in the intellect and the will's desire for the good. Just as the intellect knows by means of and through the first principles of demonstration, so does the will desire by means of and through its primary actualization with respect to the common good.[56] Although Walter does not reference Avicenna or William of Auvergne, he makes it clear that he sees the orientation of the will toward its object as active in a way that is similar to these figures.[57] We see this more clearly in his response to the third objection. Walter says that the appetible object causes a certain movement in the soul toward the object (a movement which he calls an *inclinatio*), but he firmly denies that this motion constitutes an act of the will.[58] He then answers the twelfth objection by means of the principles established in his replies to the first and the third. Although there is in the soul a natural appetite for the good in general, merely presenting to the will a good or true thing does not cause a deliberate choice in the will.[59]

At first glance, it appears that Walter's thought and Thomas's are as diametrically opposed here as Thomas's and William of Au-

54. Ibid., resp. [Longpré 37–38].

55. Ibid. [Longpré 40].

56. Ibid., ad 1 [Longpré 41].

57. See, for example, ibid., ad 14 [Longpré 45]: "voluntas est magis potentia activa vel potestativa et libera, quae non recipit ab objecto suo nisi velit."

58. Ibid., ad 3 [Longpré 41].

59. Ibid., ad 12 [Longpré 45].

vergne's were in chapter 3. But there is a level of nuance to Walter's thought that is lacking in William's thought, which brings Walter somewhat closer to Thomas on the question of natural desire. As just noted, Walter admits that the soul has a natural appetite for the good in general, and that this appetite is actualized as an inclination toward appetible objects presented to the will by the intellect. Walter will even go on to say that in this sense the will desires its object "by the will of a natural inclination, by the necessity of immutability."[60] Thomas could agree with this. The main difference between Walter and Thomas concerns what happens when the intellect identifies an object as good *in particular*.

In *Quodlibet* 5, Walter hones in on this difference. Discussing the source of the will's freedom, Walter says that there are really three possible positions. The first aligns with Thomas's position before the *Sententia libri De anima*: the will is determined by a prior judgment of reason. The second, which Walter specifically associates with *De anima* 3, aligns with Thomas's position from the *Prima pars* of the *Summa theologiae*: the will is determined simultaneously with the judgment of reason. The third is Walter's position: reason never determines the will.[61] In his response, Walter makes it clear that Thomas's earlier and later positions *both* result in some form of determinism, because the intellect, which determines the will, is not itself entirely free in its determination. When the intellect sees the truth of a matter, it must grant its assent. Consequently, only the third position safeguards the true freedom of the will.[62] Walter is aware that this makes the will more of an Avicennian impressed power than an Averroistic moved mover. One of the *sed contras* runs thus: "Avicenna in *De anima*, part 1 [says,] 'It is impossible for what is moved of itself to be moved,' therefore vice versa, that which cannot possibly be moved is moved of itself. Therefore, by the same reasoning, the will has of itself that from which it cannot possibly be separated.

60. Ibid., ad 15 [Longpré 45].
61. Ibid., 5, resp. [Longpré 51].
62. Ibid. [Longpré 52].

But freedom is of this sort. Therefore, it has freedom of itself."[63] Although he often makes a reply to each *sed contra*, this one aligns so much with his thinking that he merely concedes it.[64]

In support of his apparent critique of Thomas, Walter appeals in *Quodlibet* 6 to the difficulty of explaining the sin of Adam and Eve. Since Adam and Eve were without inordinate passions, we may recall from chapter 2 that Thomas said in his *Commentary on the Sentences* that Satan induced them to sin by convincing them to err in their intellects, while in *De veritate* Thomas had made an exception for Adam and Eve, saying that in this one case their wills could withdraw from God without a prior judgment of their intellect. Walter seemingly latches onto this latter exception as evidence that Thomas had misconstrued the nature of the will in general. Adam and Eve were not in a special situation regarding the relationship between the intellect and the will. Their wills, like ours, always had the possibility of choosing or not choosing the good presented to them by the intellect.[65]

Gerard was also involved in the controversy over the object of the will, even if he is better known for his polemical interaction with Thomas in the mendicant controversy at this time.[66] His *Quodlibet* 18 shows a similar understanding of the freedom of the will to that of Walter, but he applies that freedom both to the will and to the intellect. He does this by drawing a sharp distinction between irrational and rational creatures. Only among irrational creatures is it appropriate to say that their powers are determined to a single end, and that they are passively moved by the presence of an appetible object.

63. Ibid., s.c. 12 [Longpré 49]: "Avicenna, VI *Naturalium*, I parte: 'Quod movetur a se, impossibile est moveri'; ergo et e converso quod impossibile est moveri, movetur a se; ergo eadem ratione, quod impossibile est separari a voluntate, illud habet a se ; libertas autem est hujusmodi; ergo illam a se habet." The reference is to a corrupted version of Avicenna, *De anima* 1.2, in *Liber de anima seu Sextus de naturalibus*, ed, S. van Riet (Louvain: Peeters, 1968–72), 39: "Quicquid movetur ex seipso, impossibile est mori."

64. Walter of Bruges, *Quodlibet* 5, ad s.c. 12 [Longpré 54].

65. Ibid., 6, ad 14 [Longpré 64–65].

66. See Torrell, *Saint Thomas Aquinas*, 75–90; also see the introduction to Thomas Aquinas, *De perfectione spiritualis vitae* [Leon. 43.2:6–9].

The intellect and the will are open equally to opposed ends.[67] That being the case, the intelligible object can only change the disposition of the intellect, and the appetible object can only change the disposition of the will.[68] Neither can force its corresponding power to move. Therefore, the appetible object, apprehended by the intellect, cannot force the will to move.[69] It may be the case among irrational creatures that they cannot be the cause of their own reduction to act, but the same does not hold true among rational powers of the soul, where the will *is* the cause of its own reduction to act.[70] The will therefore has a twofold relationship to the appetible object. As an undetermined cause, it receives a disposition from the object; as a determined cause, it moves itself or does not move itself toward the object as it chooses.[71]

If there were already theologians at Paris accustomed to conflating Thomas's views with the view condemned in the ninth proposition of 1270, then whether or not Tempier intended to condemn Thomas, it behooved Thomas to state very clearly why his views ought not to be so conflated, lest someone eventually accuse Thomas of saying something that should have incurred excommunication. Thomas seems to have been aware of this need. According to Lottin, he composed *De malo, question* 6, to clarify "hastily" his understanding of the initial impetus of the will's motion.[72]

De malo, question 6, appears to be a deliberate, textual composition, rather than the fruit of a live *quaestio disputata,* in which Thomas took the opportunity to do four things:

67. Gerard of Abbeville, *Quodlibet* 18, q. 2, resp., in *L'Anthropologie de Gérard d'Abbeville: Étude préliminaire et édition critique de plusieurs* Questions quodlibétiques *concernant le sujet, avec l'édition complète du* De cogitationibus, ed. A. Pattin (Leuven: Leuven University Press, 1993), 114.80–93.

68. Ibid., ad 1 [Pattin 117.56–61]; ad 2 [Pattin 117.66–78].

69. Ibid., ad 2 [Pattin 117.62–65].

70. Ibid., q. 3, ad 2 [Pattin 120.58–65].

71. Ibid., q. 2, ad 3 [Pattin 118.95–6].

72. Lottin, *Psychologie et morale,* 1:253. Whether or not Thomas interrupted the normal course of the *De malo* in order to insert q. 6 into it remains a matter of dispute. See the introduction to Leon. 23:5*.

1) To re-articulate his response to certain objections he had raised in the *Prima pars* of the *Summa theologiae,* and so to distance himself more explicitly from the condemnation.
2) To respond to Walter of Bruges.
3) To respond to Gerard of Abbeville.
4) To position himself somewhere in between Walter and Gerard on the one hand, and the Radical Aristotelians on the other.

That these were Thomas's goals is clear from the composition of the objections raised at the start of the question. In all, there are twenty-four objections. They can be accounted for as follows:

1) Seven objections (1–4, and 21–23) are taken directly from objections raised in the *Prima pars,* affording Thomas an opportunity to re-determine his response to them.[73]
2) Eight objections are taken directly from Walter's *Quodlibet* 4. Five of these (6–10) are taken directly from objections that Walter raises. Objection 14 contains an initial reply which is taken from a respondent's reply contained in Walter's *Quodlibet.* Objection 17 is taken from another objection that Walter raises, but strips the objection of some of its supporting reasoning. Objection 18 takes the reasoning stripped from objection 17 and uses it as a respondent's reply, to which Thomas formulates an original objection.[74]

73. The sources appear to be as follows:
   1) Objection 1: *ST* Ia, q. 83, a. 1, obj. 4 [Leon. 5:307].
   2) Objection 2: *ST* Ia, q. 83, a. 1, obj. 2 [Leon. 5:307].
   3) Objection 3: *ST* Ia, q. 115, a. 4, co. [Leon. 5:544], where Thomas raises a new objection which he had not considered among the formal objections prior to the *corpus.*
   4) Objection 4: *ST* Ia, q. 83, a. 1, obj. 3 [Leon. 5:307].
   5) Objection 21: *ST* Ia, q. 115, a. 4, obj. 2 [Leon. 5:544].
   6) Objection 22: *ST* Ia, q. 83, a. 1, obj. 1 [Leon. 5:307].
   7) Objection 23: *ST* Ia, q. 83, a. 2, obj. 3 [Leon. 5:309].

74. The sources appear to be as follows:
   1) Objection 6: *Quodlibet* 4, obj. 14 [Longpré 37]. This objection contains an initial reply, and Thomas follows the original objection up to the reply.

3) Three objections (15–16 and 19) are taken directly from Gerard's *Quodlibet* 18.[75]
4) Three objections (5, 13, 24) have no textual antecedent in Thomas, Walter, or Gerard that I could find, but seem to have a Franciscan provenance.[76]
5) Three objections (11–12 and 20) have no textual antecedent in Thomas, Walter, or Gerard that I could find, but seem to have a Radical Aristotelian provenance.[77]

---

2) Objection 7: *Quodlibet* 4, obj. 3 [Longpré 34].
3) Objection 8: *Quodlibet* 4, obj. 14, and obj. 16 [Longpré 37]. Here Thomas's argument contains an initial reply. The reply is taken from the initial reply in Walter's obj. 14, and the objection to the reply is taken from Walter's obj. 16.
4) Objection 9: *Quodlibet* 4, obj. 18 [Longpré 37–38].
5) Objection 10: *Quodlibet* 4, obj. 17 [Longpré 37].
6) Objection 14: The insistence is taken from *Quodlibet* 4, ad 8 [Longpré 35]; the objection to the initial reply appears to be original.
7) Objection 17: *Quodlibet* 4, obj. 5 [Longpré 35].
8) Objection 18: The insistence is taken from some of the reasoning in *Quodlibet* 4, obj. 5, which was omitted from objection 17. The objection to the initial reply appears to be original.

75. The sources appear to be as follows:
1) Objection 15: *Quodlibet* 18, q. 3, obj. 2 [Pattin 113].
2) Objection 16: *Quodlibet* 18, q. 2, obj. 2 [Pattin 112].
3) Objection 19: *Quodlibet* 18, q. 2, obj. 4 [Pattin 112].

76. Possible sources may be as follows:
1) Objection 5: *Summa fratris Alexandri*, Ia-Iae, no. 286 [Quaracchi 1:405].
2) Objection 13: *Summa fratris Alexandri*, Ia-IIae, no. 277 [Quaracchi 2:339].
3) Objection 24: Alexander of Hales, *Glossa in II Sent.*, d. 25 [Quaracchi 2:237].

77. Significant observations are as follows:
1) Objection 11 references an axiom "dispositio primi moventis relinquitur in omnibus sequentibus." The axiom comes from Averroes, *In V Metaphysicorum* [Giunti 8:131rb–c]. The argument made from the axiom relies on the *translatio nova* of the *De anima* to say that the appetible object is the first mover of the will, and that the will is necessitated by the appetible object when it is apprehended as good by the intellect.
2) Objection 12 references the axiom from *Metaphysics* 6.4 [1027b25–29] that "bonum est in rebus, verum autem in mente." On this basis it argues that since the intellect is necessitated by its object, so likewise must the will be necessitated by its object.
3) Objection 20 relies on a very loose paraphrase of Augustine's *De Trinitate* 1.1, "nihil est sibi ipsi causa ut sit," to argue that similarly nothing can be the cause of its own motion and so to deny that the will moves itself.

In the *corpus*, Thomas begins by positioning himself with respect to the opinion he intends to criticize.

Some people claimed that the will of man is moved by necessity to choose a particular thing. Yet they did not claim that the will is compelled: for not every necessary thing is violent, but only that whose principle is external. Wherefore there also exist some necessary natural motions which are nevertheless not violent, for the violent is opposed to the natural just like it is opposed to the voluntary, since the principle of both [the natural and the voluntary] is internal, while the principle of the violent is external.[78]

If we place Thomas's *De veritate* to one side briefly, the position he summarizes could be taken almost as a summary of his own teaching from the *Sententia libri De anima* to the *Summa theologiae, Prima pars*. There is a distinction between natural and free will: the natural will follows the appetite of nature, which is authored by God, and that natural appetite constitutes the pattern according to which the will is moved by the appetible object. A similar position also appears in Walter's *Quodlibet* 4. It is placed on the mouth of the respondent, who interjects it into the middle of objection 14:

The respondent said that there is a twofold necessity: necessity of compulsion and of unchangeableness; there is also a twofold will: natural and deliberative. Now, the natural will wills the end (happiness and the good) by the necessity of unchangeableness, not of compulsion; but it wills those things which are ordered toward the end, rather than the end, by the deliberative will, because there is neither deliberation nor counsel about the end, as is said in *Ethics* 3, and it wills those things which are ordered toward the end freely, not by any necessity of compulsion or unchangeableness.[79]

78. Thomas Aquinas, *De malo* q. 6, resp. [Leon 23:147–48]: "Quidam posuerunt quod uoluntas hominis ex necessitate mouetur ad aliquid eligendum. Nec tamen ponebant quod uoluntas cogeretur: non enim omne necessarium est uiolentum, set solum illud cuius principium est extra. Vnde et motus naturales inueniuntur aliqui necessarii, non tamen uiolenti: uiolentum enim repugnat naturali sicut et uoluntario, quia utriusque principium est intra, uiolenti autem principium est extra."

79. Walter of Bruges, *Quodlibet* 4, obj. 14 [Longpré 37]: "Dixit Respondens quod duplex est necessitas, scilicet coactionis et incommutabilitatis, et duplex voluntas, scilicet naturalis et deliberativa. Finem autem, ut beatitudinem et bonum, vult voluntas naturalis necessitate immutabilitatis, non coactionis, ea vero quae sunt ad finem vult voluntate

In the response to this objection, Walter admits that the will can be said to suffer change (*pati*), but only in the sense that the natural will is necessarily borne toward the pleasingness of a good (*complacentia boni*); the deliberative will is not necessarily borne toward anything, no matter how naturally pleasing it might be.[80]

Thomas's response draws on Walter's idea that the pleasingness of a particular object has something to do with how it moves the will. Thomas no longer says that the object of the will is the appetible object (*appetibile*) or the "apprehended good" (*bonum apprehensum*); now he speaks of the object of the will as the "the good, apprehended as fitting" (*bonum conveniens apprehensum*).[81] Having said that, Thomas makes room for a subtle but important distinction that distances his own view from that of Walter. If something could appear in every particular respect as a fitting good, it would necessarily move the will.[82] Happiness is such a thing. As Boethius had said, happiness consists of a collection of every particular good. Returning to the Augustinian roots of the debate, Thomas concludes that happiness necessarily moves the will.

If Thomas had merely stated that happiness, as an appetible object, moves the will of necessity, he might have been seen to run afoul of the ninth proposition of 1270, as well as the position with which he began the *corpus* of the question. Accordingly, Thomas emphasizes the fact that the necessity spoken of here only concerns the specification of the will's act (what it wills), not its exercise (wheth-

---

deliberativa, non finem, quia de fine non est deliberatio nec consilium, ut habetur III *Ethicorum*, et haec quae ad finem sunt vult libere, non aliqua necessitate coactionis vel immutabilitatis."

80. Ibid., ad 14 [Longpré 45].

81. Thomas Aquinas, *De malo* q. 6, co. [Leon. 23:149]. When Thomas first unequivocally emphasized the freedom of the will to act or not to act in *De veritate*, he had said something similar. See *De ver.* q. 22, a. 5, co. [Leon. 22:624]: "Voluntati ipsi inest naturalis quidam appetitus boni sibi convenientis." The challenge from Walter appears to have prompted Thomas to blend his earlier language with that of the *translatio nova* of the *De anima* in order to give due emphasis to the will's freedom in the order of exercise: *bonum conveniens* (*De ver.*) → *bonum apprehensum* (*Sententia libri De anima* to the *Prima pars*) → *bonum conveniens apprehensum* (*De malo*).

82. Thomas Aquinas, *De malo* q. 6, co. [Leon. 23:150].

er it wills). Provided that the will wills to will, it necessarily wills the good specified by the intellect if and only if the good apprehended by the intellect is apprehended as fitting in every respect. However, in this life no good can be apprehended as fitting in every respect for two reasons: first, because we do not have a perfect knowledge of happiness, so there always remains some fitting aspect of happiness that we might not consider;[83] second, because even if (*per impossibile*) we were able to consider every single aspect of happiness, the will could still choose whether or not to exercise its act.[84]

Thomas's claim that the will possesses freedom of exercise irrespective of the object specified by the intellect does at least *appear* to run contrary to two of his previous commitments:

1) to his teaching from the *De veritate* onwards that the intellect is the first mover of the soul, whether directly or in virtue of its object.
2) to his teaching after the *Sententia libri De anima* that the will is a passive power.

Regarding the first, there is no other suitable explanation than that Thomas seems simply to have changed his mind.[85] He does contin-

83. ibid.

84. Ibid.; see also the ad 7 of the same question [Leon. 23:151].

85. The idea that Thomas changed his mind on the relationship between the intellect and the will around this time was originally suggested by Lottin, *Psychologie et morale*, 1:226–43, 1:252–62. Lottin only recognized two main stages of development in Thomas's thought (*De veritate* to 1270; *De malo* to *ST*, *Prima secundae*), not three as I have proposed here (*De veritate* to 1267; *Sententia libri De anima* to 1270; *De malo* to *ST*, *Prima secundae*): prior to 1270, Lottin argues that Thomas thought of the intellect as the final cause of the will's motion; after 1270, Lottin argues that Thomas thought of the intellect as the formal cause of the will's motion. The reception of Lottin's thesis has been varied. It was criticized by Rosemary Laurer, "St. Thomas's Theory of Intellectual Causality in Election," *New Scholasticism* 28 (1954): 299–319. Lottin's response is Odon Lottin, "La preuve de la liberté humaine chez saint Thomas d'Aquin," *Recherches de Théologie Ancienne et Médiévale* 23, no. 2 (1956): 323–30. More recently, Lottin's thesis was supported in a qualified manner by David Gallagher, "Free Choice and Free Judgment in Thomas Aquinas," *Archiv für Geschichte der Philosophie* 76, no. 3 (1994): 247–77, and criticized again by Daniel Westberg, "Did Aquinas Change His Mind about the Will?" *The Thomist* 58, no. 1 (1994): 41–60. The most recent contribution to the debate has been a thorough rejection of Lottin's thesis by Yul Kim, "A Change in Thomas Aquinas's Theory of the

ue to speak of the intellect and the will as exercising mutual but not reciprocal causality one another, yet from now on the will is going to enjoy pride of place among the movers in the soul, not the intellect. Regarding the second, Thomas cedes no ground whatsoever. If the will moves, it must be moved by another.

In order to claim that the will is the first mover among the powers of the soul, and yet to continue to claim that the will is a moved mover, Thomas had to identify an exterior mover of the will. He did this by appealing to a quasi-Aristotelian text, the *Liber de bona fortuna,* which was a compilation of texts from Aristotle's *Magna moralia* and *Eudemian Ethics* recently translated by William of Moerbeke.[86] In a section compiled from *Eudemian Ethics,* Book 8, Pseudo-Aristotle inquires after the principle of motion in the soul. The text says that the principle of movement in the soul is better than intellect and reason, and that God is its first mover according to a divine "impulse" (*instinctus*).[87] Since, Thomas reasons, the will is an immaterial power, the cause of the will's motion cannot be a heavenly body. By process of elimination, Thomas argues that God is therefore the first mover of the will directly in the order of exercise.[88] The will, in turn, acts as the first mover of the other powers of the soul.[89]

For Thomas to say that the will is moved directly by God ran the

---

Will: Solutions to a Long-Standing Problem," *American Catholic Philosophical Quarterly* 82, no. 2 (2008): 221–36. Kim acknowledges with Lottin the importance of reading Thomas in light of Walter and Gerard, although neither Lottin nor Kim avert to the significance of this context in light of Thomas's use of the *translatio nova* of *De anima* 3.

86. See T. Deman, "Le 'Liber de bona fortuna' dans la théologie de S. Thomas d'Aquin," *Revue des Sciences Philosophiques et Théologieque* 17, no. 1 (1928): 38–58.

87. Pseudo-Aristotle, *De bona fortuna*: "Quid motus principium in anima. Palam quemadmodum in toto deus, et omne illud: mouet enim aliquo modo omnia quod in nobis diuinum. Rationis autem principium non ratio, sed aliquid melius. Quid igitur utique erit melius et scientia et intellectu nisi deus? Virtus enim intellectus organum. Et propter hoc, quod olim dicebatur, bene fortunati uocantur qui si impetum faciant, dirigunt sine ratione existentes, et consiliari non expedit ipsis: habent enim principium tale quod melius intellectu et consilio, qui autem rationem, hoc autem non habent, neque diuinos instinctus, hoc non possunt." The extract is compiled from Aristotle, *Eudemian Ethics* 8.14 (1248a24–34).

88. Thomas Aquinas, *De malo* q. 6, co. [Leon. 23:149].

89. Ibid., ad 10 [Leon. 23:151].

risk of his appearing to say that the will is moved violently by an exterior appetible object. Thomas was aware of this objection. He had previously used it in *Summa theologiae,* Ia, q. 83, a. 1, obj. 3; and he includes it in *De malo* q. 6, obj. 4. In the *Prima pars,* Thomas had replied simply that God is the first cause of the will's motion insofar as he moves it according to its nature,[90] a nature which he understood to be moved proximately by its appetible object. In *De malo* he responds differently, emphasizing the activity rather than the passivity of the will: "The will contributes something when it is moved by God; for the will itself is that which acts, albeit moved by God. And therefore, although its motion is from an extrinsic source as from a first principle, nevertheless it is not violent."[91]

On the basis that God is the first mover of the soul by means of the will, and that the will is never necessitated with respect to exercise, Thomas goes on to consider how exactly the will chooses one good over another. He distinguishes three ways in which the will may arrive at a choice. The first is when reason judges one good to be clearly better than another. The second is when the intellect considers one circumstance and not another. The third is simply from the disposition of the will. Concerning this third category, some goods are necessary with regard to specification on account of the natural disposition of the will, like being, living, and understanding, while other goods may appear good to the will, depending on how well they accord with dispositions arising from its freely chosen habituation.[92]

90. Thomas Aquinas, *ST* Ia, q. 83, a. 1, ad 3 [Leon. 5:307–8].

91. Thomas Aquinas, *De malo* q. 6, ad 4 [Leon. 23:150]: "Voluntas aliquid confert cum a Deo mouetur: ipsa enim est que operatur, set mota a Deo. Et ideo motus eius quamuis sit ab extrinseco sicut a primo principio, non tamen est uiolentus." See also *De malo* q. 3, a. 3 [Leon. 23:73]: "actus uoluntatis nichil aliud est quam inclinatio quedam uoluntatis in uolitum, sicut et appetitus naturalis nichil est aliud quam inclinatio nature in aliquid. Inclinatio autem nature est et a forma naturali et ab eo quod dedit formam: unde dicitur quod motus ignis sursum est ab eius leuitate et a generante quod talem formam creauit. Sic igitur motus uoluntatis directe procedit a uoluntate et a Deo qui est uoluntatis causa, qui solus in uoluntate operatur et uoluntatem inclinare potest in quodcumque uoluerit."

92. Ibid., q. 6, co. [Leon. 23:150].

In *De malo,* question 3, Thomas unpacks in more detail how exactly the will relates to the apprehended object. Here again he engages the language of Walter of Bruges. Walter had described the influence of the object on the will as though it were like the influence of counselors on the king or the pope.[93] Similarly, Thomas says that the object only moves as an exterior mover by counsel and persuasion, while the origin of an act in the will lies solely within the will itself.[94] Thus the apprehended good "does not move the will of necessity."[95] Thomas concludes that there is a difference between the natural appetites of intellect and the will. Following Walter, rather than Gerard, Thomas grants a level of necessity in the natural appetite of the intellect. He says that the intellect is moved of necessity to assent to the first principles of demonstration and those things which are seen to have a necessary connection with the first principles of demonstration. Distinguishing himself from Walter on the subject of the will, as he does in question 6, Thomas says that the will is only moved of necessity in the order of specification: provided that the will wills to will, it must will happiness and to those things which appear to have a necessary connection with happiness.[96] Again, in this life we do not perceive the immediate connection between God and happiness necessarily, and so while we must always desire happiness in general, no particular object necessarily moves our will.[97]

Given the way in which Thomas now describes the relationship between the will and the appetible object, it is possible for him to account for sins against what we know in a twofold way. On the one hand, he could continue to reason in the Aristotelian tradition about sins of incontinence. More so than previously, Thomas acknowledges that Aristotle's reasoning really only applies to sins which are done

93. See Walter of Bruges, *Quodlibet* 5, ad 5 [Longpré 62].

94. Thomas Aquinas, *De malo* q. 3, a. 3, resp. [Leon. 23:72]. See also ad 5 [Leon. 23:73].

95. Ibid., ad 12 [Leon. 23:74].

96. Ibid., resp. [Leon. 23:72–73].

97. Ibid. [Leon. 23:73].

from passion.[98] Apart from sins of incontinence, there are other sins, which proceed primarily or even exclusively from a disposition of the will. These are sins of malice, in which the will "by its own motion and without any passion is inclined" to an apparent good.[99]

THE *SUMMA THEOLOGIAE, PRIMA SECUNDAE* (1271)

Thomas had a significant challenge when it came to the discussion of the desire for God in the *Prima secundae* of the *Summa theologiae.* The *Prima pars* had already begun to circulate on its own,[100] and yet Thomas's interactions with Walter of Bruges, Gerard of Abbeville, and the condemnation of 1270 had led him to a rather significant rearticulation of his thought on the relationship between the intellect and the will: he gave greater emphasis to the complete freedom of the will in the order of exercise, even if he did did not change his basic, Augustinian teaching that the soul has a natural desire for the fulfillment of its natural appetite insofar as is possible. This opened up two fundamental questions about the desire for God which could not go unanswered:

First, we saw in chapter 3 that in the *Summa contra Gentiles* Thomas used William of Auvergne's *De anima* to develop an argument based upon the intellect's natural desire to know, so as to prove that the ultimate end of man is the vision of God. However, if the intellect is dependent upon the will for some or all of the actions involved in that desire, to what extent does the argument need to be adjusted to take into account the will's influence and motion?

Second, and more fundamentally, we saw in chapter 2 how Thomas made use of Aristotle's *Nicomachean Ethics* 10.4 in order to locate the act of human happiness in the intellect. In chapter 3, we

98. Ibid., a. 9 [Leon. 23:87].

99. Ibid., a. 11, co. [Leon. 23:92]. Thomas does devote part of a previous article to sins of malice in *In II Sent.*, d. 43, q. 1, a. 1, sol. [Mandonnet 2:1094]. However, there he speaks only of a "corrupt appetite" as responsible for the sin, and in context, the most natural reading of the text would suggest that he is speaking of the sensitive appetite only.

100. Torrell, *Saint Thomas Aquinas*, 1:146.

saw how Thomas made use of the natural appetite and natural desire of the intellect in order to establish that the ultimate happiness of man is the vision of God. If Thomas is now going to say that the will is the superior mover in the soul, and not the intellect, to what extent could Thomas continue to speak of the intellect as the highest power of the soul? Indeed, to what extent could he continue to say that the perfection of man consists chiefly in intellectual vision, rather than in the love which complements that vision?

In light of these questions, it is clear that Thomas's treatment of the desire for God in the *Prima pars* could not be left to stand on its own. The most practical way to update it would be to re-articulate and/or re-write the appropriate questions and to insert them into the *Prima secundae*. Providentially, Thomas had left himself room to do this. In the *proemium* to question 84 of the *Prima pars,* he had stated his intention to reserve a formal treatment of the will for the *Prima secundae.*[101] All he had to do was to add a few articles to what he might already have planned on doing to supply the needed clarifications, emendations, and corrections.

Natural Desire

In *Summa theologiae* Ia-IIae, q. 9, a. 4, Thomas inquires after the origin of the will's movement in the order of exercise. As in *De malo,* Thomas insists on an Averroistic account of the will's motion. Given that the will at some time begins to exercise its act, it must be moved by another mover in order to do so. Thomas concludes, again following the *Liber de bona fortuna,* that the cause of this motion is an exterior *instinctus.*[102] In q. 9, a. 6, Thomas argues that the exterior principle is God. Rather than use a process of elimination which only includes heavenly bodies and God (and so leaves out the angels), as he had done in *De malo,* Thomas here borrows two positive argu-

101. Thomas Aquinas, *ST,* Ia, q. 84, proem. [Leon. 5:313]: "Actus autem appetitivae partis ad considerationem moralis scientiae pertinent: et ideo in secunda parte huius operis de eis tractabitur, in qua considerandum erit de morali materia."

102. Thomas Aquinas, *ST,* Ia-IIae, q. 9, a. 4, co. [Leon. 6:78].

ments from q. 105, a. 4, of the *Prima pars* in favor of the idea that God is the first mover of the will directly.[103] One is based on the principle from the *De potentia* that the cause of a thing's being is the cause of its motion: since the will is a power of a rational soul created directly by God, the will can only be moved by God. The other is based on the will's natural inclination. A particular cause cannot give a universal inclination; but the will has an inclination toward the universal good; ergo its inclination must be caused by a universal good, which God alone is.[104] In q. 10, a. 4, Thomas repeats the argument from *De malo* that since God moves all things in accord with their nature, and since it is of the nature of the will to be moved voluntarily, God's motion does not cause necessity in the will.[105]

In q. 10, a. 1, Thomas inquires after the origin of the will's movement in the order of specification. In *De malo,* Thomas had argued that the fact that some goods are necessary with regard to specification arises from the natural disposition of the will; his examples were being, living, and knowing. In the *Prima secundae* Thomas uses the same three examples,[106] but gives a more detailed account of how the will is naturally disposed to those objects.

> The will is distinguished from nature as one cause from another. For some things are done naturally and some are done voluntarily. Moreover, there is a different mode of causation proper to the will (which is lord of its actions), beyond the mode which befits nature (which is determined to one). Yet since the will is grounded in some nature, it is necessary that the will participate in the motion proper to its nature with respect to something; just as a posterior cause participates in what belongs to a prior cause. Now, each thing's being, which is [received] through its nature, is prior in it to its wanting, which is [caused] by its will. And it is thus that the will naturally wants something.[107]

103. Thomas Aquinas, *ST,* Ia, q. 105, a. 4 [Leon. 5:474].

104. Thomas Aquinas, *ST,* Ia-IIae, q. 9, a. 6 [Leon. 6:82].

105. Ibid., q. 10, a. 4, co. [Leon. 6:89]. See also Ia-IIae, q. 6, a. 4, ad 1 [Leon. 6:60].

106. Ibid., a. 1 [Leon. 6:83].

107. Ibid., ad 1 [Leon. 6:83]: "Voluntas dividitur contra naturam, sicut una causa contra aliam: quaedam enim fiunt naturaliter, et quaedam fiunt voluntarie. Est autem

In short, it belongs to the will, whenever it exercises itself, to seek not only its own object (the universal good), which it seeks as an undetermined power, but also the good of the whole of human nature which has a determinate end. The result, as in *De malo*, is that if the will chooses to exercise its act, it cannot *not* will those determinate goods provided that its act is specified by them.[108] It is only because the will often fails to perceive some necessary connection between a particular good and either the universal good or some determinate good of nature that the will, unlike the intellect, can be said not to desire its object of necessity.[109] In q. 9, a. 3, Thomas adds that the will's orientation toward its twofold object, the universal good and the determinate goods of nature, is fixed in the will like the first principles of demonstration are fixed in the intellect. Just like the intellect reduces itself to act in virtue of those first principles, so does the will reduce itself to act in virtue of its desire for its end.[110]

Thomas summarizes his view of the will in q. 6, a. 4, where he discusses whether violence can be brought against the will.[111] The three objections raised in this question address the three basic difficulties that Thomas had to work out in the *De malo*. The first concerns God: if God is an exterior mover of the soul, does he do violence to the

alius modus causandi proprius voluntati, quae est domina sui actus, praeter modum qui convenit naturae, quae est determinata ad unum. Sed quia voluntas in aliqua natura fundatur, necesse est quod motus proprius naturae, quantum ad aliquid, participetur in voluntate: sicut quod est prioris causae, participatur a posteriori. Est enim prius in unaquaque re ipsum esse, quod est per naturam, quam velle, quod est per voluntatem. Et inde est quod voluntas naturaliter aliquid vult."

108. Thomas explains this dynamic in a little more detail in *Sententia libri Metaphysicorum* 9.5, lect. 4, in *In Duodecim libros Metaphysicorum Aristotelis expositio*, ed Raimundo Spiazzi (Turin: Marietti, 1964), 435. Here he distinguishes between natural creatures and rational creatures on the basis that natural creatures are determined to one and rational creatures are not. Consequently, a natural creature *must* act in the presence of its appetible object, while a rational power need not. A rational power is only determined to a given appetible object by choice.

109. See also Thomas Aquinas, *ST*, Ia-IIae, q. 10, a. 2, co. [Leon. 6:86]. On the intellect, see the ad 2 of the same article.

110. Ibid., q. 9, a. 3, co. [Leon. 6:77–78]. See also q. 17, a. 6, ad 1 [Leon. 6:122].

111. Ibid., q. 6, a. 4 [Leon. 6:59–60].

will? The second concerns the appetible object: since, according to the *translatio nova* of *De anima,* Book 3, the will is moved by its appetible object, does the appetible object do violence to the will? The third concerns sins of malice: if violent motion is that which is *contra naturam,* and the will sometimes seeks what is *contra naturam,* does the will move violently in those cases?

In the *corpus* of q. 6, a. 4, Thomas states emphatically that the will is nothing other than "an inclination proceeding from an interior, knowing principle. But what is compelled or violent is from an exterior principle."[112] In neither of the three cases is the will moved by an exterior principle: in the first case, because if God were to do violence to the will, the result would cease by that very fact to be a willed act;[113] in the second case, because the appetible object only moves the will provided that the will is first disposed toward it;[114] in the third case, because the object of the will is not just something that appears good (otherwise the will would be necessitated by its object), but, as Thomas had said in the *De malo,* a good that appears *as fitting* (*conveniens*). The will chooses a good that appears to it as fitting, either in accord with the passions, or more simply in accord with the state of the will's present habituated character.[115]

Thomas's account of the will's relationship to nature gives him an opportunity in q. 68, a. 1, to return to the question of *rationes seminales.* The difficulty that faced him was that, while he could previously point to a combination of active and passive principles in the intellect in virtue of the distinction between the agent and the possible intellect, the will afforded him no such obvious distinction. In

112. Ibid., co. [Leon. 6:59]: "Voluntas nihil est aliud quam inclinatio quaedam procedens ab interiori principio cognoscente: sicut appetitus naturalis est quaedam inclinatio ab interiori principio et sine cognitione. Quod autem est coactum vel violentum, est ab exteriori principio."

113. Ibid., ad 1 [Leon. 6:59–60].

114. Ibid., ad 2 [Leon. 6:60].

115. Ibid., ad 3 [Leon. 6:60]: "Id in quod voluntas tendit peccando, etsi sit malum et contra rationalem naturam secundum rei veritatem, apprehenditur tamen ut bonum et conveniens naturae, inquantum est conveniens homini secundum aliquam passionem sensus, vel secundum aliquem habitum corruptum."

order to locate his characteristic complement of active and passive principles, Thomas pairs natural virtues with the natural appetite of the will. He argues that the natural virtues serve as "seminal predecessors [*seminalia*] … of moral virtues." This explained the possibility for development of virtue in the will, but it led to a difficulty with the intellect, because the principles in the intellect that correspond with natural virtue are the first principles of demonstration, and Thomas had consistently rejected the idea that the first principles of demonstration could serve as the active principle of the *ratio seminalis* in the intellect. Be that as it may, and seemingly to maintain consistency, Thomas also says here that the first principles of demonstration constitute the "seminal predecessors [*seminalia*] … of intellectual virtues."[116]

Thomas's treatment of the will in itself forms the basis of his discussion of the relationship between the intellect and the will. In q. 9, a. 1, Thomas asks whether the will is moved by the intellect. He had already determined a similar question in q. 82, a. 4, of the *Prima pars,* where he had asked whether the intellect is moved by the will. Against a set of objections positing various forms of intellectual determinism, Thomas had concluded that the intellect moves the will as its final cause, while the will moves the intellect in the manner of an efficient cause for those acts which concern the intellect's formal good.[117] In the *Prima secundae,* Thomas adjusts his thinking in two ways. First, he brings the *status quaestionis* up to date. The objections now all posit some form of voluntarism, while in the *sed contra* he quotes the *translatio nova* of the *De anima,* Book 3 to the effect that the appetible object is the first mover of the will. Having thus set up the parameters of the recent discussion, he determines the question

116. Ibid., q. 73, a. 1, co. [Leon. 6:406–7]: "Virtus est homini naturalis secundum quandam inchoationem. Secundum quidem naturam speciei, inquantum in ratione hominis insunt naturaliter quaedam princpia naturaliter cognita tam scibilium quam agendorum, quae sunt quaedam seminalia intellectualium virtutum et moralium; et inquantum in voluntate inest quidam naturalis appetitus boni quod est secundum rationem."

117. Thomas Aquinas, *ST,* Ia, q. 83, a. 4, co. [Leon. 5:303].

as he had in the *De malo*. He distinguishes sharply between the order of specification and the order of exercise. The good apprehended by the intellect moves the will in the order of specification; but the will itself is always free to act or not to act in the order of exercise.[118]

In q. 17, a. 6, Thomas applies this general account of specification and exercise to the particular case of the freedom of the intellect's acts. Where previously he had followed Walter on the freedom of the intellect's acts in the *De malo*, here he charts a *via media* between Walter and Gerard. The intellect has three acts in the order of specification: apprehension, judgment, and reasoning. Apprehension is never free with regard to exercise, judgment is sometimes free with regard to exercise, and reasoning is always free with regard to exercise. Apprehension is never free because it is a passive power connected to the sensory organs. Judgment is not free when it concerns the first principles of demonstration or those things which are seen immediately to be connected with them, because in those cases judgment is just as natural as apprehension. Judgment is free when it concerns things which cannot be immediately connected with the first principles of demonstration, because in that instance there is nothing in nature that impels the intellect to assent. Reasoning is always free, because by definition it involves an attempt to reach conclusions whose connection with the first principles of demonstration is not foreknown.[119]

The Natural Desire for the Vision of God

Thomas's observations about the relationship between the intellect and the will in *Prima secundae*, qq. 6–17, provide a helpful framework through which to understand his discussion of the natural desire for the vision of God in q. 5, a. 8.[120] This question asks wheth-

118. Thomas Aquinas, *ST*, Ia-IIae, q. 9, a. 1, co. [Leon. 6:74]. Concerning the manner in which the appetible object does not necessitate the will in the order of exercise, see also Ia-IIae, q. 6, a. 4, ad 2 [Leon. 6:60], where Thomas is responding directly to an objection taken from the *translatio nova* of *De anima* 3.

119. Ibid., q. 17, a. 6, co. [Leon. 6:122].

120. Ibid., q. 5, a. 8 [Leon. 6:54].

er everyone desires happiness. The first objection relates the ninth proposition condemned in 1270 to the understanding of our desire for God found in Augustine's *De trinitate,* Book 13, which, as we saw in chapter 1, had formed the basis of medieval discussions of the desire for God through Peter Lombard. Positing that the object of the will is the apprehended good (the *bonum apprehensum,* not the *bonum conveniens apprehensum*), the objection argues that since not all know where happiness is to be found, not all desire it. The second objection applies the same view of desire to a hypothetical person condemned in the first proposition of 1241. It argues that happiness consists in the vision of God; but since some people think the vision of God is impossible; therefore, those people do not desire it; ergo, etc. The third objection concerns sins of malice. When people want to want evil things, they do not desire happiness.

In the *corpus,* Thomas relies on the Augustinian relationship between natural desire and natural appetite that he developed in the *Summa contra Gentiles,* and reworks it to give motive priority to the will. The result is that there is still a power in the soul, with a natural appetite for a universal perfection, whose natural desire seeks the fulfillment of that natural appetite insofar as is possible. But that power is now the will: "Since ... the good is the object of the will, someone's perfect good is that which totally satisfies his will. Wherefore to desire happiness is nothing other than to desire that the will be sated. Everyone wants this."[121] Thomas takes this as a sufficient reply to the first objection, presumably since the first objection made no provision for the appetite of the will apart from the inclination of the intellect. He uses the reply to the second objection to discuss the question of necessity with regard to specification. Here he re-

121. Ibid., co. [Leon. 6:54]: "Cum ... bonum sit obiectum voluntatis, perfectum bonum est alicuius, quod totaliter eius voluntati satisfacit. Unde appetere beatitudinem nihil aliud est quam appetere ut voluntas satietur. Quod quilibet vult." Hütter, *Dust Bound for Heaven,* 233, notes the importance of the conditionality of our natural desire in a similar way. "The *desiderium* remains, however, an inchoate movement of the will, somewhat conditional, because it is less than a firmly realized movement of the rational appetite to a specific good."

peats what he had said in the *De malo*: provided the will wills to will, it cannot but desire happiness if it is presented to the will under every particular respect. However, given all the ways in which the intellect can fail to consider at least some particular aspect of happiness (like, for example, being wrong about which particular act it is to be found in), the will is free not to desire happiness specifically, provided that at least one particular aspect of it is missing from the intellect's specification of it. He then uses the reply to the third objection to make the consequences of the reply to the second objection clearer. The will only desires to be sated in general; it is not compelled by nature to desire anything in particular, apart from the very special case in which happiness might be presented to it in every particular respect, and even then, it could simply will not to will. Thomas then returns to Augustine's fundamental observation in *De Trinitate*, Book 13: many people's wills seek happiness in specific things which will make them miserable; but they do not for that reason fail to desire happiness in general.

Since Thomas now considers the will to be the superior mover in the soul, rather than the intellect, the will's natural inclination in the order of exercise undergirds all of the actions of the other powers of the soul which are subject to the will's command, when the will commands those other powers to perform those actions. As we saw above with regard to q. 17, a. 6, this includes some acts of the intellect. It does not include acts of apprehension; nor does it include acts of judgment concerning the first principles of demonstration and those conclusions which are seen to be immediately connected with them; but it does include all acts of reasoning, as well as judgments in which the intellect does not immediately connect the conclusion with the first principles of demonstration and/or those things which are seen as immediately connected with them. This is important, because it helps us to understand the fate of Thomas's argument from the *Summa contra Gentiles*, reworked in *Summa theologiae* Ia, q. 12, a. 1, concerning the natural desire of the intellect to know the causes of things. That argument was based upon the desire to know, as expressed through acts of reasoning. But since acts of reasoning depend upon the prior motion of the will, Thomas could preserve the substance of the argument in this new context, provided that he introduced the motion of the will into it prior to those acts of reasoning.

One aspect of this sort of argument which ultimately remains the same is that it still draws a conclusion about the intellect. In q. 3, a. 4, Thomas considers whether the highest act of man in the beatific vision resides in the intellect or in the will.[122] The third objection argues from the will's motive priority to conclude that the will is the higher power.[123] In the reply to that objection, Thomas states succinctly why the intellect should still be considered the higher power, even though the will has motive priority. Although the will moves the intellect to advance toward its end, the intellect still apprehends the end first.[124] That apprehension, like all apprehension, lies outside of the will's dominion.

Thomas reworks the argument definitively in *Summa theologiae* Ia-IIae, q. 3, a. 8.[125] Here he asks whether man's happiness is in the vision of the divine essence. Again, the context is the condemnation of 1241. The objections state in a generic form some basic objections associated with that condemnation, and are recycled from Thomas's original treatment of that condemnation in the *Commentary on the Sentences*. The first suggests, on the authority of Dionysius, that since we are united to God as "to one who is altogether unknown," our happiness does not consist in the vision of the divine essence.[126] The second argues that since it belongs properly to God to see himself, our happiness must consist in something less.[127]

122. Thomas Aquinas, *ST*, Ia-IIae, q. 3, a. 4 [Leon. 6:29].

123. Ibid., obj. 3 [Leon. 6:29].

124. Ibid., ad 3 [Leon. 6:29]. On the priority of the intellect in happiness, see also Thomas Aquinas, *Sententia libri Ethicorum* 10.10 [Leon. 47:582–85].

125. Thomas Aquinas, *ST*, Ia-IIae, q. 3, a. 8 [Leon. 6:35–36].

126. Ibid., obj. 1 [Leon. 6:35]. The antecedent is *In IV Sent.*, d. 49, q. 2, a. 1, obj. 3 [Parma 7.2:1196]. See Dondaine, "L'objet et le 'medium' de la vision béatifique," 70.

127. Thomas Aquinas, *ST*, Ia-IIae, q. 3, a. 8, obj. 2 [Leon. 6:35]. The objection is stated in three different ways in *In IV Sent.*, d. 49, q. 2, a. 1, obj. 5–7 [Parma 7.2:1196–97].

In the *corpus,* Thomas prefaces his discussion of the intellect with a discussion of the will, and bases the natural desire of the intellect to know the causes of things on the natural desire of the will to be satisfied:

Our ultimate and perfect happiness can only be in the vision of the divine essence. To give evidence for this, we should consider two things: First, that man is not perfectly happy so long as there remains something for him to desire and seek. The second is that the perfection of each potency is assigned according to the *ratio* of its object. Now, the object of the intellect is "what a thing is" [*quod quid est*], that is, the thing's essence, as is said in *De anima* 3. Wherefore the perfection of the intellect advances inasmuch as the intellect knows the essence of something. If, therefore, some intellect knows the essence of some effect, through which the essence of the cause cannot be known (such that "what it is" [*quid est*] may not be known about its cause), the intellect is not said to reach its cause simply speaking (although it can know through the effect "whether it is" [*an sit*] about the cause). And therefore, there naturally remains for man a desire, when he knows an effect, and he knows that it has a cause, to know also "what is it" about the cause. And that desire is one of wonder, and causes investigation, as is said in the beginning of the *Metaphysics*....

If therefore the human intellect, knowing the essence of some created effect, only knows "whether it is" of God, its perfection does not yet reach the first cause simply speaking; rather, there still remains for it a natural desire of seeking the cause. Wherefore it is not yet perfectly happy. Therefore, it is required for perfect happiness that the intellect reach the very essence of the first cause. And in this way, it will have its perfection through union with God as with its object, in whom alone man's happiness consists.[128]

128. Thomas Aquinas, *ST* Ia-IIae, q. 3, a. 8, co. [Leon. 6:35–36]: "Ultima et perfecta beatitudo non potest esse nisi in visione divinae essentiae. Ad cuius evidentiam, duo consideranda sunt. Primo quidem, quod homo non est perfecte beatus, quandiu restat sibi aliquid desiderandum et quaerendum. Secundum est, quod uniuscuiusque potentiae perfectio attenditur secundum rationem sui obiecti. Obiectum autem intellectus est *quod quid est*, idest essentia rei, ut dicitur in III *De anima*. Unde intantum procedit perfectio intellectus, inquantum cognoscit essentiam alicuius rei. Si ergo intellectus aliquis cognoscat essentiam alicuius effectus, per quam non possit cognosci essentia causae, ut scilicet sciatur de causa *quid est*; non dicitur intellectus attingere ad causam simpliciter, quamvis per effectum cognoscere possit de causa *an sit*. Et ideo remanet naturaliter homini desiderium, cum cognoscit effectum, et scit eum habere causam, ut etiam sciat de

If we compare this argument to all of Thomas's previous iterations of it, there are three things that stand out: the inclusion of the will, the careful way in which Thomas dissects the origin of wonder in the intellect, and the firm and certain conclusion which he draws concerning man's ultimate end.

The inclusion of the will is now necessary, because Thomas's argument depends upon the will's choice to command the intellect to perform a process of reasoning. Although Thomas had said as far back as the *Commentary on the Sentences* that such acts *could* be commanded by the will, there was no sense in any text from the *De veritate* to the *Summa contra Gentiles* that they *had* to be commanded by the will. Now it is otherwise. Since the will is the first mover in the soul, it is not only *possible* for the will to command the reasoning involved in the argument, it is *necessary*; otherwise the first act of reasoning will not take place. Consequently, before Thomas says anything at all about the intellect in particular, he attends first to the desire of "man," which desire flows from human nature into the will, as we have seen above, and includes all the perfection of that nature, including the perfection of the intellect.

The dissection of wonder is now necessary, since Aristotle identifies wonder as the first disposition of the soul that leads to inquiry, and since Thomas now needs to locate that disposition in the will. Accordingly, Thomas carefully describes wonder as that desire which remains in the will when the intellect knows an effect, knows

causa *quid est.* Et illud desiderium est admirationis, et causat inquisitionem, ut dicitur in principio *Metaphys.*...

"Si igitur intellectus humanus, cognoscens essentiam alicuius effectus creati, non cognoscat de Deo nisi *an est*; nondum perfectio eius attingit simpliciter ad causam primam, sed remanet ei adhuc naturale desiderium inquirendi causam. Unde nondum est perfecte beatus. Ad perfectam igitur beatitudinem requiritur quod intellectus pertingat ad ipsam essentiam primae causae. Et sic perfectionem suam habebit per unionem ad Deum sicut ad obiectum, in quo solo beatitudo hominis consistit."

For a similar use of the argument from natural desire, see *Sententia libri Ethicorum,* 1.2 [Leon. 47:8]. In that text, Thomas uses the fact that the argument from the natural desire for knowledge concludes to a single end to prove that there cannot be a regress to infinity in ends.

that it has a cause, and does not know the essence of the cause.[129] The certainty of the conclusion arises from the structure of the will's desire, as Thomas summarizes in q. 5, a. 8: just as the intellect cannot be perfectly satisfied until its potency is completely fulfilled, so neither can the will.[130] Thus, just as Thomas concluded in the *Summa contra Gentiles* that the ultimate perfection of the intellect necessarily consists in the vision of God, so now does he conclude in the *Prima secundae* that the ultimate perfection of the will, and of human nature as a whole, consists in the same.

The definite manner in which Thomas concludes the *corpus* of q. 3, a. 8, raises the same question with regard to the will that Thomas had to address with regard to the intellect in the *Summa contra Gentiles*: if the will has as its single, determinate end the perfection that the soul receives in the vision of God, to what extent might it be possible for the will to rest in anything short of that vision? Similarly, to what extent does the will's natural desire prove that anyone actually has, does, or will enjoy that vision?

We saw in chapters 2–4 that Thomas consistently distinguished the question of whether anyone *can* see God (the philosophical question of possibility) from the question of whether anyone *has*, *does* or *will* see God (the theological question of actuality). We also saw in chapter 3 that, at least regarding the intellect, when Thomas identified an argument that could prove that the ultimate perfection of the intellect could only be had in the vision of God, he still made provision for the intellect to come to rest in something less than the vision of God. He did this by turning the object of natural desire inward toward the fulfillment of natural appetite, and introducing the condition "insofar as is possible" from the natural desire of Avicenna's souls of heavenly bodies into the human soul. This gave him a way to understand natural desire that could balance Augustine's

129. For a description of this sort of wonder, see Malloy, "De Lubac on Natural Desire," 615.

130. Thomas Aquinas, *ST*, Ia-IIae, q. 5, a. 8 [Leon. 6:54].

anti-Pelagian concern not to identify any motion in the fallen soul directly toward the vision of God, Aristotle's concern to identify some concrete act as the goal of natural desire, as well the Christian missionary need to show that ultimate human perfection can only exist in the vision of God. Thomas does something similar in the *Prima secundae* with regard to the will. In q. 4, a. 3, Thomas asks whether comprehension is necessary for happiness.[131] In context he makes it clear that he means comprehension in a broad sense, applying both to the intellect and to the will, not just the intellect.[132] In the *corpus* of the article, Thomas describes how both the intellect and the will stand before God in this life. Concerning the intellect, he says that we have an imperfect knowledge of our end. Concerning the will, he says first that we have a certain love, which he describes in terms of natural desire, "the first motion of the will toward something." Finally, he adds that the will also has a relationship of lover to beloved, which can occur in three possible ways:

> Sometimes the beloved is present to the lover, and then [the beloved] is not sought any more. But sometimes [the beloved] is not present, rather it is impossible to reach [*adipisci*] him; and then also [the beloved] is not sought. However, sometimes it is possible to reach him, but he is elevated above the ability of the one who is reaching after him, such that he cannot immediately be possessed: and this is the relationship of one who hopes to the one he hopes for; this relationship alone makes him seek after the end.[133]

In conclusion, Thomas says that each of these three has something that corresponds with it in happiness. By "these three," he does not mean the three possible relationships between the lover and the

131. Ibid., q. 4, a. 3 [Leon. 6:39–40].

132. He distinguishes these two senses of the verb, *comprehendere*, clearly in ibid., ad 2 [Leon. 6:40].

133. Ibid., co. [Leon. 6:40]: "Quandoque enim amatum est praesens amanti: et tunc iam non quaeritur. Quandoque autem non est praesens, sed impossibile est ipsum adipisci: et tunc etiam non quaeritur. Quandoque autem possibile est ipsum adipisci, sed est elevatum supra facultatem adipiscentis, ita ut statim haberi non possit: et haec est habitudo sperantis ad speratum, quae sola habitudo facit finis inquisitionem."

beloved; rather he means the three ways in which we stand before God in this life: imperfect knowledge, love, and a relationship of a lover to a beloved being sought.

It is tempting to read the three anticipations of happiness as allusions to the theological virtues. In this way, imperfect knowledge could refer to faith; love could refer to charity; and the relationship between lover and beloved could refer to hope. Thomas could thus be read as speaking about the relationship between man and God by grace in this text, and the "possibility" he mentions could refer to grace as the means of achieving happiness. But Thomas does not say this explicitly, and in q. 5, a. 1, he suggests that he is speaking in the order of nature, not of grace. There, he asks whether man can achieve happiness. In the *corpus,* he uses the same language as q. 4, a. 3, and says that man's natural desire proves that man can achieve (*adipisci*) happiness. "'Happiness' means 'reaching the perfect good.' Whoever therefore is capable of the perfect good can arrive at happiness. Now, that man is capable of the perfect good is clear both from the fact that his intellect can apprehend the universal and perfect good, and that his will can desire it. And therefore, man can reach [*adipisci*] happiness."[134] If we read q. 4, a. 3, in the light of q. 5, a. 1, it becomes clear that the "possibility" whose presence makes us hope and whose absence makes us cease to hope is not the offer of grace; it is the passive potency in nature to receive such a gift. For someone to judge happiness impossible and so not to hope for it would be for that person to think that human nature lacks even a passive capacity for it, such as those condemned in 1241 in fact thought, if we do not grant them for the sake of argument that perfect happiness consists in something other than the vision of the divine essence.

Bearing this in mind, let us turn to what Thomas says about the

134. Ibid., q. 5, a. 1, co. [Leon. 6:47]: "Beatitudo nominat adeptionem perfecti boni. Quicumque ergo est capax perfecti boni, potest ad beatitudinem pervenire. Quod autem homo perfecti boni sit capax, ex hoc apparet, quia et eius intellectus apprehendere potest universale et perfectum bonum, et eius voluntas appetere illud. Et ideo homo potest beatitudinem adipisci."

souls in limbo in *De malo*.[135] These souls, Thomas says, possess all the knowledge which is proper to the human soul in the separated state. If we consider what Thomas says in *Summa theologiae* Ia-IIae, q. 5, a. 1, that means that they have the natural knowledge that it is possible for them to receive the vision of God. If we consider what Thomas says in q. 4, a. 3, it also means that they have a natural desire for the possession of the perfect good. The one thing they lack is Revelation.[136] As we saw above in q. 12, a. 1, of the *Prima pars*, for them to know that anyone actually has, does, or will possess the beatific vision would require that God reveal the actuality of that vision to them. On account of this lack of Revelation, they lack any sadness in what they possess according to nature.

How, then, could a rational nature whose desire finds its ultimate fulfillment in the vision of God come to rest in anything less that its complete perfection? Thomas alludes to a possible answer in Ia-IIae, q. 3, a. 6, where he takes up what he understands to be Aristotle's understanding of happiness.[137] In the *Summa contra Gentiles*, where Thomas's main purpose was to develop an argument to show that such a happiness could not serve as man's ultimate end, he took great pains to show the deficiencies of the knowledge which lies at the culmination of philosophical speculation. But here it is otherwise. Thomas places on the mouth of an objector his own argument about the natural desire to know, and has that objector argue from an exegesis of Aristotle that the desire should come to rest in the knowledge of the speculative sciences.[138] Thomas responds that Aristotelian contemplation does indeed fall under our natural desire, even if it is not the perfect happiness which completely fulfills that

135. Thomas Aquinas, *De malo* q. 5, a. 3 [Leon. 23:136]. For a more detailed exposition of this passage, particularly in regard to its importance for our understanding of the natural end of human nature, see Hütter, *Dust Bound for Heaven*, 144–50.

136. Malloy, "De Lubac on Natural Desire," 587, notes the importance of this lack of access to Revelation, although he claims on p. 586 that these souls also lack a natural desire for the vision of God.

137. Thomas Aquinas, *ST* Ia-IIae, q. 3, a. 6 [Leon. 6:32–34].

138. Ibid., obj. 2 [Leon. 6:32].

desire: since the primary object of our natural desire is our own happiness, "not only is perfect happiness naturally desired, but also any sort of similarity to or participation in it."[139] Aristotelian contemplation, Thomas adds in a reply, does in fact reduce our intellect to act; it just does not do so completely.[140]

Be that as it may, Thomas still thinks that we can know by natural reason that the particular good which causes human happiness cannot be possessed until the next life. In q. 5, a. 3, Thomas asks whether anyone can be happy in this life.[141] In the *corpus,* he gives in quick succession both the arguments that he had made in the *Summa contra Gentiles* from Aristotle's axiom that nature does nothing in vain. First, he repeats the argument from *Summa contra Gentiles* 3.48, that we cannot possess the perfect good without interruption in this life; for this reason, we must be able to possess it in the next life. Then he repeats the argument from 2.79, in which he argues that we must be able to possess perpetual existence after death. Finally, he adds a theological appendix: if we take into account that happiness consists in the vision of God, then we can know all the more so that happiness does not take place in this life, because no one can see God in this life.[142]

Nature and Grace

As in the *Summa contra Gentiles,* so also in the *Prima secundae* of the *Summa theologiae,* one can look to Thomas's treatment of grace for

139. Ibid., ad 2 [Leon. 6:33]: "Naturaliter desideratur non solum perfecta beatitudo, sed etiam qualiscumque similitudo vel participatio ipsius." See Hütter, *Dust Bound for Heaven,* 148: "different orders of providence do not entail an ontological transmutation of the human being, nor is the rational soul—while *capax dei*—becoming something else in a hypothetical order in which the human being is ordered to a lesser felicity than the vision of God. Hence, for Thomas, the creation of a rational soul, capable of and open to the vision of God, yet destined to a lesser felicity does not seem to be a contradiction in the very created nature itself, nor to constitute a punishment per se. However, in comparison to the de facto obtaining providential order, Thomas characterizes such a lesser felicity as a *defectus.*"

140. Thomas Aquinas, *ST,* Ia-IIae, q. 3, a. 6, ad 3 [Leon. 6:33].

141. Ibid., q. 5, a. 3 [Leon. 6:49].

142. Ibid., co. [Leon. 6:49].

correlations of his understanding of natural desire. Here, as previously, man's receptivity to grace is compared to matter's receptivity to form.[143] But there is a subtle difference here in the way that the analogy is presented. Thomas is trying to make the point that our receptivity to grace, that is, the material principle in us by which we are open to grace, is in our nature in a passive potency, so that although grace is supernatural, it is not above nature (*supra naturam*) for us to be able to receive grace.[144]

In some miraculous works one finds that the form induced is above the natural potency (*supra naturalem potentiam*) of such matter, as in the resurrection of the dead, life is above the natural potency of such a body. And in this respect, the justification of the impious is not miraculous, because the soul naturally has a capacity for grace; for by the very fact that the soul was made in the image of God, it has a capacity for God by grace, as Augustine says.[145]

The contrast between a corpse receiving life and us receiving grace is not a contrast between something that is passive and something that is active; it is a contrast between one thing receiving a substantial form, and another which already has a substantial form and which possesses a receptive, material potency for accidental change

143. Consequently, Thomas keeps the same distance as in the *Commentary on the Sentences* from the term, "potency for obedience." See *ST*, IIIa, q. 11, a. 1, co. [Leon. 11:157]: "Respondeo dicendum quod, sicut prius dictum est, conveniens fuit ut anima Christi per omnia esset perfecta, per hoc quod omnis eius potentialitas sit reducta ad actum. Est autem considerandum quod in anima humana, sicut in qualibet creatura, consideratur duplex potentia passiva, una quidem per comparationem ad agens naturale; alia vero per comparationem ad agens primum, qui potest quamlibet creaturam reducere in actum aliquem altiorem, in quem non reducitur per agens naturale; et haec consuevit vocari potentia obedientiae in creatura."

144. This is clear from the *sed contra* of the same article: "Opera miraculosa sunt supra potentiam naturalem. Sed iustificatio impii non est supra potentiam naturalem: dicit enim Augustinus, in libro *de Praedest. Sanct.*, quod posse habere fidem, sicut posse habere caritatem, naturae est hominum: habere autem gratiae est fidelium."

145. Thomas Aquinas, *ST*, Ia-IIae, q. 113, a. 10, co. [Leon. 7:342]: "In quibusdam miraculosis operibus invenitur quod forma inducta est supra naturalem potentiam talis materiae: sicut in suscitatione mortui vita est supra naturalem potentiam talis corporis. Et quantum ad hoc, iustificatio impii non est miraculosa: quia naturaliter anima est gratiae capax; eo enim ipso quod facta est ad imaginem Dei, capax est Dei per gratiam, ut Augustinus dicit."

by the infusion of an accidental form. As in the *Prima pars,* this form is called "superadded" or even "supernatural" because although it is natural for the soul, as a receptive principle, to receive it, the power to actualize this potency is above nature (*supra naturam*).[146]

Since man only has a receptive potency for grace, even if our natural desire can tell us that the vision of God *could* be our ultimate happiness, it tells us nothing about whether the vision of God is *actually* our happiness in the present state. Although our natural desire, insofar as it tends toward God at all, can be considered a certain "preparation" for grace, it only prepares for grace in the sense that it gives us a general motion in the will which is able to be determined, under the influence of grace, toward the vision of God.[147] Actually advancing toward the vision of God would require that there be some form in us, in virtue of which we possessed an active power in some way proportioned to the vision of God, which no creature possesses by nature.[148]

Although Thomas discusses the difference between our active and receptive potencies in the *Prima secundae,* he does not mention the idea of a *potentia obedientiae.* He reserves a discussion of this idea to a. 10 of the *Quaestio disputata de virtutibus in communi* (q. 1 of the *Quaestiones disputatae de virtutibus*), which was composed shortly after the *Prima secundae* of the *Summa theologiae.*[149] That article updates Thomas's treatment of *potentia obedientiae* from *De potentia* q. 6, a. 1, ad 18, to take into account his understanding of natural desire from the *Prima secundae* of the *Summa theologiae.* As we saw in chapter 4, *De potentia* q. 6, a. 1, ad 18, dealt with an objection raised from Averroes's idea that every passive potency in nature must have a corresponding active potency in nature. Thomas had used this argument in *Summa contra Gentiles* 2.76 to establish the existence of

146. That grace is "superadded" to nature, see ibid., q. 109, a. 1, co. [Leon. 7:290]; q. 109, a. 2, co. [Leon. 7:291]. That grace is "supernatural," see ibid., q. 110, a. 1, co. [Leon. 7:311]; q. 110, a. 2, co. [Leon. 7:312].

147. Ibid., q. 109, a. 6, co. [Leon. 7:299–300]; q. 112, a. 3, co. [Leon. 7:325].

148. Ibid., q. 109, a. 5, co. [Leon. 7:298].

149. On the dating of this question, see Torrell, *Saint Thomas Aquinas,* 1:336.

an agent intellect in the human soul as the active counterpart to the possible intellect, but then the objector in *De potentia* had used it to disprove the possibility of miracles, or even of grace. Here in the *De virtutibus*, Thomas returns to the applicability of that axiom to the powers of the soul. The objector argues: "Before acquiring virtue, man is in potency to the virtues. But a potency and its act belong to the same genus; for every genus is divided into potency and act, as is clear in *Physics* 3. Since, therefore, our potency for virtue does not arise from infusion, it seems that neither does virtue arise from infusion."[150] Thomas responds:

> When something passive is made to receive different perfections from agents which are different and ordered, there is a difference and order among the passive potencies in the passive thing according to the difference and order of the active potencies in the agents, since active potency corresponds with passive potency (just as it is clear that water or earth has one potency insofar as it is made to be moved by fire; and another insofar as it is made to be moved by a heavenly body; and still another insofar as it is made to be moved by God). For just as something can be brought to be from water or earth by the power of a heavenly body, which cannot come to be by the power of fire; in this way can something be brought to be from them by the power of a supernatural agent which cannot be brought to be by the power of some natural agent. And according to this [line of reasoning], we say that in the whole of creation there is a certain obediential potency [*obedientialis potentia*], insofar as the whole of creation obeys God in order to receive whatever God wills in it. And thus, therefore, there exists in the soul something in potency which is made to be reduced into act by a connatural agent; and in this way the acquired virtues are in potency in it. In another way, there is something in potency in the soul which is only made to be educed into act through divine power; and in this way the infused virtues are in the soul in potency.[151]

150. Thomas Aquinas, *Quaestiones disputatae de virtutibus in communi*, q. un, a. 10, obj. 13 [Odetto 734]: "Homo ante acquisitionem virtutis est in potentia ad virtutes. Sed potentia et actus sunt unius generis: omne enim genus dividitur per potentiam et actum, ut patet in III *Physic.* Cum ergo potentia ad virtutem non sit ex infusione, videtur quod nec virtus ex infusione sit."

151. Ibid., a. 1, ad 13 [Odetto 737]: "Quando aliquod passivum natum est consequi diversas perfectiones a diversis agentibus ordinatis, secundum differentiam et ordinem potentiarum activarum in agentibus, est differentia et ordo potentiarum passivarum in

There are three ways to read this response. One is to read this text as speaking only of miracles. Mark Jordan has shown that this reading is untenable in light of the fact that Thomas speaks here of infused virtues, which are a gift of grace.[152] Another is to divide passive potency into natural passive potency and obediential potency. This reading distinguishes "obediential potency," which is actualized as a supernatural effect, from natural passive potency, which is actualized as a natural effect.[153] It respects the difference and ordering among agents by associating each agent with a different potency: natural passive potency with connatural agents, and obediential potency with God. Although this is a reasonable way to read the text on the surface of it, it fails to account for miracles which are only *praeter naturam* and not also *supra naturam*. As we saw above with regard to *De potentia*, those miracles involve the actualization of a natural passive potency immediately by God, and yet they also take place according to a potency for obedience. In the *De virtutibus*, Thomas

passivo; quia potentiae passivae respondet potentia activa: sicut patet quod aqua vel terra habet aliquam potentiam secundum quam nata est moveri ab igne; et aliam secundum quam nata est moveri a corpore caelesti; et ulterius aliam secundum quam nata est moveri a Deo. Sicut enim ex aqua vel terra potest aliquid fieri virtute corporis caelestis, quod non potest fieri virtute ignis; ita ex eis potest aliquid fieri virtute supernaturalis agentis quod non potest fieri virtute alicuius naturalis agentis; et secundum hoc dicimus, quod in tota creatura est quaedam obedientialis potentia, prout tota creatura obedit Deo ad suscipiendum in se quidquid Deus voluerit. Sic igitur et in anima est aliquid in potentia, quod natum est reduci in actum ab agente connaturali; et hoc modo sunt in potentia in ipsa virtutes acquisitae. Alio modo aliquid est in potentia in anima quod non est natum educi in actum nisi per virtutem divinam; et sic sunt in potentia in anima virtutes infusae."

152. Mark Jordan, "St. Thomas, Obediential Potency, and the Infused Virtues: *De virtutibus in communi*, a. 10, ad 13," in *Thomistica*, ed. E. Manning (Leuven: Peeters, 1995), 28. Jordan corrects the readings of de Lubac, Gilson and Jorge Laporta, all of which restrict obediential potency to miracles. He cites de Lubac, *Augustinisme et théologie moderne* (Paris: Aubier, 1965), 87–88; Etienne Gilson, "Sur la problématique thomiste de la vision béatifique," *Archives d'Histoire Doctrinale et Littéraire du Moyen Âge* 31 (1964): 67–88; Laporta, *La Destinée de la nature humaine selon Thomas d'Aquin* (Paris: J. Vrin, 1965), 133–46. For a similar reading of de Lubac, which gives more thorough citations of relevant texts in de Lubac's writings, see Malloy, "De Lubac on Natural Desire," 572. For a similar conclusion about Thomas's text, see Bradley, *Aquinas on the Twofold Human Good*, 449.

153. Jordan, "St. Thomas, Obediential Potency," 32, seems inclined to this view.

reiterates that fact in the reply to the seventh objection: potencies which are actualized immediately by God in a miracle that is *praeter naturam* are one in species with potencies actualized mediately by God through nature.[154]

A third way to read Thomas's response here is to see obediential potency as in some way overlapping with natural passive potency. This reading pays deference to the history of Thomas's understanding of "material potency" as a unified potency, and reads Thomas's understanding of "obediential potency" in light of his previous understanding of a "potency for obedience." It also accounts better for the language with which Thomas actually distinguishes the different orders of agents in the example of the passive potencies of earth and water. In that example, Thomas considers three levels of agents: fire, the heavenly bodies, and God. Although he distinguishes the different agents in terms of those effects which each agent can produce above the effects which the agent below it can produce, he by no means excludes the possibility of overlap among the effects that can be produced by those agents. A creature's obediential potency is the whole of its material potency as it stands before God. The portion of that potency which can also be actualized by connatural agents can also be described as the creature's natural passive potency.

If we combine what Thomas says in the *De virtutibus* about obediential potency with what he says in the *Prima secundae* about natural desire, it would be fair to say that Thomas thinks that, in a very qualified sense, human nature has a natural desire for the fulfillment of its obediential potency, because it has a natural desire for the fulfillment of its potency insofar as is possible. How, then, does this desire relate to Aristotle's axiom that "nature does nothing in vain"? In *Summa contra Gentiles* 2.79, Thomas followed Aristotle in using that axiom to demonstrate the perpetuity of the soul: the human person has a natural desire for perpetual existence; but nature does nothing in vain; therefore, the human soul has a power capable of existing perpetual-

154. Thomas Aquinas, *Quaestiones disputatae de virtutibus in communi*, q. un, a. 10, ad 7 [Odetto 736].

ly, and this is the soul.[155] What would happen if we applied that same kind of reasoning to the natural desire for the vision of God? Could we argue that the human soul has a natural desire for its complete fulfillment; but nature does nothing in vain; therefore, the human soul has a power capable of causing its complete fulfillment? Thomas addresses this question only briefly in the *Prima secundae*, placing it in the mouth of an objector in q. 5, a. 5, obj. 1.[156] In reply, he seems to avoid saying exactly how the axiom does or does not apply to the present case:

> Just as nature does not fail in what is necessary, even though it did not give weapons and covering [to man] like it did to the other animals, since it gave him reason and hands by which he can acquire these things for himself; so neither does it fail man in what is necessary, even though it did not give him some principle by which he could achieve happiness. For this was impossible. Rather, it gave him free choice, whereby he could turn to God, who would make him happy. "For what we can do through our friends, we can in a certain way do through ourselves," as is said in *Ethics* 3.[157]

In the *De virtutibus in communi*, however, he gives a more precise answer which preserves the axiom by distinguishing what it means for God to make us happy: "Nature provided for man in what is necessary according to its power. Wherefore with respect to those things which do not exceed the ability of nature, man has from nature not only receptive principles, but also active principles. However, with respect to those things which exceed the ability of nature, man has from nature an aptitude to receive [them]."[158] Rather than carving

155. We may note a similar argument in Thomas Aquinas, *Sententia libri Ethicorum* 1.10 [Leon. 47:36–37].

156. Thomas Aquinas, *ST* Ia-IIae, q. 5, a. 5, obj. 1 [Leon. 6:51].

157. Ibid., ad 1 [Leon. 6:51]: "Sicut natura non deficit homini in necessariis, quamvis non dederit sibi arma et tegumenta sicut aliis animalibus, quia dedit ei rationem et manus, quibus possit haec sibi conquirere; ita nec deficit homini in necessariis, quamvis non daret sibi aliquod principium quo posset beatitudinem consequi; hoc enim erat impossibile. Sed dedit ei liberum arbitrium, quo possit converti ad Deum, qui eum faceret beatum. 'Quae enim per amicos possumus, per nos aliqualiter possumus,' ut dicitur in III *Ethic.*"

158. Thomas Aquinas, *Quaestiones disputatae de virtutibus in communi*, q. un., a. 10, ad 2 [Odetto 736]. "Natura providit homini in necessariis secundum suam virtutem; unde respectu eorum quae facultatem naturae non excedunt, habet homo a natura non solum principia receptiva, sed etiam principia activa. Respectu autem eorum quae facultatem

out an exception to Aristotle's axiom, as Thomas could be read as doing in the *Prima secundae,* Thomas saves the axiom in the *De virtutibus in communi* by distinguishing between active and passive potency. For God to make us happy is for us to receive from him the fulfillment of our passive potency. Aristotle's axiom proves the existence in us of a passive potency whereby we may receive the fulfillment of our nature from God. But as was the case from the very beginning of Thomas's career, this does not imply anything about whether anyone has, does or will actually receive that fulfillment. The human soul thus stands before God like the human body stands before the human soul: there are some perfections which it possesses that are connatural to it (the nutritive and the sensitive powers), and others which exceed its nature (the rational powers); so likewise are there some perfections which the human soul may possess which are connatural to it, and others which are supernatural.[159] Only through the reception of supernatural perfections from God is the human soul able to return to its origin completely, and so to reach its ultimate perfection, even though it may reach a certain participation in that perfection without the gifts of grace.[160] As Thomas had said as far back as the *Commentary on the Sentences,* the gifts of grace are part natural and part supernatural: natural according to their passive principle, and supernatural according to their active principle.

Theological Solutions from the *Secunda secundae*

The life of grace begins in the act of faith. In q. 2 of the *Secunda secundae* of the *Summa theologiae,* Thomas describes how this act occurs, and updates his previous treatments of the act of faith to include his more recent understanding of the relationship between the intellect and the will. As we may recall from chapters 2 and 3, the biggest challenge that Thomas faced from the *Commentary on the Sen-*

naturae excedunt, habet homo a natura aptitudinem ad recipiendum." The corresponding objection does not directly reference natural desire, but Thomas applies it to natural desire in the corpus.

159. Ibid., ad 1 [Odetto 736].

160. This point is made both in the *corpus* and in the ad 1 (ibid.).

tences to the *Summa contra Gentiles* was describing the act of faith in such a way that grace followed the natural order of the powers of the soul rather than subverting it. In each case, Thomas had attempted to show how there might be an act in the intellect that could present a good to the will in such a way that the will would be moved to command the intellect to assent to faith. In the *Commentary on the Sentences,* the testimony of fallible signs grounded the prudence of the will's command of the intellect; in the *De veritate,* the goods promised in faith grounded that prudence; in the *Summa contra Gentiles,* Jesus and the Apostles grounded it, insofar as their testimony was mediated through preachers.

If we read Thomas's previous work in light of his distinction in the *De malo* and the *Prima secundae* between the order of specification and the order of exercise, all of Thomas's previous treatments of the prudence of the act of faith concerned the order of specification. As noted in chapter 2, this caused a significant theological difficulty, because, since none of the acts of intellect that precede the act of faith are proportioned to the supernatural truths accepted in the act of faith, none of the preceding acts could possibly be sufficient to cause the exercise of the will's act. Thomas seems to have been aware of this difficulty, and addresses it here.

In q. 2, a. 1, Thomas locates faith among the acts of the intellect that are subject to the command of the will. He defines faith as "thinking with assent." It agrees with knowledge in the firm certitude by which it adheres to what it believes, but it differs from knowledge in that its firm certitude is not grounded in the clear perception of how what it believes is connected to the first principles of demonstration. This is important; as Thomas explains in q. 2, a. 9, if the intellect could see how the truths of faith were connected with the first principles of demonstration, then the intellect would be compelled to assent to them and the act of faith would no longer be free or meritorious.[161] Rather, as is the case with opinion, faith takes place when the will commands the intellect to assent to something in the

161. Thomas Aquinas, *ST,* IIa-IIae, q. 2, a. 9, ad 2 [Leon. 8:38].

absence of a clear perception of a connection with the first principles of demonstration.[162]

How, then, does the will command the intellect in the act of faith? Here Thomas is able to give an account of the order of grace which builds carefully on the order of nature. On the part of the intellect, in the order of specification, there are the motives of credibility, which ground the prudence of the act. Here Thomas does not list the testimony of human persons; he only lists miracles, as events which testify to the divine authority of the message of itself.[163] These, however, are not sufficient to cause the exercise of the will. As in the order of nature, so in the order of grace, there is need of a divine *instinctus* (in the language of Pseudo-Aristotle) which causes the will's exercise: "He who believes has an inducement sufficient for belief: for he is induced by the authority of divine teaching confirmed by miracles, and, what is more, by the interior impulse [*instinctus*] of God inviting [him to believe]. Wherefore he does not believe lightly, even though he does not have an inducement sufficient for knowledge."[164] Since the will can never be necessitated with regard to exercise, the "sufficiency" of its inducement to belief can never come from the reasons which ground its prudence. It can only come from the direct impulse of God, which moves the will in the order of grace like it moves the will in the order of nature.

Finally, we may turn to consider the sin of Adam and Eve. We saw in chapter 2, where Thomas did not sufficiently account for the instinct of God moving the will, how he gave two different accounts of the origin of their sin. In the *Commentary on the Sentences,* he said their sin began with an error of the intellect, in which the devil convinced them to interpret God's command not to eat of the fruit of the Tree of the Knowledge of Good and Evil in a figurative sense

162. Ibid., a 1, co. [Leon. 8:26–27].

163. Ibid., ad 1 [Leon. 8:27]; a. 9, ad 3 [Leon. 8:38].

164. Ibid., a. 9, ad 3 [Leon. 8:38]: "Ille qui credit habet sufficiens inductivum ad credendum: inducitur enim auctoritate divinae doctrinae miraculis confirmatae, et, quod plus est, interiori instinctu Dei invitantis. Unde non leviter credit. Tamen non habet sufficiens inductivum ad sciendum."

when it should have been taken in a literal sense. Already in the *De veritate* he had modified this view, and, while claiming in general that acts of the will do not proceed acts of intellect, carved out a single exception for Adam and Eve.

In the *Secunda secundae*, Thomas annexes his discussion of the sin of Adam and Eve to the discussion of pride (qq. 162–65).[165] In question 162, Thomas uses his understanding of the freedom of the will with regard to exercise, combined with his corresponding account of malice, to articulate an understanding of pride that is consistent with his view of the will after 1270. He says that pride is an "inordinate appetite of one's own excellence,"[166] which is located in the will as in its subject.[167] Unlike other sins which are located in the will, pride is the "worst of all sins," because "in other sins man averts from God on account of ignorance, or weakness, or the desire of some other good; but pride's aversion from God arises from the very fact that [the will] does not want to be subject to God and to his rule."[168] Pride, in other words, takes place particularly in virtue of the will's freedom of exercise to turn away from God, when it should be turning toward him.

Since Adam and Eve were preserved from inordinate movements of the lower appetites, as well as the possibility that any exterior creature might hurt them against their will, their resistance against the devil's temptation had first and foremost to do with whether or not they wanted to obey God.[169] In order to entice them to want to not obey God, Thomas now says that the devil played a calculated trick on their will: in the order of specification, he suggested to them an apparent good that appeared as similar as possible to the perfection

165. Ibid., qq. 162–65 [Leon. 9:310–41].

166. Ibid., q. 162, a. 2, co. [Leon. 9:314]: "[Superbia] ... est enim inordinatus appetitus propriae excellentiae."

167. Ibid., a. 3, co. [Leon. 9:316].

168. Ibid., a. 6, co. [Leon. 9:323]: "in aliis peccatis homo a Deo avertitur vel propter ignorantiam, vel propter infirmitatem, sive propter desiderium cuiuscumque alterius boni; sed superbia habet aversionem a Deo ex hoc ipso quod non vult Deo et eius regulae subiici."

169. Ibid., q. 165, a. 1, co. [Leon. 9:339].

of their nature, offering them knowledge of good and evil (seemingly a good of their nature), as well as similarity to God (seemingly its ultimate perfection);[170] he thus used Adam's and Eve's natural desire against them.[171] All that remained for Adam and Eve was to choose, in the order of exercise, whether to hold out for the true good of their nature, or to accept the substitute. They freely chose the substitute, and in so doing their wills succumbed to pride in the order of exercise.

CONCLUSION

In his second Parisian period, Thomas was thrust between two radically opposed points of view. On the one hand, scholars such as Siger of Brabant were advocating a Radical Aristotelianism which affirmed that the will is necessitated by its object. On the other hand, scholars such as Walter of Bruges and Gerard of Abbeville were opposing that Radical Aristotelianism by affirming the absolute freedom of the will; Gerard even attributed a similar freedom to the intellect. The situation was made all the more difficult by Bishop Étienne Tempier's condemnation in 1270 of the idea that the will is necessitated by the appetible object, which Thomas might have been taken as saying from the *Sententia libri De anima* to the *Prima pars* of the *Summa theologiae*. Although Thomas had already clarified in his *Sententia libri Physicorum* that the appetible object only causes necessity *ex conditione*, and not absolute necessity, Thomas's work nevertheless seems to have been interpreted by Walter and Gerard in such a way that it would run contrary to the condemnation.

Shortly after the condemnation, Thomas composed question 6 of his *Quaestiones disputatae de malo*, in which he responded to Walter and Gerard, and redetermined his responses to some questions he had already addressed in the *Prima pars*. Drawing on Walter's language that the object of the will is not just the apprehended good

170. Ibid., q. 163, a. 2, co. [Leon. 9:330].
171. Ibid., q. 165, a. 2, co. [Leon. 9:340].

(*bonum apprehensum*) but rather the good, apprehended as fitting (*bonum conveniens apprehensum*), Thomas agreed that the will possesses its own disposition and source of motion apart from the determination communicated to it by the intellect. Thomas still maintains that the will is a moved mover, but he now follows the Pseudo-Aristotelian *Liber de bona fortuna* in saying that it is moved directly by God in the manner of an impulse (*instinctus*), rather than that it is moved indirectly by God through the intellect. Consequently, the will possesses a radical freedom from the intellect, such that it can only be necessitated in the order of specification, not in the order of exercise. There are two ways for it be necessitated in the order of specification: since the will participates in human nature, the will is necessitated by the determinate goods of human nature (being, living, and knowing); since the will's proper object is the universal good, the will is necessitated by that object as well (perfect happiness), provided that perfect happiness is presented to it in every particular respect. Only the first necessitation can occur in this life. With regard to the second, our intellect can never so perfectly consider happiness in this life that there will not be some aspect of it lacking from our consideration. In the order of exercise, the will is therefore always free to choose or not to choose what is presented to it by the intellect.

Since the will is always free to choose or not to choose what is presented to it by the intellect, Thomas speaks of the will in the *De malo* as though it is now the superior mover in the soul, rather than the intellect. That does not mean that all of the actions of the intellect lie under the influence of the will. Thomas clarifies in the *Prima secundae* that the act of apprehension is not a free action, nor is an act of judgment with respect to the first principles of demonstration or those conclusions which are immediately connected with the first principles of demonstration. Any other action of the intellect, such as an act of judgment concerning matters which are not immediately connected with the first principles of demonstration or any act of reason, is subject to the influence of the will.

In the *Prima secundae*, Thomas also draws out the consequences of the *De malo* concerning our natural desire for the vision of God. Since the argument from our natural desire to know from the *Summa contra Gentiles* and the *Prima pars* was based upon acts of reasoning, and since acts of reasoning are subject to the influence of the will, Thomas now includes reference to the natural desire of the will prior to the natural desire of the intellect when discussing our natural desire for the vision of God. Once the intellect apprehends a thing, knows that it has a cause, and knows that it does not know the essence of the cause, the intellect necessitates the will in the order of specification, because knowledge is one of the determinate goods of human nature by which the will can be necessitated. Provided that the will wills to will in the order of exercise, the will commands the intellect to conduct an investigation into the first cause of the thing it has apprehended. At this point, the will behaves like the intellect. Just as the intellect uses whatever natural motion it has to pursue the perfection of its passive potency insofar as is possible, so does the will use whatever natural motion it has to pursue the perfection of human nature insofar as is possible. If God does not communicate to it any supernatural motion, then the will rests with the intellect in the analogical knowledge of God as first cause, such as Thomas says about the souls in limbo in the *De malo*. But if God does communicate to the human person a sharing in his grace, then the will uses this supernatural motion to pursue the complete perfection of human nature in the vision of God. In this way, Thomas preserves the Augustinian orientation of natural desire, which he had worked out in the *Summa contra Gentiles* and maintained in the *Prima pars*, but updates it to give motive priority to the will.

In subsequent works, Thomas draws out the implications of this new teaching about natural desire with respect to our potency for obedience, the sin of Adam and Eve, and the act of faith. Thomas says in the *De virtutibus in communi* that our obediential potency (*potentia obedientialis*) is the entirety of our passive potency. But Thomas also acknowledges a certain distinction within our passive potency between natural potency, which can be actualized by a connatural agent, and the rest of our passive potency, which can only be actualized by God. In light of the fact that our will and our intellect seek the fulfillment of our passive potency insofar as is possible, it remains the case in the *Prima secundae* as in the *Summa contra Gentiles* and the *Prima pars* that we have a natural desire not only for the fulfillment of our natural potency, but also for the fulfillment of our obediential potency insofar as is possible. It is important to note here that Thomas's use of the term "obediential potency" is subtly different than that of later Thomists, who reserve the term for that subset of our obediential potency which remains when our natural passive potency is subtracted from it, as we will see in chapter 6.

Concerning the act of faith, Thomas is able for the first time in the *Secunda secundae* to articulate a process in which the order of grace builds upon the order of nature. The act of faith is one case among many in which the intellect stands before conclusions which it cannot connect immediately with the first principles of demonstration. In the order of specification, it can base the prudence of assenting to them on motives of credibility. But like any conclusion of practical reasoning, the motives of credibility can only *dispose* the will; they cannot *move* it. In the order of exercise, only the grace of God, propelling the will by a divine *instinctus,* is sufficient to move the will so that it wants to command the intellect to believe.

Thomas is also able in the *Secunda secundae* to give a consistent account of the sin of Adam and Eve. In the *De veritate,* Thomas had said that the sin of Adam and Eve took place when their wills withdrew from God prior to their intellects, but Thomas had also admitted that this possibility was an exception to the normal rule of human actions, in which the intellect directs the will. In the *Secunda secundae,* Adam and Eve require no such exception. Their sin was a sin of pride, in which the will, motivated by no other reason than by its own disordered desire, commanded the other powers of the soul to commit an illicit action. In order to entice them to this sin, the devil appealed to their natural desire. By promising them knowledge and dei-formity, he offered them a counterfeit for some of the only goods that could necessitate their wills in the order of specification. Adam and Eve fell for the trick. But since at every moment of their temptation and sin their wills remained free in the order of exercise, the resulting sin could be fully imputed to them as a moral fault.

We see, therefore, that the solutions that Thomas reaches to questions about nature, grace, and the desire for God in the *Summa theologiae* are the result of an entire career's worth of scholarly development. That development was constant. In light of the challenges that Thomas faced in his second Paris regency, we cannot—indeed, we should not—presume an identity in Thomas's thought on nature, grace, and the desire for God from one stage of his career to the next. Thomas's interlocutors do not appear to have presumed such a constancy. Both Walther of Bruges and Gerard of Abbeville appear to have been carefully attentive to the developments in Thomas's thought from one work to the next. What is more, members of the scholarly generation immediately following Thomas's death in 1274 seem to have been similarly attentive to this nuanced context in which his thought was imbedded. However, that awareness would not last forever. As the record of Thomas's career faded from living memory, some—though not all—of the nuance of this development would be lost to the subsequent Thomistic tradition. We therefore turn now to our final chapter in order to trace some of the history of the reception of Thomas's thought, to uncover the pathways by which that tradition arrived at Henri de Lubac, and finally, to place a contextual reading of Thomas's thought in dialogue with the debate over nature, grace, and the desire for God to which de Lubac's work has given rise.

6

Henri de Lubac and the Thomistic Tradition

Although the bulk of this book has focused on the thirteenth century, we began in the introduction with reference to the twenty-first. For while the thirteenth-century conversation about nature, grace, and the desire for good is of historical interest in itself, its speculative interest lies principally in how it can make a contribution toward the resolution of the contemporary nature/grace debate. Accordingly, I would like to suggest in this final chapter how our retrieval of the thirteenth-century conversation about natural desire can help us to re-read Henri de Lubac and the Thomistic commentatorial tradition. Of necessity, any such re-reading must be provisional; each of the figures discussed herein deserves as detailed a treatment as we have given Thomas in the previous chapters. Be that as it may, we may at least indicate here the direction in which such a re-reading might take the contemporary conversation.

Our re-reading of de Lubac and the commentators will begin by uncovering the importance of the so-called "Aegidian" tradition of the Order of the Hermits of Saint Augustine. It was from this tradition that de Lubac received the interpretation of Thomas which understands Thomas to teach that nature has an active orientation toward grace, and that the natural desire for the vision of God is built on such an active orientation of nature toward grace. Consequently, I will begin by unpacking the doctrine of natural desire in the originator of this tradition, Giles of Rome. I will then examine the teachings of John Duns Scotus, Tommaso de Vio "Cajetan," and Francisco Suárez, as well as several members of the Aegidian tradition who came after Suárez. I will conclude with a study of de Lubac's understanding of natural desire, placing him within the context of the Aegidian tradition, and finally evaluating his understanding of Thomas. On the basis of the Aegidian tradition, de Lubac correctly imputed to Thomas the idea of a natural desire for the vision of God, but then incorrectly imputed to him the view that nature is active with respect to grace. A return to the delicate balance that Thomas strikes between natural appetite and natural desire can provide a way forward in present debates about de Lubac and the commentators, preserving de Lubac's commitment to our "natural desire for a supernatural end," alongside the commentators' insistence that nature is passive with respect to grace. Finally, I will also suggest how contemporary theologians might begin a return, through Thomas, to Augustine's individual and communal insights about nature, grace, and the desire for God.

GILES OF ROME

A fact well known to theologians of the early twentieth century, but now largely forgotten, is that alongside the Dominican, Franciscan, and Jesuit Orders, the Order of the Hermits of St. Augustine (OESA) developed and maintained its own theological tradition.[1] The "founder" of the tradition, if one may speak of him thus, was Giles of Rome, OESA (1246–1316), who was a student of Thomas Aquinas from 1269 to 1272 during Thomas's second Paris regency, and so had the benefit of witnessing first-hand how Thomas responded to the challenges of 1270 in the *De malo* and the *Prima secundae* of the *Summa theolo-*

1. Today the order is known simply as the Order of St. Augustine (OSA).

giae.[2] In 1287, the Augustinian Order adopted Giles as its official doctor, together with Thomas Aquinas where there was any ambiguity in the text of Giles's writing.[3] Giles thus stands at the fount of a theological tradition that might reasonably be called "Thomist" by intent, even if it gave rise to a somewhat different sort of Thomism than the Dominicans or the Jesuits would develop.

There are two principal places in which Giles treats nature, grace, and the desire for God in his mature work. The first is the *Ordinatio* of his *Commentary on the Sentences*, which was completed sometime between 1309 and the end of Giles's life in 1316;[4] the second is his *Tractatus de divina influentia in beatos*, composed around the same time.[5] In Book 2, distinction 18, of the *Ordinatio*, Giles follows the well-established custom of discussing nature in relationship to *rationes seminales*.[6] At the point where Giles explains what he thinks about *rationes seminales*, he shows deep indebtedness to Thomas's treatment of the topic. In fact, Giles seems to have used Thomas's *Commentary on the Sentences* the way that Thomas used Bonaventure's. Giles considers the very same opinions as Thomas had con-

2. Gutiérrez, *Augustinians in the Middle Ages, 1256–1356*, 139.

3. Ibid. This decree remained in effect until 1885. The only change was that for thirty years beginning in 1551, Aquinas was replaced with Thomas of Strasbourg ("Thomas de Argentina"). See David Gutiérrez, *The Augustinians from the Protestant Reformation to the Peace of Westphalia, 1518–1648*, vol. 2 of *History of the Order of St. Augustine* (Villanova, Penn.: Augustinian Historical Institute, 1979), 145.

4. On the dating of the works of Giles of Rome, I follow the exhaustive list provided in F. del Punta, S. Donati, and Concetta Luna, "*Egidio Romano*," in *Dizionario biografico degli italiani*, vol. 42 (Rome: Società Grafica Romana, 1993), 330–35. Giles's *Commentary on the Sentences* has come down to us in two forms. First, there is a *reportatio*, which gives us a shorter list of questions. This has recently been edited by Concetta Luna in Aegidius Romanus, *Opera omnia*, vol. 3, no. 2 (Florence: Edizioni del Galluzzo, 2003). An *ordinatio*, of which Giles only completed Books I and II (Book III, published in the seventeenth century, is considered by modern scholars to be a forgery), expresses a much more complete account of Giles's thought. The best editions are Giles of Rome, *Commentarius in Primum Sententiarum*, ed. Augustino Montifalconio (Venice, 1521); *Commentarius in Secundum Sententiarum*, 2 vols. (Venice, 1581).

5. Giles of Rome, *Tractatus de divina influentia in beatos*, in *Tractatus* (Rome: Antonius Bladus, 1555).

6. Giles of Rome, *Ordinatio* 2, d. 18, q. 2 [Venice 2:73–96]. There are also related *dubia* on pp. 101–2.

sidered in the same order in which Thomas had considered them, and then adds his own opinion by way of a conclusion.

Like Thomas, Giles begins by summarizing and critiquing Bonaventure's position.[7] Deploying one of the same arguments as Thomas had used against Bonaventure, Giles notes that Bonaventure's incomplete forms are impossible, because there cannot be an individual in the genus of substance without a species.[8] Also like Thomas, Giles next summarizes and critiques Bacon's position. Giles argues with Thomas that Bacon's position is similar to Bonaventure's.[9] However, rather than taking up the problem of natural generation, as Thomas does, Giles simply notes that Bacon's position can be criticized like Bonaventure's because it would make the form of a species completely separate from the form of a genus, such that there would be no essential connection between the two.[10] It is true that one can conceptualize the form of a genus and the form of a species distinctly, but what is signified by them in our mind corresponds with a single, substantial form in reality.[11]

Next, Giles discusses the position attributed by Bonaventure to Anaxagoras, the *latitatio formarum*. But this is no mere foray into antiquity for Giles:

> We heard some people with our own ears teaching at Paris in [the Faculty of] Theology, saying that those specific forms were in matter essentially, and that only being was acquired in generation. For this reason (according to them) if fire were to be made from air, the essence of the form of fire would be in air before the generation of fire, and subsequently that form would acquire the being of fire through generation.[12]

7. Ibid., a. 2, co. [Venice 2:80Ac].
8. Ibid. [Venice 2:80Ad].
9. Ibid. [Venice 2:80Bd].
10. Ibid. [Venice 2:80Bd–81Aa].
11. Ibid. [Venice 2:81Aa–d].
12. Ibid. [Venice 2:82Ac–d]: "Audivimus aliquos nostris auribus legentes Parisiis in Theologia dicentes, quod illae formae specificae secundum essentiam erant in materia, et quod per generationem non acquirebatur nisi esse: propter quod secundum eos, si ex aere fiebat ignis, essentia formae ignis erat in aere ante generationem ignis, et postea per generationem illa forma acquirebat esse ignis."

The position is problematic for Giles: any substantial form in a thing communicates being to that thing, and since a hidden form would have to communicate being to the thing in which it was hiding, the hidden form would conflict with the substantial form that the thing in which it was hiding already possessed.[13]

Next, Giles updates the discussion of Bonaventure and Bacon briefly so as to dispense with the opinion of Henry of Ghent that matter has some degree of actuality in it, and that pure potentiality is somehow distinct from and below matter.[14] According to Giles, the only thing below matter is nothingness at all.[15]

Finally, Giles arrives at Thomas's position. He begins by accurately summarizing the text of Thomas's commentary on Book 2, distinction 18. "Therefore, there are others who say, coming nearer to the truth, that *rationes seminales* are the active and passive powers in things, by which natural effects are produced."[16] Giles may perhaps have given his former *magister* a kind introduction, saying that he came *nearer* to the truth, but Giles continues by forcefully rejecting Thomas's opinion. For Giles, "it is necessary that what desires have some similarity with what it desires."[17] Thus, if matter is to desire form, it must be the case that matter has some similarity with the form which it desires. Accordingly, one can distinguish two appetites in matter. The first is completely unspecific. In virtue of the fact that matter with one form is partially actualized, it possesses a similarity with the form that could completely actualize it.[18] This confers on matter only a general desire for the complete actualization of its

13. Ibid.

14. On Henry's doctrine of matter, see Raymond Macken, "Le Statut de la matière première dans la philosophie d'Henri de Gand," *Recherches de Théologie Ancienne et Médiévale* 46 (1979): 130–82.

15. Giles of Rome, *Ordinatio* 2, d. 18, q. 2, a. 2, co. [Venice 2:82Ba–b].

16. Ibid.: "Sunt ergo alii dicentes, et magis veritati appropinquantes, quod rationes seminales sunt virtutes activae, et passivae in rebus, per quas producuntur naturales effectus."

17. Giles of Rome, *Ordinatio* 2, d. 12, q. 3, dub. lat. 2 [Venice 1:549Ac]: "Oportet, quod appetens habeat aliquam similitudinem cum eo, quod appetit."

18. Ibid. [Venice 1:549Ad–Ba].

unactualized potency, without any specific orientation toward this or that specific actualization.[19] The second is specific. In virtue of the fact that opposites are in the same genus, matter with one form (for example, white) has in it a generic similarity with matter informed by the opposite form (for example, black). For this reason, matter can be said to desire not only complete actualization in general, but also actualization by a form opposite to the one it presently possesses in particular.[20]

In each of these categories of appetite, one can distinguish two elements. There is the element of negation, which implies a lack of form and actuality, and a positive aptitude toward subsequent formation, which Giles calls the principle of "transmutation" (*transmutatio*).[21] Both are necessary, because without an active aptitude for form, the passive receptivity conferred upon it by negation would be pointless; any subsequent formation would be completely contrary to the form already possessed.[22] This explains why, although Giles adopted Thomas's critique of Bonaventure, he did not adopt Thomas's critique of Bacon. Giles's own account of nature, while not identical to that of Bacon, relies on a similar principle: there must be in matter some positive principle toward form in order for form to be received in matter naturally. For Bacon, it was an incomplete active potency. For Giles, it is a positive aptitude.

Distinguishing between negation and the positive aptitude conferred by *transmutatio* enabled Giles to develop a reading of Genesis 1 which he considered more faithful to the literal sense of the text of Scripture, as well as to Augustine's *De genesi ad litteram*.[23] Following Bonaventure's *Breviloquium* and the *Prima pars* of Thomas's *Summa theologiae*, Giles says that the creation of the elements in Genesis preceded the creation of the plants and animals, which means that

19. Ibid. [Venice 1:549Ba].
20. Ibid. [Venice 1:549Bb–550Aa].
21. Ibid., a. 2 [Venice 1:548Aa–c].
22. Ibid., q. 2, a. 2, dub. lat. 1 [Venice 2:83Bd]; dub. lat. 3. [Venice 2:85Ad–a].
23. What follows here is a summary of ibid., a. 2, co. [Venice 1:82Bb–83Ba].

there were already active and passive powers present in nature prior to the creation of plants and animals. But elements do not undergo all of their change of their own accord. Hence, Giles argues that Thomas cannot be correct that the active and passive powers in nature are *rationes seminales,* because otherwise the "seeds" of all things would be in the elements. Yet the elements are powerless of themselves to bring forth the variety of Creation on their own.[24] Rather, on the third day of creation, when by "a certain blessing"[25] God put seeds in the earth and the earth began to give forth plants and trees,[26] God added *rationes seminales* to the elements. The elements thus received the negations and positive aptitudes necessary to bring forth the variety of created things that we know today.[27]

On the basis of his account of the relationship between matter and form, as well as his corresponding account of Creation, Giles proceeds to a detailed criticism of Thomas's understanding of *rationes seminales.* The critique of Thomas is masked as a critique of Aristotle's concept of privation, which, as we saw in chapter 2, Thomas relied upon at the beginning of his career in the treatise, *De principiis naturae.* As Giles summarizes Thomas, matter still remains in potency to the reception of new forms after it has received a form, because it stands in privation to the forms which it has not received.[28] However, Giles argues, privation means first of all a lacking of something before it means any openness to what is lacking. Insofar as privation is a principle at all, it can only be associated with matter as passive, not form as active.[29] Privation's association with passivity therefore makes it an incomplete principle of nature.[30] But since *rationes sem-*

24. Ibid., dub. lat. 5 [Venice 2:88Ac–d].
25. Ibid., dub. lat. 6 [Venice 2:91Bc].
26. Ibid., dub. lat. 4 [Venice 2:87Ac].
27. Ibid., dub. lat. 6 [Venice 2:90Bd].
28. Immediately after his initial critique of Thomas and giving his own opinion on *rationes seminales,* Giles devotes several *dubia lateralia* to issues stemming from the question of privation, setting out his own doctrine in response to that of Thomas. The particular *dubium* concerning privation is the first, ibid. [Venice 2:83Bb].
29. Ibid. [Venice 2:83Bd–84Aa].
30. Ibid. [Venice 2:84:Ab].

inales, conceived as Giles interprets them, posit first and foremost an "aptitude toward form,"[31] Giles argues that *rationes seminales* can serve as a more potent principle of nature than privation, as well as a more complete one.[32]

Affirming that *rationes seminales,* rather than privation, constitute the principle according to which the distinction of natures occurred in Genesis 1 led to a particular difficulty concerning nature's relationship to grace. Since Thomas had affirmed that one and the same privation accounts both for a creature's openness to natural change as well as its openness to grace, Thomas had no need to adopt a separate potency for obedience to account for nature's openness to grace; his understanding of passive potency already included the openness to divine action which previous generations of theologians had tried to account for with a potency for obedience. Giles, on the other hand, by criticizing Thomas's use of privation and positing positive aptitudes in creatures for specific forms alongside privation, in a sense closed off the openness to grace in Thomas's understanding of privation. Indeed, Giles affirms explicitly that *rationes seminales,* such as he understands them, can only account for what is done in creatures and by creatures.[33] For that reason, Giles affirms the existence of "obediential properties" (*rationes obedientiales*), distinct from *rationes seminales,* in order to account for how a creature, endowed with *rationes seminales,* remains open to the continued influence of God.[34]

31. Ibid. [Venice 2:83Bc]: "Nam privatio est carentia cum aptitudine. Sed carentiam dicit privatio ex vi nominis primo, et principaliter, quia idem est carere quod privari. Si autem dicat aptitudinem ad formam: hoc est ex consequenti, sed ratio seminalis econverso. Quia ex vi nominis per se, et primo dicit aptitudinem ad formam. Si autem potest importare carentiam formae, hoc erit ex consequenti, sed cum carentia: secundum quod huiusmodi non videatur habere rationem principii. Aptitudo vero videtur de se rationem principii importare: magis ergo congrue, et magis convenienter locutus est Augustinus ponens rationem seminalem esse principium naturae, quam philosophus, tale principium esse privationem."

32. Ibid. [Venice 2:84Aa–c].

33. Ibid., a. 3, co. [Venice 96Ad].

34. Ibid., a. 2, co. [Venice 2:83Aa]; a. 3, co. [Venice 2:92Ba, 95Ab, 96Ad].

Concerning miracles, Giles notes that when something occurs above what nature can achieve as concerns the substance of the act, it is above nature (*supra naturam*). When it occurs above what nature can achieve as concerns the mode of action, it is beyond nature (*praeter naturam*). When it is contrary to the aptitudes in nature, it is said to be against nature (*contra naturam*).[35] Here one sees the consequence of Giles's understanding of *rationes seminales*. For Thomas, at least from the time of the *Summa contra Gentiles*, nothing God does can be said to be against nature, because nature is always open to divine action in virtue of its passive potency. For Giles, on the other hand, God can act against the *rationes seminales* in nature, and so act against nature properly speaking.[36]

Giles's understanding of natural desire follows his understanding of nature. For Thomas, the natural desire of the will does not presuppose any positive ordering in the will toward a particular end; it can be known by natural reason that the natural desire of the will for complete satisfaction can only be satisfied by the vision of God, but any question of an actual, positive ordering toward the vision of God by grace requires a knowledge of revealed truth. For Giles, it is otherwise; natural desire possesses "in hope" (*in spe*) an end toward which deliberation chooses the means "in actual fact" (*in re*).[37] While Giles refers to the end possessed by the natural will *in spe* as the good in "general" or in "common," the sense is more that the will is disposed positively toward a specific end that its subject does not know specifically, and hence cannot desire specifically, not that

35. Ibid., dub. lit. 13 [Vence 2:101Aa–Bc].

36. Even so, for Giles as for Thomas, the reception of grace does not fit into any of these categories completely, because nature can prepare for grace. See ibid., dub. 15 lit [Venice 2:102Ad–Ba].

37. Ibid., d. 41, q. 2, a. 3, co. [Venice 2:633Bd]: "Prout voluntas movetur ad formam, et activatur, et fit gravis per amorem finis: potest dici motus naturalis: sed, prout activata naturaliter per amorem finis in spe movet se deliberative ad ea, quae sunt ad finem, et ad ipsum finem in re: potest dici motus deliberativus, et sicut ille motus dicitur naturalis, et iste deliberativus: ita voluntas mota illo, et isto motu, potest dici naturalis, et deliberativa."

the will is ordered negatively toward any number of goods, of which only the best and most perfect would completely satisfy it.[38]

On account of his doctrine of *rationes seminales,* Giles effectively returns to the earlier, Avicennian-Augustinian doctrine of an active, determinate, natural desire, which has the vision of God as its specific end. Thomas had opposed the expression of this doctrine he had found in William of Auvergne, arguing that deliberate desires are restricted within the bounds of natural desires, and that if our natural desire had a fixed end, we could not sin, since our will would be fixed in the good. Giles is aware of this objection. Consequently, Giles gives an alternative account of the possibility of sin: we can sin not because of the indeterminacy of our will simply speaking, but because of the weakness with which our will pursues its end. Since our natural desire is "imperfect" in this way, it is still possible for us to make a deliberate choice which is contrary to it.[39]

Confirmation of the difference between Thomas's and Giles's respective understandings of natural desire can be seen in Giles's *Tractatus de divina influentia in beatos,* where Giles discusses the terminal development of man's natural desire in a question on whether the beatific vision in angels is mediated through a celestial hierarchy or whether the angels are beatified immediately by God.[40] Giles, fol-

38. Thus Giles of Rome, *Ordinatio* 2, d. 41, q. 2, a. 3, co. [Venice 2:633Ab–d]. See also d. 39, q. 2, a. 1, ad 1 [Venice 2:587Ab]. The distinction between possession *in spe* and possession *in re* is present in both Albert and Thomas. However, both Albert and Thomas use it to describe the ordering of humanity to the beatific vision by grace, not by nature. See Jacob W. Wood, "The Study of Theology as a Foretaste of Heaven: The Influence of Albert the Great on Aquinas's Understanding of *Beatitudo Imperfecta,*" *Nova et Vetera* (English) 16, no. 4 (2018): 1108, 1131.

39. Ibid., d. 39, q. 2, a. 1, ad 3 [Venice 2:587Ad]: "Ut tactum est in his, quae sunt determinata ad unum, semper sequitur actus nisi impediantur, et impedimentum est in minori parte. Sed voluntas loquendo simpliciter non est sic determinata ad unum: sed homines habent quandam generalem inclinationem ad bonum, sed ista inclinatio non est perfecta, ut homines bene faciant in maiori parte, sed perficitur per assuetudinem, quantum ad virtutes acquisitas, vel per gratiam quantum ad infusas."

40. Giles of Rome, *De divina influentia in beatos,* 1, in *Tractatus* (Rome: Antonius Bladus, 1555), 21ra. The question arises from Pseudo-Dionysius, *Celestial Hierarchy* 13 (301C), where Pseudo-Dionysius claims that higher angels mediate happiness to lower angels. See also *Ecclesiastical Hiearchy* 2 [445A], 5 [504C–D].

lowing his *magister*,[41] answers that the angels are beatified immediately by God. But Giles explicitly broadens his response to include human beings as well, even though he acknowledges that the question was not supposed to concern them. Evoking the famous proofs for the existence of God from the *Prima pars* of his *magister's Summa theologiae*, Giles gratuitously offers "five ways" (*quinque viae*) from natural reason why only the vision of God can satisfy the human person's desire for God.[42]

Of most interest for the present purposes are the first and fifth arguments that Giles offers in support of his conclusion. The first proceeds thus:

> It is self-evident (*per se notum*) that if a vessel can hold so much wine, less wine than that cannot fill the vessel. For example, if a vessel can hold a bottle's worth of wine, or a couple of gallons, or however much wine, less wine than that cannot fill that vessel. Since, therefore, the soul and an angel can hold as much good as God himself is, less good than God himself can fill neither the soul, nor an angel, and according to Augustine in *Confessions* 10, "we are not happy until we say 'it is enough,'" that is, until we are filled with the joy and the goodness of God. Therefore, since we can hold as much good as God is, less good than God cannot make us happy and fulfill us. Moreover, the fact that we can hold as much good as God is, is clear from the fact that we are in the image and likeness of God. For according to Augustine, the soul is the image God because it is capable of and can be a participant in him.[43]

41. Thomas Aquinas, *Summa contra Gentiles*, 3.49–52 [Leon. Man. 279–84]. See also *In IV Sent.*, d. 45, q. 3, a. 1, co. [Parma 7.2:1150], where Thomas argues that inferior angels receive some knowledge from superior ones in the beatific vision, but only such knowledge as does *not* pertain to the essence of happiness. Thomas is following Albert the Great, *In II Sent.*, d. 10, a. 3, ad 2 [Bourgnet 27:214]. One may also consult Thomas's *In II Sent.*, d. 9, q. un., a. 2, co. [Mandonnet 2:229–30], and *In II Sent.*, d. 26, q. un., a. 2, co. [Mandonnet 2:671–72], which touch on the same question, as well as *In III Sent.*, d. 19, a. 5, qc. 3, ad 4 [Moos 3:605], where, on a related question, Aquinas describes angels as *ministri mediatoris* (ministers of the mediator) rather than mediators simply speaking.

42. Giles of Rome, *De divina influentia in beatos*, 1 [Bladus 21ra–21vb]. Thomas's *quinque viae* can be found in *ST*, Ia, q. 2, a. 3, co. [Leon. 4:31–32].

43. Giles of Rome, *De divina influentia in beatos*, 1 [Bladus 21rb]: "Est enim per se notum, quod si aliquod vas potest capere tantum vinum, minus vinum quam illud, non potest illud vas replere: ut si potest capere vas aliquod quintam vini, vel modium, vel quantumcunque vinum, minus vinum quam illud non potest vas illud replere. Cum ergo

Initially, one sees nothing very different here from what Thomas had argued. The soul has a capacity for God; therefore, less than the possession of God will not completely satisfy the soul. Thomas employed this argument with respect to the intellect in the *Summa contra Gentiles* and the *Prima pars* of the *Summa theologiae,* and with respect to both the intellect and the will in the *Prima secundae.* Yet one can note a certain shift in tone here. Even if Thomas did not think that anything less than the vision of God could completely satisfy us, he did not hesitate to say that there were many, lesser participations of that happiness. Giles is somewhat more radical than this in his insistence that *only* the complete possession of God can make us happy, and that nothing short of it can satisfy us in any meaningful respect.

The shift in Giles's tone indicated by the first argument foreshadows a mode of argumentation in Giles's fifth argument that parts company with Thomas more definitively:

The fifth way ... is taken from God's rest and fulfillment. For as long as something is in motion, it is not resting. Since, therefore, we tend toward our end itself by way of those things which are [ordered] toward our end, we are in motion and not resting as long as we remain among those things which are [ordered] toward our end. Since, therefore, all creatures are ordered toward God as toward their end, there cannot be rest, simply speaking, in any creature, since no creature is an end simply speaking, or the end of all things. Rather, God alone is the end of all things, since, as the Commentator says concerning *Metaphysics* 1, God alone exists in a threefold genus of cause with respect to all things, because God is the efficient cause of all, the formal exemplar cause of all, and God alone is the final cause, or end of all. Therefore, our rest and happiness can be in God alone. For, since every creature is something liable to slip away, and something mobile, our rest

anima et angelus possit capere tantum bonum quantum est ipse Deus, minus bonum quam ipse Deus non potest nec animam nec angelum replere: et secundum Augustinum 10 Confessionum non sumus beati donec dicamus satis est, idest donec sumus gaudio et bonitate Dei impleti: ideo potentes capere tantum bonum quantum est Deus, minus bonum quam Deus nos beatificare et replere non potest. Quod autem nos possimus tantum bonum capere quantum est Deus, patet ex hoc quod sumus ad imaginem et similitudinem Dei. Nam secundum Augustinum anima est imago Dei ex eo quod eius capax et particeps esse potest."

cannot be in any creature simply speaking, because whoever tries to lean on something slipping away, necessarily slips away with it.[44]

Instead of arguing from the will's desire for the complete fulfillment of its potency, Giles here emphasizes the determined nature of our natural desire toward a single object in order to show that our happiness can only be in God.

Giles's treatment of infants who die in original sin only confirms his understanding of *rationes seminales* and natural desire, but it must be treated very carefully. Giles holds that these children will not experience any pain on account of not having reached the vision of God because "their state is at its *terminus* [*in termino*], on account of which their natural appetite is at its *terminus,* because they possess nature left to itself, such that they cannot desire [*appetere*] more than they have."[45] He also says that "after death, the children do not have an appetite beyond their natural appetite in itself, and left to itself. But that good, which they lack, is altogether above nature [*supra naturam*]. For this reason, they cannot have a natural appetite for the vision of God, and they cannot be sad about it."[46] Although the latter argument appears before the former in the text, it must be read in light of the former. The reason for this is Giles's insistence that the children are "*in termino.*" Since Giles thinks that *rationes seminales* were added to nature after nature began, Giles also thinks that *ratio-*

44. Ibid. [Bladus 21vb]: "Quinta via ... sumitur ex divina quietatione et satietate: nam quandiu aliquid est in motu non quiescit: cum ergo per ea quae sunt ad finem tendimus in ipsum finem, quandiu sistimus in his quae sunt ad finem, tandiu sumus in motu et non quiescimus. Cum ergo omnes creaturae ordinentur ad Deum tanquam ad finem, in nulla creatura simpliciter loquendo potest esse quies: quia nulla creatura est finis simpliciter vel finis omnium: solus autem Deus est finis omnium, quia solus ipse, ut vult Comment. in primo *Metaphy.*, se habet in triplici genere causae respectu omnium, quia ipse est omnium causa efficiens, omnium causa formalis exemplaris, et ipse solus est causa finalis vel finis omnium. In ipso ergo solo potest esse quies et beatitudo nostra: nam cum omnis creatura sit quid labile, et quid mobile, in nulla creatura potest simpliciter esse quies: quia qui labenti innitur, oportet quod cum labente labatur."

45. Giles of Rome, *Ordinatio* 2, d. 33, q. 2, a. 2, co. [Venice 2:492Aa]: "status eorum est in termino, propter quod appetitus eorum naturalis, quia habet naturam sibi derelictam, est in termino, ut non possint amplius appetere, quam habeant."

46. For Latin text, see ibid. [Venice 2:491Bd].

nes seminales will pass away at the end of time.[47] Since, moreover, *rationes seminales* are that by which Giles thinks that human nature was oriented toward the beatific vision, this means that if Giles thinks of these children as *in termino,* as in the first argument, he thinks of them as having lost their *rationes seminales,* and consequently their positive aptitude for the beatific vision, as he expresses in the second argument. Hence, Giles will draw a similar conclusion as Thomas does about these infants, even if he reaches it by a significantly different means: they do indeed have a privation with respect to the vision of God, but since they lack any positive aptitude for that vision, they do not suffer at not having received it.[48]

Giles's understanding of *rationes seminales* also affects his understanding of a hypothetical state of "pure nature." In his *Ordinatio* Giles explicitly imagines man "if God had created him in a purely natural state" (*si Deus fecisset hominem in puris naturalibus*).[49] Giles is thinking of man with *rationes seminales,* and so with a positive aptitude for the vision of God, but without any means of achieving that vision. For Giles, such a situation would be unthinkable for two reasons. First, a man would not be able to attain his end *a priori* because, "the end of a rational creature is the vision of God, which is above nature."[50] Moreover, and lest the reader have any doubt that Giles excludes any possibility of a lesser end for man, Giles adds: "And I do not say that our happiness is *chiefly* in the vision of God, but rather I say that without the vision of God there can be no hap-

47. Ibid., d. 18, q. 2, a. 2, co. [Venice 2:83Aa].

48. See ibid., d. 33, q. 2, a. 1, co. [Venice 2:489Bd–90Aa]: "Ex actuali culpa Adae infecta est natura nostra, per cuius infectionem contrahimus peccatum originale, et quia parvuli non per actum suum, sed per actum primi parentis contrahunt originale peccatum, quod est carentia boni supernaturalis, ipsi Adae pro actuali suo peccato debebatur poena sensus: parvulis autem, quos peccatum Adae non plus potuit attingere per se, et directe nisi quia potuit eos privare, et privavit quodam bono supernaturali. Ideo pro tali privatione, sola privatio, et sola carentia alicuius boni supernaturalis debet esse competens, et debita poena. Hoc autem est carentia divini boni, vel carentia visionis illius boni, quod videndo adipiscimur omne bonum."

49. Ibid., d. 31, q. 1, a. 1, corp. [Venice 2:443Ad].

50. Ibid. [Venice 442Bd]: "Finis creaturae rationalis est divina visio, quae est supra naturam."

piness for us."[51] Pure nature is not possible *a priori*, because humanity would be condemned to a perpetual state of unhappiness on account of his inability to reach its only end.

Giles not only finds pure nature unthinkable on the basis of our natural desire's end; he also considers it unthinkable on the basis of our nature's weakness. Without the gift of original justice, man would be subject to the natural antipathy of flesh and spirit. In this state, Giles thinks we would not be able to persevere in moral goodness of our own accord, because he thinks that our natural desire for the good is too weak and too imperfect. For this reason, he argues that if humanity had been created without original justice, it would have been "not only avertible, but already averse," from God.[52] Not only would we be unhappy for not having reached our end, but we would also be, in a certain sense, unable not to sin by nature. The unfortunate result would be that, after already having been deprived of our only possible happiness, we would certainly be condemned to a worse fate for our inability to persevere in basic moral goodness.

Although Giles's picture of pure nature may be closer to Thomas's understanding of wounded nature than of human nature as such,[53] what is most important for the present purposes is not what

51. See ibid., d. 33, q. 2, a. 1, co. [Venice 2:490Aa]: "Nec dicimus, quod in visione divina sit principaliter beatitudo nostra, sed dicimus, quod sine visione divina non potest esse beatitudo nostra."

52. Ibid. [Venice 2:443Ad–Ba]: "si fuisset creatus in puris naturalibus, quia haberet necessitatem se avertendi, deberet dici creatus non solum avertibilis, sed aversus."

53. Thomas thought that man could avoid sin in a state of integral nature even without grace. See *ST*, Ia-IIae, q. 109, a. 8, co. [Leon. 7:303]: "Secundum statum ... naturae integrae, etiam sine gratia habituali, poterat homo non peccare nec mortaliter nec venialiter: quia peccare nihil aliud est quam recedere ab eo quod est secundum naturam, quod vitare homo poterat in integritate naturae." See also *In II Sent.*, d. 24, q. 1, a. 4, co. [Mandonnet 2:599]. Likewise, see *In II Sent.*, d. 20, q. 2, a. 3, ad 5 [Mandonnet 2:517], where Thomas acknowledges the possibility of Adam's resisting temptation without grace, as well as *In II Sent.*, d. 28, q. 1, a. 2, co. [Mandonnet 2:722]; *De veritate*, q. 26, a. 6, ad 12 [Leon. 22:770]; *Summa contra Gentiles* 3.160 [Leon. Man. 420].

Although Thomas thought that man could avoid sin without grace in a state of integral nature, that does not mean that he denied all natural concupiscence of the flesh against the spirit. See *In II Sent.*, d. 31, q. 2, a. 1, ad 3 [Mandonnet 2:810]; *De malo*, q. 5, a. 1 [Leon. 23:131]; *ST*, Ia, q. 95, a. 1 [Leon. 5:420]; Hütter, *Dust Bound for Heaven*, 146; Nicholas Lombardo, *The Logic of Desire: Aquinas on Emotion* (Washington, D.C.: The Catholic

Giles says, but how he defends it. Since humanity in a state of pure nature would neither be able to persevere in moral goodness, nor reach his happiness, Giles argues that the gift of original justice can be said to be "due" (*debitum*) to human nature, lest it be deprived of the possibility of reaching its only end.

Let us conclude, therefore, and say... that human nature was made at its institution with a debt of original justice (this is a debt [*debitum*], and we call this a debt, because someone ought [*debet*] to have it). For original justice was due to human nature at its institution, even if not absolutely and simply speaking, yet according to a certain fittingness of God's goodness and justice, lest man were created averse from God without fault.[54]

In applying the word *debitum* in such a strong sense to any grace, even the grace of original justice, Giles clearly develops, if not supersedes the thought of his *magister*, who was very cautious to avoid the word *debitum* with respect to God's gifts.[55] Yet such was the delicate balance that Giles struck in the light of his commitment to the unicity of man's final end, and his rejection of any possible resting place for our heart's desire short of the vision of God.

University of America Press, 2011), 122. The main difference between Thomas and Giles is that Thomas thought that man in integral nature but without grace could withstand natural concupiscence, while Giles did not.

54. Ibid. [Venice 2 :444Bc]: "Concludamus ergo, et dicamus... quod natura humana in sui institutione producta est cum debito originalis iustitiae, hoc est enim debitum, et hoc vocamus debitum, quod quis debet habere. Debebatur enim naturae humanae in sui institutione originalis iustitia, etsi non absolute et simpliciter, tamen secundum quandam decentiam divinae bonitatis, et iustitiae, ne homo sine culpa produceretur a Deo aversus."

55. When Thomas use the word "*debitum*" in relation to original justice, he is discussing a *debitum ex parte subiecti*, that is, the debt on our part of keeping our souls in order, not any debt on God's part of giving us that right ordering. While examples of this usage abound, we may note in particular *In II Sent.*, d. 20, q. 2, a. 3, co. [Mandonnet 2:516–17]; *De malo*, q. 5, a. 4, ad 7 [Leon. 23:139]; *ST*, Ia-IIae, q. 89, a. 5, ad 3 [Leon. 7:146]. In one text, namely, *Quodlibet* IV, q. 11, a. 2, ad 2 [Leon. 25.2:344], Thomas does use the phrase, "*debitum originalis iusticie*," but his language is rather more reserved than that of Giles. The question to which Thomas is responding is whether the first motion of the soul in unbelievers is a mortal sin. In the *corpus* of the article, Aquinas argues emphatically in the negative. This suggests a more positive view of human nature without grace than Giles would allow, since Giles thinks that man without original justice would be created averse from God.

JOHN DUNS SCOTUS

As Bonaventure was the backdrop against which Thomas formulated his understanding of nature, grace, and the desire for God, John Duns Scotus can be considered the backdrop against which many subsequent Thomists formulated their own understandings of these subjects.[56] The reason for this is that Scotus changed the debate on nature, grace, and the desire for God in two significant ways: he abandoned the use of *rationes seminales,* and he thought that the passive "second nature" which Thomas had borrowed from Averroes should replace its active counterpart in discussions of nature and natural desire.

Scotus discusses *rationes seminales* at three points during his career, marking roughly the beginning, the middle, and the end of it respectively: the *Lectura Oxoniensis,*[57] the *Quaestiones super libros Metaphysicorum Aristotelis,*[58] and the *Reportatio Parisiensis.*[59] In all three works, Scotus maintains that it is unnecessary to posit some active element in matter in order to account for natural change, be it Bacon's incomplete potency, Bonaventure's incomplete form, or any number of other variations that scholars had proposed in the interim.[60] Change, for Scotus, is natural only on account of the passive

56. Hütter, *Dust Bound for Heaven,* 184, makes a similar observation, following William O'Connor, *The Eternal Quest: The Teaching of St. Thomas Aquinas on the Natural Desire for God* (New York: Longman, Green, and Co., 1947). For an introduction to Scotus's life and works, see Thomas Williams, "Introduction: The Life and Works of John Duns the Scot," in *The Cambridge Companion to John Duns Scotus,* ed. Thomas Williams (New York: Cambridge University Press, 2003), 1–14; Richard Cross, *Duns Scotus on God* (Burlington, Vt.: Ashgate, 2005), 1–14; Antoine Vos, *The Philosophy of John Duns Scotus* (Edinburgh: Edinburgh University Press, 2006).

57. John Duns Scotus, *Lectura Oxoniensis* 2, d. 18, in *Opera Omnia* (Vatican City: Vatican Polyglott Press, 1993), 19:155–80.

58. Scotus, *Quaestiones super libros metaphysicorum Aristotelis,* ed. R. Andrews et al. (St. Bonaventure, N.Y.: The Franciscan Institute, 1997), 7, q. 12 [Andrews 2:195–214].

59. Scotus, *Reportata Parisiensia* 2, d. 18, in *Opera Omnia* (Paris: Vivès, 1894), 23:83–90.

60. For a list of these positions, see the editors' notes to Scotus, *Quaestiones super libros Metaphysicorum Aristotelis* 7, q. 12, nos. 12–22 [Andrews 2:197–201].

principle receiving it, not any active principle expecting it.[61] It is useless to posit a separate active principle in things in order to account for the possibility of natural change in them, since that would multiply causes without necessity.[62]

Emphasizing the importance of the passive principle in nature brought Scotus very close to Thomas's understanding of nature as such, but Scotus saw an exegetical problem with the use of this view as an interpretation of Augustine, such as Thomas had initially proposed it: Augustine plainly did not intend a passive principle by the term *rationes seminales*.[63] If the term implies an active principle, but there is no need for an active principle in order to give an account of natural change, then Scotus argues that we should dispense with the term entirely. The term no longer serves the purpose for which previous generations of theologians had appealed to it.

If Scotus comes conceptually close to Thomas on the question of matter's passive receptivity toward form, he is closer to Rufus than to Thomas on form's activity in matter,[64] for although Scotus holds with Thomas that matter's receptive potency explains its pluripotentiality toward substantial forms, he holds with Rufus that substances are individuated by individual forms.[65] There cannot be substantial change in a creature without either adding and/or destroying some form in it.[66] That being the case, matter must serve as the principle undergirding the addition and destruction of forms in order to ac-

61. Scotus, *Quaestiones super libros Metaphysicorum Aristotelis* 7, q. 12, no. 47 [Andrews 2:209]; *Reportatio Parisiensis* 2, d. 18, q. 1, ad 1 [Vivès 23:86B].

62. Scotus, *Lectura Oxoniensis* 2, d. 18, no. 61 [Vat. 19:169–70]; *Quaestiones super libros Metaphysicorum Aristotelis* 7, q. 12, no. 30 [Andrews 2:204]; *Reportatio Parisiensis* 2, d. 18, q. 1, co. [Vivès 23:87B].

63. Scotus, *Lectura Oxoniensis* 2, d. 18, no. 20 [Vat. 19:200]; *Reportatio Parisiensis* 2, d. 18, co. [Vivès 23:84A].

64. See Rega Wood, "Individual Forms," 251–72, in which Wood provides a helpful summary of similarities and differences between Rufus and Scotus. For a more detailed discussion of Scotus, see Richard Cross, *The Physics of Duns Scotus: The Scientific Context of a Theological Vision* (Oxford: Clarendon Press, 1998), 35–41.

65. Rega Wood, "Individual Forms," 263–66.

66. Cross, *The Physics of Duns Scotus*, 44, provides a detailed engagement with the primary texts in Scotus.

count for the continuity of created existence as those changes take place.[67] This gives matter a degree of separability from form that it could not have for Thomas: Scotus thinks that matter, absent any form, could exist on its own.[68]

Scotus defends his view that matter could exist apart from form by distinguishing between two kinds of potentiality: subjective and objective.[69] Subjective potentiality describes the potency of things that exist to take on forms, while objective potentiality describes the potentiality of things that do not exist to begin to exist. Since matter exists, it must have subjective potentiality, and some nature of its own without form. Hence, Scotus holds together two views on matter that would have been considered irreconcilable by many previous thinkers: (1) matter is pure subjective potentiality; (2) matter, while remaining pure potentiality, has some level of actuality from its nature apart from that which is communicated to it by form.

For Scotus, the will is a nature, and so the will has an inclination toward its perfection like matter.[70] This inclination is, as it was for Thomas, toward its *highest* or *most perfect* perfection.[71] This is the case even if, like matter, the will stands in a position of pure passivity toward the reception of its perfection. But since Scotus thinks that matter does not receive all of its actuality from form, Scotus can posit in matter not just what Thomas would have called a natural appetite for form, but also a natural desire for it; similarly he can posit not just what Thomas would have called a natural appetite in the will for the vision of God, but also a natural desire for it. As Scotus explains, every nature has a specific perfection; therefore every nature must have a natural desire for its specific perfection.[72] Scotus

67. Ibid., 22.

68. Ibid., 23–26.

69. In what follows, I summarize Cross, *The Physics of Duns Scotus*, 17–18.

70. Scotus, *Reportatio Parisiensis* 4, d. 49, q. 9, co. [Vivès 24:659B]; *Ordinatio* 4, d. 49, q. 10 [Vivès 21:318A–B].

71. Scotus, *Reportatio Parisiensis* 4, d. 49, q. 9, co. [Vivès 24:660A]; *Ordinatio* 2, d. 1, p. 1, q. 1, no. 10 [Vat. 2:5].

72. Scotus, *Reportatio Parisiensis* 4, d. 49, q. 9, co. [Vivès 24:660B, 661B]; *Ordinatio* 4, d. 49, q. 10 [Vivès 21:319B].

calls this desire an "appetite," but the understanding of matter undergirding Scotus's use of the term means that what Scotus calls an "appetite" includes part of what Thomas means by the word "desire." This is important to note, because it is Scotus's understanding of appetite as in some way active, not Thomas's understanding of appetite as purely passive, which will predominate in the subsequent Thomistic tradition.

If the will seeks its end in a particular perfection, that does not mean that every act of the will necessarily seeks that one, particular perfection. Like Thomas emphasized after 1270, Scotus says that the natural will influences the free will in the sense that whenever one decides to elicit an act concerning happiness, one cannot help but to will that happiness, and not to will its opposite.[73] But one always remains free to suspend judgment altogether and not to will anything at all,[74] or to choose that which has nothing to do with human happiness, if one wills not to think about happiness when making such a choice.[75]

Since our intellect and our will are in receptive potencies to their objects just like matter is in a receptive potency for form, Scotus thinks that whether an act is *secundum naturam* or *contra naturam* depends not so much on the active power of our souls to produce it, as whether or not it is in accord with the natural inclination of our passive potency to receive it.[76] In this way, even the vision of God can be called "natural" in a certain respect: it is entirely in accord with our natural inclination to be perfected by God as the highest possible object to receive it.[77] What makes the vision of God ultimately supernat-

73. Scotus, *Reportatio Parisiensis* 4, d. 49, q. 9, co. [Vivès 24:664A]; *Ordinatio* 4, d. 49, q. 10 [Vivès 21:319B].

74. Ibid. [Vivès 24:664B]; *Ordinatio* 4, d. 49, q. 10 [Vivès 21:332B–333A].

75. On choosing an object that seems contrary to our natural inclination, see Scotus, *Reportatio Parisiensis* 4, d. 49, q. 9, co. [Vivès 24:662B]; *Ordinatio* 4, d. 49, q. 10 [Vivès 21:331B]. On choosing an object that is not objectively ordered to happiness, see *Reportatio Parisiensis* 4, d. 49, q. 9, co. [Vivès 24:664B].

76. Allan Wolter, "Duns Scotus on the Natural Desire for the Supernatural," *The New Scholasticism* 23, no. 3 (1949): 286–87.

77. Scotus, *Reportatio Parisiensis* 4, d. 49, q. 10 [Vivès 24:674A–B]. Scotus will argue

ural is not that it is above the active power of our nature to produce such an act, as it was for Thomas, but that the agent which produces this act in us does so not as a consequence of its own natural action.[78] The vision of God is supernatural because it is above what follows of necessity from God's nature to cause it.

Saying that we have a natural inclination toward supernatural happiness raised for Scotus, as it had for Thomas, the question of the applicability of Aristotle's *dictum*: "nature does nothing in vain." Scotus avoids treating the axiom from a purely philosophical point of view. Since we know by Revelation that some people *do* enjoy the vision of God, it is not a problem if some individuals in the species lack the vision of God. That is enough to show that the desire is not in vain.[79]

Here one might ask whether Scotus's treatment of Aristotle's *dictum* perhaps implies that Scotus has confused the philosophical question of the possibility of the vision of God with the theological question of its actuality, two questions which Thomas carefully distinguished at all times. That would be the case if Scotus thought that he was responding to a philosophical question. But since Scotus does not consider an active counterpart to our passive potency when discussing what it means for something to be natural, he does not think that natural reason can demonstrate what the specific *terminus* of our natural desire in a given order of Providence is; the end at which we ultimately hope to arrive depends entirely upon God's free decision.[80] In this state (*pro statu isto*), we experience the limitation of our knowledge by our encounter with the material world,[81] which

as a corollary that, according to this logic, charity is not necessary in the will for the beatific vision. He thinks that the only reason we posit charity in the will as the necessary condition to receiving the vision of God is because it is revealed in Scripture as necessary.

78. See Wolter, "Duns Scotus on the Natural Desire," 287, 294–95.

79. Scotus, *Ordinatio* 4, d. 49, q. 10 [Vivès 21:379A–B].

80. Wolter, "Duns Scotus on the Natural Desire," 308, notes that many generations of theologians were misled about Scotus on this point on account of an error in the manuscripts.

81. Ibid., 292–94.

actually seems to suggest to unaided reason that the end of human nature is naturally achievable.[82] But even if we were able to overcome the seeming appearance of naturality, another difficulty would arise: since the soul is an intellectual nature, it is capable of receiving intuitive knowledge; but that knowledge has to be caused in the soul by its object, and we can never know by natural reason whether God would choose to cause in us the vision of himself.[83]

Confirmation of the fact that Scotus considers the end of our natural desire as a theological and not as a philosophical topic can be seen in his discussion of our need for supernatural knowledge in the prologue to his *Ordinatio*. There, he raises the following objection:

> Some active natural potency corresponds with every natural passive potency, otherwise it would seem that a passive potency were vain in nature if it could not be reduced to act by something in nature; but the possible intellect is a passive potency with respect to whatever is intelligible; therefore, some active, natural potency corresponds with it.... The minor premise is clear, because the possible intellect naturally desires the knowledge of whatever is knowable; it is also naturally perfected by any sort of knowledge; therefore, it is naturally receptive of any sort of understanding.[84]

Scotus gives three arguments in response to this objection. The first suggests that Aristotle's *dictum* only applies when there is a positive ordering in nature toward a given end; since there is no positive ordering in nature toward the vision of God, the argument does not apply.[85] The second suggests that Aristotle's *dictum* only applies to

82. Scotus, *Ordinatio* prol., p. 1, q. un. [Vat. 1:10]. See Wolter, "Duns Scotus on the Natural Desire," 311–13.

83. Wolter, "Duns Scotus on the Natural Desire," 291, 298–99. See Scotus, *Ordinatio* 1, prol. p. 1, q. un. [Vat. 1:11].

84. Scotus, *Ordinatio* prol., p. 1, q. un., no. 7 [Vat. 1:5–6]: "Omni potentiae naturali passivae correspondet aliquod activum naturale, alioquin videretur potentia passiva esse frustra in natura si per nihil in natura posset reduci ad actum; sed intellectus possibilis est potentia passiva respectu quorumcumque intelligibilium; ergo correspondet sibi aliqua potentia activa naturalis.... Minor patet, quia intellectus possibilis naturaliter appetit cognitionem cuiuscumque cognoscibilis; naturaliter etiam perficitur per quamcumque cognitionem; igitur est naturaliter receptivus cuiuscumque intellectionis."

85. Scotus, *Ordinatio* prol., p. 1, q. un., no. 76 [Vat. 1:46–47].

TABLE 4. Comparison of Thomas Aquinas and John Duns Scotus on natural desire

Thomas	Scotus
Form is educed from matter.	Form is placed in matter.
Matter cannot exist apart from form.	Matter can exist apart from form.
What is natural is measured by active and passive potencies.	What is natural is measured by passive potencies only.
Natural desire exercises a positive influence on the activity of the will.	Natural desire exercises a negative influence on the activity of the will.
Aristotle's dictum that "nature does nothing in vain" is of philosophical importance.	Aristotle's dictum that "nature does nothing in vain" is of theological importance only.

potencies that are called "natural" with respect to an act caused, not an act received. Since there is no positive ordering of our powers toward this act, the principle does not apply.[86] The third contends that the principle does not apply in this state (*pro statu isto*), in which our mind has been restricted to knowledge drawn from the material world.[87] Setting aside the third argument's talk of states, which is particular to Scotus, there is nothing in the first two arguments which is at odds with what we find in Thomas.

In summary, while Scotus and Thomas differ on much concerning natural desire, they are not entirely different from one another on some fundamental questions. The differences are summarized in table 4.

However much Scotus and Thomas may differ on these points, they agree on Thomas's principal contribution to the thirteenth-century conversation about nature, grace, and the desire for God:

86. Ibid., no. 77 [Vat. 1:47].

87. Ibid., no. 78 [Vat. 1:47]: "Posset etiam tertio modo faciliter dici ad minorem, negando, quia licet absolute intellectus possibilis sit naturaliter receptivus talis intellectionis, non tamen pro statu isto."

grace is received according to a passive potency in the soul. Consequently, there is not much reason to posit a separate obediential potency in man in order to account for our receptivity to grace. Thomas may have drawn a sharper distinction between what is *secundum naturam* and what *supra naturam,* owing to his pairing of active principles with passive ones in *rationes seminales,* but that distinction is not absent in Scotus, even if it is not at the forefront. Thomas and Scotus also agree that grace is partly natural and partly supernatural, because it is received in nature according to a passive potency, but caused directly by God (even if for Thomas its supernaturality comes from its enabling us to achieve an act above the active principles of our nature, while for Scotus it comes from God's doing something above the necessity of his own nature). Hence, when both Thomas and Scotus follow Aristotle in affirming that the highest perfection of man must be according to the highest act of our highest power oriented toward its highest object, they may disagree about which power should be accounted highest (the intellect for Thomas and the will for Scotus), but they both agree that the ultimate perfection of human nature as such is to be found in the immediate vision of God.

TOMMASO DE VIO "CAJETAN"

Tommaso de Vio "Cajetan" (1469–1534) was born Giacomo de Vio,[88] but took the name "Thomas" when he entered the Dominican Order in 1484, and received the nickname "Gaetano" ("the gentleman from Gaetà") when he went for studies at the University of Padua in 1491, since he had come to the university from the Dominican convent at Gaetà.[89] At Padua, he took the Dominican chair as a master of theology in 1494, though he would not remain in the post for long. In spite

88. Eckehart Stöve, "De Vio, Tommaso," in *Dizionario biografico degli italiani,* vol. 39 (Rome: Istituto della Enciclopedia Italiana, 1991), 568.

89. Jared Wicks, "Thomas de Vio Cajetan (1469–1534)," in *The Reformation Theologians: An Introduction to Theology in the Early Modern Period,* ed. Carter Lindberg (Malden, Mass.: Blackwell, 2002), 269–70.

of his absence from a regular university chair, Cajetan continued to publish throughout his life, and his *magnum opus* was a commentary on the entire *Summa theologiae*, published successively: *In Primam partem* (1507), *In Primam secundae* (1511), *In Secundam secundae* (1511), *In Tertiam partem* (1520). This commentary was influential on its own merits for its content and its scope. However, it gained additional notoriety when Pope Pius V had it printed alongside the post-Tridentine Roman edition of the *Summa theologiae*,[90] a practice which was continued when Pope Leo XIII had it printed alongside the Leonine edition of the *Summa theologiae* just prior to and at the start of the twentieth century.[91]

The desire for God was a central question for Cajetan. He discusses it in his commentary on the very first article of the *Summa theologiae*. There, he draws a stark contrast between himself and Scotus.

> We say that that end [that is, the vision of God] is naturally hidden from us, because it is the supernatural end of our soul.... But [Scotus] holds that that end is the natural end of our soul, although it is supernaturally reached. And nevertheless, it is naturally unknown, since our soul is not naturally known to us, at least in this state, under the proper and special *ratio* by which it is ordered to that end.[92]

The contrast that Cajetan draws between himself and Scotus forces the question of natural desire into a framework that omits some of the subtlety both of Thomas's and of Scotus's treatments of the question. For Thomas, the vision of God is "above nature" or "supernatural" in the sense that nature cannot produce the act from its

90. Thomas Aquinas, *Opera omnia*, vols. 9–11 (Rome, 1569–70). This edition is the so-called *Editio Piana*, which is named after Pius V, who ordered it printed. It omitted Cajetan's commentary on the *tertia pars*.

91. Thomas Aquinas, *Opera omnia*, vols. 4–12 (Rome, 1888–1906).

92. Cajetan, *In Primam partem*, q. 1, a. 1, no. 7 [Leon. 4:7]: "Nos enim dicimus quod ideo finis ille est nobis naturaliter occultus, quia est supernaturalis finis animae nostrae.... Ipse vero tenet illum finem esse naturalem nostrae anime, quamvis supernaturaliter adipiscendum. Et tamen esse naturaliter incognitum: quia anima nostra non nobis naturaliter est nota, saltem pro statu isto, sub illa propria et speciali ratione, qua ordinatur ad illum finem."

active powers, but it is nevertheless natural for the soul to receive the act in view of its passive potency. What is unknown about the vision of God is not whether it is possible, but whether it is actual. For Scotus, the argument that Cajetan references here is a secondary, theological confirmation of a more basic philosophical point: even if we were to come to the knowledge of the soul as it is in itself, Scotus agrees with Thomas that this would only allow us to know the possibility and not the actuality of the vision of God.

In lieu of giving a complete explanation of his thought on the desire for God at this point in his text, Cajetan refers the reader to a short *Quaestio de potentia neutra,*[93] which he intended to be read alongside this article.[94] It is paired with a *Quaestio de natura receptivae potentiae,* which explains Cajetan's position on the manner in which receptive potency relates to supernatural actions.[95] In the first *quaestio,* Cajetan opposes the Scotistic idea that a passive potency could be indifferent to the forms received in it. Lurking in the background is the question of matter's relationship to form, which Cajetan treats by analogy with a blank surface. Scotus, says Cajetan, thinks that a blank surface has a neutral potency toward color, because it is open to accidental formation by this or that color.[96] Cajetan responds that Scotus has failed to distinguish between acts which are *per se primo* (in a genus) and acts which are *per se secundo* (in a species). A blank surface desires to be informed with color *per se primo* and to be informed with this or that color *per se secundo*. We cannot say that the surface's potency is neutral, therefore, because of its generic desire for color.[97] It is similar with prime matter. Prime matter is not neutral with respect to form. It has a desire to be

93. It was most recently reprinted in Tommaso de Vio Cajetan, *Opuscula omnia* (Lyons, 1587; repr. Hildesheim: Georg Olms, 1995), 206–7.

94. Cajetan, *In Primam partem,* no. 10 [Leon. 4:8].

95. Cajetan, *De potentia neutra,* in *Opuscula omnia,* 207.

96. Cajetan, *Quaestio de potentia neutra,* p. 1 [Lyons 206b3]: "Si poneremus aliquam superficiem receptivam albi et nigri, et tamen ad neutrum inclinatam . . . proprie vocatur potentia neutra."

97. Ibid., p. 4 [Lyons 206b79].

formed *per se primo,* and a desire to be formed by this or that form *per se secundo.*[98] On this basis, Cajetan concludes that there is no such thing as a neutral potency. Every potency is inclined toward some act, but some potencies are inclined toward a genus of act before they are inclined to any species of act within that genus.[99]

The *Quaestio de potentia neutra* seems at first glance to say nothing different than what Thomas says about natural desire. Thomas had said that matter has a desire for form on account of its capacity for form, and had based his account of our natural desire on this account of matter's desire for form. Yet if we look closely, a certain tension with Thomas's thought also begins to appear. For Thomas, matter does not have a generic desire for form, which is indifferent to a given species of form. Matter has a single desire for the actualization of all of its potency *insofar as is possible.* But since it is impossible for prime matter to receive contrary forms at the same time, it reaches its perfection *gradually*: at one time it actualizes its potency for one thing; at another time it actualizes its potency for the opposite. Cajetan in a way gets this backwards. Where Thomas identifies in human nature an unconditional, passive natural appetite for a specific end and a conditional, active natural desire for a generic end, Cajetan identifies in human nature a conditional natural appetite for a generic end and an unconditional natural desire for a specific end.

Cajetan's misreading of Thomas in the *Quaestio de potentia neutra* paves the way for a larger misreading in the *Quaestio de natura receptivae potentiae.* There Cajetan inquires about our receptive potency for supernatural acts. First, he defines a "supernatural act," that "which cannot be achieved according to the course of nature."[100] Here he follows Thomas, who had described such acts as "above nature" (*supra naturam*) or "supernatural" (*supernaturalis*). But Cajetan parts company with Thomas when he explains what it means for a potency to

98. Ibid. [Lyons 207a1]. Cajetan later makes the same argument in *In Primam partem,* q. 82, a. 1, no. 9 [Leon. 5:295].

99. Ibid. [Lyons 207a4].

100. Cajetan, *Quaestio de natura receptivae potentiae,* p. 1 [Lyons 207a38]: "Actus supernaturalis dicitur, quem non potest secundum naturae cursum adipisci."

be "natural": "'natural potency,'" he says, "is not said subjectively, that is, as a potency of nature, but formally, that is, as a potency naturally inclined."[101] That is, natural potency is "natural" insofar as it arises from a formal, active potency, and not a material passive one. By defining his terms in this way, Cajetan effectively returns to Albert's understanding of natural desire, and omits any reference to the passive "second nature," which Thomas shares with Scotus.

When it comes to Aristotle's *dictum* that nature does nothing in vain, Cajetan combines his Albertine understanding of natural desire with a new premise, which is found neither in Thomas nor in Scotus: a potency is "vain" if a creature has an active inclination toward a specific act, but lacks the proportionate active power to achieve that act.[102] This premise confuses the two very separate uses of Aristotle's *dictum* that we identified above in chapter 3 in Thomas's *Summa contra Gentiles* 2.79 and 3.48, respectively; it thus leads Cajetan to confuse the question of the possibility of an act (3.48) with the question of the actuality of a power (2.79), and so to use Aristotle's *dictum* to attempt to attempt to prove the actuality of an act:

101. Ibid. [Lyons 207a40]: "Potentia naturalis vocatur non subiective, id est, potentia naturae, sed formaliter, id est, potentia naturaliter inclinata."

102. See ibid., p. 3 [Lyons 207b2], where Cajetan uses the word "proportion" apposite to "inclination." For Cajetan, the one implies the other. Also see *In Primam partem*, q. 82, a. 1, no. 12 [Leon. 5:295]: "Nos appelamus naturalem appetitum, non solum inclinationem voluntatis in obiectum etc., sed illum actum elicitum determinatum quoad specificationem: ipse [Scotus] vero non vult vocare illum appetitum naturalem, propter libertatem quae est in exercitio eius; ex qua parte nec nos dicimus naturalem."

Here, one should compare the doctrine of Cajetan to the doctrine of Francis de Sylvestris Ferrariensis. As Feingold, *Natural Desire to See God*, 183n1, notes, Francis published his commentary on Thomas's *Summa contra Gentiles* shortly after Cajetan's commentary on the *Summa theologiae*. We see the same use of Aristotle's *dictum* in Francis's *In Summam contra Gentiles*, 3.51 [Leon. 14:141], as we do in Cajetan: "Si enim in individuis non esset talis potentia, nunquam naturae desiderium adimpleretur: sed si in illis sit capacitas rei desideratae, naturae desiderium quandoque in aliquo individuo adimpletur; et hoc sufficit ad hoc ut non sit inane et frustra." Francis goes on to develop a novel idea: that we have an active, specific desire for the vision of God as first cause.

Feingold appears to suggest that Francis's solution is to be preferred to this particular text (196). However, he does not treat Suárez's criticism of the view in *De fine hominis*, disp. 5, §3, nos. 7–14, in *Opera Omnia* (Paris: Vivès, 1856), 4:52–55; and again at disp. 15, §145, no. 4 [Vivès 4:145].

Quidditative knowledge of something is a sufficient *ratio* of all its properties, and every question concerning a thing is resolved by [this knowledge], as is said in *Physics* 4. Consequently, when something is known quidditatively, all of its natural potencies can be known from it. And since the knowledge of a potency depends on its act, as is said in *Metaphysics* 9, consequently, the acts to which its potencies correspond are known. And since these sorts of acts are supernatural, according to Scotus, it follows from first to last that from the quidditative knowledge of something natural, supernatural things are known. This is obviously false. And this is confirmed, because we certainly know this major premise: that no natural potency is in vain. Therefore, if we know this minor premise: that there is a natural potency for a supernatural act in matter, or the soul, or whatever else, we have to grant that we know that those supernatural things must exist. And thus we would know the future resurrection of the dead, and the grace that justifies the impious, etc. This is ridiculous![103]

Cajetan's argument makes sense if one accepts the premise upon which Cajetan bases it, namely, that a natural desire for a specific act arises from the formal, active principle in nature. What would be the point of a nature actively inclined to one specific act, which lacked the power to achieve that act? That was the problem that Giles had faced. Giles actually *had* affirmed that nature is positively inclined to the vision of God as toward one, specific act, and consequently could not see any way in which a providential God could create man without the possibility of achieving that end. Yet neither Thomas nor Scotus understood Aristotle's *dictum* in the manner

103. Cajetan, *Quaestio de natura receptivae potentiae*, p. 4 [Lyons 270b42]: "Quidditativa cognitio alicuius [est] sufficiens ratio omnium proprietatum eius, et ex ea solvantur omnes difficultates contingentes rei, ut in quarto *Phys.* dicitur. Consequens est, quod cognita quidditative re aliqua, cognosci ex ea possint omnes eius naturales potentiae: et quum potentiae cognitio ex actu pendeat, ut dicitur 9. *Meta.*, consequens est, quod actus, ad quos sunt naturales potentiae, cognoscantur, et cum huiusmodi actus sint supernaturales apud Scotum, sequitur de primo ad ultimum, quod ex cognitione quidditativa alicuius naturalis cognoscuntur supernaturalia: quod est manifeste falsum. Et confirmatur: quia certe scimus hanc maiorem, quod nulla naturalis potentia est frustra: ergo si scimus hanc minorem quod in materia vel anima, vel quacunque alia re est naturalis potentia ad actum supernaturalem, oportet concedere quod scimus supernaturalia illa debere esse: et sic sciemus resurrectionem mortuorum futuram, et gratiam iustificantem impium, etc. quod est ridiculum."

that Cajetan suggests. For Thomas and Scotus, since the specificity of our natural desire arises from the passive principle in our nature, not the active one, for a potency to be vain means that it is necessarily unable *to be fulfilled* (in the passive voice), not that a creature is unable *to fulfill it* (in the active voice). Thomas never said that we would know by natural reason that someone has, does, or will enjoy the vision of God. Questions of actuality were always theological, because the active power by which we achieve the fulfillment of our passive potency is given to us by a free gift of grace. All the more so was this the case for Scotus, for whom it is not even clear that we know by natural reason *pro statu isto* that our intellect is capable of the vision of God, and for whom, even if we could, this would only prove what it does for Thomas: that we *could* receive the beatific vision, *if* God chose to grant it.

Cajetan's doctrine of a specific, active, natural desire had two further consequences for his thought about how nature relates to grace: the adoption of a specific natural end for man apart from the vision of God, and the re-adoption of a potency for obedience. Of these, only the second is dealt with in any detail in the *Quaestio de natura receptivae potentiae*. There, since Cajetan had suggested that our natural inclination is restricted only to those specific acts which nature can achieve on its own, he has to add that our active, specific inclination only tends toward the fulfillment of passive potencies to which active powers in our nature correspond.[104] In order to account for our openness to grace, there must be some other potency in the soul, toward whose specific actualization our natural, active inclination cannot tend.[105] As Cajetan had otherwise arrived at something close to Albert's understanding of the desire for God, so now does he alight on something close to Albert's understanding of the relationship between nature and grace. He preserves Thomas's

104. Ibid., p. 4 [Lyons 207b30].

105. Ibid., p. 4 [Lyons 207b13]. One should note that Cajetan speaks customarily of a *potentia obedientialis* rather than a *potentia obedientiae*, where the medieval authors at times used one or the other of the two terms. There seems to have been a gradual shift in preference over several centuries from one to the other.

firm commitment to nature's passivity with respect to grace, but he does so by abandoning Thomas's natural appetite for the vision of God.[106]

In light of Cajetan's understanding of natural desire, he had a difficult time explaining those passages in the *Summa theologiae* where Thomas says that we have a natural desire for the vision of God. One such example is *Summa theologiae,* Ia, q. 12, a. 1, where Thomas argues from the impossibility that a natural desire be in vain that the vision of God must be possible. Cajetan comments on this article, "It does not seem true that a created intellect would naturally desire to see God, because nature does not bestow an inclination for that which the whole power of nature cannot produce."[107] Continuing, he supports this view with an exegesis of Thomas: "according to St. Thomas's ... doctrine, as was said in the first article of this work, man is ordered not naturally but obedientially to that happiness."[108] Cajetan concludes that our natural desire would be vain if the created intellect "could not" see God,[109] but his use of the verb *posse* refers to our active, not our passive potency.

Cajetan's argument, which circumvents Thomas's by confusing the question of possibility with the question of actuality, curious-

106. Bradley, *Aquinas on the Twofold Human Good,* 456.

107. Tommaso de Vio Cajetan, *In Primam partem,* q. 12, a. 1, no. 9 [Leon. 4:116]: "Non enim videtur verum quod intellectus creatus naturaliter desideret videre Deum: quoniam natura non largitur inclinationem ad aliquid, ad quod tota vis naturae perducere nequit."

108. Ibid.: "Apud s. Thomae ... doctrinam, ut dictum est in primo articulo huius operis, homo non naturaliter, sed obedientialiter ordinatur in felicitatem illam."

109. Ibid., no. 10: "Creatura rationalis potest dupliciter considerari: uno modo absolute, alio modo ut ordinata est ad felicitatem. Si primo modo consideretur, sic naturale eius desiderium non se extendit ultra naturae facultatem: et sic concedo quod non naturaliter desiderat visionem Dei in se absolute. Si vero secundo modo consideretur, sic naturaliter desiderat visionem Dei: quia, ut sic, novit quosdam effectus, puta gratiae et gloriae, quorum causa est Deus, ut Deus est in se absolute, non ut universale agens. Notis autem effectibus, naturale est cuilibet intellectuali desiderare notitiam causae. Et propterea desiderium visionis divinae, etsi non sit naturale intellectui creato absolute, est tamen naturale ei, supposita revelatione talium effectuum. Et sic tam ratio hic allegata, quam reliquae rationes ad idem collectae in cap. L. tertii Contra Gentes, concludunt inane fore desiderium intellectualis naturae creatae, si Deum videre non possit."

ly combines elements of Cajetan's own synthesis with elements of Thomas's. First, Cajetan denies natural knowledge of the possibility of the vision of God because he restricts both natural appetite and natural desire to a connatural end: since our natural desire does not concern the fulfillment of our obediential potency, the existence of our obediential potency first has to be revealed to us, and only then can we can desire its fulfillment. From there, Cajetan transposes Thomas's argument from the *Summa contra Gentiles* onwards about our natural desire for the vision of God from a natural to a supernatural basis. But Feingold points out a glaring inconsistency here. To be consistent, Cajetan would have had to have said that our subsequent natural desire for the vision of God would make the vision owed to nature in actual fact.[110]

A second text which Cajetan has difficulty interpreting is *Prima secundae*, q. 3, a. 8, where Thomas updates the argument *Prima pars*, q. 12, a. 1, to include the natural desire of the will:

> And note in the eighth article that those words of the text, that the human intellect, knowing only whether the first cause is, has a natural desire to know what the first cause is, do not lack ambiguity. The reason for this is that a natural desire does not exceed the power of nature, nor [is there a natural desire] of human nature's or any created nature's intellect for a supernatural operation.[111]

Cajetan's response is surprising. Having declined to consider natural potency subjectively and passively in the *Quaestio de natura receptivae potentiae*, here he uses that manner of considering natural potency as the solution to the argument: if we consider our nature insofar as it has been ordered by divine Providence to the vision of God, then we can say that we "naturally" desire the vision of God,

110. Feingold, *Natural Desire to See God*, 171.

111. Tommaso de Vio Cajetan, *In Primam secundae*, q. 3, a. 8, no. 1 [Leon. 6:36]: "Et averte in octavo articulo quod illa verba litterae, quod intellectus humanus, non cognita prima causa nisi an est, habet naturale desiderium ad cognoscendam primam causam quid est, etc., non carent ambiguitate; propterea quia naturale desiderium non excedit vim naturae, nec est ad supernaturalem operationem, non solum ipsius, sed omnis intellectus creati."

so long as the adverb "naturally" does not apply to the mode of that desire, since this would mean we had an active, specific desire for the vision of God arising from our nature.[112]

If Cajetan's view of natural desire differs from that of Thomas, this does not mean that Cajetan diverges from Thomas in every respect. Cajetan's adoption of a doctrine of obediential potency preserved Thomas's consistent teaching that man is absolutely passive with respect to grace.

> The soul's potency for grace is in a certain manner natural, insofar as the act of the free will, by which it is prepared for grace, is educed from the natural potency of the free will. But, it is supernatural insofar as that act, as a disposition for grace, can only occur solely from the gratuitous motion of God. And this form, namely grace, is of the highest order, above every order of nature.[113]

Cajetan here preserves an essential element of Thomas's understanding of the relationship between nature and grace, even if it places grace *supra totum naturae ordinem,* and so upsets the matter/form analogy which Thomas used for the relationship between nature and grace from the beginning of his career, as well as the idea that acts of grace are partly *secundum naturam* in their material principle, even if they are otherwise *supra naturam* in their formal principle.

Accordingly, Cajetan left Thomism with a mixed legacy. In one

112. Ibid.: "Sed haec citius solvuntur, si desiderium naturale distinguitur iuxta praedicta in I Libro, in principio. Desiderium namque potest dici naturale a natura ut subiecto tantum: et sic naturaliter desideramus visionem Dei. Et a natura ut subiecto et modo: et sic procedunt obiectiones." Cajetan goes on to add, "Posset quoque dici quod Auctor tractat de homine ut theologus.... Et sic, licet homini absolute non insit naturale huiusmodi desiderium, est tamen naturale homini ordinato a divina providentia in illam patriam, etc."

113. Ibid., q. 103, a. 10, no. 5 [Leon. 7:343]: "Potentia animae ad gratiam est quodammodo naturalis, pro quanto actus liberi arbitrii quo praeparatur ad gratiam, educitur de potentia naturali liberi arbitrii. Est autem supernaturalis, pro quanto actus ille, ut dispositio ad gratiam, a sola gratuita Dei motione esse potest; et forma ipsa, scilicet gratia, supremi ordinis est, super totum naturae ordinem...." See Ralph McInerny, *Praeambula Fidei: Thomism and the God of the Philosophers* (Washington, D.C.: The Catholic University of America Press, 2006), 80–81.

sense, he radically altered Thomas's doctrine of natural desire by confusing the soul's natural appetite and its natural desire. Where Thomas thought that generality should be attributed to our natural desire and specificity to our natural appetite, Cajetan thought that generality should be attributed to our natural appetite and specificity to our natural desire. For this reason, Cajetan argues that if we had a natural desire for the vision of God, it would prove the *actuality* of the vision of God and make that vision owed to nature. However, Cajetan did not diverge from Thomas in all respects. By positing a doctrine of obediential potency to account for nature's receptivity to grace, Cajetan saved Thomas's commitment to the idea that nature is passive with respect to grace, even if Cajetan lost sight of the fact that nature's passivity with respect to grace was intended by Thomas to be *natural.*

FRANCISCO SUÁREZ

However much influence Cajetan may have had on the Thomistic tradition, Francisco Suárez, SJ (1548–1617), had significantly more. As Feingold notes, most Thomists after Suárez would follow in broad terms his understanding of the desire for God, whether they read Suárez directly in the Jesuit tradition or they read his teaching mediately through John of St. Thomas in the Dominican tradition.[114]

Suárez begins his discussion of the desire for God with a little terminological housekeeping. Where Thomas distinguished passive natural appetite from active natural desire, and then distinguished natural desire from free desire, and where Scotus had used the term "natural appetite" in such a way as to refer to some of the activity which Thomas reserved for "natural desire," while distinguishing "natural appetite" from "elicited appetite," Suárez follows his Jesuit confrère and predecessor Gabriel Vasquez in banishing any use

114. Feingold, *Natural Desire to See God,* 267.

of the word "natural" from the discussion of the desire for God. Suárez's linguistic shift is purely pragmatic. He thinks that "natural" is susceptible to so many different possible meanings that it can easily be misunderstood.[115] Instead, Suárez prefers to speak of two kinds of appetites: innate and elicited.[116]

Suárez describes an innate appetite thus: "Properly, . . . it is nothing other than the natural propensity, which each and every thing has toward some good. In passive potencies, this inclination is nothing other than a natural capacity, and a proportion to its perfection, but in active potencies, it is the natural ability to act itself."[117] By including both active and passive potencies under the term "innate appetite," Suárez reveals his indebtedness to Scotus: innate appetite covers roughly the same conceptual territory as natural appetite does for Scotus. But since Scotus's natural appetite includes all of what Thomas understood by the term "natural appetite," as well as some of what Thomas understood by the term "natural desire," it might be more accurate to say that the combination of active and passive principles implied by Suárez's "innate appetite" is more akin to Thomas's *ratio seminalis* than to any other Thomistic term. Also following Scotus, Suárez also attributes positive existence to matter apart from form.[118] Suárez thus has no difficulty attributing to matter an innate appetite for form, just like Scotus.

Where Suárez comes closer to Thomas is in ascribing an innate

115. Francisco Suárez, *Disputationes Metaphysicae*, disp. 1, §6, no. 4, in *Opera Omnia* (Paris: Vivès, 1877), 25:54.

116. On this terminological shift, see Feingold, *Natural Desire to See God*, 218–21.

117. Suárez, *Disputationes metaphysicae*, disp. 1, §6, no. 3 [Vivès 25:53]: "Proprie . . . nihil aliud est quam naturalis propensio, quam unaquaeque res habet in aliquod bonum, quae inclinatio in potentiis passivis nihil aliud est quam naturalis capacitas, et proportio cum sua perfectione, in activis vero est ipsa naturalis facultas agendi." See also ibid., disp. 15, §6, no. 3 [Vivès 25:519]; *De fine hominis*, disp. 16, §1, no. 1 [Vivès 4:149]: "Omnis . . . potentia naturaliter inclinatur ad actum sibi connaturalem, praesertim ad perfectissimum: omne enim perfectibile appetit suam perfectionem."

118. Suárez, *Disputationes metaphysicae*, disp. 13, §4, nos. 8–9 [Vivès 25:411–12]. In no. 10 [Vivès 25:412], he goes on to support this doctrine with the same argument that Scotus had used.

appetite to the intellect and to the will for their respective ends.[119] Thomas had long identified a *ratio seminalis* in each. But the reduction of disparate active and passive components to a single term, implying complete correspondence between the active and passive powers in nature, was to have a similar effect on Suárez's understanding of innate appetite as it did on Cajetan's understanding of natural appetite. For both Suárez and Cajetan, innate appetites (to use Suárez's terminology), while they arise from the powers of nature, cannot exceed the faculties of nature. In Suárez, this is evident from the use of the word "proportion" in his definition of an innate appetite to describe the relationship between a passive potency and its act; it is also evident when he describes an active potency as a natural "ability" (*facultas*) to act. Here again, therefore, one sees the true extent of Thomas's synthesis of natural appetite and natural desire excluded by definition. The inclination of any passive potency toward the vision of God is excluded, because the vision of God is not proportioned to any passive potency in nature. The inclination of any active potency toward the complete fulfillment of such a passive potency is excluded, because there is no such thing as a natural, active power to see God.

If Suárez aligns with Cajetan in restricting innate desires by naturally achievable ends, Suárez's and Cajetan's respective accounts of innate desire are not alike in all respects. Suárez criticizes the manner in which Cajetan conceives of the innate appetite of the will, because when Cajetan says that a natural appetite posits no antecedent inclination of the will, but only a necessity with respect to specification (*necessitas quoad specificationem*), there are two ways that this could be understood: in the first way, the intellect presents an end to the will, which necessarily prompts the will to act of its own accord; in the second way, the object presented to the will acts as a partial efficient cause of the will's action.[120] The first is impossible,

119. Ibid., disp. 1, §6, no. 14 [Vivès 25:57]; disp. 13, §11, no. 14 [Vivès 25:444]; *De fine hominis*, disp. 16, §1, no. 3 [Vivès 4:150].

120. For what follows, see Suárez, *Tractatus de anima* 5, cap. 3, nos. 3–8, in *Opera*

Suárez argues, because it would destroy the freedom of the will if the will could be moved of necessity by an extrinsic object. The second, which Suárez takes to have been Cajetan's position, suggests that the will requires the intellect in order to be constituted in its first act. But the will, like every other power, is sufficient to constitute itself in its first act; it does not require the intellect in order simply to exist. Our historical reading of Thomas in chapters 2–5 confirms this insight: the position he associates with Cajetan is effectively that of Thomas from the *De veritate* to the *Quaestiones disputatae de anima*; the other position is the one which was imputed to Thomas from the *Sententia libri De anima* until just before the *De malo*. The position upon which Suárez alights represents the mature teaching of Thomas in the *Prima secundae* of the *Summa theologiae*.

By freeing the innate appetite of the will from determination by the intellect, Suárez, like Thomas and Scotus, was then able to assign it a specific *terminus*. Following Cajetan's misinterpretation of Thomas, Suárez interprets Aristotle's *dictum* that nature does nothing in vain to imply that it is not only possible for us to achieve the happiness which satisfies our innate appetite,[121] but also possible that some members of our species have, do, or will enjoy it.[122] The reason for this is:

> What never happens among any individuals of some species, no matter how much the species is multiplied, is rightly said to be impossible, if not physically or metaphysically, at least morally and in a human manner of speaking. Moreover, it pertains to the Author of Nature's Providence, and is in a certain manner due [*debitum*] to human nature itself that it be so guided toward its end that it can reach it.[123]

Omnia (Paris, Vivès, 1856), 3:758–61. Suárez provides several other arguments against Cajetan than the ones I will discuss here, but for reasons of space, I will include the ones most pertinent to the question of natural desire.

121. Suárez, *De fine hominis*, disp. 4, §3, no. 4 [Vivès 4:42].

122. Ibid., no. 6 [Vivès 4:42].

123. Ibid.: "Quod nunquam accidit in omnibus individuis alicujus speciei etiamsi quamplurima multiplicentur, merito dici potest impossibile, si non omnino physice, seu metaphysice, saltem moraliter, et humano modo loquendo: pertinet autem ad providentiam auctoris naturae, et quodammodo debitum est ipsi humanae naturae ita dirigi in suum finem, ut possit illum consequi." See also ibid., disp. 1, §4, no. 2 [Vivès 4:7].

Here, as in Giles, one encounters the language of "debt" applied to God with respect to creatures. Giles used it in a qualified sense to describe a necessity of fittingness for God to make man with the gift of original justice, lest humanity be created in such a way that it could not reach its final end. In Suárez, the word appears at least initially to be used in a less qualified and more definitive manner. However, Suárez goes on to issue the same sort of qualifier: "I did not say that the arguments just made were demonstrations, but rather extremely compelling moral arguments, which show the manner of Providence most befitting God's wisdom and goodness."[124] Suárez, like Giles, wants to avoid any hint of giving humanity Pelagian rights before God.

If Suárez thinks that his argument concerning the actuality of happiness is only an argument from fittingness, that does not stop him from employing it in other discussions of nature and grace. Describing the supernatural character of the vision of God, Suárez notes:

> If that happiness is supernatural, then God could, without a miracle, make man without ordering him to that happiness or providing him the mode or means by which he could reach it. [God] would do nothing against or beyond that which is due [*debitum*] to such a nature, but man, created thus, would necessarily have some natural happiness [*beatitudo naturalis*], at which he could arrive if he wished. Therefore it is necessary that some natural happiness in human nature be granted beyond its supernatural happiness.[125]

124. Ibid., disp. 4, §2, no. 7 [Vivès 4:43]: "Non dixi rationes factas esse demonstrationes, sed morales rationes multum suadentes et ostendentes modum providentiae maxime consentaneum divinae sapientiae et bonitati."

125. Ibid., disp. 4, §3, no. 3 [Vivès 4:44]: "Si beatitudo illa supernaturalis est, potuit ergo Deus absque miraculo condere hominem non ordinando illum ad illam beatitudinem, nec providendo illi modum, aut media, quibus illam consequi possit, in quo nihil ageret contra, vel praeter id, quod debitum est tali naturae; sed homo sic conditus necessario habiturus esset aliquam beatitudinem naturalem ad quam, si velit, possit pervenire: ergo necesse est praeter supernaturalem beatitudinem dari in humana natura aliquam beatitudinem naturalem."

Suárez's statement here seems to be at odds with the qualifier he had just issued about the language of debt. On the one hand, if God has no debt to creatures, then the argument advanced by Suárez can only be construed as an argument of fittingness, not a demonstration. Nevertheless, Suárez says that the conclusion is "necessary," and explains the minor term by arguing from the fact that human nature is "capable of some proportionate happiness that is connatural with it," to the idea that "it is necessary that some natural happiness in human nature be granted beyond its supernatural happiness."[126] Either Suárez has spoken imprecisely, or there is some further layer of subtlety to his argument.

If one considers again that Suárez thinks that innate appetites are always proportionate to natural powers, the missing term in the above argument emerges more clearly. Suárez fills it in a bit later on:

> It is possible for man to reach this natural happiness by means which are proportionate and suitable to nature. This conclusion can be proved first by common arguments: that the means must be proportionate to the end, hence we gather that supernatural means must be necessary in order to reach supernatural happiness; likewise, since nature does not incline toward an end except by sufficient means, and the Author of Nature does not institute or order the one [that is, nature] except by the other [that is, proportionate means to its end], since Providence would be very diminished [otherwise]; likewise, since every other created nature can reach its natural end by means befitting the nature—why therefore would human nature be in a worse condition in this matter?[127]

126. Ibid., no. 4 [Vivès 4:44]: "Homo sic creatus haberet aliquem finem ultimum, et illum posset suis actionibus aliquo modo attingere cognoscendo et amando illum: ergo esset capax alicujus beatitudinis proportionatae et connaturalis sibi: ergo in humana natura datur aliqua beatitudo naturalis praeter superanturalem."

127. Ibid., disp. 15, §2, no. 6 [Vivès 4:147–48]: "Possibile est hominem consequi hanc beatitudinem naturalem per media naturae proportinata et consentanea. Haec conclusio probari potest primo rationibus communibus, quod media esse debent proportionata fini, hinc enim colligimus ad superanturalem beatitudinem assequendam necessaria esse superanturalia media. Item, quia natura non inclinat ad finem nisi per sufficientia media: neque auctor naturae unum instituit, seu ordinat nisi per aliud, quia esset valde diminuta providentia. Item quia omnes aliae naturae creatae possunt assequi suos fines naturales per media consentanea naturae; cur ergo natura humana erit in hoc pejoris conditionis?"

According to Suárez, since innate desires are proportionate to naturally achievable ends, if man has an innate desire for happiness, it must be the case that man has the natural means of obtaining that happiness. Consequently, if God were to establish man in a state without the call or the means to the vision of God, man would be able to use the means provided by nature to achieve the happiness to which those means are proportioned.[128]

However, saying that human nature has the means to reach a proportionate end and that human nature could choose to apply those means to that proportionate end is not the same as saying that human nature would, if established without any grace, actually reach a proportionate natural happiness. Suárez recognizes that any number of impediments could, in fact, prevent human nature from successfully reaching that proportionate happiness.[129] God would not be bound in a strict sense to govern human affairs so as to remove these impediments and to ensure that man *actually* reached the happiness which he otherwise *could* reach.

> This providence would not be due to man, properly speaking, but would come from a certain liberality of God, which, if I may so speak, God would owe to himself, that is, to his Providence, his wisdom, and his goodness. But it would differ from the Providence of grace in this: man would not be elevated to a supernatural end or to supernatural means by it; rather, only impediments would be removed so that man could carry out his natural activity well. Yet God did provide better for man, and take away every difficulty, by conferring grace and supernatural gifts upon him.[130]

Suárez's argument is very subtle. Like Thomas, Suárez holds that our capacity for happiness proves only the possibility, not the actuality, of achieving it. However, unlike Thomas, Suárez holds that our

128. Ibid., disp. 16, §1, no. 10 [Vivès 4:153].

129. Ibid., disp. 15, §2, no. 9 [Vivès 4:148].

130. Ibid., no. 11: "Haec autem providentia non esset debita homini, proprie loquendo, sed esset ex quadam liberalitate Dei, quam, ut ita dicam, Deus sibi ipsi deberet, id est, suae providentiae et sapientiae, ac bonitati. Differret autem a providentia gratiae in hoc, quod per eam non elevaretur homo ad finem, vel media supernaturalia, sed tantum tollerentur impedimenta, ut posset bene naturaliter operari: melius autem Deus homini providit, et omnes difficultates abstulit, gratiam et supernaturalia dona illi conferendo."

desire for happiness is restricted to a naturally achievable happiness. Thus, while for Suárez it can be demonstrated that man could be created without grace, with a natural end, and with natural means to that end (which would otherwise seem to be the same as saying that he would *actually* achieve that end), Suárez relies on the freedom of God's Providence to argue that God would not be bound to bring humanity to that natural end in actual fact.

Given his insistence that man's natural desire must have a naturally achievable end, Suárez encounters the difficulty, with Cajetan, of explaining what Thomas was supposed to have meant when he describes man as having a natural desire (or in Suárez's language, an "innate appetite") for the vision of God. Here Suárez makes his own the common recognition: "Thomas's discussion here is very difficult. . . ."[131] Suárez's solution is to put aside the question of innate appetite and to focus only on elicited appetite ("free desire" in thirteenth-century parlance). By his own power man can elicit a conditional appetite for the vision of God, "if it were possible."[132] This desire can proceed from two sources. If it proceeds from a judgment of natural reason, then failing to achieve it causes no harm, since natural reason does not know that God has chosen to provide the means toward this vision; the vision of God thus appears as something impossible. If it proceeds from an encounter with Revelation, which reveals to us the existence of our obediential potency for the vision of God as well as the existence of grace, then, as for Cajetan, the desire becomes in some way insatiable without the possession of that vision.[133] But even here Suárez distinguishes himself from Cajetan. The insatiability of the desire does not proceed principally from the Revelation of the existence of our obediential potency. To say so would be the equiva-

131. Suárez, *De divina substantia ejusque attributis* 2, cap. 9, in *Opera Omnia (Paris:* Vivès, 1856), 1:66: "Hic discursus D. Thomae est valde difficilis. . . ." Suárez makes this comment when discussing the text of *ST*, Ia, q. 12, a. 1, although he elsewhere distances himself from other scholastics who proclaim, "D. Thomas autem non videtur satis clare in hac materia locutus." See Suárez, *De fine hominis*, disp. 16, §1, no. 6 [Vivès 4:152].

132. Suárez, *De fine hominis*, disp. 16, §2, no. 7 [Vivès 4:155].

133. Ibid., no. 8 [Vivès 4:156].

lent of admitting an innate desire for the fulfillment of an obediential potency, something which Suárez is careful to avoid.[134] Rather, the insatiability comes principally from the revelation of the existence of the end, together with the offer of the necessary means. Man's natural, elicited appetite for the vision of God always contains the condition, "if it were possible." But revelation tells us that it is possible, thus changing the character of the appetite.

Like Cajetan, Suárez left Thomism with a mixed legacy. Agreeing with Cajetan's premise that innate appetites (in Suárez's language) must be able to be fulfillable by natural active powers, Suárez argued that humanity could be created in a state without grace, called "pure nature," in which it was left to seek the end of its innate appetite with natural powers. The conclusion is consistent with Thomas's view of the souls of unbaptized infants, but the means of drawing that conclusion are somewhat inconsistent with Thomas's understanding of natural appetite and natural desire. For Suárez, man's "natural" desire for the vision of God can only be a conditional, elicited desire, which seeks the vision of God "if it were possible." The conditionality of the desire is consistent with Thomas, who in the *Summa contra Gentiles* adopted the same condition from Avicenna's account of the natural desire of the souls of the heavenly bodies in order to show how human nature seeks a higher perfection than Aristotelian contemplation. But the location of the condition is not consistent with Thomas. Distinguishing in what Suárez calls "innate appetite" between a passive natural appetite and an active natural desire, Thomas located the condition in the active component of what Suárez calls "innate appetite," not in the free desire which Suárez calls "elicited appetite." This allowed Thomas to show with Augustine that the vision of God is not only the explicit desire of those who have come to think about it, but also the implicit desire of all human persons, who are propelled by their nature to seek the fulfillment of their natural appetite insofar as it is possible.

134. Ibid., no. 4 [Vivès 4:155].

THE AEGIDIAN TRADITION

Each of the figures discussed above gave rise to a tradition about nature, grace, and the desire for God. Among Thomists, the Dominican and Jesuit traditions are well known; Feingold has given us a summary of them which is difficult to surpass for its clarity and breadth. But as the principal purpose of the present chapter is ultimately to arrive at Henri de Lubac, we must turn now to a tradition which is less well-known today, but nevertheless exercised a decisive influence on de Lubac's thought: the scholastic tradition arising from within the Order of the Hermits of Saint Augustine.

The theological tradition of the Augustinian Order was for a long time known as "Aegidian," after Giles of Rome ("Aegidius Romanus" in Latin).[135] This tradition had a difficult history. It suffered severe academic decline in the fourteenth and fifteenth centuries.[136] Following the excommunication of Martin Luther, who was himself a member of the Order, it was yet more severely wounded when entire provinces of the Order were lost at the Protestant Reformation.[137] Nevertheless, in spite of difficulties in numbers and in influence, the Aegidian tradition continued to exist in the Post-Tridentine period as a theological alternative to the Dominican and Jesuit Thomistic traditions.

The chief difficulty facing the Aegidian tradition in the Post-Reformation period was the advent of two extreme Augustinianisms: those of Michel de Bay ("Baius") (1513–89),[138] and of Cor-

135. It was at times also known as "Augustinian." But given the variety of "Augustinianisms" in the medieval and early modern periods, I will refer to it exclusively as "Aegidian."

136. David Gutiérrez, *The Augustinians in the Middle Ages, 1357–1517*, vol. 1, pt. 2, of *History of the Order of St. Augustine* (Villanova, Penn.: Augustinian Historical Institute, 1983), 123–26.

137. Gutiérrez, *Augustinians from the Protestant Reformation*, 19–42.

138. The works of Baius relevant to this controversy are collected in Michael Baius, *Opuscula theologica* (Louvain: Joannes Bogard, 1566). The propositions censured by Pius V can be found in *Enchiridion Symbolorum*, 43rd. ed., ed. Heinrich Denzinger and Peter Hünermann (San Francisco: Ignatius Press, 2012), *nos.* 1901–80.

nelius Jansen (1585–1638).[139] Both of these Augustinianisms shared important commitments with the Aegidian tradition: first, the beatific vision is the only possible end for human nature;[140] second, human nature is subject to a certain natural rebellion of the body against the soul, such that the human person is not able to persevere in the good on his or her own, even if created in a hypothetical state of pure nature.[141] But there were also two significant differences between the new Augustinianisms and the Aegidian tradition: first, Baius and Jansen absolutized Giles's notion of *debitum*; second, they applied it to the gifts of supernatural grace and glory instead of preternatural justice. For Baius, God would not only be constrained to grant us original justice in a state of pure nature but also the beatific vision as our reward for keeping the natural law.[142] For Jansen, God would at least not be constrained to grant the beatific vision to purely natural acts, but God would be constrained in strict justice to create us in original grace in order for us to have the opportunity of reaching our final end.[143] In either case, what were for Giles and the other scholastics God's gifts became his strict debts: glory for Baius,[144] and grace for Jansen.[145]

Opinions diverged within the Aegidian tradition over how best to continue to defend the natural desire for a supernatural end after the work of Baius and Jansen. One approach was to deny the application of *debitum* to supernatural grace by conceding to the Dominican and Jesuit traditions the idea that human nature can come to rest in a natural end which differs from its supernatural end. This approach is found in the work of Michael Paludanus, OESA (1593–

139. The main work of Jansen relevant to this controversy is the posthumously published *Augustinus*, 3 vols. (Louvain: Jacques Zegers, 1640).

140. For Baius, see *De meritis operum*, lib. 1, cap. 2–3, in *Opuscula theologica*, 3–7. For Jansen, see *De statu purae naturae*, lib. 2, cap. 2–3, in *Augustinus*, vol. 2, col. 681–92.

141. For Baius, see *De prima hominis iustitia*, lib. 1, cap. 4, in *Opuscula theologica*, 52. For Jansen, see *De statu purae naturae*, lib. 2, cap. 20–21 [Zegers, vol. 2, col. 867–76].

142. Baius, *De meritis operum*, lib. 1, cap. 2, in *Opuscula theologica*, 5–7.

143. Jansen, *De statu purae naturae*, lib. 1, cap. 2 [Zegers vol. 2, col. 685].

144. Baius, *De prima hominis iustitia*, lib. 1, cap. 9–11, in *Opusculum theologica*, 61–66.

145. Jansen, *De statu purae naturae*, lib. 1, cap. 15 [Zegers vol. 2, col. 745–52].

1653). In his *Treatise on Our End and on Happiness,*[146] Paludanus borrows from Suárez and teaches that man has an innate, natural desire, which terminates in naturally achievable knowledge of God.[147] Paludanus adds that this naturally achievable end cannot be called our "final end," nor can it be called a "different" end from our supernatural end, as though our natural end and our supernatural end were two parallel ways of fulfilling our human nature. Rather, our natural end is an imperfect participation of our final end, which, though it does not satisfy all of our capacity for God, is still satisfying in a certain respect.[148] Paludanus's position had the advantage of avoiding any difficulty with the gratuity of the vision of God. Yet his conciliatory approach hardly won over fellow Aegidians, who sought a more faithful preservation of their Aegidian patrimony.

A second approach was to concede the application of *debitum* to supernatural grace, but to reintroduce Giles's distinction between an absolute debt and a debt of fittingness. This more common approach can be found in the works of Enrico Noris, OESA (1631–1704), Fulgenzio Bellelli, OESA (1675–1742), and Giovanni Lorenzo Berti, OESA (1696–1766). Berti gave the most complete systematic pre-

146. Michael Paludanus, *Tractatus de fine et beatitudine* (Louvain: Andrea Bouvetius, 1664).

147. Ibid., disp. 13, part. 2 [Louvain 254B–55A]. On Suárez, see Francisco Suárez, *De ultimo fine hominis ac beatitudo,* disp. 16 § ult., no. 2, in *Opera Omnia* (Paris, Vivès, 1856), 4:154. As for the nature of that happiness, see disp. 15, § 1, no. 3 [Vivès 4:145].

148. See Paludanus, *Tractatus de fine et beatitudine,* disp. 13 [Louvain 247A], where Paludanus makes an explicit association between *beatituto imperfecta* and *beatitudo naturalis,* contrasting them with *beatitudo perfecta/supernaturalis.* Subsequently, in part 2 of this *disputatio* [Louvain 255A], he explains the nature of the distinction between *beatitudo naturalis* and *beatitudo supernaturalis*: "Respondeo, omnino nos eam [distinctionem] admittere, non tamen tamquam eam, quae sit generis in species, aut alicuius alterius univoci in sua univocata, sed analogi in sua analogata, et quae sit similis divinisioni, qua aliquid divideretur in id quod est simpliciter tale, et in id quod non est tale nisi secundum quid." In part 3 of the *disputatio* [Louvain 256B–57A], he describes the act of *beatitudo naturalis* in greater detail: "Respondeo, in beatitudine naturali Deum se non habere sicut formam aut actum beatificantem, qui immediate sic nobis coniungatur ut eum possideamus nosque se ipso perficiat (quo modo se habet in beatitudine supernaturali). Nullum enim donum ordinis naturalis eo modo Deum homini potest coniungere; sed habet se solummodo tamquam obiectum alicuius nostri actus, illius scilicet cognitionis abstractivae, quae ad naturalem beatitudinem requiritur."

sentation of their thought.[149] As Berti reasons, man cannot be said to have a right to grace and glory under any circumstances because those gifts lay outside our natural faculties; we have no right and title to what we cannot achieve of our own accord.[150] However, even if there is no need to postulate a natural happiness for man, a state of pure nature is not altogether unthinkable. God could *de potentia absoluta* create humanity in a state in which our only final end, the beatific vision, would be outside our reach.[151] Persons created in this state would be called by desire to see God, but not ordered by grace to do so.[152] Nevertheless, we can hardly imagine a state in which God would do this if we consider *de potentia ordinata* the Providence by which God arranges all things for the good.[153]

A third approach was to concede the application of Giles's *debitum* to supernatural grace but to relativize human nature's end. This approach can be found in the works of Fulgence Lafosse, OESA (c. 1640–*post*-1684).[154] On the surface of things, Lafosse and Berti seem to agree: God could create man and not order him to the beatific vision; this would not be contrary to God's justice absolutely, even if it would be contrary to his Providence.[155] But where, for

149. Giovanni Berti, *De theologicis disciplinis,* 10 vols. (Naples: Gaetano Migliaccio, 1776–84). The main works of Noris and Bellelli, while still of intellectual value, are more polemical in nature. See Enrico Noris, *Vindiciae Augustinianae* (Brussells: Lambert Marchant, 1675); Fulgenzio Bellelli, *Mens Augustini de statu creaturae rationalis ante peccatum* (Lucerne: Anna Felicitas Hauttin, 1711); and *Mens Augustini de modo reparationis humanae naturae post lapsum adversus Baium et Jansenium,* 2 vols. (Rome: Bernabò, 1737). For a more thorough bibliography of primary sources for this period, including unpublished works, see Bocxe, *Introduction to the Teaching of the Italian Augustinians,* 6–10.

150. See Berti, *Additamentum* lib. 12, cap. 2, in *De theologicis disciplinis* (Naples: Gaetano Migliaccio, 1776), 3:79B.

151. A similar position to that of Berti was already foreseen by Suárez, who, though he thought it unlikely, at least affirmed that it was possible. See Suárez, *De ultimo fine hominis ac beatitudo,* vol. 4, disp. 4, § 2, no. 7 [Vivès 4:43].

152. Berti, *Additamentum* lib. 12, cap. 3 [Naples 3:83A].

153. Ibid. [Naples 3:83B–84B].

154. Jean-Robert Armogathe, "Histoire des idées religieuses et scientifiques dans l'Europe moderne," *Annuaire de l'École pratique des hautes études (EPHE), Section des sciences religieuses* 117 (2008–9), 330. Lafosse's main contribution to the Aegidian tradition is his *Augustinus theologus,* 3 vols. (Toulouse: Guillaume Bosc, 1676–83).

155. Lafosse, *Augustinus theologus,* 3:52.

Berti, being called to the vision of God by desire is a necessary feature of human nature, even if being ordered to it by grace is not, Lafosse argues—in a way more faithfully to Giles—that even our call to the beatific vision is contingent. In every state, humanity desires that end which God has assigned to us; but since God has called us *in the present, historical state* to the beatific vision, human nature has a natural desire for its supernatural end.[156] The contingency of this desire's end opens up for Lafosse, as for Paludanus, the possibility of a natural happiness for man in a state in which humanity has been neither called by desire nor ordered by grace to the beatific vision. But where Paludanus thinks that human nature as we presently experience it could be satisfied by such a natural happiness, Lafosse thinks that human nature as we presently experience it has been so altered by its call to the beatific vision that it cannot be satisfied by a natural happiness. This does not mean that the beatific vision is in any way owed to human nature once humanity has been called to it. Similar to Berti, Lafosse argues that having a natural desire for the vision of God does not make the vision owed to human nature, because the fulfillment of that desire lays outside our nature's reach.[157]

A fourth approach was to concede the application of a *debitum* to supernatural grace, even in an absolute sense, but to relativize human nature itself even more radically. This approach can be found in the *Institutiones theologicae* of Michelangelo Marcelli, OESA (d. 1804).[158] Like Berti and unlike Lafosse, Marcelli sees a necessary connection between God's creating human nature and his calling it to himself with a natural desire for the vision of God.[159] Yet unlike Berti and somewhat like Jansen, Marcelli radicalizes the debt arising from that call. According to Marcelli, when God made intellectual creatures with a desire to see him, God was "bound" (*tenebatur*)

156. Ibid., 3:169.

157. Ibid., 3:174, 182–83.

158. Michelangelo Marcelli, *Institutiones theologicae,* 7 vols. (Foligno: Francesco Xavier Tomassino, 1847–51).

159. Ibid., 3:345–46.

to order them to that desire's fulfillment by grace.[160] Contrast that statement with Berti, who explicitly states that God "was in no way bound" (*nullo titulo teneretur*) to give us grace at all.[161]

To preserve the gratuity of grace in view of the debt arising from God's choice to make an intellectual creature, Marcelli suggests that while God can *de potentia absoluta* create man and not call him to the vision of God, this would entail having not to create man in the *imago Dei*.[162] Since, however, being made in the *imago Dei* is synonymous with having a reason and free will,[163] the unstated conclusion—which was understood by others to have been implied by Marcelli's argument—is that for God to make man in a state of pure nature would require that God *de potentia absoluta* perform the impossible by an extraordinary act of divine power: make an irrational-rational creature.[164] Theologically, at least, God is not constrained to grant us the beatific vision. But the metaphysical means of avoiding that constraint require a voluntarist extremism which the rest of the Aegidian tradition had carefully avoided.

HENRI DE LUBAC

De Lubac's Early Work

Henri de Lubac, SJ, was aware of the Aegidian tradition and relied upon it throughout his career to help him articulate his doctrine of a natural desire for a supernatural end. The importance of this tra-

160. Ibid., 3:344–45: "Quod antequam argumentis confirmare incipiamus, animadvertimus non loqui nos de potentia Dei absoluta. Si namque Deus alterius ordinis hominem produceret, non dubitamus quin posset illi suae gratiae donum denegare. Sed loquimur de potentia, ut inquiunt, ordinaria. Supposito nempe quod hominem ad imaginem ac similitudinem suam condiderit, quum ratio imaginis ordinationem importet ad Deum ipsum intuitive videndum tamquam ad ultimum finem, quem absque gratiae auxilio assequi non valet, tenebatur Deus aliquo titulo supernaturalis gratiae ornamento illum fulcire. Dixi, *aliquo titulo*: hoc est, *non propter exigentiam rei creatae, sed propter decentiam Creatoris*, ut verbis utar Eminentissimi Norisii" (emphasis in original).

161. Berti, *Additamentum* lib. 12, cap. 3 [Naples 3:83A].

162. Marcelli, *Institutiones theologicae* 3:344–45.

163. Ibid., 3:345.

164. See Sestili, *De naturali intelligentis animae capacitate*, 150.

dition in questions of natural desire had been known and discussed throughout his formation, and in the first article de Lubac wrote on nature and grace (1931),[165] he explicitly references Berti's branch of the Aegidian tradition as a helpful means of upholding the natural desire for a supernatural end without lapsing into Baius's and Jansen's "strict debt" of grace.[166] The topic addressed in that article concerned the possibility of a state of pure nature, defined as a state in which man is neither called by desire nor ordered by grace to the beatific vision. By maintaining the call but denying the ordering, Berti's branch of the Aegidian tradition protected the supernaturality and gratuity of the vision. By contrast, Baius denied the possibility of a state of pure nature because he denied that the call has a properly natural end; Jansen denied the possibility of a state of pure nature because he denied that the ordering to our final end is properly gratuitous.

De Lubac returned to the Aegidian tradition in his second article on nature and grace (1934) in order to defend the tradition from criticism by Réginald Garrigou-Lagrange, OP.[167] Garrigou-Lagrange had effectively accused Berti's branch of the Aegidian tradition of Baianism for failing to distinguish between a natural order with a naturally achievable end and a supernatural order with a supernaturally achievable end; anyone who postulates a natural desire for a supernatural end naturalizes the vision of God.[168] In response, de

165. Henri de Lubac, "Deux Augustiniens fourvoyés: Baïus et Jansénius," *Recherches de Science Religieuse* 2, nos. 4–5 (1931): 422–33; 513–40.

166. Ibid., 400, especially n. 38. This text was included in de Lubac, *Surnaturel*, 33–34. De Lubac is describing the historical circumstances of challenges to the Aegidian tradition. Bellelli, de Lubac observes, was criticized for denying the possibility of pure nature, as though his doctrine were no different from that of Baius. De Lubac argues that Berti rightly defended Bellelli, because while Bellelli and Berti both denied the possibility of pure nature in order to preserve the supernatural character of nature's destiny, Baius (and later Jansen) denied it in order to form an anthropology in which all of human existence is effectively carried out in a state of pure nature.

167. Henri de Lubac, "Remarques sur l'histoire du mot 'Surnaturel,'" *Nouvelle revue théologique* 61 (1934): 225–49, 350–70.

168. Réginald Garrigou-Lagrange, "La possibilité de la vision béatifique peut-elle se démontrer?" *Revue Thomiste* 38, no. 80 (1933): 669–88. Cf. de Lubac, "Deux Augustiniens

Lubac added to his previous support for Berti's Aegidianism an argument from authority: not only had Berti's branch of the Aegidian tradition denied a strict debt of grace on God's part, but in combining the affirmation of a natural desire for a supernatural end with the denial of a strict debt of grace, it gave the authentic interpretation of Thomas Aquinas.[169] Quoting a text of Robert Bellarmine, which de Lubac takes as a summary of the entire scholastic tradition, de Lubac notes that the vision of God "is natural with respect to desire, but not with respect to achievement."[170] The implication is that it was Garrigou-Lagrange (following Cajetan) who naturalized the end of man, not Berti.

Surnaturel

When in 1946 de Lubac republished the two aforementioned articles on nature and grace in part one of *Surnaturel*,[171] he bolstered his previous support of the Aegidian tradition with a more detailed defense against the criticism of Garrigou-Lagrange. Calling the Aegidian tradition "the Augustinian School *par excellence*,"[172] De Lubac claims

fourvoyé," 400. In *Surnaturel*, the reference to the Aegidian tradition was moved to the discussion of pure nature (101n1), and was separated from the reference to Garrigou-Lagrange.

169. De Lubac, "Remarques sur l'histoire du mot 'Surnaturel,'" 248n2.

170. Robert Bellarmine, *De gratia primi hominis* 1.4, in *Opera omnia*, vol. 5, ed. Justin Fèvre (Paris: Vivès, 1873), 191, cited in De Lubac, "Remarques sur l'histoire du mot 'Surnaturel,'" 248n2: "Respondeo beatitudinem finem hominis naturalem esse quoad appetitum, non quoad consecutionem."

171. For a helpful chart, which indicates how and where de Lubac's early work on nature and grace was included in his later work, see Michel Sales, preface to Henri de Lubac, *Surnaturel: Études historiques* (Paris: Lethielleux, 2010), xiv.

172. De Lubac, *Surnaturel*, 164–65: "L'école augustinienne par excellence, ou du moins par dénomination propre—celle que forment les ermites de saint Augustin—est plus formelle encore. Illustrée successivement par Frédéric Gavardi, par Henri Noris, par Fulgence Belleli [sic] et par [Jean] Laurent Berti, elle maintient au milieu des contradictions sa doctrine inchangée. C'est par erreur qu'on lui prête communément, dans l'intention de la distinguer de l'école janséniste, l'idée d'une possibilité métaphysique de la 'pure nature' et d'une nécessité seulement 'morale,' du surnaturel, en raison de la sagesse et de la bonté du Créateur. Du moins cette nécessité morale—*attenta Dei providentia*—concerne-t-elle chez eux non pas la fin, mais le moyen; le secours de grâce et la lumière de gloire, non la destinée elle-même; ou, si l'on préfère, le don effectif de la béatitude à

that Garrigou-Lagrange's criticism confuses two distinct questions: the supernaturality of man's end and the gratuity of the means of obtaining it. The Aegidian tradition had never called into question the supernaturality of man's final end nor had its members ever suggested that God has any "debt" of offering glory to humanity (that was Baius's position). The whole question of a "debt" (albeit a debt of fittingness) concerned the means (grace), not the end (glory).[173]

If all de Lubac did in *Surnaturel* was continue his support of Berti, there would have been significantly less controversy in the years that followed. However, where in his previous articles de Lubac relied on Berti's branch of the Aegidian tradition exclusively, he includes in *Surnaturel* several positive references to Marcelli. With Marcelli, de Lubac acknowledges a distinction between man considered "as a species" and man considered "in the image of God."[174] As a species, man can be considered apart from a supernatural end, but insofar as human nature is created in the image of God, it must be a) endowed with reason, and b) called to the vision of God. De Lubac does not explicitly attribute this position to Marcelli. But based upon this Marcellian distinction de Lubac goes on to quote Marcelli thus: "from the fact that God ordered man to the vision of himself as to his ultimate end, by establishing [man] in his image, it follows that a state of pure nature is impossible."[175] Following this application of the species/image distinction to Marcelli's understanding of human

l'individu, non l'ordination de la nature à cette béatitude. La créature raisonnable, dit par example Gavardi, ne peut avoir d'autre fin dernière que la possession de Dieu; tel est son principal point de départ pour établir que Dieu doit la créer 'dans la grâce.' Selon Noris, il serait moralement impossible que, dans l'état d'innocence, l'appétit sensible ne fût point soumis à la raison. Selon Belleli [sic] et Berti, Dieu doit pareillement à sa sagesse et à sa bonté d'accorder à l'homme la grâce, c'est'à-dire le moyen qui seul lui permettra d'atteindre sa fin; car, étant donné que l'homme est fait à l'image de Dieu, c'est-à-dire doué de raison, il est ordonné à voir Dieu. Aucun d'eux ne met en doute que la fin d l'être spirituel ne soit en toute hypothèse la béatitude, telle que la définissait saint Thomas, c'est-à-dire ce que nous appelons et ce qu'ils appellent eux-mêmes la fin surnaturelle."

173. Ibid., 168–70.

174. Ibid., 168.

175. Marcelli, *Institutiones theologicae*, 3:146, quoted in de Lubac, *Surnaturel*, 166: "ex quo Deus, ad imaginem suam condendo illum, ad suipsius ordinaverit visionem, tanquam ad ultimum finem, sequitur impossibilem esse statum purae naturae."

nature, de Lubac proceeds to deploy the distinction between God's *potentia absoluta* and God's *potentia ordinata* distinction in support of the gratuity of grace:

> We could not dream of contesting, [Marcelli] says in the name of his entire school, that God could, by his absolute power, designate such an other end for man as pleases him; that is enough for man not to have any right to require anything [from God], since if the introduction of the concept of "ordered power" renders hypotheses objectively realizable, it does not confer any new title at all to a creature of which it could boast.[176]

With the deployment of the *absoluta/ordinata* distinction in concert with the species/image distinction, de Lubac thus sets up the first two steps of Marcelli's argument. He does not, however, draw the conclusion explicitly.

De Lubac's use of Marcelli leaves de Lubac's thought subject to a certain ambiguity at this point in his career. Does de Lubac intend for us to draw a conclusion that he is unwilling to state, namely, that a man who was not called to the vision of God would be a man who was not made in the image of God? Or has he not read Marcelli thoroughly enough so that a) he confuses Marcelli's position with that of Berti, or b) he does not realize the full extent of the consequences of Marcelli's position? De Lubac does not answer these questions in *Surnaturel.* In fact, the difficulty of answering them is compounded by the fact that his earlier defenses of Berti also appear in *Surnaturel.* Intellectual charity suggests that we not accuse de Lubac of embracing an extreme position without sufficient evidence to do so. But his use of Marcelli does at least raise an important question as to his precise understanding of the natural desire for a supernatural end.

176. De Lubac, *Surnaturel,* 169: "Nous ne songeons pas à contester, dit-il au nom de toute son école, que par sa puissance absolue Dieu puisse désigner à l'homme telle autre fin qu'il lui plaît; cela suffit pour que l'homme ne soit en droit de rien exiger, car, si l'introduction du concept de 'puissance ordonnée' réduit les hypothèses objectivement réalisables, elle ne confère pour autant à la créature aucun titre nouveau dont celle-ci pourrait se prévaloir."

"Duplex hominis beatitudo" and "Le mystère du surnaturel"

After *Surnaturel,* de Lubac clarified his thinking about nature, grace, and the desire for God in two articles that appeared before the end of the 1940s. The first, "Duplex hominis beatitudo," published in 1948, defends his Aegidian reading of Thomas.[177] The second, "Le mystère du surnaturel," published the following year, develops de Lubac's relationship with the Aegidian tradition by shifting his primary emphasis from Berti and Marcelli to Lafosse.

In "Duplex hominis beatitudo," de Lubac takes up the question of those passages in the Thomistic corpus in which Thomas seems to speak of the possibility of a happiness that is proportioned to human nature.[178] Calling into question the idea that these passages can be thought of as describing the end of man in a hypothetical state of pure nature,[179] de Lubac argues that the only "natural" happiness of which Thomas speaks "is an imperfect, worldly, and temporal happiness."[180] By isolating natural happiness within the context of the present life, and thus identifying the vision of God as the only possible end for man in Thomas's writings, the article supports de Lubac's Aegidian reading of the Thomistic tradition.

Although de Lubac does not devote a large amount of space in "Duplex hominis beatitudo" to his own argumentation, preferring to let the array of texts he references from the Thomistic corpus speak largely for itself, we can see how the article contributes to de Lubac's Aegidian reading of Thomas if we compare what de Lubac says in it to the exegesis of Thomas given above in chapters 2–5. As we saw above in chapter 2, Thomas used the earthly nature of Aristotelian beatitude as an initial means of harmonizing Aristotle's vision of hu-

177. Henri de Lubac, "Duplex hominis beatitudo (Saint Thomas, 1a 2ae, q. 62, a. 1)," *Recherches de Science Religieuse* 35 (1948): 200–99.

178. De Lubac had already given many of these passages an initial treatment in *Surnaturel,* 451–65.

179. De Lubac, "Duplex hominis beatitudo," 291.

180. Ibid., 293: "C'est une béatitude imparfaite, terrestre et temporelle ..."

man happiness with Christian revelation in his *Commentary on the Sentences.*[181] In this sense, de Lubac is right to point out the temporal nature of Aristotelian beatitude. However, we saw above in chapter 3 that while Thomas realized as a matter of historical record that Aristotle's understanding of happiness was confined to this world, Thomas did not think that Aristotle's understanding of the act which constitutes human happiness, taken in itself, needed to be confined to this world. Since Thomas admitted that it was possible for separated substances (whether angels or separated souls) to know God by analogical contemplation, Thomas had to develop his understanding of natural desire precisely to exclude the possible objection that such contemplation constitutes the final end of the human person. While Thomas was ultimately able to do so by introducing Avicenna's condition, "insofar as possible," into natural desire, thereby developing a uniquely Augustinian approach to our desire for God, the very conditionality of that desire allowed for the possibility that, absent the gift of grace, our natural desire might in actual fact come to rest in the terminal development of the active principle in human nature.

Thomas's acknowledgement that Aristotelian beatitude need not be confined to this world brings us to a second difficulty with "Duplex hominis beatitudo." Although de Lubac's citation of texts in the article is fairly comprehensive, there are two important texts which de Lubac does not cite: *In II Sent.*, d. 33, q. 2, a. 2, and *De malo*, q. 5, a. 3. In both of these texts, Thomas addresses the fate of children who die in original sin only. In spite of the differences between these two texts concerning Thomas's explanation of how these infants do not suffer, we saw above in chapters 2 and 5 respectively that the texts are consistent in their description of the act that Thomas supposes these children to perform: Thomas supposes that children who die in original sin only occupy a state after this life in which they enjoy perpetually the good which Aristotle thought we could only enjoy

181. For a fuller discussion of this complementarity, see my "The Study of Theology as a Foretaste of Heaven," 1119–20.

temporally. Although Thomas does not describe these children as occupying a state of "pure nature," since he envisions them within the present order of Providence, it is not entirely correct to say that all instances of natural happiness in Thomas's writings are therefore confined to this world. Even if one does not agree with Thomas on the fate of unbaptized children, it remains true as a matter of Thomistic exegesis that Thomas *thought* that they occupied a historical state of perpetual analogical contemplation, rather than a hypothetical one. This means that Thomas could and did envision an historical state in which human natural desire reached the terminal development of the active principle in human nature.[182]

Be that as it may, de Lubac proceeds in "Le mystère du surnaturel" to apply his Aegidian reading of Thomas to a resolution of the ambiguities with his use of Marcelli in *Surnaturel*. As in *Surnaturel*, de Lubac continues to see the context for his discussion of a natural

182. De Lubac later responded to this objection in *Augustinisme et théologie moderne*, 236. His argument is textual: although he acknowledges that Thomas sees these infants as occupying the sort of state I have described, he denies that Thomas ever described this state as a "natural end" or "natural beatitude." While this is true in the strict sense that Thomas does not use either of those terms in the two texts in which he discusses the fate of unbaptized infants, the trouble with de Lubac's argument is that de Lubac had already cited an abundance of texts in "Duplex hominis beatitudo" where Thomas describes the sort of act that he envisions the infants performing alternately as a "beatitudo imperfecta ... quae potest ab homine acquiri per sua naturalia" (Ia-IIae, q. 5, a. 5, co. [Leon. 6:51], quoted on p. 292); "qua[e]dam felicita[s] quam homo natus est acquirere per propria naturalia ..." (*De virtutibus*, a. 9, ad 6 [Odetto 2:732], quoted on p. 294); a "felicitas ad quam homo per naturalia sua potest devenire ..." (*In III Sent.*, d. 27, q. 2, a. 2, co. [Moos 3:877], quoted on p. 295n11); a "fin[is] ... ultim[us] ... proportionat[us] ... humanae facultati ..." (*In II Sent.*, d. 41, q. 1, a. 1, co. [Mandonnet 2:1036], quoted on p. 295n10); a "bonum ultimum ... proportionatum naturae" (*De veritate*, q. 14, a. 2, co. [Leon. 22:441], quoted on p. 295n13); and even a "naural[is] perfecti[o] hominis" (*De veritate*, q. 20, a. 3, co. [Leon. 22:536], quoted on p. 297n20). In "Duplex hominis beatitudo," de Lubac is aware that the description of the act in question as a *finis* is the most problematic assertion for his case, and so he argues that the word *finis*, applied to the act of Aristotelian contemplation, refers to the common end of creation, not to the specific end of a rational creature; the specific end of a rational creature must be considered in light of the separated state of the soul (p. 299n25). However, it is precisely the idea that the happiness which the philosophers identify in this life could be enjoyed perpetually in the separated state of the soul which led to the developments in the *Summa contra Gentiles* already mentioned, and to Thomas's description of the fate of unbaptized infants.

desire for a supernatural end in sixteenth-century responses to the errant Augustinianisms of Baius and Jansen;[183] he continues to employ a distinction between man considered "in his species" and man considered as made in the image of God;[184] he alludes to the distinction between God's *potentia absoluta* and God's *potentia ordinata* to describe God's ability to make humanity in a state of pure nature.[185] As in *Surnaturel*, therefore, this line of thought would seem to bring de Lubac to the doorstep of Marcelli's impossible possibility. De Lubac even goes beyond *Surnaturel* and rejects out of hand Berti's idea that human nature's calling to the vision of God is necessary; he affirms unequivocally with Marcelli the idea that human nature's calling to the vision of God is contingent.[186] It would seem, therefore, as if "Le mystère du surnaturel" should be read as a clarification in which de Lubac solidified a commitment to Marcelli.

However, there is reason to take caution before suggesting that de Lubac's articulation of the natural desire for a supernatural end in "Le mystère du surnaturel" should be aligned with Marcelli. If we look beneath the surface of words that appear to align with Marcelli, we find very quickly that the conceptual framework undergirding those words is no longer that of Marcelli; it is that of Lafosse.

Spiritual nature, de Lubac now explains, radically differs from lower natures. Other natures have a fixed end which they achieve by their natural powers, while spiritual nature lacks a determined end in itself.[187] When God chooses to create a spiritual creature, he therefore has to do two things: 1) decree an end for that spiritual nature;[188] 2) create concrete individuals (that is, persons) who share in that nature and desire its end.[189] This process results in a certain

183. De Lubac, *Augustinisme et théologie moderne*, 90.

184. Ibid., 105–6.

185. On God's *potentia absoluta*, see the reference to God's "sourveraine liberté" at ibid., 104; on God's *potentia ordinata*, see ibid., 92: "Et par conséquent, semble-t-il, le Dieu juste et bon ne saurait m'en frustrer, si ce n'est pas moi qui par ma propre faute me détourne librement de Lui."

186. Ibid., 87.

187. Ibid., 106.

188. Ibid., 101.

189. Ibid., 103.

tension between nature and the persons who possess it. Their nature, considered in itself, lacks an end and so is a mystery;[190] the persons with that nature, on the other hand, have a single, determined end, which gives definition to their nature insofar as it has been received by them in history.[191] To consider humanity "in its species" is not to consider human nature apart from its intellectuality; it is to consider human nature apart from the decree of God establishing an end for human nature, and so to consider human nature apart from any natural or supernatural call.[192] To consider human nature "in the image of God" is not, as it was for Marcelli, to consider human nature with the addition of intellectual powers; it is to consider the consequences arising from creating individual members of an intellectual species who possess the powers inherent in that species: they have intellect and will, as they would in any hypothesis, but they also possess an element of mystery arising from the primary indetermination of the nature which they have received.[193]

Two consequences follow from this Lafossian view of human nature. The first is that even though de Lubac now clearly acknowledges the possibility of a state of pure nature in which humanity is neither called nor ordered to the vision of God, reflection by natural reason on that *hypothetical* state is rendered practically useless for the purpose of expounding the natural law in this *historical* state.[194]

190. Ibid., 113.

191. Ibid., 92. It is in this sense that de Lubac can say, "Le désir de Le voir est en nous, il est nous-mêmes." (111).

192. Ibid., 105: "Considérée en elle-même, statiquement pour ainsi dire, ou encore 'dans son espèce,' ma nature n'est que ce qu'elle est: il n'y a pas en elle, répétons-le, le moindre élément surnaturel. Mais pas plus qu'on n'avait le droit d'envisager sinon par manière de dire un sujet réel avant sa position dans l'être par l'acte créateur, pas davantage on ne pourrait réellement envisager cette nature avant d'y voir inscrite sa finalité surnaturelle."

193. Ibid., 118: "Une doctrine chère aux Pères de l'Église est que l'homme est à l'image de Dieu non seulement par son intelligence, sa liberté, son immortalité, sa domination sur la nature, mais encore et surtout, en fin de compte, par ce qu'il y a d'incompréhensible en lui."

194. Ibid., 99: "Donc l'idée d'une 'pure nature' . . . appairaît inapte au service qu'on en attendait."

... When you postulate another order of things, then whether you like it or not, you postulate at the same time another humanity, another human being and, if I may so speak, another me.... Between this man who, according to the hypothesis, is not destined to see God and the man who I am in reality, between this futurible [man] and this existing [man], there is nothing more than an entirely ideal, an entirely abstract identity. Then again, perhaps this is already conceding too much. For the difference between these two does not just concern individuality; it concerns nature itself.[195]

In that other state, man technically possesses the same nature as we do in this state, provided that we abstract our consideration of human nature from the question of nature's end and view the nature itself as a mystery. But since any rational reflection on a nature has to be based upon the end which God has decreed for it, and since God has decreed a different end for human nature in that state, there is next to nothing that nature in that state can tell us about nature in this state.

Although de Lubac's Lafossian anthropology therefore makes it impossible to derive an account of the natural law by reflection on pure nature, it would be open to the possibility of deriving an account of the natural law by reflection on nature as we presently experience it, were it not for a second consequence. The second consequence is that even in this historical state it is not possible to demonstrate by natural reason that the end of human nature is the vision of God. Since, as for Scotus, the end of human nature depends upon a voluntary decree of God, Revelation is a necessary precondition in order for us to give a teleological account of human nature

195. Ibid., 93: "En posant un autre ordre de choses, on pose du même coup, qu'on le veuille ou non, une autre humanité, un autre être humain et, si l'on peut dire, un autre moi.... Entre cet homme qui, par hypothèse, n'est pas destiné à voir Dieu, et l'homme que je suis en réalité, entre ce futurible et cet existant, il n'y a encore qu'une identité tout idéale, tout abstraite. Peut-être même est-ce là déjà trop concéder. Car la différence entre l'un et l'autre n'affecte pas seulement l'individualité, mais la nature même." See also ibid., p. 95: "Si l'on me parle d'une autre nature hypothétiquement réalisable avec une autre finalté dans un autre univers, je ne me sens plus avec elle qu'un lien purement abstrait, quoi qu'il en soit des traits de ressemblance qu'on lui confère, peut-être d'ailleurs arbitrairement, avec la nôtre." See also ibid., pp. 88–89.

with any certainty.[196] To unaided human reason, human nature possesses an irreducible air of mystery.[197] Any attempt to reduce this mystery to a "system," such as had been the case in the great systems of the Dominican and Jesuit Thomists,[198] necessarily compromises some essential aspect of it.[199]

This second consequence seems to ignore the fact that the Aegidian doctrine of a natural desire for a supernatural end was founded upon arguments which Giles of Rome thought were metaphysically demonstrable and, in his words, "unassailable." It similarly seems to ignore the fact that two of the principal representatives of the Aegidian tradition referenced in the course of de Lubac's career drew up systems which were every bit as elaborate as those of the Dominicans and Jesuits: Berti (in 10 volumes) and Marcelli (in 7 volumes). But, as we shall see with reference to de Lubac's future work, it was an essential—if peculiar—feature of Lafosse's understanding of human nature's indeterminacy, and one which de Lubac, in his embrace of Lafosse, came to accept.

Humani Generis and "the Twins"

In 1950, the year after "Le mystère du surnaturel," Pope Pius XII weighed in on the controverted question about the natural desire for a supernatural end by censuring those who "corrupt the true gratuity of the supernatural order, since they affirm that God cannot establish beings endowed with intellect, without ordering and calling them to the beatific vision."[200] Although de Lubac was widely interpreted as the intended object of this condemnation, he himself denied that his thought fell within it.[201] Apart from the question

196. Ibid., 105.

197. Ibid., 113.

198. On the prevalence of these systems, see ibid., 81. On the limits thereof, see ibid., 109.

199. Ibid., 114–16.

200. Pius XII, *Humani generis*, no. 26, in *Acta Apostolicae Sedis* 42 (1950): 570: "Alii veram 'gratuitatem' ordinis supernaturalis corrumpunt, cum autumnent Deum entia intellectu praedita condere non posse, quin eadem ad beatificam visionem ordinet et vocet."

201. For a list of quotations and passages in which de Lubac made this denial, see

of the personal intention of Pius XII, which is difficult if not impossible to ascertain,[202] part of the difficulty in assessing de Lubac's place with respect to this condemnation concerns the nuanced tradition upon which he was relying, and the manner in which his thought had already undergone three stages of development with respect to this tradition. As we have seen, the entire Aegidian tradition affirmed the existence of a natural desire for a supernatural end, but that tradition did not universally agree as to how such a desire should be articulated. To review:

- In his early articles, de Lubac voiced support for Berti. Berti relativizes the *debitum*. Humanity would be endowed with intellect and *called* by desire to the beatific vision in any hypothesis, but would not necessarily be *ordered* to it by grace; *de potentia absoluta*, God might create humanity for the beatific vision without giving it the means of attaining that end.

Susan Wood, *Spiritual Exegesis and the Church in Henri de Lubac* (Grand Rapids, Mich.: Eerdmans, 1998), 15. Cf. Sales, preface, xi.

202. De Lubac recounts that Pius XII spoke positively of his teaching when he met the pontiff in 1946. See de Lubac, *At the Service of the Church*, 61, cited in Andrew Swafford, *Nature and Grace: A New Approach to Thomistic Ressourcement* (Eugene, Ore.: Pickwick, 2014), 59. The pontiff's words were ambiguous: "Ah! I know your doctrine very well." De Lubac says they were spoken in a "friendly tone," and that the newly elected superior general assured him, after meeting with the Holy Office and the pontiff, that his work was not in question.

In his address to the entire delegation of the Society of Jesus, the pontiff counseled the members of the Society to "accommodate" themselves to the character of the people of their day, but exhorted them not to change what is immutable. While he spoke of a "new theology" as something which primarily compromises the immutability of dogma, he never names any theologian in association with this theology. According to the pontiff, the members of the Society should take care that "in proponendis et proferendis quaestionibus, in argumentationibus ducendis, in dicendi quoque genere deligendo, oporteat sui saeculi ingenio et propensioni sapienter orationem suam accommodent. At quod immutabile est, nemo turbet et moveat. Plura dicta sunt, at non satis explorata ratione, 'de nova theologia' quae cum universis semper volventibus rebus, una volvatur, semper itura, numquam perventura. Si talis opinio amplectenda esse videatur, quid fiet de numquam immutandis catholicis dogmatibus, quid de fidei unitate et stabilitate?" See Pius XII, "Allocutio ad Patres Societatis Iesu In XXIX Congregatione generali electores" (September 17, 1946), in *Acta Apostolicae Sedis* 38 (1946): 384–85. Balanced though they may have been, Pius XII's words were taken as a warning, and this "warning" was published on the front page *L'Osservatore Romano* the following day. See Henri de Lubac, *Mémoire sur l'occasion de mes écrits* (Namur: Culture et Vérité, 1989), 62.

- In *Surnaturel,* de Lubac voiced an ambiguous support for Marcelli. Marcelli relativizes nature itself. In any hypothesis in which humanity is endowed with intellect, it must be *called* by desire and *ordered* by grace to the beatific vision; *de potentia absoluta,* God might create humanity without calling or ordering it to the beatific vision, but that would require making humanity without intellect.
- In "Le mystère du surnaturel," de Lubac followed Lafosse. Lafosse relativizes the *debitum* as well as nature's end. Humanity would be endowed with intellect in any hypothesis, but would be neither *called* by desire nor *ordered* by grace to the beatific vision in every hypothesis. Even if God created human nature and called it to the vision of himself, *de potentia absoluta,* God might create humanity for the beatific vision without giving it the means of attaining that end.

Carefully read, *Humani generis* condemns the view that humanity, in any hypothesis in which it is endowed with intellect, must be both *ordered* and *called* to the beatific vision. This view was not universally shared among the theologians of the Aegidian tradition. Only Marcelli falls under the condemnation in a strict sense. Berti allows for a state in which humanity is not *ordered* to the beatific vision by grace even if it is *called* there by desire.[203] Lafosse allows for a state in which humanity is neither *called* by desire nor *ordered* by grace. Marcelli, however, requires that in every hypothesis in which humanity is endowed with intellect, God must call and order it to the beatific vision—and that is precisely what *Humani generis* condemns.

Was de Lubac's natural desire for a supernatural end condemned by *Humani generis*? As expressed in the publication nearest to its

203. It is upon this distinction that Agostino Trapè, OSA (1915–87), perhaps the last great theologian of the Aegidian tradition, sought to defend the tradition after the promulgation of *Humani generis*. See Agostino Trapè, "De gratuitate ordinis supernaturalis apud theologos augustinienses litteris encyclicis 'Humani Generis' praelucentibus," *Analecta Augustiniana* 21 (1947–50): 217–65.

promulgation, "Le mystère du surnaturel," certainly not. With Lafosse, de Lubac acknowledged the possibility of a state in which man, endowed with intellect, is neither called nor ordered to the vision of God. As expressed previously in *Surnaturel,* perhaps. If de Lubac intended fully to support Marcelli's idea that in any state in which human nature is endowed with intellect it must be called and ordered to the beatific vision, then yes; if de Lubac did not realize the consequences of Marcelli's position (as we may suspect from his failure to state the conclusion at that time or to reject Berti), then no. A more careful interpretation would be to say that *Humani generis* condemned what in actual fact is Marcelli's position, that there is a chance that de Lubac supported Marcelli in 1946, and that whatever the case may be about de Lubac's support for Marcelli in 1946, he had moved on by 1950 and abandoned Marcelli for Lafosse.[204]

De Lubac's shift from Marcelli toward Lafosse is developed in his subsequent works on the natural desire for a supernatural end, "the Twins": *Augustinisme et théologie moderne* (1965), and *Le mystère du surnaturel* (1965).[205] Those works were originally intended to be elaborations of de Lubac's previous publications: *Augustinisme et théologie moderne* was supposed to be an expansion of part one of *Surnaturel,* in which de Lubac's ambiguous support for Marcelli originally appeared; *Le mystère du surnaturel* was supposed to be an expansion of the article by the same name, in which de Lubac made the turn from Marcelli toward Lafosse. Looking back on these texts, de Lubac later reflected that although he had expanded them he had not changed "the least point of doctrine."[206] That may be true with

204. While the compositional history of *Humani generis* is not known, it is plausible that a Roman theologian, assisting in the drafting process and hostile to the natural desire for a supernatural end, might suggest censuring what he took to be the conclusion implied by *Surnaturel.* But de Lubac never actually states the condemned conclusion, and even if he at one time held it—which cannot be proved from the text of *Surnaturel*—he had moved on by the time *Humani generis* was promulgated.

205. Henri de Lubac, *Augustinisme et théologie moderne* (Paris: Aubier, 1965); *Le mystère du surnaturel* (Paris: Aubier, 1965).

206. De Lubac, *Mémoire sur l'occasion de mes écrits,* 124: "L'un, *le Mystère du surnaturel,* développe dans le même ordre, et sans y changer le moindre point de doctrine,

respect to *Le mystère du surnaturel,* but it is certainly not the case with respect to *Augustinisme et théologie moderne.*

While large sections of *Surnaturel* are repeated *verbatim* in *Augustinisme et théologie moderne,* de Lubac actually went back and substantially edited the section in which he praises the Aegidian tradition so as to soften his references to Marcelli.[207] His references to Marcelli remain intact materially: he still refers to the species/image distinction;[208] he still associates being made in the image of God with being called to the vision of God;[209] he still deploys the *potentia absoluta/ordinata* distinction while leaving the conclusion to be drawn from it unspoken.[210] Yet if we read de Lubac's "additions" carefully, we find that he uses them to empty Marcelli's terms of any force that they might have had, by introducing the Lafossian understanding of the species/image distinction he had developed in "Le mystère du surnaturel":

> For someone like Lafosse, like Bellelli, like Berti, the [image of God] is above all, as it was for St. Augustine and for all the Fathers, as well as for St. Thomas, the soul itself, considered in its superior part, with its natural powers of reason and free will.... If the consideration of "image" adds anything to the consideration of "species," it is solely in the sense that it is a more complete and more concrete view *of the same reality.*[211]

More tellingly, de Lubac also eliminates the necessary connection between possessing intellect and will and being called to the vi-

l'article publié sous ce titre ... en 1949.... Le second, *Augustinisme et théologie moderne,* reproduit de même fidèlement, en la grossissant de textes nouveaux, la première partie du vieux *Surnaturel.*"

207. De Lubac, *Augustinisme et théologie moderne,* 293–305.

208. Ibid., 301.

209. Ibid., 301–2.

210. Ibid., 302–3.

211. Ibid., 302 (emphasis added): "Pour un Lafosse, pour un Belleli [sic], pour un Berti, elle est avant tout, comme pour saint Augustin et pour tous les Pères, comme aussi bien pour saint Thomas, l'âme elle-même, considérée dans sa partie supérieure, avec ses puissances naturelles de raison et de libre vouloir.... Si la considération de l' 'image' ajoute quelque chose à la considération de l' 'espèce,' c'est en ce sens seulement qu'elle est une vue plus complète et plus concrète de la même réalité."

sion of God. Immediately after he refers to the Aegidians as Augustinians "par excellence," we read, concerning their tradition:

> They also do not preoccupy themselves with drawing up a system of thought; like Giles of Rome long ago, they base themselves on Scripture and hardly seek to know what can or cannot be demonstrated by reason. When they discuss this last point, they are happy to be restrained: "Our opinion is this: the possibility of the beatific vision cannot be proven demonstrably by the light of natural reason alone."[212]

This observation develops the critique of metaphysical demonstrations and of systems which de Lubac first suggested in "Le mystère du surnaturel." There, it was confined to a series of general critiques of the Dominicans and Jesuits. Here, de Lubac goes so far as to suggest that Giles of Rome himself was unconcerned about metaphysical arguments, and that the Aegidian tradition as a whole was unconcerned about systematizing in theology.

At this point, de Lubac commits two historical errors. The first is with regard to Giles of Rome. As we saw above, Giles was intentional about engaging in the very kind of metaphysical demonstrations from which de Lubac seeks to dissociate him. The second is with regard to the Aegidian tradition. Systematization was as much a concern of that tradition as any other; Aegidians could boast such systematizers as Berti and Marcelli, both of whom bequeathed to the Order multi-volume systematizations for use in seminary education covering all of the scholastic treatises, and written in the same style as the scholastic treatises of Dominican and Jesuit Thomists from the same era. Where, then, does de Lubac get the idea that "the possibility of the beatific vision cannot be proven demonstrably by the light of natural reason alone"? If we follow up the reference for the quotation he uses to support the idea, we find that it is taken from

212. Ibid., 294: "Ils ne se préoccupent pas non plus d'un effort de pensée intégrale; comme jadis Gilles de Rome, ils se fondent sur l'Écriture et ne cherche guère à savoir ce qui peut ou ne peut pas être démontré par la raison. Quand ils traitent de ce dernier point, ils sont volontiers restrictifs: 'Sententia nostra sit ista : possibilitas visionis beatificae non potest probari demonstrative solo lumine naturali.'"

Lafosse,[213] and that on the page preceding it, Lafosse had expressed the same idea as de Lubac.[214] Lafosse's opinion represents not the common opinion of the entire Aegidian tradition, but the particular thought of Lafosse as distinct from other significant members of the tradition. Thus Lafosse says, as quoted in a footnote by de Lubac:

> Since, therefore, this elevation cannot be known naturally, neither consequently can our innate appetite for the beatific vision [be known naturally]. Wherefore the arguments, which we make to prove this sort of appetite, are not purely physical and natural arguments, but theological and radically supernatural [arguments], insofar as they are based upon revelation and the faith by which we believe that man has been elevated by God to the supernatural order and to the level of grace and glory. They are nevertheless partly physical and natural: insofar as it is shown by probable argument that man ought to have been elevated to a supernatural end, and consequently that he desires it naturally.[215]

In short, Lafosse thinks that we cannot demonstrate by natural reason the concrete possibility that human nature has been called to beatific vision, because there is nothing in human nature which necessitates its having been called to the beatific vision. Arguments seeking to demonstrate that we have in fact been so called, and based on our present experience of natural desire, can and will only

213. Lafosse, *Augustinus theologus*, 3:139.

214. Ibid., 3:138. Recounting three opinions about the demonstrability of the possibility of the vision of God, he concludes, "Tertia tandem sententia defendit possibilitatem visionis Beatificae nullatenus nec ex ulla suppositione probari posse naturaliter demonstrative: haec est mens omnium fere Theologorum, maxime vero Thomistarum, ex nostris quoque eandem opinionem tutantur quamplurimi, Aegidius Rom[anus]; [Thomas] Argentinas, Aegidius Lusitanus, [Johannes] Puteanus, [Andreas] Landon, [Augustinus] Gibbon [de Burgo]." He acknowledges that others in the Aegidian tradition think that the possibility can be proven demonstratively, but thinks that they first require an encounter with Revelation.

215. Ibid., 3:184, in de Lubac, *Augustinisme et théologie moderne*, 294n2: "Cum igitur haec elevatio non possit naturaliter cognosci, nec consequenter appetitus innatus ad visionem beatificam. Quare argumenta, quae nos ad probandum hujusmodi appetitum, non sunt argumenta pure physica, et naturalia, sed theologica et radicaliter supernaturalia, in quantum fundantur supra revelationem et fidem, qua credimus hominem esse elevatum a Deo ad ordinem supernaturalem et gradum gratiae et gloriae. Sunt tamen ex parte physica et naturalia: quatenus probabili ratione ostenditur hominem debuisse elevari ad finem supernaturalem, et consequenter ipsum appetere naturaliter."

ever be probable. Our elevation to the beatific vision is a supernatural mystery; only faith can teach us about it with certainty.[216]

A more systematic and overt presentation of de Lubac's Lafossian anthropology can be found in *Le mystère du surnaturel.* Here again, de Lubac makes clear that he agrees with Lafosse that the calling of human nature to the beatific vision is contingent and that this calling creates in man a natural desire for the vision of God. This enables de Lubac to take up the question of *Humani generis* explicitly.[217] Need humanity in all hypotheses be called to the beatific vision? De Lubac's response is negative. All the same, does a natural desire for the vision of God, which results from an ontological call, constitute a positive ordering to the beatific vision? De Lubac's response is *emphatically* negative. There is an infinite distance between our capacity for the vision of God with the desire that results from it, and the sanctifying grace which orders us to that end.[218] God remains free in every hypothesis in which he has called us to the beatific vision not to give us the means of fulfilling a call which has been contingently imprinted on our nature.

Since Lafosse admitted the possibility of a state in which humanity is not called to the vision of God, de Lubac also feels constrained to speculate as to what our end in such a state might look like. He suggests two possibilities, both of which he acknowledges to be inconclusive. In the first hypothesis, human life would culminate in the natural knowledge of God. However, this knowledge cannot constitute a final *terminus* to human nature because abstractive knowledge in fact *increases* our desire for vision rather than quieting it.[219] Human nature would therefore terminate in a limitless

216. Lafosse, *Augustinus theologus*, 139. After the sentence quoted by de Lubac in the body of the text, Lafosse continues: "Visio Beatitifica non potest probari etiam ut possibilis argumento demonstrativo naturali: consequentia valet, quia Apostolus eo textu [Rom 6:23 'Gratia Dei vita aeterna'] probat visionem Beatificam, quae est vita aeterna esse mysterium fidei supernaturale, inquantum est mysterium gratiae."

217. De Lubac, *Le mystère du surnaturel*, 111.

218. Ibid., 116–17.

219. Ibid., 247.

search, spurred on by its unfulfilled desire. There could be "a certain joy" in this search, but then again, it would seem ultimately frustrating to search forever without growing closer to the object of our search.[220] In the second hypothesis, man would not be spurred on by his knowledge of God, but rather by his ignorance of God. We would wait in the darkness of expectation, hoping that we might one day achieve the satisfaction of our soul's capacity for the vision of God, without knowing whether such a satisfaction were possible.[221] This too is problematic because if the goal of this natural hope is not reached, the result will be despair.[222] Human nature not called to the beatific vision must have as its *telos* some definite act,[223] but de Lubac ultimately acknowledges that he is unable to come to a definite conclusion as to what that act is supposed to be.[224] Lafosse had never said what he thought the end of human nature would be in a state in which it was not called to the beatific vision. De Lubac is unable to do so either.

CONCLUSION

I would like to conclude this relecture of the Thomistic commentators and of de Lubac by proposing a constructive answer to the question with which we began in the introduction: to what extent can the two sides in the contemporary nature/grace debate be brought together? In order to answer this question, we need to distinguish, as in the introduction, between the historical question of what Thomas Aquinas thought, and the speculative questions about nature, grace, and the desire for God which Thomas Aquinas, the Thomistic commentators, and de Lubac all considered. I will begin by discussing the extent to which de Lubac's historical studies accurately represent Thomas and the Thomist tradition. Then I will proceed to consider

220. Ibid., 247–49.
221. Ibid., 252.
222. Ibid., 253.
223. Ibid.
224. Ibid., 254–55.

the extent to which de Lubac's thought can be reconciled with that of the Thomistic commentators.

De Lubac's Relationship to the Thomistic Tradition

De Lubac's relationship to Thomas and the Thomistic tradition can best be considered in terms of several theological themes:

The end of man's natural desire. De Lubac was correct to note a certain divergence in Cajetan's work from that of Thomas on the question of natural desire: Thomas ultimately affirmed the existence of a natural desire for the vision of God, while Cajetan, and a number of scholastics after him, denied it.[225] However, de Lubac's account of this divergence was not entirely accurate. Cajetan did not err in suggesting that natural desire (to use Thomas's language) has a naturally achievable act as its terminal development, provided that God leaves it unassisted by grace. Cajetan did err in his understanding of how Thomas related natural desire to natural appetite. Cajetan thought that the formal, active principle in nature has a specific desire, and the material, passive principle in nature has a conditional appetite. Thomas, following Augustine, thought the reverse. Cajetan thereby restricted natural desire to a naturally achievable end in a way that Thomas, from the *Summa contra Gentiles* onwards, had not. For Thomas, the soul naturally desires the complete fulfillment of its natural appetite insofar as is possible; explicitly, it desires its own happiness, while implicitly it desires the vision of God.

Activity and causality. Insofar as de Lubac's doctrine of natural desire posits an *activity* in man toward the vision of God, his doctrine bears the strongest affinity with the Aegidian tradition. Giles

225. De Lubac begins to identify Cajetan as the origin of the natural desire for a natural end in *Surnaturel*, 105–7. The corresponding section of *Augustinisme et théologie moderne* can be found on pp. 144–47. Thereafter, the identification of Cajetan as the primary originator of a natural desire for a natural end becomes something of a refrain in de Lubac's work. In *Le mystère du surnaturel*, 26, de Lubac even goes so far as to say that "Le tournant dans l'histoire de la pensée thomiste est marqué principalement par l'exégèse de Cajetan ..." and that even Suárez could not find a source closer to Thomas himself for the natural desire for a natural end.

of Rome agreed with Thomas that man has a natural desire for the vision of God, but criticized Thomas for not affirming any positive aptitude in matter for form, nor any positive aptitude in the human soul for the vision of God. De Lubac explicitly embraced the Aegidian tradition and used it in support of his understanding of natural desire, but he seems to have been unaware of the fact that its doctrine of natural desire was developed—at least initially—by a student of Thomas Aquinas in conscious *distinction* from Thomas. Consequently, de Lubac thought that Thomas and the Aegidian tradition had the same doctrine of a natural desire for the vision of God, when in fact they do not.

Obediential potency. De Lubac suggests that obediential potency was a later development misattributed to Thomas.[226] As a matter of historical record, obediential potency preceded Thomas in the Parisian tradition from Philip the Chancellor to Bonaventure, although de Lubac is correct that Thomas seldom used the term. Since Thomas affirmed matter's complete passivity with respect to form, and nature's complete passivity with respect to grace, he had no need for a separate potency in nature to account for its openness to grace.[227] Thomas does very occasionally use the term *potentia obedientialis* and its cognate, *potentia obedientiae*. But it is always synonymous with the whole of our passive potency, not a certain subset of it. The term is similarly rare in Scotus, who accounted for

226. De Lubac, *Surnaturel*, 135–38. The corresponding section of *Augustinisme et théologie moderne* can be found on pp. 242–57, although it has been significantly expanded.

227. Ibid., 135–36: "Loin de parler de puissance obédientielle à propos de l'aptitude au surnaturel, à la béatitude et à la vue de Dieu, il avait au contraire déclaré que 'l'âme est naturellement capable de la grâce.'" In the corresponding section of *Augustinisme et théologie moderne*, de Lubac turns this statement into a generalization. Words in italics represent insertions to the text of *Surnaturel*; words which are stricken through represent deletions: "Loin de parler *habituellement* de puissance obédientielle à propos de l'aptitude au surnaturel, à la béatitude, et à la ~~vue~~ *vie* de Dieu, il avait au contraire déclaré *plus d'une fois, dans une formule générale*, que 'l'âme est naturellement capable de la grâce." The change from *vue* to *vie* appears to be a simple typographical correction to the manuscript of *Surnaturel*; the other changes turn de Lubac's single citation of Thomas into a citation which is intended to be representative of the broader pattern of Thomas's thought.

natural change entirely by means of a similar passive potency. For Thomas and Scotus, matter's passivity with respect to form and nature's passivity with respect to grace, although not generally called "obediential," are the lynchpin of any account of the relationship between nature and grace.

Thus, de Lubac's accusation that Cajetan bears the primary responsibility for making obediential potency the hinge of man's openness to grace is not entirely appropriate.[228] Cajetan did not err in suggesting that, for Thomas, man is absolutely passive with respect to the reception of grace; here Cajetan preserves a common doctrine of Thomas and Scotus. But Cajetan did err, at least in emphasis, in suggesting that the best way to account for nature's receptivity to grace is by postulating an obediential potency in nature for grace. For Thomas, man is naturally *capax Dei* in that man has a "material" potency whereby he stands in privation to accidental perfections received from God. These accidental perfections are suitable objects of natural desire insofar as they are included in the complete actualization of the human intellect and will. Cajetan, by contrast, limits man's natural desire to an end which is naturally known. He thus separates obediential potency from natural potency, placing the fulfillment of obediential potency outside the bounds of natural desire. De Lubac rightly criticized Cajetan's sole reliance on the concept of obediential potency to establish nature's receptivity to grace, though greater awareness of those few texts where Thomas shows an openness to the concept would have been beneficial to his argument.

The possibility of a natural end for man. Another consequence of de Lubac's ignorance of the difference between Thomas and Giles is in de Lubac's account of the possibility of a natural end for man.

228. See de Lubac, *Surnaturel,* 137: "[I]l était réservé à Cajetan, conformément à sa distinction première, d'opposer décidément puissance naturelle et puissance obédientielle dans l'âme ..." In the corresponding section of *Augustinisme et théologie moderne,* on p. 247, de Lubac, acknolwedges the influence of Denys the Carthusian in the development of obediential potency in the Thomistic tradition; and so he softens this statement somewhat: "C'est la même tendance qui amène enfin Cajetan à opposer constamment puissance naturelle et puissance obédientielle dans l'âme humaine...."

De Lubac tends to associate the claim that a natural desire must be naturally fulfillable with the hypothesis that a natural end for man is possible and consequently with the possibility of a state of pure nature. However, the question of whether a natural desire must be naturally fulfillable and the question of whether man has a natural end are logically distinct, and have a different historical provenance. De Lubac correctly observed that the restriction of natural desires to natural ends arises primarily in Cajetan. However, Thomas proposes that a natural end for man is nevertheless possible, because although human nature desires the complete fulfillment of its natural appetite insofar as is possible, the terminal development of that natural desire is the analogical knowledge of God as first cause, provided that God does not communicate any higher motion to human nature. Thomas shows this in his later treatment of infants who die in original sin only. Thomas's final position is that these infants are aware of the possibility of the vision of God from a reflection on the potential of their nature to receive this vision, but are unaware of whether or not God has chosen to grant this vision to them; accordingly, they are contented with the terminal development of the active principle of their nature, even though their receptive potential remains partially unfulfilled. In short, they desire happiness, they find something that makes them happy, and, since their desire for happiness is a desire for the fulfillment of their natural appetite insofar as is possible and they possess as great a fulfillment of that appetite as they know themselves to be capable of, they are happy. De Lubac's emphasis on the impossibility of such an end is more akin to the teaching of Giles than to Thomas, although even Giles admitted that the souls in limbo were happy, because he thought that they had lost their positive aptitude for the vision of God by entering into a terminal state.

The natural knowability of man's final end. There is one particular point at which de Lubac parts company with much of the Aegidian tradition. Giles argues that it can be demonstrated by natural reason that, since the human soul is capable of the vision of God, the vision of God is the final end of man. While acknowledging the force of this argument, de Lubac expresses some hesitancy concerning the natural knowability of the specific term of man's natural desire. A similar hesitancy can be found in Fulgence Lafosse, and de Lubac expressly relies on Lafosse for it. But that hesitancy is peculiar to Lafosse and based upon his peculiar understanding of the contingency of human nature's end; it is not the common teaching of the Aegidian tradition as a whole.

Toward the Reconciliation of the Nature/Grace Debate

The nature/grace debate is important in itself. It is an exercise in *disputatio,* in which faith seeks understanding about what it means to be a human person with a restless heart before God. While this debate may have come a long way from its origins, it arose in history out of a *lectio* of Scripture, considering those truths about human nature's relationship to God which are revealed in Creation, the Fall, the Passion of Christ, and the struggle that fallen nature experiences to accept the grace poured out through that Passion. This was certainly the case for Augustine. Augustine's original account of our restless heart in the *Confessions* arose out of a consideration for the struggle that fallen nature experiences to accept the grace poured out through Christ's Passion, and his anti-Pelagian work on the Fall and the Passion developed into his mature teaching on the restless heart in *De Trinitate* and *De civitate Dei.* It was also the case for the medievals, who used Augustine's account of Creation—formulated in terms of *rationes seminales*—to explain the relationship between fallen nature and redemptive grace. Nevertheless, the nature/grace debate is not important *for* itself. As a *disputatio* about Scripture, it possesses within itself a teleological orientation toward the proclamation of the truths which it considers in the Church's *praedicatio*. That proclamation requires that Christians consider not only the questions that arise from their own contemplation of nature, grace, and the desire for God, but also those questions which non-Christians raise about these subjects from outside the Christian Faith.

In the second quarter of the thirteenth century, Christian *prae-*

dicatio about nature, grace, and the desire for God had to come to grips with a long list of new questions posed to it from within the Aristotelian tradition—not just the texts of Aristotle, but also the text of his Greek, Arabic, and Hebrew commentators. Until that point, medieval Latins had tended to think about nature with Augustine in terms of God as its cause, and the desire for God in terms of Augustine's desire for happiness; the relationship between nature and grace posed no particular difficulty for them. But the Aristotelian tradition challenged Latin Christians to think about nature in terms of some act as its end. This meant that in proclaiming a Christian answer to the question "what does the human heart long for?" they now had two different sets of answers before them: those of the Augustinian tradition, and those of the Aristotelian tradition. The challenge in the second quarter of the thirteenth century was to figure out in *disputatio* how to unite those disparate answers into a single, coherent message, which could acknowledge with the Aristotelian tradition the integrity of nature in relation to some end, but maintain with the Augustinian tradition nature's openness to and need for the grace of Christ.

In the period after 1231, Latin theologians sought the closest parallel to Christianity that they could find among the Aristotelian tradition; they looked not to Aristotle but to Avicenna, whose *dator formarum* they identified with God, and whose account of natural places and natural inclinations they used to argue that human nature has a natural desire for the vision of God. This protected the integrity of nature to a certain extent, and easily accounted for nature's openness to and need for grace, but even the medievals sensed that it might not protect in every respect the gratuity of grace. In the 1240s and early 1250s, Albert the Great and Bonaventure each tried to overcome that difficulty by making use of Averroes. Albert restricted natural desires to natural ends, which had the benefit of protecting the integrity of nature and the gratuity of grace, but not of explaining how nature is open to grace; Bonaventure allowed natural desires to transcend their natural ends, but this raised a number of questions about the integrity of nature which he was not initially able to solve.

Faced with an Avicennian tradition, which leaned toward a natural desire for a supernatural end, and an Averroistic tradition, which leaned toward a natural desire for a natural end, Thomas Aquinas found himself in a very similar position to one in which we find ourselves today. The Avicennians emphasized the transcendence of desire and the need for grace, but struggled with the integrity of nature and the gratuity of grace; the Averroists emphasized the integrity of nature and the gratuity of grace, but struggled with the transcendence of desire and the need for grace. Neither side was able to give a single answer to the question "what does the human heart long for?" which took into account the insights of the Aristotelian tradition while preserving the commitments of the Augustinian tradition. At a distance of nearly eight centuries from the beginning of that controversy, we find ourselves similarly situated. Perhaps Thomas's solution may therefore suggest to us not only the process by which we might arrive at one today, but also some indication of what that solution might be.

We can affirm, with de Lubac, man's orientation toward the vision of God as a final end, but acknowledge, with the commentators, that a natural end for man is possible. We can affirm, with de Lubac, that human nature as such is open to the vision of God and that this openness need not be considered as an obediential potency, but acknowledge, with the commentators, that our receptivity to the vision of God is purely passive. We can affirm, with de Lubac, that a natural desire for the vision of God does not make the vision of God owed to nature, but we can acknowledge, with the commentators, that one reason why the vision of God is not owed to nature is that God could *reasonably* withhold it. When confronted with the basic question "what does the human heart long for?" the Christian can answer with Augustine, "happiness." When confronted with the Aristotelian question of nature's end, the Christian can answer with Thomas: human natural desire seeks the fulfillment of human natural appetite insofar as is possible. Left unaided, our natural desire comes to rest in the analogical knowledge of God as first cause; but raised by grace, that same desire comes to rest in the vision of the divine essence. This answer protects the integrity of nature by allowing its active principle to come to rest in a naturally achievable teleological act; it protects the gratuity of grace by ensuring that God could reasonably withhold it; it protects nature's openness to grace by showing how and in what way human nature can be said to have a natural desire for the vision of God; and it protects nature's need for grace because it is a subjective desire for self-fulfillment, rather than an objective desire that can claim any right before God.

Commentatorial Objections

From the perspective of the commentators, there are four principal questions that this solution is liable to raise:

1) How is this not a restatement of Suárez's thesis? Did not Suárez already propose that human nature has a conditional desire for the vision of God?

As we saw above, Suárez distinguishes between innate and elicited appetites. He argues that human nature has an innate, absolute appetite for a natural end, and a conditional, elicited appetite for a supernatural end. Suárez intended the categories of "innate" and "elicited" appetites to cover the same conceptual ground as the thirteenth-century categories of "natural" and "free" desires. But we also saw above that they do not. Suárez's innate appetite includes Thomas's passive natural appetite as well as a portion of Thomas's active natural desire; Suárez's elicited appetite is roughly analogous to Thomas's free desire. If we translate what Thomas says into the language of Suárez, Thomas introduces a condition into the active component of Suárez's innate appetite.

2) How can we introduce a condition into Suárez's "innate" appetite?

While Suárez's innate appetite is roughly analogous to Thomas's combination of passive natural appetite and active natural desire, it is not completely equivalent. Suárez's innate appetite includes all of a creature's active potency, as well as that portion of a creature's passive potency which corresponds with its active potency. By contrast, Thomas's passive natural appetite includes all of a creature's passive potency, not just that portion of it which corresponds with the creature's active potency. While we can make a conceptual distinction, based upon our knowledge of the terminal development of a creature's active potency, between that portion of a creature's passive potency which corresponds with its active potency and that portion which does not, Thomas does not usually make this distinction, even when speaking of human nature's *potentia obedientiae,* as shown above in chapters 2–5. In order to bring natural appetite and natural desire together, and bearing in mind that they are not precisely equivalent, Thomas borrowed a condition from Avicenna's account of the natural desire of the souls of the heavenly bodies for their complete perfection *insofar as is possible,* and he introduced that condition in the *Summa contra Gentiles* into the active component of what would later become Suárez's innate appetite. This allowed Thomas to say going forward in his career that the natural desire of the soul seeks the complete fulfillment of the natural appetite of the soul, and that the natural desire of the soul comes to rest in either a natural or a supernatural end depending on whether God chooses to communicate grace to the soul or not.

3) Is it not the case that a natural desire for the vision of God makes that vision owed to nature?

Thomas never thought so. For Thomas, the natural desire for the vision of God (conceived in terms of a natural desire for the fulfillment of our natural appetite insofar as is possible) proves that the vision of God is metaphysically possible, but not that anyone has, does, or will receive it. In order to argue that the natural desire for the vision of God makes that vision owed to nature, one has to amend Thomas's thought in one of two ways: a) by re-orienting natural desire so that it seeks the vision of God directly and unconditionally, or b) by using the Aristotelian *dictum* "nature does nothing in vain" to argue that a natural desire for an end means that the act which constitutes that end must actually occur. Thomas carefully and scrupulously avoids doing either of these things. The first would have been a return to William of Auvergne's Avicennianism; the second would have been a conflation of two arguments he found in Jean de la Rochelle, where Aristotle's *dictum* proves that i) an act is possible (see *SCG* 3.48), and ii) a power of the soul exists (see *SCG* 2.79), but not iii) an act has, does, or will take place.

Thomas's concern was to establish in nature what we might call a "preferential option for the vision of God" with the Augustinian tradition, without therefore precluding the possibility of a naturally achievable end with the Aristotelian tradition. Since Thomas achieved that synthesis by means of a condition taken from Avicenna, Thomas was able, from the *Summa contra Gentiles* onwards, to give priority to the Augustinian tradition from *within* the Aristotelian tradition. Cajetan's restriction of natural desires to naturally achievable ends, which Suárez adopted, wounded this synthesis by placing nature's openness to grace outside of nature *qua* nature. Even if that does not necessarily make grace extrinsic to nature, it introduces a level of extrinsicism of which Thomas was aware in figures such as Albert the Great, and which he worked much of his career to overcome.

4) Does the natural desire for the vision of God violate the integrity of nature, and so the integrity of human communities apart from the Church?

It need not. The way that Thomas formulates it (as a natural desire for the fulfillment of our natural appetite insofar as is possible), it always allows for the possibility that God might not choose not to offer grace to humanity. In that state—the state which Thomas in fact supposes the souls in limbo to be—natural desire reaches the terminal development to which the active principle in human nature can bring it: the analogical knowledge of God as first cause, which fulfills that portion of the soul's passive potency which corresponds with its active potency. Human persons, as well as human communities, always have a conceptual integrity arising from the ordering of human nature toward this end. In the order of moral action, the natural law is founded upon this conceptual integrity, as well as on the fact that human nature communicates to the will a determination in the order of specification toward certain goods of nature (see chapter 5).

Lubacian Objections

From the perspective of de Lubac, there are three principal questions that this solution is liable to raise:

1) How is this not a restatement of de Lubac's thesis? Did not de Lubac already propose that human nature has a natural desire for a supernatural end?

As we saw above, de Lubac based the scholastic formulation of his understanding of natural desire not on Thomas directly, but on Thomas mediated through the Aegidian tradition of the Order of the Hermits of St. Augustine. The founder of that tradition, Giles of Rome, was a student of Thomas Aquinas, and consciously disagreed with the way in which Thomas understood nature and natural desire. For Thomas, nature is passive toward grace like matter is passive toward form; for Giles, matter and nature have a positive aptitude toward form and grace respectively. These positive aptitudes were placed in nature at Creation as part of a *ratio seminalis*. Consequently, while Thomas allowed for the possibility that our natural desire, which seeks the fulfillment of our natural appetite insofar as is possible, might come to rest in the terminal development of is active potency, Giles did not.

Within the Aegidian tradition, theologians did not always agree as to how best to articulate Giles's natural desire for a supernatural end. Initially, de Lubac followed Giovanni Lorenzo Berti: human nature's only end is the vision of God; *de potentia absoluta* God could withhold the means to our only end; but *de potentia ordinata* we could hardly imagine God doing so. Shortly after the publication of *Surnaturel* in 1946, de Lubac shifted toward Fulgence Lafosse, who introduced a further contingency: human nature desires in any state that end which God has decreed for it; but in this state God has decreed that the vision of God is the end of human nature; therefore in this state we have a natural desire for a supernatural end. In some other state, we might have had a natural end and a natural desire for it; but human nature, such as we concretely experience it, does not.

2) Does allowing a natural end for human nature close off nature, *qua* nature, to grace?

If we think about natural desire the way that Albert the Great, Cajetan, and Suárez did, then in a certain sense, yes: having a natural desire for a natural end closes off nature *qua* nature to grace. For these figures, natural desire seeks the terminal fulfillment of that portion of a creature's passive potency which corresponds to its active potency. Consequently, nature *qua* nature only seeks a natural end. There remains an obediential potency in human beings for divine elevation, but the fulfillment of that obediential potency cannot be sought by a person's natural desire (or in Suárez's language, "innate appetite"). However, Thomas did not think about natural desire that way. Although he followed Albert on the question of our natural desire's end in his *Commentary on the Sentences,* he followed Bonaventure on the question of our natural appetite's end, and Bonaventure sees the whole of human nature *qua* nature as oriented toward the vision of God. In the *Summa contra Gentiles,* Thomas found a way of bringing the two together, and so of achieving a synthesis of Augustine's subjective desire for happiness with the Aristotelian tradition: nature *qua* nature does not seek some particular act first and foremost; it seeks with its natural desire the fulfillment of its natural appetite insofar as is possible. Depending on whether God chooses to offer grace to humanity, one and the same desire can come to a terminal rest in either the analogical knowledge of God or the beatific vision of God.

3) Does allowing a natural end for human nature promote a secular vision of human nature, and of human community?

For Thomas, to suggest that human nature and human communities have a structural integrity is not to suggest that they are in any way closed off from grace. Let us recall from chapter 3 that the natural desire for the fulfillment of our natural appetite insofar as possible was not merely supposed to balance Augustine's anti-Pelagianism with Aristotle's philosophy; it was also supposed to support Christian missionary efforts in answer to the questions raised by the Aristotelian tradition as a whole. It was in view of this latter goal that Thomas showed how the very same natural desire, which seeks the fulfillment of human natural appetite insofar as is possible, seeks implicitly the vision of God which the grace of Christ alone can bestow. Granted, then, that unaided human reason can never know which end God has in fact chosen to offer human nature, even if it can know what the terminal development of the active principle in human nature looks like, as well as some aspects of what the complete fulfillment of the passive principle in human nature would look like, a question still arises: which end of human nature should we take as normative in our accounts of the natural law and in our paradigms for the human communities based upon it: the terminal development of our unassisted natural desire (the analogical knowledge of God as first cause), or the ultimate end of our natural appetite (the vision of God)? As important as the question of an individual's perfection is, it is this more overtly political question which tends to raise the nature/grace debate to the feverish pitch at which it can often arrive. However, if we follow carefully the solution that Thomas suggests, we find that it is actually a trick question, because it is based on a false dichotomy. Thomas's principal contribution to the thirteenth-century discussion of nature, grace, and the desire for God was to show, with Augustine, that nature's desire is inwardly turned: it seeks happiness first and foremost, not this or that happiness. One and the same natural desire, like the nature from which it arises, terminates in one of two ends depending upon God's choice concerning the grace of Christ. Any description of the natural law which wants to account for the whole of human *nature* must therefore take into account both aspects of human finality: that which it can achieve by its natural desire, and that which it can receive by its natural appetite.

It might seem from an Aristotelian perspective that our natural end should have priority, since Aristotle contended that form is more properly called "nature" than matter; while it might seem from an Augustinian perspective that our supernatural end should have priority, because the receptivity in human nature which natural appetite describes was a mid-thirteenth-century attempt at articulating Augustine's understanding of nature in Aristotelian terms. But in point of fact, neither can answer the question "what does the human heart long for?" completely without the other. Thomas shows us by means of Aristotle that no system of moral theology or political theology can be so derived in relation to the end of our "second nature" that it closes the door to the legitimate speculative and moral truths that can be known by reflecting on the terminal development of our "first nature." But Thomas also shows us with Augustine that no ethics or politics can be so derived in relation to this "natural end" that it can afford to ignore the fact that the very restlessness with which it pursues the goods of nature always bespeaks another possibility: that God may stir our restless hearts by grace, pierce us with his love, and so draw us up by Christ into the mystical ascent in which Augustine took part at Ostia, and at whose apex the Church Triumphant now rejoices in the praise and glory of God. What is more, these two possibilities do not sit on equal footing. They may have done so in Thomas's *Commentary on the Sentences*. But from the *Summa contra Gentiles* onwards, Thomas imagined a very different sort of Aristotle than the one which scholars on either side of the nature/grace debate tend to envision. Avicenna's account of the natural desire of the souls for the heavenly bodies helped Thomas to imagine an Aristotle who shared Augustine's restless heart. That Aristotle sought his own happiness among the highest intellectual goods of this world, but in that very search, he always implicitly longed by nature to have what Augustine found by grace.

Bibliography

MANUSCRIPTS

Ann Arbor, Michigan. Alfred Taubman Medical Library. Ms. 201.
Vatican City. Vat. Lat. 1098.

PRIMARY SOURCES

Aegidius Romanus. *Opera omnia.* Vol. 3, no. 2. Florence: Edizioni del Galluzzo, 2003.

Albert the Great. *Opera Omnia.* Edited by Auguste Borgnet, Jacques Echard, and Jacques Quétif. 38 vols. Paris: Vivès, 1890–99.

———. *Opera Omnia. Editio Coloniensis.* Edited by Bernhard Geyer et al. 41 vols. Münster: Aschendorff, 1951–.

Alexander of Aphrodisias. *De anima libri mantissa* [*De intellectu*]. In *Alexandri Aphrodisiensis praeter commentaria scripta minora,* Supplement 2.1 to *Commentaria in Aristotelem Graeca,* edited by I. Bruns, 101–86. Berlin: Reimer, 1887.

———. *De intellectu.* Translated by Frederic Schroeder. Toronto: PIMS, 1990.

Alexander of Hales. *Glossa in quatuor libros Sententiarum Petri Lombardi.* Quaracchi: Collegium S. Bonaventurae, 1951–57.

———. *Summa theologica* [*Summa fratris Alexandri*]. With prolegomena by Victorin Doucet. 4 vols. Quaracchi: Collegium S. Bonaventurae, 1924–48.

Aristotle. *Aristoteles Latinus.* 32 vols. Paris: Desclée de Brouwer; Boston: Brill, 1961–.

———. *The Basic Works of Aristotle.* Edited by Richard McKeon. New York: Modern Library, 2001.

Augustine. *Confessionum libri XIII.* Edited by L. Verheijen. Corpus Christianorum Series Latina 27. Turnhout: Brepols, 1981.

———. *De civitate Dei.* Edited by B. Dombart and A. Kalb. 2 vols. Corpus Christianorum Series Latina 47–48. Turnhout: Brepols, 1955.

———. *De doctrina christiana, De vera religione*. Edited by Joseph Martin and K.-D. Daur. Corpus Christianorum Series Latina 32. Turnhout: Brepols, 1962.

———. *De genesi ad litteram libri XII eiusdem libri capitula, De genesi ad litteram inperfectus liber, Locutionum in heptateuchum libri septem*. Edited by J. Zycha. Corpus Christianorum Series Latina 28. Vienna: F. Tempsky, 1894.

———. *De peccatorum meritis et remissione et de baptismo parvulorum, De spiritu et littera, De natura et gratia, De natura et origine animae, Contra duas epistulas Pelagianorum*. Edited by K. F. Urba and J. Zycha. Corpus Scriptorum Ecclesiasticorum Latinorum 60. Vienna: F. Tempsky, 1913.

———. *De trinitate libri XV*. Edited by W. J. Mountain and F. Glorie. Corpus Christianorum Series Latina 50. Turnhout: Brepols, 1968.

———. *Epistulae*. 2 vols. Edited by A. Goldbacher. Corpus Christianorum Series Latina 34, nos. 1–2. Vienna: F. Tempsky, 1895.

———. *On the Trinity*. Translated by Edmund Hill. Brooklyn, N.Y.: New City Press, 1991.

———. *Selected Writings on Grace and Pelagianism*. Translated by Roland Teske. Hyde Park, N.Y.: New City Press, 2011.

Averroes [Ibn Rushd]. *Commentarium magnum in Aristotelis De anima libros*. Edited by F. Stuart Crawford. Cambridge, Mass.: Medieval Academy of America, 1953.

———. *On Aristotle's "Metaphysics": An Annotated Translation of the So-called "Epitome."* Edited by Rüdiger Arnzen. Berlin: Walter de Gruyter, 2010.

———. *Opera Omnia*. 12 vols. Venice: Giunti, 1562.

Avicebron [Ibn Gebirol]. *Avicebrolis Fons Vitae*. Vol. 1, nos. 2–3 of *Beiträge zur Geschichte der Philosophie des Mittelalters*, edited by Clemens Baeumker. Münster: Aschendorff, 1895.

Avicenna [Ibn Sīnā]. *Liber de anima seu Sextus de naturalibus*. Edited by S. van Riet. 2 vols. Louvain: Peeters, 1968–72.

———. *Liber de philosophia prima*. Edited by S. van Riet. 2 vols. Leuven: Peeters, 1977–80.

———. *Liber primus naturalium*. Edited by S. van Riet, with introduction by Gérard Verbeke. 2 vols. Louvain: Peeters, 1996–2006.

Bacon, Roger. *Opera hactenus inedita*. Edited by Robert Steele et al., with introductions by Robert Steele and Ferdinand Delorme. 16 vols. Oxford: Clarendon Press, 1909–40.

———. *Quaedam hactenus inedita*. Vol. 1. Edited by J. Brewer. London: Longman, Green, Longman, and Roberts, 1859.

———. *Roger Bacon's Philosophy of Nature: A Critical Edition, with English Translation, Introduction, and Notes, of* De multiplicatione specierum *and* De speculis comburentibus. Edited by David Lindberg. New York: Oxford University Press, 1983.

Baius, Michael. *Opuscula theologica*. Louvain: Joannes Bogard, 1566.

Bellarmine, Robert. *Opera omnia*. Edited by Justin Fèvre. 12 vols. Paris: Vivès, 1870–74.

Bellelli, Fulgenzio. *Mens Augustini de modo reparationis humanae naturae post lapsum adversus Baium et Jansenium.* 2 vols. Rome: Bernabò, 1737.

———. *Mens Augustini de statu creaturae rationalis ante peccatum.* Lucerne: Anna Felicitas Hauttin, 1711.

Berti, Giovanni. *De theologicis disciplinis.* 10 vols. Naples: Gaetano Migliaccio, 1776–84.

Biblia sacra cum glossa ordinaria. 4 vols. Strassburg: A. Rusch, 1480–81.

Boethius. *De consolatione philosophiae.* Translated by H. F. Stewart, E. K. Rand, and S. J. Tester. Loeb Classical Library 74. Cambridge, Mass.: Harvard, 1973.

———. *Opuscula theologica.* Edited by Claudio Moreschini. Munich: K. G. Saur, 2000.

Bonaventure, *Opera Omnia.* 10 vols. Quaracchi: Collegium S. Bonaventurae, 1882–1902.

David of Dinant. *Quaternulorum fragmenta.* Edited by Marian Kurdziałek. Warsaw: Polska Akademia Nauk, 1963.

Denifle, Heinrich, et al., eds. *Chartularium Universitatis Parisiensis.* 4 vols. Paris: Delalain, 1889–97.

Dominicus Gundissalinus. "The Treatise De anima of Dominicus Gundissalinus." Edited by J. T. Muckle. *Mediaeval Studies* 2 (1940): 23–103.

Gerard of Abbeville. *L'Anthropologie de Gérard d'Abbeville: Étude préliminaire et édition critique de plusieurs* Questions quodlibétiques *concernant le sujet, avec l'édition complète du* De cogitationibus. Edited by A. Pattin. Leuven: Leuven University Press, 1993.

Gilbert of Poitiers. *The Commentaries on Boethius by Gilbert of Poitiers.* Edited by Nikolaus Häring. Toronto: PIMS, 1966.

Giles of Rome. *Commentarius in Primum Sententiarum.* Edited by Augustino Montifalconio Venice, 1521.

———. *Commentarius in Secundum Sententiarum.* 2 vols. Venice: 1581.

———. *Giles of Rome's On Ecclesiastical Power: A Medieval Theory of World Government* [*De ecclesiastica potestate*]. Edited and translated by Robert Dyson. New York: Columbia University Press, 2004.

———. *Opera Omnia.* 4 vols. Edited by Francesco del Punta and Gianfranco Fioravanti. Florence: Leo S. Olsckhi, 1985–.

———. *Tractatus.* Rome: Antonius Bladus, 1555.

Humbert of Romans. *Opera Omnia.* 2 vols. Rome: A. Befani, 1889.

James of Viterbo. *De regimine christiano: A Critical Edition and Translation.* Edited by Robert Dyson. Boston: Brill, 2009.

Jansen, Cornelius. *Augustinus.* 3 vols. Louvain: Jacques Zegers, 1640.

Jean de la Rochelle. *Summa de anima.* Edited and introduction by Jacques Bougerol. Paris: J. Vrin, 1995.

———. *Tractatus de multiplici divisione potentiarum animae.* Edited by Pierre Michaud-Quantin. Paris: J. Vrin, 1964.

Jean Quidort [John of Paris]. *Jean de Paris et l'ecclésiologie du XIIIe siècle* [*De potes-*

tate regia et papali]. Edited by Jean Leclercq. Paris: J. Vrin, 1942. Translated by J. A. Watt as *On Royal and Papal Power* (Toronto: PIMS, 1971).

Jerome. *Contra Iohannem*. Edited by J. L. Feiertag. Corpus Christianorum Series Latina 79A. Turnhout: Brepols, 1999.

John Damascene. De Fide Orthodoxa: *Versions of Burgundio and Cerbanus*. Edited by Eligius Buytaert. St. Bonaventure, N.Y.: The Franciscan Institute, 1955.

John Duns Scotus. *Opera Omnia*. 26 vols. Paris: Vivès, 1891–95.

———. *Opera Omnia*. 21 vols. Vatican City: Vatican Polyglott Press, 1950–2015.

———. *Quaestiones super libros metaphysicorum Aristotelis*. 2 vols. Edited by R. Andrews et al. St. Bonaventure, N.Y.: The Franciscan Institute, 1997.

Lafosse, Fulgence. *Augustinus theologus*. 3 vols. Toulouse: Guillaume Bosc, 1676–83.

Lectura in librum de anima a quodam discipula reportata. Edited by R.-A. Gauthier. Grottaferrata: Collegium S. Bonaventurae ad Claras Aquas, 1985.

Maimonides, Moses. *Dux dubitantium*. Venice: Iodoco Badío Ascensio, 1520.

———. *Guide of the Perplexed*. Translated and introduction by Shlomo Pines. 2 vols. Chicago: University of Chicago Press, 2010.

Marcelli, Michelangelo. *Institutiones theologicae*. 7 vols. Foligno: Francesco Xavier Tomassino, 1847–51.

Migne, Jean-Paul, ed. Patrologiae curus completus. Series Graeca. 161 vols. Paris: Migne, 1857–66.

———. Patrologiae curus completus. Series Latina. 221 vols. Paris: Migne, 1844–1902.

Noris, Enrico. *Vindiciae Augustinianae*. Brussells: Lambert Marchant, 1675.

Paludanus, Michael. *Tractatus de fine et beatitudine*. Louvain: Andrea Bouvetius, 1664.

Peter Cantor. *Verbum abbreviatum: Textus conflatus*. Edited by M. Boutry. Corpus Christianorum Continuatio Mediaevalis 196. Turnhout: Brepols, 2004.

Peter Lombard. *Sententiae in IV libris distinctae. Prolegomena* by Ignatius Brady. 2 vols. 3rd ed. Grottaferrata: Collegium S. Bonaventurae ad Claras Aquas, 1971–81.

Philip the Chancellor. *Summa de bono*. Edited and introduction by Nicolai Wicki. 2 vols. Bern: Editiones Francke, 1985.

Piché, David, ed. *La condamnation parisienne de 1277: Nouvelle édition du texte latin, traduction, introduction et commentaire*. Paris: J. Vrin, 1999.

Richard Rufus. *Contra Averroem*. Transcribed by Rega Wood. Unpublished manuscript.

———. *Lectura Oxoniensis*. Transcribed by Rega Wood. Unpublished manuscript.

Siger of Brabant. *Quaestiones in tertium de anima, de anima intellectiva, de aeternitate mundi*. Edited and introduction by Carlos Bazán. Louvain: Publications universitaires, 1972.

Suárez, Francisco. *Opera Omnia*. 26 vols. Paris: Vivès, 1856–78.

Themistius. *On Aristotle on the Soul*. Translated by Robert Todd. New York: Bloomsbury, 2013.

———. *Themistii in libros Aristotelis de anima paraphrasis* [*De anima*]. Vol. 5, pt. 3, of *Commentaria in Aristotelem Graeca*, edited by R. Heinze. Berlin: Reimer, 1899.

Thomas Aquinas. *Commentary on Aristotle's Physics*. Translated by Kenneth Thomas. Notre Dame, Ind.: Dumb Ox Books, 1999.

———. *Contra Gentiles: Texte de l'édition Léonine*. Translated by Réginald Bernier and Maurice Coverz, with historical introduction by R. A. Gauthier. 4 vols. Paris: Lethielleux, 1961.

———. *In Duodecim libros Metaphysicorum Aristotelis expositio*. Edited by Raimundo Spiazzi. Turin: Marietti, 1964.

———. *Lectura romana in primum Sententiarum Petri Lombardi*. Edited by Leonard Boyle and John Boyle, introduction by John Boyle. Toronto: PIMS, 2006.

———. *The Literal Exposition on Job: A Scriptural Commentary Concerning Divine Providence*. Translated by Anthony Damico, and "Interpretive Essay" and notes by Martin D. Yaffe. Atlanta: Scholars Press, 1989.

———. *Opera omnia*. 18 vols. Rome: Antonio Blado, 1570–71.

———. *Opera omnia*. 27 vols. Parma: Pietro Fiaccadori, 1852–73.

———. *Opera omnia*. 50 vols. Rome: Commissio Leonina, 1882–.

———. *Opuscula Theologica*. Edited by Raymundo Verardo. 2 vols. Turin: Marietti, 1954.

———. *Quaestiones disputatae de potentia*. Edited by Paul Pession. In *Quaestiones disputate*, edited by P. Bazzi, vol. 2, 1–276. Turin: Marietti, 1954.

———. *Quaestiones disputatae de virtutibus in communi*. Edited by P. A. Odetto. In *Quaestiones disputate*, edited by P. Bazzi, vol. 2, 707–51. Turin: Marietti, 1954.

———. *Scriptum super libros Sententiarum Magistri Petri Lombardi Episcopi Parisiensis*. 4 vols. Edited by Pierre Mandonnet and Fabien Moos. Paris: Lethielleux, 1929–47.

———. *Summa contra Gentiles: Editio Leonina Manualis*. Rome: Commissio Leonina, 1934.

———. *Super Evangelium S. Matthaei Lectura*. Edited by R. Cai. Turin: Marietti, 1951.

Tommaso de Vio "Cajetan." *Opuscula Omnia*. Lyons, 1587; reprint: New York: Olms, 1995.

Walter of Bruges. *Quaestiones disputatae*. Edited by E. Longpré. Louvain: Institut Supérieur de Philosophie de l'Université, 1928.

William of Auvergne. *Opera Omnia*. 2 vols. Orleans: F. Hotot, 1674.

SECONDARY SOURCES

Acar, Rahim. *Talking about God and Talking about Creation: Avicenna's and Thomas Aquinas's Positions*. Boston: Brill, 2005.

Aertsen, Jan. "Avicenna's Doctrine of the Primary Notions and Its Influence on Medieval Philosophy." In *Islamic Thought in the Middle Ages: Studies in Text,*

Transmission and Translation, in Honour of Hans Daiber, edited by Anna Akasoy and Wim Raven, 21–42. Boston: Brill, 2008.

———. "The Transformation of Metaphysics in the Middle Ages." In *Philosophy and Theology in the Long Middle Ages: A Tribute to Stephen F. Brown*, edited by Kent Emery et al., 17–40. Boston: Brill, 2011.

———. *Medieval Philosophy as Transcendental Thought: From Philip the Chancellor (ca. 1225) to Francisco Suarez*. Boston: Brill, 2012.

Alfaric, Prosper. *L'évolution intellectuelle de Saint Augustin*. Paris: Noury, 1918.

d'Alverny, Marie-Thérèse. "Translations and Translators." In *Renaissance and Renewal in the Twelfth Century*, edited by Robert Benson and Giles Constable, 421–62. Toronto: University of Toronto Press, 1991.

Andrée, Alexander. "Anselm of Laon Unveiled: The *Glosae super Iohannem* and the Origins of the *Glossa Ordinaria* on the Bible." *Mediaeval Studies* 73 (2011): 217–60.

———. "Magisterial *auctoritas* and Biblical Scholarship at the School of Laon in the Twelfth Century." In *Auctor et Auctoritas in Latinis medii aevi litteris. Author and Authorship in Medieval Latin Literature*, edited by E. D'Angelo and J. Ziolkowski, 3–16. Florence: Edizioni del Galluzzo, 2014.

———."Peter Comestor's Lectures on the *Glossa 'Ordinaria'* on the Gospel of John: The Bible and Theology in the Twelfth-Century Classroom." *Traditio* 71 (2016): 1–32.

Anzulewicz, Henryk. "Pseudo-Dionysius Areopagita und das Strukturprinzip des Denkens von Albert dem Grossen." In *Die Dionysius-Rezeption im Mittelalter: Internationales Kolloquium in Sofia vom 8. bis 11. April 1999 unter der Schirmherrschaft de Société Internationale pour l'Étude de la Philosophie Médiévale*, edited by Tzotcho Boiadjiev, Georgi Kapriev, and Andreas Speer, 251–95. Turnhout: Brepols, 2000.

———. "Person und Werk des David von Dinant im literarischen Zeugnis Alberts des Grossen." *Mediaevalia Philosophica Polonorum* 24 (2001): 15–58.

———. "The Systematic Theology of Albert the Great." In *A Companion to Albert the Great: Theology, Philosophy, and the Sciences*, edited by Irven Resnick, 13–67. Boston: Brill, 2013.

Armogathe, Jean-Robert. "Histoire des idées religieuses et scientifiques dans l'Europe moderne." *Annuaire de l'École pratique des hautes études (EPHE), Section des sciences religieuses* 117 (2008–9), 325–30.

Bäck, Allan. "The Islamic Background: Avicenna (b. 980; d. 1037) and Averroes (b. 1126; d. 1198)." In *Individuation in Scholasticism: The Later Middle Ages and the Counter-Reformation 1150–1650*, edited by Jorge Gracía, 39–67. Albany, N.Y.: SUNY Press, 1994.

Bazán, Carlos. "The Human Soul: Form *and* Substance? Thomas Aquinas' Critique of Eclectic Aristotelianism." *Archives d'Histoire Doctrinale et Littéraire du Moyen Âge* 64 (1997): 95–126.

———. "13th Century Commentaries on *De anima*: From Peter of Spain to

Thomas Aquinas." In *Il commento filosofico nell'occidente latino (secoli XIII–XV), atti del colloquio Firenze-Pisa, 19–22 ottobre 2000, organizzato dalla SISMEL*, edited by Gianfranco Fioravanti, Claudio Leonardi, and Stefano Perfetti, 119–84. Turnhout: Brepols, 2002.

Bejczy, István. Introduction to *Virtue Ethics in the Middle Ages: Commentaries on Aristotle's Nicomachean Ethics, 1200–1500*, edited by István Bejczy, 1–10. Boston: Brill, 2008.

Benedict XVI. *Spe salvi.* encyclical letter (November 30, 2007).

Bernardi, Peter. *Maurice Blondel, Social Catholicism, and Action Française: The Clash over the Church's Role in Society during the Modernist Era.* Washington, D.C.: The Catholic University of America Press, 2009.

Berschin, Walter. *Greek Letters and the Latin Middle Ages: From Jerome to Nicholas of Cusa.* Washington, D.C.: The Catholic University of America Press, 1988.

Bertolacci, Amos. "On the Latin Reception of Avicenna's Metaphysics before Albertus Magnus: An Attempt at Periodization." In *The Arabic, Hebrew and Latin Reception of Avicenna's Metaphysics*, edited by Dag Nikolaus Hasse and Amos Bertolacci, 197–223. Boston: De Gruyter, 2012.

Blanchette, Oliva. *Maurice Blondel: A Philosophical Life.* New York: Fordham University Press, 2010.

di Blasi, Fulvio. "Natural Law as Inclination to God." *Nova et Vetera* (English) 7, no. 2 (2009): 327–60.

Blondel, Maurice. *L'action; Essai d'une critique de la vie et d'une science de la pratique (1893)*. 2nd ed. Paris: Presses Universitaires de France, 1950.

Bochet, Isabelle. *Saint Augustin et le désir de Dieu.* Paris: Études Augustiniennes, 1982.

Bocxe, Winfried. *Introduction to the Teaching of the Italian Augustinians of the 18th Century on the Nature of Actual Grace.* Louvain: Augustinian Historical Institute, 1958.

Boersma, Hans. *Nouvelle Théologie and Sacramental Ontology: A Return to Mystery.* New York: Oxford University Press, 2012.

Bonino, Serge-Thomas, ed. *Surnaturel: A Controversy at the Heart of Twentieth-Century Thomistic Thought.* Translated by Robert Williams and revised by Matthew Levering. Ave Maria, Fla.: Sapientia Press, 2009.

Boone, Mark. *The Conversion and Therapy of Desire.* Cambridge: J. Clark and Co., 2017.

Bougerol, Jacques. *Introduction à Saint Bonaventure.* 2nd ed. Paris: J. Vrin, 1988.

Boyle, Leonard. "Notes on the Education of the *Fratres communes* in the Dominican Order in the Thirteenth Century." In *Xenia medii aevi historiam illustrantia oblata Thomae Kaeppeli, O.P.*, edited by Raymond Creytens and Pius Künzel, 249–67. Rome: Edizioni di storia e letteratura, 1978.

———. *The Setting of the Summa theologiae of Saint Thomas.* Toronto: PIMS, 1982.

———. "Alia lectura fratris Thome." In *Lectura romana in primum Sententiarum*

Petri Lombardi. edited by Leonard Boyle and John Boyle, 58–69. Toronto: PIMS, 2006.

Bradley, Dennis. *Aquinas on the Twofold Human Good: Reason and Human Happiness in Aquinas's Moral Science.* Washington, D.C.: The Catholic University of America Press, 1997.

———. "Thomas Aquinas on Weakness of the Will." In *Weakness of Will from Plato to the Present,* edited by Tobias Hoffmann, 82–114. Washington, D.C.: The Catholic University of America Press, 2008.

Brandi, Salvatore. Review of *In Summam Theologicam S. Thomae Aquinatis I. P. Q. XII a. I—De naturalis intelligentis animae capacitate atque appetitu intuendi divinam essentiam, Theologica disquisitio,* by Gioacchino Sestili. *Civiltà Cattolica* 6, no. 1125 (May 1, 1897): 323–26.

Brock, Stephen. *Philosophy of Saint Thomas Aquinas: A Sketch.* Eugene, Ore.: Cascade Books, 2015.

Burns, J. Patout. *The Development of Augustine's Doctrine of Operative Grace.* Paris: Études Augustiniennes, 1980.

Burrell, David. "Maimonides, Aquinas and Gersonides on Providence and Evil." *Religious Studies* 20, no. 3 (1984): 335–51.

———. *Aquinas: God and Action,* 2nd ed. Scranton, Penn.: University of Scranton Press, 2008.

Bushlack, Thomas. "The Return of Neo-Scholasticism? Recent Criticisms of Henri de Lubac on Nature and Grace and Their Significance for Moral Theology, Politics, and Law." *Journal of the Society of Christian Ethics* 35, no. 2 (2015): 83–100.

Callus, David. "The Origin of the Problem of the Unity of Form." *The Thomist* 44 (1961): 257–85.

Capelle, G. C. *Amaury de Bène: Étude sur son panthéisme formel.* Paris: J. Vrin, 1931.

Catechism of the Catholic Church. Second ed. Vatican City: Libreria Editrice Vaticana. 2000.

Cavanaugh, William. *The Myth of Religious Violence: Secular Ideology and the Roots of Modern Conflict.* New York: Oxford University Press, 2009.

———. *Migrations of the Holy: God, State, and the Political Meaning of the Church.* Grand Rapids, Mich.: Eerdmans, 2011.

Chantraine, Georges. *Henri de Lubac.* 4 vols. Paris: Cerf, 2007–.

Chenu, Marie-Dominique. *Toward Understanding Saint Thomas.* Translated by A.-M. Landry and D. Hughes. Chicago: Henry Regnery and Co., 1964.

Clark, Mark. "The Biblical Gloss, the Search for the Lombard's Glossed Bible, and the School of Paris." *Mediaeval Studies* 76 (2014): 57–114.

———. *The Making of the Historia Scholastica, 1150–1200.* Toronto: PIMS, 2015.

———. "Peter Lombard, Stephen Langton, and the School of Paris: The Making of the Twelfth-Century Scholastic Biblical Tradition." *Traditio* 72 (2017): 171–274.

Coakley, Sarah, and Charles Stang, eds. *Re-Thinking Dionysius the Areopagite.* Malden, Mass.: Wiley-Blackwell, 2009.

Colish, Marcia. "From the Sentence Collection to the Sentence Commentary and the Summa: Parisian Scholastic Theology, 1130–1215." In *Manuels, programmes de cours et techniques d'enseignement dans les universités médiévales*, edited by Jacqueline Hamesse, 9–29. Louvain-la-Neuve: Université Catholique de Louvain, 1994.

———. *Peter Lombard.* 2 vols. Boston: Brill, 1994.

———. "The Development of Lombardian Theology, 1160–1215." In *Centres of Learning and Location in Pre-modern Europe and the Near East*, edited by Jan Willem Drijvers and Alasdair A. MacDonald, 207–16. Boston: Brill, 1995.

Compendium: Catechism of the Catholic Church. Washington, D.C.: U.S. Conference of Catholic Bishops. 2006.

Conybeare, Catherine. *The Irrational Augustine.* New York: Oxford University Press, 2006.

Courcelle, Pierre. *Recherches sur les* Confessions *de saint Augustin.* Paris: De Boccard, 1950.

Cross, Richard. *The Physics of Duns Scotus: The Scientific Context of a Theological Vision.* Oxford: Clarendon Press, 1998.

———. *Duns Scotus on God.* Burlington, Vt.: Ashgate, 2005.

Cunningham, Stanley. *Reclaiming Moral Agency: The Moral Philosophy of Albert the Great.* Washington, D.C.: The Catholic University of America Press, 2008.

Davidson, Herbert. *Alfarabi, Avicenna and Averroes on Intellect.* New York: Oxford University Press, 1992.

Davies, Brian. *The Thought of Thomas Aquinas.* Oxford: Clarendon Press, 2009.

Delmas, Sophie. *Un franciscain à Paris au milieu du XIIIe siècle: Le maître en théologie Eustache d'Arras.* Paris: Cerf, 2010.

del Punta, F., S. Donati, and Concetta Luna. "Egidio Romano." In *Dizionario biografico degli italiani*, vol. 42, 330–35. Rome: Società Grafica Romana, 1993.

de Lubac, Henri. "Deux Augustiniens fourvoyés: Baïus et Jansénius," *Recherches de Science Réligieuse* 2, nos. 4–5 (1931): 422–33; 513–40.

———. "Remarques sur l'histoire du mot 'Surnaturel,'" *Nouvelle revue théologique* 61 (1934): 225–49, 350–70.

———. *Le drame de l'humanisme athée.* Paris: Spes, 1944.

———. *Surnaturel: Études historiques.* Paris: Aubier, 1946.

———. "Duplex hominis beatitudo (Saint Thomas, 1a 2ae, q. 62, a. 1)." *Recherches de Science Religieuse* 35 (1948): 200–99.

———."Le mystère du surnaturel," *Recherches de Science Religieuse* 36, no. 1 (1949): 80–121.

———. *Histoire et esprit: l'Intelligence de l'Écriture d'après Origène.* Paris: Aubier, 1950.

———. *Exégèse médiévale: Les quatre sens de l'Écriture.* 4 vols. Paris: Aubier, 1959–64. Translated by E. M. Macierowski as *Medieval Exegesis*, 3 vols. (Grand Rapids: Eerdmans, 1998–2009).

———. *Augustinisme et théologie moderne.* Paris: Aubier, 1965.

———. *Le mystère du surnaturel.* Paris: Aubier, 1965.

———. *L'Écriture dans la tradition.* Paris: Aubier, 1966.

———. *Mémoire sur l'occasion de mes écrits.* Namur: Culture et Vérité, 1989.

———. *Scripture in the Tradition.* Translated by Luke O'Neill. New York: Crossroad, 2000.

———. *History and Spirit: The Understanding of Scripture according to Origen.* Translated by Anne Englund Nash. San Francisco: Ignatius Press, 2007.

———. *Surnaturel: Études historiques.* Paris: Lethielleux, 2010.

———. *Vatican Council Notebooks.* Vol. 1, translated by Andrew Stefanelli and Anne Englund Nash, introduction by Jacques Prévotat. San Francisco: Ignatius Press, 2015.

Deman, T. "Le 'Liber de bona fortuna' dans la théologie de S. Thomas d'Aquin." *Revue des Sciences Philosophiques et Théologiques* 17, no. 1 (1928): 38–58.

Dobell, Brian. *Augustine's Intellectual Conversion: The Journey from Platonism to Christianity.* New York: Cambridge University Press, 2009.

Dodaro, Robert. *Christ and the Just Society in the Thought of Augustine.* New York: Cambridge University Press, 2004.

Donati, Silvia. "Pseudoepigrapha in the *Opera hactenus inedita Rogeri Baconi*? The Commentaries on the Physics and on the Metaphysics." In *Les débuts de l'enseignement universitaire à Paris (1200–1245 environ)*, edited by Jacques Verger and Olga Weijers, 153–203. Turnhout: Brepols, 2013.

———. "Is Celestial Motion a Natural Motion?" In *Averroes' Natural Philosophy and Its Reception in the Latin West*, edited by Paul Bakker, 89–126. Leuven: Leuven University Press, 2015.

Dondaine, H. F. "Hugues de Saint-Cher et La Condamnation de 1241." *Revue des Sciences Philosophiques et Théologieque* 33 (1949): 170–205.

———. "L'objet et le 'medium' de la vision béatifique chez les théologiens du XIIIe siècle." *Recherches de Théologie Ancienne et Médiévale* 19, no. 1 (1952): 60–130.

———. *Le corpus dionysien de l'Université de Paris au XIIIe siècle.* Rome: Edizioni di storia e letteratura, 1953.

———. "Guerric de Saint-Quentin et La Condamnation de 1241." *Revue des Sciences Philosophiques et Théologiques* 44, no. 2 (1960): 225–42.

Doolan, Gregory. *Aquinas on the Divine Ideas as Exemplar Causes.* Washington, D.C.: The Catholic University of America Press, 2008.

Dunne, Michael. "Peter of Ireland, the University of Naples and Thomas Aquinas' Early Education." *Yearbook of the Irish Philosophical Society* 3 (2006): 84–96.

Eardley, Peter. "Giles of Rome's Theory of the Will." Ph.D. diss., University of Toronto, 2003.

Evans, G. R. *Philosophy and Theology in the Middle Ages.* New York: Routledge, 1993.

Faes de Mottoni, Barbara. "Les manuscrits du commentaire des Sentences d'Hugues de Saint-Cher." In *Hugues de Saint-Cher (+1263): Bibliste et théologien*, edited by Louis-Jacques Bataillon, Gilbert Dahan, and Pierre-Marie Gy, 273–98. Turnhout: Brepols, 2004.

Feingold, Lawrence. *The Natural Desire to See God according to St. Thomas Aquinas and His Interpreters*. Rome: Apollinare Studi, 2001.

———. *The Natural Desire to See God according to St. Thomas Aquinas and His Interpreters*. 2nd ed. Naples, Fla.: Sapientia Press, 2010.

Gallagher, David. "Free Choice and Free Judgment in Thomas Aquinas." *Archiv für Geschichte der Philosophie* 76, no. 3 (1994): 247–77.

Gardner, Patrick. "Thomas and Dante on the *Duo Ultima Hominis*." *The Thomist* 75, no. 3 (2011): 415–59.

Garrigou-Lagrange, Réginald. "La possibilité de la vision béatifique peut-elle se démontrer?" *Revue Thomiste* 38, no. 80 (1933): 669–88.

Gibson, Margaret. "The *Opuscula Sacra* in the Middle Ages." In *Boethius: His Life, Thought, and Influence,* edited by Margaret Gibson, 214–34. Oxford: Basil Blackwell, 1981.

Gilson, Étienne. "Pourquoi saint Thomas a critiqué saint Augustin." *Archives d'Histoire Doctrinale et Littéraire du Moyen Âge* 1 (1926–27): 111–27.

——— "Les sources gréco-arabes de l'augustinisme avicennisant." *Archives d'Histoire Doctrinale et Littéraire du Moyen Âge* 4 (1929): 5–149.

———. "Roger Marston: Un cas d'augustinisme avicennisant." *Archives d'Histoire Doctrinale et Littéraire du Moyen Âge* 8 (1933): 37–42.

———. "Sur la problématique thomiste de la vision béatifique," *Archives d'Histoire Doctrinale et Littéraire du Moyen Âge* 31 (1964): 67–88.

Giraud, Cédric. *Per verba magistri: Anselme de Laon et son école au xii*[e] *siècle*. Turnhout: Brepols, 2010.

Glasner, Ruth. *Averroes' Physics: A Turning Point in Medieval Philosophy*. New York: Oxford University Press, 2012.

Grabmann, Martin. *Die Geschichte der scholastischen Methode*. 3 vols. Freiburg im Breisgau: Herder, 1909–11.

Grant, Edward. *The Nature of Natural Philosophy in the Late Middle Ages*. Washington, D.C.: The Catholic University of America Press, 2010.

Gregory, Eric. *Politics and the Order of Love: An Augustinian Ethic of Democratic Citizenship*. Chicago: University of Chicago Press, 2010.

Gratry, Auguste. *De la connaissance de Dieu*, 2 vols. 2nd ed. Paris: C. Douniol, 1854.

Gutiérrez, David. *The Augustinians from the Protestant Reformation to the Peace of Westphalia, 1518–1648*. Vol. 2 of *History of the Order of St. Augustine*. Villanova, Penn.: Augustinian Historical Institute, 1979.

———. *The Augustinians in the Middle Ages, 1357–1517*. Vol. 1, pt. 2, of *History of the Order of St. Augustine*. Villanova, Penn.: Augustinian Historical Institute, 1983.

———. *The Augustinians in the Middle Ages, 1256–1356*. Vol. 1, pt. 1, of *History of the Order of St. Augustine*. Villanova, Penn.: Augustinian Historical Institute, 1984.

Hackett, Jeremiah. "Roger Bacon: His Life, Career, and Works." *In Roger Bacon and the Sciences: Commemorative Essays,* edited by Jeremiah Hackett, 9–23. Kinderhook, N.Y.: Brill, 1997.

Hammond, Jay. "The Textual Context." In *Bonaventure Revisited: Companion to the Breviloquium,* edited by Dominic Monti and Katherine Wrisley-Shelby, 29–72. St. Bonaventure, N.Y.: The Franciscan Institute, 2017.

Harrison, Carol. *Rethinking Augustine's Early Theology: An Argument for Continuity*. New York: Oxford University Press, 2006.

Hasse, Dag Nikolaus. *Avicenna's* De anima *in the Latin West: The Formation of a Peripatetic Philosophy of the Soul 1160–1300*. London: The Warburg Institute, 2000.

———. "Avicenna's 'Giver of Forms' in Latin Philosophy, Especially in the Works of Albertus Magnus." In *The Arabic, Hebrew and Latin Reception of Avicenna's Metaphysics,* edited by Dag Nikolaus Hasse and Amos Bertolacci, 225–49. Boston: Walter de Gruyter, 2012.

———. "Latin Averroes Translations of the First Half of the Thirteenth Century." In *Università della Ragione, Pluralità delle Filosofie nel Medioevo. XII Congresso Internazionale di Filosofia Medievale, Palermo 17–22 settembre 2007,* vol. 1, edited by A. Musco, 149–78. Palermo: Officina di Studi Medievali, 2012.

Healy, Nicholas. "Henri de Lubac on Nature and Grace: A Note on Some Recent Contributions to the Debate." *Communio* 5, no. 4 (2008): 535–64.

Hendrikx, E. "La date de composition du *De Trinitate* de saint Augustin." *L'année théologique augustinienne* 12 (1952): 305–16.

Hillebert, Jordan, ed. *The T&T Clark Companion to Henri de Lubac*. Edinburgh: T&T Clark, 2017.

Hissette, Roland. *Enquête sur les 219 articles condamnés à Paris le 7 mars 1277*. Louvain: Publications universitaires, 1977.

———. "Thomas d'Aquin compromis avec Gilles de Rome en mars 1277?" *Revue d'histoire ecclésiastique* 93 (1998): 5–26.

Hochschild, Joshua. *The Semantics of Analogy: Rereading Cajetan's* De nominum analgoia. Notre Dame, Ind.: University of Notre Dame Press, 2010.

Hoffmann, Tobias. "Aquinas on the Moral Progress of the Weak Willed." In *The Problem of Weakness of Will in Medieval Philosophy,* edited by Tobias Hoffman, Jörn Müller, and Matthias Perkams, 221–47. Leuven: Peeters, 2006.

———. "Aquinas and Intellectual Determinism: The Test Case of Angelic Sin," *Archiv für Geschichte der Philosophie* 89, no. 2 (2007): 122–56.

Hütter, Reinhard. *Dust Bound for Heaven: Explorations in the Theology of Thomas Aquinas*. Grand Rapids: Eerdmans, 2012.

Janz, Denis. *Luther and Late Medieval Thomism: A Study in Theological Anthropology*. Waterloo, Ont.: Wilfrid Laurier University Press, 1983.

Jones, Andrew. "The Preacher of the Fourth Lateran Council." *Logos* 18, no. 2 (2015): 121–49.

———. *Before Church and State: A Study of the Social Order in the Sacramental Kingdom of St. Louis IX*. Steubenville, Ohio: Emmaus Academic, 2017.

Jordan, Mark. "St. Thomas, Obediential Potency, and the Infused Virtues: *De virtutibus in communi,* a. 10, ad 13." In *Thomistica,* edited by E. Manning, 27–34. Leuven: Peeters, 1995.

Karfíková, Lenka. *Grace and the Will according to Augustine.* Boston: Brill, 2012.

Kent, Bonnie. *Virtues of the Will: The Transformation of Ethics in the Late Thirteenth Century.* Washington, D.C.: The Catholic University of America Press, 1995.

Kerr, Fergus. *After Aquinas: Versions of Thomism.* New York: Wiley Blackwell, 2008.

Kim, Yul. "A Change in Thomas Aquinas's Theory of the Will: Solutions to a Long-Standing Problem." *American Catholic Philosophical Quarterly* 82, no. 2 (2008): 221–36.

Knobel, Angela McKay. "Aquinas and the Pagan Virtues." *International Philosophical Quarterly* 51 (September 2011): 339–54.

Komonchak, Joseph. "Theology and Culture at Mid-Century: The Example of Henri de Lubac." *Theological Studies* 51, no. 4 (1990): 579–602.

Kretzmann, Norman. *The Metaphysics of Creation: Aquinas's Natural Theology in Summa Contra Gentiles II.* New York: Oxford University Press, 1999.

Laporta, Jorge. *La Destinée de la nature humaine selon Thomas d'Aquin.* Paris: J. Vrin, 1965.

Laumakis, John. "Aquinas' Misinterpretation of Avicebron on the Activity of Corporeal Substances: *Fons Vitae* II, 9 and 10." *The Modern Schoolman* 81, no. 2 (2004): 135–49.

Lemay, Richard. "Roger Bacon's Attitude towards the Latin Translations and Translators of the Twelfth and Thirteenth Centuries." In *Roger Bacon and the Sciences: Commemorative Essays,* edited by Jeremiah Hackett, 25–48. Leiden: Brill, 1997.

Laurer, Rosemary. "St. Thomas's Theory of Intellectual Causality in Election." *New Scholasticism* 28, no. 3 (1954): 299–319.

Lennerz, Heinrich. *De deo uno.* 5th ed. Rome: Gregorian University, 1955.

Levy, Ian. *Introducing Medieval Biblical Interpretation: The Senses of Scripture in Premodern Exegesis.* Grand Rapids: Baker, 2018.

Ligeard, Hippolyte. "Le rapport de la nature et du Surnaturel d'après les théologiens scolastiques du XIIIe au XVIIIe siècles." *Revue Pratique de l'Apologétique* 5 (1908): 543–51, 621–48, 773–84, 861–77.

Lombardo, Nicholas, *The Logic of Desire: Aquinas on Emotion.* Washington, D.C.: The Catholic University of America Press, 2011.

Long, D. Stephen. *Speaking of God: Theology, Language, and Truth.* Grand Rapids: William B. Eerdmans, 2009.

Long, R. James. "Adam's Rib: A Test Case for Natural Philosophy in Grosseteste, Fishacre, Rufus, and Kilwardby." In *Robert Grosseteste and His Intellectual Milieu: New Editions and Studies,* edited by John Flood, James Ginther, and Joseph Goering, 153–64. Toronto: PIMS, 2013.

Long, Steven. "Obediential Potency, Human Knowledge, and the Natural Desire for the Vision of God." *International Philosophical Quarterly* 37, no. 1 (1997): 45–63.

———. *Natura Pura: On the Recovery of Nature in the Doctrine of Grace.* New York: Fordham, 2010.

———. "Creation *ad imaginem Dei*: The Obediential Potency of the Human Person to Grace and Glory." *Nova et Vetera* (English) 14, no. 4 (2016): 1175–92.

Lottin, Odon. *Psychologie et morale aux XIIe et XIIIe siècles*. 6 vols. Gembloux: J. Duculot, 1948–60.

———. "La preuve de la liberté humaine chez saint Thomas d'Aquin." *Recherches de Théologie Ancienne et Médiévale* 23, no. 2 (1956): 323–30.

Louth, Andrew. *Maximus the Confessor.* New York: Routledge, 1996.

MacIntyre, Alasdair. *God, Philosophy, and Universities: A Selective History of the Catholic Philosophical Tradition.* Lanham, Md.: Rown and Littlefield, 2011.

Macken, Raymond. "Le Statut de la matière première dans la philosophie d'Henri de Gand." *Recherches de Théologie Ancienne et Médiévale* 46 (1979): 130–82.

Malloy, Christopher. "De Lubac on Natural Desire: Difficulties and Antitheses." *Nova et Vetera* (English) 9, no. 3 (2011): 567–624.

Mandonnet, Pierre. *Siger de Brabant et l'averroïsme latin.* Fribourg: Librairie de l'Université, 1899.

Mansini, Guy. "The Abiding Theological Significance of Henri de Lubac's *Surnaturel*." *The Thomist* 73, no. 4 (2009): 593–619.

Markus, Robert. *Saeculum: History and Society in the Thought of St. Augustine.* New York: Cambridge University Press, 1970.

McAleer, Graham. "The Presence of Averroes in the Natural Philosophy of Robert Kilwardby." *Archiv für Geschichte der Philosophie* 81, no. 1 (1999): 33–54.

———. "Who Were the Averroists of the Thirteenth Century?: A Study of Siger of Brabant and Neo-Augustinians in respect of the Plurality Controversy." *The Modern Schoolman* 76, no. 4 (1999): 273–92.

McCool, Gerald. *From Unity to Pluralism: The Internal Evolution of Thomism.* New York: Fordham University Press, 2002.

McInerny, Ralph. *Aquinas and Analogy.* Washington, D.C.: The Catholic University of America Press, 1996.

———. *Praeambula Fidei: Thomism and the God of the Philosophers.* Washington, D.C.: The Catholic University of America Press, 2006.

Meinert, John. "In Duobus Modis: Is Exemplar Causality Instrumental According to Aquinas?" *New Blackfriars* 95, no. 1 (2014): 57–70.

Mensching, Günther. "Metaphysik und Naturbeherrschung im Denken Roger Bacons." In *Mensch und Natur im Mittelalter*, vol. 1, edited by Albert Zimmermann and Andreas Speer, 129–42. Berlin: Walter de Gruyter, 1991.

Milbank, John. *The Suspended Middle: Henri de Lubac and the Debate concerning the Supernatural.* Grand Rapids: Eerdmans, 2005.

———. *Beyond Secular Order: The Representation of Being and the Representation of the People.* Malden, Mass.: Wiley Blackwell, 2013.

Milbank, John, and Catherine Pickstock. *Truth in Aquinas.* London: Routledge, 2001.

Milbank, John, Catherine Pickstock, and Graham Ward, eds. *Radical Orthodoxy: A New Theology.* New York: Routledge, 2006.

Montagnes, Bernard. *The Doctrine of the Analogy of Being according to Thomas Aquinas*. Translated by M. Macierowski, edited by Andrew Tallon. Milwaukee: Marquette University Press, 2004.

Mulchahey, Michèle. "More Notes on the Education of the *fratres communes* in the Dominican Order: Elias de Ferreriis of Salagnac's *Libellus de doctrina fratrum*." In *A Distinct Voice: Medieval Studies in Honor of Leonard E. Boyle, O.P.*, edited by Jacqueline Brown and William Stoneman, 328–69. Notre Dame, Ind.: University of Notre Dame Press, 1997.

———. *"First the Bow Is Bent in Study . . ." Dominican Education before 1350*. Toronto: PIMS, 1998.

Mulcahy, Bernard. *Aquinas's Notion of Pure Nature and the Christian Integralism of Henri de Lubac: Not Everything Is Grace*. New York: Peter Lang, 2011.

Oakes, Edward. "The *Surnaturel* Controversy: A Survey and a Response." *Nova et Vetera* (English) 9, no. 3 (2011): 627–34.

O'Carroll, Mary. *A Thirteenth Century Preacher's Handbook: Studies in MS Laud Misc. 531*. Toronto: PIMS, 1997.

O'Connell, James. *St. Augustine's Early Theory of Man*. Cambridge, Mass.: Harvard University Press, 1968.

O'Connor, William. *The Eternal Quest: The Teaching of St. Thomas Aquinas on the Natural Desire for God*. New York: Longman, Green, and Co., 1947.

O'Donovan, Oliver. *The Desire of Nations: Rediscovering the Roots of Political Theology*. New York: Cambridge University Press, 1996.

Pasnau, Robert. "The Latin Aristotle." In *The Oxford Handbook of Aristotle*, edited by Christopher Shields, 666–85. New York: Oxford University Press, 2012.

Patfoort, Albert. *Saint Thomas d'Aquin. Les clefs d'une théologie*. Paris: FAC, 1983.

Pecknold, C. C. "Church and Politics." In *The Oxford Handbook of Catholic Theology*, 457–75. New York: Oxford University Press, 2019.

Pius XII. "Allocutio ad Patres Societatis Iesu In XXIX Congregatione generali electores." September 17, 1946. *Acta Apostolicae Sedis* 38 (1946): 381–85.

———. *Humani generis*. *Acta Apostolicae Sedis* 42 (1950): 562–578.

Porro, Pasquale. *Thomas Aquinas: A Historical and Philosophical Profile*. Translated by Joseph Trabbic and Roger Nutt. Washington, D.C.: The Catholic University of America Press, 2016.

Portalié, E. "Augustinianisme." In *Dictionnaire de théologie catholique*, vol. 1, no. 2, edited by Alfred Vacant, E. Mangenot, and Emile Amann, cols. 2485–501. Paris: Letouzey et Ané, 1903.

Pseudo-Dionysius. *Pseudo-Dionysius: The Complete Works*. Translated by Colm Luibheid, introductions by Jaroslav Pelikan, Jean Leclercq, and Karlfried Froehlich. New York: Paulist Press, 1987.

Quinn, John Francis. *The Historical Constitution of St. Bonaventure's Philosophy*. Toronto: PIMS, 1973.

Raedts, Peter. *Richard Rufus of Cornwall and the Tradition of Oxford Theology*. New York: Oxford University Press, 1987.

Raffel, Charles. "Providence as Consequent Upon the Intellect: Maimonides' Theory of Providence." *AJS Review* 12, no. 1 (1987): 25–71.

Ramellini, Carlo. Review of *In Summam Theologicam S. Thomae Aquinatis I. P. Q. XII a. I—De naturalis intelligentis animae capacitate atque appetitu intuendi divinam essentiam, Theologica disquisitio*, by Gioacchino Sestili. *Divus Thomas* 6 (1897): 273–75, 327–31, 355–60, 423–27, 515–20.

Ratzinger, Joseph. *Church, Ecumenism, and Politics: New Endeavors in Ecclesiology*. Translated by Michael Miller et al. San Francisco: Ignatius Press, 1987.

———. "Communio: A Program." Communio 19, no. 3 (1992): 436–49.

Renan, Ernest. *Averroès et l'Averroïsme*. Vol. 3 of *Oeuvres Complètes*. Paris: Calmann-Lévy, 1949.

Renwart, Léon. "Augustiniens du XVIIIe siècle et 'Nature Pure." S.T.D. diss., Institut Catholique de Paris, 1948.

Riches, Aaron. "Christology and *duplex hominis beatitudo*: Re-sketching the Supernatural Again." *International Journal of Systematic Theology* 14, no. 1 (2012): 44–69.

Robiglio, A. A. "'Neapolitan Gold': A note on William of Tocco and Peter of Ireland." *Bulletin de Philosophie Médiévale* 45 (2002): 107–11.

Rocca, Gregory. *Speaking the Incomprehensible God: Thomas Aquinas on the Interplay of Positive and Negative Theology*. Washington, D.C.: The Catholic University of America Press, 2004.

Roest, Bert. *A History of Franciscan Education (c. 1210–1517)*. Boston: Brill, 2000.

Roland-Gosselin, Marie-Dominique. "Le principe de l'individualité. In *Le "De ente et essentia" de St. Thomas d'Aquin: Texte établi d'après les manuscrits parisiens: Introduction, Notes et Études historiques*. Edited by Marie-Dominique Roland-Gosselin, 49–134. Paris: J. Vrin, 1948.

Rombs, Ronnie. *Saint Augustine and the Fall of the Soul: Beyond O'Connell and His Critics*. Washington, D.C.: The Catholic University of America Press, 2006.

Rorem, Paul. *Pseudo-Dionysius: A Commentary on the Texts and an Introduction to Their Influence*. New York: Oxford, 1993.

Rosemann, Philipp. *Peter Lombard*. New York: Oxford University Press, 2004.

———. *The Story of a Great Medieval Book: Peter Lombard's* Sentences. New York: Broadview Press, 2007.

Russo, Antonio. *Henri de Lubac: Biographie*. Turin: San Paolo, 1994.

Saak, Eric. *High Way to Heaven: The Augustinian Platform between Reform and Reformation, 1292–1524*. Boston: Brill, 2002.

———. "Augustine in the Western Middle Ages to the Reformation." In *A Companion to Augustine*, edited by Mark Vessey, 465–77. Somorset: Wiley-Blackwell, 2012.

———. *Creating Augustine: Interpreting Augustine and Augustinianism in the Later Middle Ages*. Oxford: Oxford University Press, 2012.

———. *Luther and the Reformation of the Later Middle Ages*. New York: Cambridge University Press, 2017.

Schindler, David. *Heart of the World, Center of the Church: Communio Ecclesiology, Liberalism and Liberation.* Grand Rapids: Eerdmans, 2001.

Schlosser, Marianne. "Bonaventure: Life and Works." In *A Companion to Bonaventure,* edited by Jay Hammond, Wayne Hellmann, and Jared Goff, 7–59. Leiden: Brill, 2014.

Sestili, Gioacchino, *In Summam theologicam S. Thomae Aquinatis Ia. Pe., Q. XII, A. I.: De naturali intelligentis animae capacitate atque appetitu intuendi divinam essentiam: Theologica disquisitio.* Rome: A. and Salvatore Festa, 1896.

———. *Il desiderio naturale d'intuire la divina essenza, in risposta ad una critica della Civiltà Cattolica.* Rome: F. Setth, 1897.

———. *De possibilitate desiderioque primae caussae* [*sic*] *substantiam videndi a criticis animadversionibus vidiciae.* Rome: Hospitii S. Hieronymi Aemiliani, 1900.

Shanley, Brian. *The Thomist Tradition.* London: Springer, 2011.

Sicari, Antonio. "'Communio' in Henri de Lubac." *Communio* 19, no. 3 (1992): 450–64.

Sílva, José. *Robert Kilwardby on the Human Soul: Plurality of Forms and Censorship in the Thirteenth Century.* Boston: Brill, 2012.

Sirilla, Michael. *The Ideal Bishop: Aquinas's Commentaries on the Pastoral Epistles.* Washington, D.C.: The Catholic University of America Press, 2017.

Smalley, Beryl. *The Study of the Bible in the Middle Ages.* Notre Dame, Ind.: University of Notre Dame Press, 1989.

Smith, Lesley. *The Glossa Ordinaria: The Making of a Medieval Bible Commentary.* Boston: Brill, 2009.

Spatz, Nancy. "Approaches and Attitudes to a New Theology Textbook: The Sentences of Peter Lombard." In *The Intellectual Climate of the Early University: Essays in Honor of Otto Gründler,* edited by Nancy van Deusen, 27–52. Kalamazoo: Medieval Institute Publications, 1997.

van Steenberghen, Fernand. *Maître Siger de Brabant.* Louvain: Publications universitaires, 1977.

———. *La philosophie au xiii*[e] *siècle.* 2nd ed. Louvain: Peeters, 1991.

Stöve, Eckehart. "De Vio, Tommaso." in *Dizionario biografico degli italiani,* vol. 39, 567–78. Rome: Istituto della Enciclopedia Italiana, 1991.

Swafford, Andrew. *Nature and Grace: A New Approach to Thomistic Ressourcement.* Eugene, Ore.: Pickwick, 2014.

Taylor, Richard. "Aquinas and 'the Arabs': Aquinas's First Critical Encounter with the Doctrines of Avicenna and Averroes on the Intellect: *In 2 Sent.,* d. 17, q. 2, a. 1." In *Philosophical Psychology in Arabic Thought and the Latin Aristotelianism of the 13th Century,* edited by Luis Xavier López-Farjeat and Jörg Alejandro Tellkamp, 141–83. Paris: J. Vrin, 2013.

Thijssen, Hans. "1277 Revisited: A New Interpretation of the Doctrinal Investigations of Thomas Aquinas and Giles of Rome." *Vivarium* 35, no. 1 (1997): 72–101.

———. *Censure and Heresy at the University of Paris, 1200–1400.* Philadelphia: University of Philadelphia Press, 1998.

Torrell, Jean-Pierre. *Saint Thomas Aquinas.* 2 vols. Translated by Robert Royal. Washington, D.C.: The Catholic University of America Press, 2000–2003.

Trapè, Agostino. "De gratuitate ordinis supernaturalis apud theologos augustinienses litteris encyclicis 'Humani Generis' praelucentibus," *Analecta Augustiniana* 21 (1947–50): 217–65.

———. "Scuola teologica e spiritualità nell'Ordine Agostiniano." In *S. Augustinus vitae spiritualis magister*, vol. 2, 7–75. Rome: Analecta Augustiniana, 1956.

Trottmann, Christian. *La vision béatifique: Des disputes scolastiques à sa définition par Benoît XII.* Rome: École française de Rome, 1995.

Turner, Denys. *Faith, Reason and the Existence of God.* New York: Cambridge University Press, 2004.

Van Geest, Paul, Harm Goris and Carlo Leget, eds. *Aquinas as Authority: A Collection of Studies Presented at the Second Conference of the Thomas Instituut te Utrecht, December 14–16, 2000*. Leuven: Peeters, 2002.

Voderholzer, Rudolf. *Meet Henri de Lubac: His Life and Work.* Translated by Michael J. Miller. San Francisco: Ignatius Press, 1988.

Vos, Antoine. *The Philosophy of John Duns Scotus.* Edinburgh: Edinburgh University Press, 2006.

Wagner, Jean-Pierre. *Henri de Lubac.* Paris: Cerf, 2001.

Weisheipl, James. "The Life and Works of Saint Albert the Great." In *Albertus Magnus and the Sciences: Commemorative Essays (1980)*, edited by James A. Weisheipl, 12–51. Toronto: PIMS, 1980.

———. *Friar Thomas d'Aquino: His Life, Thought and Works.* Washington, D.C.: The Catholic University of America Press, 1983.

Westberg, Daniel. "Did Aquinas Change His Mind about the Will?" *The Thomist* 58, no. 1 (1994): 41–60.

Wetzel, James. *Augustine and the Limits of Virtue.* New York: Cambridge University Press, 2008.

Wicks, Jared. "Thomas de Vio Cajetan (1469–1534)." In *The Reformation Theologians: An Introduction to Theology in the Early Modern Period*, edited by Carter Lindberg, 268–83. Malden, Mass.: Blackwell, 2002.

Wielockx, Robert. "Autour du processus de Thomas d'Aquin." In *Thomas von Aquin: Werk und Wirkung im Licht neurerer Forschungen*, edited by A. Zimmermann, 413–38. New York: Walter de Gruyter, 1988.

———. "A Separate Process against Aquinas. A Response to John F. Wippel." In *Roma, Magistra Mundi: Iteneraria culturae medievalis (Mélanges offerts au Père L. E. Boyle à l'occasion de son 75e anniversaire*, 1009–30. Louvain-la-neuve: Fédération internationale des instituts d'études médiévales, 1998.

———. "Procédures contre Giles de Rome et Thomas d'Aquin. Réponse à J. M. M. H. Thijssen," *Revue des Sciences Philosophiques et Théologiques* 83 (1999): 293–313.

———. "Henry of Ghent and the Events of 1277." In *A Companion to Henry of Ghent*, edited by Gordon Wilson, 25–62. Boston: Brill, 2010.

Williams, Thomas. "Introduction: The Life and Works of John Duns the Scot." In *The Cambridge Companion to John Duns Scotus*, edited by Thomas Williams, 1–14. New York: Cambridge University Press, 2003.

Wippel, John. "The Condemnations of 1270 and 1277 at Paris." *The Journal of Medieval and Renaissance Studies* 7 (1977): 169–201.

———. "Thomas Aquinas and the Condemnation of 1277." *The Modern Schoolman* 73 (1995): 233–41.

———. "Bishop Stephen Tempier and Thomas Aquinas: A Separate Process against Aquinas?" *Freiburger Zeitschrift für Philosophie und Theologie* 44, nos. 1–2 (1997): 117–36.

———. *The Metaphysical Thought of Thomas Aquinas*. Washington, D.C.: The Catholic University of America Press, 2000.

———. *Metaphysical Themes in Thomas Aquinas II*. Washington, D.C.: The Catholic University of America Press, 2007.

———. "Thomas Aquinas and the Unity of Substantial Form." In *Philosophy and Theology in the Long Middle Ages: A Tribute to Stephen F. Brown*, edited by Kent Emery et al., 117–54. Boston: Brill, 2011.

Wolter, Allan. "Duns Scotus on the Natural Desire for the Supernatural." *The New Scholasticism* 23, no. 3 (1949): 281–317.

Wood, Benjamin. *The Augustinian Alternative: Religious Skepticism and the Search for a Liberal Politics*. Minneapolis: Fortress, 2017.

Wood, Jacob. "The 500th Anniversary of the Reformation: A Catholic Perspective." In *Reformation Observances: 1517–2017*, edited by Philip Krey, 69–93. Eugene, Ore.: Cascade, 2017.

———. "Ressourcement." In *The T&T Clark Companion to Henri de Lubac*, edited by Jordan Hillebert, 93–119. New York: T&T Clark, 2017.

———. "The Study of Theology as a Foretaste of Heaven: The Influence of Albert the Great on Aquinas's Understanding of *Beatitudo Imperfecta*." *Nova et Vetera* (English) 16, no. 4 (2018): 1103–34.

Wood, Rega. "Individual Forms: Richard Rufus and John Duns Scotus." In *John Duns Scotus: Metaphysics and Ethics*. Edited by Ludger Honnefelder, Rega Wood, and Mechthild Dreyer, 251–72. New York: Brill, 1996.

———. "Richard Rufus and English Scholastic Discussion of Individuation." In *Aristotle in Britain during the Middle Ages: Proceedings of the International Conference at Cambridge 8–11 April 1994 Organized by the Société Internationale pour l'Étude de la Philosophie Médiévale*, edited by John Marenbon, 117–43. Turnhout: Brepols, 1996.

———. "Richard Rufus." In *A Companion to Philosophy in the Middle Ages*, edited by Jorge J. E. Gracia and Timothy B. Noone, 579–78. Malden, Mass.: Blackwell, 2006.

———. "Indivisibles and Infinites: Rufus on Points." In *Atomism in Late Medieval Philosophy and Theology*, edited by Christophe Grellard and Aurélien Robert, 39–64. Boston: Brill, 2009.

Wood, Susan. *Spiritual Exegesis and the Church in Henri de Lubac*. Grand Rapids, Mich.: Eerdmans, 1998.

Young, Spencer. *Scholarly Community at the Early University of Paris: Theologians, Education, and Society, 1215–1248*. New York: Cambridge University Press, 2014.

Zumkeller, Adolar. *Theology and History of the Augustinian School in the Middle Ages*. Translated by John Rotelle. Villanova, Penn.: Augustinian Press, 1996.

Index

ALSO IN THE
THOMISTIC RESSOURCEMENT SERIES

Series Editors: Matthew Levering
Thomas Joseph White, OP

Aquinas on Transubstantiation
The Real Presence of Christ in the Eucharist
Reinhard Hütter

Bound for Beatitude
A Thomistic Study in Eschatology and Ethics
Reinhard Hütter

Analogy after Aquinas
Logical Problems, Thomistic Answers
Domenic D'Ettore

The Metaphysical Foundations of Love
Aquinas on Participation, Unity, and Union
Anthony T. Flood

The Cleansing of the Heart
The Sacraments as Instrumental Causes in the Thomistic Tradition
Reginald M. Lynch, OP

The Ideal Bishop
Aquinas's Commentaries on the Pastoral Epistles
Michael G. Sirilla